# THE NEW AMERICAN COMMENTARY

An Exegetical and Theological Exposition of Holy Scripture

# THE NEW AMERICAN COMMENTARY

Volume
28

## 1 CORINTHIANS

Mark Taylor

B&H
PUBLISHING GROUP
Brentwood, Tennessee

ISBN 978-0-8054-0128-8
Dewey Decimal Classification: 227.2
Subject Heading: BIBLE. N.T.—Commentaries\BIBLE. N.T. 1 Corinthians\BIBLE—STUDY AND TEACHING
Printed in China
5 6 7 8 9 10 • 29 28 27 26 25

To

my wife, Ann,

and my daughters,
Mary, Audrey, and Anna Ruth,

for their love and support

# Editors' Preface

God's Word does not change. God's world, however, changes in every generation. These changes, in addition to new findings by scholars and a new variety of challenges to the gospel message, call for the church in each generation to interpret and apply God's Word for God's people. Thus, THE NEW AMERICAN COMMENTARY is introduced to bridge the twentieth and twenty-first centuries. This new series has been designed primarily to enable pastors, teachers, and students to read the Bible with clarity and proclaim it with power.

In one sense THE NEW AMERICAN COMMENTARY is not new, for it represents the continuation of a heritage rich in biblical and theological exposition. The title of this forty-volume set points to the continuity of this series with an important commentary project published at the end of the nineteenth century called AN AMERICAN COMMENTARY, edited by Alvah Hovey. The older series included, among other significant contributions, the outstanding volume on Matthew by John A. Broadus, from whom the publisher of the new series, Broadman and Holman, partly derives its name. The former series was authored and edited by scholars committed to the infallibility of Scripture, making it a solid foundation for the present project. In line with this heritage, all NAC authors affirm the divine inspiration, inerrancy, complete truthfulness, and full authority of the Bible. The perspective of the NAC is unapologetically confessional and rooted in the evangelical tradition.

Since a commentary is a fundamental tool for the expositor or teacher who seeks to interpret and apply Scripture in the church or classroom, the NAC focuses on communicating the theological structure and content of each biblical book. The writers seek to illuminate both the historical meaning and contemporary significance of Holy Scripture.

In its attempt to make a unique contribution to the Christian community, the NAC focuses on two concerns. First, the commentary emphasizes how each section of a book fits together so that the reader becomes aware of the theological unity of each book and of Scripture as a whole. The writers, however, remain aware of the Bible's inherently rich variety. Second, the NAC is produced with the conviction that the Bible primarily belongs to the church. We believe that scholarship and the academy provide an indispensable foundation for biblical understanding and the service of Christ, but the editors and authors of this series have attempted to communicate the findings of their research in a manner that will build up the whole body of Christ. Thus, the commentary concentrates on theological exegesis while providing practical, applicable exposition.

THE NEW AMERICAN COMMENTARY's theological focus enables the reader to see the parts as well as the whole of Scripture. The biblical books vary in content, context, literary type, and style. In addition to this rich variety, the editors and authors recognize that the doctrinal emphasis and use of the biblical books differs in various places, contexts, and cultures among God's people. These factors, as well as other concerns, have led the editors to give freedom to the writers to wrestle with the issues raised by the scholarly community surrounding each book and to determine the appropriate shape and length of the introductory materials. Moreover, each writer has developed the structure of the commentary in a way best suited for expounding the basic structure and the meaning of the biblical books for our day. Generally, discussions relating to contemporary scholarship and technical points of grammar and syntax appear in the footnotes and not in the text of the commentary. This format allows pastors and interested laypersons, scholars and teachers, and serious college and seminary students to profit from the commentary at various levels. This approach has been employed because we believe that all Christians have the privilege and responsibility to read and seek to understand the Bible for themselves.

Consistent with the desire to produce a readable, up-to-date commentary, the editors selected the New International Version as the standard translation for the commentary series. The selection was made primarily because of the NIV's faithfulness to the original languages and its beautiful and readable style. The authors, however, have been given the liberty to differ at places from the NIV as they develop their own translations from the Greek and Hebrew texts.

The NAC reflects the vision and leadership of those who provide oversight for Broadman Press, who in 1987 called for a new commentary series that would evidence a commitment to the inerrancy of Scripture and a faithfulness to the classic Christian tradition. While the commentary adopts an "American" name, it should be noted some writers represent countries outside the United States, giving the commentary an international perspective. The diverse group of writers includes scholars, teachers, and administrators from almost twenty different colleges and seminaries, as well as pastors, missionaries, and a layperson.

The editors and writers hope that THE NEW AMERICAN COMMENTARY will be helpful and instructive for pastors and teachers, scholars and students, and for men and women in the churches who study and teach God's Word in various settings. We trust that for editors, authors, and readers alike, the commentary will be used to build up the church, encourage obedience, and bring renewal to God's people. Above all, we pray that the NAC will bring glory and honor to our Lord who has graciously redeemed us and faithfully revealed himself to us in his Holy Word.

SOLI DEO GLORIA
The Editors

# Author's Preface

Writing a commentary is a daunting and humbling task. I am keenly aware of my own inadequacies, but I eagerly accepted the assignment when asked to do it and will be forever grateful for the opportunity to spend hour upon hour wrestling with the interpretation of this important New Testament letter. I have written primarily for the church with the goal of producing a clear exposition of the text. I have not attempted to solve every exegetical problem, but I have tried to provide the reader with interpretive options and a lucid presentation of the argument and theological themes of the letter. Complex exegetical issues abound at almost every turn, but the theological principles that undergird Paul's pastoral concerns and the moral exhortations to be obeyed are rather transparent.

The literature on 1 Corinthians is vast and continues to grow with no end in sight. The past fifteen years or so have witnessed a new round of major commentaries on the letter with most approaching a thousand pages or more in length. I have learned much from them, which is evident in the footnotes, but I still find myself drawn to the shorter commentaries, which are a bit more accessible to the teaching pastor. My goal has been to produce an up-to-date commentary of mid-range length that interacts representatively with the most recent scholarship.

I am grateful to all who played a role in what is now the finished product. My family is a source of constant strength and encouragement. The prayers and support of my parents, Mahlon and Sue Taylor, and my in-laws, Bill and Betty Jones, have sustained me through the process. A Christian heritage is a priceless gift to a child. Opportunities to teach 1 Corinthians in both the classroom and the church have shaped my thinking and writing in many ways. I am indebted to numerous mentors along the way who instilled in me a love for studying the Word of God in the original languages. I think especially of Richard Melick and Kendall Easley, my New Testament professors from seminary days at Mid-America Baptist Seminary, and the late Thomas Lea and Curtis Vaughan of Southwestern Baptist Seminary, where it has been my privilege to teach for the past fifteen years. I owe a special debt of gratitude to the administration of Southwestern Seminary, who granted a generous yearlong sabbatical leave in 2012–13 that enabled the completion of the final manuscript.

Thank you, Ray Clendenen, for asking me to contribute this volume to the NEW AMERICAN COMMENTARY series and for your patient editorial work. Thank you, Southwestern colleagues, for the genuine fellowship that we share in our common task. Thank you, students, for asking great questions and challenging me to become a better interpreter and teacher of God's Word.

Thank you, Ann, for your love and support. Thank you, Mary, Audrey, and Anna Ruth, for the joy that you bring to our home each day. First Corinthians 10:31 expresses my heart's desire for you, that "whatever you do, do it all to the glory of God."

Mark Taylor<br>Southwestern Baptist Theological Seminary<br>Fall 2013

# Abbreviations

## Bible Books

| | | |
|---|---|---|
| Gen | Isa | Luke |
| Exod | Jer | John |
| Lev | Lam | Acts |
| Num | Ezek | Rom |
| Deut | Dan | 1, 2 Cor |
| Josh | Hos | Gal |
| Judg | Joel | Eph |
| Ruth | Amos | Phil |
| 1, 2 Sam | Obad | Col |
| 1, 2 Kgs | Jonah | 1, 2 Thess |
| 1, 2 Chr | Mic | 1, 2 Tim |
| Ezra | Nah | Titus |
| Neh | Hab | Phlm |
| Esth | Zeph | Heb |
| Job | Hag | Jas |
| Ps (pl. Pss) | Zech | 1, 2 Pet |
| Prov | Mal | 1, 2, 3 John |
| Eccl | Matt | Jude |
| Song | Mark | Rev |

## List of Abbreviations

AB Anchor Bible

AGJU Arbeiten zur Geschichte des antiken Judentums und des Urchristentums

AnBib Analecta biblica

ANTC Abingdon New Testament Commentaries

ASNU Acta seminarii neotestamentici upsaliensis

*BAR* *Biblical Archaeology Review*

*BBR* *Bulletin of Biblical Research*

BDAG W. Bauer, F. W. Danker, W. F. Arndt, and F. W. Gingrich, *Greek-English Lexicon of the New Testament and Other Early Christian Literature,* 3rd ed.

BECNT Baker Exegetical Commentary on the New Testament

BETL Bibliotheca ephemeridum theologicarum Iovaniensium

*Bib* *Biblica*

*BR* *Biblical Research*

| | |
|---|---|
| *BRev* | *Bible Review* |
| *BSac* | *Bibliotheca Sacra* |
| *BTB* | *Biblical Theology Bulletin* |
| *BZ* | *Biblische Zeitschrift* |
| BZNW | Beihefte zur Zeitschrift für die neutestamentliche |
| CBET | Contributions to Biblical Exegesis and Theology |
| *CBQ* | *Catholic Biblical Quarterly* |
| ConBNT | Coniectanea biblica, New Testament |
| *CTR* | *Criswell Theological Review* |
| *CurBS* | *Currents in Research: Biblical Studies* |
| *CV* | *Communio viatorum* |
| *DPL* | *Dictionary of Paul and His Letters*, ed. G. F. Hawthorne, Ralph P. Martin, Daniel G. Reid |
| *EQ* | *Evangelical Quarterly* |
| *ExpTim* | *Expository Times* |
| FF | Foundations and Facets |
| *GOTR* | *Greek Orthodox Theological Review* |
| *HAR* | *Hebrew Annual Review* |
| HNTC | Harper's New Testament Commentaries |
| *HTR* | *Harvard Theological Review* |
| ICC | International Critical Commentary |
| *Int* | *Interpretation* |
| *JAAR* | *Journal of the American Academy of Religion* |
| *JBL* | *Journal of Biblical Literature* |
| *JETS* | *Journal of the Evangelical Theological Society* |
| *JSNT* | *Journal for the Study of the New Testament* |
| JSNTSup | Journal for the Study of the New Testament Supplement Series |
| *JTS* | *Journal of Theological Studies* |
| LNTS | Library of New Testament Studies |
| Louw-Nida | *Greek-English Lexicon of the New Testament Based on Semantic Domains*, ed. J. P. Louw and E. A. Nida |
| LXX | Septuagint |
| MNTC | Moffatt New Testament Commentary |
| NAC | New American Commentary |
| NCB | New Century Bible |
| *Neot* | *Neotestamentica* |
| NICNT | New International Commentary on the New Testament |
| NIGTC | New International Greek Testament Commentary |
| NIVAC | New International Version Application Commentary |
| *NovT* | *Novum Testamentum* |
| NovTSup | Novum Testamentum Supplement |
| *NTS* | *New Testament Studies* |
| PNTC | Pillar New Testament Commentary |

| | |
|---|---|
| *Presb* | *Presbyterion* |
| *PRSt* | *Perspectives in Religious Studies* |
| *RB* | *Revue biblique* |
| *ResQ* | *Restoration Quarterly* |
| *RevExp* | *Review and Expositor* |
| *RTR* | *Reformed Theological Review* |
| SBLDS | Society of Biblical Literature Dissertation Series |
| SBT | Studies in Biblical Theology |
| *SJT* | *Scottish Journal of Theology* |
| SNTSMS | Society of New Testament Studies Monograph Series |
| SP | Sacra Pagina |
| *SwJT* | *Southwestern Journal of Theology* |
| *TDNT* | *Theological Dictionary of the New Testament,* ed. G. Kittel and G. Friedrich |
| TNTC | Tyndale New Testament Commentaries |
| *TQ* | *Theologische Quartalschrift* |
| *TrinJ* | *Trinity Journal* |
| *TynBul* | *Tyndale Bulletin* |
| *WTJ* | *Westminster Theological Journal* |
| WUNT | Wissenschaftliche Untersuchungen zum Neuen Testament |
| *WW* | *Word and World* |
| *ZNW* | *Zeitschrift für die neutestamentliche Wissenschaft und die Kunde der älteren Kirche* |

**Bible Translations**

ESV
HCSB
KJV
NASB
NEB
NET
NIV2011
NRSV

# Contents


Editors' Preface . . . . . 7
Author's Preface . . . . . 9
Abbreviations . . . . . 11
Introduction . . . . . 17

I. Letter Opening (1:1–9) . . . . . 33
II. God's Wisdom for a Divided Church (1:10–4:21) . . . . . 47
III. Sexual Immorality, the Civil Courts, and Issues of Marriage and Singleness (5:1–7:40) . . . . . 129
IV. Christian Freedom, the Priority of Love, and the Peril of Idolatry (8:1–11:1) . . . . . 195
V. The Church Gathered for Worship (11:2–14:40) . . . . . 251
VI. The Resurrection of the Dead (15:1–58) . . . . . 365
VII. The Collection for the Saints in Jerusalem and Travel Plans (16:1–12) . . . . . 417
VIII. Letter Closing (16:13–24) . . . . . 427

Selected Bibliography . . . . . 437

Name Index . . . . . 451

Subject Index . . . . . 457

Scripture Index . . . . . 459

# 1 Corinthians

## *INTRODUCTION OUTLINE*

1. The City and Its Citizens
2. The Church and Her Apostle
3. The Occasion of the Letter, Structure, and Main Themes
   (1) The Letter Opening: God's Grace and Faithfulness in Christ (1:1–9)
   (2) The Wisdom of God: Embracing the Values of the Cross (1:10–4:21)
   (3) Issues of Purity, Both Corporate and Individual (5:1–7:40)
   (4) The Freedom of the Gospel: Loving God and Loving One's Neighbor (8:1–11:1)
   (5) Worship in Community (11:2–14:40)
   (6) Bodily Resurrection: Certainty, Possibility, and Necessity (15:1–58)
   (7) The Continuing Work of the Gospel (16:1–24)
4. Outline of the Letter

## INTRODUCTION

### 1. The City and Its Citizens

The location of Corinth virtually guaranteed its success as a major cosmopolitan city in the ancient world. Situated on the narrow Isthmus which connects Southern Greece (Peloponnesus) with the mainland, Corinth rose to prominence as a strategic crossroads of trade and commerce. The city boasted two ports, Lechaeum, located two miles to the north on the west side of the Isthmus overlooking the Gulf of Corinth, and Cenchreae, six miles to the east on the Saronic Gulf. Today a canal cuts across the Isthmus in order for ships to pass through,[1] but in ancient times, due to the treacherous journey around the Peloponnesus, ships unloaded cargo on one side of the Isthmus to be hauled overland and unloaded on the other side. Smaller ships were transported on a

[1] The canal was completed in 1893.

paved road, called the *diolkos*, meaning "haul-across." The Acrocorinth, a towering nineteen-hundred-foot summit adjacent to the city, dominates the local landscape.[2]

The history of ancient Corinth is the story of two cities, the old Greek city and the new Roman Corinth of Paul's time. The old Corinth dates back to prehistoric times that, by the eighth century BC, grew to be one of the wealthiest and most prominent cities in Greece and a rival to Athens located approximately fifty miles to the east. Ancient ruins of the old city are still standing today, including the famed columns of the temple of Apollo, dating back several hundred years prior to Paul's arrival in the early to mid AD 50s. In 146 BC the Roman general Lucius Mummius invaded Corinth and reduced the city to rubble. Most of the citizens were killed or sold into slavery, and the city lay in ruins for a little over one hundred years until Julius Caesar founded the new Corinth as a Roman colony in 44 BC.[3] Corinth soon regained the prominence of the old Greek city, serving as the capital of the Roman province of Achaia and the residence of the governor, called the proconsul.[4] Even though Corinth was a Greek city, the customs, laws, and political structures were of Roman character as evidenced by the extensive extant Latin inscriptions, the official language of Rome. Although Latin was the formal, administrative language of Corinth, Greek was the common language of the people. Recent studies of 1 Corinthians highlight the importance of understanding the letter against a Roman cultural background.[5]

The Roman Corinth of the New Testament era was a large, cosmopolitan city boasting a population surpassed only by Rome and Alexandria.[6] Julius Caesar colonized the city with freed slaves, soldiers, and urban laborers.[7] Over

---

[2] On the geography and economy of Corinth see D. Engels, *Roman Corinth: An Alternative Model for the Classical City* (Chicago: University of Chicago Press, 1990), 8–21; J. Murphy-O'Connor, *St. Paul's Corinth: Texts and Archaeology* (Glazier: Wilmington, 1983), 3–44, 51–70. O'Connor provides excerpts and commentary on the relevant classical ancient sources, especially Strabo, *Geography*, and Pausanius, *Description of Greece*.

[3] Horrell and Adams point out that the destruction of Corinth by the Romans was far from complete. Archaeology provides evidence of inhabitants in Corinth between 146–44 BC, and Cicero (*Tusculanae Disputationes*, 3.53) gives a firsthand account of people living among the ruins when he visited the city around 79–77 BC, but there was clearly no formal political and civic life in the city between its destruction and rebuilding. See E. Adams and D. G. Horrell, *Christianity at Corinth: The Quest for the Pauline Church* (Louisville: WJK, 2004), 3.

[4] Gallio was the proconsul during Paul's missionary visit to Corinth (Acts 18:12–17).

[5] In addition to Engels' groundbreaking study see D. W. J. Gill, "Corinth: A Roman Colony in Achaea," *BZ* 35 (1991): 233–41; B. W. Winter, "The Achaean Federal Imperial Cult II: The Corinthian Church," *TynBul* 46 (1995): 169–78. Corinth would have been Roman in its layout and organization and its political and cultural makeup (so Adams and Horrell, *Christianity at Corinth*, 6).

[6] Population estimates range from 400,000 to 700,000 inhabitants.

[7] A. C. Thiselton, *The First Epistle to the Corinthians: A Commentary on the Greek Text*, NIGTC (Grand Rapids: Eerdmans, 2000), 3.

time many different ethic groups migrated to Corinth, including Jews,[8] resulting in a society of cultural and religious pluralism.[9] The city's location, cosmopolitan character, and tourism[10] all contributed to its wealth and status, issues that clearly plagued the Corinthian church.[11] Fee draws a modern-day parallel by suggesting that "Paul's Corinth was at once the New York, Los Angeles, and Las Vegas of the ancient world."[12]

Like other ancient Greek cities, Corinth was notoriously wicked, given over to the vices of idolatry and sexual immorality (cf. Rom 1:18–32) and associated sins (cf. 1 Cor 5:9–11; 6:9–11).[13] The old Corinth boasted the temple of Aphrodite, the Greek goddess of lust and love. It is uncertain if the worship of Aphrodite was revived in the rebuilding of the city in 44 BC, but it is possible that the ancient religion thrived in shrines located throughout the city. Scholars dispute the accuracy of the famed remark made by the Greek geographer Strabo concerning the one thousand temple prostitutes who served the temple of Aphrodite on the Acropolis.[14] In any case, his remarks refer to the old city, not the re-founded Roman Corinth. Nevertheless, immorality was entrenched in the city and was typical of large seaport and commercial cities of the day.

## 2. The Church and Her Apostle

Acts 18 lays out the sequence of events of the beginnings of the church at Corinth. Paul arrived in Corinth during his second missionary journey sometime in the early AD 50s. He took up residence with Aquila and Priscilla, who had recently moved from Rome, working with them in their common trade (18:1–3).[15] Paul spent his Sabbaths dialoguing with both Jews and Greeks in

[8] Upon his arrival in the city Paul reasoned in the synagogue with both Jews and Greeks (Acts 18:4).

[9] Several passages in the letter attest to the pagan setting of Corinth and the pagan past of some of the members of the church. Cf. 6:9–11; 12:1–3; and esp. Paul's lengthy argument regarding food sacrificed to idols in 8:1–11:1.

[10] Corinth hosted the biennial Isthmian games, which was second only to the famed Olympic games.

[11] See esp. Paul's confrontation of the social stratification that dishonored the Lord's Supper (11:17–34; cf. also 1:26–31). Issues of status and wealth may inform the background of many of the problems that Paul confronts in the letter, such as factions (1:10–4:21), the toleration of the incestuous man (5:1–13), litigation (6:1–11), food sacrificed to idols (8:1–11:1), etc.

[12] G. D. Fee, *The First Epistle to the Corinthians*, NICNT (Grand Rapids: Eerdmans, 1987), 3. On the character of Corinth in Paul's times see Murphy-O'Connor, *St. Paul's Corinth*; Engels, *Roman Corinth*.

[13] Sexual immorality and idolatry are given extended treatment in the letter (5:1–13; 6:12–20; 8:1–11:1).

[14] *Geography* 8:6.20. For a critique of Strabo's claim see Murphy-O'Connor, *St. Paul's Corinth*, 55–56. "Sacred prostitution was never a Greek custom and, were Corinth an exception, the silence of all other ancient authors becomes impossible to explain."

[15] The mention of Gallio, the proconsul of Achaia (18:12), provides a relatively fixed date for Paul's ministry in Corinth at AD 51–52. For a discussion of the Edict of Claudius (18:2) and the

the synagogue (18:4) until he was able to devote himself exclusively to evangelistic work upon the arrival of Silas and Timothy from Macedonia (18:5). The Jews vigorously opposed Paul, but he found a more receptive audience at the home of Titius Justus, who lived next door to the synagogue (18:6). Crispus, the synagogue ruler, and his entire household, along with many other Corinthians, believed Paul's message and were baptized (18:7–8). The Lord appeared to Paul in a night vision, assuring him of protection and of the success of the gospel in the city (18:9–10). Paul remained in Corinth for eighteen months, a longer stay than in any other city up to that time in his missionary journeys (18:11). The persecution of Paul by the Jews continued (18:12–17), and he eventually departed for Syria, along with Priscilla and Aquila (18:18). At some point after Paul's departure, Apollos arrived in Corinth (18:27–19:1). In addition to Paul the names of four men in Acts 18 reappear in 1 Corinthians: Timothy (4:17; 16:10), Crispus (1:14), Sosthenes (1:1), and Apollos (1:12; 3:4–6,22; 4:6; 16:12).[16] Although Jews numbered among the Corinthian believers, the membership of the church was predominantly Gentile, some of whom had lived formerly shameful lives (6:9–11; 12:2). Most of the Corinthians were of low social status although there was a core group of persons of rank among them.[17]

Paul's contentious relationship with the Corinthians produced the most extensive correspondence between an apostle and a local church preserved in the New Testament.[18] As a result we know more about the inner workings of this Christian community than any other and possess a rich storehouse of

proconsul Gallio in light of the relevant ancient texts see Murphy-O'Connor, *St. Paul's Corinth*, 130–52.

[16] We cannot know with certainty if the Crispus and Sosthenes mentioned in Acts 18 are the same men appearing in 1 Corinthians.

[17] Erastus, the city treasurer in Corinth, is mentioned in Rom 16:23, and Sosthenes (1:1) and Crispus (1:14), both synagogue rulers, may be the same men mentioned in Acts 18. Paul mentions the household of Stephanas (1:16; cf. also 16:17) and the household of Chloe, who may have been a Corinthian (see comments on 1:11). Aquila and Priscilla, who were among the original members of the Corinthian church, traveled extensively (see comments on 16:19). Regarding social stratification in Corinth see comments on 1:26–31.

[18] There were other letters that are no longer extant (see 1 Cor 5:9; 2 Cor 2:1–11). The exact number of letters written by Paul to the Corinthians is a matter of debate, but most concede a minimum of four. Thiselton (*First Corinthians*, 45) observes that the length of Paul's stay in Corinth and his extensive correspondence with the church underlies his concern as a missionary-pastor. Paul is not merely a theological thinker, nor is he someone preoccupied with his own experience in Christ. He is a pastor-theologian.

The length of Paul's Corinthian correspondence indicates something of the nature of his relationship with the church, not only the extent of their problems, but of their attitude toward their own behavior, which needed correction, and of their attitude toward their founder, Paul. In other words, Paul does not give concise answers to this church, but rather goes to great lengths to reason with them and to guide them pastorally through a theological answer to their problems. But herein lies the great value of 1 Corinthians for the church today. However complex the issues may be and distant the historical situation from our own, Paul's theological response demonstrates the shape that our own thinking should take toward similar (or perhaps even vastly different) problems.

Paul's theology, a thoroughgoing application of the gospel to a litany of real life situations, such as the wisdom of the cross and church leadership, the perils of sexual immorality and idolatry, marriage and divorce, evangelism and worship, and the greatest enemy of all, death. In 1 Corinthians we encounter a church still beguiled by the wisdom of the world, and we see Paul's firm commitment to mold their thinking and behavior into conformity with who they are in Christ, those set apart from the world to be God's holy people. Paul unashamedly reminds them of his manner of life in Christ and calls them to reject worldly values and to replace them with the values of the cross. In a nutshell, Paul teaches them (and us) how to live in this present world in community with other believers and in relation to unbelievers in light of the age to come. In 1 Corinthians we learn as much about Paul, if not more, than we do about the Corinthians as he fulfilled his apostolic mission to bring the light of the gospel to the Gentiles.

### 3. The Occasion of the Letter, Structure, and Main Themes

At some point after Paul left Corinth he received information about the church by way of oral report (1:11; 5:1; 11:18)[19] and through written correspondence from the Corinthians themselves (7:1). In 5:9 Paul mentions a prior letter he wrote to the Corinthians. This earlier letter, which is no longer extant, probably occasioned the Corinthians' letter to Paul mentioned in 7:1. First Corinthians is Paul's response both to what he had heard about the church and to the content of their letter to him, which likely contained both questions and challenges to his prior instruction. The Corinthian letter to Paul was probably delivered to him in Ephesus by Stephanas, Fortunatus, and Achaicus (16:8,17), and from Ephesus Paul wrote his response, either in the spring of AD 54 or 55.[20]

A simplified approach to the structure of the letter linked closely to its occasion divides the body of the letter into two major components, namely, Paul's response to oral reports (1:10–6:20) followed by his response to their questions

[19] We could possibly include 15:12, "But if it is preached that Christ has been raised from the dead, how can some of you say that there is no resurrection of the dead?" In 1:11 Paul identifies the source of information regarding divisions in the church as coming from "some from Chloe's household." The other references leave the source(s) unnamed. Paul's letter closings give evidence of a strong network of Paul's personal relationships in ministry (see comments on 16:13–24).

[20] The unity and literary integrity of 1 Corinthians as a genuine Pauline letter is well established. In the modern era challenges to Pauline authorship take the form of theories of non-Pauline interpolations of various sections within the letter (e.g., 2:6–16; 11:2–16; 14:33–36). See especially the series of articles collected and revised in W. O. Walker, *Interpolations in the Pauline Letters*, JSNTSup 213 (London: Sheffield Academic Press, 2001). For an analysis and critique see J. Murphy-O'Connor, "Interpolations in 1 Corinthians," in *Keys to First Corinthians: Revisiting the Major Issues* (New York: Oxford University Press, 2009), 257–87. We do not know who delivered Paul's letter to the Corinthians. The three mentioned in 16:17 and Sosthenes (1:1), the co-sender, are probable candidates.

(7:1–16:4).[21] As attractive as this option may be, it is not the case that Paul's response to oral reports is relegated entirely to roughly the first part of the letter (11:18; 15:12), and similarly, Paul's clarification of what he wrote in a previous letter in 5:9 may be a response to the letter from Corinth. Furthermore, although the formula in 7:1 that introduces the matters about which the Corinthians wrote recurs in 7:25; 8:1; 12:1; 16:1; and 16:12,[22] it does not introduce Paul's discussion of head coverings and the Lord's Supper (11:2–34) nor does it initiate the final major discourse of the letter concerning the resurrection of the dead (15:1–58).

Since Paul alternates between oral reports and answers to their questions,[23] the evidence strongly suggests an intentional thematic arrangement of the letter. Mitchell offers a thoroughgoing rhetorical analysis in support of the overarching theme of unity.[24] Garland detects a topical organization that warns against various perils.[25] And Ciampa and Rosner submit that the arrangement of the material reflects Paul's main concern for the purity of the church and the glory of God as the Corinthian church, God's eschatological temple, fulfills the Old Testament expectation of the worldwide worship of the God of Israel.[26] Thematic approaches vary in their emphases but demonstrate the vital relationship between the structure of the letter and the discernment of its main theme or themes. While Mitchell argues that Paul writes to reunify the Corinthians,[27] Ciampa and Rosner give more weight to four themes that emerge from "Paul's identity, aims, and agenda in his relations to the church at Corinth," which

---

[21] So C. K. Barrett, *A Commentary on the First Epistle to the Corinthians*, HNTC (New York: Harper & Row, 1968); Fee, *First Corinthians*; C. L. Blomberg, *1 Corinthians*, NIVAC (Grand Rapids: Zondervan, 1994).

[22] Gk. περί δέ, rendered by the NIV as "Now" (7:1) or "Now about" (8:1; 12:1; 16:1,12). On the use of the περί δέ formula and its implications see the discussion introducing 7:1–40.

[23] So R. B. Terry, *A Discourse Analysis of First Corinthians* (Dallas: University of Texas Press, 1995).

[24] M. M. Mitchell, *Paul and the Rhetoric of Reconciliation: An Exegetical Investigation of the Language and Composition of 1 Corinthians* (Louisville: WJK, 1991). For a rhetorical approach among the commentaries see R. F. Collins, *First Corinthians*, SP (Collegeville, MN: Liturgical Press, 1999); B. Witherington, *Conflict and Community in Corinth: A Socio-Rhetorical Commentary* (Grand Rapids: Eerdmans, 1994). The rise of rhetorical criticism has changed the focus of the study of 1 Corinthians with less attention to the historical situation and more on the arrangement of Paul's argument. Partition theories are now less acceptable to scholars and 1 Corinthians is widely received as a literary unity. So W. Willis, "1 Corinthians 8–10: A Retrospective after Twenty-Five Years," *ResQ* 49 (2007): 104–5.

[25] D. E. Garland, *1 Corinthians*, BECNT (Grand Rapids: Baker, 2003), 21–22.

[26] R. E. Ciampa and B. S. Rosner, "The Structure and Argument of 1 Corinthians," *NTS* 52 (2006): 205–18. More recently, R. E. Ciampa and B. S. Rosner, *The First Letter to the Corinthians*, PNTC (Grand Rapids: Eerdmans, 2010), 21–35. Ciampa and Rosner argue that 1 Corinthians is fundamentally of Jewish character, that purity concerns outweigh concerns for communal harmony, and that the central portion of the letter is structured around the parallel commands to flee from the two chief Gentile vices, sexual immorality and idolatry, and to glorify God (6:18–20; 10:14,31).

[27] Mitchell, *Rhetoric of Reconciliation*, 1.

include "the lordship of Christ, worldwide worship, the eschatological temple, and the glory of God."[28]

I concur that a careful thematic analysis is the best approach to the letter's structure. Aside from the letter's opening (1:1–9) and closing (16:13–24), six sections constitute the letter's body (1:10–4:21; 5:1–7:40; 8:1–11:1; 11:2–14:40; 15:1–58; 16:1–12).[29] In some cases, an overarching theme of a section is apparent, such as the wisdom of God over against human wisdom (1:10–4:21), food sacrificed to idols (8:1–11:1), and the resurrection of the dead (15:1–58). In other sections various topics are put together because they stand in thematic relation to one another in some way, such as Paul's treatment of sex and marriage and related ethical concerns within the community (5:1–7:40), his discussion of various topics that have to do with the church gathered corporately for worship (11:2–14:40), and his instructions concerning the collection for the saints in Jerusalem and travel plans (16:1–12). It would be a mistake, however, to identify only the common element that binds each section together without also giving due consideration to the relationship of sections to one another that demonstrate the core theological concerns that cut across sections and permeate the letter as a whole. Sometimes a concern raised in one section recurs throughout the letter,[30] or a major theme introduced early in the letter receives fuller treatment elsewhere,[31] or a particular overarching theological concern governs two adjoining sections.[32] Thus, in the commentary, I give attention not only to the flow of argument within each section but also provide an analysis of the relationship of major discourse units to one another in order to highlight Paul's overarching pastoral and theological concerns. I concur with Barrett that the "theology that underlies the counsel contained in 1 Corinthians is best studied as it emerges

[28] Ciampa and Rosner, *First Corinthians*, 32–33. Thielman, in his recent New Testament theology, suggests that 1 Corinthians focuses on three critical issues: (1) peace within the church (unity), (2) holiness in the world, and (3) fidelity to the gospel. F. Thielman, *Theology of the New Testament: A Canonical and Synthetic Approach* (Grand Rapids: Zondervan, 2005), 278.

[29] The first five sections are of substantial length. The sixth (16:1–12) is brief and properly belongs adjacent to the letter's formal closing (16:13–24).

[30] In 1:10–4:21 Paul confronts the arrogance of the Corinthians, using the key term "puffed up" (φυσιόω) that recurs throughout the letter (4:6,18–19; 5:2; 8:1; 13:4).

[31] In 2:4 Paul first mentions the Spirit that becomes the emphasis of the ensuing unit (2:6–3:4) that anticipates the more extensive treatment in 12:1–14:40. The key term "spiritual" (πνευματικός) appears in 2:13,15; 3:1; 9:11; 10:3–4; 12:1; 14:1,37; 15:44,46.

[32] I have separated 8:1–11:1 and 11:2–14:40 as distinct sections in their own right but recognize the chief theological concerns that bind the two sections together (see introductory comments on 11:2–14:40). Thiselton (*First Corinthians*, 799) recognizes the relationship, combines the two, and comments, "It is very surprising how readily virtually all commentators appear to ignore the fundamental continuity between the arguments and themes of 8:1–11:1 and the application of these very same themes to issues concerning public or corporate worship in 11:2–14:40."

in the course of the epistle."[33] Nevertheless, I offer the following brief summary of the letter's flow of thought and main themes.

### *(1) The Letter Opening: God's Grace and Faithfulness in Christ (1:1–9)*

The letter opens (1:1–9) in typical Hellenistic letter style with a salutation followed by thanksgiving. Both the salutation and thanksgiving are theologically rich and set the tone for the entire letter. Paul's identity is wrapped up in his calling as an apostle of Jesus Christ through God's will (1:1). As such he was personally commissioned by the risen Lord to preach the gospel (1:17) and held status as the founder and father of the community in Corinth (3:10–11; 4:14–15). The imitation of Paul as Christ's representative is a major emphasis in the letter, captured succinctly in the parallel commands to "imitate me" that conclude two of the major sections (4:16–17; 11:1).[34] Paul's mandate to the Corinthians to imitate her apostle is grounded in his own imitation of Christ and their obligation to live out a calling as God's holy people set apart in Christ (1:2). Throughout the letter Paul shows concern for behavior that is consistent with Christian identity.[35] Paul's collective address of the church in Corinth as "the church of God" stresses their unity and identity as an assembly belonging solely to God, and his reminder that they are only one such assembly among many others (1:2b) anticipates the attention given in the letter to the continuity of Paul's teaching among the churches (4:17; 7:17; 11:16; 14:33b,36; 15:11).

The thanksgiving portion of the letter opening (1:4–9) extols God's grace given in Christ and God's faithfulness to establish his people blameless on the Day of the Lord. Everything is positive with no hint of the problems plaguing the Corinthian church and the confrontation to come in the letter's body. Paul's first concern is praise since God's actions in Christ elicit nothing less than unqualified gratitude and confidence. He and they are both recipients of God's grace, fully equipped to be God's people in the world until the return of Christ. Pervasive references to God and Christ in the letter opening disclose Paul's rich

---

[33] Barrett, *First Corinthians*, 17. While Barrett concedes that Paul's practical advice is grounded in discernable theological principles, he views the letter as a practical discourse "aimed at telling its readers not so much what they ought to think as what they ought to do—or ought not to do." I agree with the first statement but would contest the second, or nuance it differently. That is, Paul *is* concerned to correct their thinking in order to correct their behavior. To offer just one example, at four points in the letter, Paul confronts the Corinthians' way of thinking introduced by the conditional clause, "If anyone thinks," followed by a command or an evaluation of such thinking (see 3:18; 8:2; 11:16; 14:37).

[34] The imitation theme extends beyond the two summary commands and is emphasized throughout the commentary (see e.g., 2:1–5; 9:1–18).

[35] A concern captured succinctly in 5:7a, "Get rid of the old yeast that you may be a new batch without yeast—as you really are."

theological framework that informs the letter as a whole. Key themes touched on in the letter opening are a precursor of things to come.[36]

### *(2) The Wisdom of God: Embracing the Values of the Cross (1:10–4:21)*

The first major section of the letter (1:10–4:21) addresses the problem of Corinthian factions head-on. Divisions in the church, fueled by boasting in men, demonstrate a profound absence of God's wisdom. For this reason Paul confronts their utter failure to grasp and embody the values of the cross in a lengthy and sustained argument that explains the wisdom of God in relation to the message of a crucified Messiah (1:18–25), their calling as believers (1:26–31), his apostolic ministry of proclamation (2:1–5), the revelatory work of the Spirit (2:6–16), and church leadership (3:5–4:13). As their spiritual father, Paul sternly warns the Corinthians concerning their pride and urges them to imitate his manner of life in Christ (4:14–21).

A primary focus of this section is the death of Jesus as the content of gospel preaching (1:17–18), the embodiment of God's wisdom and power to effect salvation (1:23,30), and the paradigm for proper Christian behavior (2:1–5; 4:6–13,16–17).[37] The truly wise person embraces the foolishness of the cross because the wisdom of the world is foolishness to God (3:18–19). The Holy Spirit also occupies a significant place in Paul's exposition of God's wisdom. The Spirit empowers Paul's ministry of proclamation (2:4) and reveals the hidden things of God (2:6–16). The Spirit not only indwells believers individually but also inhabits the church corporately as God's sacred temple (3:16). For this reason Paul sternly warns, "If anyone destroys God's temple, God will destroy him" (3:17). The role of the Spirit in the church and the meaning of "spiritual" (2:13–15), a probable Corinthian catchword, receives a more extensive treatment in chaps. 12–14.[38] The first major argument of the letter employs six citations of Scripture (1:19; 1:31; 2:9; 2:16; 3:19–20).[39]

### *(3) Issues of Purity, Both Corporate and Individual (5:1–7:40)*

In the next major section (5:1–7:40) Paul addresses a variety of topics that are bound together by recurring references to sexual immorality. The only unit

[36] Themes such as calling, holiness, the church, enrichment in gifts (esp. speech and knowledge), the Day of the Lord, God's faithfulness, fellowship, etc. Paul does not touch on every theme that he will develop in the letter, but the letter opening is clearly specific to the Corinthian situation.

[37] Christ's death "for us" is highlighted in 5:7; 6:20; 7:23; 8:11; 11:24–26; and 15:3 ("for our sins"). Paul especially emphasizes Christ's death as a pattern of Christian behavior in community in chaps. 8–14, namely the edification of others rather than self. Paul focuses on the resurrection of Christ as a key component of the gospel in chap. 15.

[38] In addition to chaps. 12–14, references to the Spirit appear elsewhere in 6:11,19, and 7:40. Cf. also "spirit" language in 5:3–5 and 6:17.

[39] All but one citation (2:9) is signaled by the formula, "It is written."

that does not relate directly to this issue is the matter of civil lawsuits (6:1–11),[40] but even here the concluding vice list enumerating those sins that exclude the unrighteous from the kingdom of God includes *porneia* (6:9–11).[41] The community's toleration of an incestuous man demonstrated the ramifications of unchecked arrogance in the church (5:1–13).[42] Equally appalling was the matter of believers taking one another to court before unrighteous judges who have no part in the kingdom of God (6:1–11). Was there no one wise enough in the church in Corinth to handle their disputes (6:5)? Going to the prostitutes is also an egregious breach of Christian identity, a fundamental misuse of the body that violates the believer's vital union with Christ (6:12–20).[43] Sexual union in marriage, however, is the biblical norm and the positive counterpart to sexual immorality (7:1–7). Paul urges the Corinthians to keep their marriages intact, even in the case of a believer married to an unbeliever (7:10–16). The guiding theological principle for both married and unmarried is to be content in one's present calling in life, to "remain as you are" (7:17–24).

Paul's end-time perspective looms large in his responses throughout 5:1–7:40. He calls for the expulsion of the incestuous man, in part, in light of the Day of the Lord (5:5) and reasons that if God's people will participate in the final judgment of the world and angels, then surely they are competent to settle trivial disputes in this life (6:1–3). The present use of the body has a bearing on the life to come since God will raise up believers from the dead bodily as he did the Lord (6:14),[44] and Paul's guiding theological maxim for decision-making in chap. 7, "to remain as you are" (7:17–24), derives to some extent from the reality that "this world in its present form is passing away" (7:31).

The death of Jesus also figures prominently in the arguments of 5:1–7:40. In dealing with the incestuous offender Paul instructs the Corinthians, on the analogy of the Passover, to purge sin from the community and become what they already are, that is, an unleavened lump of dough "for Christ, our Passover lamb, has been sacrificed" (5:7b). Furthermore, the theological basis for honoring God with the body and serving him faithfully in one's present calling has to do with "belonging" to him, captured in the repeated phrase, "You were bought at a price" (6:20; 7:23).

---

[40] Some, however, have linked the lawsuits in 6:1–11 with the incident of incest in 5:1–13. See discussion on 6:1–11.

[41] The Greek term πορνεία (sexual immorality) occurs in every unit in 5:1–7:40 (5:1; 6:13,18; 7:2). The verb form πορνεύω occurs in 6:18.

[42] The use of the term φυσιόω (puffed up) in 5:2 carries over from the previous section (4:6,18–19).

[43] The body as both individual and corporate (church as Christ's body) receives further emphasis in chap. 12. Cf. also the emphasis on the church as God's Spirit-indwelt temple in 3:16–17.

[44] The first mention of the resurrection of the body from the dead in 6:14 anticipates the comprehensive treatment of this topic in chap. 15.

### *(4) The Freedom of the Gospel: Loving God and Loving One's Neighbor (8:1–11:1)*

In 8:1–11:1 Paul again takes up a lengthy discussion of one main topic. The subject is food sacrificed to idols, but the theological issues at stake include Christian freedom, the priority of love, and the spiritual peril of idolatry. The thematic statement of 8:1b sets the agenda, "Knowledge puffs up, but love builds up."[45] Paul concurs that the core Christian belief in only one God effectively rules out that an idol is anything in the world (8:4–6), but love for one's fellow believer with a weak conscience, for whom Christ died, takes priority over knowledge (8:7–13). Food may be neutral in terms of one's relationship to God (8:8), but idol food is not harmless when there are clear idolatrous associations (8:10; 10:14–22). Paul himself is the example of giving up one's "rights" for the cause of the gospel (9:1–23). To this end Paul disciplines himself (9:24–27). The Corinthians should follow suit and learn from their spiritual predecessors, the Israelites, who enjoyed great spiritual privileges yet perished in the wilderness for their disobedience (10:1–13). Just as sexual immorality is incompatible with union with Christ (6:15–17) so also believers cannot participation in the table of demons and the table of the Lord (10:20–21). Just as Paul warned the Corinthians in 6:18–20 to flee sexual immorality and to glorify God in their bodies, here too he implores them to flee idolatry (10:14) and to do all things for the glory of God (10:33).[46] The most apparent core theological convictions that underly Paul's response to the issue of idol food is complete allegiance to the one true God and loving one's neighbor as oneself.[47] Believers who deal with idols arouse the Lord's jealousy (10:22), and the gospel demands seeking the welfare of others. In a nutshell, to live Christianly is to do everything for the good of others and for the glory of God (10:23–11:1). The gospel defines and sets the boundaries of Christian freedom. Paul concludes this section by repeating the exhortation to imitate his example as he imitates Christ (11:1; cf. 4:16–17).

### *(5) Worship in Community (11:2–14:40)*

All topics in the next section have to do with the church assembled for worship. The themes of behaving in consideration of others and bringing glory to God, prominent in the previous section, carry forward in 11:2–14:40. The hierarchical relationship that exists between husbands and wives, symbolized

[45] Yet another use of the verb φυσιόω indicating the core problem of arrogance (cf. 4:6,18–19; 5:2).

[46] The proverbial, "Everything is permissible," appears in both sections (6:12; 10:23).

[47] Cf. the teaching of Jesus in Matt 22:36–40 and par., known as the "double love command." Paul quotes neither from Deut 6 or Lev 19 but the theological principle is obvious. Chapter 8 refers to love for God (8:3) and the mention of "one God" (8:4–6) echoes the Shema of Deut 6. Doing what is best for others is the epitome of love for one's neighbor. See further discussion in the commentary on 8:1–11:1.

by the attire of both when praying and prophesying, reflects the relationship between God and Christ and the order of creation (11:3,8–9). Each brings glory to another. "A man ought not to cover his head, since he is the image and glory of God; but the woman is the glory of man" (11:7). However, in the Lord and according to the design of creation since the first human couple, a fundamental interdependence exists between men and women (11:11–12).

Although Paul praises the Corinthians for holding fast to the traditions he handed down to them (11:2), he cannot praise them for their appalling behavior at the Lord's Supper (11:17–34). The actions of the rich toward the poor show contempt for the church of God (11:21–22) and demonstrate a profound lack of insight into the significance of the meal that proclaims the death of Jesus (11:23–26). Presently, they are eating and drinking judgment to themselves (11:27–34).

In 12:1–14:40 Paul gives an extended discussion of the things pertaining to the Spirit in a reprise and expansion of previous themes.[48] All believers are "spiritual" (12:1–3), and the manifestations of the Spirit are given for the common good (12:7). The body of Christ is composed of individually gifted members (12:12–31). The controlling principle for the exercise of spiritual gifts is the more excellent way of love (13:1–13). Paul makes an extended case for prophecy over uninterpreted tongues since only the former edifies the church (14:1–19) and provides opportunity for the conversion of unbelievers (14:20–25). Those who are truly "spiritual" will acknowledge and live by the principle of doing all things decently and in order for the edification of all (14:26–40).

In addition to the themes of God's glory, the edification of others, the manifestations of the Spirit, and ordered worship, Paul broaches the theme of unity again as he addresses factious behavior in each unit of this section. In 11:16 he appeals to the widespread practice of the churches regarding head coverings for those who might be contentious over this issue (11:16). First Corinthians 11:18 specifically mentions their divisions, and throughout chaps. 12–14 unity is emphasized as the chief purpose of spiritual gifts. Ordered and edifying worship brings glory to God.

#### *(6) Bodily Resurrection: Certainty, Possibility, and Necessity (15:1–58)*

The last major discourse of the letter is the most comprehensive treatment anywhere in Scripture of the resurrection of the dead (15:1–58). Paul had learned, presumably by way of oral report, that some in Corinth were denying the resurrection of the dead (15:12). He responds by showing that to deny the resurrection of the dead generally is to deny the resurrection of Christ specifically, which amounts to a rejection of a core tenet of the gospel, namely, the uniform apostolic testimony that Christ was raised from the dead (15:1–11). If

[48] Namely, the revelatory work of the Spirit (2:6–16), believers as members of Christ's body (6:15), and the edifying purpose of spiritual gifts (8:1).

Christ has not been raised from the dead, then serious theological (15:12–19) and practical (15:29–34) consequences ensue. But Christ has, in fact, been raised from the dead, which has set in motion a sequence of events, including the future resurrection of all believers and the ultimate subjugation of all things to God the Father so that God might be all in all (15:20–28). In 15:35–49 Paul responds to objections regarding the possibility of bodily resurrection and explains that the resurrection body will be imperishable, glorious, and powerful, patterned after the resurrection body of Jesus. The transformation of our present earthly bodies is necessary in order to enter the imperishable kingdom of God (15:50–53). Even though death still possesses a deadly sting, Paul gives thanks unto God who gives victory over death in Christ (15:54–57). Since there is still much work to be done in this present life, however, Paul concludes with an exhortation to abound confidently in the Lord's work (15:58).

Eschatology is the most apparent theological contribution of chap. 15, but as the brief apocalyptic narrative of 15:20–28 shows, the doctrine of last things is vast in scope, taking into account the all-encompassing story of God's redemptive plan for the world from the first Adam, through whom sin and death entered the word, to Christ, the last Adam, who died for our sins and triumphed over death itself in his resurrection. The full humanity of Christ is a core presupposition of Paul's argument in this chapter (15:13,16,21). The hope of resurrection impinges profoundly on present Christian service (15:58).

### *(7) The Continuing Work of the Gospel (16:1–24)*

Paul concludes the letter by addressing matters of practical concern (16:1–12) and giving final exhortations, commendations, and greetings (16:13–24). Paul frequently mentions travel plans and co-workers in his letters as a means of keeping other churches informed of the ongoing work of the gospel. In the formal letter closing (16:13–24), Paul exhorts the Corinthians one final time to do everything in love (16:14) and reminds them of his love for all of them (16:24) but pronounces a curse on anyone who does not love the Lord (16:22). The letter's concluding chapter is no less significant theologically than the rest of the letter. We know from other passages in Paul's writings of the theological motivations for the Jerusalem offering (16:1–4), and Paul's interaction with co-workers demonstrates his commitment to partnership in ministry. Others carry out the work of the Lord with integrity and are worthy of imitation (16:10,15–18). Paul always opens his letters with a grace greeting and closes with a grace benediction. From beginning to end, the gospel is about grace.

## OUTLINE OF THE LETTER

I. Letter Opening
  1. Salutation (1:1–3)
  2. Thanksgiving (1:4–9)

II. God's Wisdom for a Divided Church (1:10–4:21)
  1. An Appeal for Unity in the Light of Corinthian Factions (1:10–17)
  2. The Wisdom of God and the Cross (1:18–2:5)
    (1) The Wisdom of God and a Crucified Messiah (1:18–25)
    (2) The Wisdom of God and the Corinthians' Calling (1:26–31)
    (3) The Wisdom of God and Paul's Ministry in Corinth (2:1–5)
  3. The Wisdom of God and the Spirit (2:6–3:4)
    (1) Wisdom as Revealed by the Spirit (2:6–16)
    (2) Application: Factions Demonstrate a Lack of God's Wisdom (3:1–4)
  4. The Wisdom of God and His Servants (3:5–4:13)
    (1) The Church, Its Leaders, and God's Fiery Test (3:5–17)
    (2) The Wisdom of God vs. the Wisdom of the World (Reprise) (3:18–23)
    (3) Faithfulness as the Criterion of Judgment (4:1–5)
    (4) Application: God's Servants as Paradigms of the Cross (4:6–13)
  5. Paul's Warning and Appeal as Their Spiritual Father (4:14–21)

III. Sexual Immorality, the Civil Courts, and Issues of Marriage and Singleness (5:1–7:40)
  1. Directives to the Church Regarding an Incestuous Man (5:1–13)
  2. The Shame of the Righteous Taking Disputes Before the Unrighteous (6:1–11)
  3. The Sanctity of the Body (6:12–20)
  4. Issues of Marriage and Singleness (7:1–40)
    (1) General Principles for the Married: Maintain Sexual Relations (7:1–7)
    (2) Various Situations: Both Unmarried and Married (7:8–16)
    (3) The Guiding Theological Principle: "Remain as You Are" (7:17–24)
    (4) Concerning the Virgins (7:25–40)

IV. Christian Freedom, the Priority of Love, and the Peril of Idolatry (8:1–11:1)
  1. The Priority of Love over Knowledge (8:1–13)
  2. Paul's Apostolic Rights (9:1–12a)
  3. Giving Up Rights for the Sake of the Gospel (9:12b–23)
  4. Application and Transition: Run to Win! (9:24–27)

5. The Negative Example of Israel in the Wilderness (10:1–13)
6. Do Not Provoke the Lord to Jealousy—Flee Idolatry! (10:14–22)
7. Summary and Application: Do All for the Good of Others and the Glory of God (10:23–11:1)

V. The Church Gathered for Worship (11:2–14:40)
1. Husbands and Wives and the Glory of God (11:2–16)
2. Disorder and Divisions at the Lord's Table (11:17–34)
   (1) Paul's Sharp Rebuke for Their Behavior at the So-Called Lord's Supper (11:17–22)
   (2) The Received Tradition of the Lord's Supper (11:23–26)
   (3) Eating and Drinking Unworthily (11:27–34)
3. The Manifestation of the Spirit for the Common Good (12:1–31)
   (1) Confession of Jesus as Lord by the Spirit (12:1–3)
   (2) The Distribution of Gifts by the One and the Same Spirit (12:4–11)
   (3) One Body, Many Members (12:12–31)
4. Controlling Principle of Love (13:1–13)
   (1) Love: The More Excellent Way (13:1–3)
   (2) What Love Does and Does Not Do (13:4–7)
   (3) Love's Permanence (13:8–13)
5. Do All Things for the Edification of the Church (14:1–40)
   (1) The Case for Prophecy over Uninterpreted Tongues (14:1–5)
   (2) The Vital Link between Intelligibility and Edification (14:6–19)
   (3) The Negative Effect of Tongues on Unbelievers (14:20–25)
   (4) Do All Things Decently and in Order (14:26–40)

VI. The Resurrection of the Dead (15:1–58)
1. The Centrality of the Resurrection to the Gospel (15:1–11)
2. The Consequences of No Resurrection, Part 1 (15:12–19)
3. The Defeat of Death So That God Might Be All in All (15:20–28)
4. The Consequences of No Resurrection, Part 2 (15:29–34)
5. The Nature of the Resurrection Body (15:35–49)
6. The Necessity of Transformation and Death's Final Defeat (15:50–58)

VII. The Collection for the Saints in Jerusalem and Travel Plans (16:1–12)
1. The Collection for the Jerusalem Saints (16:1–4)
2. Travel Plans (Paul, Timothy, Apollos) (16:5–12)

VIII. Letter Closing (16:13–24)
1. General Exhortations (16:13–14)
2. Commendation of the Household of Stephanas and Others (16:15–18)
3. Greetings (16:19–20)
4. Paul's Greeting and Conclusion: Warning and Affirmation of Love (16:21–24)

## SECTION OUTLINE

I. Letter Opening
   1. Salutation (1:1–3)
   2. Thanksgiving (1:4–9)

## I. LETTER OPENING (1:1–9)

Letters in the first century typically opened with a salutation followed by a prayer or thanksgiving.[1] The salutation identified the sender and recipient of the letter followed by a brief greeting. Paul's letter introductions generally follow this pattern,[2] but the content is always uniquely Christian. In this letter, for example, Paul writes as an apostle of Jesus Christ to the church of God in Corinth and extends greetings of grace and peace from God and Christ (1:1–3). Furthermore, in contrast to the routine prayer or thanksgiving for good health or prosperity typical of secular letters of the time, Paul offers an expansive thanksgiving for the grace of God given in Christ (1:4–8) and extols the faithfulness of God, who called them into fellowship with his Son (1:9).

One of the outstanding features of this particular thanksgiving is the remarkable optimism that precedes Paul's response to divisions in the church (1:10–4:21), an incident of egregious immorality (5:1–13), civil litigation before the unrighteous (6:1–11), libertine attitudes toward sexual immorality and idolatry (6:12–20; 8:1–11:1), a deficient understanding of the function of spiritual gifts in building up the church (12:1–14:40), and the denial by some of the resurrection of the dead (15:12). Throughout the letter Paul repeatedly mentions the poisonous sin of pride that had gripped the community.[3] Yet, in spite of their failures, Paul offers continual thanks to God for them (1:4), their enrichment in Christ (1:5–6), and their sufficient endowment of spiritual gifts (1:7), and he expresses confidence that God will establish them blameless in the Day of the Lord (1:8). How are we to reconcile Paul's favorable attitude with the wide-ranging problems that needed correction?

---

[1] See F. X. J. Exler, *The Form of the Ancient Greek Letter of the Epistolary Papyri* (Washington: Catholic University of America, 1923), 60–66; J. L. White, *Light from Ancient Letters*, FF (Philadelphia: Fortress, 1986), 198–200; S. K. Stowers, *Letter-Writing in Greco-Roman Antiquity* (Philadelphia: Westminster, 1986).

[2] The salutation-thanksgiving pattern appears in 1 and 2 Thessalonians, Romans, Philippians, and Colossians, as well as Paul's letters to individuals (see 2 Tim 1:1–7). The thanksgiving stanza is absent in Galatians due to Paul's consternation over their departure from the truth of the gospel (Gal 1:6–10). In 2 Corinthians, the language of blessing and encouragement replaces thanksgiving (2 Cor 1:3–7). Ephesians includes both doxology (Eph 1:3–14) and thanksgiving (Eph 1:15–23).

[3] Captured especially by the repetition of the verb φυσιόω, meaning "to puff up," in 4:6,18–19; 5:2; 8:1; and 13:4. Cf. also "boasting" language in 1:29,31; 3:21; 4:7.

Some suggest Paul's affirmative stance in the letter opening serves a rhetorical purpose to establish good will between the author (Paul) and the recipients (the church at Corinth) while at the same time encapsulating the main themes of the letter.[4] Certainly Paul accomplishes both, yet he does so sincerely with a pastoral purpose without irony or flattery.[5] He does not commend the Corinthians directly for their faith and love as he does other churches[6] but rather "boasts" for what God has done for them in Christ (cf. 1:31).[7] The theological focus of the letter opening, coalescing around the twin themes of God's grace (1:4–8) and God's faithfulness (1:9), explains Paul's gratitude and confidence.

## 1. Salutation (1:1–3)

**1Paul, called to be an apostle of Christ Jesus by the will of God, and our brother Sosthenes,**

**2To the church of God in Corinth, to those sanctified in Christ Jesus and called to be holy, together with all those everywhere who call on the name of our Lord Jesus Christ—their Lord and ours:**

**3Grace and peace to you from God our Father and the Lord Jesus Christ.**

All letters attributed to Paul begin with a three-part structure of sender, recipient, and greetings. Paul often adds a further descriptor to his name, such

---

[4] So B. Witherington, *Conflict and Community in Corinth: A Socio-Rhetorical Commentary* (Grand Rapids: Eerdmans, 1994), 87; R. F. Collins, *First Corinthians*, SP (Collegeville, MN: Liturgical Press, 1999), 58.

[5] R. Ciampa and B. Rosner note that Paul's thanksgivings are only loosely comparable to the *exordium* of ancient rhetoric that function to secure the goodwill of the recipients. Furthermore, since Paul's thanksgiving is directed toward God "to do so in any way other than sincerely would be to mock him" (*The First Letter to the Corinthians*, PNTC [Grand Rapids: Eerdmans, 2010], 61). See also P. T. O'Brien, *Introductory Thanksgivings in the Letters of Paul* (Leiden: Brill, 1977), 113–15; A. C. Thiselton, *The First Epistle to the Corinthians: A Commentary on the Greek Text*, NIGTC (Grand Rapids: Eerdmans, 2000), 94; D. E. Garland, *1 Corinthians*, BECNT (Grand Rapids: Baker, 2003), 31.

[6] A prime example is the church at Thessalonica, which excelled in faith, love, and hope in spite of severe suffering. The Thessalonian believers became examples to others and possessed a faith renowned throughout the region (1 Thess 1:3,6–9). Paul affirmed the Thessalonians for becoming "imitators of us and of the Lord" (1 Thess 1:6). By way of contrast, he exhorts the Corinthians twice to "become imitators of me" (4:16; 11:2). See also Phil 1:5; Col 1:4; 1 Thess 1:3,6–8; 2 Thess 1:3–4; Phlm 5,7. We should note, however, that Paul does praise the Corinthians in 11:2 "for remembering me in everything and for holding to the teachings, just as I passed them on to you." See also 2 Cor 8:7, "But just as you excel in everything—in faith, in speech, in knowledge, in complete earnestness and in your love for us—see that you also excel in this grace of giving."

[7] So Ciampa and Rosner, *First Corinthians*, 62. Paul uses the passive voice five times when describing God's action. The forms are ἡγιασμένοις (1:2), δοθείσῃ (1:4), ἐπλουτίσθητε (1:5), ἐβεβαιώθη (1:6), and ἐκλήθητε (1:9). The first two are passive participles, and the remaining three are verb forms. The Corinthians have been set apart (1:2), grace was given (1:4), they were enriched (1:5), the testimony of Christ was confirmed (1:6), and they were called into fellowship with God's Son (1:9).

as apostle[8] or servant,[9] but not always.[10] Slight variations also occur in the description of the recipients and the manner of greeting.[11] Additionally, Paul sometimes expands on any one of the three standard components. Romans 1:2–7, for example, develops the "gospel of God" theme following the identification of the sender. Galatians 1:3 extends the greeting of grace and peace, focusing on Christ's saving work. In 1 Cor 1:2 Paul expands on the recipients more than in any other of his letters to the churches (1:2).[12] Other noteworthy adaptations to the salutation in 1 Corinthians include the epithet "called apostle," found elsewhere only in Rom 1:1, and the mention of Sosthenes as the co-sender of the letter. The differences and elaborations among the salutations in Paul's letters is best explained by the occasional nature of his correspondence with the churches.[13]

**1:1** By identifying himself as a called apostle through the will of God, Paul emphasizes that his apostolic call was a matter entirely of God's choice. Similarly, Gal 1:11–17 accentuates the revelatory nature of Paul's conversion and his summons to preach Christ among the Gentiles,[14] that his call was according to God's purpose, even before birth, like the call of the Old Testament prophets.[15] Further insight into Paul's conversion and call appears in his autobiographical accounts in Phil 3:3–17 and 1 Tim 1:12–16 as well as Luke's accounts in the book of Acts.[16] At various points in the letter Paul mentions the

---

[8] See also Rom 1:1,2; 2 Cor 1:1; Gal 1:1; Eph 1:1; Col 1:1; 1 Tim 1:1; 2 Tim 1:1.

[9] Phil 1:1; Rom 1:1; Titus 1:1.

[10] 2 Thess 1:1; 2 Thess 1:1.

[11] In the Thessalonian correspondence, for example, Paul writes to "the church of the Thessalonians in God the Father and the Lord Jesus Christ," but here to "the church of God in Corinth." The most uniform part of the salutation in Paul's letters is the greeting. In 1 and 2 Timothy he adds "mercy" to the usual "grace and peace."

[12] The salutation in Romans is longer, but Collins (*First Corinthians*, 41) notes that the salutation in 1 Corinthians as a whole "is the most lavish among the letters written by Paul to communities he personally evangelized."

[13] So also G. D. Fee, "In each case the elaborations reflect, either directly or subtly, many of the concerns about to be raised in the letter itself. Even as he formally addresses the church in the salutation, Paul's mind is already at work on the critical behavioral and theological issues at hand" (*The First Epistle to the Corinthians*, NICNT [Grand Rapids: Eerdmans, 1987], 28).

[14] Gal 1:12, "I did not receive it from any man, nor was I taught it; rather I received it by revelation from Jesus Christ." The essence of the gospel, that Jesus was the Messiah, was by revelation. In terms of received traditions, Paul passed on what was handed down to him by others (see 15:1–4; see also the discussion on 11:23, "For I received from the Lord what I also passed on to you."). Garland (*1 Corinthians*, 25) notes that Paul not only passed on traditions about Jesus, he continued "to interpret for them the meaning of these traditions (7:10–16) as one who has received mercy from God to be a trustworthy interpreter (7:25), guided by the Spirit of God (7:40), and having insights into the mystery of God (2:7–13; Eph 3:5) and the mind of Christ (2:16)."

[15] See Isa 6:8–9; 49:1–5; Jer 1:5; Amos 7:14–15. Paul mentions his apostolic commission in 1 Cor 1:17, that Christ sent him to preach the gospel. In 9:16 he professes his compulsion to preach, "Woe to me if I do not preach the gospel!"

[16] Acts 9:1–20; 22:1–21; 26:2–23.

fruit of his apostolic labors (see 1:17; 3:6; 4:15; 9:1–2).[17] Because he formerly persecuted the church Paul deemed himself unworthy of his calling and considered himself to be the least of the apostles; yet, by God's grace he claimed, "I worked harder than all of them" (15:9–11; cf. also 3:10).

Since Paul does not always include his apostolic credentials in the salutation of other letters,[18] why does he do so here? Fee detects evidence of a crisis between Paul and the Corinthians and thinks he intends to defend his apostleship and re-establish his authority.[19] Apostleship possesses inherent authority by virtue of the divine call, and we cannot rule out the possibility that Paul's authority was in question among some in Corinth.[20] Thiselton, however, draws attention to another perspective in the history of interpretation, namely, that apostles not only uniquely bear witness to Christ's death and resurrection but also endure the practical experience of suffering as a necessary sign of apostleship.[21] Paul patterned his life and preaching according to a crucified Messiah (2:1–5; 4:6–13), and he urged others to follow his example (4:16; 11:1; see also 9:1–18). The Corinthians, on the other hand, were boasting in men, as the lengthy exposition in 1:10–4:21 demonstrates. Perhaps they expected Paul to "boast" like the great public speakers of the day in order to elevate his worldly status, but he would have none of it.[22] Such ostentatious motives would have been completely out of line for one commissioned by a crucified Messiah.

Sosthenes, the co-sender of the letter,[23] may be the "synagogue ruler" mentioned in Acts 18:17, who was beaten by the Jews when the Roman proconsul

[17] Regarding Paul's Gentile mission see also Acts 9:15; 22:21; 26:17; Rom 1:1–5; 11:13; Gal 2:7; 2 Cor 10:13–16. For the founding of the church in Corinth see Acts 18:1–11; also 3:10; 4:14–21; 9:1–5; 2 Cor 3:2–3; 10:13–14; 12:12.

[18] E.g., Philippians and the Thessalonian correspondence.

[19] Fee, *First Corinthians*, 28. "The Corinthians are a church at odds with their founder: they are judging him (4:1–5) and examining him as to his apostleship (9:1–23). Later (4:15; 9:1–2) he will present further evidence for his apostleship (he founded the church; he saw the Risen Lord), but because this church is questioning that apostleship, he begins by asserting its divine origins." Fee's commentary is a thoroughgoing treatment of 1 Corinthians as an apologetic letter. More recent commentators question whether or not this is the case, suggesting that such a view over-reads the situation in light of 2 Corinthians. Witherington (*Conflict and Community*, 78–79) notes, "We are not yet at the stage where Paul believes that his apostolic authority is in serious question and must be defended at length. He would hardly argue for the Corinthians to imitate him and assume (chap. 9) that his apostolic example could spur them to right conduct if he believed he was dealing with a crisis of apostolic authority. The situation is markedly different when 2 Corinthians is written, which helps to explain its more strident tone."

[20] So Ciampa and Rosner (*First Corinthians*, 54), "In 1 Corinthians, as in Galatians, it functions to bolster his standing in a community where at least some were questioning his authority."

[21] Thiselton (*First Corinthians*, 66) notes that this view extends from the patristic era (Chrysostom, AD 390) to the present time, calls attention to God's grace (1 Cor 15:9–10), and is associated with lowliness (1 Cor 4:9).

[22] See comments on 1:17.

[23] The phenomenon of a co-sender of a letter is rare in antiquity outside of Paul. See G. J. Bahr, "Paul and Letter Writing in the First Century," *CBQ* 28 (1966): 476–77; E. R. Richards, *The Secretary in the Letters of Paul*, WUNT 2:42 (Tübingen: Mohr, 1992), 47n138. The Greek reads

Gallio refused to hear their complaint against Paul.[24] If this is the same person, then presumably he was converted to Christ and was with Paul in Ephesus at the time of the writing of 1 Corinthians. Since the name Sosthenes occurs only twice in the New Testament, we know nothing further about him. Apparently, he was well-known to the Corinthians and co-labored in ministry with Paul in some way. It is uncertain if he participated in some way in the writing of the letter, although not out of the question.[25] In Romans, the name of Paul's scribe, Tertius, appears at the end of the letter (Rom 16:22) rather than at the beginning as the co-sender. The mention of a co-sender highlights the collaborative nature of Paul's ministry.[26]

**1:2** Paul elaborates more on the recipients of this letter, the church of God in Corinth, than he does in any of his other letters. His description of the believers in Corinth is replete with Old Testament imagery and phrases, and he addresses the church as a whole without any mention of its factions or leaders.[27] In addition to the usual identification of the church's location, Paul describes the recipients as "those sanctified in Christ Jesus[28] and called to be holy,[29] together with all those everywhere who call on the name of our Lord

---

literally, "Sosthenes, the brother" (Σωσθένης ὁ ἀδελφὸς). It is possible that "brother" is used in a technical sense here designating an official leadership role, or it may only indicate that he was well-known among the Corinthians. Apollos is also designated as "the brother" in 16:12, and in 16:20, "all the brothers" send greetings.

[24] Luke does not tell us why the Jews turned on Sosthenes. Perhaps the reason is simple; he took Paul's side!

[25] It is possible that Sosthenes was Paul's scribe for the writing of 1 Corinthians. See M. Prior, *Paul the Letter Writer*, JSNTSup 23 (Sheffield: JSOT Press, 1989). J. Murphy-O'Connor ("Co-Authorship in the Corinthian Correspondence," *RB* 100 [1993]: 562–79) thinks that Sosthenes occupied some role in writing the letter. Recently, Oxford University Press has republished a one volume collection of sixteen prior articles by Murphy-O'Connor with up-to-date postscript responses by the author to the subsequent scholarly discussion per the views presented in the original articles. See J. Murphy-O'Connor, *Keys to First Corinthians: Revisiting the Major Issues* (Oxford: Oxford University Press, 2009).

[26] On Paul's network of ministry relationships see the discussion on 16:1–24.

[27] So also Fee, *First Corinthians*, 32. Collins (*First Corinthians*, 49) comments that "Paul describes the church as a gathering. He describes it in biblical terms as God's very own. He describes it as one and many. He describes it as a community that is related to other communities that similarly confess the name of the Lord Jesus Christ."

[28] The perfect passive participle, ἡγιασμένοις, indicates a completed action with ongoing results. They have been and are "set apart" in Christ. Fee (*First Corinthians*, 32n20) thinks the Greek construct is an instrumental dative, meaning set apart "by Christ." The broader context, however, suggests that the NIV rendering is correct. As Thiselton (*First Corinthians*, 76) explains, "Elsewhere Paul places strong theological emphasis on being-in-Christ as a concept of corporate status which provides the ground for Christian life and destiny." The noun "sanctification" (ἁγιασμός) appears in 1:30 and the verb "to sanctify" (ἁγιάζω) in 6:11. In Pauline usage these instances of "sanctification" refer to conversion rather than to the progress of the Christian life. Believers are "set apart" for God's purposes at conversion. The Christian life flows from the prior action of having been set apart. See also Rom 15:16 and Paul's use "sanctification" language in his description of his apostolic ministry.

[29] The NIV rendering of the Greek κλητοῖς ἁγίοις, "called to be holy," should not be read as though Paul is asserting here that holiness is something to which the Corinthians and other

Jesus Christ." This last phrase does not identify other co-senders (the whole church) or a second group of recipients to whom the letter was written.[30] Paul simply asserts that the Corinthians are God's holy people by calling, as are all other believers everywhere who call on the name of the Lord. The statement that Jesus is both "their Lord and ours,"[31] reminds the Corinthians of their solidarity with other believers and prepares the way for the exhortation to unity in 1:10. To "call on the name of the Lord" is an Old Testament expression for the worship of Yahweh as the God of Israel, which in the New Testament context refers to an acknowledgement of the Lordship of Christ, the confession of all believers.[32] In using the term Lord with reference to Jesus, "Paul acknowledges along with the rest of early Christians that the risen Christ is on a par with Yahweh of the OT."[33]

In classical Greek the word translated "church" denoted a political assembly.[34] In the LXX the term describes the people of Israel.[35] The New Testament usage emphasizes the idea of the people of God gathered in the Lord's presence.[36] Here, Paul speaks of the church "of God," that is, an assembly of believers that is God's sole possession (cf. 3:9). The use of the term translated "set apart" occurs only here in a Pauline greeting.[37] This, along with the designation "holy ones,"[38] reflects the Old Testament background of God's people

---

believers should aspire. Clearly they should, but already they have been set apart and are "holy ones," just as Paul is an apostle by calling. The NASB more accurately translates the phrase, "saints by calling," and the HCSB, "called as saints." The juxtaposition of the singular (church) and the plural (called saints, those who have been sanctified) emphasizes the unity of the church. Ciampa and Rosner (*First Corinthians*, 55) explain, "By referring first to the church as a whole and then collectively Paul excludes any form of individualism and one-upmanship."

[30] An interpretation that would rest on whether or not σὺν πᾶσιν modifies Παῦλος καὶ Σωσθένης, or τῇ ἐκκλησίᾳ, or κλητοῖς ἁγίοις. The phrase could be read this way, but everything in this letter points to local situations in Corinth. Nothing suggests a general audience.

[31] It is also possible that αὐτῶν καὶ ἡμῶν modifies "place," which is the most natural reading of the Greek text (so Witherington, *Conflict and Community*, 80), but translations uniformly render the phrase as modifying Lord, as does the NIV. Jesus is "their Lord and ours."

[32] Acts 9:14,21; Rom 10:12–13; 1 Cor 12:3; Phil 2:1–11; 2 Tim 2:22.

[33] J. A. Fitzmyer, *First Corinthians: A New Translation with Introduction and Commentary*, AB 32 (New Haven and London: Yale University Press, 2008), 127.

[34] The term carries this sense in the New Testament in Acts 19:32,39–40. Paul uses ἐκκλησία (church) to describe a local gathering of believers. The term is especially frequent in 1 Corinthians, occurring twenty-two times (1 Cor 1:2; 4:17; 6:4; 7:17; 10:32; 11:16,18,22; 12:28; 14:4–5,12,19,23,28,33–35; 15:9; 16:1,19).

[35] A search on Accordance Bible Software indicates that the term ἐκκλησία occurs 100 times in the LXX, including the Apocryphal books Sirach, Judith, and Maccabees. For representative uses of the term see Deut 4:10; 9:10; 18:16; 23:2–4,9; 31:30; Josh 8:35; Judg 20:2; 21:5. The term does not always refer to the assembly of God's people (see Ps 26:5 [LXX 25:5], which speaks of the "assembly of evildoers").

[36] So Thiselton, *First Corinthians*, 75. See especially 1 Cor 11:18, "When you gather together in assembly" (NIV, "When you come together as a church").

[37] Gk. ἁγιάζω. For other uses of the verb in 1 Corinthians see 6:14; 7:14.

[38] Gk. ὁι ἅγιοι.

as holy, that is, set apart unto the Lord's purposes.[39] Likewise, the notion of calling on the name of the Lord has Old Testament roots.[40] Furthermore, Paul locates the Corinthians with other believers "everywhere," which may be a reference to the world-wide worship of God spreading throughout the world in the Gentile mission.[41]

That Paul strikes such a universal tone in his elaboration on the recipients is no accident in light of the self-sufficiency that plagued the Corinthian church. His intent is to strike at the independent spirit among those in Corinth who wanted to go their own way. He reminds them that they are under the Lordship of Jesus Christ and they exist in relation to other churches. Throughout the letter Paul gives instructions with reference to the commonly held teachings of all the churches.[42] What he says to the Corinthians he says to all. They are part of a much larger picture. Paul speaks collectively to the church of God in Corinth, not to any one house church, and he reminds them that they are only one assembly of believers among many.

**1:3** Paul always extended greetings of grace and peace to his readers,[43] even in his letter to the Galatians when he was quite displeased with what was occurring there (Gal 1:6–9).[44] The terms "grace" and "peace" are theologically significant and appropriate to those who have received the gospel. Grace

---

[39] Ciampa and Rosner (*1 Corinthians*, 56) comment, "The term derives from Exodus 19:5–6, where Israel is called 'a holy nation' set apart by God for himself through the events of the exodus (cf. Deut 7:6; 26:19; Jer 2:3). In later writings it was used more narrowly to refer to the elect within Israel who were destined to share in the blessings of the messianic kingdom (Dan. 7:18–27; *Psalms of Solomon* 17)." Hays likewise observes that "when Paul applies this language to the Corinthians, he is echoing God's call to Israel." R. B. Hays, *First Corinthians* (Louisville: John Knox, 1997), 16. Cf. Lev 19:1–2.

[40] Ps 98:6; Joel 2:28–32; 3:5; Acts 2:21; Rom 10:13. In the Old Testament the "name" refers to one's character (Exod 3:13–14) and to call on the name of the Lord is "to commit oneself in trust to the one whose nature and character have been disclosed as worthy of this trust" (Thiselton, *First Corinthians*, 78–79).

[41] See especially Ciampa and Rosner (*1 Corinthians*, 57), who think that the phrase "in every place" echoes Mal 1:11 and evokes a significant scriptural tradition going back to Deuteronomy, which contains repeated references to the place where the Lord would have people call on his name (LXX Deut 12:11,21,26; 14:23–24; 16:2,6; 17:8; 26:2). In the Old Testament context the place was Jerusalem, but Paul now envisions believers calling on the name of the Lord in every place (see 2 Cor 2:14; 1 Thess 1:8; 1 Tim 2:8). See also M. M. Mitchell, *Paul and the Rhetoric of Reconciliation: An Exegetical Investigation of the Language and Composition of 1 Corinthians* (Louisville: WJK, 1991), 194 n 42.

[42] See 4:17; 7:17; 11:16; 14:33–36; 15:1–11. Thiselton (*1 Corinthians*, 75) comments, "Whether a given local group genuinely reflects Christ and the apostolic gospel is not left to be determined by criteria internal to the group in question, but also relates to translocal counterchecks such as the apostles, Paul's fellow workers, and creeds, practices, and traditions followed in all the churches."

[43] The typical Hellenistic letter began with χαίρειν, "greetings" (cf. Acts 15:23; Jas 1:1). Paul used the related term, χάρις, "grace." Paul also concludes all of his letters with a grace benediction.

[44] In 1 and 2 Timothy the greeting is "grace, mercy, and peace" (1 Tim 1:2; 2 Tim 1:2; cf. 1 Pet 1:2; 2 Pet 1:2; 3 John 3; Rev 1:4).

indicates God's unmerited favor[45] and peace flows from grace, presupposing a former state of rebellion.[46] The combination of grace and peace may echo the blessing uttered by the sons of Aaron over the Israelites in Num 6:24–26.[47] Porter contends that since there is little evidence of superscriptions with "peace" in Hellenistic Jewish letters of the time, "Paul has consciously created his own superscription to emphasize the comprehensive work of God: it is one of gracious giving and forgiveness for previous hostility."[48]

Paul's greeting of grace and peace extends from both God the Father and the Lord Jesus Christ, a juxtaposition that occurs throughout the salutation. Paul is an apostle of Jesus Christ, through the will of God (1:1). He writes to the church of God, which has been set apart in Christ (1:2). The designation of Jesus as "Lord" in 1:2 and 1:3 evokes a title ascribed to Yahweh in the Old Testament. It is hard to miss the profound theological implications of the divine functions accorded to both God the Father and Jesus the Son. As Fee explains, "If in 8:6; 11:3, and 15:26–28 there is a functional subordination of the Son to the Father in terms of his work, texts such as this one, and 1 Thess 3:11 and 1 Cor 12:4–6, make it clear that in Paul's mind the Son is truly God and works in cooperation with the Father in the redemption of his people."[49] The salutation as a whole emphasizes God's action in and through Christ, which carries forward to the thanksgiving in 1:4–9 and sets the tone for the remainder of the letter. The work of the Father and the Son are inseparable.[50]

## 2. Thanksgiving (1:4–9)

**4I always thank God for you because of his grace given you in Christ Jesus. 5For in him you have been enriched in every way—in all your speaking and in all your knowledge—6because our testimony about Christ was confirmed in you. 7Therefore you do not lack any spiritual gift as you eagerly wait for our Lord Jesus Christ to be revealed. 8He will keep you strong to the end, so that you will be blameless on the day of our Lord Jesus Christ. 9God, who has called you into fellowship with his Son Jesus Christ our Lord, is faithful.**

45 1 Cor 4:7, "What do you have that you did not receive?"

46 Eph 2:1–3.

47 So Collins, *First Corinthians*, 47; Fitzmyer, *First Corinthians*, 128.

48 S. E. Porter, "Peace, Reconciliation," *DPL*, 699.

49 Fee, *First Corinthians*, 35. Collins (*First Corinthians*, 48) notes that almost all references to the God the Father and Jesus are found in Paul's salutations and doxologies (see Rom 6:4; 8:15; 15:6; Gal 1:3–4; 4:6; Phil 2:11; 4:20; 1 Thess 3:11,13). See also Thiselton, *First Corinthians*, 84. Ciampa and Rosner (*First Corinthians*, 59) draw attention to the messianic overtones of "Lord" and "Christ" in relation to Jesus, which point to the universal lordship of the Davidic king and Son of God and the associations of the exodus and second exodus (eschatological redemption) in the Old Testament with the fatherhood of God (Exod 4:22; Deut 32:5–20; Isa 63:16; 64:8; Jer 3:19; 31:9; Hos 11:1–11).

50 Cf. John 5:16–19.

The extended thanksgiving in 1:4–9 captures Paul's profound gratitude to God for the grace given to the Corinthians in Christ.[51] The NIV punctuates 1:4–9 into five sentences, but in Greek the paragraph is structured around two main clauses: "I thank God" (1:4) and "God is faithful" (1:9). The thanksgiving is comprehensive in scope, taking into account the Corinthians' past enrichment (1:5–6), present giftedness (1:7), and future standing on the Day of the Lord (1:8).[52] Paul's affirmation of God's faithfulness (1:9) is the crowning statement of the letter's opening. Although the word "faithful" occurs last in the NIV rendering of 1:9, in Greek it is in the emphatic position, drawing attention to the character of God as one who keeps his promises.[53] The notion of "calling" closes the letter opening, forming an inclusio with the calling language of the salutation (1:1–2).[54]

**1:4** O'Brien observes that although God's activity in the gospel recurs in Paul's thanksgivings,[55] "in no other introductory thanksgiving is the grace of God found to be the basis or ground for the giving of thanks."[56] Here Paul affirms, however, that he continually offers thanks to God for the Corinthians because of God's grace given to them in Christ.[57] Thiselton recognizes the significance of Paul's perspective: "Not only the churches which bring him unmixed joy, such as the Philippians, invite regular thanksgiving on Paul's part, but even troublesome Corinth. For the very existence of their faith as Christians

---

[51] For extended treatments of Paul's thanksgivings, see P. Schubert, *Form and Function of the Pauline Thanksgivings*, BZNW 20 (Berlin: Topelmann, 1939); O'Brien, *Introductory Thanksgivings*; P. Arzt, "The 'Epistolary Introductory Thanksgiving' in the Papyri and in Paul," *NovT* 36 (1994): 29–46. O'Brien (*Introductory Thanksgivings*, 134–37) concludes that Paul's thanksgiving in 1 Corinthians serves to touch on some of the main themes of the letter, to remind the Corinthians of prior teaching by emphasizing God as the source of their spiritual endowments, to exhort them to continue to wait for the Day of the Lord, and to communicate his pastoral concern. For a thorough treatment of thanksgiving as a major theme in Paul in its larger biblical and theological context, see D. W. Pao, *Thanksgiving: An Investigation of a Pauline Theme*, New Studies in Biblical Theology (Downers Grove: InterVarsity, 2002).

[52] See also 1 Cor 15:57 where Paul gives thanks for the victory of future resurrection in Christ.

[53] Gk. πιστὸς ὁ θεός. God's faithfulness is an Old Testament theme (see Deut 7:9; Ps 144:13; Isa 49:7). In 1 Cor 10:13 Paul again reminds the Corinthians of God's faithfulness in the hour of testing. Cf. also 1 Thess 5:24; 2 Thess 3:3.

[54] Ciampa and Rosner (*1 Corinthians*, 62) suggest that this paragraph supplies several definitions of what it means to be a Christian: one who has received grace, who has been enriched in spiritual endowments, who waits eagerly for the Lord's return, and who will stand blameless on that day and who is in fellowship with God's Son, Jesus Christ.

[55] Phil 1:6; Col 1:4–6; Phlm 5–6.

[56] O'Brien, *Introductory Thanksgivings*, 111.

[57] The NIV rightly captures the causal sense of the preposition ἐπί, "because of his grace given you . . ." (so BDAG). The basis of the thanksgiving is God's grace, which had been expressed concretely to the Corinthians. See also Titus 2:11–13. That Paul "always" gives thanks is characteristic of his thanksgivings (cf. Rom 1:8; Phil 1:3; Col 1:3; 1 Thess 1:2; 2:13; 2 Thess 1:3; 2:13; Phlm 4). The combination of "grace" and "given" often occurs in the context of Paul's evangelization of the Gentiles (see Rom 12:3,6; 15:15; 1 Cor 3:10; 2 Cor 8:1; Gal 2:9; noted by O'Brien, *Introductory Thanksgivings*, 110–11; so also Fitzmyer, *First Corinthians*, 131).

outweighs any personal inconvenience, disappointment, or anguish which their less-than-appropriate attitudes and at times lifestyles also bring."[58] Similarly Fee observes, "To delight in God for his working in the lives of others, even in the lives of those with whom one feels compelled to disagree, is sure evidence of one's own awareness of being the recipient of God's mercies."[59]

Paul was thankful for specific manifestations of grace among the Corinthians, such as speech and knowledge (1:5), but he was also grateful for the totality of their experience of salvation past, present, and future (1:6–8). Paul himself had an extraordinary experience of God's grace in his conversion and call, which surely played a large role in his thanksgiving for God's grace in the conversion of others. Paul sustained a deep sense of God's grace following his conversion and attributed his missionary work in Corinth "to the grace of God given to me" (3:10). Although he considered himself to be the least of all the apostles as one who formerly persecuted the church, he affirmed God's abundant and effective grace in his apostolic work (15:10).[60] Grace profoundly shaped Paul's outlook in every way, and his gratitude for grace anticipates a major emphasis of the letter.[61]

**1:5** Paul elaborates on God's grace given to them by acknowledging their enrichment in Christ,[62] particularly in the areas of speech and knowledge, in conjunction with the confirmation of the gospel among them, and by stating that they come short in no gift as they eagerly wait for the revelation of Jesus Christ (1:5–7).[63] That Paul singles out the enrichments of "speech" and "knowledge," surely has to do with the misuse of these gifts in Corinth, which becomes apparent in the

---

[58] Thiselton, *First Corinthians*, 89. Thiselton (90) further notes that only overfamiliarity with the text can obscure the remarkable repetition of references to Christ in the thanksgiving.

[59] Fee, *First Corinthians*, 37.

[60] Cf. also Paul's perspective toward the end of his life in 1 Tim 1:12–16.

[61] Representative passages include 1:30; 4:7; 5:7; 6:11,19–20; 7:23. Particularly noteworthy is the statement in 6:11 following the vice list of 6:9–10: "Such were some of you, but you were washed, sanctified, and justified in the name of the Lord Jesus Christ and by the Spirit of our God." With all of their faults, the transformation of some of the Corinthians must have been quite remarkable.

[62] The verb "to enrich" occurs in the New Testament only in the Corinthian correspondence (here and 2 Cor 6:10; 8:9). Fee (*1 Corinthians*, 38–39) points out that the imagery of "enrichment" occurs in contrast to the poverty of Christ who effected their enrichment (2 Cor 8:9) or of Paul whose preaching made it possible (4:8–13; 2 Cor 6:10). Given its sarcastic use in 4:8, this may have been a Corinthian term that Paul turns around in a positive sense. O'Brien (*Introductory Thanksgivings*, 117) thinks the data suggests that the Corinthians themselves had informed Paul of their spiritual wealth.

[63] Paul's elaboration on God's grace is expressed by three conjunctions: ὅτι (1:5), καθὼς (1:6), and ὥστε (1:7). The first conjunction explains the content of Paul's thanksgiving (an "explicative" use of the ὅτι; so NASB, "I thank God *that* . . . ; so also Thiselton, *First Corinthians*, 90; O'Brien, *Introductory Thanksgivings*, 116). Collins (*1 Corinthians*, 56, 62) thinks the conjunction is causal, explaining Paul's reasons for gratitude. But a causal notion in the preposition ἐπί would render a causal reading of ὅτι in 1:5 redundant. Grace (χάρις) manifests itself concretely in the gifts (χαρίσματα). In 15:57 the term χάρις is used of thanksgiving (*thanks* be to God) and in 16:3 with reference to the Jerusalem collection (your *gift*).

letter.[64] The most prized gifts among the Corinthians likely contributed to their divisions in some way, yet Paul recognizes the genuineness of these gifts and their divine origin. Paul never disparages the sovereign work of the Spirit in the church (12:4–11), only improper attitudes toward and abuses of the gifts and the failure to exercise the gifts in love. The use of "all" with reference to speech and knowledge is qualitative, that is, the Corinthians had been enriched in every kind of speaking and knowledge. However, Paul's criticism of their boasting later in the letter shows that he did not consider all speech in Corinth to be a product of grace, and as 13:8 makes clear, spiritual gifts are limited. The content of the letter suggests that the Corinthians failed to act properly on the knowledge they had.[65] In 1:5, Paul seems to have in mind Spirit-endowed speech and knowledge that serves to build up the body of Christ.[66]

**1:6–7** The Corinthians' enrichment in spiritual gifts validated the genuineness of their reception of the gospel message, that the "testimony about Christ"[67] had been confirmed among them. "Testimony" in this context is synonymous with the gospel and refers to the apostolic witness to the gospel proclaimed by Paul in his mission in Corinth.[68] The term "confirm" appears again in 1:8 taking into account not only what God did in the past but what he will also do in the future in establishing them blameless on judgment day.[69] As a result of their reception of the gospel the Corinthians did "not lack any spiritual gift."[70] The meaning may be that they did not fall short in the gifts they had, not that they had every gift available. In other words, in no gift of grace were they any less rich than others.[71] "Gift" may be a term coined by

---

[64] This is the first occurrence in the letter of the term λόγος (speech), which anticipates the programmatic contrast in 1:17–18 between preaching "in wisdom of word" (ἐν σοφίᾳ λόγου), and "the word of the cross" (Ὁ λόγος γὰρ ὁ τοῦ σταυροῦ; cf. also 2:1–4). The abuse of the speech gift of tongues is apparent in chap. 14 (cf. also 13:1–3). Regarding knowledge see especially 8:1–13.

[65] Captured in the repeated question, "Do you not know?" See 3:16; 5:6; 6:2,3,9,15,16,19; 9:13,24; 12:2.

[66] In the listing of manifestations of the Spirit, 12:8 refers to a "word of wisdom" and a "word of knowledge." In 1:17, λόγος refers to rhetorical eloquence, something prized by the Corinthians but depreciated by Paul. In 8:1, Paul strictly warns that "knowledge puffs up."

[67] The conjunction καθὼς is rendered causally by the NIV. The NASB renders "just as," but the meaning is essentially the same (cf. 1 Thess 1:5).

[68] So also O'Brien, *Introductory Thanksgivings*, 120–21.

[69] Gk. βεβαιόω. For other uses see Mark 16:20; Rom 15:8; 2 Cor 1:21; Col 2:7; Heb 2:3; 13:9. The term was frequently used in the papyri in a technical sense of guaranteeing legal contracts, but it is not certain if it retains this sense here. O'Brien (*Introductory Thanksgivings*, 121–22) explains, "It is possible that Paul has taken a metaphor from the language of contracts and guarantees and pressed it into service in this thanksgiving passage underlining that God has indeed confirmed the gospel in the Corinthians."

[70] The Gk. conjunction ὥστε plus the infinitive indicates the actual outcome, not a contemplated result.

[71] So O'Brien, *Introductory Thanksgivings*, 123n69. Garland (*1 Corinthians*, 34) thinks that Paul's wording is "a deft swipe at their undue pride. Instead of congratulating them for their abundant spiritual endowment, he says that they do not fall short in this area."

Paul.[72] Outside of Paul the word *charisma* occurs only in 1 Pet 4:10.[73] The term does not always specify spiritual gifts. The use of the adjective "spiritual" with "gift" appears only in Rom 1:11. In the same letter Paul uses the term broadly to refer to God's gift of salvation (see Rom 5:15–16; 6:23). Some think, therefore, that the term need not specify spiritual gifts in 1 Cor 1:7,[74] but it seems probable that it does since it follows so closely after the mention of their enrichment in speech and knowledge, both identified as gifts in 12:8.[75]

Paul qualifies his affirmation of their giftedness with the phrase "as you wait eagerly for our Lord Jesus Christ to be revealed." Some think that by emphasizing their anticipation of the future revelation of Jesus, Paul intends to undermine the Corinthians' overemphasis on their present state; that is, he combats an "over-realized eschatology" that was the source of some of their problems.[76] But since eschatological references appear elsewhere in Paul's thanksgivings we should exercise due caution in reading too much into the Corinthian situation.[77] Every Corinthian problem was not due to their "over-realized eschatology." It is certain, however, that an eschatological perspective pervades the letter and is central to Paul's theology.[78] For believers, the present era is one of eager expectation of things to come. The term rendered "eagerly wait"[79] always occurs in eschatological contexts in Paul.[80] Thiselton perceptively comments, "God in Christ has won the decisive battle which assures victory for his people; but the war still drags on. Christians cannot yet behave as if sin and death were simply behind them."[81] Paul does not mention the Spirit specifically at this point in the letter, only the gifts, but his mention of the gifts implies the Spirit and anticipates the full discussion of chaps. 12–14.[82]

---

[72] Gk. χάρισμα.

[73] Collins (*1 Corinthians*, 63) claims, "There is no unassailable earlier textual evidence of its use before Paul." Similarly Thiselton (*1 Corinthians*, 98) observes, "One cannot say whether it was Paul himself who brought χαρίσματα into use as a term for πνευματίκα, but there can be no question about the difference of emphasis here between Paul and some of the 'gifted spiritual people' at Corinth.

[74] So Ciampa and Rosner, *First Corinthians*, 65.

[75] So also Fee, *First Corinthians*, 42. Fee notes that the syntax of the sentence, namely, the verb "lacking" modified by a prepositional phrase (in no gifts) rather than the typical genitive object, has been influenced by 1:5, and thus, the word "gift" is to be understood more specifically to special endowments of the Spirit mentioned in chaps. 12–14. O'Brien (*Introductory Thanksgivings*, 124) reads in the more general sense of spiritual endowments, which includes the gifts and anticipates the discussion of chaps. 12–14.

[76] So Fee, *First Corinthians*, 34. 4:6–13 has also been read this way.

[77] See Phil 1:10; 1 Thess 1:10; 2:12; 3:11–13; 2 Thess 1:6–10.

[78] See 3:12–17; 4:1–5; 5:1–5; 6:1–3,14; 7:31; 9:24–27; 10:11; 11:26; 13:8–12, the whole of chap. 15 (but esp. 15:20–28); 16:21–23.

[79] Gk. ἀπεκδέχομαι. Cf. also 1 Thess 1:10, "to wait," but a different Greek term (ἀναμένω).

[80] See Rom 8:19,23,25; Gal 5:5; Phil 3:20. Cf. also Heb 9:28 and 1 Pet 3:20.

[81] Thiselton, *First Corinthians*, 99.

[82] See also 2:5; 6–16; 3:16; 6:19. In Paul's theology, God's people are uniquely marked by the Spirit. See also 1 Thess 1:4–9 regarding the experience of the Spirit in the reception of the gospel.

**1:8** Paul expands on the thought of the Day of the Lord by affirming, "He will keep you strong to the end." The verb translated "to keep strong" is the same verb translated "to confirm" in 1:6.[83] In context, this confirmation is further explained as being "blameless," that is, without accusation on the Day of the Lord.[84] Colossians 1:22 provides further insight on Paul's meaning: "But now he has reconciled you by Christ's physical body through death to present you holy in his sight, without blemish and free from accusation."[85] First Corinthians 1:8 is truly a remarkable statement since the Corinthians were anything but blameless in their behavior! Yet, Paul's anticipation of their blameless standing on the Day of the Lord is entirely consistent with their present status as "called saints," and as those "set apart in Christ" (1:2), and his confidence was grounded in God's faithfulness (1:9).[86] Paul expressed the same kind of confidence in his thanksgiving for the believers in Philippi, "that he who began a good work in you will carry it on to completion until the day of Christ Jesus" (Phil 1:6) and prayed for them to be "pure and blameless until the day of Christ" (Phil 1:10).

One of the interpretive questions of 1:8 is the antecedent of the pronoun "he." Does this refer to God or to Jesus? The ambiguity exists even in the Greek.[87] While the closest referent, both in the English and Greek text, is Jesus, most recent commentators think that "he" refers to God, who is the agent of all of the passive verbs in 1:4–9.[88] Although not decisive, Paul uses the same

---

[83] Gk. βεβαιόω.

[84] The phrase, "Day of the Lord," is an Old Testament eschatological expression, which can refer to the day as a day of judgment (Amos 5:18–20) and salvation (Joel 2:32 [LXX 3:5]). Fee (*1 Corinthians*, 43) points out that Paul appropriates the Old Testament phrase but makes it christological. "It is still 'the day of the Lord,' but 'the Lord' is none other than Jesus Christ."

[85] The phrase "free from accusation" (NIV) translates the same Greek term rendered "blameless" in 1 Cor 1:8 (ἀνέγκλητος). BDAG notes the occurrence of this term with "holy" and the related term ἄμωμος (blameless/spotless) in Col 1:22. The term ἀνέγκλητος appears in the Pastoral letters with reference to the overseer who is to be "blameless/above reproach" (1 Tim 3:10; Titus 1:6–7). See also Rom 8:33 and the use of the cognate verb, ἐγκαλέω (to charge, to accuse), "Who will bring any charge against those whom God has chosen?" Collins (*1 Corinthians*, 65) notes Paul's characteristic judicial language in 1 Cor 1:8 (see 2 Cor 5:10; Phil 1:10; 1 Thess 3:13; 5:23).

[86] In other contexts Paul speaks of God strengthening and establishing believers. See Rom 1:11; 16:25; 1 Thess 3:2,13; 2 Thess 2:17; 3:3. Fee (*1 Corinthians*, 43) observes, "If Paul's confidence lay in the Corinthians themselves, then he is in trouble. But just as in 5:6–8 and 6:9–11, in Paul's theology the indicative (God's prior action of grace) always precedes the imperative (their obedience as response to grace) and is the ground of his confidence." Cf. also Phil 1:6–10; 2:16.

[87] Which has only the relative pronoun ὅς.

[88] Contra C. K. Barrett, *A Commentary on the First Epistle to the Corinthians*, HNTC (New York: Harper & Row, 1968), 39; A. Robertson and A. Plummer, *A Critical and Exegetical Commentary on the First Epistle of St. Paul to the Corinthians*, ICC, 2nd ed. (Edinburgh: T&T Clark, 1914), 7. Fitzmyer (*First Corinthians*, 133) notes that Jesus as the antecedent of the pronoun was also the view of Origen and Chrysostom. Thiselton (*First Corinthians*, 101) comments, "The Greek leaves the matter open. This need not trouble us since Paul's language here concerns the promises of God-in-Christ."

verb meaning, "to make strong/confirm," in 2 Cor 1:21 with reference to God: "Now it is God who makes both us and you stand firm in Christ."[89]

**1:9** Paul concludes the thanksgiving with particular accent on the faithfulness of God,[90] an emphasis missed by the NIV translation in putting the descriptor "faithful" at the end of the sentence, when in Greek, the word occurs first. That God is faithful means that he is worthy of our belief, trust, and devotion. Faithfulness is covenant language that underscores God's trustworthiness to keep all of his promises. In linking God's faithfulness to their call into fellowship with the Son, Paul is thinking of their past conversion. The faithful God who saved them will be the one who "keeps them strong" to the end (1:8). The calling language recalls the epithet "called saints" in the opening salutation (1:2).[91] "Fellowship" means much more in Greek than it does in current English idiom. In Pauline usage the term carries the idea of participation and sharing,[92] expressed also as being "in Christ." Their calling into participation with the Son sets the stage for the opening exhortation of the letter body to follow in 1:10, where Paul addresses the looming problem of a divided church, which is the antithesis of those called into intimate union with God's Son.[93]

---

[89] For further discussion see O'Brien, *Introductory Thanksgivings*, 127–28.

[90] Gk. πιστὸς ὁ θεός. The word order stresses faithfulness as an attribute of God. See also 1 Cor 10:13; 2 Cor 1:18; 1 Thess 5:24; 2 Tim 2:13; Heb 10:23.

[91] Cf. also 1:24 and the language of "choosing" in 1:26–31.

[92] Gk. κοινωνία. "Participation, sharing" is the fourth definition given in BDAG, which also references 46 1 Corinthians 1:9 under the definition, "close association involving mutual interests and sharing, *association, communion, fellowship, close relationship*." The term appears again in 1 Cor 10:16 with reference to the Lord's Supper, a "sharing" in the blood and the body of Christ, and the cognate term (κοινωνός) is used in 10:20 to describe Israel's idolatry, when they became "participants" with demons. See also 2 Cor 13:13 and Phil 2:1. Ciampa and Rosner (*1 Corinthians*, 68) note, "Verses 8–9 demonstrate that for Paul the judicial and participationist ways of looking at salvation are not exclusive alternatives, as sometimes thought. He moves effortlessly from speaking of forgiveness on the day of Christ to fellowship with Christ in the present."

[93] The title "Son" for Jesus is not all that frequent in Paul, except in contexts that stress the close work between the Father and the Son in salvation. The title appears again in 15:28. See also Rom 1:9; 8:29; 2 Cor 1:18.

## SECTION OUTLINE

II. God's Wisdom for a Divided Church (1:10–4:21)
   1. An Appeal for Unity in the Light of Corinthian Factions (1:10–17)
   2. The Wisdom of God and the Cross (1:18–2:5)
      (1) The Wisdom of God and a Crucified Messiah (1:18–25)
      (2) The Wisdom of God and the Corinthians' Calling (1:26–31)
      (3) The Wisdom of God and Paul's Ministry in Corinth (2:1–5)
   3. The Wisdom of God and the Spirit (2:6–3:4)
      (1) Wisdom as Revealed by the Spirit (2:6–16)
      (2) Application: Factions Demonstrate a Lack of God's Wisdom (3:1–4)
   4. The Wisdom of God and His Servants (3:5–4:13)
      (1) The Church, Its Leaders, and God's Fiery Test (3:5–17)
      (2) The Wisdom of God vs. the Wisdom of the World (Reprise) (3:18–23)
      (3) Faithfulness as the Criterion of Judgment (4:1–5)
      (4) Application: God's Servants as Paradigms of the Cross (4:6–13)
   5. Paul's Warning and Appeal as Their Spiritual Father (4:14–21)

## II. GOD'S WISDOM FOR A DIVIDED CHURCH (1:10–4:21)

The first major section of the letter opens with an appeal for unity (1:10–17) and closes with an appeal to imitate Paul, their father in the gospel (4:14–21).[1] The first appeal identifies the problem, a divided church, while the second points toward the solution, namely, the imitation of Paul, Christ's apostle, who not only proclaimed the gospel but lived out its message. In the opening unit of this section, 1:10–17, Paul renounces any misguided attachments to himself, and, by implication, to any human leader (1:13). In the closing unit, however, he urges the Corinthians to follow his way of life in Christ (4:16–17). In other words, although they do not "belong" to anyone, including Paul (1:12), he is

[1] Commentators routinely recognize the presence of an *inclusio* built around the repetition of the word παρακαλῶ, occurring in 1:10 ("I appeal") and 4:16 ("I urge"). An *inclusio* is a structural device, commonly employed by ancient writers, that begins and ends a unit of thought with the same word, collection of words, or a common phrase. There is a wide consensus that 1:10–4:21 constitutes the first major unit of the letter. A few suggest that 4:18–21 belongs with the following section (so R. Ciampa and B. Rosner, *The First Letter to the Corinthians*, PNTC [Grand Rapids: Eerdmans, 2010], 189–91); K. E. Bailey, "The Structure of 1 Corinthians and Paul's Theological Method with Special Reference to 1 Cor 4:17," *NovT* 25 [1983]: 152–81). In my view, 4:18–21 is a transitional unit belonging to both what precedes and what follows.

an apostle who represents Christ and is worthy of imitation. Between these twin exhortations Paul expounds the nature of the gospel as divine wisdom over against human wisdom since the latter lies at the source of their divisions (1:18–4:13).

The issues raised in this section of the letter are immensely complex and subject to a broad diversity of scholarly opinion. That the church was divided is clear. That the divisions had something to do with their leaders in relation to wisdom and involved boasting in men is equally clear. There is, however, a long-standing debate over the exact nature of the "splits";[2] how many "parties" actually existed, if any;[3] how "theology" plays into it,[4] if at all; how the persons mentioned in 1:11 (Paul, Apollos, Cephas, and Christ) factored into the situation,[5] and how 1:10–4:21 functions in the letter as a whole.[6]

---

[2] F. C. Baur famously argued for two parties in Corinth representing a Jewish/Gentile theological rift in the church that mirrored the opposing forces of Gentile and Jewish Christianity. The Gentile group claimed allegiance to Paul and Apollos and the Jewish group to Cephas and Christ (F. C. Baur, "Die Christuspartei in der Korinthischen Gemeinde, der Gegensatz des paulinischen und petrinischen Christentums in der altesten Kirche, der Apostle Petrus in Rom," *Tubinger Zeitschrift für Theologie* 4 [1831]: 61–206). J. Munck challenged Baur's historical reconstruction and the evidence from 1 Corinthians supporting the existence of parties with clear-cut theological positions (J. Munck, "The Church Without Factions," in *Paul and the Salvation of Mankind*, trans. F. Clarke [Atlanta: John Knox, 1977], 135–67). For an accessible analysis of the history of scholarship on this issue, see E. Adams and D. G. Horrell, *Christianity at Corinth: The Quest for the Pauline Church* (Louisville: WJK, 2004), 51–70. Adams and Horrell (61–62) note that Munck's argument, while a bit overstated in his desire to refute Baur, anticipated widespread trends in recent scholarship that attribute the Corinthian quarrels to "customs attested in the wider culture" and the view that "the controversy between Paul and the Corinthians over wisdom had to do in part with the rhetorical conventions of that age."

[3] The view of John Chrysostom (*On the First Epistle of the Corinthians, Homily* 3.1), that Paul tactfully used the four names as substitutes for the real offenders, based on his interpretation of 4:6, still lingers in modern scholarship. Some think that Paul employs rhetorical exaggeration that would have been unmistakable to the original hearers (see discussion on 1:12 below).

[4] G. D. Fee notes the tendency of scholars to read the entire letter in the light of chaps. 1–4, that divisions in the church underlie every issue. Although the Corinthians were divided over leaders, there is no evidence in the letter that they were also "theologically" divided over issues (*The First Epistle to the Corinthians*, NICNT [Grand Rapids: Eerdmans, 1987], 47). Without question, theological differences existed among the Corinthians (15:12), but the problem lies in clearly delineating the shape or form of actual parties in Corinth, if they existed at all. Fee (50) notes further that while "theological" divisions may be impossible to detect, the "nature of this particular strife had as its root cause their false theology, which had exchanged the theology of the cross for a false triumphalism that went beyond, or excluded, the cross."

[5] A. C. Thiselton observes that "a consensus has emerged that subsequent references in the epistle to wisdom (chs. 1–2), to boasting (1:29–31; 3:21; 4:7), and perhaps also to what counts as being 'spiritual' (3:1–3; chs. 12–14) lie behind some or all of the factors involved" (*The First Epistle to the Corinthians: A Commentary on the Greek Text*, NIGTC [Grand Rapids: Eerdmans, 2000], 123).

[6] N. A. Dahl ("Paul and the Church at Corinth According to 1 Corinthians 1:10–4:21," in *Christian History and Interpretation: Studies Presented to John Knox* [Cambridge: University Press, 1967]), and more recently, J. A. Fitzmyer (*First Corinthians: A New Translation with Introduction and Commentary*, AB 32 [New Haven: Yale University Press, 2008], 137–38), view

Following the opening exhortation to unity (1:10), Paul describes the present situation in Corinth as reported to him (1:11–12), whether in terms of actual slogans bandied about or caricatures that accurately represented the facts, and evaluates their discord in light of the gospel (1:13–15), which Christ sent him to preach (1:17). A lengthy critique of human wisdom follows (1:18–4:21), drawing on the Old Testament in support of the argument.[7] In light of their boasting in men, Paul's most urgent task in this section is to completely rehabilitate the Corinthians' perception of leadership (3:5–4:13). But first he has to reintroduce the first principles of the cross (1:18–2:5) and the Spirit (2:6–3:4) in relation to God's wisdom in order to redirect their focus. This is because, whatever the precise nature or source of the divisions in Corinth, the core problem was a misunderstanding of the nature of the gospel, what it means to be "spiritual," and, relatedly, a false conception of Christian ministry.[8] Indeed, "The most astonishing feature of 1:18–4:21 is its clear implication that even the self-styled 'spiritual' who had presumably begun with the cross had come to regard it, in effect, as foolish."[9]

The three imperatives in the thematic reprise of 3:18–23 provide a concise summary of Paul's response to the Corinthian divisions. He warns of self-deception (3:18a) and advises that if anyone thinks he is wise in this age, he should become a "fool," in order that he might become truly wise (3:18b). In other words, they should embrace the ideals of the cross and boast only in the Lord (1:31). Thus the third command, "So then, no more boasting in men!" (3:21).[10]

## 1. An Appeal for Unity in Light of Corinthian Factions (1:10–17)

**[10]I appeal to you, brothers, in the name of our Lord Jesus Christ, that all of you agree with one another so that there may be no divisions among you and that you**

1:10–4:21 as Paul's apologetic seeking to justify his apostolic authority and ministry. See also J. B. Chance, "Paul's Apology to the Corinthians," *PRSt* 9 (1982): 145–55. Fitzmyer suggests that the scandal of "preacher-factions" is only a surface problem. The real issue was Paul's attempt to re-establish his apostolic authority as the founder of the church (cf. also Fee, *First Corinthians*, 48–49). B. Witherington articulates a different view: "These chapters are not a defense but rather an exposition of true wisdom (as offered in the gospel) meant to cause the Corinthians to decide to change their factious behavior" (*Conflict and Community in Corinth: A Socio-Rhetorical Commentary* [Grand Rapids: Eerdmans, 1994], 98). The "apostolic defense" view has increasingly come under scrutiny in modern scholarship.

[7] A string of Old Testament quotations introduced by the formula, "It is written," occur throughout 1:18–3:23 (1:19,31; 2:9; 3:19–20; see also 2:16 and 4:6). Other literary features that provide cohesion to this section include (1) the heavy use of wisdom language in 1:18–3:23, where the terms σοφία (wisdom) or σοφός (wise) occur; collectively twenty-six times, and (2) the mention of Christian leaders by name in 1:12; 3:4–5,23; and 4:6.

[8] The slogans in 3:4, "I follow Paul" and "I follow Apollos," hark back to 1:10–17. The intervening material, 1:18–3:4, is critical to Paul's discussion of leadership in 3:5–4:13.

[9] Thiselton, *First Corinthians*, 147.

[10] The three imperatives, all third person, are ἐξαπατάτω (to deceive), γενέσθω (to become), and καυχάσθω (to boast).

**may be perfectly united in mind and thought. [11]My brothers, some from Chloe's household have informed me that there are quarrels among you. [12]What I mean is this: One of you says, "I follow Paul"; another, "I follow Apollos"; another, "I follow Cephas"; still another, "I follow Christ."**

**[13]Is Christ divided? Was Paul crucified for you? Were you baptized into the name of Paul? [14]I am thankful that I did not baptize any of you except Crispus and Gaius, [15]so no one can say that you were baptized into my name. [16](Yes, I also baptized the household of Stephanas; beyond that, I don't remember if I baptized anyone else.) [17]For Christ did not send me to baptize, but to preach the gospel—not with words of human wisdom, lest the cross of Christ be emptied of its power.**

On the basis of a report of divisions in the church, Paul urges the Corinthians to unity "in the name of our Lord Jesus Christ."[11] He swiftly denounces their splits and disavows their wrong-headed attachment to human leaders by using himself as the example, which serves to point out the incongruity of their behavior with the gospel. That Paul repudiates personal allegiances by asking rhetorically, "Was Paul crucified for you?" and "Were you baptized into the name of Paul?" is not at odds with his later instruction to "imitate me" (4:16; 11:1). In all instances he is turning their focus to Christ. Paul's qualification in 1:17 that Christ sent him to preach the gospel,[12] "not with words of human wisdom," sets the stage for his exposition of God's wisdom versus human wisdom in 1:18–4:13.

**1:10** Paul appeals to the Corinthians in familial language[13] with the authority of Christ.[14] To make an appeal in the name of Jesus is to evoke his

---

[11] For the most thoroughgoing argument that unity is the fundamental theme of the letter, see M. M. Mitchell, *Paul and the Rhetoric of Reconciliation: An Exegetical Investigation of the Language and Composition of 1 Corinthians* (Louisville: WJK, 1991). See also R. B. Hays, *First Corinthians* (Louisville: John Knox, 1997), 21; Witherington, *Conflict and Community*, 94. R. Ciampa and B. Rosner represent the most recent challenge to the view that 1:10 is the theme statement of the entire letter. "While it is true that disunity is a major theme of the letter, extending beyond chaps. 1–4, to give it primacy obscures other equally important concerns" (*The First Letter to the Corinthians*, PNTC [Grand Rapids: Eerdmans, 2010], 73). Ciampa and Rosner read 1 Corinthians through the lens of the Old Testament and Jewish frames of reference rather than through the lens of Greco-Roman rhetoric. Disunity is only one of several Corinthian misbehaviors, and Paul's goal is larger than having them live harmoniously. Certainly Paul seeks to unify the Corinthians, "but, just as importantly, to rid them of pagan influences other than disunity, in particular sexual immorality (cf. 6:18), idolatry (cf. 10:14), and greed."

[12] The second reference in the letter to Paul's apostolic commission (cf. 1:1, "called apostle").

[13] This is the first occurrence of the vocative, ἀδελφοί (brothers), in the letter (see also 1 Cor 1:11,26; 2:1; 3:1; 4:6; 7:24,29; 10:1; 11:33; 12:1; 14:6,26,39; 15:1,31,50,58; 16:15). Here the vocative occurs consecutively in 1:10 and 1:11. Paul also uses father/child language in referring to himself and the Corinthians in 4:14–16.

[14] This is the tenth use of the name of Christ since 1:1, eleven if one takes into account the personal pronoun αὐτῷ in 1:5. See also 1 Cor 5:4 and 6:11 for references to the "name" of Jesus." A. Robertson and A. Plummer state, "The genitive makes the Name the instrument of the appeal" (*A Critical and Exegetical Commentary on the First Epistle of St. Paul to the Corinthians*, ICC, 2nd ed. [Edinburgh: T&T Clark, 1914], 6). Garland suggests that the name of Jesus may invoke Christ's meekness and gentleness (cf. 2 Cor 10:1) (*1 Corinthians*, BECNT [Grand Rapids: Baker,

person and character and to speak authoritatively as the Lord's representative. The call to unity is linked tightly and logically to the previous section where Paul reminded the Corinthians that they not only number themselves among others who call up the name of the Lord (1:2), but that they also were called by God into fellowship with his Son (1:9).[15] Their disunity is the very antithesis of their fellowship with the Son and status as God's holy people. In 1:13, Paul reminds them that they were not baptized into the "name" of Paul, which would have signified allegiance and devotion to a mere man. Since Christ alone was crucified for them and they were baptized only in his name, their allegiance is to Jesus and to him alone (1:13).[16]

The exhortation itself consists of three parallel statements, each underscoring the nature of Christian unity. Paul urges (1) that "all of you agree with one another,"[17] (2) "so that there may be no divisions among you," and (3) "that you may be perfectly united in mind and thought." The NIV translation misses the threefold repetition of the word "same" in the Greek text that underscores the need for unity. The text reads literally, "that you speak the *same* thing and that you be joined together in the *same* mind and *same* outlook." The word translated "divisions"[18] recurs in 11:18 in reference to factious behavior at the Lord's Supper, which was social in nature rather than doctrinal,[19] and again in

2003], 41). Witherington (*Conflict and Community*, 95) notes that Paul uses the verb παρακαλῶ ("I appeal") to introduce crucial ideas in the letter (here, 4:16, and 16:15), all tied to "rhetorical strategies he uses in the letter to overcome divisions: direct exhortation to the offending parties, modeling, and the attempt to set up effective local leadership." A nonrhetorical use of the verb, merely a "request formula," appears widely in the papyri, inscriptions, and early Christian literature. See C. J. Bjerkelund, *Parakalō: Form, Funktion und Sinn der parakalō-Sätze in den paulinischen Briefen* (Oslo: Universitetsforlaget, 1967). In 1:10, the addition of "brothers" and "in the name of the Lord Jesus Christ" creates the effect of a command (so Fee, *First Corinthians*, 52; R. F. Collins, *First Corinthians*, SP [Collegeville, MN: Liturgical Press, 68]).

[15] In Gk. 1:10 is joined to 1:9 by the particle δέ.

[16] The recurrence of "name" in 1:2,10,13 contributes to the cohesion of Paul's argument, linking the letter opening (1:1–9) to the present paragraph (1:10–17).

[17] Gk. ἵνα τὸ αὐτὸ λέγητε πάντες, literally, "that you all say the same thing." Mitchell (*Rhetoric of Reconciliation*, 68) observes that this is a stock phrase that describes the "opposite of factionalism." There is a strong emphasis on speech in this section: there are quarrels in the community, and Paul describes their divisions in terms of what each one "says." Paul is thankful that he baptized so few of them lest any "say" that they had been baptized in his name. The implication is that their inappropriate allegiance to leaders is expressed in what they say, which is confirmed by further references to "boasting" (see 1:31; 3:21). Ciampa and Rosner (*1 Corinthians*, 75–76) consider that "the same thing" that Paul wants them to say may well be, "I follow Christ," depending on how the fourth slogan in 1:12 is understood. More likely, the third parallel statement explains the first. "To say the same thing" is "to be perfectly united in mind and thought."

[18] Gk. σχίσματα. Collins (*First Corinthians*, 77) points out that in terms of political rhetoric the term was used figuratively of a division of opinion "or a cleft in political consciousness" (Herodotus, *Persian Wars*, 7.219).

[19] On the "social" aspect of the divisions see Munck, "The Church Without Factions"; Mitchell, *Rhetoric of Reconciliation*, 71; B. W. Winter, *Philo and Paul Among the Sophists*, SNTSMS 96 (Cambridge: Cambridge University Press, 1997), 180–202.

12:25 in reference to God's arrangement of the members of the body "so that there should be no division in the body." In the Synoptics the term is used of a tear in a garment (Matt 9:16; Mark 2:21). John's use of the word to describe various groups with divided opinions about Jesus (John 7:40–43; 9:16; 10:19–21) is probably close to what Paul implies here. A competitive party-spirit centered on personalities persisted in Corinth that erupted into quarrels and provoked jealousy.

In contrast to division, Paul urges the Corinthians to be "perfectly united in mind and thought." The word translated "perfectly united" carries with it the notion of reconciliation that brings about the restoration of relationships.[20] "Mind" and "thought" are probably synonymous terms in this context[21] and anticipate Paul's emphasis in the ensuing argument on God's wisdom expressed in the gospel. He wants them to embrace the "mind of Christ" (cf. 2:16), that is, to take up a perspective conditioned by the cross. In 7:25, Paul refers to giving a "judgment" as one who by the Lord's mercy is trustworthy and in 7:40 to his "opinion" that is guided by the Spirit of God.[22] In Phil 2:1–11 Paul expresses the same idea in exhorting the church at Philippi to "think" in a certain way, that is, to be like-minded" (Phil 2:2),[23] and to take up the humble attitude of Christ (Phil 2:5–8). Similarly, his appeal to the Corinthians is that they take up a Christian mindset and a common perspective. The appeal to unity, however, is not an appeal to uniformity at all costs. There is no room for disagreement on the fundamental nature of the gospel,[24] which is the heart of Paul's argument to follow in 1:18–4:13.

**1:11** The basis of Paul's appeal for unity is a report received from Chloe's household regarding "quarrels among you." The mention of the informants gives credibility to the report.[25] Since Chloe is mentioned only here in the New Testament we know nothing about her, but the Corinthians would have been well-acquainted with her and/or her household. The NIV translation, "Chloe's household" renders the Greek expression, "those of Chloe,"[26] which

---

[20] Gk. *καταρτίζω*. Commentators often noted that the word was a surgical term for the resetting of a broken bone, thus metaphorical for the restoration of broken relationships. The word occurs again in 2 Cor 13:11.

[21] So also Collins (*First Corinthians*, 69), "The repetition has the rhetorical effect of emphasizing Paul's point."

[22] In both instances the word is *γνώμη*, the same Greek term as "thought" in 1:10. In addition to the occurrences of *νοῦς* (mind) in 1:10 and 2:16 (2x), the term occurs in 14:14,15, and 19.

[23] Although a different Greek term is used, the idea is the same; "to think the same thing" (Gk. *τὸ αὐτὸ φρονῆτε*). Thiselton (*First Corinthians*, 119) translates *νοῦς* as "mind-set," "which in the present context draws out the meaning of *outlook, stance, orientation,* or *attitude,* without entirely losing the dimension of *rational judgment* which is nearly always implicit."

[24] Cf. also Gal 2:1–10.

[25] The verb "to inform" is *δηλόω*, which means "to make clear" or "to reveal." The verb recurs in 3:13 with reference to the Day of the Lord that will "bring to light" the quality of work of those who labor in ministry.

[26] Gk. *τῶν Χλόης*.

could indicate family and extended household members, such as slaves, or those who acted on behalf of Chloe as business agents. Some think that since Paul was in Ephesus at the time of the writing of the letter, Chloe may have been a wealthy Asian with business interests that required her representatives to travel to Corinth.[27] We do not know for certain that she was a believer, but it is probable since she had a presence in Corinth and was known to the church, even if through her business agents.[28] The report itself regarding the Corinthian quarrels does not come from Chloe but rather from her household. The term for "quarrels" is used only by Paul in the New Testament and frequently appears in vice lists.[29] The word appears again in 1 Cor 3:3 alongside the term "jealousy."[30]

**1:12** As noted in the introduction to this section, the interpretation of this verse is complex and moves in many different directions.[31] Fee calls 1:12 "a crux in terms of how one is going to understand 1 Corinthians as a whole."[32] The most straightforward reading of the Greek grammar indicates that individuals in Corinth were split long four party lines, claiming to "follow" either Paul, Apollos, Cephas, or Christ.[33] Scholars, however, frequently call into question the existence of four actual parties in Corinth since only Paul and Apollos figure prominently into the argument of 1:10–4:21 (cf. 3:4–9 and 4:6),[34] and it is uncertain that Cephas ever visited Corinth.[35] Furthermore, Paul never addresses the factions directly but rather speaks to the entire church. Most puzzling of all is the reference to the so-called Christ party. Why would Paul have a problem with this group since "all belong to Christ" (3:23)? Would they not be in full agreement with the rhetorical questions that follow in 1:13? Or is this fourth slogan Paul's own rhetorical flourish, a bit of sarcasm wherein he claims his own allegiance to Christ?[36] That the language employed by Paul

[27] So Fee, *First Corinthians*, 54; Thiselton, *First Corinthians*, 121.

[28] Collins (*First Corinthians*, 78) suggests further that Chloe was probably a patron of a house-church.

[29] Gk. ἔρις. See Rom 1:29; 13:13; Gal 5:20; 1 Tim 6:4; Titus 3:9.

[30] See also 2 Cor 12:20 for a similar context. The other occurrence of the term is Phil 1:15.

[31] For a discussion of the history of interpretation of 1:12 see Thiselton, *First Corinthians*, 123–33. For a concise summary of the different views see Collins, *First Corinthians*, 72. Ciampa and Rosner (*First Corinthians*, 78) warn that one can become overwhelmed by the scholarly discussion on this issue and must beware of tying their exegesis too closely to any one particular historical reconstruction.

[32] Fee, *First Corinthians*, 55.

[33] Gk. ἐγὼ μέν εἰμι Παύλου, ἐγὼ δὲ Ἀπολλῶ, ἐγὼ δὲ Κηφᾶ, ἐγὼ δὲ Χριστοῦ. Literally, "I am of Paul, but I am of Apollos," etc., with the meaning, "I belong to Paul . . ."

[34] Apollos appears six times in the argument of 1:10–4:21 (1:12; 3:4–6,22; 4:6; see also 16:12). This may suggest that the Apollos party, in Paul's view, was the key player in the divisions in Corinth, but this is not certain.

[35] In the present argument the name "Cephas" reappears only in the thematic reprise of 3:18–23.

[36] Along the lines of, "As for me, I, Paul, belong to Christ!"

in 1:12 as a whole is a "forceful piece of rhetoric"[37] rather than a rehearsing of actual slogans by various groups in Corinth has become an increasingly popular view among the commentators. The matter is complicated even further by those who hold the view that Paul has substituted names in 1:12 as a covert allusion for the actual perpetrators.[38]

On the assumption that some actually claimed to "belong" to Paul, it is easy to understand how some in Corinth might have developed an unhealthy allegiance to the founder of the community. Although Paul baptized only a few, he did baptize Crispus, Gaius, and Stephanus (1:14–16), who all were undoubtedly leading figures in the community. Crispus is probably the synagogue ruler mentioned in Acts 18:8. In Rom 16:23 Paul sends greetings to the Roman church from Gaius and commends him for his hospitality for the whole church. Stephanus was among the first converts in Corinth and was part of the delegation sent to Paul in Ephesus by the Corinthians (16:17). There is no firm evidence that any of these men had anything to do with the Corinthian factions or that they contributed in any way to a party spirit.[39] People do tend, however, to develop certain loyalties to individuals, and one can easily conceive how Paul would have had his own defenders if other rival factions emerged.[40] Was Paul's unimpressive style of speaking an issue (2 Cor 10:10)? Did Paul's refusal to accept financial support factor into the situation and create tensions in Corinth (1 Cor 9:1–6)?

We know from Acts 18:24–19:1 that Apollos was in Corinth following Paul's departure, a fact corroborated by the statement, "I planted, Apollos watered, but God gave the increase" (1 Cor 3:6). Luke does not indicate why Apollos visited Corinth but describes him as a learned Alexandrian Jew, who was mighty in the Scriptures and a powerful speaker.[41] These qualities, especially his rhetorical skills, may have contributed to some rallying around the name of Apollos. Barrett comments that it is "easy to understand where the gifts of speech were highly prized that the appearance of an eloquent speaker such as Apollos would awaken partisanship."[42] Did Apollos teach a form of Jewish wisdom that some in Corinth found attractive? There is not enough

---

[37] Collins, *First Corinthians*, 73.

[38] A view based on the meaning of the Greek verb, μετασχηματίζω, ("to transform/disguise") in 4:6.

[39] Although Garland (*1 Corinthians*, 55) thinks that Crispus and Gaius were key figures in the dispute.

[40] C. K. Barrett suggests the very mention of those who lay claim to Paul represented in the slogan, "I follow Paul," in and of itself implies opposition to Paul in Corinth (*A Commentary on the First Epistle to the Corinthians*, HNTC [New York: Harper & Row, 1968], 43).

[41] The Gk. ἀνὴρ λόγιος (Acts 18:24) is translated by the NASB as "an eloquent man." The phrase δυνατὸς ἐν ταῖς γραφαῖς in the same verse means "mighty/powerful in the Scriptures." The NIV translates Acts 18:24, "He was a learned man, with a thorough knowledge of the Scriptures."

[42] Barrett, *First Corinthians*, 44.

evidence to know for sure, but it is possible.[43] Since Paul refers repeatedly to Apollos in the argument (3:4–9,22; 4:6), Fee concludes that "the most natural understanding of 4:6 is that Paul for all practical purposes has narrowed the issue in chaps. 1–4 to himself and Apollos and that the Corinthians are 'puffed up' in favor of the one (Apollos) against the other (Paul)."[44]

The reference to Cephas[45] is a bit more mysterious since there is no direct evidence that he ever visited Corinth. Although there is no record in Acts that Peter spent time there, some think that the four references to Cephas in the letter make more sense if, in fact, he had visited Corinth. The mention of Cephas in 1:12, along with Paul and Apollos, may indicate that Cephas and Apollos both baptized converts in Corinth as did Paul. The mention of Cephas again in 3:22, along with Paul and Apollos, may suggest that he too was a teacher revered by some in Corinth. Furthermore, in 9:5, Paul mentions the right of Cephas and others to take along a wife with the financial support of the church, and in 15:5, Paul singles out Cephas as one of the apostolic eyewitnesses of the resurrection, which he may have done because Cephas was someone with whom they were familiar.[46]

Without a doubt, the most enigmatic reference of all is to the supposed "Christ-party."[47] After noting the difficulties with this "slogan,"[48] Fee suggests that the popular view may still be the best one: "here are some people who form no distinct group at all, but who in their own attempt to rise above the rest, those boasting in mere men, have fallen into their own brand of spiritual elitism that makes them no better than others."[49] Others tend to question the

[43] Ciampa and Rosner (*First Corinthians*, 79) comment, "As a learned Alexandrian Jew, Apollos may have taught a form of Jewish wisdom which may well have had considerable appeal in Corinth. Perhaps some of those whom he had influenced also disparaged Paul on the grounds that, unlike Apollos, Paul had not taught them in this manner."

[44] Fee, *First Corinthians*, 56.

[45] Peter's Aramaic name. With the exception of Gal 2:7–8, Paul refers to Peter as "Cephas."

[46] See Fitzmyer, *First Corinthians*, 144; Ciampa and Rosner, *First Corinthians*, 79. Ciampa and Rosner note, however, that "if Peter had been to Corinth, and some Corinthians had used his name as a rallying point, Paul's silence in regard to him in his response to Corinthian factionalism, except in 3:22, indicates that the Peter group was not as much a problem as the Apollos party. If Peter himself had somehow been at fault in the Corinthian situation facing Paul, we would have expected a direct and robust response from Paul, as in his disagreement with Peter reported in Galatians 2."

[47] Thiselton (*First Corinthians*, 129–33) lists six different interpretations of the phrase.

[48] Namely, "(1) the placing of Christ's name alongside others; (2) the probability that all groups would think they were following Christ; (3) the fact that this is what Paul would want all of them to do; (4) the lack of another explicit reference to this group; (5) the fact that the rhetorical questions in v. 13 that are intended to show the absurdity of their quarreling in this fashion could in each instance be answered favorably by such a group" (Fee, *First Corinthians*, 58).

[49] Ibid., 59. See also Robertson and Plummer (*First Corinthians*, 12), who think that the Christ-party may be explained in terms of 2 Cor 10:7–11 and possibly 11:4,23 where there appears to be a reference to a prominent leader in rebellion against Paul and who claimed that Christ belonged exclusively to his group rather than Paul in connection with genuine apostleship in knowing Christ during his life on earth. Garland (*1 Corinthians*, 47), however, thinks that Robertson and

view that there was a fourth party in Corinth, the "Christ-party," since "belonging to Christ" is exactly what Paul wants to affirm (3:23) and the rhetoric of the passage may indicate that Paul was not citing actual Corinthian slogans at all. Rather, the slogans are caricatures created by Paul in order to highlight the Corinthians' childish behavior,[50] and he possibly employs rhetorical crescendo by adding his own "ironic" touch in stating his own allegiance to Christ, "I follow Christ." Later references to the so-called parties that allude back to 1:12 do not mention Christ (3:4–5,22; 4:6), and Paul later emphasizes his good relationship with Apollos (3:5–9; 16:12). Garland explains that Chloe's people only reported the fact that there were quarrels among the Corinthians. "Paul does not say that Chloe's people reported that they were rallying around these names and spouting these slogans." It is Paul himself that interprets the implications of the report and "exaggerates when he claims 'each one' is saying these things."[51] It is Paul's way of underscoring their ludicrous behavior. The main objection to this view is the grammatical symmetry that suggests four distinct groups with no indication that the fourth slogan is Paul's.[52] Ciampa and Rosner contend, however, that this objection is not decisive, "for if the Corinthians knew of some basis to the slogans of attachment to the three human leaders, then *I follow Christ* would have been understood immediately as Paul's own ironic dig."[53]

In the final analysis it is helpful to keep in mind that the scholarly debates seek only to resolve the *nature* of the divisions in Corinth,[54] not the *fact* of divisions. Even if the slogans are caricatures created by Paul, his rhetorical

Plummer's contention that there are "local streams of influence which show themselves at work elsewhere in the New Testament," should be rejected.

[50] So Mitchell, *Rhetoric of Reconciliation*, 83–86; Collins, *First Corinthians*, 73; Garland, *1 Corinthians*, 47–49; Ciampa and Rosner, *First Corinthians*, 80–81.

[51] Garland, *1 Corinthians*, 48.

[52] One might also expect the strong adversative, ἀλλά, instead of δέ before the last slogan, "I belong to Christ!"

[53] Ciampa and Rosner, *First Corinthians*, 80. Similarly, Garland (*1 Corinthians*, 49), "There is no hint in the text that some Corinthians are claiming a unique relationship to Christ. If there was a Christ party, Paul seems to play into their hands by naming Christ ten times in the previous verses and by declaring that no one can boast except in Christ, who is wisdom from God (1:29–31). In 3:21–22, he rejects boasting in human leaders—Paul, Apollos, Cephas—and follows in 3:23 with an expression corresponding to 'I belong to Christ' that he clearly understands in a positive sense and not as a boisterous slogan: 'And you [plural] belong to Christ, and Christ belongs to God.'"

[54] Although the nature of the divisions is difficult to pin down, the answer probably lies somewhere in the social stratification in the church between the rich and the poor (see 11:28), or to their allegiance to the various leaders who may have baptized them or served as leaders or patron-hosts of house groups, or to a cultural milieu that promoted a competitive spirit and attachment to various leaders. For important studies on the interpretation of 1 Corinthians against the background of the social milieu in Corinth, see W. A. Meeks, *The First Urban Christians: The Social World of the Apostle Paul* (New Haven: Yale University Press, 1983); P. Marshall, *Enmity in Corinth: Social Conventions in Paul's Relation with the Corinthians*, WUNT 23 (Tübingen: Mohr, 1987); D. G. Horrell, *The Social Ethos of the Corinthian Correspondence: Interests and Ideology from 1 Corinthians to 1 Clement* (Edinburgh: T&T Clark, 1996).

flourish works precisely because it accurately sheds light on the true situation. If Paul created the slogans to drive home his point, this does not necessarily imply that the factions did not, in fact, attach themselves in some way to Paul, Apollos, and Cephas, for the reasons mentioned above. What is crystal clear is that a party spirit plagued the church in Corinth, and their boasting in men contradicted the very essence of the gospel. The root problem was pride, the worst of sins, especially for those identified with a crucified Christ.

**1:13** However one perceives the historical situation and the meaning of 1:12, Paul expresses his displeasure over the situation in a series of three questions that function to show the absurdity of their attachment to human leaders: "Is Christ divided? Was Paul crucified for you? Were you baptized into the name of Paul?" The second and third questions are clearly rhetorical and expect a "no" answer in response. Paul was not crucified for them, Christ was, and they were baptized in the name of Christ, not Paul. The first question, however, could be read as an indicative statement, "Christ has been divided!"[55] In context, a question is more likely, but it may carry the force of a statement. In other words, the answer to the question, "Is Christ divided?" is "Yes, Christ has been divided."[56]

Another interpretive issue has to do with the meaning of the verb translated "divided."[57] Barrett notes that the verb means not just to divide but to divide and to distribute. In this case Paul would be asking, "Do you suppose that there are fragments of Christ that can be distributed among different groups?"[58] Or as Fee puts it, "Has Christ been distributed/apportioned out as one among many."[59] If Paul is still thinking about the so-called Christ-party, then the meaning might be, "Has Christ been divided up and distributed only to some?"[60] Some think that Paul's language here evokes the metaphor of the body of Christ,[61] which he will develop later in the letter (12:12), and that Paul shocks them by portraying Christ's body as torn to pieces. "The vivid imagery of Christ sliced into fragments is Paul's first move decrying the divisions among them."[62]

In the second and third questions, Paul tactfully refers to himself rather than Apollos or Cephas in order to underscore his displeasure with their actions and make clear that he will have no part in their rivalries. The mention of

---

[55] So translated by the GNB and NEB. The Greek has only μεμέρισται ὁ Χριστός, which could be read as a statement. The grammatical structure of the second and third statements clearly indicate a question with the expected negative response (μή plus the indicative verb).

[56] So Garland, *1 Corinthians*, 51.

[57] Gk. μερίζω.

[58] Barrett, *First Corinthians*, 46.

[59] Fee, *First Corinthians*, 60. So also Hays, *First Corinthians*, 23.

[60] See Robertson and Plummer, *First Corinthians*, 13; Thiselton, *First Corinthians*, 136.

[61] So H. Conzelmann, *1 Corinthians: A Commentary,* trans. J. Leitch, Hermeneia (Philadelphia: Fortress, 1975), 35; Collins, *First Corinthians*, 81.

[62] Garland, *1 Corinthians*, 52. Cf. also Ciampa and Rosner, *First Corinthians*, 82.

crucifixion anticipates a major emphasis on the death of Jesus in the letter, beginning with 1:18. That Paul was not crucified "for them" implies, of course, that Christ was and is the first mention in the letter, by way of implication, that Jesus died as a substitute for others. The Greek construct indicates one acting on behalf of another.[63] That Christ was crucified for them and that they were baptized in his name underscores that Jesus is the only possible object of their allegiance.[64]

**1:14–16** Paul's reference to baptism leads to a brief digression regarding his own practice of baptism during his missionary days in Corinth. Surprisingly, and somewhat ironically, Paul exclaims, "I am thankful that I did not baptize any of you except Crispus and Gaius." He then recalls that he also baptized the household of Stephanas but cannot remember if he baptized others. These were presumably among the early converts in Corinth, and it is likely that all three mentioned by name were wealthy and prominent people in the community.[65] The reason for Paul's statement is rather apparent. He is grateful, in retrospect, that he did not engage in the ministry of baptism lest some claim special allegiance to him on this basis.[66] Paul's statement may suggest that baptism played some role in the rivalries, but we cannot be certain.[67] There is no indication that Apollos or Cephas baptized anyone in Corinth, although it is not impossible. Who did the baptizing seems to be of little importance to Paul. Perhaps baptism was carried out primarily by his missionary co-workers.

**1:17** Paul is clear that Christ sent him to herald the gospel, not to baptize. The language of sending recalls Paul's apostolic commission mentioned already in the salutation (1:1). Paul's clarification that his primary calling is to preach rather than baptize in no way minimizes the importance or the significance of baptism.[68] However, while this verse does not speak primarily to the issue of Paul's "theology" of baptism, it does provide some insight into his understanding of the practice in relation to the gospel. Clearly, Paul

---

[63] Gk. ὑπὲρ ὑμῶν. On the use of the preposition to express the vicarious nature of Jesus' death see 11:24; 15:3. Cf. also references to the death of Jesus for others in 1 Cor 5:7; 6:20; 7:23; 8:11. Elsewhere in Paul see Rom 5:8; 8:32; 14:15; 2 Cor 5:14–15; Gal 1:4; Eph 3:1,13; Col 1:24; 2:1.

[64] To be baptized in the name of Jesus indicates "entrance into fellowship and allegiance" (so Robertson and Plummer, *First Corinthians*, 13). On baptism in Paul see Rom 6:4; Gal 3:27; Eph 4:5; Col 2:12. In 1 Corinthians see especially 12:12–14.

[65] For inscriptional evidence that "ruler of the synagogue" was an honorific title bestowed on wealthy patrons, see J. Murphy-O'Connor, *Paul: A Critical Life* (Oxford: Oxford University Press, 1996), 267. The home and those who served as patrons of the church performed an important role in the early church. In 1 Corinthians references to the "home" occur in 11:22,34; 14:35; 16:19. For scholarship regarding the ancient "household" see Thiselton, *First Corinthians*, 141.

[66] That Paul delegated baptism to others generally followed the similar practice of Jesus (John 4:2).

[67] Fee (*First Corinthians*, 61–62) thinks that the Corinthians held a somewhat "magical" view of baptism, based on Paul's arguments in 10:1–6 and 15:29, but, again, this is speculation.

[68] See Rom 6:3–7.

distinguishes baptism from the gospel, which should dispel any notions of baptismal regeneration, that is, that the act of baptism itself effects salvation.[69] But Paul's emphasis in this verse lies elsewhere, as seen in the phrase qualifying his commission to preach, "not with words of human wisdom, lest the cross of Christ be emptied of its power." The next unit expands on the theme of human wisdom versus the cross as God's power (1:18–25).

The gospel shaped Paul's outlook comprehensively and constitutes a major theme in the letter, not only in the first and last major discourses of the letter (1:10–4:21 and 15:1–58) but especially in chap. 9 (esp. 9:19–23).[70] Paul's qualification in 1:17, that he did not preach the gospel "with words of human wisdom," leads into his extended exposition of the gospel as God's wisdom and the solution to their problem of divisions. In 1:17 Paul explains how he did not preach the gospel, and in 2:1–5 he reminds the Corinthians how he did come to them—"in weakness and fear, and with much trembling" (2:3), yet "with a demonstration of the Spirit's power" (2:4). To preach the gospel in "wisdom of word" is to empty the cross of Christ (1:17b), but to preach in the Spirit's power is to anchor one's faith in the power of God rather than the wisdom of men (2:5).

The introduction of the term "wisdom" sets the tone for the ensuing argument[71] and raises key interpretive issues, beginning with the phrase rendered by the NIV as "not with human words of wisdom," which is literally, "wisdom of word."[72] Pogoloff has produced the most recent comprehensive study of how the two key terms "wisdom" and "word" function in Paul's rhetorical situation, and he makes the case that the phrase refers to the sophisticated and cultured speech of those of high status.[73] What Paul denies in 1:17 is preaching in a "status-conferring manner," rather than a denial of rhetorical sophistication as such. Paul is concerned with the ethical dimensions of speech that promote rivalries rather than a competing content-driven philosophical or theological wisdom that is contrary to the message of the cross.[74] The ensuing argument presumes that the message of the cross is antithetical to the status-seeking

---

[69] So also ibid., 62. Paul uses baptismal language in the letter in interesting ways, referring to the Israelites' "baptism into Moses" (10:2), the fact that all believers are "baptized by one Spirit into one body" (12:13), and the intriguing reference to those who "baptized for the dead" (15:29).

[70] The noun "gospel" occurs six times and the verb "to preach the gospel" three times in chap. 9 alone. The noun occurs sixty times in the Pauline corpus, and the verb occurs twenty-one times. Ciampa and Rosner (*First Corinthians*, 86), drawing on the work of John Dickson, claim that Paul's use of the verb "to preach the gospel" refers to an eschatological, divinely commissioned activity as shown in Paul's use of Isa 52:7 in Rom 10:15. See J. P. Dickson, *Mission Commitment in Ancient Judaism and in the Pauline Communities* (Tübingen: Mohr-Siebeck, 2003), 176.

[71] The term "wisdom" occurs sixteen times from 1:17–3:23.

[72] Gk. ἐν σοφίᾳ λόγου.

[73] S. M. Pogoloff, *Logos and Sophia: The Rhetorical Situation of 1 Corinthians* (Atlanta: Scholars Press, 1992).

[74] Ibid., 108–19.

cultural expectations associated with wise speech.[75] In other words, Paul is attacking the use of rhetoric as a value system, not rhetoric per se.[76] In the Corinthian context, Pogoloff suggests that competing rivalries developed around Paul and Apollos as the Corinthians sought to enhance their status by association with wise rhetors.[77]

Rhetoric, however, was not the only issue at stake in Corinth. The key term, "wisdom," can have a wide range of meaning, and in the present context is not altogether void of content. Paul was equally concerned about the content of his message as he was about the motivations behind it. He preached a "Christ crucified," who was God's power and wisdom (1:23–24; also 1:30; 2:2), deemed by the world as "foolishness" (1:18,25). The world has not "known" God through its own wisdom (1:21). Furthermore, the content of God's wisdom is hidden, unknown to the "rulers of this age," and cannot be known apart from revelation (2:6–16). Paul describes "wisdom" as God's plan of salvation and the content of salvation itself.[78]

Paul explains that he refused to preach according to human wisdom "lest the cross of Christ be emptied of its power."[79] It is quite astounding to imagine that how Paul preached, or that his underlying motivations in preaching, would have rendered his preaching ineffectual. For Paul, the effectiveness of proclamation lay not in the manipulative rhetorical devices of the speaker but rather in the persuasive message of the cross proclaimed in the power of the Spirit (2:1–5).[80]

---

[75] Three parallel verses (2:1,4,13) further explain and expand on 1:17.

[76] Collins (*First Corinthians*, 75) notes that despite Paul's disavowal of rhetoric he, in fact, employs rhetoric in his denial. "His manner of arguing his point is clearly an appeal expressed in the language of persuasive rhetoric with its conventions and rhetorical devices." Furthermore, regarding 1:18–25, "the message of the cross is phrased in powerful rhetoric" (91). See, however, Litfin's important study that argues that Paul disavowed ancient rhetoric because of the values embodied by it, and limited himself to the role of herald rather than persuader. D. A. Litfin, *St. Paul's Theology of Proclamation: 1 Corinthians 1–4 and Greco-Roman Rhetoric* (Cambridge: Cambridge University Press, 1994).

[77] Pogoloff, *Logos and Sophia*, 129–72. Winter (*Philo and Paul Among the Sophists*) also ties Paul's discussion in chaps. 1–4 heavily to the cultural context as a refutation of the persuasive rhetoric of the sophists of the day. What Paul means in 1:17 is that he came to Corinth with an "antisophistic strategy." So Witherington, *Conflict and Community*, 101; Ciampa and Rosner, *First Corinthians*, 86.

[78] Barrett (*First Corinthians*, 49) observes that "... wisdom as a formal characteristic of skillful speech is not far from describing also the content of a preaching in which the cross may come to look like a foolish error.

[79] The Greek does not include the term "power," which the NIV picks up from the following verse (1:18). The text only reads, "That the cross might be emptied/made of no effect." The NASB translates, "So that the cross of Christ would not be made void."

[80] Regarding Paul's "theology" of proclamation see especially Litfin, *Paul's Theology of Proclamation*.

## 2. The Wisdom of God and the Cross (1:18–2:5)

The mention of preaching the gospel and the cross of Christ in 1:17 sets in motion the ensuing argument concerning the wisdom of God and the wisdom of the world beginning in 1:18. There is general agreement that 1:18–2:5 constitutes the first rhetorical unit in Paul's argument regarding God's wisdom as it applies to the Corinthian situation.[81] Taking into account the transitional verse, 1:17, the unit begins and ends with a contrast between eloquent words of human wisdom and the powerful proclamation of Christ crucified, who is the power of God (cf. 1:17 and 2:4–5). The unit further divides into three subunits (1:18–25; 1:26–31; 2:1–5), each uncovering a different aspect of God's wisdom that stands in complete contradiction to the wisdom of the world. Paul begins with the message of the cross, which is offensive and foolish to the wise of the world but at the same time power and wisdom to those who believe (1:18–25). In 1:26–31, the focus shifts to the recipients[82] of the message as further evidence of God's "contrary-to-the world" wisdom. That God chooses foolish, weak, and despised things to shame the wise and the strong eliminates human boasting and is consistent with the proclamation of a crucified Christ. Finally, in 2:1–5, Paul reminds the Corinthians of his initial ministry of proclamation in Corinth, that it too was a demonstration of God's wisdom and was consistent with the message he preached. The first two quotes from the Old Testament occur in the first and third units respectively (1:19 and 1:31). The first quote from Isa 29:14 announces God's judgment on human wisdom. The second quote from Jer 9:22–23 corroborates the point that their very existence contradicts their present boasting.[83]

### *(1) The Wisdom of God and a Crucified Messiah (1:18–25)*

**18For the message of the cross is foolishness to those who are perishing, but to us who are being saved it is the power of God. 19For it is written:**

> **"I will destroy the wisdom of the wise;**
> **the intelligence of the intelligent I will frustrate."**

**20Where is the wise man? Where is the scholar? Where is the philosopher of this age? Has not God made foolish the wisdom of the world? 21For since in the wisdom of God the world through its wisdom did not know him, God was pleased through the foolishness of what was preached to save those who believe. 22Jews**

---

[81] So Thiselton, *First Corinthians*, 148. The NIV misses the play on words, σοφίᾳ λόγου ("wisdom of word"; 1:17) and ὁ λόγος γὰρ ὁ τοῦ σταυροῦ ("the word of the cross"; 1:18). As Fee (*First Corinthians*, 68) puts it, "There is a *logos* (speech) that belongs to wisdom and there is a *logos* (message) whose content is the cross; but they are mutually exclusively." The main point is that the gospel is not human wisdom; it is wisdom (2:6ff.) but not human wisdom.

[82] Expressed in terms of their "calling," the fourth occurrence of calling language in chap. 1 (see 1:1–2,9,24).

[83] Fee, *First Corinthians*, 66.

**demand miraculous signs and Greeks look for wisdom, 23but we preach Christ crucified: a stumbling block to Jews and foolishness to Gentiles, 24but to those whom God has called, both Jews and Greeks, Christ the power of God and the wisdom of God. 25For the foolishness of God is wiser than man's wisdom, and the weakness of God is stronger than man's strength.**

Through careful repetition and parallelism, three main themes emerge in this unit:[84] (1) the proclamation of the cross, (2) the two basic human responses to the gospel message, and (3) the decisive triumph of God's wisdom over the wisdom of the world. All three themes appear in the first two verses (1:18–19), which are then restated in various ways with elaboration in the remainder of the paragraph. Initially, Paul categorizes humanity not as unbelievers and believers but rather as "those who are perishing" and those "who are being saved."[85] The former are the wise of this age (1:19–21) who stand under God's judgment and who deem the message of a crucified Messiah as foolish (1:18,21,23) or scandalous (1:23). The latter are those who believe the message (1:21), who are "called,"[86] whether Jews or Gentiles. For them the proclamation of Christ crucified is something entirely different, namely, God's wisdom and God's power (1:24). Verse 25 presents the summarizing conclusion: "The foolishness of God is wiser than man's wisdom and the weakness of God is stronger than man's strength."[87]

Within the framework of these three main themes, four features of 1:18–25 deserve further comment. First, the term "wisdom" carries both positive and negative connotations in Paul's use. In the same verse he speaks of the wisdom of the world and the wisdom of God (1:21).[88] In order to grasp the gist of Paul's argument it is unnecessary to locate this "worldly wisdom" with a

[84] Due to the high literary quality and skillful arrangement of 1:18–25, some think that Paul crafted this material prior to its insertion in the letter, or that he adapted pre-existing material since he seems to digress from his immediate concern regarding divisions (1:13–17). The paragraph, however, is critical to Paul's argument regarding the cross as the solution to the Corinthians' problem of boasting in men (so also Fee, *First Corinthians*, 67n1; Ciampa and Rosner, *1 Corinthians*, 89). Lampe submits that Paul opens this section with "covert speech" that causes the audience to puzzle over the relevance of the topic at hand as he builds his case for the application that comes later in 3:18–23. Paul's main points are that human wisdom will perish (1:18–2:5) and God's wisdom is a gift (2:6–16). See P. Lampe, "Theological Wisdom and the 'Word About the Cross': The Rhetorical Scheme in 1 Corinthians 1–4," *Int* 44 (1990): 117–31. Followed by Garland, *1 Corinthians*, 59. While Lampe's insights are helpful regarding the shape of Paul's argument, it is questionable whether or not Paul is attacking the problem "covertly" in light of his already strong denunciation of their factions in 1:13 (cf. also the strong rebuke of 3:1–4).

[85] Both present participles describing their present state. The participle "those who believe" occurs also in 1:21 as the object of the verb "to save"; God "saves those who believe."

[86] Cf. 1:2,9.

[87] Ciampa and Rosner (*First Corinthians*, 89) observe that Paul's main point in this section is "not just that humans cannot grasp God's wisdom through their own wisdom, but that human wisdom is under God's eschatological judgment," a verdict he learns from Scriptures (Isa 29:14 quoted in 1:19). Garland (*1 Corinthians*, 59) describes 1:18–25 as a reproclamation of the cross.

[88] The phrases "of this age" and "of the world" are synonymous (see 2:6–8).

particular historical expression or belief system.[89] The chief concern is the nature of the two contrasting wisdoms; one is "of the world" and the other is "of God." Paul is countering a value system, a particular "worldview." Just as there are essentially only two categories of people, those who are perishing and those who are being saved, so also there are only two kinds of wisdom, the wisdom of God and the wisdom of the world. Second, Paul cites the Old Testament for the first time in the letter in 1:19 that launches a series of scriptural quotations that play a large role in the argument through 3:23.[90] All citations support Paul's point that God's wisdom and human wisdom are mutually exclusive.[91] Third, the first person plural appears for the first time in the letter in 1:23, "*We* preach Christ crucified," in contrast to the first person singular in 1:17, "Christ sent *me* to preach," setting up an alternating pattern of singular and plural references throughout the argument of 1:18–4:21 by which Paul conveys that he is one among other duly appointed heralds of the gospel.[92] Finally, and perhaps most importantly, the function of 1:18–25 in the overall

[89] Attempts have been made to locate the "wisdom of the world" within the Jewish wisdom tradition, Hellenistic wisdom found in Philo, or a form of incipient Gnosticism. As noted in 1:17 and related texts (2:1,4,13), the context suggests the association of wisdom and rhetoric that led to excessive pride. See Collins, *First Corinthians*, 77; Thiselton, *First Corinthians*, 166; Garland, *1 Corinthians*, 60–66; Fitzmyer, *First Corinthians*, 139; Ciampa and Rosner, *First Corinthians*, 69–70.

[90] In this section alone Paul utilizes texts from Isaiah, Jeremiah, Psalms, and Job.

[91] The six citations of Scripture occur in 1:19,31; 2:9,16; and 3:19–20. All but one (2:16) include the introductory formula, "It is written." For further insight on the use and function of Scripture in 1:18–3:23 see H. H. D. Williams, *The Wisdom of the Wise: The Presence and Function of Scripture within 1 Cor. 1:18–3:23*, AGJU 49 (Leiden: Brill, 2001). Regarding the six quotations R. B. Hays observes that they are "all taken from passages that depict God as the one who acts to judge and save his people in ways that defy human imagination" (*Conversion of the Imagination: Paul as Interpreter of Israel's Scripture* [Grand Rapids: Eerdmans, 2005], 13). For the most recent full-length treatment of all scriptural quotations in 1 Corinthians, see J. P. Heil, *The Rhetorical Role of Scripture in 1 Corinthians*, Studies in Biblical Literature (Atlanta: Society of Biblical Literature, 2005). See also C. D. Stanley, *Paul and the Language of Scripture: Citation Technique in the Pauline Epistles and Contemporary Literature*, SNTSMS 74 (Cambridge: Cambridge University Press, 1992). Collins (*First Corinthians*, 94–96) helpfully summarizes how Paul cites and uses the Scriptures in this section. Paul appeals to the authority of Scriptures, generally quotes from the LXX but may sometimes use a minority textual tradition, sees the Scriptures as actualized in the present situation, sometimes applies to Christ as Lord Old Testament references to God, and usually takes note of the original context.

[92] Compare 1:18–25 (pl.); 2:1–5 (sg.); 2:6–16 (pl.); 3:1–4 (sg.); 3:5–17 (sg. and pl.); 4:1–13 (sg. and pl.). In 15:1–11 (sg. and pl.) Paul emphasizes that the gospel he preached to the Corinthians is the same gospel preached by all of the apostles (cf. the summarizing statement in 15:11, "Whether, then, it was I, or they, this is what we preach, and this is what you believed."). 1:18–25 emphasizes the death of Jesus as central to the gospel. In chap. 15, the emphasis falls on the centrality of the resurrection. Neither passages excludes the other. The present argument assumes a risen Christ (1:17, "Christ sent me . . ."). Likewise, in 15:3, Paul includes the death of Jesus as a key component of the gospel.

argument lays the foundation for Paul's ethical exhortations to follow.[93] The death of Jesus, which is "for us" (see 1:13; 5:7; 6:20; 7:23; 11:24) and "for our sins" (15:3) impinges on Christian behavior.[94] The cross is presented "as both the way of salvation and the way of life."[95] The cross is both the remedy for past sins and the basis of Christian identity.[96] In this initial section, which has to do primarily with Paul's exhortation to unity (1:10–17), the approach to factions in Corinth is precisely the same as his approach to the brewing problem of disunity in the church at Philippi (Phil 4:1–2), where he urged them to take up the same attitude of Christ, who humbled himself to death on a cross (Phil 2:5–11).[97] The cross is the interpretive framework for Christian living.

**1:18** The conjunction "for" ties this verse to the preceding (1:17) and launches the lengthy exposition of God's wisdom with the cross as the focal point.[98] Structurally, 1:18 functions as a thesis statement, not only of 1:18–25 but extending to at least 3:23.[99] The phrase "word of the cross" (NASB) may itself refer to either the content of the message or the act of preaching itself, but Paul probably has the former in mind (1:23). Commentators frequently and correctly point out that the offense of the cross in Paul's context is often lost to the modern Christian for whom the cross is now a symbol of the faith.[100] The Roman orator and philosopher Cicero called crucifixion a "most cruel and disgusting penalty."[101] From a Jewish perspective the one crucified was under God's curse.[102] Yet, a "Christ crucified" was the object of Paul's proclamation

---

[93] So also Fee (*First Corinthians*, 68), who notes that 1:18–25 "is crucial not only to the present argument (1:10–4:21) but to the entire letter as well."

[94] See 5:8; 6:7–8,20; 7:23; and the extended argument of 8:1–11:1; 11:17–34; and 12:1–14:40 with its emphasis on living in love for the edification of others. The theology of the death of Jesus is very rich in this letter. The command to imitate Paul as Paul imitates Christ (4:16–17; 11:2) refers to the self-giving pattern exemplified in Jesus' death for others.

[95] Ciampa and Rosner, *First Corinthians*, 91–92.

[96] Thiselton, *First Corinthians*, 147. Garland (*1 Corinthians*, 63) states, "What makes the story of the cross even more offensive to humans is that it is not simply the foundation of human redemption but is also to become the way of life for believers. They, too, will endure the wounds from slander, mockery, and affliction as they live for others (4:8–10; 2 Cor. 4:7–12; 6:4–10; 11:24–29)." See also Rom 8:17 and Phil 3:10.

[97] The phraseology of 2:16, "We have the mind of Christ," is similar to Phil 2:5, "Let this mind be in you which was also in Christ Jesus." Cf. also Jas 3:13–18, which speaks of a "wisdom from below" that leads to jealousy and strife, which in turn leads to disorder and every evil practice. The solution to factionalism is God's wisdom in the cross.

[98] On the specific use of "cross" terminology elsewhere in Paul see Gal 5:11; 6:12,14; Eph 2:16; Phil 2:8; 3:18; Col 1:20; 2:14. For the verb form, see Rom 6:6; Gal 2:19.

[99] 3:18–23 is a summary and reprise of the wisdom/folly contrast that begins with 1:18–25.

[100] Garland (*1 Corinthians*, 61) comments, "It was not yet the 'old rugged cross' sentimentalized in hymns, embalmed in stained-glass windows, perched on marble altars, or fashioned into gold charms."

[101] Cicero, *In C. Verrem* 2.5.65 (quoted in Fitzmyer [*First Corinthians*], 154). For a thorough study of the cross in its historical context, see M. Hengel, *Crucifixion in the Ancient World and the Folly of the Message of the Cross*, trans. J. Bowden (Philadelphia: Fortress, 1977).

[102] See Deut 21:22–23; cf. Gal 3:10–14.

(1:23; 2:2), which brings into focus the sharp distinction between those who belong to this age and those who belong to the age to come. The gospel is a message of foolishness "to those who are perishing" but the power of God "to us who are being saved," which are eschatological descriptors that look forward to end-time judgment.[103] The present age is doomed and is already in the process of passing away (7:31).[104] For this reason, those who belong to this age and deem the cross as nonsense are on their way to ultimate ruin. Paul uses present tense participles to describe both groups, thus commenting here only on their present state rather than their final destiny. In other words, those who are perishing are on their way to ultimate ruin apart from repentance and faith.[105] Similarly, those who are being saved are reminded that they are still on the way and have not yet arrived. Paul's choice of the present tense to describe salvation in 1:18 may be due to the parallel present tense description of those perishing,[106] or he may have chosen the present to counter a Corinthian self-congratulatory mood "which is entirely at odds with the proclamation of the cross."[107]

Since Paul's argument in 1:18–25 coheres around the concepts of folly and wisdom,[108] the contrast between "foolishness" and "power" in 1:18 is somewhat surprising. One would expect Paul to affirm that the gospel is the wisdom of God, the opposite of folly. But the claim is that the message of the cross is the "power" of God to the ones being saved.[109] The explanation lies in the close association between "word" and "power"[110] in the larger argument of

---

[103] In addition to the "perishing/saved" language, Barrett (*First Corinthians*, 51) notes other eschatological terms, such as "this age" and "signs," and the fulfillment of Scripture (1:19). Similarly, Fee (*First Corinthians*, 69) suggests that this division of humanity is predicated on the "event" of the cross, rather than one's response to it. That is, the cross marks the "turn of the ages" whereby God judged this present age.

[104] Cf. 1 John 2:15–17.

[105] Cf. 2 Cor 4:6–7. The voice of the verb in 1:18 could be middle (destroying themselves) or passive (being destroyed). The translation "perishing" is ambiguous regarding the agent.

[106] Paul speaks of salvation in all three tenses: past, present, and future. In similar fashion to 1:18, Paul refers to the gospel in 15:2 as that through which "you are being saved." But Paul can also speak of salvation as a past occurrence. In 1 Corinthians, Paul speaks of the Corinthians as "those sanctified in Christ Jesus" (1:2), as those who were "washed," "sanctified," and "justified" at conversion (6:11; see also Eph 2:8). However, in 3:15 and 5:5, "saved" is used in a future sense in the context of the Day of the Lord. Elsewhere in Paul, of salvation as past, see Rom 8:24; 2 Tim 1:9; Titus 3:5; of future see Rom 5:9–10; 9:27; 10:9,13; 11:14,26; 2 Tim 4:18. Past and future are combined in Rom 5:9, "Since we have now been justified by his blood, how much more shall we be saved from God's wrath through him!" Paul refers to salvation in a timeless, proverbial sense in 1 Cor 1:21, "God was pleased . . . to save those who believe" (see also 1 Tim 1:15). Robertson and Plummer (*First Corinthians*, 18) think that the force of the verb in 1:18 is axiomatic as well, referring to either past, present, or future.

[107] Thiselton, *First Corinthians*, 156. So also Garland, *1 Corinthians*, 64.

[108] Note the repetition of the term "foolishness" or "foolish" in 1:18,20,21,23,25 and the corresponding emphasis on "wisdom" or "wise" in 1:19,20,21,22,24,25.

[109] Paul affirms that Christ is both God's power and wisdom in 1:24. Cf. also 1:30, "Christ became wisdom to us from God," and 2:6–16.

[110] Gk. λόγος and δύναμις.

1:18–4:21 and in the juxtaposition of "wisdom" and "power" in the immediate context (see 1:24,25,26). In addition to 1:17–18, the word/power combination occurs also in 2:4–5 and 4:19–20. In contrast to human wisdom, Paul's message was powerfully effective, a demonstration of the Spirit (1:17–18; 2:4–5). In 4:14–21, Paul informs the Corinthians that he is not impressed with their arrogant speech but rather wants to know what kind of power they had since the kingdom of God is not a matter of speech[111] but of power (4:19–20). Thus, the term "power" in 1:18 is particularly suited to the Corinthian context in that it counters their tendency to boast in human achievement. The mention of power in 1:18 anticipates the affirmation of Christ as God's power to those who seek after signs (1:22–24). In 1:24, power is paired with wisdom, which is further developed in 1:25 and 1:26–27: God is wiser and stronger (more powerful) than men (1:25), and, in contrast to the wise and influential[112] of the world (1:26), God chooses foolish and weak things (1:27).[113] Thus, the concept of "power" is developed in relation to both "word" and "wisdom" in Paul's argument.

The term "power," in this context, has to do with the effectiveness of the cross to make God known, to accomplish salvation, and to transform lives. Thiselton argues that the term "effective" more accurately captures Paul's intent and avoids secular notions of that which is miraculous or overwhelming.[114] Ciampa and Rosner concur and further note the close connection between God's word and power in the Old Testament, citing Jer 29:23 as an example. "In v. 18 the word of the cross is the *power of God* in the sense that God's intention to defeat evil, to make himself known, and to save those who believe will certainly be brought to completion. In other words, he is able to deliver on his promise that is the gospel."[115] The use of power in 1:18 is analogous to its use in Rom 1:16 where Paul announces the gospel as "the power of God for the salvation of everyone who believes: first for the Jew, then for the Gentile." In terms of Christian living, Paul rejects the world's perspective and "personally adopts a cruciform posture in relation to 'power'."[116] The

[111] In context we should understand the phrase "not a matter of talk" in 4:20 in the sense of boastful human speech. The message of the cross, by way of contrast, is the power of the kingdom of God.

[112] The word underlying the NIV translation, "influential" (1:26), is δυνατός (powerful), which corresponds to δύναμις (power).

[113] In 1:18, Heil (*Rhetorical Role of Scripture*, 25) links the use of "power" also with the destruction of wisdom announced in the quote from Isaiah in the next verse, "Paul employs the word 'power' rather than 'wisdom' here in accord with his use of the scriptural quote, which serves as an emphatic expression of God's power to destroy wisdom."

[114] Thiselton (*First Corinthians*, 155), "God's promise and transforming activity becomes operative, effective, and actualized." So also Garland, *1 Corinthians*, 62. On the association of "power" with rhetoric and eloquence in Hellenistic literature, see Marshall, *Enmity in Corinth*, 387.

[115] Ciampa and Rosner, *First Corinthians*, 92.

[116] Thiselton, *First Corinthians*, 157. See also 2 Cor 4:7–10; 13:4.

Corinthians, on the other hand, wanted to avoid the humiliation associated with the apostolic way of life (cf. 4:9–13).

**1:19** Paul cites Isa 29:14, slightly altered from the LXX,[117] possibly under the influence of Ps 33:10 (LXX 32:10) and 89:34 (LXX 88:35),[118] to show that God's sentence against human wisdom is supported by the Scriptures. This is the first in a series of occurrences of the formula, "It is written,"[119] in the present argument (see also 1:31; 2:9; 3:19–20; and 4:6). The Scriptures speak accurately and powerfully to the present situation and show that God's modus operandi has not changed concerning human wisdom. God's actions in the present are consistent with his actions in the past. Here, the quote from Isaiah carries forward the notion of destruction from 1:18 in the use of the same Greek term that underlies the translation "to perish."[120] The wise of this world are on their way to destruction (1:18) because the Scriptures declare that God will destroy the "wisdom of the wise"[121] and will frustrate the plans of the self-styled intelligent (1:19). God's power both to save and to destroy[122] is a theme developed further in the next unit, 1:26–31; God shames the wise and the strong, and he brings to nothing the things that are (1:27–28).

Ciampa and Rosner suggest the possibility that Isa 29:14 has influenced Paul's language and thought in the surrounding verses, not only the destruction language of 1:18 but also the language of empty speech mentioned in Isa 29:13, which is the essence of Paul's criticism of the Corinthians in chaps. 1–4.[123] More significantly, however, "the 'wonderful' yet 'shocking' things (Isa 29:13–14) the prophet foretells, with messianic overtones, are what Paul

[117] The wording is identical to the LXX with the exception of the last word, κρύψω, "I will hide," altered to ἀθετήσω, "I will frustrate" (NIV). Scholars offer various explanations for the slight change: this is Paul's own free rendering, it is a combination with other texts, the explanation is found in midrashic traditions, Paul's word captures the sense of the word in the Hebrew text behind the LXX, or Paul has simply changed and adapted to this context. See the discussion in ibid., 160. Also Stanley, *Paul and the Language of Scripture*, 186. Ciampa and Rosner (*First Corinthians*, 93) note a wide range of Jewish texts that treat the theme of the absence and judgment of human wisdom (see Williams, *Wisdom of the Wise*, 61–73). These texts have affinities with Isa 29:14 and occur in situations where strife and division are plaguing a community. Isaiah 29:14 is quoted also in Matt 15:18–19 and Mark 7:6–7.

[118] So Heil, *Rhetorical Role of Scripture*, 17–19. "The Pauline version of the Isaian text evokes for the audience not just the text and context of Isa 29:14b but all of the other texts in the scriptures that speak of a similar theme and that are often interrelated by catchword connections (19). For the possible allusion to Ps 33:10, see also Barrett, *First Corinthians*, 52; Fee, *First Corinthians*, 70.

[119] In Greek, the perfect tense verb, γέγραπται, denoting the continuing validity, relevance, and authority of the Scriptures.

[120] Gk. ἀπόλλυμι.

[121] Barrett (*First Corinthians*, 52) notes that the sense of "wisdom" has changed from 1:17, that it is no longer a way of speaking but a way of thinking, yet the two are closely related in their man-centeredness.

[122] Cf. Jas 4:12.

[123] Ciampa and Rosner, *First Corinthians*, 93.

declares have now transpired through Christ-crucified."[124] In keeping with the eschatological tenor of the passage, Fee suggests that in the use of the Isaianic text Paul asserts, "In the cross, the promised 'great reversal' has been played out before human eyes in its ultimate way."[125]

**1:20** The use of Isa 29:14 raises the likelihood of the influence of Scripture at other points in Paul's argument, a feature typical of Jewish interpretive techniques. Many think that the influence of Isa 33:18 on this verse is likely.[126] The wording is different, but both texts contain three questions beginning with the word "where," as Paul derides the learned of this world: the wise man, the scholar,[127] and the philosopher. Paul probably does not have fine distinctions in mind with these three categories but employs a series of terms that are typically associated with the learned of this world, that is, the experts or professionals. What is more significant is the descriptive phrase "of this age," which modifies all three.[128] In other words, the experts to whom Paul refers belong to this age and not to the age to come and are thus unable to rightly discern the ways of God (cf. 2:14). God hides his plans from the wise and the learned and reveals them to little children (cf. Matt 11:25). Like "the rulers of this age" to be mentioned in 2:6, they are "coming to nothing." Paul will counsel further in 3:18 that "If any one of you thinks he is wise by the standards of this age, he should become a 'fool' so that he may become wise." The experts of 1:20 are those whose intellect operates solely at the human level and whose values, influence, and admiration are tied to this world. The phrase "of this age" helps up to see that Paul does not denigrate wisdom or human reason as such (see 2:6) but rather wisdom that is wedded to the value system and the motivations of this present world order.[129]

The follow-up question, "Has not God made foolish the wisdom of the world?" confirms the overthrow of human wisdom mentioned in 1:19 and counters the world's evaluation of the cross as foolishness in 1:18. In the cross God has "turned the tables" on the wise by turning their wisdom into its very opposite—foolishness.[130] Those who are perishing consider the cross foolish-

---

[124] Ibid.

[125] Fee, *First Corinthians*, 70.

[126] Barrett (*First Corinthians*, 53) notes other similar OT texts (Job 12:17; Isa 19:11–12; 33:18; 44:25). On the use of Isa 19:11–12 see also Fee, *First Corinthians*, 70. These questions continue the point of 1:19 and reflect the same kind of sarcasm found in Isa 19:12. Ciampa and Rosner (*First Corinthians*, 94) read Isa 33:18 as a messianic text and suggest that the echo of this text in 1 Cor 1:20 "recalls the overthrow by the Messiah of all those who oppose God and his people in the End Time, reinforcing both the passage's Christology and eschatology."

[127] Other translations read, "scribe." Thiselton (*First Corinthians*, 163–64) thinks "scribe" is too specific and prefers "expert."

[128] The phrase "of this age" presumes a two-age perspective: "this age and the age to come." See 2 Cor 4:4; Gal 1:4. Thiselton (*First Corinthians*, 165) translates "this age" as "this world order."

[129] So Thiselton, *First Corinthians*, 166; Garland, *1 Corinthians*, 66.

[130] So Fee, *First Corinthians*, 72.

ness, but now God has "made foolish" the "wisdom of the world," a phrase synonymous with "this age." Both phrases point to the transitory nature of human wisdom.[131]

**1:21** In 1:21–24, Paul explains further why and how God has made foolish the world's wisdom and why he (Paul) numbers himself among those who proclaim Christ crucified.[132] Simply stated, it is a matter of God's own wisdom and pleasure that the world did not come to know him through its own wisdom.[133] To put it another way, God determines how it is that people come to know him, and God is pleased to save those who believe "through the foolishness of what was preached." The NIV translation suggests that Paul has in mind specifically the content of the message of salvation, not the form of preaching. Litfin contends, however, that both content and form are included, that "what was preached" is synonymous with "the message of the cross" in 1:18, which stands in contrast to preaching "words of human wisdom" in 1:17. "Paul has intentionally chosen a term which collapses form and content into one."[134]

The chief point is that God prevents the wise from knowing him through their own wisdom but rather saves "those who believe," an expression parallel to those "being saved" in 1:18.[135] This is the second mention of the preaching of the cross in conjunction with salvation and the first mention of faith (believing) in the letter. Faith stands in contrast to human wisdom as the means of the knowledge of God. Fee puts it this way: "A God discovered by human wisdom will be both a projection of human fallenness and a source of human pride, and this constitutes the worship of the creature, not the Creator."[136] Thus, the wise and the powerful are in no better position to know God than anyone else. In fact, their self-sufficiency and supposed wisdom stands in the way.[137] Ciampa and Rosner think that this verse has a specific connection to Isa 28:16 regarding the cornerstone with the consequence of perdition or salvation, depending on one's response to the stone (1 Cor 1:23–24). "Along with developing these

---

[131] So L. Morris, *1 Corinthians*, TNTC (Grand Rapids: Eerdmans, 1985), 44.

[132] In Greek, the conjunction γὰρ is explanatory. The causal conjunction ἐπειδή occurs twice, in 1:21 and again in 1:22, linking these two verses and leading up to the climactic statement of 1:23–24, "We preach Christ crucified."

[133] Thiselton (*First Corinthians*, 168–69) notes the various interpretations of the enigmatic phrase, "in the wisdom of God": wisdom as revealed in the Law and Prophets, wisdom as that which reverses the values of the world, divine wisdom as God's self-revelation, wisdom as a prophetic critique of human achievement and pride, and wisdom as grace freely given in contradistinction to self-sufficiency. All of these may assist us in understanding Paul's use of the phrase. For an apt commentary on the state of those who "claimed to be wise" but became "fools," see esp. Rom 1:18–31.

[134] Litfin, *Paul's Theology of Proclamation*, 198–99. So also Garland, *1 Corinthians*, 68.

[135] Again, the present participle is used. Here a proverbial (gnomic) sense is likely.

[136] Fee, *First Corinthians*, 72.

[137] Knowing God is connected to God's self-revelatory acts. Garland (*First Corinthians*, 68) posits, "The problem for the 'wise' is that God's acts in history are so unexpected and so enigmatic that they fail to recognize them as God's acts."

same themes, 1 Corinthians 1:21–24 has some terms that overlap with the Isaiah text: it shares the participial form of the verb 'to believe' in 1:21 (in both texts God saves 'those who believe'). The use of the word 'stumbling block' in 1:23 may also have been picked up from the broader associated 'stone' tradition (that emerges in 1 Cor. 3:10–15); the word appears in Romans 9:33 in connection with Isaiah 28:16 and 8:14."[138]

**1:22–24** Barrett calls these verses "Paul's most brilliant epigrammatic description of the world in which the gospel is preached, and of the gospel itself."[139] The NIV misses a nuance of the Greek in 1:22 by omitting the causal conjunction "since," which parallels the same conjunction in 1:21. A better translation would be "since also Jews ask for a sign." Both 1:21 and 1:22 further explain 1:18–20 and connect logically to the statement of 1:23, "But we preach Christ crucified."[140] In other words, Paul's commitment to preach Christ crucified is grounded in God's determination to save those who believe the message of the cross (1:21), even though Jews and Gentiles alike reject the message (1:22–23b). The message does not fall on deaf ears, however, since to those whom God has called, both Jews and Gentiles, Christ is God's power and God's wisdom (1:24).

The Jews' demand for miraculous signs refers to Jewish messianic expectations,[141] God's extraordinary intervention on behalf of his people. After all, since God has shown himself mighty on behalf of his people in times gone by, why should they now expect anything less?[142] Thiselton notes that Jews already had access to wisdom in the Scriptures, "but required signs to locate their situation within the promised purposes of salvation history."[143] Jesus refused to offer signs to those who asked for it, yet ultimately he provided the greatest of all signs, the "sign of Jonah" that prefigured his resurrection from the dead (Matt 12:28–42).

The terms "Greeks" (1:22,24) and "Gentiles" (1:23) are probably synonymous in this context. Paul may have used the former as a cultural descriptor since the Greeks were renowned for their love and pursuit of wisdom.[144] Together, these two portrayals of humanity, the demand for power and the pursuit of wisdom, constitute what Fee calls "the basic idolatries of our fallen

---

[138] Ciampa and Rosner, *First Corinthians*, 98.

[139] Barrett, *First Corinthians*, 54.

[140] Robertson and Plummer (*First Corinthians*, 21) translate, "Since—while Jews and Gentiles alike demand something which suits their unsympathetic limitations—we, on the other hand, preach,' etc."

[141] The NIV interprets by supplying the word "miraculous."

[142] See also Num 14:11,22; John 6:30. Fitzmyer (*First Corinthians*, 158) notes that the phrase "signs and wonders" frequently occurs in the LXX to describe God's mighty acts (see Exod 7:3; Deut 4:34; 28:46; 34:11; Ps 135:9; Isa 8:18).

[143] Thiselton, *First Corinthians*, 170.

[144] So Collins, *First Corinthians*, 106; Garland, *1 Corinthians*, 70; Ciampa and Rosner, *First Corinthians*, 99.

world."[145] They are self-centered expressions of man in rebellion against God.[146] Although Paul still distinguishes between Jew and Gentile in 1:22–24, the categories of real significance are "those who are perishing" and those "who are being saved" (1:18), or those who believe (1:21) and, by implication, those who do not, or those who deem the message of the cross to be a stumbling block or foolishness (1:23) and those who are "called," for whom Christ is God's power and God's wisdom (1:24).

The emphatic, "But we,"[147] sets Christian proclamation in stark contrast to the human quest for signs and wisdom. The cross is the solution to the world's quest for power and wisdom but only to "the called" for whom Christ is God's power and God's wisdom. To the unbelieving Jew a crucified Messiah[148] is the epitome of weakness and defeat, a flat-out contradiction and a stumbling block[149] that goes against all expectations of a royal, conquering king. Similarly, to the Greeks, distinguished by their quest for wisdom, the notion of an executed criminal as the locus of God's wisdom amounted to sheer nonsense. The "stumbling block" and "foolishness" language ascribed to Christ in his crucifixion is difficult for the modern Christian to grasp, but we have to keep in mind how the proclamation of an executed criminal as "good news" would have played out in the first-century context to the Jew with fervent messianic expectations and to the Greek who coveted honor, esteem, and success.[150]

The emphatic construction "to the called" (1:24)[151] further defines "those who believe" in 1:21, which is synonymous with "the ones being saved" in 1:18. The gospel is for all without distinction, both Jews and Greeks. It is the power of God to everyone who believes (Rom 1:16), yet the divine initiative in salvation, rather than human achievement or decision, explains the positive response to the message of the cross.[152] God's sovereignty in salvation

---

[145] Fee, *First Corinthians*, 75.

[146] So Barrett, *First Corinthians*, 54–55.

[147] In Greek, the personal pronoun subject is used with the verb for emphasis (ἡμεῖς δὲ κηρύσσομεν).

[148] Literally, "Christ, having been crucified," a perfect participle. The risen Christ is still the "crucified one." Thiselton (*First Corinthians*, 171) notes that to translate simply as "Christ-crucified" loses some of its force.

[149] The Greek term σκάνδαλον occurs only here in 1 Corinthians but is used in a similar context in Rom 9:33 and 11:11–12. Thiselton (*First Corinthians*, 171) prefers the translation "affront." Ciampa and Rosner (*First Corinthians*, 100) contend, however, that the use of the term in Romans with connections to Isa 8:14 and Ps 69:23–24 suggests something more serious is at stake. There are disastrous consequences.

[150] Fee (*First Corinthians*, 75) comments that we must appreciate the depth of this scandal and folly "if we are to understand both why the Corinthians were moving away from it toward wisdom and why it was well over a century before the cross appears among Christians as a symbol of their faith."

[151] Gk. αὐτοῖς δὲ τοῖς κλητοῖς.

[152] "Called" is a passive adjective, placing emphasis on God's action rather than human decision. The passive verb form is used in 1:9, "You were called into fellowship with his Son, Jesus Christ." The adjective "called" appears in Paul only in 1 Corinthians and Romans (cf. Rom 1:6,

receives further emphasis in the next section, where, in addition to the fourth reference in this chapter to "called" (1:26), Paul refers three times to God's choice of the foolish and weak things as the means of bringing down the powerful and the wise of the world. The language of salvation is decidedly against human performance and undermines the Corinthians' present attitude of self-sufficiency.[153] To this group of "called," both Jews and Greeks, Christ is God's power and God's wisdom. The mention of Christ in 1:24 is parallel grammatically to "Christ" in 1:23.[154] The meaning is that the proclamation of Christ crucified is, to the called, God's power and God's wisdom.[155] Paul thus recasts worldly perceptions of power and wisdom (1:22) in terms of God's purposes in salvation, a point that receives further elaboration in 1:26–31 (see esp. 1:30).[156] God's wisdom and power rest on a completely different basis from that of the world.

**1:25** The final verse of this unit recaps Paul's initial argument about God's wisdom in the cross of Christ, and points forward to the next section with emphasis on God's strength (power) in weakness. The phrase "foolishness of God" occurs for the first time, recapping the "foolish gospel" theme of the entire paragraph. This is also the first mention of the "weakness of God," a key term in the next two units (1:26–31; 2:1–5), describing both the Corinthian believers and Paul. Although 1:25 functions as a summary of 1:18–24, grammatically, it most likely relates back directly to 1:23, "We preach Christ crucified."[157] In other words, Paul preaches a crucified Messiah because this supposed foolishness of God is wiser than men, and his apparent weakness is stronger than men.[158] Barrett comments, "What God has done in Christ

---

"You also are among those who are called to belong to Jesus Christ"; Rom 8:28, "And we know that in all things God works for the good of those who love him, who have been called according to his purpose"). The verb/participle form is far more frequent and carries different meanings in different contexts (for all uses of the verbal forms see Rom 4:17; 8:30; 9:7,12,24–26; 1 Cor 1:9; 7:15,17–18,20–22,24; 10:27; 15:9; Gal 1:6,15; 5:8,13; Eph 4:1,4; Col 3:15; 1 Thess 2:12; 4:7; 5:24; 2 Thess 2:14; 1 Tim 6:12; 2 Tim 1:9). In Paul's usage of the verb, we cannot divorce God's calling from human responsibility. God's calling is the basis of and presumes a positive Christian response in a life of holiness. In Gal 1:6 Paul writes, "I am astonished that you are so quickly deserting the one who called you by the grace of Christ and are turning to a different gospel."

[153] Thiselton (*First Corinthians*, 172) comments, "Any version of the gospel which substitutes a message of personal success for the cross is a manipulative counterfeit."

[154] Both are anarthrous and in the accusative case.

[155] The genitive construction is emphatic, repeating and placing the genitive construct "of God" before "power" and "wisdom." Ciampa and Rosner (*First Corinthians*, 101) suggest that the response of the "called" echoes Daniel's prayer in Dan 2:20–22.

[156] See also 2:6–3:4.

[157] The explanatory conjunction ὅτι could refer back to 1:21 ("God was pleased to save those who believe, because . . .) or 1:24b ("Christ is God's power and God's wisdom, because . . .).

[158] Strictly speaking, since the adjectives are neuter, the phrase is "the foolish thing of God" and "the weak thing of God," which may refer, in context, to the cross.

crucified is a direct contradiction of human ideas of wisdom and power, yet it achieved what human wisdom and power fail to achieve."[159]

### *(2) The Wisdom of God and the Corinthians' Calling (1:26–31)*

**26Brothers, think of what you were when you were called. Not many of you were wise by human standards; not many were influential; not many were of noble birth. 27But God chose the foolish things of the world to shame the wise; God chose the weak things of the world to shame the strong. 28He chose the lowly things of this world and the despised things—and the things that are not—to nullify the things that are, 29so that no one may boast before him. 30It is because of him that you are in Christ Jesus, who has become for us wisdom from God—that is, our righteousness, holiness and redemption. 31Therefore, as it is written: "Let him who boasts boast in the Lord."**

The main point of 1:26–31, which extends the argument of 1:18–25, is that God's choice of individuals is consistent with the message of the cross. Both exclude human boasting and both defy human wisdom.[160] By human standards the Corinthian church consisted primarily of the foolish, the weak, and the insignificant. The mention of their calling in 1:26, along with the threefold emphasis on God's choosing (1:27–28) and the assertion that it is "because of him that you are in Christ Jesus" (1:30) places strong emphasis on the sovereignty of God in salvation and leads to the conclusion that the Lord is the only proper object of boasting (1:29,31).[161] As in 1:18–25, Paul appeals to Scripture (1:31), which supports the claim that human criteria are of no consequence to God.[162] There are two equally likely sources of the citation, Jer 9:22–23

---

[159] Barrett, *First Corinthians*, 56.

[160] The shift to the second person plural, along with the vocative ἀδελφοί, indicates a shift in the argument. The Greek conjunction γάρ (untranslated by the NIV) links 1:26–31 to the previous section, especially 1:23–25. The "calling" language in 1:26 (κλῆσις) connects thematically to the mention of "the called" in 1:24 (κλητός), and the reference to the "foolish things" and "weak things" of the world (1:27) follows closely on the summarizing reference in 1:25 to the "foolish thing of God" and "weak thing of God." The explanatory γάρ indicates that Paul is calling attention to the circumstances of their coming to faith as a living paradigm of the principle that the foolishness of God is wiser than men and the weakness of God is stronger than men. So also F. W. Grosheide, *Commentary on the First Epistle to the Corinthians*, NICNT (Grand Rapids: Eerdmans, 1953), 50n49; Barrett, *First Corinthians*, 56.

[161] The NIV translation misses the two occurrences of "flesh" (Gk, σάρξ). Not many of the Corinthians were wise "by human standards" (1:26); the end result of God's activity in salvation is that "no one" may boast before God (1:29).

[162] 1:31 is the second use of the formulaic, γέγραπται, "It is written." If the verb βλέπετε (1:26) is indicative rather than imperative, then the reference to the Old Testament in 1:31 is the first command of the letter, "Let him who boasts boast in the Lord." In 3:19–20 Paul appeals again to Scripture (Job 5:12; Ps 93:11) and follows with the imperative, "Stop boasting in men!"

(LXX) and 1 Sam 2:10 (LXX), both of which may have influenced the vocabulary, structure, and theme of 1 Cor 1:26–31.[163]

The importance of this passage concerning the question of the social makeup of the early Hellenistic Christian communities is self-evident since Paul comments on the social status of the Corinthians at the time of their conversion. The traditional understanding of this passage posits that, for the most part, the Christian faith appealed primarily to the lower classes.[164] Some have argued just the opposite, reading 1:26b as a question ("Were not many of you wise . . . ?), and interpret Paul's statement as rhetoric intended as theological critique and warning.[165] More recent sociological approaches emphasize the nonhomogeneous character of early Christianity, a mixture of social classes, a more complex social history.[166] The traditional reading understands 1:26b as forthright appraisal that "not many" among the Corinthians were wise, influential, and of noble birth, implying that "some" in the community enjoyed esteemed social standing. Those in Corinth who might have been among the upper class include Crispus (1:14; cf. Acts 18:18), Gaius (1:14; cf. Rom 16:23), Erastus, the city treasurer (Rom 16:23), Phoebe of Cenchreae (16:1–2), and Aquila and Priscilla (16:19–20; cf. Rom 16:3–5a).[167] Paul's discussion of the Lord's supper in chap. 11 implies divisions along social lines (see 11:17–22), and the social stratification within the community may have played a large role

[163] So Ciampa and Rosner, *First Corinthians*, 110–11; Heil, *Rhetorical Role of Scripture*, 37–39. Heil argues that whatever the source of the quotation, Paul evokes any and all of the scriptural texts that refer to "boasting" or trusting in God alone. Paul's version is not an exact, verbatim quote of either text. See also G. R. O'Day, "Jeremiah 9:22–23 and 1 Corinthians 1:26–31: A Study in Intertextuality," *JBL* 109 (1990): 259–67. On "sophistic boasting" as a possible cultural background to 1:26–31, see Winter, *Philo and Paul*, 187–95.

[164] A. Deissmann, *Light from the Ancient Near East* (London: Hodder & Stoughton, 1927), 144. More recently, see J. J. Meggit, *Paul, Poverty, and Survival* (Edinburgh: T&T Clark, 1998).

[165] W. Wuellner, "The Sociological Implications of 1 Corinthians 1:26–28 Reconsidered," in *Studia Evangelica*, ed. E. A. Livingstone, Texte Und Untersuchungen (Berlin: Akademie Verlag, 1973). See also O'Day, "Jeremiah 9:22–23 and 1 Corinthians 1:26–31: A Study in Intertextuality." Wuellner reads the ὅτι clause as interrogative, yielding, "Were not many of you wise, were not many strong, were not many noble?" This is the exact opposite of traditional English translations. Following Wuellner, O'Day reads the passage as an example of Pauline irony characteristic of 1 Cor 1–4. Paul acknowledges that many of the Corinthians were wise, powerful, and of noble birth, and does so with a theological purpose. The categories are "essential elements in a theological critique" (264). Paul's purpose is to critique their false sources of security that promote human boasting. Paul's words are not a commendation of the community but a warning. His primary concern is not their social location but a critique of "wisdom, power, and wealth as false sources of identity that violate the covenant" (266). Collins (*1 Corinthians*, 110) counters, however, that Paul does not use the interrogative ὅτι elsewhere. Regarding social status, Judge argued, "Far from being a socially depressed group, if the Corinthians are at all typical, the Christians were dominated by a socially pretentious section of the population of the big cities." See E. A. Judge, *The Social Pattern of the Christian Groups in the First Century* (London: Tyndale, 1960), 60.

[166] See the studies by G. Theissen, *The Social Setting of Pauline Christianity: Essays on Corinth,* trans. J. H. Schutz (Philadelphia: Fortress, 1982); Meeks, *First Urban Christians*.

[167] For a full analysis see Theissen, *Social Setting*, 69–120.

in other problems in the church, including legal disputes (6:1–11) and the issue of food sacrificed to idols (8:1–11:1).[168]

**1:26** The NIV translation, "Think of what you were when you were called," is an interpretive rendering of the Greek that takes into account both the Corinthians' station in life as well as their call to salvation.[169] Witherington thinks that the primary sense of the term "calling" in this verse has to do with their social standing, as the modifying clause indicates, "not many of you were wise by human standards; not many were influential; not many were of noble birth."[170] The term "calling" can refer to one's station in life as well as to God's call to salvation. Both senses occur in 7:20.[171] Previous occurrences of "calling" language in this chapter, however, relate to the divine initiative (1:2,9,24), and 1:27–28 emphasize God's choice. In this context, "calling" and "choosing" seem to be interchangeable terms.

In this second stage of his argument regarding the character of God's wisdom, Paul invites the Corinthians to take into consideration their identity in terms of worldly wisdom or merit when they received the message of the cross. By human standards,[172] few of the Corinthians were learned, influential, or born with a pedigree of high social standing. The descriptive clause in Greek is a verbless construction, and most translations supply a past tense, such as the NIV, "Not many of you *were* wise . . . ." But a present tense is also possible, rendering "Not many of you *are* wise."[173] On this reading, Garland comments that their coming to Christ has "done nothing to enhance their social estate."[174]

**1:27–29** The literary and stylistic effects makes 1:27–29 "an especially powerful passage."[175] The emphatic Greek word order and repetition draw attention to God's choice, the objects of his choosing, and the outcome. First Corinthians 1:27 begins with an emphatic conjunction,[176] punctuating the fact that not many of the Corinthians were esteemed by human standards. In each successive

[168] Social scientific studies of the New Testament have proliferated in New Testament studies over the last several decades. For the history of scholarship with reference to 1 Corinthians and the relevant literature, including excerpts from the history of scholarship, see Adams and Horrell, *Christianity at Corinth*, 26–34.

[169] The Greek reads, βλέπετε γὰρ τὴν κλῆσιν ὑμῶν, "For consider your calling." The NIV renders "calling" as a passive verb rather than as a noun ("when you were called"). Most translations render the verb βλέπετε (think, or consider) as an imperative. The verb could also be indicative (KJV and AV), and if so, Paul would be making an affirmation, "You see your calling, brothers."

[170] Witherington, *Conflict and Community*, 113.

[171] NIV, "Each one should remain in the situation [Gk. κλῆσις, "calling"] which he was in when God called" (Gk. καλέω) him. The only two occurrences in the letter of the noun "calling" are in 1:26 and 7:20.

[172] Gk. κατὰ σάρκα, "according to the flesh." The HCSB renders, "from a human perspective."

[173] So HCSB.

[174] Garland, *1 Corinthians*, 73.

[175] Thiselton, *First Corinthians*, 186.

[176] Gk. ἀλλά. Thiselton (*First Corinthians*, 183) comments that "The threefold repetition of ἐξελέξατο ὁ θεός, God chose, dominates the flow of thought and syntax."

parallel line, the object of God's choice occurs first for emphasis: "the foolish things God chose . . . the weak things God chose. . . the lowly things and the despised things God chose. . . ." The parallelism corresponds to the wise, the influential, and those of noble birth mentioned in 1:26. The threefold repetition of the phrase, "God chose," sets up three result clauses,[177] which indicate the outcome of God's choice; God shames the wise and the strong (1:27) and he brings to nothing the "things that are" (1:28),[178] so that "no one may boast before him" (1:29).[179] This last statement answers the question of why God, in his own wisdom, has disallowed access to himself via the "wisdom of the world" (1:21). In Greek the words translated "shame," "nullify," and "boast" all begin with the same letter, heightening the rhetorical impact.[180]

Thus, the emphasis of 1:27–29 falls on God's freedom and purpose to choose as he pleases, just as he acted in the past with respect to Israel: "The LORD did not set his affection on you and choose you because you were more numerous than other peoples, for you were the fewest of all peoples" (Deut 7:7). This also accords with the teaching of Jesus, "I praise you, Father, Lord of heaven and earth, because you have hidden these things from the wise and learned, and revealed them to little children" (Matt 11:25), and his half-brother James, who derived much of his teaching from Jesus: "Has not God chosen those who are poor in the eyes of the world to be rich in faith and to inherit the kingdom he promised those who love him?" (Jas 2:5). First Corinthians 1:18–31 presents a very strong theology of grace.[181]

**1:30–31** The paragraph climaxes with a succinct statement that refers more positively to what the Corinthians are "in Christ Jesus" (1:30) followed

---

[177] Each clause begins with the Greek conjunction ἵνα.

[178] The concept of "shame" (καταισχύνω) reflects the Old Testament theme of God's righteous judgments and vindication over his enemies (see Pss 6:10; 31:17; 35:4,26–27; 40:15; 83:16–18; Isa 41:11; Jer 2:26). The term "nullify" (καταργέω) occurs throughout 1 Corinthians in eschatological contexts (2:6; 6:13; 13:8,10–11; 15:24,26) "to express Paul's conviction that in Christ God has already set the future in motion, whereby the present age is 'on its way out,' is being done away with by God himself" (Fee, *First Corinthians*, 83).

[179] Literally, "that all flesh may not boast before God." The use of the term "flesh" may hark back to the previous use in 1:26, "not many wise *according to the flesh*." The NIV does not translate "flesh" in either case (Gk. σάρξ). God's choice excludes all human boasting absolutely.

[180] καταισχύνω (to shame), καταργέω (to nullify, to render void), and καυχάομαι (to boast). To this list we might also note the word "world" (κόσμος) also begins with the Greek letter kappa.

[181] Thiselton (*First Corinthians*, 184) notes the fundamental commonality between Paul and Jesus on this point, citing the many parables of Jesus about invitations to a great banquet that "turned on the primacy of grace over religious and social degrees of status and achievement (Matt 9:10–13; 11:25–27; 18:10–14; 20:1–16; 21:28–41; 22:1–10; Mark 2:15–17; 7:1–8; 10:23–27; 12:1–12; Luke 5:29–32; 7:36–50; 10:21–22,29–37; 11:45–53; 14:12–24; 15:1–32; 18:9–13,24–27)." Furthermore, Thiselton comments, "Jesus had 'nowhere to lay his head' (Matt 11:20). His sayings about the ambiguity of 'signs' (Mark 8:11), about wisdom (Matt 11:25–27; Luke 10:21–23), about rejection, suffering, and the cross (Mark 8:31–38), and above all about grace (Matt 20:1–16; Luke 15:1– 32) offer very close affinities with Pauline themes in this and similar passages."

by a command to "boast in the Lord" (1:31).[182] What really matters are not the categories of the wise, the influential, and those of noble birth acclaimed by the world (1:27), but rather God's saving power in the gospel (recall 1:18,21,24), that "Christ became for us wisdom from God," which Paul explicates in terms of "righteousness, sanctification, and redemption." These three terms are not coordinate with wisdom, but rather "denote aspects of the wisdom which believers find in Christ, in whom they are justified, sanctified, and redeemed (cf. 6:11)."[183] Thus, the NIV translation, "Christ . . . has become for us wisdom from God—that is, our righteousness, holiness and redemption." Paul does not expand on these aspects of salvation here, but he touches on them at various points in the letter.[184] Believers have these things because of their union with Christ, and believers are in union with Christ because of God: "It is because of him that you are in Christ Jesus."[185] Thus Paul reminds the Corinthians that they owe everything to God, that their very existence as the people of God is predicated on the activity of God in Christ. There are grounds for boasting but only in Christ's redemptive work. "Let him who boasts boast in the Lord" (1:31).[186]

### *(3) The Wisdom of God and Paul's Ministry in Corinth (2:1–5)*

**[1]When I came to you, brothers, I did not come with eloquence or superior wisdom as I proclaimed to you the testimony about God. [2]For I resolved to know nothing while I was with you except Jesus Christ and him crucified. [3]I came to you in weakness and fear, and with much trembling. [4]My message and my preaching were not with wise and persuasive words, but with a demonstration of the Spirit's power, [5]so that your faith might not rest on men's wisdom, but on God's power.**

In 2:1–5 Paul describes the content, the manner, and the results of his preaching during the time of the establishment of the Corinthian church. Having shown that God's wisdom upends human wisdom in the proclamation of a crucified Messiah (1:18–25), which is further illustrated in God's choice of the foolish and insignificant things of the world (1:26–31), Paul now describes his own ministry among them as a ministry that exemplified the wisdom of God (2:1–5).[187] He did not come to Corinth preaching with all the embellishments

---

[182] Thus the term "boast" can carry both positive (1:31) and negative connotations (1:29), depending on the object of one's boast or the attitude behind it.

[183] F. F. Bruce, *1 and 2 Corinthians*, NCB (Grand Rapids: Eerdmans, 1971), 36.

[184] Cf. 1:2; the Corinthians have been "set apart in Christ." In 3:17 Paul refers to the Corinthians as the holy temple of God, the dwelling place of the Holy Spirit and in 6:11 to their justification and sanctification at conversion. The language of redemption, which evokes the image of the slave market, is captured twice in the phrase, "You were bought for a price" (6:20; 7:23).

[185] In Gk. a very terse, "of him (ἐξ αὐτοῦ) you are in Christ Jesus." The NASB, "But by His doing you are in Christ Jesus." See also Rom 11:36; 1 Cor 8:6; Eph 2:8–9.

[186] The citation of Jer 9:23–24 (LXX 1 Sam 2:10) appears also in 2 Cor 10:17.

[187] So also Thiselton, *First Corinthians*, 204, "Paul's own experience in Corinth confirms precisely the same point as 1:26–31."

of human eloquence and wisdom but rather as one bearing witness to Christ crucified (2:2; cf. 1:23). In short, Paul's manner of preaching and way of life was consistent with the message he preached.[188]

Beginning with 2:1 Paul references his initial ministry in Corinth at various points in the remainder of the argument through 4:21.[189] In addition to this present paragraph concerning how he came to them, Paul recounts his initial instruction (3:1–4), his role as a church planter (3:6) and his work as a wise builder in laying the foundation according to God's grace (3:10–11).[190] In 4:14–15 Paul warns the Corinthians as his spiritual children since he alone fathered them in Christ through the gospel. Collectively these self-references lead to the climactic exhortation in 4:16–17 to "imitate me." The self-references are balanced, however, by the use of the first person plural to call attention to the shared proclamation of Christ crucified (1:23) and instruction in God's wisdom (2:6). Furthermore, Paul refers to Apollos as his co-worker (3:9), counts himself among other servants and stewards of the mysteries of God (4:1), and identifies with other apostles who represented Christ and patterned their life after the cross in suffering (4:9–13).

The NIV leaves untranslated the emphatic "and I,"[191] which occurs twice in this section, setting up a contrast between how Paul did *not* come to them preaching (2:1), that is, in excellence of speech or wisdom, and how he *did* come (2:3), that is, in weakness, fear, and with much trembling, yet with powerful results (2:4b). Thus, in terms of structure, 2:1–2 and 2:3–4 are parallel sections.[192] In both sections Paul denies preaching according to words of human wisdom; the second denial (2:4a) stands in contrast with how Paul did preach, "in demonstration of the Spirit's power" (2:4b). First Corinthians 2:5 explains why Paul preached in this way: "So that your faith might not rest on men's wisdom, but on God's power." Although Paul does not quote Scripture in 2:1–5, as he does in the previous two units, Williams suggests that this section echoes Zech 4:6, "'Not by might nor by power, but by my Spirit,' says the LORD Almighty."[193]

---

[188] See also 2 Cor 1:12 where Paul "boasts" that he conducted himself in holiness and sincerity, "not according to worldly wisdom but according to God's grace."

[189] This is the first use of the first person singular since 1:17, "Christ did not send *me* to baptize but to preach the gospel."

[190] The NIV translates 3:10 "expert builder," but the term for "expert" is σοφός (wise), which can carry the connotation of "skilled." The term is obviously carefully chosen in context and should be rendered "wise" builder, which supports the point that Paul's ministry was a ministry of the wisdom of God.

[191] Gk. κἀγώ. A combination of the Greek conjunction καί with the personal pronoun ἐγώ.

[192] In addition to the emphatic κἀγώ, both sections mention Paul's "coming" to them, both mention proclamation, and both use the key terms λόγος and σοφία.

[193] Williams, *Wisdom of the Wise*, 156. Followed by Ciampa and Rosner, *First Corinthians*, 112. Ciampa and Rosner note further the connection that "Paul and Zechariah are both layers of foundation of a new temple (Zech 4:6–10; 1 Cor 3:10–11)."

**2:1–2** Paul's claim that he came preaching not in "eloquence or superior wisdom"[194] should be read in light of 1:17, which clarifies that he was faithful to Christ's commission to preach the gospel apart from the values embodied in Greco-Roman rhetoric.[195] His manner of preaching did not conform to a desire to win the approval of his audience, nor was it based on the schemes of human intelligence. Both empty the cross of its effectiveness. Winter sees Paul's language as specifically "anti-sophistic," repudiating the sophistic method of presenting oneself in competitive rhetoric.[196] Paul took issue with a certain strain of rhetoric, born and nurtured by human wisdom, but not rhetoric or wisdom per se. Thiselton notes that Paul "constantly strove for wise argument," both using and at the same time opposing rhetoric in his own writing. "His respect for reason precludes any anti-intellectualism as such."[197] What Paul rejects is self-presentation and haughty speech. Garland puts it this way: "The gospel always points beyond humans to God and Christ and becomes garbled whenever humans exploit it instead to headline themselves as its stars."[198] The content of Paul's message was simple and straightforward, "For I resolved to know nothing while I was with you except Jesus Christ and him crucified,"[199] and delivered with full confidence in the Spirit's power to produce results.[200]

---

[194] Cf. also 2 Cor 10:10, "For some say, 'His letters are weighty and forceful, but in person he is unimpressive and his speaking amounts to nothing.'"

[195] The adjective "superior" (ὑπεροχὴν) likely modifies both speech (λόγου) and wisdom (σοφίας). Speech and wisdom are separated by the comparative "or," whereas in 1:17 the two are linked ("not in wisdom of word"). See also 2:13, "not in taught words of human wisdom." There are numerous lexical parallels between 2:1–5 and 1:17–25. Paul's claim that he came preaching not in excellence of speech or wisdom in 2:1, nor by persuasive words of wisdom in 2:4, parallels 1:17. In 1:17 Christ sent Paul to preach the gospel, not ἐν σοφίᾳ λόγου (in wisdom of word), where in 2:1, Paul claims that his manner of coming to them was not according to ὑπεροχὴν λόγου ἢ σοφίας (excellence of word or wisdom). The content of Paul's message, Christ crucified (2:2), repeats the claim of 1:23. Paul's coming to them in "weakness" (2:3) recalls the same term in 1:25. And the notion that Paul's preaching was a demonstration of God's power so that the Corinthians' faith would rest on the power of God rather than the wisdom of men captures the whole of 1:17–25. Finally, the term, δύναμις (power) occurs in 1:18,24, and 2:5.

[196] Winter, *Philo and Paul*, 147–49, 155–59.

[197] Thiselton, *First Corinthians*, 208. See also S. K. Stowers, "Paul on the Use and Abuse of Reason," in *Greeks, Romans, and Christians: Essays in Honour of J. Malherbe,* ed. D. L. Balch, E. Ferguson, W. Meeks (Minneapolis: Augsburg, 1990), 253–86; M. A. Bullmore, *St. Paul's Theology of Rhetorical Style: An Examination of I Corinthians 2.1–5 in Light of First Century Graeco-Roman Rhetorical Culture* (San Francisco: International Scholars, 1995), 224–25.

[198] Garland, *1 Corinthians*, 82.

[199] Cf. 1:23. Paul uses the perfect participle, "crucified," in both 1:23 and 2:2 as the modifier of "Christ." See also Gal 3:1, "Before your very eyes Jesus Christ was clearly portrayed as crucified."

[200] See the discussion in Litfin, *Paul's Theology of Proclamation*, 204–9; Winter, *Philo and Paul*, 158–59. The term Paul uses to describe his missionary preaching, "to proclaim" (Gk. καταγγέλλω), occurs eleven times in Acts (Acts 3:24; 4:2; 13:5,38; 15:36; 16:17,21; 17:3,13,23; 26:23) and seven times in Paul's letters (Rom 1:8; 1 Cor 2:1; 9:14; 11:26; Phil 1:17–18; Col 1:28), in almost all instances of proclaiming the word of God or proclaiming Christ/the gospel. Thiselton (*First Corinthians*, 209) observes that the term often occurs in contexts that carry nuances of

In 2:1, the critical editions of the Greek New Testament read "mystery of God" instead of "testimony of God." The difference in spelling between the two terms in Greek is very minimal.[201] "Testimony" has wider manuscript support but "mystery" is attested in some of the important early manuscripts. One can make the case either way according to internal evidence since "testimony" either looks back to 1:6 or "mystery" looks forward to 2:6. Among modern commentators, Fee supports the NIV reading, "testimony,"[202] while others opt for "mystery."[203]

The mystery of God, in context, is that the proclamation of "Christ crucified" is the wisdom of God (2:2; cf. 1:23; 2:6–8). The term "mystery" as used by Paul underscores the revelatory dimension of Christian proclamation.[204] In 2:6–16, Paul elaborates further on the nature of this "mystery" with particular emphasis on the Spirit as the necessary means of revelation. In 4:1 Paul describes himself as a "steward" of the mysteries of God.[205] In short, mystery is a revelatory term that denotes the disclosure of God's truth and the revelation of something previously unknown. Garland puts it this way, "The mystery is truth revealed by God, not truth discovered by human investigation and argument. Humans do not find this truth; it finds them."[206]

**2:3–4** With another emphatic "I," the focus shifts to how Paul did come to them, "in weakness and fear, and with much trembling." In Greek the terms "weakness," "fear," and "trembling" occur first, perhaps for emphasis. By using the term "weakness" Paul numbers himself among the "weak things of the world" chosen by God in order to shame the strong" (1:28; recall also 1:25), but he does not elaborate further on the circumstances to which the terms refer. Weakness could imply a physical ailment, or any number of things, such as poverty, laboring to support oneself in ministry, or persecution, all mentioned in the context of Paul's scathing rebuke and ironic contrast of the

---

solemnity. In Rom 1:8 Paul uses the term of the believers in Rome whose "faith is being reported all over the world."

201 μυστήριον (mystery) and μαρτύριον (testimony).

202 Fee, *First Corinthians*, 91.

203 Thiselton, *First Corinthians*, 208; Garland, *1 Corinthians*, 83; Fitzmyer, *First Corinthians*, 171.

204 Of the twenty-eight occurrences of "mystery" (μυστήριον) in the New Testament, twenty-one are found in Paul's letters: Rom 11:25; 16:25; 1 Cor 2:1,7; 4:1; 13:2; 14:2; 15:51; Eph 1:9; 3:3–4,9; 5:32; 6:19; Col 1:26–27; 2:2; 4:3; 2 Thess 2:7; 1 Tim 3:9,16 (see also Matt 13:11; Mark 4:11; Luke 8:10; Rev 1:20; 10:7; 17:5,7).

205 See also Eph 3:2–13; Col 1:24–28. Collins (*First Corinthians*, 115) notes the eschatological dimension of mystery in Jewish apocalyptic literature, referring to salvific events revealed in the last time. For the most recent and thorough investigation of the term "mystery" in Paul against its Jewish background, see B. Gladd, *Revealing the Mysterion: The Use of Mystery in Daniel in Second Temple Judaism with its Bearing on First Corinthians*, BZNW 160 (Berlin: Walter de Gruyter, 2008).

206 Garland, *1 Corinthians*, 83.

"weak" apostles with the "strong" Corinthians (4:10–12).[207] Regarding fear, Acts 18:9–10 records a vision of encouragement from the Lord to Paul following persecution, "Do not be afraid; keep on speaking, do not be silent. For I am with you and no one is going to attack and harm you, because I have many people in this city." But "fear and trembling" may have little to do with human circumstances of peril and more to do with Paul's demeanor in carrying out his apostolic commission.[208] In Phil 2:12 Paul exhorted the believers in Philippi to "work out your salvation with fear and trembling."[209]

There may be no difference between "my message" and "my preaching" (2:4), unless the first term refers to the manner of Paul's presentation and the latter to the content of his preaching. The key point is that he did not rely on persuasive words of human wisdom, restating the essence of 2:1 and adding "with a demonstration of the Spirit's power." This verse marks the third time that Paul has denied preaching according to human wisdom (cf. 1:17; 2:1) and it is the first mention of the Spirit in the letter,[210] which sets the stage for the fuller treatment of the Spirit's revelatory role concerning wisdom of God in the next unit (2:6–16). The NIV takes the reference to "Spirit" and "power" as an expression of the same reality and renders "the Spirit's power." It is possible to also translate "Spirit" and "power." Either way, the meaning is that Paul's preaching was effective for God's purposes because of the empowerment of the Spirit. The Spirit bore witness to the truth of the message (see Gal 3:1; 1 Thess 1:5).[211] No one is able to say, "Jesus is Lord," except by the Holy Spirit (12:3).

**2:5** The final clause, "so that your faith might not rest on men's wisdom, but on God's power," is, in substance, a recasting of the climactic statement of the previous unit, "Let him who boasts boast in the Lord" (1:31). If we take into account the summarizing statement of 1:18–25, that God is wiser and stronger than men (1:25), taken together, the three concluding statements of each unit in 1:18–2:5 provide a succinct summary of Paul's main emphasis throughout. The mention of the Corinthians' faith in 2:5 is the first specific

[207] For a thorough study of the theme of "weakness" in Paul, see the recently revised D. A. Black, *Paul, Apostle of Weakness: Astheneia and Its Cognates in the Pauline Literature*, rev. ed. (Eugene: Wipf and Stock, 2012).

[208] Cf. 2 Cor 5:11, "Since, then, we know what it is to fear the Lord, we try to persuade men." Cf. also 1 Cor 9:24–27. See T. B. Savage, *Power Through Weakness: Paul's Understanding of the Christian Ministry in 2 Corinthians*, SNTSMS 86 (Cambridge: Cambridge University Press, 1996), 73.

[209] Cf. also 2 Cor 7:1.

[210] Although cf. 1:7 (lit.), "So that you come short in no gift," which, in the broader context of the letter, implies the reception of spiritual gifts.

[211] For other passages relating to the manner of Paul's ministry, see 2 Cor 1:12; 2:17; 4:2,7; 10:3–4 and the brief analysis in Litfin, *Paul's Theology of Proclamation*, 210–12. On the "power through weakness" theme, see also Savage, *Power Through Weakness*; D. Ortlund, "'Power Is Made Perfect in Weakness' (2 Cor. 12:9): A Biblical Theology of Strength through Weakness," *Presb* 36 (2010): 86–108.

reference to their faith in the letter.[212] The parallel between "faith" in 2:5 and "boasting in the Lord" in 1:31 is instructive to Paul's meaning of "faith" in this context. To "boast" in the Lord is to depend on, to trust, to declare one's allegiance, and to rely on. To trust in the wisdom of men is a dead-end street, a guaranteed failure (cf. 1:19).

## 3. The Wisdom of God and the Spirit (2:6–3:4)

The mention of the Spirit in 2:4 paves the way for the fuller exposition of the role of the Spirit in relation to God's wisdom in 2:6–3:4. In many respects 2:6–3:4 is parallel to 1:18–2:5. In both sections Paul contrasts God's wisdom with human wisdom (1:18–25; 2:6–16), and in both sections Paul shifts from the plural "we" to the first person singular as he recounts his initial ministry in Corinth (2:1–5; 3:1–4).

Even though the interpretation of this section hinges on a number of factors, Paul's overall intent becomes clear in the strong rebuke in 3:1–4 of the Corinthians' factious behavior, recalling the whole reason for the lengthy discussion of God's wisdom in the first place (cf. 3:4; 1:12). Paul affirms that he (and others) do indeed speak wisdom but not as the Corinthians suppose. First, there are important questions raised by key terms in 2:6–3:4. Who are the "mature" (2:6), the "spiritual," and the "natural" man (2:14–15; 3:1), the "worldly" (3:1), and the "infants" (3:1)? Are these Pauline terms, Corinthian terms, or both in the sense that the Corinthians have taken up but misconstrued Paul's language? To what extent, if at all, does Paul employ irony? Second, what is the content of the "wisdom" that Paul and others speak? Is it the gospel, something different from the gospel, or something different yet related, such as the fuller implication of or application of the gospel? Third, how do the "mature" and the "infants" (2:6; 3:1), along with the metaphors of "milk" and "solid food" (3:2), relate to this wisdom? Fourth, what is the relation of this passage to analogous passages in Ephesians and Colossians that employ similar language regarding wisdom? Fifth, what does this passage have to say about spiritual maturity, that is, what constitutes a "spiritual" person in Paul's view? While the Corinthians may have defined maturity in terms of knowledge, Paul is far more interested in defining maturity according to behavior in community. The passage aims at defining who is mature/wise and who is not. At the present time, based on their internal rivalries, the Corinthians are not.

### *(1) Wisdom as Revealed by the Spirit (2:6–16)*

**6We do, however, speak a message of wisdom among the mature, but not the wisdom of this age or of the rulers of this age, who are coming to nothing. 7No, we**

[212] 1:21 is a more generic statement, (lit.) "God was pleased to save those who believe through the foolish message."

**speak of God's secret wisdom, a wisdom that has been hidden and that God destined**
**for our glory before time began. 8None of the rulers of this age understood it, for if**
**they had, they would not have crucified the Lord of glory. 9However, as it is written:**

> **"No eye has seen,**
> **no ear has heard,**
> **no mind has conceived**
> **what God has prepared for those who love him"—**

**10but God has revealed it to us by his Spirit.**
**The Spirit searches all things, even the deep things of God. 11For who among**
**men knows the thoughts of a man except the man's spirit within him? In the same**
**way no one knows the thoughts of God except the Spirit of God. 12We have not**
**received the spirit of the world but the Spirit who is from God, that we may under-**
**stand what God has freely given us. 13This is what we speak, not in words taught**
**us by human wisdom but in words taught by the Spirit, expressing spiritual truths**
**in spiritual words. 14The man without the Spirit does not accept the things that**
**come from the Spirit of God, for they are foolishness to him, and he cannot under-**
**stand them, because they are spiritually discerned. 15The spiritual man makes**
**judgments about all things, but he himself is not subject to any man's judgment:**

> **16"For who has known the mind of the Lord**
> **that he may instruct him?"**

**But we have the mind of Christ.**

In 2:6–16 the contrast between God's wisdom and human wisdom continues but in a heightened sense and with a different focus.[213] Here Paul expands on the hidden nature of God's wisdom in relation to this age (2:6–9)[214] and in connection to the Spirit (2:10–16). What has been inferred up to this point in the argument is now made explicit, namely, that one's apprehension of the gospel as the wisdom of God comes only through divine revelation.[215] Simply stated, the wisdom of God cannot be known unless God makes it known. More specifically, God's wisdom is revealed through the Spirit, who searches the deep things of God (2:10). God's wisdom is not a matter of human intelligence or discovery but rather of divine disclosure. Paul's exposition of God's wisdom

---

[213] This unit is marked by a number of emphatic constructions, including the emphatic placement of σοφίαν (wisdom) twice in 2:6, the use of the emphatic conjunction ἀλλά (NIV, "We do, however, speak . . ." and "However, as it is written . . ."), the emphatic placement of the personal pronoun ἡμῖν ("to us") in 2:10, the use of the pronoun ἡμεῖς ("we") for emphasis in 2:12 and again in 2:16, and the more emphatic reference to the Spirit of God by repetition of the Greek definite article (τὸ πνεῦμα τὸ ἐκ τοῦ θεοῦ; NIV, "the Spirit, who is from God") in contrast to the less emphatic "spirit of the world" in 2:12. Garland (*1 Corinthians*, 90) also notes the antitheses expressed in "not/but" language that pervades Paul's argument.

[214] Picking up the same expression from 1:21. In 2:6–8, there are four occurrences of the term αἰών (age).

[215] This has been implied previously in the claims that the cross is foolishness to unbelievers (1:21,23–24), that the world did not know God through its own wisdom (1:21), and that Paul proclaimed the mystery of God (2:1).

in relation to the gospel and the Spirit provides us with one of the truly great trinitarian passages in the New Testament.[216]

As noted in the introduction to this unit (2:6–3:4), the interpretation of this passage is not without challenges.[217] The shift from the first person singular in 2:1–5 to the first person plural in 2:6–16[218] along with what some perceive as differences in content from the surrounding context has led to various suggestions regarding its origin and purpose. Some propose that this section is non-Pauline and was inserted by an editor at a later time after the original composition.[219] Ellis suggests that 2:6–16 is a pre-formed exposition created within a Pauline group and adapted by Paul into its present context.[220] Still others think Paul gives his own exposition of true wisdom from God, but, in doing so, he likely takes up concepts and phraseology in Corinth that account for the unique language.[221]

The uniqueness of this section, however, is often overstated, and what Paul actually writes coheres quite well with the literary and theological context of the letter.[222] Additionally, Paul's description of the nature of his ministry here

---

[216] Note especially 2:10–11, that the Spirit searches all things, even the depths of God and the claim, "We have the mind of Christ" (2:16) in conjunction with an Old Testament "Yahweh" text (Isa 40:13), "Who has known the mind of the Lord?"

[217] Murphy-O'Connor claims, "Of all the passages in 1 Corinthians the exegesis of 2:6–16 is perhaps the most complicated" ("Interpolations in 1 Cor," *CBQ* 48 [1986]: 81).

[218] The first person plural occurs throughout the passage: λαλοῦμεν ("we speak") in 2:6,12,13; also ἐλάβομεν ("we received"), εἰδῶμεν ("we know") in 2:12, and ἔχομεν ("we have") in 2:16; also the use of plural pronouns "we" or "us" in 2:7,10,12,16. Paul reverts back to the first person singular in 3:1 and addresses the Corinthians directly with the second person plural in 3:2–4, thus clearly distinguishing 3:1–4 from 2:6–16 linguistically.

[219] M. Widmann, "1 Kor 2 6–16: Ein Einspruch gegen Paulus," *ZNW* 70 (1979): 44–53; W. O. Walker, "1 Cor. 2:6–16: A Non-Pauline Interpolation?," *JSNT* 47 (1992): 75–94. Conzelmann (*1 Corinthians*, 57) claims that 2:6–16 contradicts Paul's previous statements.

[220] E. E. Ellis, "Traditions in 1 Corinthians," *NTS* 32 (1986), 490.

[221] So Thiselton (*First Corinthians*, 224) "But Paul takes up the major catchwords which had become embedded in the life of the church in Corinth." Paul's "most urgent task at this point is neither to reject their validity nor to bypass what was important for his readers, but to reclaim the terms for the gospel by redefining them in the light of the nature of God and of the gospel." So also Fee, *First Corinthians*, 100.

[222] There are numerous parallels with material both preceding and following this unit that allow for a fluid contextual interpretation. These parallels include (1) There is a stylistic precedent for the use of the first person plural ("we") in 1:23. (2) The "wisdom of God" in 2:7 parallels the mention of the same in 1:21,24,30. (3) God's wisdom is tied to the cross in 2:8 (cf. 1:23; 2:2). (4) God's wisdom is defined in terms of a "mystery" (2:2; 2:7). (5) God's wisdom is proclaimed in demonstration of the Spirit (2:4,10–14); note esp. the similar concepts between 1:17; 2:4,13, that is, Paul's claim that his words were not rooted in human wisdom. (6) The eschatological judgment on representatives of human wisdom in 2:6 parallels 1:28 with the use of the term καταργέω in both places (see also 6:13; 13:8–11; 15:24–26). (7) God's wisdom in relation to "this age," mentioned three times in 2:6–8, parallels the same expression in 1:20 and anticipates the same in 3:18. (8) The reference to the "world" in 2:12 corresponds to 1:20,21,27. (9) The reference to Jesus as the *Lord of Glory* and *our glory* anticipate numerous occurrences of the term "glory" in the letter (10:31; 11:7,15; 15:40–43).

and elsewhere in 1 Corinthians is analogous to Eph 3:9–13 and Col 1:25–29. The Colossian parallels are especially noteworthy. Paul refers to himself as a servant of the church according to a stewardship entrusted to him by God (Col 1:24; cf. 1 Cor 3:5; 9:17). The word of God is a mystery, which has been hidden from the ages and from generations, but now is manifested to his saints (Col 1:26; 1 Cor 2:7; also 2:1; 4:1). In Col 1:27, the glory of this mystery is "Christ in you, the hope of glory" (cf. 1 Cor 2:7–8). Furthermore, Paul proclaims Christ by warning, admonishing, and teaching every man in all wisdom in order to present every man mature in Christ (Col 1:28–29), using virtually identical language to 1 Cor 2:6. Finally, Paul claims in Col 1:29 that he labors according to the power of God (cf. 1 Cor 1:18,24; 2:4).[223]

**2:6** In light of the aforementioned parallels and the prior assertion that the message of Christ crucified is God's power and God's wisdom (1:24) and that Christ became wisdom for us from God (1:30), the claim in 2:6, "We do, however, speak a message of wisdom,"[224] flows well with the context, even if the first impression is a bit surprising since Paul has repeatedly disavowed wisdom in the proclamation of the gospel (1:17; 2:1,4). Yet Paul does not reject all wisdom, only the wisdom belonging to this age and the rulers of this age. Here he speaks of God's wisdom.

The shift to plural pronouns throughout 2:6–16 in contrast to the singular "I" in 2:1–5 and 3:1–4 presents one of the key interpretive questions of the passage. Morris claims that the plural "links Paul with other Christian teachers in a common understanding and proclamation of wisdom."[225] Ciampa and Rosner are more specific and contend that "we" is "a reference to Paul and the other apostles and prophets/preachers in Corinth who instruct the congregation."[226] Already Paul has used the plural in 1:23—"But we preach Christ crucified"—and he characteristically shifts between the first singular and the first plural elsewhere in the letter (3:7–9; 4:1–5,9–15; 9:1–5). In 15:1–11 Paul reminds the Corinthians that the gospel he preached to them was the uniform gospel preached by all the apostles.[227] Likewise, in Col 1:28 (NASB) Paul uses the

[223] Garland (*1 Corinthians*, 103) notes that other occurrences of "wisdom" language in Ephesians and Colossians, if authentically Pauline, undermine the thesis that Paul has adopted Corinthian terminology and filled it with his own content. This thesis is often built on the fact that most of his uses of the term coalesce in 1 Cor 1–3. There are different ways, however, to read the evidence. Even if Paul picks up on "catchwords" in Corinth, the language may still have originated with Paul and later been distorted.

[224] "Wisdom" occurs first in the sentence for emphasis. The particle δέ connects 2:6 with what precedes and indicates contrast. The NIV captures the contrast well. Thiselton (*First Corinthians*, 225) translates, "yet we do [indeed] communicate a wisdom . . . but it is a wisdom that is not of this present world order."

[225] Morris, *1 Corinthians*, 52. So also Garland, *1 Corinthians*, 91.

[226] Ciampa and Rosner, *First Corinthians*, 121. They clarify, however, that this is not the case with every "we" or "us" in the passage since 2:10 and 12 refers to all believers (121n10).

[227] Compare 15:1–2, "I preached," with 15:11, "We preach." The focus in 15:1–11 is on the uniform preaching of the resurrection of Jesus as an integral component of the gospel.

plural, "Him *we* proclaim, warning every man and teaching every man in all wisdom, in order that *we* may present every man mature in Christ," and in Eph 3:2–5 Paul refers to what has been revealed to the holy apostles and prophets by the Spirit.

But what is the content of this "message of wisdom" that Paul and others speak, and who are the mature? Is "wisdom" in this context the gospel or something more? Are the "mature" all believers, or does Paul have in mind more discerning, spiritually advanced Christians? Here Paul does not unfold the content of wisdom, as he does God's "mystery" in Ephesians and Colossians; he only specifies that the rulers of this age would not have crucified Jesus had they known it (2:7–8). Rather, Paul focuses on the nature of wisdom as "hidden in mystery" and its source; it is God's wisdom (2:7) disclosed by the Spirit (2:10–16). Bruce comments, "It is evident that the mystery of which Paul speaks here is not something additional to the saving message of Christ crucified; it is in Christ crucified that the wisdom of God is embodied. It consists rather in the more detailed unfolding of the divine purpose summed up in Christ crucified."[228] Ciampa and Rosner think that the "message of wisdom" is not to be associated with the gospel in the sense of the message of salvation for all and that "mature" refers to more experienced Christians. "God's secret wisdom" in 2:7 is to be equated with the "mind of Christ" in 2:16 and "both refer in context to the wisdom of the cross applied to everyday life," which is "precisely what Paul offers to the Corinthians in the letter as a whole."[229] This position, they claim, does not entail a two-tiered view of the gospel or the introduction of any sort of elitism into the church.[230] The problem is behavioral, not an issue of one's "status."[231] The context clearly indicates that behavior is

---

[228] Bruce, *1 and 2 Corinthians*, 38. Bruce comments further, "There is substance in H. Schlier's remark that it is in the Epistle to the Ephesians that the secret and hidden wisdom of God, on which Paul does not enlarge here to the Corinthians, is imparted 'among the mature' (*Der Brief and die Epheser* [1965], 21)." Ciampa and Rosner (*First Corinthians*, 123) note that "Lightfoot makes the intriguing suggestion that Colossians, Ephesians, and to a lesser extent Romans reflect the content of this wisdom."

[229] Ciampa and Rosner, *First Corinthians*, 122–23. Ciampa and Rosner go on to show how the death of Jesus pervades Paul's teaching in the letter beyond chaps. 1–4. "In chaps. 1–4 the wisdom of God is the recognition that the cross spells the end of the world's power and wisdom and provides a solid basis for Christian unity. In chap. 5 the sacrifice of Christ our Passover lamb (5:7) is the reason for purifying the assembly by removing the incestuous man. In 6:1–11 righteous suffering instead of self-assertion is recommended with the implicit example of the crucified Christ. In 6:12–20 the redemption achieved by Christ is a major reason to honor God with your body (6:20). Likewise in chap. 7 being 'bought with a price' is the reason not to 'become slaves of human beings' (7:22). In 8:1–11:1 it is because Christ died for our weaker brother (8:11) that we imitate Christ (11:1) and avoid causing our brother to stumble. In 11:17–34 the recollection of Christ's sacrifice for us reveals the utter unacceptability of behavior that demeans those who are members of his body."

[230] For the view that 2:6–16 speaks of a higher class of believer see Conzelmann, *1 Corinthians*, 60.

[231] Ibid., 123.

a primary issue and that the distinction Paul makes is between maturity and immaturity as 3:1–4 shows (see also 14:20). Others, however, make the case that "mature" is a term applicable to all believers, just as Paul speaks elsewhere of all Christians as "saints," "beloved," "elect," "called," and "faithful." The "mature" are those who love God (2:9) and those who have received the Spirit (2:12), who enables them to understand God's wisdom. The only wisdom Paul preaches is the wisdom of the cross, not more sophisticated instruction for a select group. It is the same wisdom for beginners and more advanced Christians, but the measure of this wisdom is one's grasp of the deep things of God embodied in the cross that manifests itself in behavior.[232]

Paul's reference to the mature[233] in 2:6 is the first in a series of terms critical to the argument running through 3:4. Verses 14–15 contrasts the "man without the Spirit,"[234] who cannot understand the things of God, with the "spiritual man,"[235] who discerns all things. In 3:1–3 Paul employs "flesh"[236] and "infant" language to describe the Corinthians since he could not, he claims, speak to them as "spiritual." It is this collection of terms in the overall argument that provides the best clue to the meaning of "mature," a term that finds its opposite in the term "infants" in 3:2. In context, "mature" is parallel to and synonymous with "spiritual," and perhaps somewhat interchangeable with "wise" as used in Corinth.[237] As noted in the introduction to this passage, "mature" may have been a Corinthian catchword or a Pauline term misunderstood and misapplied. Thiselton thinks it probable that the term "mature" had gained currency in Corinth among self-styled elite leaders and what Paul does is redefine spiritual maturity in terms of being like Christ. Christian maturity is "the flowering of those qualities which characterize the God who reveals himself in the humiliation of the cross and the love of Christ for others." This

---

232 Garland, *1 Corinthians*, 92–93. See also Fitzmyer, *First Corinthians*, 175; W. Willis, "'The Mind of Christ' in 1 Corinthians 2, 16," *Bib* 70 (1989): 110–22.

233 Gk. τέλειος. On Paul's use of the term elsewhere see Rom 12:2; 1 Cor 2:6; 13:10; 14:20; Eph 4:13; Phil 3:15; Col 1:28; 4:12. Williams (*Wisdom of the Wise*, 205–06) suggests that the term refers to "Christians who are looking towards the endpoint of their faith," on the basis of passages such as 1 Cor 13:10 that looks to endtime expectation and Phil 3:12–15 where he refers to himself and the Philippians as τέλειοι, as those in process of the pursuit of their heavenly calling. "Mature" in his view is not a higher maturity level but rather "a faith that anticipates perfection." Louw-Nida (11.18) note that the term can refer to one who is initiated into a community of faith, a technical meaning related to its use for persons initiated into the mystery religions. But, it is also possible "to interpret τέλειος in Phil 3:15 and Col 1:28 as mature spirituality or a state of being spiritually mature." Paul is clear in Phil 3:12–14 that he himself has not yet "arrived," that he presses on toward the goal of the heavenly call in Christ Jesus.

234 Gk. ψυχικός (NASB, "natural man").

235 Gk. πνευματικός.

236 Two terms are employed, σάρκινος (*sarkinos*, "made of flesh") and σαρκικός (*sarkikos*, "characterized by flesh"). The NIV translates both as "worldly."

237 Although Paul associates "foolish," the opposite of "wise," with the unbeliever, the one who cannot know the things of God (2:14). However, Paul concludes in 3:18, "If anyone thinks he is wise in this age, let him become a fool so that he may become wise."

receives further elaboration in 3:1–4.[238] If there is a tinge of sarcasm in Paul's choice of the term in this context, then, in using this language, Paul reshapes the Corinthians' perceptions of what it means to be mature (wise) in relation to true Christian maturity (wisdom). The Corinthians may have considered themselves mature and wise, and, as those who had believed the message of the cross and received the Spirit, they were mature and wise. The term itself, in principle, can refer to all believers, who have received the message of the cross, but the Corinthians' behavior was not in keeping with who they were in Christ as the letter so ably demonstrates.[239] While Paul does not advocate a two-tiered gospel, a distinction in different "classes" of believers, he does recognize stages of growth in Christlikeness as manifested in the fruit of the Spirit.[240] Paul does not advocate a wisdom beyond the cross, but he does urge the Corinthians to embody the message of the cross. The Corinthians' failure to live out the reality of the cross in their relations to one another deemed them as mere "infants" in Christ. Maturity is related to behavior, living out the paradigm of the cross in love, rather than knowledge.

In 2:6b Paul clarifies that the wisdom he speaks does not belong to this age (cf. 1:20) "or of the rulers of this age, who are coming to nothing." Opinions differ on the precise identity of the these rulers. Are these rulers the unseen demonic forces of this world,[241] or simply the worldly rulers, who put Jesus to death?[242] Is there a dual reference, both to earthly rulers and to the demonic forces that inspire them?[243] Whatever the identity of the rulers, the outcome remains the same. These "rulers," who embody the wisdom of this age are

[238] Thiselton, *First Corinthians*, 225. See also Fitzmyer (*First Corinthians*, 174–75), who thinks that Paul could be speaking in "no little irony."

[239] Morris (*1 Corinthians*, 53) states, "Those who have welcomed the message of the cross are *mature*, whereas the worldly minded who reject it are not." So also Fee, *First Corinthians*, 102; Garland, *1 Corinthians*, 91–93; C. L. Blomberg, *1 Corinthians*, NIVAC (Grand Rapids: Zondervan, 1994), 63.

[240] In 3:3 Paul rebukes them specifically for jealousy (ζῆλος) and quarreling (ἔρις), two works of the flesh appearing in tandem elsewhere in Paul (see Rom 13:13; 2 Cor 12:20; Gal 5:20). In Gal 5 these two vices stand in contrast to the fruit of the Spirit.

[241] Barrett, *First Corinthians*, 70.

[242] Morris (*1 Corinthians*, 53–54) makes the following points: (1) The contrast is the wisdom of God and the wisdom of the world. The notion of demonic powers introduces something extraneous to the context and is out of harmony with 2:9, which refers to humans. (2) The word for rulers is consistently used of Jewish and Roman leaders (cf. Acts 3:17; 4:5,8,26; Rom 13:3). (3) Earthly rulers carried out the crucifixion in ignorance, but the demons knew the identity of Jesus (Mark 1:24,34).

[243] So Bruce (*1 and 2 Corinthians*, 38–39) and, more recently Ciampa and Rosner (*First Corinthians,* 125) who think "the biblical and Jewish apocalyptic background sees evil supernatural figures behind such acts against God." They further note comparable themes elsewhere in Paul's letters (Eph 3:10; 6:10–12; Col 1:26; 2:2,15). See also O. Cullmann, *Christ and Time* (London: SCM, 1951), 191–201.

"coming to nothing," the same word used in 1:28 to refer to God's choice of the foolish things of the world in order to *nullify* the things that are.[244]

**2:7–8** In 2:7 Paul differentiates the wisdom of God with the wisdom of this age, which is on its way out (2:6),[245] and qualifies the former in three ways. First, God's wisdom is "hidden in mystery."[246] This reading takes the phrase "in mystery" with the perfect tense participle rather than the verb "we speak."[247] "Mystery," as noted in the discussion on 2:1–2, is a common Pauline term used to describe something previously unknown but now disclosed by revelation. Paul develops the term more fully in Colossians and Ephesians and explains the mystery as the inclusion of Gentiles in God's salvation. God's mystery is not a riddle that men can solve but rather a secret that the human mind by itself is wholly unable to penetrate. God's wisdom remains hidden until he chooses to disclose it. As 2:9–10 clarifies, God's wisdom is known to those who love God by revelation from the Spirit. Second, God's wisdom was predestined[248] before the ages for our glory (2:7b), that is, God purposed before the ages to bring his people to glory through the wisdom of Christ crucified. This is a recasting of 1:21, that God, in his wisdom, was pleased to save those who believe the foolish message. Yet, here, in 2:7b, Paul's perspective is vast, taking into account what God determined "before the ages" all the way to the consummation of the ages "for our glory." Third, this wisdom is unknown by the rulers of this age, that is, the representative "wise" of the world (cf. 1:20).[249] That the rulers did not know God's secret is demonstrated in the crucifixion (see Acts 3:17; 4:25–28; Luke 23:34) of Jesus, the "Lord of glory," a title applied to Christ by Paul only here.[250] In referring to "our glory" and Jesus as the "Lord of glory," Paul implicitly connects the destination of God's people with Jesus. This is the first mention of "glory" in the letter, which anticipates Paul's emphasis on glory elsewhere, culminating in the focus on

---

[244] Gk. *καταργέω*. In 2:8 Paul refers to Jesus as the Lord of glory. The Greek terms *καταργέω* and *δόξα* often occur in close proximity in Paul's letters: see Rom 3:3–7; 6:4–6; 2 Cor 3:7–18; 2 Thess 2:8–14. See also Heb 2:10–14.

[245] The emphatic *ἀλλά* introduces the contrast.

[246] NIV, "God's secret wisdom, a wisdom that has been hidden." Gk. *θεοῦ σοφίαν ἐν μυστηρίῳ τὴν ἀποκεκρυμμένην* (lit., "God's wisdom in mystery having been hidden").

[247] So also Garland, *1 Corinthians*, 95–96. The force of the participle is that wisdom has been and remains hidden in mystery. The implication is that this wisdom remains hidden until God reveals it. Fee (*First Corinthians*, 104–5) takes the phrase "in mystery" as modifying "wisdom."

[248] Gk. *προορίζω*. The term occurs elsewhere in the New Testament in Acts 4:28; Rom 8:29; and Eph 1:5,11.

[249] See on 2:6 the view that rulers could also refer to demonic powers.

[250] See also Jas 2:1. Fitzmyer (*First Corinthians*, 177) notes, "In applying 'glory' to the risen Christ, Paul implicitly is putting him on the same level as Yahweh (see Ps 29:3, quoted in Acts 7:2)."

resurrection in chap. 15 (see esp. 15:40–42).[251] The glory of Jesus remains hidden to the rulers of the world, as does the final destination of God's people.

**2:9** Another use of the strong adversative conjunction brings the first phase of Paul's argument to conclusion with the citation of Scripture.[252] The source of this scriptural citation, however, is quite the challenge. Although Paul uses the typical introductory formula citing Scripture, "It is written," there is no exact correspondence to an Old Testament text, which has led to a host of proposals regarding the antecedent text.[253] A common suggestion is that Paul paraphrases the Greek version of Isa 64:3 (MT 64:4) in combination with 65:16 (MT 65:17), since the Hebrew idiom "to ascend upon the heart" appears in the Greek of 65:16 but not in 64:3. Thiselton thinks this connection is possible but "too imprecise for certainty."[254] Heil is of the opinion that the Greek of Isa 52:13–15 is a better candidate for the precursor text, but he also shows how the language of the quote resonates with a wide range of Old Testament texts and concludes that "the scriptural quote is not meant to evoke any single text from the OT."[255] First Corinthians 2:9 brings "together various formulations and concepts found in a number of different places in the OT."[256] While

[251] Cf. also Rom 6:4,8; 2 Cor 3:18; Phil 2:5–11; 3:21. See C. C. Newman, *Paul's Glory-Christology: Tradition and Rhetoric* (Leiden: Brill, 1992).

[252] Gk. ἀλλά. If parallel to the same conjunction in 2:7, then Paul continues to contrast the wisdom he speaks with the wisdom of this age in 2:6. Thus, λαλοῦμεν continues to function as the main verb, "We speak . . . what God prepared" (so Thiselton, *First Corinthians*, 249; Garland, *1 Corinthians*, 97; Ciampa and Rosner, *1 Corinthians*, 128). The introductory formula (ἀλλὰ καθὼς γέγραπται) draws attention to the previous argument rather than advancing to another subject as in Rom 15:3,21. See Fee, *First Corinthians*, 108; Williams, *Wisdom of the Wise*, 202. On the difficulties of the grammar and syntax of 2:9 see B. Frid, "The Enigmatic ἀλλά in 1 Cor 2:9," *NTS* 31 (1985): 603–11.

[253] Stanley (*Paul and the Language of Scripture*, 189) states that all solutions are too uncertain for any to gain widespread approval.

[254] Thiselton, *First Corinthians*, 251. So also Ciampa and Rosner, *First Corinthians*, 127–28.

[255] Heil, *Rhetorical Role of Scripture*, 53–57. The quote is from p. 57. Heil further proposes that Sirach 1:1–10 provides significant background to 1 Cor 2:9. Williams (*Wisdom of the Wise*, 168) suggests that in the surrounding context, 1 Cor 2:6–8 and 10–11, there is an echo of Dan 2:19–23. Williams bases his case on common vocabulary between 1 Cor 2 and Dan 2 and common concepts and themes between Dan 2, 1 Cor, and Isaianic texts quoted in 1 Cor 2. "The concepts from Daniel 2:19–23 are a fitting, positive response to Paul's attack against human wisdom that he established previously by the Scripture citation of Isa 29:14 in 1 Cor 1:19."

[256] Heil, *Rhetorical Role of Scripture*, 66. This accords with the judgment of others. Fitzmyer (*First Corinthians*, 177) suggests Isa 64:3 and 52:15; also 65:16 or Jer 3:16 (LXX). Morris (*1 Corinthians*, 56) thinks this is a "free citation of Isaiah 64:4 (MT), with reminiscences of other scriptural passages." Garland (*1 Corinthians*, 103) suggests a loose association of Isa 64:3 (LXX) with several other passages (Job 28:12–28; Isa 48:6; 52:15; 65:17; Jer 3:16; Sir 1:10). Since the passage does occur in the same form in the *Ascension of Isaiah* 8:11, a first- or second-century Jewish writing, this suggests to Fee (*First Corinthians*, 108–9) that Paul is not paraphrasing the Old Testament but is probably referring to an amalgamation of texts that had already been joined together and reflected on in apocalyptic Judaism, which Paul knew either directly or indirectly. Thiselton (*First Corinthians*, 251) notes, however, that Christian editing of the document makes the origin of the material uncertain.

the source of the quote is up for discussion, its function in context is not difficult to discern. The citation emphasizes the hiddenness of God's plans and the incapacity of humans to know them, which sets up the emphasis on the revelation of the Spirit to follow in the succeeding verses (2:10–13).[257]

**2:10–11** In 2:10 the plural pronoun translated "to us" is in the emphatic position in Greek, occurring first in the sentence. But how does 2:10a relate back to what precedes, and to whom does the plural pronoun refer in context? Some Greek manuscripts include the adversative conjunction,[258] implying a contrast between those who cannot fathom God's plan for his people (2:9) and those who now know God's plan for his people through the revelation of the Spirit (2:10a). Other manuscripts have an explanatory conjunction,[259] stating the reason why others cannot understand God's plan, that is, God's wisdom is available only to those to whom he has revealed it. If the "us" is parallel with "we" in 2:6, then the more specific reference may be to the apostles and prophets. If "us" refers back to the more immediate "those who love him" in 2:9, then all believers are in view rather than an inner circle in the early church.[260] The contrast is not so much between "us" and "them" as it is why they cannot know and we can.[261]

Spirit language dominates the remainder of the section through v. 15.[262] The fact that God has revealed his plan to us through the Spirit once again strikes at any notion of boasting or self-sufficiency, which is critical to Paul's overall argument (recall 1:29–31). The Spirit is able to reveal these things because the Spirit "searches all things, even the deep things of God." In context, "all things" and the "deep things of God" correlate to God's hidden wisdom (2:7a), to what God predestined before the ages (2:7b), and to what God has prepared for those who love him (2:9). Paul does not elaborate further here on the content

[257] Williams (*Wisdom of the Wise*, 200–01) notes that the "things" refer broadly to the blessings of God's plan of salvation. God's whole plan of redemption is in view, from creation to salvation to judgment to new creation. Williams' suggestion corresponds to the grand perspective set forth in 2:7, that is, God's wisdom predestined before the ages unto our glory.

[258] Gk. δέ.

[259] Gk. γάρ. The NIV opts for the adversative, "but." The TNIV has changed to the explanatory, "for."

[260] So Thiselton, *First Corinthians*, 255. Thiselton further notes that the "our" in 2:7b (our glory) and "we" (we received the Spirit of God) in 2:12 signify all Christians, without a doubt (229). However, a more specific reference for the dative pronoun "to us" in 2:10 does not mean that all believers are not privy to God's mystery. Col 1:26 indicates a broader focus of revelation in that God's mystery has been disclosed to "all the saints." This revelation, however, comes through the mediation of the Spirit through God's gifted servants that is now available to all through the written word of God.

[261] So Fee, *First Corinthians*, 109. Fee goes with the explanatory "for" as the correct reading. This does not, however, rule out the implied contrast between 2:9 and 2:10. There are some "in the know" and some who aren't. The difference is the Spirit.

[262] The Greek word πνεῦμα occurs eight times in 2:10–16, used of both the Holy Spirit and the human spirit. The adjective πνευματικός (spiritual) occurs three times and the adverb πνευματικῶς (spiritually) occurs once.

of the revelation as he does elsewhere (Col 1:24–28; Eph 3:8–13) because this is not his intent in the present argument, which focuses more on the fact and the means of revelation rather than the content. The context, however, supplies that Paul is speaking of God's plan of salvation in Christ crucified. Furthermore, what God has prepared for those who love him is "glory" (2:8; cf. also 15:20–28). Paul's language of the "deep things" of God corresponds to his analogous exclamation in Rom 11:33, "Oh, the depth of the riches of the wisdom and knowledge of God! How unsearchable his judgments, and his paths beyond tracing out!" In Eph 3:8 he speaks of preaching to the Gentiles "the unsearchable riches of Christ," and in 3:18 of the same letter he prays that believers might be able to grasp "how wide and long and high and deep is the love of Christ." Others note the possible Old Testament background of Dan 2:19–23 with its vocabulary relating to mystery, revelation, and the deep things of God.[263] Paul's own explanation of 2:10, which has to do with the fact of the Spirit's knowledge, appears in 2:11 and works off of the analogy of "like is known by like."[264] Just as no one knows the inner thoughts of another, so only the Spirit of God knows the things of God. Paul's explanation "ascribes full deity to the Spirit."[265]

**2:12** Once again, in 2:12, the emphatic structures of the sentence in Greek indicate Paul's stress on the recipients of God's revelation ("we") and its source, that it is not the spirit of the world but the Spirit who is from God.[266] The "we" in 2:12 is parallel to the plural "us" in 2:10 and either refers to all believers or to a more specific group such as the apostles and prophets as the means of God's revelation by the Spirit (see discussion on 2:10 above). That all believers possess the Spirit of God is abundantly clear in the broader context of the letter.[267] In the immediate context (2:13–3:1) Paul introduces the term "spiritual person," who is set in contrast to the "natural person." The distinction is between those who have the Spirit and those who do not, although Paul may be addressing self-styled "spirituals" in the church at Corinth.[268]

---

[263] See Williams, *Wisdom of the Wise*, 168. Also Fee, *First Corinthians*, 111.

[264] See Garland, *1 Corinthians*, 98.

[265] Morris, *1 Corinthians*, 57.

[266] Several matters of the Greek sentence structure are worth noting: (1) The personal pronoun ἡμεῖς (we), not required by the Greek, is included. (2) The phrase "not the spirit of the world" occurs next in the sentence before the main verb and is set in contrast to the "Spirit of God" by the emphatic contrasting conjunction, ἀλλά (but). (3) The phrase "the Spirit who is from God" is more emphatic than the phrase "spirit of the world" in the use of the definite article, literally, "the Spirit, the one who is from God." The full Greek main clause reads, ἡμεῖς δὲ οὐ τὸ πνεῦμα τοῦ κόσμου ἐλάβομεν ἀλλὰ τὸ πνεῦμα τὸ ἐκ τοῦ θεοῦ. Fitzmyer (*First Corinthians*, 181) takes the second occurrence of "spirit" to mean the human "spirit" that we received from God as in Zech 12:1. The parallel is closer, however, to 2:10 where the Holy Spirit is clearly in view.

[267] See especially 6:19 and the full discussion of the work of the Spirit in chaps. 12–14.

[268] Note 14:37, "If anyone thinks that he is a prophet or spiritual, let him recognize that what I am writing to you is the command of the Lord." See also 7:40, "But I think I also have the Spirit of

**2:13** The phrase "This is what we speak" refers back to the scriptural citation in 2:9 to the things revealed by the Spirit, yet unseen and unknown by men.[269] The use of the first person plural continues ("we speak") with the use of the same verb that occurred in 2:6–7.[270] What is spoken by Paul and others is the hidden wisdom of God (2:6–7) now revealed by the Spirit (2:10). As such Paul's teaching proceeds from the Spirit rather than from human wisdom.[271] This is now the fourth time in the present argument that Paul has denied human wisdom as the source of his speech (1:17; 2:1,4). Verse 13 is especially close to 2:4 where Paul claims that his preaching was not in persuasive words of human wisdom but in demonstration of the Spirit's power.

The phrase rendered by the NIV, "expressing spiritual truths in spiritual words," is difficult to translate and interpret.[272] The more recent NIV2011 has "explaining spiritual realities with Spirit-taught words." The NASB translates, "combining spiritual thoughts with spiritual words," and the HCSB, "explaining spiritual things to spiritual people."[273] All are possible renderings of the Greek, and it is difficult to decide between these options. Part of the difficulty resides in the fact that the first occurrence of the word "spiritual"[274] in the Greek text could be either masculine or neuter. Does the term refer to Spirit-taught words just mentioned in 2:13a, or does the word mean "spiritual people" in anticipation of 2:14–15? Furthermore, the meaning of the participle, translated "expressing" by the NIV,[275] is uncertain. Does it mean to "explain," "combine," or "compare"? The only other occurrence of the term in the New Testament is 2 Cor 10:12 with the meaning "to compare." But the context here indicates something more along the lines of "explain" or "interpret," as the word is used in the LXX.[276] Fee suggests, "explaining spiritual things by means of spiritual words taught us by the Spirit."[277] The implication in this

God." In other words, Paul is targeting a certain group of individuals in the church at Corinth, those either self-designated as mature/wise/spiritual or perceived as such by the church.

[269] As the Greek neuter pronoun, ἅ, makes clear. The same form of the pronoun occurs twice in 2:9.

[270] Gk. λαλέω. The verb appears frequently in Paul's discussion of the Spirit in chaps. 12–14 (see 1 Cor 12:3,30; 13:1,11; 14:2–6,9,11,13,18–19,21,23,27–29,34–35,39).

[271] A subjective genitive reading.

[272] Gk. πνευματικοῖς πνευματικὰ συγκρίνοντες. Louw-Nida (33.154) render the verb συγκρίνω, "to explain, primarily by means of comparison," and the phrase πνευματικοῖς πνευματικὰ συγκρίνοντες, "we explain spiritual truths by means of spiritual matters." They also note, however, that the expression is highly ambiguous and may mean, "we explain spiritual truths to those who have the Spirit" or "we explain spiritual truths with words given by the Spirit."

[273] Similarly ESV, "interpreting spiritual truths to those who are spiritual."

[274] πνευματικοῖς. Meaning either "to spiritual persons" (masc.) or "with spiritual words" (neut.). The same ambiguity exists in 1 Cor 12:1, meaning either, "Now about spiritual persons" or "Now about spiritual things (gifts)."

[275] Gk. συγκρίνω.

[276] Garland (*1 Corinthians*, 100) notes several LXX occurrences with the meaning "interpret" in the sense of unlocking truth revealed by God. See Gen 40:8,22; 41:12; Judg 7:15; Dan 5:8,12.

[277] Fee, *First Corinthians*, 115. So also Garland, *1 Corinthians*, 100.

translation would be that "spiritual people" are the ones who receive the explanation of spiritual things (so the HCSB). Either way, the very next verse picks up the contrast between the *natural man* and the *spiritual man*, where there is no ambiguity in Greek on the gender of the adjective.

**2:14–16** In 2:14, Paul introduces a new term for the worldly wise man, translated by the NIV as "the man without the Spirit,"[278] usually rendered as the "natural man" in other translations in contrast to the "spiritual man."[279] The natural man does not accept the things of the Spirit of God.[280] How can he? The things of God are foolishness to him (1:18,21,23). The natural man is the unconverted and unregenerate, the person who is void of the Spirit and who belongs to this age (1:20; 2:6). The absence of the Spirit renders the natural man unable to know the things of the Spirit of God since the Spirit is the one who searches the deep things of God (2:10). The natural man is unable to penetrate spiritual things because spiritual things are evaluated spiritually, that is, they are examined by means of the Spirit.[281] The natural man, therefore, is unable to make spiritual judgments or comprehend spiritual truths. The spiritual man, on the other hand, is able to evaluate all things because the Spirit of God is guiding him. In context, "all things" primarily refers to an examination of/inquiry into God's hidden wisdom; "all things that pertain to the work of salvation, matters formerly hidden in God but now revealed through the Spirit."[282] The truly spiritual believer is likewise able to truly examine the unbeliever (see 14:24).

But what is intended in 2:15b by the statement "he himself is not subject to any man's judgment"? Certainly Paul does not mean to convey that the "spiritual person" is beyond critique or scrutiny, which would be exactly the sort of attitude that would wreak havoc in the church.[283] In the very next paragraph (3:1–4), not to mention the rest of the letter, Paul renders his own evaluation

---

[278] Gk. ψυχικός. The term is not all that frequent in the New Testament. In Jude 19, the term is defined as those "not having the Spirit." James uses the term to describe a wisdom that is not from God (Jas 3:15). The term denotes humanity in its natural, physical existence. In context, it refers to the natural human existence apart from the illumination of the Holy Spirit. Paul uses the term exclusively of the unbeliever. When he refers to the Corinthians as those who act like unbelievers, he prefers the term σαρκικός (3:3).

[279] The ψυχικός/πνευματικός contrast occurs again in 15:44–46.

[280] Gk. δέχομαι. BDAG references 1 Cor 2:14 under the meaning, "to indicate approval or conviction by accepting, be receptive of, be open to, approve, accept."

[281] The Greek term translated "discern" by the NIV is ἀνακρίνω. In Paul's letters the term occurs only in 1 Corinthians (2:14–15; 4:3–4; 9:3; 10:25,27; 14:24). Louw-Nida (30.109) explain that the term means "to make a judgment on the basis of careful and detailed information—to judge carefully, to evaluate carefully." In 1 Cor 2:15, the phrase ὁ δὲ πνευματικὸς ἀνακρίνει [τὰ] πάντα means "the spiritual person makes careful judgments about all things." Garland (*1 Corinthians*, 101) suggests a better translation is "investigate" or "examine," and thinks that it is close to the notion of "search" in 2:10. The natural person analyzes divine truth with limited earthbound faculties. Although see Thiselton (*First Corinthians*, 273) who prefers "discern" in his translation.

[282] Fee, *First Corinthians*, 118.

[283] So ibid., "There are always some who consider themselves full of the Spirit in such a way

of the Corinthians and assesses them to be "worldly" rather than "spiritual."[284] Thiselton, somewhat cautiously, treats 2:15 as a Corinthian quotation representing a Corinthian viewpoint. He explains that "many at Corinth saw themselves as 'judging everything' but as 'being judged by no one'."[285] Others think that "no one," in context, is the person without the Spirit, the "natural man." In other words, the spiritual person cannot be evaluated by a "nonspiritual" person, who does not have the Spirit of God and who is therefore incapable of evaluating spiritual things (2:14).[286] Garland thinks that 2:15 looks forward to the next paragraph (3:1–4) and means something like, "If they were truly spiritual in their behavior, he would not be provoked to judge them as *sarkikoi*" (worldly).[287] This would be similar to what Paul writes in Gal 5:18, "But if you are led by the Spirit, you are not under law." Perhaps the best commentary and solution lies with 4:3–4, a parallel passage where the same Greek term for "discern"/"judge" appears three times.[288] Here Paul clarifies that the evaluations of others, even self-examination is ultimately inconsequential. Only one assessment matters. "It is the Lord who judges me" (4:4).[289]

Paul's conclusion in 2:16, based on Isa 40:13,[290] amplifies not only the previous statement (2:15) but also provides a succinct summary of the unit as a whole;[291] God's ways are inscrutable (2:9), yet his hidden plans have been revealed through the Spirit (2:10). The implied answer to the question raised by Scripture, "Who has known the mind of the Lord that he may instruct him?" is,

as to be beyond the discipline and counsel of others. Such a reading of the text is an unfortunate travesty, since these people are usually among those most needing such discipline."

[284] See also 1 Cor 14:37, "If anybody thinks he is a prophet or spiritually gifted, let him acknowledge that what I am writing to you is the Lord's command." "Spiritually gifted" translates "πνευματικός," the same term in 2:15.

[285] Thiselton, *First Corinthians*, 272. In taking this view Thiselton clarifies that "this by no means implies that Paul necessarily dissents from it, provided that it is contextualized within his wider theology of the Holy Spirit and the Christian life." On the issue of Corinthian slogans, which can at times involve a great deal of speculation, see the discussion on 1 Cor 6:12.

[286] So Robertson and Plummer (*First Corinthians*, 50), "This perhaps means 'by no nonspiritual person' (cf. 1 John 4:1)." Similarly Ciampa and Rosner (*First Corinthians*, 137) who suggest that 2:15b reinforces the argument of 1:18–2:5 by placing "the spiritual" beyond the assessment of worldly wisdom. "Those who are spiritual are not examined by the world's false wisdom."

[287] Garland, *1 Corinthians*, 101.

[288] ἀνακρίνω.

[289] Barrett, *First Corinthians*, 78.

[290] Paul does not use the introductory formula, "It is written," and he does not quote the whole of Isa 40:13, omitting the middle clause, "Who has become his counselor?" Furthermore, the Hebrew reads the "Spirit of the Lord" rather than the "mind" of the Lord, although the NIV translates the Hebrew רוח (Spirit) in Isa 40:13 as "mind." "Spirit" and "mind" appear to be somewhat synonymous terms. 1 Cor 2:16 agrees with the LXX in the use of νοῦς (mind). In light of the Old Testament context of Isa 40:1–11 of God's intention to save his people, Williams (*Wisdom of the Wise*, 214) suggests the meaning of Isa 40:13a is, "Who is able to comprehend the salvific plan of God?" For a full discussion of the use of Isa 40:13 in early Jewish literature see Williams, *Wisdom of the Wise*, 216–25. Paul quotes Isa 40:13 again in Rom 11:34.

[291] 2:16 is connected to the previous verse with an explanatory γὰρ.

of course, "No one."[292] Yet in response to the question, Paul states surprisingly and boldly, "But we have the mind of Christ."[293] Strikingly, Paul does not say, as he does in 2:12, "We have received the Spirit that comes from God," but rather, "We have the mind of Christ," which, in context, is synonymous with God's hidden wisdom. One cannot help but note the strong trinitarian focus in Paul's interplay with the Old Testament text. Furthermore, the reference to the "mind" of Christ recalls Paul's initial exhortation in 1:10, "to be of the same mind." Garland notes that Paul particularly appeals to the mind of Christ when a community is rent by divisions (cf. Phil 2:1–5; 4:2).[294]

### (2) *Application: Factions Demonstrate a Lack of God's Wisdom (3:1–4)*

**1Brothers, I could not address you as spiritual but as worldly—mere infants in Christ. 2I gave you milk, not solid food, for you were not yet ready for it. Indeed, you are still not ready. 3You are still worldly. For since there is jealousy and quarreling among you, are you not worldly? Are you not acting like mere men? 4For when one says, "I follow Paul," and another, "I follow Apollos," are you not mere men?**

In 3:1 the argument transitions from the nature, revelation, and recipients of God's wisdom (2:6–16) to a direct application of this wisdom to the Corinthian factions. There are significant parallels between 3:1–4 and 2:1–5. Both sections begin with the emphatic expression "And I,"[295] both address the Corinthians with the affectionate "brothers," both refer to Paul's initial missionary preaching and teaching in Corinth, and both make application of the immediately preceding units (1:18–31; 2:6–16).[296] The contrast, however, between 2:1–5 and 3:1–4 is striking. Whereas 2:1–5 portrays Paul's preaching as a powerful, Spirit-inspired proclamation of Christ crucified, Paul's claim in 3:1–4 is that he was not able and is still not able to speak to the Corinthians as spiritual people but as "worldly," as "mere infants in Christ."[297] In introducing these terms Paul confronts head-on the Corinthian pursuit of worldly wisdom by sharply rebuking their childish behavior.[298] The re-mention of personality-centered factions

[292] Heil (*Rhetorical Role of Scripture*, 71) calls attention to various uses of the verb "to know" (Gk. γινώσκω) in the antecedent context (1:21; 2:7–8,11,14). These expressions reach their climax in the rhetorical question of 2:16a.

[293] Again the personal pronoun, ἡμεῖς, is included for emphasis (cf. 2:12).

[294] Garland, *1 Corinthians*, 102. Thiselton (*First Corinthians*, 275) prefers the translation "mind-set." In context, the reference to "Christ" is to "Christ-crucified." Paul's reference to the "mind of Christ" is thus a way of thinking commensurate with the revelation of God's wisdom in Christ-crucified. See also Collins, *First Corinthians*, 137; Willis, "'The Mind of Christ' in 1 Corinthians 2, 16," 121.

[295] Gk. κἀγώ (not reflected in the NIV translation).

[296] Thus, 2:1–5 and 3:1–4 are parallel in both content and function, both serving as the conclusion of their respective sections (1:18–2:5 and 2:6–3:4).

[297] Thiselton (*First Corinthians*, 286) gives the following heading to 3:1–4: "The Inapplicability of the Term 'Spiritual' in the Face of Infantile Status-Seeking."

[298] The terms are σάρκινος and σαρκικός, both translated with no distinction by the NIV as "worldly," and νήπιος, rendered as "infants." Other translations distinguish the first two terms, such

in 3:4 shows that the disunity addressed in 1:10–13 has shaped Paul's response all along. In terms of the structure of the argument, 3:1–4 is a transitional unit, completing the argument of 2:6–16 and looking ahead to the following emphasis on the wisdom of God and his servants.[299]

**3:1–2** In 3:1 Paul drops the comparison between the "man without the Spirit" (natural man) and the "spiritual man" (2:14–15) and pinpoints a different contrast between those who are "spiritual" and those who are "worldly—mere infants in Christ." That he is addressing believers is clear from the designation "in Christ." The Greek term translated "man without the Spirit"[300] is reserved for unbelievers and refers to those who do not accept the things of the Spirit of God, who consider spiritual things as foolishness, and who are not able to know the things of God (2:14). Paul does not say that the Corinthians are not spiritual, only that he was not able to speak to them as spiritual. In principle they are spiritual by virtue of their reception of the Spirit of God, but in practice the designation "spiritual" is not an appropriate term for them in their present condition. In context the opposite of "spiritual" is "infant," which means that "spiritual" is synonymous with "mature" (2:6). Paul is seeking to adjust their attitudes and change their behavior. As a direct application of his exposition of God's wisdom for the mature (2:6–16), Paul retorts that he cannot speak to them as spiritual (mature) because of their childish behavior evidenced by their jealousy and quarrels.

The NIV renders two different Greek terms as "worldly" (3:1,3), apparently adopting the stance that there is not a significant discernible difference in meaning between the two.[301] Other translations distinguish the terms, such as the NASB, rendering *sarkinos* in 3:1 as "men of flesh"[302] and *sarkikos* in

---

as the NASB's "men of flesh" (σάρκινος) and "fleshly" (σαρκικός). In context, the term σάρκινος seems to be synonymous with "infants" and the phrase "acting like mere men" (3:3) is synonymous with σαρκικός (fleshly, or "characterized by the flesh").

[299] In addition to the parallels between 3:1–4 and 2:1–5, the use of the verb λαλέω (to speak) and πνευματικός (spiritual) establish a direct connection to 2:6–16. The mention of Paul and Apollos in 3:4 introduces the discussion of the role and function of God's servants in the church (3:5–4:13), followed by a concluding warning and exhortation (4:14–21). That Paul's topic continues to be divine vs. human wisdom in the following sections is confirmed by (1) Paul's reference to himself as a "wise" master-builder in 3:10, (2) Jesus Christ as the only proper foundation of anything Christian in 3:11 (recall 2:1), and (3) the thematic reprise of 3:18–23 that forms an *inclusio* with 1:18–31 thereby reiterating all the key themes 1:18–3:23. On the nature of 3:1–4 as a transition unit see also Fee, *First Corinthians*, 121–22; Thiselton, *First Corinthians*, 290.

[300] Gk. "natural man," ψυχικός.

[301] The terms are σάρκινος and σαρκικός. Garland (*1 Corinthians*, 109) mentions a number of interpreters who contend that the two terms are essentially synonymous. Barrett (*First Corinthians*, 79n1) recognizes a distinction between the words but doubts that Paul intends any difference between the two in this context. Thiselton (*First Corinthians*, 292) comments that "The three terms ψυχικός (2:14), σάρκινος (3:1), and σαρκικός (3:3) all draw their semantic nuances from their mutual interaction with one another within a single semantic field in which the term of major contrast to all three is πνευματικός, *spiritual* or *pertaining to the Spirit*."

[302] Or "people of the flesh" (so HCSB, NRSV, ESV).

3:3 as "fleshly,"[303] which follows the common suggestion that *sarkinos* carries the idea of "made of flesh," that is, human, and *sarkikos* means something a bit different, such as "characterized by flesh."[304] The term "infant" carries a negative connotation in many contexts but not always.[305] There is nothing blameworthy in being an "infant in Christ" at the beginning stages of Christian experience, yet when Paul claims in 3:2 that they are still not ready for solid food, the term "infant" becomes pejorative in this context. The "infant"/"adult" metaphor occurs two more times in the letter, 13:11 and 14:20.

Commentators understand the comparable metaphors of "milk" and "solid food" differently, depending on the interpretation of the content of Paul's "wisdom for the mature" (see 2:6). The metaphor itself was commonly employed in the ancient world to refer to elementary versus advanced teaching, an image that depicted progression in knowledge. In the New Testament the metaphor carries this apparent sense in Heb 5:12–14 (cf. also 1 Pet 2:2). If the same holds for 1 Cor 3:2, then milk represents Paul's initial missionary preaching centered on the cross and solid food portrays more advanced teaching, God's wisdom that unveils the meaning of the cross.[306]

Others suggest, however, that this meaning is difficult to maintain contextually in 1 Corinthians. In other words, the view that Paul's initial instruction in the gospel (milk) proclaimed the cross and that the Corinthian's behavior prevented him from moving to more extensive, advanced instruction misses Paul's intention.[307] To be sure, the Corinthians failed to make progress, but it was not a failure of knowledge but a failure to comprehend and incarnate the

---

[303] ESV and NRSV, "of the flesh."

[304] Robertson and Plummer (*First Corinthians*, 52) explain the difference, "The termination -ινος denotes a material relation, while -ικος denotes an *ethical* or dynamic relation, to the idea involved in the root. In 2 Cor 3:3 the tables are *made* of stone, the hearts are *made* of flesh . . . we are all σαρκίνοις, but we are not to live κατὰ σάρκα" (according to flesh). Similarly, Fee (*First Corinthians*, 124) notes that σάρκινος emphasizes their humanness and physical side of existence over against the spiritual. σαρκικός, on the other hand, has clear ethical overtones of living from the perspective of the present age. This meaning holds in the context of 1 Cor 3:1–4, but the term does not always carry this sense. Paul uses the term to refer to "material" things in Rom 15:27 and 1 Cor 9:11. Regarding the term σάρκινος see also Rom 7:14 and Heb 7:16. In Rom 7:14 the term occurs in contrast to πνευματικός, "We know that the law is spiritual; but I am unspiritual, sold as a slave to sin."

[305] Gk. νήπιος. Paul uses the term affectionately of a nursing mother in 1 Thess 2:7. This familial image is not entirely absent from the present passage for Paul goes on to say, "I gave you milk to drink" (3:2).

[306] Robertson and Plummer, *First Corinthians*, 52–53; Bruce, *1 and 2 Corinthians*, 42; C. Vaughan and T. D. Lea, *1 Corinthians*, Bible Study Commentary (Grand Rapids: Zondervan, 1983), 39–40. More recently, Ciampa and Rosner, *First Corinthians*, 140.

[307] Thiselton (*First Corinthians*, 292) makes the following excellent observation, "If Paul meant that even now you still cannot manage something more complex than the milk of proclamation, it is difficult to see what he expects them to make of his rigorous arguments about ethical conduct, marriage and celibacy, the nature of freedom in relation to food offered to idols, the eucharist, spiritual gifts or persons in a corporate setting, and the resurrection."

wisdom of the cross. The evidence for this was their strife and jealousy.[308] By referring to "solid food" Paul uses their language that means that the contrast in this case is not between two different diets but between "the true food of the Gospel (whether milk or meat), and the synthetic substitutes which the Corinthians have preferred."[309] Paul knows only one kind of wisdom, Christ and him crucified. It is not that Paul does not or cannot give them wisdom in the form of solid food; it is that they do not recognize what he gives them to be wisdom.[310] Paul wants them to abandon their present behavior so that they can appreciate the milk for what it really is, "solid food."

**3:3–4** If we maintain the distinctions mentioned above between *sarkinos* and *sarkikos*, then Paul's characterization of them as *sarkikoi* carries the notion of "characterized by flesh." Thiselton proposes a further nuancing between the two occurrences of *sarkikos* in 3:3. The first he translates "unspiritual" and the second, "centered on yourselves."[311] In Gal 5 Paul contrasts the works of the flesh and the life in the Spirit using the terms "jealousy" and "quarreling" in the vice list of fleshly deeds (Gal 5:19). What is at issue, Thiselton claims, "is the anomaly of Christians who are nominally or in principle focused on Christ but in practice and in stance still focused on the interests of the self."[312] For the Corinthians to behave in this manner is "acting like mere men" (3:3),[313] a phrase that is repeated in 3:4 and is the equivalent of "walking according to the flesh." Paul stops short of calling them "natural" (cf. 2:14, "the person without the Spirit"), but his use of the term "man" comes close. They are acting no different from people who belong to the world, human beings who tend toward strife and envy. Factionalism gives evidence of a fleshly mindset rather than the "mind of Christ" (2:16).

## 4. The Wisdom of God and His Servants (3:5–4:13)

The rhetorical questions of 3:3–4, which implicate the Corinthians for their worldly behavior, pave the way for a more extended and focused analysis of the status and role of church leaders in the light of God's wisdom.[314] Paul uses

---

[308] Garland, *1 Corinthians*, 106–8.

[309] M. Hooker, "Hard Sayings: 1 Cor. 3:2," *Theology* 69 (1966): 21. See also J. Francis, "As Babes in Christ—Some Proposals Regarding 1 Cor. 3:1–3," *JSNT* 7 (1980): 41–60. Fee (*First Corinthians*, 125) quips, "the Corinthians do not need a change in diet but a change in perspective."

[310] Garland, *1 Corinthians*, 109.

[311] Thiselton, *First Corinthians*, 292–93.

[312] Ibid., 293.

[313] Literally, "Are you not walking according to man" (Gk. κατὰ ἄνθρωπον περιπατεῖτε).

[314] Fee (*1 Corinthians*, 128) comments that "their radically misguided perception of the nature of the church and its leadership, in this case especially the role of teachers." Further (131), "The cross is not only the paradigm of the gospel, and of God's ways that stand in contradiction to human ways, but it also serves as the basic model for ministry."

himself and Apollos as the examples,[315] but what he has to say targets the local leadership in Corinth. The argument of 3:5–4:13 divides into four units. First, in 3:5–17, Paul explains the relative insignificance of the church's leaders and stresses their accountability before God with a strong emphasis on God's ownership of the church and his activity with respect to its leaders.[316] God sovereignly assigns tasks to each worker in his field, and God alone causes the growth (3:6–7). The workers are mere servants and co-workers, who belong to God, the owner of the field/building (3:9). God will evaluate the leaders and will determine the quality of their work (3:12–15). He will also destroy anyone who destroys his temple (3:16–17). Second, in 3:18–23, Paul warns of self-deception, recapitulates the wisdom/folly contrast of 1:18–31, and urges the Corinthians to become truly wise since the wisdom of this world is foolishness with God. In this unit Paul turns the Corinthians' perspective inside out. They do not belong to the church's leaders, the leaders belong to them, and they belong to Christ who belongs to God! Third, Paul takes up the proper way to view God's servant/stewards in 4:1–5 and the insignificance of human evaluations. The Lord's judgment is the only one that matters. In the course of Paul's argument there are three statements in the first three subunits, all introduced by the same Greek conjunction, that trace and summarize Paul's progression of thought:[317] (1) God's servants are inconsequential; it is God who causes the growth (3:7). (2) Thus, the third imperative of 3:18–21, "So then, no more boasting about men!" (3:21). (3) The Corinthians are to judge nothing before the time of the coming of the Lord, who will expose the motives of men's hearts (4:5). Only then will God praise his workers. Finally, in the last unit of this section, 4:6–13, Paul pulls out all the stops and with scathing irony reproves the Corinthians for their arrogance. His confrontation, however, is rooted in a father's love for his children (4:14–15).

### *(1) The Church, Its Leaders, and God's Fiery Test (3:5–17)*

**5What, after all, is Apollos? And what is Paul? Only servants, through whom you came to believe—as the Lord has assigned to each his task. 6I planted the seed,**

[315] Paul and Apollos are mentioned three times in this section (3:5,22; 4:6).

[316] References to God occur eleven times from 3:6–17 (reminiscent of 1:1–9). Note also the use of the emphatic conjunction ἀλλά (3:6–7) and the emphatic placement of θεός (3:9). Kuck notes that the four parallel statements in 3:5–8 place emphasis on God and the servants' dependence on God. See D. W. Kuck, *Judgment and Community Conflict: Paul's Use of Apocalyptic Judgment Language in 1 Corinthians 3:5–4:5*, NovTSup 66 (Leiden: Brill, 1992), 164. The emphasis on the individual workers in the church is captured by the repetition of "each one" (5 times in 3:5–13) and the condition "if anyone" (4 times in 3:12–17). Paul is not setting forth an individualistic concept of ministry, but rather emphasizing assigned roles within corporate ministry and individual accountability.

[317] The Greek conjunction is ὥστε, which in three instances introduces an independent clause meaning, "for this reason" or "therefore." The NIV translates "so" (3:7), "so then" (3:21), "therefore" (4:5).

**Apollos watered it, but God made it grow. [7]So neither he who plants nor he who waters is anything, but only God, who makes things grow. [8]The man who plants and the man who waters have one purpose, and each will be rewarded according to his own labor. [9]For we are God's fellow workers; you are God's field, God's building.**

**[10]By the grace God has given me, I laid a foundation as an expert builder, and someone else is building on it. But each one should be careful how he builds. [11]For no one can lay any foundation other than the one already laid, which is Jesus Christ. [12]If any man builds on this foundation using gold, silver, costly stones, wood, hay or straw, [13]his work will be shown for what it is, because the Day will bring it to light. It will be revealed with fire, and the fire will test the quality of each man's work. [14]If what he has built survives, he will receive his reward. [15]If it is burned up, he will suffer loss; he himself will be saved, but only as one escaping through the flames.**

**[16]Don't you know that you yourselves are God's temple and that God's Spirit lives in you? [17]If anyone destroys God's temple, God will destroy him; for God's temple is sacred, and you are that temple.**

**3:5** In reply to the questions, "What is Paul? What is Apollos?", Paul answers, "Servants through whom you came to believe."[318] The term "servants" applies not only to Paul and Apollos but to anyone else who assumes a leadership role in the church.[319] In this particular context, since the image is that of laborers in the field, the word stresses the lowly character of the service rendered.[320] The image of a lowly minister would have conveyed a value system completely opposite the value system of the status-hungry Corinthians. Morris suggests the term "ridicules the tendency to make much of preachers."[321] Emphasis falls on the fact that Paul and Apollos were merely those *through whom* the Corinthians believed and that it was the Lord himself who gave a certain role to each one.[322] Paul and Apollos were mere instruments of the Lord's work. While it is possible to interpret the phrase "as the Lord has assigned to

---

[318] An ingressive aorist, "through whom you came to faith."

[319] The word rendered "servants" (NIV) or "ministers" (KJV) is διάκονος. The word "deacon" is a transliteration of the Greek, but it rarely functions with such a technical nuance in the New Testament (see Phil 1:1; 1 Tim 3:8,12). In Col 1:7, Paul identifies Epaphras as a servant of the church at Colossae, and in 1 Tim 4:6, Paul calls Timothy a servant. The term appears only here in 1 Corinthians. Paul even applies the term to the governing authorities (Rom 13:4), to Christ (Rom 15:8), and to servants of Satan (2 Cor 11:15).

[320] Garland (*1 Corinthians*, 111) notes that the servant image does not detract from the authority of God's agents, but the image does lower status in keeping with Jesus' view of the disciple's leadership roles (see esp. Mark 10:41–45; Luke 22:25–27). Along these lines Rupert Davies notes that 1 Cor 3–4 save us from both too high and too low a doctrine of the ministry. The minister is not the person who makes the church, but they are more than full-time servants. They are God's agents. R. E. Davies, *Studies in 1 Corinthians* (London: Epworth, 1962), 42.

[321] Morris, *1 Corinthians*, 63.

[322] "Lord" in this context (κύριος) likely refers to the Lord Jesus Christ.

each" as referring to the faith of the Corinthians,[323] the context demands that the reference is to the different tasks assigned by God to the workers.[324] Thus the NIV expands the Greek, "As the Lord has assigned *to each his task*." That the Lord gives to "each one" anticipates the rich discussion of the gifts of the Spirit in chap. 12, which extends the teaching of God's assigned tasks beyond the leadership to all the members of the church, Christ's body. The Spirit distributes gifts as he wills (12:11), and God places members in the body as he pleases (12:18; cf. also 12:28).[325]

Commentators often note that Paul uses the neuter pronoun "what" instead of "who" in the question, "What is Apollos, what is Paul?"[326] Morris may be correct to note that the neuter draws attention to the function of the preachers rather than focusing on their persons.[327] Thiselton suggests that the neuter pronoun points back to 3:3 (cf. 1:10–12) with reference to the jealousy and strife arising from political sloganing. "What does all this Apollos-language and Paul-language amount to? What is Apollos or Paul? What is their role?"[328] Another solution is that the neuter interrogative, "what" in 3:5, corresponds to the following neuter indefinite pronoun, "anything" in 3:7.[329] What do the servants amount to? Not much of anything when compared to God, who alone causes the growth. Of course, Paul's low estimation of church leaders must be read in context. Paul will exhort the Corinthians in 4:16 to "become imitators of me." In the letter closing he commends the household of Stephanas and urges the Corinthians to "submit to such as these and to everyone who joins in the work, and labors at it" (16:16). And of Stephanas, Fortunatus, and Achaicus, Paul states, "Such men deserve recognition" (16:18).[330]

**3:6–8** In order to press home the different functional roles assumed by servants, Paul employs an agricultural metaphor.[331] The Corinthians are God's cultivated field (3:9),[332] and Paul and Apollos are humble field hands, who

[323] The Greek reads, "and to each one as the Lord gave," following immediately on the verb "believed."

[324] So also Fee, *First Corinthians*, 131.

[325] The word "each one" appears three times in 1 Cor 12 (12:7,11,18).

[326] Some manuscripts read, "Who?" This is followed by the KJV.

[327] Morris, *1 Corinthians*, 63.

[328] Thiselton, *First Corinthians*, 299.

[329] In Greek the spelling of the interrogative and the indefinite pronoun is identical except for the accent mark (what, τί; anything, τι).

[330] Cf. also 1 Thess 5:12–13, "Now we ask you, brothers, to respect those who work hard among you, who are over you in the Lord and who admonish you. Hold them in the highest regard in love because of their work."

[331] Does Paul employ three metaphors (field, building, temple) or two (field and building/temple) or an even tighter association of images (a garden-like temple)? See G. K. Beale, *The Temple and the Church's Mission: A Biblical Theology of the Dwelling Place of God* (Downers Grove: InterVarsity, 2004), 245–50. Ciampa and Rosner (*First Corinthians*, 142) give 3:5–23 the heading, "Metaphors for the Church and Its Leaders: God's Garden Temple."

[332] Gk. γεώργιον. According to Louw-Nida (1.96) the term is "normally restricted to tilled fields or orchards, in contrast with pasture land . . . in the NT γεώργιον is used only figuratively of

labor in conjunction with one another in a common purpose. It is often suggested that the image of a field echoes the tradition of Israel as God's vineyard in Isa 5 and related texts.[333] The metaphor allows Paul to emphasize a number of things relevant to the Corinthian situation.[334] First, different activities lead to the growth of the church (3:6–7). Each laborer performs a task assigned by the owner of the field. Paul planted the church in Corinth and Apollos watered, that is, he came along after Paul and ministered there for an unspecified period of time (Acts 19:1). Although Apollos was not part of the original missionary team that founded the church, Paul readily acknowledges Apollos' subsequent role of cultivation. The metaphor should not be pressed to indicate that Paul never engaged in a teaching ministry and Apollos never evangelized. Paul spent eighteen months in Corinth (Acts 18:11) and would have devoted extensive time teaching new converts. Likewise, 3:5b identifies Apollos, along with Paul, as a servant through whom the Corinthians came to faith.[335]

Second, Paul stresses God as the cause of the growth of the church, mentioned twice (3:6–7) and in both cases preceded by the emphatic conjunction.[336] The tense of the verb shifts from aorist to imperfect[337] with the meaning, "God was causing the growth." God's work is always behind the scenes, and even when human work is finished, God's work continues. Paul is not claiming that human endeavors are of no consequence whatsoever. God himself has assigned certain tasks to those who work in the field, and as Paul will warn in 3:10–15, using the metaphor of a building, each minister must construct the building with proper materials. Verses 16–17 explicitly warn the church leaders (and others) of the dire consequences of inflicting damage on God's temple.

Third, Paul underscores the unity of purpose between the one who plants and the one who waters. The Greek of 3:8 reads, "The one who plants and the one who waters are one." The NIV captures one possible sense of Paul's meaning with the translation "have one purpose." Thiselton notes that the Greek leaves open the question whether or not Paul meant "one in purpose" or "one in status."[338] In context Paul's point has to do primarily with unity, which

---

people whom God cares for and nurtures." The word occurs in the LXX eight times (Gen 26:14; Prov 6:7; 9:12; 24:5,30; 31:16; Sir 27:6; Jer 28:23).

[333] See Hays (*1 Corinthians*, 53) and the discussion in Thiselton (*1 Corinthians*, 302). Ciampa and Rosner (*First Corinthians*, 143) point out that Isa 5:2 mixes building and planting metaphors (see also Jer 18:9; 24:6; Ezek 36:9–10).

[334] Garland (*1 Corinthians*, 111–12) suggests four applications of the image of planter and waterer: (1) The labor of one without the other is useless. (2) Both roles are essential to the task. (3) Rivalry between servants is absurd. (4) God is the life force that produces the harvest. Whether or not Paul intends to press the metaphor in all four directions is uncertain.

[335] So Thiselton, *First Corinthians*, 302.

[336] Gk. ἀλλά.

[337] ἐγὼ ἐφύτευσα ("I planted," aorist), Ἀπολλῶς ἐπότισεν ("Apollos watered," aorist), ἀλλὰ ὁ θεὸς ηὔξανεν ("but God was causing the growth," imperfect).

[338] Ibid., 303. Ciampa and Rosner (*First Corinthians*, 147) think that Paul has status in view; Paul and Apollos are both servants, neither is responsible for the growth, and neither is anything. In

stands in stark contrast to the divisiveness of the Corinthians and renders their competitive spirit completely absurd. The Corinthians were bogged down in the mire of unhealthy allegiances based on human criteria resulting in a completely distorted view of the gospel. Paul and Apollos, on the other hand, were stellar examples of ministers who were "perfectly united in mind and thought" (cf. 1:10).

In 3:8b Paul interjects that just as "each one" receives his own assignment from God, so also "each one" will receive his own reward[339] according to his own labor. The mention of reward anticipates the further elaboration in 3:13–15 and 4:1–5. Paul does not elaborate on the nature of the reward. In the context of the metaphor of the field-worker the term denotes pay received for labor performed, but Paul does not have anything of material substance in mind, such as remuneration from the church. His use of the term in 3:14 is strictly eschatological. This suggests that the reward is God's affirmation of the quality of work performed by means of his fiery test, which shows the enduring quality of what has been built on the foundation of Jesus Christ (3:10). In 9:17–18 Paul speaks of his own earthly reward as preaching the gospel free of charge. First Corinthians 4:1–5 supports the idea that the reward is praise that comes to each one from God. Reward is given according to the quality of one's labor, not success by worldly standards, as revealed on the day of judgment.[340] Thiselton believes the image of pay or reward "serves primarily to intensify the point that Paul and Apollos are responsible to God, their employer, for judgments about their success or failure, not the community." This gives to the concept of reward the sense of worth as determined by God not by man.[341] In 15:58 Paul exhorts the Corinthians to give themselves fully to the Lord knowing that their labor in the Lord is not in vain.[342]

**3:9** Paul describes himself and Apollos as God's fellow-workers,[343] followed by the claim that the Corinthians are God's field, God's building. In every clause, God is placed in the emphatic position, literally, "God's fellow-workers we are, God's field, God's building you are." The emphatic place-

---

context, a case can be made either way, and the point may be that they are "one" (united) because they share the same lowly status. However, other contexts suggests that Paul held a different status within the church as its founder (cf. 4:15, "Even though you have ten thousand guardians in Christ, you do not have many fathers, for in Christ Jesus I became your father through the gospel").

[339] Gk. μισθός.

[340] 4:1–5, which also employs servant imagery, emphasizes the relationship between present faithfulness and future judgment, when God discloses human motives. Garland (*First Corinthians*, 112), notes, "The idea of rendering to each according to each one's work runs throughout the NT (Matt 16:27; Rom 2:6; 2 Cor 11:15; 2 Tim 4:14; 1 Pet 1:17; Rev 2:23; 20:12–13; 22:12)."

[341] Thiselton, *First Corinthians*, 304.

[342] See also 1 Cor 9:24–25 where Paul employs the image of the "crown," drawing from the athletic metaphor.

[343] Gk. συνεργοί. NIV2011, "co-workers." The term occurs once here in 1 Corinthians but twelve other times in Paul's writings (Rom 16:3,9,21; 1 Cor 3:9; 2 Cor 1:24; 8:23; Phil 2:25; 4:3; Col 4:11; 1 Thess 3:2; Phlm 1:1,24; cf. also 3 John 1:8).

ment of "God" stresses divine initiative and divine ownership. Paul shifts the image from the field to the building, from agriculture to architecture.[344] In the claim to be God's fellow-workers, Paul means either that he and Apollos are co-workers *belonging to* God[345] or that they labor along *with* God.[346] The context strongly suggests the former, taking the genitive as possessive with the meaning "We are fellow-workers belonging to God."[347] The whole argument emphasizes the unity of the workers in their labor *under* God.[348] Servants are not co-workers with their master. They serve under the master and work for the master. Furthermore, the subsequent clauses are clearly possessive. The Corinthians, God's field and God's building, belong to the Lord. They are God's possession.

**3:10–11** In 3:10 Paul develops the image of the building introduced in 3:9. There are differences of interpretation regarding the meaning and significance of the building. The mention of the construction materials (gold, silver, and precious stones) along with the reference to the temple in 3:16 suggests to some that the building in 3:10–15 is, in fact, the temple of 3:16–17. Ciampa and Rosner, following Beale, suggest that Paul has in mind Solomon's garden-like temple and the end-time temple of Mal 3–4. "In terms of specific connections, Paul echoes Isaiah 3:3 in 3:10, 1 Chronicles 29:2 in 3:10, and Malachi 3:2–3 in 3:12–15. As 'God's temple' (3:16), the Corinthians are the antitype of the imposing temple of Solomon and the fulfillment of Malachi's vision of an end-time temple."[349] Garland, following Kuck, thinks that there is no particular building in mind in 3:10–15, that the background of Solomon's temple "would not have been obvious to the readers, and the inclusion of hay and straw would seem anomalous."[350] Mitchell argues that both "building" and "temple" are images of unity, which is Paul's essential point.[351] On all accounts Paul is saying something of great significance about the nature of the church: God is the owner of the building, the Holy Spirit dwells in the temple, and God will destroy those who destroy his temple.

For the most part, the analogy of the building corresponds in detail to the analogy of the field. The building represents the church, God is the owner, Paul

[344] The images of a field and a building do appear together in the Old Testament (see Jer 1:10; 18:9; 24:6).

[345] A possessive genitive.

[346] A genitive of association.

[347] See also D. B. Wallace, *Greek Grammar Beyond the Basics: An Exegetical Syntax of the New Testament* (Grand Rapids: Zondervan, 1996), 130. ". . . the apostle is not claiming that he and Apollos are God's partners, but his servants."

[348] So Fee, *First Corinthians*, 134. Most recent commentators take the possessive view (so Thiselton, Garland, Ciampa and Rosner). For the associative view see Robertson and Plummer, *First Corinthians*, 58.

[349] Ciampa and Rosner, *First Corinthians*, 150; Beale, *The Temple and the Church's Mission*, 246.

[350] Garland, *1 Corinthians*, 116; Kuck, *Judgment and Community Conflict*, 177–78.

[351] Mitchell, *Rhetoric of Reconciliation*, 99–105. Also Garland, *1 Corinthians*, 120.

is the founder, and workers are rewarded according to their labor (cf. 3:6; 4:5). But on the last point there is added emphasis on the quality of the materials used in the construction. Indeed, the main point of the unit is expressed in 3:10, "each one should be careful how he builds."[352] All work does not receive equal pay; in fact, some work will be rendered useless on judgment day and will go up in the flames when submitted to God's fiery test. Paul presents himself as the "expert builder" who, according to God's grace, laid the only proper foundation that one can lay, Jesus Christ (cf. 2:1–5). The NIV translation, "expert builder," while correct, misses a not-so-subtle nuance in the Greek text. The term translated "expert" is the adjective "wise" (cf. NIV2011), which, in this context, can have the meaning of "skilled," or "cxpert" as a modifier of the noun "builder."[353] The choice of the term reminds the Corinthians that Paul is still on the topic of ministry constructed according to God's wisdom rather than human wisdom.[354]

The mention of "another who builds" on the foundation laid by Paul, in context, could refer to Apollos (cf. 3:6),[355] but the use of indefinite pronoun "anyone" in the following verses (3:12–17) suggests that Paul has in view any who are involved in the building up of the church,[356] as he launches a frontal attack against those responsible for division in the church and those culpable for the current "wood, hay, and straw" of human wisdom.[357] However, while the reference in the immediate discussion is to the leaders involved in the building of the church, the participation of the whole church is in view in chaps. 8–14, particularly in the discussion of spiritual gifts.[358]

**3:12–15** Paul develops the metaphor further as the argument shifts from the foundation to the superstructure, which will undergo an inspection on judgment day in order to determine its quality.[359] Unlike the foundation, he

[352] So also Garland, *1 Corinthians*, 115. The verb is βλέπω in the imperative mood that constitutes a warning. See also 8:9; 10:12,18.

[353] Gk. σοφός (wise). The phrase σοφὸς ἀρχιτέκτων occurs in the LXX in Isa 3:3.

[354] The adjective σοφός has not occurred since 1:27, and the noun σοφία since 2:13. In 3:18 σοφός appears again, "If anyone among you thinks that he is wise in this age let him become a fool that he may become wise."

[355] See Thiselton, *First Corinthians*, 309n54. There is considerable amount of discussion whether Apollos is the referent of someone else, or whether this excludes Apollos. Thiselton thinks Apollos cannot be excluded, even if he is not the primary or sole referent.

[356] The conditional particle with the indefinite pronoun ("if anyone"; εἴ τις) dominates the argument from 3:12–18, appearing in 3:12,14,15,17,18.

[357] So Fee, *First Corinthians*, 136.

[358] The thematic link between 3:10–17 and chaps. 8–14 is in the "building" language. To "build upon" (ἐποικοδομέω) occurs only in 3:10–14 in 1 Corinthians (elsewhere in Paul in Eph 2:20; Col 2:7; cf. Jude 20). The term "building" (οἰκοδομή) used figuratively in the sense of "edification" appears throughout chap. 14 (14:3,5,12,26). The verb form "to build up" (οἰκοδομέω) appears in 8:1,10; 10:23; 14:4,17. Garland (*1 Corinthians*, 115) notes that "to build upon" refers to preaching and instruction (cf. 2 Cor 10:8; 12:19; 13:10; cf. Eph 2:19–22).

[359] In addition to the repetition of "if anyone," this section (3:12–15) coheres around the theme of God's testing "fire."

envisions different kinds of materials that one might use in the construction of the building. There is only one kind of foundation possible; if the foundation is not Jesus Christ, then the building is not the church. Even if Paul's language evokes the image of Solomon's temple, either in the identification of the building or in the anticipation of the mention of the temple in 3:16–17, the essential point has do to with materials that are imperishable versus those that are perishable. Paul probably does not have in mind specific meanings for the individual items of gold, silver, costly stones, wood, hay and straw. Thiselton notes that the position taken by the overwhelming majority of commentators is that Paul simply sets forth two categories of material of different quality.[360] One is perishable and the other is not. One withstands the fire, but the other burns up. Anything that is not of the quality of the wisdom of God is wood, hay, and straw and will be consumed in the final judgment.

The time of testing reveals the quality of the materials used in building the church of God. The "day" refers to the eschatological day of judgment, when the work of each one will become evident.[361] Fire is an appropriate image associated with the last day.[362] In this context, the purpose of the fire is not punitive but rather serves the purpose of testing and disclosing the true value of one's work for God. The subject of the verb in 3:13 is ambiguous, "It will be revealed." Either "day," the closest noun to the verb, is the subject, or the subject is the "work" of each one. If "day" is the subject, then the meaning is either, "The Day is revealed in fire," or "The Day reveals itself in fire." The difference is the voice of the verb, which could be either passive or middle in Greek. Either way, the meaning is that God's testing fire is a key feature of the Day of the Lord. Collins takes the view that the subject is "work" since, he claims, "day" never appears elsewhere in the extant literature as the subject of the verb "to reveal" and 3:13d refers to the testing of one's work by fire.[363]

The fire determines the reward (pay), but the issue is not the salvation versus the ruin of the workman. The worker is saved, but the works are burned up. Paul is clear that his work as the builder who laid the foundation was "by the grace God has given me." The notion of "work" is easy to grasp within the analogy of the building. One either does good work or not, using quality materials or that which is inferior and subject to destruction by fire. But exactly what Paul means by the term "work" is not immediately apparent.[364] In 5:2, "work" refers to the sinful deed of the incestuous man, in 9:1 Paul refers to the

---

[360] Thiselton, *First Corinthians*, 311.

[361] For other references to the Day of the Lord see Rom 13:12; 1 Cor 1:8; 5:5; 2 Cor 1:14; Phil 1:6,10; 2:16; 1 Thess 5:2,4; 2 Thess 2:2.

[362] See 2 Thess 1:7–8; 2 Pet 3:12. In the Gospels see Matt 3:10–12; 5:22; 7:19; 13:40,42,50; 17:15; 18:8–9; 25:41; Mark 9:43,48–49; Luke 3:9,16–17; 9:54; 12:49; 17:29; John 15:6. In the Old Testament see Isa 66:15; Dan 7:9–10; Mal 3:1–3; 4:1.

[363] Collins, *First Corinthians*, 158–59.

[364] Gk. ἔργον.

Corinthians as his "work" in the Lord, and in the conclusion to chap. 15 Paul exhorts the church to full devotion to the "work" of the Lord (cf. also 16:10). In 3:10–17 "work" applies to the leadership of the church in relation to the wisdom of God. Any work that exalts men or that arises out of a self-serving motive will perish on the Day of the Lord. Paul often links his own success in ministry to the faithfulness of others, who are his work in the Lord.[365] Garland observes that Paul's "reward will be that his churches will be saved with him."[366] In 1 Thess 2:19–20, Paul explicitly connects reward with the final outcome of his converts, "For what is our hope, our joy, or the crown in which we will glory in the presence of our Lord Jesus when he comes? Is it not you? Indeed, you are our glory and joy."

It is possible that saved "as through fire" is a proverbial expression indicating salvation and nothing more. The phrase may have become a metaphor like "brand plucked from the burning" (Amos 4:11), meaning something like "saved at the last moment." Witherington suggests it is a metaphor for escaping "by the skin of one's teeth."[367] The main point, however, is that God's verdict is comprehensive, definitive, and final. There are no revisions possible because God knows comprehensively all motivations and intentions of the human heart.

**3:16–17** The imagery shifts yet again to a temple, unless, as noted above, all three images refer to the same thing. The temple language, however, more explicitly links the gathered church to the very presence of God. The corporate dimensions of Paul's thought can be quite complex yet of great significance for his ethical instructions.[368] The church is God's temple, and the image applies because "God's Spirit lives in you."[369] Jesus associated the temple with his body (John 2:19–21), and Paul refers to the church as the "body of Christ," which is constituted by the Spirit (1 Cor 12:12–13,27). The reference to the Spirit in 3:16–17 continues what has already been emphasized from 2:4,6–16 and prepares for further teaching on the Spirit in relation to the church in 6:12–20; 12:1–14:40; and 15:42–49.[370]

---

[365] See Gal 2:2; 4:11; Phil 2:16; 1 Thess 3:5. See also 1 Cor 9:24–27.

[366] Garland, *1 Corinthians*, 119. Garland suggests that this idea lies behind 2 Cor 1:12–14.

[367] Witherington, *Conflict and Community*, 134.

[368] Paul's thought is both corporate and individual. In 6:19, Paul refers to the individual bodies of the Corinthians as members of Christ and the temple of the Holy Spirit.

[369] Could also be rendered, "The Spirit of God dwells among you" or "in your midst" (NIV2011). See also 2 Cor 6:16–18. For the concept of the community as a temple in the Old Testament see Exod 25:8; 29:45; Lev 26:11–12; Ezek 11:16; 37:26–28.

[370] Ciampa and Rosner (*First Corinthians*, 159) propose that "The identification of the Corinthian believers as God's temple also sets the scene for the expulsion in chapter 5, where the incestuous man is 'destroyed' because he has destroyed God's temple. Presumably it is because the Corinthians are God's temple that their consumption of the bread and wine in the Lord's Supper is understood in terms of participation in a sacrifice offered at an altar (10:16–22) and that Paul thought it essential for the church to be 'built up' through the Spirit in chapters 12–14 (picking up on the theme from 3:10–12)."

Paul's question, "Don't you know?" is an indictment. This is the first of ten occurrences of the question in the letter.[371] No doubt many in Corinth took great pride in their knowledge (8:1) and linked the possession of wisdom to their knowledge rather than behavior. If so, then the question, "Don't you know?" repeated throughout the letter constitutes a rebuke. From the question, Paul issues a stern warning, and the application of the analogies intensifies. He warns that if anyone destroys the temple of God, then God will destroy that person. Some suggest that Paul's meaning refers only to inflicting damage on the church or to corrupt the church since God's church cannot ultimately be destroyed.[372] Yet, local manifestations of the church can and do become extinct. The warning is severe and real and similarly harsh injunctions appear elsewhere in the letter (see 10:1–13). The reason that God's judgment comes to those who profane the temple is simple: "God's temple is sacred." This statement recalls the letter's opening, where Paul identified the Corinthians as God's church, "those sanctified in Christ Jesus and called to be holy" (1:2). In context, the reference to destroying the temple has a more specific reference to those causing and stoking divisions.[373] To engage in such behavior is to destroy the temple of God.[374]

### *(2) The Wisdom of God vs. the Wisdom of the World (Reprise) 3:18–23*

**18Do not deceive yourselves. If any one of you thinks he is wise by the standards of this age, he should become a "fool" so that he may become wise. 19For the wisdom of this world is foolishness in God's sight. As it is written: "He catches the wise in their craftiness"; 20and again, "The Lord knows that the thoughts of the wise are futile." 21So then, no more boasting about men! All things are yours, 22whether Paul or Apollos or Cephas or the world or life or death or the present or the future—all are yours, 23and you are of Christ, and Christ is of God.**

The concluding exhortation of 3:18–23, marked by three commands,[375] rounds out the discussion begun in 1:18.[376] Once again, Paul quotes Scripture

[371] See 5:6; 6:2–3,9,15,16,19; 9:13,24.

[372] The term for "destroy" is φθείρω. Elsewhere in Paul the meaning is "to corrupt" (see 1 Cor 15:33; 2 Cor 7:2; 11:3; Eph 4:22). BDAG, however, gives 1 Cor 3:17b the meaning, "to inflict punishment, to destroy," in the sense "punish with eternal destruction."

[373] Ciampa and Rosner (*First Corinthians*, 160) suggest a broader application that Paul may be "talking more generally of those who may not be in leadership doing damage to the church. The 'destruction of the flesh' of the immoral man in chapter 5, or the members taking one another to secular court in 6:1–11, or the men making use of prostitutes in 6:12–20 may be in his sights. In chapter 8 Paul warns the Corinthians not to destroy a brother or sister in Christ by acting on their so-called knowledge, as by eating in an idol's temple (8:11)."

[374] On the "temple" language see J. R. Lanci, *A New Temple for Corinth: Rhetorical and Archaeological Approaches to Pauline Imagery* (New York: Lang, 1997).

[375] 3:18a ("Do not deceive yourselves); 3:18b ("become a fool" in order to become wise); 3:21 ("no more boasting about men!").

[376] 3:18–23 forms an *inclusio* with 1:18–31 by reiterating key terms such as "wise," "foolish," "in this age," and "boasting." So also Collins, *First Corinthians*, 87.

(Job 5:13; Ps 94:11) and inverts previous statements in order to drive home the point. In 1:18–25, for example, the message of the cross is "foolishness" to the unbelieving world, but in 3:19, the wisdom of the world is foolishness in God's sight. The way to become truly wise is to become a "fool," which is to embrace the cross not only as the object of faith but as a value system, a way of thinking and behaving. The opposite, the wisdom of this age, enshrined in "boasting in men" (3:21), should be completely discarded.

The rhetorical crescendo of 3:18–23 is analogous to the climactic crescendo of Rom 8:38–39. There is no reason to boast in men because all things belong to them in Christ, who belongs to God. Paul's declaration, "All things are yours!", followed by "whether Paul or Apollos or Cephas, etc." is the exact opposite of the rhetorical caricature of 1:12, "I follow Paul, I follow Apollos, I follow Cephas." The Corinthians do not belong to these men; these men belong to them, that is, the church, and all belong to Christ, who belongs to God.[377] This supports the key point of 3:5–17, that Paul and Apollos are servants of the church who labor under their master. The boasting language recalls 1:26–31. Boasting has its place but only in the Lord.

### *(3) Faithfulness as the Criterion of Judgment (4:1–5)*

**[1]So then, men ought to regard us as servants of Christ and as those entrusted with the secret things of God. [2]Now it is required that those who have been given a trust must prove faithful. [3]I care very little if I am judged by you or by any human court; indeed, I do not even judge myself. [4]My conscience is clear, but that does not make me innocent. It is the Lord who judges me. [5]Therefore judge nothing before the appointed time; wait till the Lord comes. He will bring to light what is hidden in darkness and will expose the motives of men's hearts. At that time each will receive his praise from God.**

A number of literary features of 1:18–3:23 appear to suggest that chap. 4 begins a new line of thought. First, the ending of chap. 3 (3:18–23) clearly parallels 1:18–31 and brings to conclusion Paul's discussion of the folly of human wisdom in the light of God's wisdom, Christ crucified.[378] Second, the terms "wise" and "wisdom," occurring collectively twenty-six times in chaps. 1–3 disappear altogether in chap. 4. And third, Paul's sustained use of the Old Testament in support of his argument related to divine/human wisdom concludes in 3:19–20.[379] Yet, upon closer examination we discover that a fluid relationship exists between chap. 4 and the preceding material.

In its immediate context, chap. 4 continues the theme of 3:5–17 concerning how one should regard ministers in the church. As in chap. 3, Paul applies

---

[377] On Christ and his relation to God see also 8:6 and 15:20–28.

[378] Collins (*First Corinthians*, 87) identifies 1:18–3:23 as a distinct subunit within the larger rhetorical unit of 1:10–4:21.

[379] The use of γέγραπται in 4:6 refers to Scripture but points back to the prior uses of Scripture in the argument of 1:18–3:23.

the servant image to those who lead the church and refers to them as "those entrusted with the secret things of God." The word translated "those entrusted" picks up on the "building" language of 3:5–17,[380] and the term "mystery" harks back to the use of the same term in 2:1,7. The judgment language in 4:3–4 recalls previous uses of the same term in 2:14–15.[381] Furthermore, the verb in 4:1,[382] translated by the NIV, "ought to regard" is the fifth in a series of third person imperatives beginning with 3:10.[383] Finally, the mention of "each one" in 4:5 recalls the five uses of the same term in 3:8–13, and the plural "us" carries over from 3:22.[384]

In 4:1–5 Paul recounts how human judgments are a very small matter to him. In saying this he is not trying to challenge the Corinthians in an arrogant way as though he is beyond human scrutiny, nor does it seem that his primary motivation is personal self-defense, a response to those in Corinth seeking to judge him.[385] Rather, Paul's chief aim is related to the command of 3:21, to persuade the Corinthian believers to cease from boasting in men, whether it be Paul, Apollos, Cephas, or their local leaders. Paul wants the Corinthians to become imitators of him as he imitates Christ (4:6–13,16–17) and to understand that the only examination that counts is God's judgment on the Day of the Lord. God alone appraises and discerns accurately the motives of the heart. All human appraisals, including self-appraisals, always fall short. For this reason final judgments must be withheld until the Lord comes (cf. 3:13–17) when God will bring to light the secret things of darkness and will expose the counsels of the heart. The only "praise" that counts is the praise that comes from God.

**4:1–2** The Greek adverb translated, "So then,"[386] can refer either to what precedes or what follows. The NIV translation implies that Paul draws an inference from the previous section (3:18–23). Other translations take the adverb as

---

[380] The Greek, *οἰκονόμος* (translated by others as "steward" or "manager"), is from the same root as the word used for building in 3:9 (οἰκοδομή) and the verbs used in 3:10,12,14 (ἐποικοδομέω, "to build upon") and 3:16 (οἰκέω, "to dwell").

[381] Gk. ἀνακρίνω, occurring three times in 4:3–4 and three times in 2:14–15.

[382] Gk. λογιζέσθω.

[383] The imperative mood verbs are βλεπέτω (3:10, "each one should be careful"); ἐξαπατάτω (3:18a, "do not deceive yourselves); γενέσθω (3:18b, "he should become a 'fool'"); καυχάσθω (3:21, "no more boasting about men!").

[384] Kuck (*Apocalyptic Judgment Language*, 159), followed by Garland (*1 Corinthians*, 122), argues that 3:18–4:5 constitutes a "double recapitulation of previous themes." The first recapitulation, 3:18–23, is a climactic summary of the first major rhetorical unit, 1:18–2:16, and concerns how to regard oneself. The second, 4:1–5, recites the argument of 2:6–3:17 and concerns how to regard God's servants.

[385] Contra Fee (*First Corinthians*, 158–59), who sees a decidedly apologetic purpose in 4:1–5. Collins (*First Corinthians*, 157) comments, "Paul is obviously making an apology (see 9:3) for his ministry, but one must not assume that his ministry has been under attack at Corinth or that some of the Corinthians had accused Paul of doing evil. It may be that this 'apology,' like that of ch. 9, is an element in the rhetorical strategy adopted by Paul to enhance his ethos."

[386] Gk. οὕτως.

forward referring and correlative with "as servants of Christ."[387] The NASB, for example, translates, "Let a man regard us *in this manner*, as servants of Christ and stewards of the mysteries of God" (emphasis added).[388] Commentators, like the modern translations, differ on this issue.[389] Either way, 4:1–5 extends the argument of the previous section. The plural "us" carries over from 3:22 with primary reference to Paul, Apollos, and Peter but likely extends also to the local Corinthian leaders.[390] Leaders are servants of Christ, "those entrusted with the secret things" (NIV) of God (cf. 2:1,7). The word for servants in 4:1 is a different word from the "servants" of 3:5.[391] The term used in 4:1 occurs frequently in the Gospels and Acts and refers to many diverse kinds of servants, "such as attendants to a king, officers of the Sanhedrin, attendants of magistrates, and, especially in the Gospel of John, Jewish Temple guards."[392] Since this is the only occurrence of the word in Paul, it is difficult to know if he intends any significant difference in meaning between "servants" and the companion term in the same verse translated "those entrusted with."[393] In this context the two terms may be somewhat synonymous.[394] Both stress the servile role of leaders in relation to God and Christ, and both also can indicate a large measure of responsibility associated with the humble task.

The NIV translates the second term, *oikonomos*, as "those entrusted" in 4:1 and "those who have been given a trust" in 4:2.[395] The word denotes one who has authority and responsibility for something such as an administrator or manager of a household.[396] The term denotes a person in a position of trust and who is accountable to others.[397] Paul's description in 4:1 complements and balances the previous reference to himself and Apollos as humble

---

[387] Gk. ὡς. Cf. NIV2011.

[388] Similarly, HCSB, "A person should consider us in this way: as servants of Christ and managers of God's mysteries," and ESV, "This is how one should regard us, as servants of Christ and stewards of the mysteries of God."

[389] The evidence suggests that οὕτως refers forward when followed by ὡς. See 1 Cor 3:15 and 9:26 (elsewhere in Paul 2 Cor 9:5; Eph 5:33; 1 Thess 2:4). Thus the NASB and similar translations are correct. BDAG also classifies the usage of οὕτως in 1 Cor 4:1 as pertaining to what follows in discourse material. So also Fee, *First Corinthians*, 158n3; Fitzmyer, *First Corinthians*, 212. Contra Garland (*First Corinthians*, 125), who takes οὕτως with what precedes.

[390] So Fee, *First Corinthians*, 159.

[391] Gk. ὑπηρέτης (4:1) instead of διάκονος (3:5).

[392] Louw-Nida, 35.20. BDAG defines as "one who functions as a helper or assistant."

[393] Gk. οἰκονόμος.

[394] Fee (*First Corinthians*, 156) distinguishes the two by suggesting that ὑπηρέτης is a general term and refers to one who administers the affairs of another, while οἰκονόμος may carry more of the sense of responsibility in the assigned task.

[395] For other uses of the term in Paul see Rom 16:23; Gal 4:2; Titus 1:7. Cf. also 1 Pet 4:10.

[396] NASB translates as "stewards" and the HCSB as "managers." Louw-Nida (37.39) define as "one who has the authority and responsibility for something" (1 Cor 4:1; 1 Pet 4:10). Also 46.4, "one who is in charge of running a household" (Luke 16:1), and 57.231, as an idiom of one in charge of the finances of the city; see Rom 16:23, "Erastus, the city treasurer sends his greetings."

[397] Cf. Luke 12:42 where Jesus speaks of a "faithful and wise manager."

field-workers in 3:5. Their service is lowly service as unto the Lord but entails enormous responsibility, accountability, and dignity. Paul is saying that apostles and gifted teachers have been entrusted with nothing less than the secret things of God, that is, God's plan of salvation revealed in Christ.[398] Thiselton translates *oikonomos* as "estate manager" and comments, "This office normally included responsibility for overseeing a household budget, purchasing, accounts, resource allocation, collection of debts, and general running of the establishment, but only as instructed within guidelines agreed by the employer or the head of the house."[399]

In 4:2 Paul draws inferences concerning the role of servant/stewards.[400] The foremost requirement and the chief criterion of God's judgment of a household manager is faithfulness, which entails dependability and trustworthiness.[401] That the one entrusted with God's secret things "must prove faithful" complements what has already been said in 3:8 and 3:14–15 regarding "reward" for labor and the testing of one's work. Paul has in mind fidelity to the gospel as received (cf. 15:1–11),[402] but he also has in view the faithfulness of God's steward to God's call of suffering that goes along with it (4:6–13). Garland thinks that Paul's comments are to be understood as a direct application to the local situation in Corinth: "The gist of Paul's argument is this: if they are to regard ministers such as Paul, Apollos, and Cephas as menial underlings who belong to them and as God's household managers whose chief duty is faithfulness, then they also need to regard their local leaders in the same way."[403] God requires faithfulness, not eloquence or any other form of human wisdom.

**4:3–4** Thiselton comments that 4:3 is "one of the memorably liberating statements of Paul."[404] Only the owner of the household can determine if the steward has been trustworthy in the management of the estate. In the same way, only the Lord determines the faithfulness of his servant/steward.[405] Ultimately Paul, all other Christian stewards, and all believers will give an account to God for their service. The phrase "to me" is placed in the emphatic position in Greek. The Corinthians valued human judgments, but Paul did not. Preachers are servants of the church, but God is their master. So, for Paul, all human judgments are ultimately of little importance. The use of the term "day" in

---

398 This is now the third mention of the term μυστήριον (mystery) in the letter. In 2:1 and 2:7, the mystery refers to the preaching of Christ crucified, the wisdom of God that has been hidden but revealed to the apostles and prophets.

399 Thiselton, *First Corinthians*, 336.

400 Gk. ὧδε λοιπὸν, a marker of additional comment (see Louw-Nida, 89.98).

401 Cf. 1 Tim 1:12.

402 So Fee, *First Corinthians*, 160.

403 Garland, *1 Corinthians*, 126–27.

404 Thiselton, *First Corinthians*, 338.

405 Cf. Rom 14:4, "Who are you to judge someone else's servant? To his own master he stands or falls."

Greek,[406] translated "court," recalls the imagery of the "day" of fiery testing in 3:13–15. A human "day" in court is quite insignificant in comparison with the judgment day of God. Morris insightfully notes, "Often people think they know exactly what their spiritual state is and just what their service for God has effected. The result may depress beyond reason or exalt beyond measure; neither is relevant."[407]

Not only did Paul depreciate human judgments; he understood that he could not accurately assess his own motives. He confesses that he knows[408] nothing against himself,[409] but he also acknowledges, "that does not make me innocent."[410] Thus, Paul forthrightly numbers himself among others as one incapable and unqualified to make a final determination concerning his ministry.[411] He knows that only the Lord rightly discerns, and that even one's own conscience is not an accurate measure. Paul distances himself from any notion that he goes it alone, judging himself to be right without any accountability whatsoever. Garland notes Paul's own prior inaccurate assessment of his righteousness before God (cf. Phil 3:6).[412] Even though Paul ministers with a clear conscience, God alone weighs the intent and motives of the heart.[413] Thiselton observes that "Paul does not therefore advocate a thick-skinned indifference to public opinion; his point is a different one, namely, its fallibility, relativity, and limits that make it an unreliable guide on which to depend. Everything must be left with God in the final analysis, and one should not give privilege to one's own introspective assessments."[414]

**4:5** If humans are incapable of rendering final judgments, then all should cease from premature judgments.[415] The present imperative could carry the force of "stop judging before the time," or it could indicate a general admonition such as, "Make it your habit not to judge prematurely." In 4:5 there is a shift in terminology, from the Greek term meaning "to examine" (4:3–4) to

[406] Gk. ἡμέρα. Literally, "That I might be judged by you or by a human day." The implication is a "human day in court."

[407] Morris, *1 Corinthians*, 73.

[408] The word is σύνοιδα; to be aware of something; to be conscious of something.

[409] Note the emphatic ἀλλ' οὐδὲ (but neither).

[410] Literally, "I am not justified [δεδικαίωμαι] by this." Here the Greek verb "to justify" is not used in the same sense of "justification" elsewhere in Paul, the declaration of righteousness by faith. In context, the term refers to vindication as a faithful steward of the mysteries of God. Fee (*First Corinthians*, 162) notes that final judgment is in view. "I have not been acquitted by my own estimation of my trustworthiness as God's apostle."

[411] In 2 Tim 4:6, in the face of impending death, Paul expresses confidence that he has "fought the good fight, finished the race, and kept the faith." The crown that awaits him is righteousness, which the Lord gives to all who have longed for his appearing.

[412] Garland, *1 Corinthians*, 128.

[413] Cf. 1 Thess 2:4. Also Jas 4:11–12, "There is only one Lawgiver and Judge, the one who is able to save and destroy."

[414] Thiselton, *First Corinthians*, 341. Fitzmyer (*First Corinthians*, 213), notes the parallel of Job 27:6 (LXX) to Paul's claim that he knows nothing against himself (οὐ γὰρ σύνοιδα ἐμαυτῷ).

[415] 4:5 begins with a result clause introduced by ὥστε.

a term meaning "to judge" (4:5),[416] a reference to the final judgment when the Lord will render ultimate verdicts. The time of judgment is the Day of the Lord (cf. 3:13). God alone brings to light the secrets of darkness and discloses the counsels of the heart. Praise that comes "to each one" from God indicates the substance of the "reward" that Paul envisions in 3:8,14.[417] The time for final verdicts has not yet arrived. This, of course, does not demand the suspension of all judgment in the present so that there is no discernment whatsoever. Paul explicitly renders judgment against the incestuous man in the next chapter (see 5:3–5). He asks the Corinthians in 5:12, "Are you not to judge those inside?" And in 6:1–11 he scolds them for taking matters before the secular courts rather than before believers. In 4:1–5, Paul is speaking of the evaluation of one's ministry, of faithfulness to the master in the assigned task. Even here there is the necessity of some discernment provided that due consideration is given to its fallible and limited nature before the final judgment.[418]

### *(4) Application: God's Servants as Paradigms of the Cross (4:6–13)*

**6Now, brothers, I have applied these things to myself and Apollos for your benefit, so that you may learn from us the meaning of the saying, "Do not go beyond what is written." Then you will not take pride in one man over against another.**
**7For who makes you different from anyone else? What do you have that you did not receive? And if you did receive it, why do you boast as though you did not?**
**8Already you have all you want! Already you have become rich! You have become kings—and that without us! How I wish that you really had become kings so that we might be kings with you! 9For it seems to me that God has put us apostles on display at the end of the procession, like men condemned to die in the arena. We have been made a spectacle to the whole universe, to angels as well as to men.**
**10We are fools for Christ, but you are so wise in Christ! We are weak, but you are strong! You are honored, we are dishonored! 11To this very hour we go hungry and thirsty, we are in rags, we are brutally treated, we are homeless. 12We work hard with our own hands. When we are cursed, we bless; when we are persecuted, we endure it; 13when we are slandered, we answer kindly. Up to this moment we have become the scum of the earth, the refuse of the world.**

Paul's argument regarding human wisdom and the exaltation of church leaders, which began in 1:10, reaches a climactic point in 4:6–13,[419] which is then followed immediately by warning and exhortation (4:17–21). In 3:5–17, Paul described himself and Apollos as servants and co-workers belonging to God, a ministry team with one purpose. In 4:1–5 Paul explained that they should be regarded as assistants of Christ and managers of God's mysteries. It

---

416 Gk. ἀνακρίνω (used also in 2:14–15) and κρίνω. The NIV renders both terms as "to judge," making no distinction.

417 Note the previous use of "each one" in 3:5,8,10,13.

418 Thiselton, *First Corinthians*, 342. Cf. Matt 7:1–4; Rom 2:16; 14:13; Col 2:16–19.

419 The emphatic placement of "these things" (ταῦτα) and the use of the vocative, "brothers" (ἀδελφοί), indicates a shift in argument.

now becomes clear in 4:6 that everything Paul has said regarding himself and Apollos has a direct bearing on the Corinthian situation.[420] He wants them to stop exaggerating the importance of human leaders, whether it be Paul, Apollos, or Cephas, or their own local leaders. The intent of the lengthy discourse regarding the cross and human wisdom has been to bring the Corinthians into conformity with what the Scriptures say about human wisdom (1:19,30; 2:9; 3:19–20), to reject all tendencies to become inflated with pride in human leaders, which has led to their rivalries and divisions. The Corinthian problem of arrogance must cease.

In light of their proud stance toward human leaders and their love of human wisdom, Paul offers a stiff rebuke in the form of stinging sarcasm. Apostolic suffering stands in sharp relief to the Corinthians' pride. There are things that they need to learn from Paul and other apostles. Since genuine apostleship is measured according to the standard of the cross, Paul compares the present realities of apostolic service over against the present state of affairs in Corinth and by doing so shows just how far they have missed the mark. From their own point of view, they are full, rich, and reigning (4:8)! But to this frame of mind Paul sarcastically retorts, "How I wish that you really had become kings so that we might be kings with you!" The apostolic perspective is radically different. A life measured by the cross holds to a profoundly different standard. God has put the apostles on display as men condemned to die. In a series of emphatic contrasts Paul sizes up the Corinthians to see how they measure up to the cruciform way of life (4:10). Apostolic life is far from the ease and comfort coveted by the world; presently the apostles "have become the scum of the earth, the refuse of the world" (cf. 2 Cor 11:16–30).[421]

**4:6** In 4:6 Paul explains why he has used himself and Apollos as examples. This verse is riddled with a number of difficult interpretive issues. The use of the term "brothers" marks a new unit of thought, but the antecedent to "these things" is uncertain. Does "these things" refer to the immediately preceding paragraph (4:1–5), or does it reach back to 3:5 where Paul and Apollos are paired together?[422] Or is the reference even broader in scope, taking in the whole argument from 1:10–4:5?[423] Further uncertainty surrounds Paul's use

[420] Of this section Fee (*First Corinthians*, 166) notes, "Paul here is applying the theology of the cross, set forth in 1:18–2:16, to the Christian life."

[421] Note especially the terms "foolish" and "weak" in 4:10, which hark back to the description of those belonging to the crucified one in 1 Cor 1. Note also the parallels between 4:12 and Jesus' teaching in the Sermon on the Mount in Matt 5:1–11.

[422] So Robertson and Plummer, *First Corinthians*, 80; Fee, *First Corinthians*, 165–66.

[423] So Fitzmyer, *First Corinthians*, 214; B. Fiore, "'Covert Allusion' in 1 Corinthians 1–4," *CBQ* 47 (1985): 94. Garland (*1 Corinthians,* 131) notes, "If this verse applies to his argument in 1:10–4:5, then unpacking its meaning is critical for understanding what Paul is doing in the opening section of the letter." By this Garland has in mind whether or not their were actual parties within the church with loyalties to Paul, Apollos, and Peter, or if, in fact, the divisions in Corinth centered on local leaders in Corinth who go unnamed.

of the term translated "I have applied"[424] and the phrase "Do not go beyond what is written."[425]

The word translated "I have applied" is used only by Paul in the New Testament. The verb appears three times in 2 Cor 11:13–15 to describe those who disguise themselves, whether false apostles masquerading as Christ's apostles or Satan appearing as an angel of light. In Phil 3:21, Paul uses the term to describe the future transformation of our human bodies. Thus, in these occurrences the word means to change the form of something into something else. However, in 1 Cor 4:6, modern translations render the term differently, as "applied" (NIV, NRSV, HCSB, ESV) or "figuratively applied" (NASB), inferring that Paul has in mind the servant and steward imagery related to planting, building, and judgment in 3:5–4:5.

There is a long tradition, however, extending back to the church fathers, that understands the Greek term to have essentially the same meaning in 1 Cor 4:6 as in other New Testament occurrences, and several scholars of the modern era follow this understanding. Robertson and Plummer, for example, argue that in 4:6 Paul indicates a "veiled allusion," with the meaning "I have transferred these warnings to myself and Apollos for the purpose of a covert allusion, and that for your sakes, that in our persons you may get instruction."[426] This view has found further support among more recent scholars.[427] In this view, the source of division in Corinth was "an overzealous allegiance to local leaders, who go unnamed."[428] As Hall puts it, "When Paul describes the relationship between himself and Apollos, what he is really concerned about is certain unnamed teachers who were at work in the church at Corinth, and competing for allegiance of church members."[429] In other words, the cause of division was not centered around Paul, Apollos, and Cephas. The Paul, Apollos, and Cephas parties did not exist. Instead, Paul replaced the names of the local leaders with his own and Apollos in order to avoid direct and personal rebuke. Fee does not think this view is correct and argues that it is the figures that have changed form, not the persons. He attributes this to context and the emphatic position of "these things." According to Fee's interpretation Paul "has gone from metaphor to metaphor, changing images as he went along, but always intending them (at least most of them), as he now says, to apply 'to myself

---

[424] Gk. μετασχηματίζω.

[425] Put in quotation marks by the NIV. In Greek, a cryptic phrase, τὸ μὴ ὑπὲρ ἃ γέγραπται.

[426] Robertson and Plummer, *First Corinthians*, 81.

[427] See Fiore, "Covert Allusion"; D. R. Hall, "A Disguise for the Wise: ΜΕΤΑΣΧΗΕΜΑΤΙΣΜΟΣ in 1 Corinthians 4:6," *NTS* 40 (1994): 143–49; Winter, *Philo and Paul*, 196–202; Garland, *1 Corinthians*, 131–33; Collins, *First Corinthians*, 176, 179. Hall puts forth impressive linguistic evidence for maintaining a consistent meaning for μετασχηματίζω, "to change the form of."

[428] Garland, *1 Corinthians*, 132.

[429] Hall, "A Disguise for the Wise," 144.

and Apollos.'"[430] The different views have important implications for the historical reconstruction of the actual situation in Corinth, whether the cause of divisions centered around Paul, Apollos, and Peter or mainly around other unnamed local leaders.[431] There are good arguments on both sides. In the end, however, the main point of Paul's argument regarding the Corinthian's pride and the corrections that need to occur remains the same as seen in the two purpose clauses of 4:6.

Paul amplifies the basic premise in 4:6a with a prepositional phrase and two purpose clauses.[432] The lessons that Paul laid out for them, either using himself and Apollos as a covert allusion in place of the local leaders or simply as illustrations using various metaphors has been "for your benefit" and with the express purpose, "that you may learn from us the meaning of the saying, 'Do not go beyond what is written.'" This statement is then followed by a second purpose/result clause, "Then you will not take pride in one man over against another."

The first purpose clause is obscure in Greek, which reads literally, "in order than you may learn in us the 'not beyond what has been written',"[433] and has been the subject of a variety of interpretations. The most widely held view and the one that is most probable is that the phrase, "It is written," refers back to the previous occurrences of the same phrase in chaps. 1–3, that is, the Scriptures. In other words, the Corinthians should learn in the example of Paul and Apollos to live within the boundaries prescribed by Scripture, to live in a way consistent with what the Scripture has to say about human wisdom.[434] The second

[430] Fee, *First Corinthians*, 167, 55n37. Thiselton (*First Corinthians*, 351) translates, "I have allusively applied all this to myself and to Apollos." He explains, "Clearly the examples are *allusive* to those whom Paul does not mention by name; but it goes beyond the evidence to claim that Paul and Apollos themselves are necessarily only *ciphers of rhetorical fiction* whom Paul himself exempts from his own warnings. Indeed, his reference to his own self-knowledge or conscience (4:4) suggests the opposite. Mere *example* undertranslates; *covert* rhetoric *overtranslates*; **allusive application** identifies the issue."

[431] Do we, for example, understand 4:6b, "Then you will not take pride in one man over against another," as referring specifically to Paul and Apollos or to local leaders in Corinth?

[432] The prepositional phrase is δι' ὑμᾶς (because of you, NIV, "for your benefit"). Both purpose clauses are introduced by the Greek conjunction ἵνα. The two clauses could be parallel, or the second could be subordinate to the first (so the NIV translation; so also Barrett, *First Corinthians*, 107; Kuck, *Judgment and Community Conflict*, 212; Garland, *1 Corinthians*, 136; Fee, *First Corinthians*, 166n6). Garland notes Paul's use of the double ἵνα clause in Rom 7:13; Gal 3:14; 4:5; Eph 5:26–27.

[433] Gk. ἵνα ἐν ἡμῖν μάθητε τὸ μὴ ὑπὲρ ἃ γέγραπται.

[434] So M. Hooker, "'Beyond the Things Which are Written': An Examination of 1 Cor. iv.6," *NTS* 10 (1963); Fee, *First Corinthians*, 168–69; Hays, *First Corinthians*, 68–69; Garland, *1 Corinthians*, 135–36; Ciampa and Rosner, *First Corinthians*, 176. Garland (*1 Corinthians*, 133–36) lists four other interpretations of the phrase: (1) It is completely unintelligible, which might indicate that it is a marginal gloss and not original to the text (so Conzelmann, *1 Corinthians*, 86). (2) The definite article signals a quotation of a proverbial idiom, which is reflected in the NIV translation. A variant of this view is that Paul refers to a well-known maxim, a recognized principle. See L. L. Welborn, *Politics and Rhetoric in the Corinthian Epistles* (Macon, GA: Mercer University

purpose clause follows from the first and expresses Paul's main concern: "He wants to promote concord and harmony and dissuade individual Corinthian Christians from their arrogance in forming rivalries to one or another preacher . . . The general meaning of the verse is clear, even if its formulation is complicated."[435] If the Corinthians would live within the boundaries of Scripture, then they would not boast in men, the specific point made by Paul in 3:21 following the use of Scripture in 3:19–20. This is the first occurrence of the term "puffed up,"[436] which sustains an important use throughout the letter (see 4:18; 5:2; 8:1; 13:4). The root cause of most, if not all, of their problems was pride.

**4:7** With three questions (Who? What? and Why?) Paul launches a stern, ironic rebuke.[437] The switch to the singular "you" is unexpected and may be a rhetorical device, a dialogue with a typical "puffed up" Corinthian as a means for Paul to give the proper perspective on the matter.[438] The NIV translates the first question, "For who makes you different from anyone else?" The NASB renders, "Who regards you as superior?" and the HCSB, "For who makes you so superior?" BDAG defines the Greek verb in the sentence "to differentiate, to make a distinction, to evaluate or to judge, even to dispute with someone" and suggests for 4:7 the translation "Who concedes you any superiority?"[439] Thiselton translates as "Who defines you?"[440] The sense of the phrase, in context, seems to be "Who elevates you to a place of rightful boasting? Who has given you the right to assume a position of such arrogance? Who makes these determinations about your exalted status?" The previous section (4:1–5) spelled out how humans are incapable of distinguishing or differentiating one's

Press, 1997), 56; Fitzmyer, *First Corinthians*, 215. (3) The phrase refers to some foundational document of the community that spelled out the rules by which the community could prosper, meaning something like, "Don't go beyond the rules." (4) The phrase is a general warning against extravagant behavior due to arrogance. See Marshall, *Enmity in Corinth*, 190–95; R. Pickett, *The Cross in Corinth: The Social Significance of the Death of Jesus*, JSNTSup 143 (Sheffield: Sheffield Academic Press, 1997), 57–58.

[435] Fitzmyer, *First Corinthians*, 216.

[436] Gk. φυσιόω.

[437] 4:7 begins with an explanatory γάρ.

[438] Fee (*First Corinthians*, 170n27) suggests that the singular may pick up on the "each one" of 4:6 and at the same time reflect Paul's semitic background in which the OT legal materials given to Israel appeared in the singular. This same kind of movement, from second singular to second plural, occurs again in 7:27–28; 8:9–10; 14:16–17; and 15:36.

[439] The verb is διακρίνω, its first appearance in the letter (see also 6:5; 11:29,31; 14:29). It is another term consonant with "judgment" language (cf. previous uses of ἀνακρίνω in 2:14–15; 4:1–5 and κρίνω in 4:5). Louw-Nida (30.99) translate the phrase, "Who judges you to be superior?" They comment further, "Superiority is often expressed in terms of 'being better,' but in some languages it is designated by means of a phrase meaning 'to surpass,' so that the question in 1 Cor 4:7 may be rendered as 'who judges that you surpass others?'" Kuck (*Apocalyptic Judgment Language*, 215) suggests the translation, "Who made you so special?"

[440] Thiselton, *First Corinthians*, 356. In this reading the first two questions are virtually identical; question 2 would drive home the point of question 1.

true status before God. Fee understands the question as directly related to 4:6 and their pride vis-a-vis Paul. The question would mean, "Who distinguishes *you*?" "On what possible grounds do you boast in this manner?" Fee suggests that the English equivalent would be, "Who in the world do you think you are, anyway? What kind of self-delusion is it that allows you to put yourself in a position to judge another person's servant?"[441]

The second and third questions go together. Paul reminds them that there is absolutely nothing that they presently have that they did not receive. The question emphasizes the undeserved grace of God, which is the very ground of their existence in the first place.[442] Everything they possess came from God (cf. 1:5; 3:10), which rules out all boasting.[443] All that they have comes by virtue of their relationship to Christ (3:23). Paul has transformed the slogan "I belong to Paul" (1:12) to "Paul and others belong to you" (3:22) to "You belong to Christ" (3:23) to "You don't have anything that you did not receive!" (4:7). The third question, "If you received it, then why are you boasting as though not receiving?" goes back to the heart of the issue of human wisdom and the theme of boasting (1:29–31; 3:21). To boast implies human achievement and fails to recognize the free grace of God.

**4:8–9** In 4:8 Paul switches back to the second person plural and with scathing irony contrasts the present suffering of the apostles with the Corinthians' own perceptions of their supposed exalted status. Garland comments, "The apostles live according to the wisdom of the cross; the Corinthians imbibe the wisdom of this age and pass themselves off as kings."[444] The perfect participle describes their satiated attitude.[445] BDAG renders, "You think you already have all the spiritual food you need." The notion is that of self-assurance, a sense that one needs nothing. In other words, Paul presents them as those who think they have arrived! Already they have become rich.[446] Fitzmyer com-

---

[441] Fee, *First Corinthians*, 171.

[442] Cf. Rom 12:3, "For by the grace given me I say to every one of you: Do not think of yourself more highly than you ought, but rather think of yourself with sober judgment, in accordance with the measure of faith God has given you."

[443] Fee (*First Corinthians*, 171) comments, "This is an invitation to experience one of those rare moments of total honesty, where in the presence of the eternal God one recognizes that everything—absolutely everything—that one 'has' is a gift. All is of grace; nothing is deserved, nothing earned."

[444] Garland, *1 Corinthians*, 137.

[445] Gk. κεκορεσμένοι. Collins (*First Corinthians*, 186) notes connections of satiation with licentiousness. For traditional associations of satiation with arrogance, see Marshall, *Enmity in Corinth*, 208.

[446] The NIV translates as an ingressive aorist. Note Paul's stark contrast to a realized eschatology in the sense of having already arrived in Phil 3:12–14, " Not that I have already obtained all this, or have already been made perfect, but I press on to take hold of that for which Christ Jesus took hold of me. Brothers, I do not consider myself yet to have taken hold of it. But one thing I do: Forgetting what is behind and straining toward what is ahead, I press on toward the goal to win the prize for which God has called me heavenward in Christ Jesus."

ments, "The Corinthian Christians in their wisdom may be persuaded that they have already a prominent part in God's kingdom, because they have been richly evangelized by noted preachers."[447] Maybe so, but Paul claims that they have become kings "without us!" Does this mean "without our aid"[448] or "without our company"?[449] The latter would have the notion of deliberately turning away from the preachers.

To the three statements of 4:8a Paul adds an unattainable wish: "How I wish that you really had become kings so that we might be kings with you!"[450] But, in fact, this is not the case, so in stark contrast to the Corinthians' attitude regarding their own status, Paul unfolds the actual plight of the apostles (4:9). The list of apostolic hardships is an ironic critique of the Corinthians' present attitudes and a paradigm for their own Christian calling.[451] That Paul follows this section with the exhortation to "become imitators of me" indicates that apostolic suffering is not the lot of a select few but also the lot of all believers (cf. Phil 1:29–30).

The Greek of 4:9a is more compact than the NIV translation.[452] The Greek reads, "God appointed us, the apostles, last, as men given over to death." The NIV interprets, "God has put us apostles on display at the end of the procession, like men condemned to die in the arena." This conveys the sense that "Paul sees himself as someone engaged by God in the service of Christ-crucified and cast in a situation analogous to that of the crucified Christ, perhaps like a

---

[447] Fitzmyer, *First Corinthians*, 218.

[448] So Barrett, *First Corinthians*, 108.

[449] So Robertson and Plummer, *First Corinthians*, 84; Garland, *1 Corinthians*, 138; Fitzmyer, *First Corinthians*, 218. Fee (*First Corinthians*, 173) suggests the meaning, "They reign without the apostles having a share in it."

[450] In Greek the construction is καὶ ὄφελόν γε. BDAG translates, "Indeed, I wish you had become kings." This verse has been key for the view that the Corinthians held an aberrant view of "realized eschatology." However, Garland (*1 Corinthians*, 138–39) argues against the notion that the Corinthians were living as if the eschatological age has already consummated. Paul draws a contrast between the abased apostles and the Corinthian boasters. He corrects their worldly arrogance, not their mistaken eschatological outlook. The notions of being filled, rich and reigning were widespread in the ancient world, ideas common in wisdom literature without any eschatological overtones (Wis 6:20; 7:8; 8:14,18). See also Kuck, *Judgment and Community Conflict*, 216–18. Thiselton (*First Corinthians*, 357–59), on the other hand, still maintains that an overrealized eschatology lies behind this verse. See also the discussion in Barrett, *First Corinthians*, 109; Fee, *First Corinthians*, 172.

[451] Cf. other hardship lists in Paul (2 Cor 4:7–12; 6:4–10; 11:23–29). Garland (*1 Corinthians*, 139n18) comments that the hardship lists become increasingly specific and are not a rhetorical convention. See also J. T. Fitzgerald, *Cracks in an Earthen Vessel: An Examination of the Catalogues of Hardships in the Corinthian Correspondence*, vol. 99, SBLDS (Atlanta: Scholar's Press, 1988), 148.

[452] The verse begins with the explanatory conjunction γάρ followed by the verb δοκέω, "I think." The same verb appeared in 3:18, "If any of you thinks he is wise." The contrast may be intentional as Paul sets forth in 4:9 the way to "think" in line with God's wisdom rather than the wisdom of the world. For the construction "if anyone thinks" (εἴ τις δοκεῖ) see also 8:2; 11:16 and 14:37.

gladiator."[453] The term "last" in context could refer to social status.[454] While the Corinthians craved social standing, the apostles were at the end of the line, the only possible place for those who represent a crucified Messiah. Like their Lord, the apostles are "men condemned to die,"[455] objects of derision. Just as God put his Son on public display in the crucifixion, so also the apostles have become "a spectacle[456] to the whole universe, to angels as well as to men." A servant is not greater than his Lord (cf. Luke 20:26–27).

**4:10** Paul's irony continues with an emphatic use of the first person plural pronoun in three antithetical verbless constructions, a contrast between "we" (the apostles) and "you" (the Corinthians).[457] The contrast between the apostles and the Corinthians echoes previous themes in 1:18–2:5 and 3:18–19.[458] The NIV reads, "We are fools for Christ, but you are so wise in Christ! We are weak, but you are strong! You are honored, we are dishonored!" The word translated "wise" is not the same as previous uses of "wise" in the wisdom/ folly contrast.[459] Paul definitely is not passing out compliments. He is bringing to their attention with the strongest possible language the inappropriateness of their boasting and arrogance and their misapprehension of what it means to live a cruciform existence.

**4:11–13** The conclusion of Paul's ironic rebuke is framed by an inclusio, "to this very hour" (4:11) and "until the present moment" (4:13).[460] Paul now abandons irony and describes the present reality of the apostolic vocation, detailing his suffering in a "tribulation list."[461] The emphasis on the "present" is parallel to the three "alreadys" of 4:8. "Already" the Corinthians are full, but at the present time the apostles find themselves in a state of hunger and thirst, poor clothing, mistreatment, and homelessness (cf. Heb 11:13–16). Although treated exactly like Jesus, they also respond like Jesus in blessing those who curse, enduring hardship, and answering kindly when slandered (cf.

---

[453] Fitzmyer, *First Corinthians*, 218. See also 2 Cor 2:14.

[454] See Garland, *1 Corinthians*, 140. Also Fitzgerald, *Cracks in an Earthen Vessel*, 136n58.

[455] Gk. ἐπιθανάτιος. A rare term, appearing only here in the New Testament. Paul often employed "death" language in describing his ministry (1 Cor 15:31; 2 Cor 4:10–11; Gal 6:17).

[456] Gk. θέατρον.

[457] Collins (*First Corinthians*, 184) notes an A, B, A' pattern in 4:10–13. A—Three contrasts between Paul and the Corinthians (4:10); B—Six tribulations (4:11–12a); A'—Three contrasting actions (4:12b–13a).

[458] In the contrasts between "fools" and "wise" (prudent), "weak" and "strong," "honored" and "dishonored," Fee (*First Corinthians*, 176) notes the connection to 1:26. Garland (*1 Corinthians*, 140–41) also notes that foolish, weak, and dishonored echoes the Beatitudes. 4:10–13 likely draws on the teaching of Jesus.

[459] Here the word is φρόνιμοι, translated by the NASB as "prudent." Paul uses the term with the reflexive pronoun in Rom 11:25 and 12:16 with the meaning of conceited (wise in yourselves). However, in 1 Cor 10:15, Paul uses the term positively, appealing to their sense of reason.

[460] Gk. ἄχρι τῆς ἄρτι ὥρας (4:11) and ἕως ἄρτι (4:13).

[461] See R. Hodgson, "Paul the Apostle and First Century Tribulation Lists," *Zeitschrift für die Neutestmentlicher Wissenschaft* 74 (1983): 59–80. For similar passages that describe Paul's condition see 2 Cor 4:8–10; 6:4–5,8–10; 11:23–29; 12:10. See also Rom 8:35.

Rom 12:14; 1 Pet 2:23; 3:9,15–16). There is a significant connection between Paul's description of suffering and the teaching of Jesus at this point, which paves the way for the exhortation of imitation in 4:16–17.[462] Paul's catalog of tribulations puts Christian values in stark contrast to worldly values. The world's opinion of the apostles may be summed up in two phrases, translated by the NIV as "scum of the earth" and "refuse of the world,"[463] terms used metaphorically for anything contemptible. Apostles were regarded by the world as the most detestable of all people, but, as such, the apostles incarnated the scandal of the cross.

### 5. Paul's Warning and Appeal as Their Spiritual Father (4:14–21)

**14I am not writing this to shame you, but to warn you, as my dear children. 15Even though you have ten thousand guardians in Christ, you do not have many fathers, for in Christ Jesus I became your father through the gospel. 16Therefore I urge you to imitate me. 17For this reason I am sending to you Timothy, my son whom I love, who is faithful in the Lord. He will remind you of my way of life in Christ Jesus, which agrees with what I teach everywhere in every church.**

**18Some of you have become arrogant, as if I were not coming to you. 19But I will come to you very soon, if the Lord is willing, and then I will find out not only how these arrogant people are talking, but what power they have. 20For the kingdom of God is not a matter of talk but of power. 21What do you prefer? Shall I come to you with a whip, or in love and with a gentle spirit?**

The shift in tone from 4:13 to 4:14 is striking. Paul explains that his profound concern for them is the reason for writing to them so sternly.[464] What he has written has, in a sense, shamed them, thus the clarification "I am not writing this to shame you."[465] This is how they would have taken it. But Paul's purpose is not to demean them but rather to admonish them since he is their spiritual father. The father/child metaphor reminds the Corinthians of Paul's role as the founder of the community and brings a measure of balance to their understanding of Paul's previous use of servant language in 3:5–4:5. The metaphor affirms the familial relationship they enjoy "in Christ" and Paul's responsibility to warn them of spiritual dangers and sets the stage for the key exhortation in 4:16, "I urge you to imitate me." The father image is appropriate

---

[462] So also Fee, *First Corinthians*, 179. Cf. Matt 5:44; Luke 6:28a; Rom 12:17–21. On the sayings of Jesus in 1 Corinthians see F. Neirynck, "The Sayings of Jesus in 1 Corinthians," in *The Corinthian Correspondence*, BETL 75, ed. R. Bieringer (Leuven: University Press, 1996), 141–76.

[463] The two terms, περικάθαρμα and περίψημα may be synonymous terms. Some think that Paul may have intended to evoke pictures of vicarious suffering for others in his choice of the terms, that the apostles' suffering was for the benefit of others (cf. Phil 2:17). For further discussion see Fee, *First Corinthians*, 180; Garland, *1 Corinthians*, 142. Conzelmann (*First Corinthians*, 90) thinks this interpretation is unlikely. The terms are derisive, consonant with the description of the apostles as "men condemned to die" in 4:9.

[464] 4:14–21 opens and closes with the balance of warning motivated by love (4:14,21).

[465] The words "not shaming you" (οὐκ ἐντρέπων ὑμᾶς) are first in the Greek for emphasis.

for what Paul wants to do in this section: admonish, exhort, and, if necessary, discipline (4:18–21).

The focus of 4:14–17, which is closely linked to 4:6–13, is apostolic imitation. To this point in the argument Paul has established that his ministry among them embodied the wisdom of God (2:1–5,13–16; 3:10), that he and other apostles are living examples of Christ crucified (4:9–13). In 4:17 he explains that he sent Timothy for the purpose of reminding them of Paul's manner of life in Christ. Again in 11:1 Paul will exhort the Corinthians to "follow my example, as I follow the example of Christ." The cross is the measure of genuine apostleship, but it is also the standard of all things Christian (4:17). The Corinthians must embrace the wisdom of the cross exemplified by the apostles in order to rid themselves of arrogance that leads to divisions and other vices. In the concluding verses of this section, 4:18–21, Paul admonishes the arrogant yet again and warns that he will come and discover how effective they are for the kingdom of God. But how will he come to them; "with a whip, or in love with a gentle spirit"?

**4:14** The phrase "I am not writing this,"[466] at a bare minimum, refers to the preceding rebuke (4:6–13) but may reach all the way back to 1:10, taking into account all that has been said regarding their factionalism as a result of their devotion to human wisdom rather than God's wisdom. Fee observes that Paul never refers to his converts as disciples but rather as his children (cf. 2 Cor 6:13; 12:14; Gal 4:19; 1 Thess 2:11).[467] His purpose is to correct their behavior, not put them to shame.[468] There are, of course, occasions when shame is appropriate. In the next chapter Paul boldly confronts scandalous behavior occurring in the community (5:1–13) and specifically indicates his intent to shame in 6:5 and 15:34. Honor (glory) and shame are important motifs in chap. 11.[469] The word translated by NIV as "warn" is rendered "admonish" in other translations (NASB).[470] The cognate noun is used in Eph 6:4 of fathers, who are to instruct their children in the Lord.[471]

**4:15** Paul strengthens the ground of his warning in 4:14 and the forthcoming appeal in 4:16 by contrasting himself with other teachers. The implication of the "child" metaphor in 4:14 is now made more explicit in 4:15. Paul is their

---

[466] Gk. ταῦτα, "These things."

[467] Fee, *First Corinthians*, 184.

[468] Gk. ἐντρέπω. In certain contexts, the term means "respect," in the sense of turning toward something, giving deference to someone (see Mark 12:6; Luke 18:2,4; 20:13). But here the meaning is to cause embarrassment. Outside of 1 Corinthians Paul uses the term in 2 Thess 3:14 and Titus 2:8.

[469] 11:2–16,22–27. Note especially the question of 11:22, "Or do you despise the church of God and humiliate those who have nothing?"

[470] Gk. νουθετέω. Louw-Nida (33.231, 33.418, 3.424) note that the meaning of the word ranges from providing instruction in order to correct behavior and belief to admonishing someone for wrongdoing to warning of dangerous consequences for some course of action. For occurrences of the term in the New Testament, see Acts 20:31; Rom 15:4; Col 1:28; 3:16; 1 Thess 5:12,14; 2 Thess 3:15.

[471] Gk. νουθεσία. See also 1 Cor 10:11; Titus 3:10.

spiritual father, whereas other local leaders are only "guardians."[472] The term is difficult to render precisely into English since it is set in a certain cultural context. The NASB renders as "tutors." The guardian was a trustworthy slave of the upper class charged with the responsibility of the supervision of the children. They served an important role, supervising the education, life, and morals of the child. Garland suggests that Paul's use of the term implies that the local leaders of the competitive factions and the Corinthians are still in a childish state.[473] The guardians were important, but they were replaceable. There was no comparison between the guardian and the father.[474] The use of the number "ten thousand" is hyperbole. The number was regularly used in Greek for the highest number imaginable.[475] The mention of their birth through the "gospel" recalls yet again Paul's apostolic call (1:17) and his role in the founding of the church (2:1–5; 3:10) and thus his unique relationship to the Corinthian Christians.[476]

**4:16–17** In light of all that Paul has argued to this point in the letter and in light of his role as the founder of the church in Corinth, their father in the gospel, he has established his right to say (lit.), "Become imitators of me."[477] He has not written to shame but to admonish. But how are they to imitate Paul? Verse 17 explains that it has to do with his way of life in Christ. The most immediate example is 4:9–13, which includes not only the reality of suffering for the gospel but also the proper response to those who inflict it (4:12–13). To imitate Paul would be to walk in the way of humility and suffering and godliness for the cause of Christ. Imitation is not the same as saying, "I belong to Paul!" Rather, Paul wants them to incarnate the cross, to live out their Christian identity in a real and meaningful way, to become true disciples of Christ. This teaching, Paul claims, is universal to all the churches and not specific only to the church at Corinth (see also 7:17; 11:16; 14:33–36). There was a consistency of apostolic teaching and expectation of imitation in all the churches. Paul's sending Timothy was not a special case in the sense that unusual demands would be made of the Corinthians. The Corinthians are part of a greater whole (cf. 1 Cor 1:1–2).

---

[472] Gk. παιδαγωγός.

[473] Garland, *1 Corinthians*, 146.

[474] Along these lines Thiselton (*First Corinthians*, 370) notes, "The main function was a guardian, teacher, and corrector, but the motivation of the παιδαγωγός would be either one of paid duty or one of obedience to the instructions of the master, not the love for the child." Thiselton also notes a similar contrast in John 10:11–14, between the "good shepherd" and the "hired help."

[475] The NASB renders, "countless." See also the use of this hyperbole with reference to speaking in tongues in the church (14:19).

[476] Paul uses the same imagery in Phlm 10, "I appeal to you for my son Onesimus, who became my son while I was in chains."

[477] For the notion of "imitation" see also 11:2; Gal 4:12; Phil 3:17; 2 Thess 3:7–9. Fee (*First Corinthians*, 186n24) notes that "imitation" means more than to "mimic," or even to follow someone as a disciple. What Paul has in mind is one who internalizes and lives out the model set before him/her. Phil 3:17 uses the term συμμιμητής, one who joins others in imitating.

The NIV translates the aorist tense verb in 4:17 as a present, "I am sending," whereas other translations render as a past tense, either "I have sent" (so NASB, HCSB) or simply "I sent" (so ESV). The NIV interprets the tense as an epistolary aorist with the apparent meaning that Paul plans to send Timothy but he writes from the viewpoint of the recipients, that is, Timothy will have already left Ephesus by the time the Corinthians receive the letter (but cf. NIV2011). In light of 16:10, which expresses some uncertainty about Timothy's arrival ("If Timothy comes"),[478] and since Timothy is not mentioned as the co-sender of the letter (cf. 2 Cor 1:1; 1 Thess 1:1; Phil 1:1; Phlm 1:1), Paul probably had already sent Timothy from Ephesus for further missionary work with plans to visit Corinth.[479] Paul himself plans to visit Corinth in person (4:18–21), but until he comes he wants Timothy's actual presence in Corinth to remind them of his pattern of life in Christ.[480] The implication that "presence" is a necessary component of "imitation" is hard to miss. Timothy, like the Corinthians, is also Paul's "beloved child" (NASB), but to this descriptor Paul adds "and faithful in the Lord."[481] Timothy is a trustworthy child. Paul desires the same in his children in Corinth.[482]

**4:18–21** Paul's sternness returns in 4:18–21, a transitional section that leads into the bold confrontation of 5:1–13. Paul's words are aimed directly at the lofty speakers, the trouble-makers in the community, who possibly had become arrogant[483] *because* of Paul's prolonged absence. There is some uncertainty in the phrase "as if I were not coming." Had Paul indicated that he would come, yet he did not fulfill the expectation?[484] The mention of their arrogance anticipates the confrontation of 5:1–13 regarding the arrogance of some regarding blatant sexual sin in the community. The use of the same verb in 4:6 may indicate that the arrogance existed primarily among the church leaders.[485]

If the Lord wills, Paul will certainly come to them,[486] and upon his arrival he warns that he will discover how much power (effectiveness) the arrogant actually possess.[487] Their rhetorical skills are completely irrelevant for the

---

[478] Cf. ESV, "When Timothy comes . . ."

[479] See Robertson and Plummer, *First Corinthians*, 90; Barrett, *First Corinthians*, 116; Fee, *First Corinthians*, 188; Thiselton, *First Corinthians*, 375; Garland, *1 Corinthians*, 147.

[480] Thiselton, *First Corinthians*, 374.

[481] Recall 4:2, "Now it is required that those who have been given a trust must prove faithful."

[482] Robertson and Plummer (*First Corinthians*, 90) comment that Timothy was sent "to remind children who were equally beloved, but not equally faithful, of their duties towards the Apostle who was the parent of both."

[483] An ingressive aorist. This is the second use of the verb "to be arrogant" (φυσιόω).

[484] See 2 Cor 1:15–17.

[485] Gk. φυσιόω (4:6,18; 5:2)

[486] Cf. 1 Cor 16:5–9 for the details of Paul's plans. The Greek phrase "I will come to you soon" probably has in mind certainty rather than a specific time frame (so Fee, *First Corinthians*, 191).

[487] Paul uses the perfect tense of the verb to describe the arrogant; they are in a state of arrogance (contrast the aorist in 4:18, "Some have become arrogant").

kingdom of God. Paul is not impressed with words but rather with deeds. Are they effective for the kingdom of God? Arrogance and power (or lack of it) are linked again in 5:1–4. Paul's reference to power recalls the previous uses of the term in his description of the gospel (1:18,24) and of his ministry of power through the Spirit (2:4). Perhaps Paul intends to link his challenge to their power in 4:19 with the exhortation to "imitate me" in 4:16–17. Paul came to them, not in excellence of word, but in demonstration of the Spirit and of power. So now he wants to know, "You have lofty words, but do you have the power of the Spirit of God?"[488] This is one of the few places that Paul uses the phrase "kingdom of God" in his letters.[489] In sum, the question is not will Paul come, but how he will come to them. Paul threatens the possibility of discipline by the "whip" (NIV), which depicts reproof and correction. Will Paul have to come as a disciplining father, or can he come as he prefers, in a spirit of love and humility?

[488] As Fee (*First Corinthians*, 191) puts it, "Will they evidence what for Paul is the crucial matter, namely the powerful, dynamic presence of the Spirit among them to save and to sanctify (cf. 5:1–5)?" So also Thiselton (*First Corinthians*, 376–77), "When he comes to Corinth, he will discover whether those concerned are mere windbags who merely talk or whether there are *solid effects* that indicate what they can do." Cf. also 1 Thess 1:5 for the "word/power" combination. The gospel came to them not in word only but also in power. In context, "word" refers to boastful rhetoric (see on 1:17–18).

[489] In 1 Corinthians see 6:9–10 and 15:24,50. Hays (*First Corinthians*, 75) notes, "His use of terminology in 1 Cor 4:20 may be dictated in part by his desire to present a polemical rejoinder to the Corinthians' talk about already reigning as kings (4:8). If so, the force of verse 20 would be to reassert that God alone is king, and that God's kingdom operates in a way very different from what the Corinthian boasters imagine."

## *SECTION OUTLINE*

III. Sexual Immorality, the Civil Courts, and Issues of Marriage and Singleness (5:1–7:40)
   1. Directives to the Church Regarding an Incestuous Man (5:1–13)
   2. The Shame of the Righteous Taking Disputes Before the Unrighteous (6:1–11)
   3. The Sanctity of the Body (6:12–20)
   4. Issues of Marriage and Singleness (7:1–40)
      (1) General Principles Concerning Marriage (7:1–7)
      (2) Principles for Diverse Situations, Both Unmarried and Married (7:8–16)
      (3) The Guiding Principle for Decision-Making: "Remain as You Are" (7:17–24)
      (4) Concerning the Virgins (7:25–40)

## III. SEXUAL IMMORALITY, THE CIVIL COURTS, AND ISSUES OF MARRIAGE AND SINGLENESS (5:1–7:40)

Having addressed reports of factionalism in 1:10–4:21 Paul moves on to reports of immorality and litigation (5:1–6:20) before addressing other topics, including questions raised by the Corinthians in a letter to Paul (7:1–16:4). As noted in the introduction (see The Occasion of the Letter, Structure, and Main Themes), since everything following 7:1 does not pertain to a question raised by the Corinthians, the evidence suggests that Paul arranged the letter thematically. It seems best, therefore, to include 7:1–40 with 5:1–6:20 and recognize 5:1–7:40 as the next major section of the letter. Each unit within this section addresses a different topic. Garland observes how 5:1–6:20 is bound together by an eschatological focus (5:5; 6:2,14), a concern for how ethical lapses impact those outside the church (5:1; 6:6,18–20), sharp commands to desist and flee from sin (5:13; 6:4,18), and instruction anchored in the Deuteronomic code. Furthermore, two similar vice lists appear in 5:9–11 and 6:9–10.[1] Paul's concern regarding immorality and the eschatological focus carries forward in 7:1–40 (see 7:2,29–31).

[1] D. E. Garland, *1 Corinthians*, BECNT (Grand Rapids: Eerdmans, 2003), 150–51. On the underlying Deuteronomic code Garland comments, "Incest is specifically condemned in Deut. 22:30; 27:20. The command to purge any evil from the midst of God's people is found in Deut. 13:5 [6]; 17:7; 19:19–20a; 21:21; 24:7. Appointing judges to render just decisions when disputes arise among the people is found in Deut. 16:18–20. A connection to prostitution is declared to be abhorrent to God in Deut. 23:17–18." Garland thinks that the three units (5:1–13; 6:1–11; 6:12–20) are independent and that those who detect an A B A' chiastic arrangement are mistaken (so R. F. Collins, *First Corinthians*, SP [Collegeville, MN: Liturgical Press, 1999], 225).

In 5:1, Paul clearly transitions to a new topic,[2] yet there is a close relationship between 5:1–13 and the preceding material.[3] First, the term "puffed up,"[4] which occurs in 5:2, recalls the prior uses in 4:6 and 4:18–19. As in 4:19, the perfect participle is used in 5:2, reflecting a settled state of arrogance. Similarly, the noun "boasting"[5] in 5:6 recalls uses of the cognate verb form in 1:29,31; 3:21; and 4:7.[6] So, even though there is a shift of topic, Paul continues to address the core problem of pride. Second, judgment language, which occurs at numerous junctures in chaps. 1–4,[7] continues in 5:3 and 5:12–13.[8] In their examination of others, including Paul, they have failed to render proper judgments within their own community. Third, Paul appeals to the authority of the name of the Lord Jesus Christ in 5:4 as he did in the opening exhortation in 1:17. Furthermore, in the same verse, Paul refers to the "power" of the Lord Jesus in delivering the offender to Satan, which ties directly to Paul's statement of the lack of "power" among the arrogant in 4:19 and the previous descriptions of the gospel in terms of power (1:18,24; 2:4–5). They had not demonstrated the power of the Lord Jesus in dealing with the immoral man. Fourth, the eschatological focus of 5:5 with reference to the Day of the Lord recalls other references to the "Day" in 3:13 and 4:3. Fifth, Paul continues his interaction with the Old Testament Scriptures as he did in chaps. 1–3.[9]

## 1. Directives to the Church Regarding an Incestuous Man (5:1–13)

**[1]It is actually reported that there is sexual immorality among you, and of a kind that does not occur even among pagans: A man has his father's wife. [2]And you are proud! Shouldn't you rather have been filled with grief and have put out of your**

[2] A. Robertson and A. Plummer comment that the indictment of 5:1 following on 4:20 with no connecting particle "bursts upon the reader like a thunder clap" (*A Critical and Exegetical Commentary on the First Epistle of St. Paul to the Corinthians*, ICC, 2nd ed. [Edinburgh: T&T Clark], 95).

[3] M. M. Mitchell suggests that the man who committed the act of sexual immorality as described in 5:1–13 contributed to the community's divisiveness. In this view, unity remains an overarching concern throughout the letter (*Paul and the Rhetoric of Reconciliation: An Exegetical Investigation of the Language and Composition of 1 Corinthians* [Louisville: WJK, 1991], 112).

[4] Gk. φυσιόω.

[5] Gk. καύχημα.

[6] Gk. καυχάομαι.

[7] The Gk. terms include κρίνω (2:2; 4:5), ἀνακρίνω (2:14–15; 4:3–5), and διακρίνω (4:7).

[8] In every instance in chap. 5 the word is κρίνω, providing clear evidence that "to judge nothing before the time" (4:5) does not exclude rendering judgments against ethical violations within the community. Paul declares in 5:3, "I have already passed judgment on the one who did this." And he asks in 5:12, "What business is it of mine to judge those outside the church? Are you not to judge those inside?"

[9] Paul does not employ the formula "It is written" in 5:1–13, but the interaction with the Old Testament is significant. On the Old Testament underpinnings of Paul's ethics in chaps. 5–7, see especially B. S. Rosner, *Paul, Scripture and Ethics: a Study of 1 Corinthians 5–7*, vol. 22, AGJU (Leiden: Brill, 1994).

**fellowship the man who did this? [3]Even though I am not physically present, I am with you in spirit. And I have already passed judgment on the one who did this, just as if I were present. [4]When you are assembled in the name of our Lord Jesus and I am with you in spirit, and the power of our Lord Jesus is present, [5]hand this man over to Satan, so that the sinful nature may be destroyed and his spirit saved on the day of the Lord.**

**[6]Your boasting is not good. Don't you know that a little yeast works through the whole batch of dough? [7]Get rid of the old yeast that you may be a new batch without yeast—as you really are. For Christ, our Passover lamb, has been sacrificed. [8]Therefore let us keep the Festival, not with the old yeast, the yeast of malice and wickedness, but with bread without yeast, the bread of sincerity and truth.**

**[9]I have written you in my letter not to associate with sexually immoral people— [10]not at all meaning the people of this world who are immoral, or the greedy and swindlers, or idolaters. In that case you would have to leave this world. [11]But now I am writing you that you must not associate with anyone who calls himself a brother but is sexually immoral or greedy, an idolater or a slanderer, a drunkard or a swindler. With such a man do not even eat.**

**[12]What business is it of mine to judge those outside the church? Are you not to judge those inside? [13]God will judge those outside. "Expel the wicked man from among you."**

Chapter 5 divides into two sections. In 5:1–8, Paul acknowledges that immorality is being reported among the Corinthians, confronts their complacent attitude toward the sin, and directs the church to carry out appropriate disciplinary action. In 5:9–13, Paul clarifies a misunderstanding from a previous letter regarding associations with immoral people and concludes with a final injunction to expel the wicked man from the community. There are four directives to take decisive action regarding outrageous sin in their midst (5:2,5,7,13). There are three issues at hand: (1) the sin of the offender, (2) the corporate responsibility of the church toward the sinner, and (3) their present arrogance. Ultimately Paul's concern is for the purity of the church, which is God's sacred temple inhabited by the Holy Spirit (3:16–17).

**5:1** The precise contextual meaning of the Greek adverb that begins this section is not entirely clear.[10] The word can mean "completely," or "wholly," indicating that the case of incest was widely known, a matter of general knowledge.[11] The NIV translates "actually," which has the sense of pertaining to reality.[12] Translated this way, the word might indicate a sense of shock and outrage. The report, as appalling as it is, is in fact true.[13] Garland adopts a neglected sense of the adverb, "in short," as a possible meaning in this context,

[10] Gk. ὅλως (cf. 6:7; 15:29). Fee thinks the meaning is closer to "altogether" or "actually" (*The First Epistle to the Corinthians*, NICNT [Grand Rapids: Eerdmans, 1987], 199).

[11] So the HCSB, "It is widely reported."

[12] So most modern English translations (NASB, ESV, NET, NRSV).

[13] Louw-Nida (70.1) take "actually" and "widely" as rather close in meaning: "pertaining to reality, with the implication of being generally known." BDAG places 1 Cor 5:1 under both definitions as possible meanings.

making the transition from chap. 4 to 5 less abrupt and linking this section more directly to the previous chapter. "The report of incest, 'in short,' knocks the props out from under their grandiosity (4:18). It betrays that they are not wise, that they should not be held in honor (4:10), and that he needs to come to them like an irate *paidagōgos*, rod in hand, to punish them (4:21)."[14]

It is possible that the news of immorality among the Corinthians,[15] like the report of divisions, came also from those of Chloe's household (cf. 1:11). It is just as likely that Paul received the information from Stephanas, Fortunatus, and Achaicus, who are mentioned in 16:17. Since Paul does not indicate the source, we cannot know for sure. The term translated by the NIV as "sexual immorality" is broad in meaning, referring to any unlawful sexual intercourse.[16] Here Paul applies the term more specifically to incest,[17] an immoral act of such character that even the pagans are appalled![18] It is a particularly severe case of immorality. But what is even more egregious in Paul's mind is the church's tolerance of blatant sin. Paul does not confront the individual directly but rather directs the church to take immediate action. The Old Testament condemned incest, but so did Roman law.[19] The fact that even pagans disapproved of the sin allowed Paul to appeal to a universal norm of decency and added all the more to the shame of the Corinthian attitude and lack of disciplinary action.[20]

Paul provides no details other than the bare facts of the case, "A man has his father's wife."[21] "To have" someone, in this context, indicates a sexual union, and commentators concur that the use of the present tense infinitive suggests

---

[14] Garland, *1 Corinthians*, 156. Cf. also *The First Epistle of Paul to the Corinthians*, Cambridge Greek Testament, ed. J. Parry (Cambridge: University Press, 1916), 86.

[15] Paul uses the present passive of ἀκούω (to hear), which in this context means "is being reported." The present tense verb could mean "the report is continually spreading," or it could draw attention to the fact that the immorality is going on presently (So Fee, *First Corinthians*, 199n17). The phrase "among you" (ἐν ὑμῖν) could modify the verb with the meaning "Immorality is being reported among you," or the noun "immorality" (πορνεία), resulting in the translation "Immorality among you is being reported." The latter seems more likely. Paul's concern is the very presence of this sin in the community. So C. K. Barrett, *A Commentary on the First Epistle to the Corinthians*, HNTC (New York: Harper & Row, 1968), 121; Fee, *First Corinthians*, 159.

[16] Gk. πορνεία. BDAG defines as "every kind of unlawful sexual intercourse."

[17] Paul will use the term again in 6:13,18, and 7:2, with other meanings. For other Pauline uses of the term, see 2 Cor 12:21; Gal 5:19; Eph 5:3; Col 3:5; 1 Thess 4:3.

[18] Gk. τοιαύτη πορνεία, "immorality of such kind." This is an especially egregious kind of sexual aberration.

[19] See A. C. Thiselton for the Greco-Roman sources indicating the universal rejection of incest as socially unacceptable (*The First Epistle to the Corinthians: A Commentary on the Greek Text*, NIGTC [Grand Rapids: Eerdmans, 2000], 385).

[20] So Garland, *1 Corinthians*, 157. There is no verb in the clause ἥτις οὐδὲ ἐν τοῖς ἔθνεσιν ("which [is] not among the Gentiles"). South suggests "tolerated" as the supplied verb. J. T. South, "A Critique of the 'Curse/Death' Interpretation of 1 Cor. 5:1–8," *NTS* 39 (1993): 539–61. Followed by Thiselton (*First Corinthians*, 385).

[21] Gk. γυναῖκά τινα τοῦ πατρὸς ἔχειν. Fee (*First Corinthians*, 200) thinks the language "father's wife" is taken directly from the LXX (Lev 18:7–8).

an ongoing, habitual relationship, not a one-time affair. Beyond this statement, however, Paul does not elaborate further on the circumstances or the reasons for the cohabitation. Nothing is said about the father, who is either deceased or divorced from his wife. Paul makes no mention about taking action against the woman, indicating that she is not a believer (5:12). Rather, Paul's primary focus is on the church's attitude and their failure to carry out their corporate responsibility as God's holy people.

Interpreters puzzle over the source of the Corinthians' pride and the reason they allowed such an egregious sin to continue unpunished. Were they arrogant, and did they permit the offender to maintain fellowship because of an aberrant view of a supposed Christian freedom that sanctioned such behavior? Did some hold to a form of exalted spirituality or a view of human bodily existence that regarded all bodily actions as of no ultimate consequence? In other words, was their lack of discipline theologically motivated?[22] Or was the problem primarily social in nature? Was the perpetrator of high social standing, perhaps a rich patron or benefactor, and the church feared action due to the person's status?[23] Either way, Paul's mandate to the church is crystal clear. Since he does not dwell on the particulars, we have to concede that all historical reconstructions remain speculative as to what led to this disastrous situation. The circumstances that allowed the sin would have been of concern, but Paul focuses on the present reality and the necessity of confrontation. Nothing less than the sanctity of God's temple is at stake (cf. 3:16–17).

**5:2** Paul's response to the news of their toleration of the immoral man is direct and emphatic as seen in the inclusion of the personal pronoun "you" along with the perfect tense verb "puffed up,"[24] which the NIV renders as an exclamation, "And you are proud!" The only possible response to the circumstance should have been corporate mourning and the removal of the unrepentant sinner. The term used here for mourning occurs in other contexts indicating genuine anguish of soul over sin, whether one's own sin or the sin

[22] In 6:12, for example, the catch-phrase "all things are lawful" appears in the context of sexual immorality. The phrase reappears in 10:23 in the context of Paul's argument regarding Christian liberty (8:1–11:1). One possible reading of 5:3–4 is that the perpetrator committed this deed "in the name of our Lord Jesus" (see discussion on 5:3–5 below).

[23] Recent scholarship emphasizes the social background in understanding the reasons the Corinthians overlooked such behavior, which challenges the view that the heinous sin was somehow theologically motivated. See A. D. Clarke, *Secular and Christian Leadership in Corinth: A Socio-Historical and Exegetical Study of 1 Corinthians 1–6*, AGJU 18 (Leiden: Brill, 1993), 76–87; J. K. Chow, *Patronage and Power: A Study of Social Networks in Corinth*, JSNTSup 75 (Sheffield: Sheffield Academic Press, 1992), 130–41. Among the most recent commentators Garland (*1 Corinthians*, 159–62) and Ciampa and Rosner (*The First Letter to the Corinthians*, PNTC [Grand Rapids: Eerdmans, 2010], 202–3) agree that the Corinthians were puffed up in spite of the sin rather than because of it. Ciampa and Rosner point out that Paul has already warned them about their arrogant state (1:31; 3:21; 4:6,18–19) and view the statement in 5:6, "Your boasting is not good," as a more general reference "rather than a specific and direct reaction to the case of incest."

[24] Gk. καὶ ὑμεῖς πεφυσιωμένοι ἐστὲ.

of others. Paul uses the term again in 2 Cor 12:21 to refer to his grief "over many who have sinned earlier and have not repented of the impurity, sexual sin and debauchery in which they have indulged" (cf. also Matt 5:4; Jas 4:9). The term is used in Mark 16:10 of those who mourned the death of Jesus[25] and three times in Revelation (18:11,15,19) for the grief one experiences over an enormous loss. Ciampa and Rosner call attention to the corporate dimension of Paul's rebuke and the six appearances of the term in the LXX with reference to sin,[26] particularly Ezra who mourned over the sins of others.[27] In our own contemporary setting rarely do we think of the ramifications the sins of others have on the whole. Corporate responsibility entails corporate guilt and thus corporate punishment. The intended outcome of their mourning should be to "put out of your fellowship the man who did this."[28]

**5:3–6a** Paul's attitude stands in sharp contrast to theirs.[29] Although Paul is not present physically, he is present "in spirit." But what does Paul intend by the phrase "present in spirit"? In Greek, "spirit" has the article.[30] Does this mean, "in my spirit" or "by the Holy Spirit," or some combination of the two? Barrett represents those who hold the view that Paul is speaking psychologically, referring to his concern for the Corinthian church, as in Col 2:5.[31] Others argue, however, that Paul intends something more in light of his threefold

[25] Cf. also Matt 9:15; BDAG gives other examples outside of the New Testament where the word described the kind of mourning one experiences for one who is dead.

[26] Ezra 10:6; Neh 1:4; 8:9; 1 Esdras 8:72; 9:2; Dan 10:2. The term itself (πενθέω) occurs 65 times in the LXX, but Ciampa and Rosner draw attention to these specific texts that connect mourning with sin.

[27] Ciampa and Rosner (*First Corinthians*, 201) comment, "It is an Ezra-like Paul who deals with the expulsion of the sinner. Just as Ezra 'mourned' over the sins of the community, so Paul enjoined the Corinthians to 'mourn' over the sin of the incestuous man. Just as Ezra demanded that the sinners separate from their foreign partners or else suffer expulsion themselves (10:8), so Paul demanded the expulsion of the sinner, unless he separate from his illicit partner." See the brief article, B. S. Rosner, "'οὐχὶ μᾶλλον ἐπενθήσατε': Corporate Responsibility in 1 Corinthians 5," *NTS* 38 (1992): 470–73. R. B. Hays likewise asserts, "Paul assumes the reality of corporate responsibility" and draws attention to the Old Testament narrative of Achan, the Levitical holiness code, Ezra's mourning, and other examples of national grief (*First Corinthians* [Louisville: John Knox, 1997], 82).

[28] Expressed by a subordinate ἵνα clause in Greek, ἵνα ἀρθῇ ἐκ μέσου ὑμῶν ὁ τὸ ἔργον τοῦτο πράξας. The clause may have imperatival force here. Garland (*1 Corinthians*, 164) views 5:2 and 5:13 an an *inclusio*, lending support to the view that 5:2 is a command.

[29] As noted above, the additional personal pronoun adds emphasis, "*You* are puffed up, but *I* have already judged." Gk. καὶ ὑμεῖς πεφυσιωμένοι ἐστὲ καὶ . . . ἐγὼ μὲν γάρ . . . ἤδη κέκρικα. So also Fee, *First Corinthians*, 203.

[30] Gk. τῷ πνεύματι.

[31] Barrett, *First Corinthians*, 123. Barrett does not altogether rule out a reference to the Holy Spirit but thinks that this is not Paul's primary emphasis. In Col 2:5, Paul writes, "For though I am absent from you in body, I am present with you in spirit." The parallel, though close, is not exact since the term translated "body" by the NIV in Colossians is σάρξ (flesh) whereas in 1 Cor 5:3 Paul uses σῶμα (body).

emphasis on his presence with them (5:2–5).[32] Even though Paul plans to come to them, if the Lord wills (4:18–21), he also is able to render judgment, along with the gathered church, by the authority and power of Jesus.[33] Paul's use of the perfect tense in 5:3 parallels and stands in contrast to the use of the perfect in 5:2. They have become puffed up, but Paul has already judged the situation. They are settled in arrogance. Paul is settled in judgment.

Even though there is more than one way to understand the complex Greek grammar and syntax of vv. 3–5, the overall thrust of the passage is clear. There is no ambiguity regarding the verdict Paul expects when the church assembles. They should expel the incestuous man for his own sake and for the sake of the church. The grammatical issues have to do with what certain phrases modify, such as "in the name of our Lord Jesus," and "with the power of our Lord Jesus."[34] For example, the first phrase could go with the immediately preceding participle, translated "the man who did this,"[35] conveying the notion that the one who committed this deed did so in the name of Lord. This reading of the text would support the idea that the act of incest and the boasting of the church was theologically motivated, that it was predicated on mistaken notions about Christian freedom. Second, the same phrase could refer to the gathering of the church, as in the NIV translation, "When you are assembled in the name of our Lord Jesus." Third, the phrase could modify the main verb, "I have judged . . . in the name of the Lord." [36] Fourth, "in the name of the Lord Jesus" could modify the infinitive phrase "hand this man over to Satan." In sum, is the sin committed in the name of the Lord, are they gathered in the name of the Lord, has Paul cast judgment in the name of the Lord, or has Paul judged to deliver the man to Satan in the name of the Lord? The same kinds of options pertain also to the phrase "together with the power of the Lord Jesus."[37] In

[32] Thiselton, *First Corinthians*, 391.

[33] Fee (*First Corinthians*, 204–5) thinks that what Paul says in some way relates to life in the Spirit, but also refers to Paul's spirit, translating πνεῦμα as S/spirit. Clearly, Paul refers to "my spirit" in 5:4. Garland (*1 Corinthians*, 165) notes a parallel with 6:17, those united with Christ are "one spirit" with him. "United to Christ in spirit, he is present with them through Christ's presence."

[34] L. Morris lists seven options (*1 Corinthians*, TNTC [Grand Rapids: Eerdmans, 1985]), 84–85).

[35] Gk. τὸν οὕτως τοῦτο κατεργασάμενον.

[36] So Fee, *First Corinthians*, 207.

[37] Garland (*1 Corinthians*, 167) argues for two roughly parallel statements: (1) He is present with them in spirit and pronounces judgment "in the name of the Lord" on the one who has done this deed; (2) When they assemble together, he is present with them in spirit, and "with the power of the Lord Jesus" they are to hand this one over to Satan. Thiselton (*First Corinthians*, 394) thinks that "in the name" could go with both "gathered together" and "with the power." Morris leans toward "in the name" modifying "hand over to Satan." Furthermore, since Paul stresses the real efficacy of his presence, Thiselton (392; also Garland, 168) argues that ὡς παρὼν should not be rendered "as if" or "as though," but "being present, as one who is present." There is a collective judgment carried out by the power of the Lord Jesus. One of the keys here is Paul's expectation of community involvement. Paul has rendered judgment, but they are all to be participants in the process. They are to reach a decision and carry out judgment with Paul.

the end, whatever conclusions one draws regarding these various grammatical options, the overall tenor of the passage is clear. Paul has already rendered judgment, and he is present with the gathered church as they turn the man over to Satan. The collective judgment of the gathered church, along with Paul, carries the weight of the authority and power of Jesus.

But what are we to make of the latter part of Paul's instruction to "hand this man over to Satan,[38] so that the sinful nature may be destroyed and his spirit saved on the day of the Lord"? The NIV translation, "so that the sinful nature may be destroyed" is rendered by other translations more literally, "for the destruction of the (his) flesh."[39] South observes that the most widespread critical understanding of this passage is what he calls the "curse/death" interpretation, meaning that "Paul is enjoining the pronouncement of a curse on the offender in question with the expectation that he will die as a result."[40] The evidence for this view, as summarized by South,[41] includes: (1) alleged parallels with Greek and Jewish curse formulae that Paul drew on and used in the context of church discipline; (2) examples of the curse/death phenomenon in the New Testament itself, such as the death of Ananias and Sapphira in Acts 5:1–11, and, more significantly, Paul's reference to the death of some Corinthians due to their behavior at the Lord's Supper (1 Cor 11:30);[42] (3) the force of the meaning of the Greek term translated "destruction";[43] a very strong word used in the LXX to denote utter ruin,[44] and (4) the use of curses in connection with the death penalty in the Old Testament.[45]

South follows with a thorough critique of the "curse/death" interpretation of 1 Cor 5:1–8 that calls into question the evidence used to support this understanding.[46] Another way to read the passage understands the phrase "hand over

[38] The infinitive (παραδοῦναι) functions as an imperative.

[39] Gk. εἰς ὄλεθρον τῆς σαρκός. NIV2011 moved to a more literal translation.

[40] South, "A Critique of the 'Curse/Death' Interpretation," 540. South notes the assertion of H. Conzelmann as typical, "The destruction of the flesh can hardly mean anything else but death" (*1 Corinthians: A Critical and Historical Commentary on the Bible*, Hermeneia, trans. J. Leitch [Philadelphia: Fortress, 1975], 97). South also notes variations within this view such as Barrett (*First Corinthians*, 126–27) and F. F. Bruce (*1 and 2 Corinthians*, NCB [Grand Rapids: Eerdmans, 1971], 54–55), who "envision the death of the offender, but do not connect with a curse."

[41] South, "A Critique of the 'Curse/Death' Interpretation," 541–44.

[42] In a nondisciplinary text, 2 Cor 12:7, Paul links his physical suffering with a "messenger of Satan."

[43] Gk. ὄλεθρος. The NIV translates as a verb, "may be destroyed."

[44] For examples of the use of the noun in the LXX with this meaning, see 1 Kgs 13:34; Jer 28:55; 31:3,8,32; 32:31; Ezek 6:14; 14:16; Obad 1:13. For the use of the related verb ὀλεθρεύω, see Exod 12:23; 22:19 (22:20); Num 4:18; Josh 3:10; 7:25; Jer 2:30; 5:6; 22:7; 32:36. In the New Testament the term occurs three times outside of its use in 1 Cor 5:5 (see 1 Thess 5:3; 2 Thess 1:9; 1 Tim 6:9). The verb ὀλεθρεύω appears in Heb 11:28 and the cognate noun ὀλοθρευτής in 1 Cor 10:10. Both of these texts describe physical deaths associated with Israel's exodus from Egypt.

[45] See Deut 27:15–26.

[46] South, "A Critique of the 'Curse/Death' Interpretation," 544–61. South asserts that the Greek and Jewish curse formulae and Acts 5:1–11/1 Cor 11:30 are not genuine parallels to 1 Cor 5:5.

to Satan" as expulsion from the church, ejecting the offender out of the community and back into the world, thus removing him from the care and concern of the church[47] for the purpose of final salvation. Paul uses similar language in 1 Tim 3:19–20 with reference to Hymenaeus and Alexander, "whom I have handed over to Satan to be taught not to blaspheme," where correction rather than death seems to be in view. Furthermore, the "curse/death" interpretation understands "flesh" to refer to the man's physical body, which is destroyed in order that his "spirit" may be saved. Yet, this view violates Paul's doctrine of the resurrection of the body (6:12–14; 15:20–58).[48] Furthermore, Paul employs the flesh/spirit contrast in other contexts to denote "a contrast in tendencies and loyalties which compete for dominance as powers within each person."[49] Or, to put it another way, "spirit" refers to the orientation of the whole person toward God and, conversely, "flesh" refers to the orientation of the whole person away from God.[50] Paul applies "death" language metaphorically with reference to the flesh in other contexts (Rom 8:23; Gal 5:24; Col 3:5). Thiselton explains that what Paul hopes will be destroyed "is his attitude of self-congratulation, which deprivation from the respect and support of the church is likely to bring about."[51] Thus, the meaning in 1 Cor 5:5 would be to excommunicate the offender from the community in order to destroy his sinful orientation so that he himself might be saved on the Day of the Lord.[52]

This interpretation assumes that Paul is speaking primarily of the individual. Paul is equally concerned, however, for the sanctity of the church, which is expressed in the analogy that follows of the leaven that infects the whole batch of dough (5:6–8). Since the Greek leaves open the meaning of "his spirit" in 5:5 where there is no possessive pronoun, only the definite

Paul's use of ὄλεθρος does not require the curse/death interpretation and the Old Testament curse/death situations do not fully explain 1 Cor 5:5. South thinks that Job 1:12 and 2:6, in spite of the contextual differences, is the probable source of Paul's language "to hand over to Satan." While it is clear that there are sins that lead to death (see also 1 Cor 10:8–10; 1 John 5:16–17), the question is whether or not this is Paul's intention in this context.

[47] Note Col 1:13, which refers to the rescue of believers from the dominion of darkness.

[48] See also 1 Thess 5:23, "May your whole spirit, soul and body be kept blameless at the coming of our Lord Jesus Christ."

[49] South, "A Critique of the 'Curse/Death' Interpretation," 552. See Rom 8:5–17 and Gal 3:13; 5:13,16–24. Note also Paul's previous contrast between the "spiritual person" and the person "characterized by flesh," and his confrontation in 3:3, "You are still worldly. For since there is jealousy and quarreling among you, are you not worldly? Are you not acting like mere men?" The term translated "worldly" is σαρκικός.

[50] Fee, *First Corinthians*, 212. Fee comments that in 1 Cor 5:5 "we have a typically Pauline contrast between 'flesh' and 'spirit,' although not necessarily typically expressed." On the "flesh/spirit" language see A. C. Thiselton, "The Meaning of ΣΑΡΧ in 1 Corinthians 5:5: A Fresh Approach in the Light of Logical and Semantic Factors," *SJT* 26 (1973): 204–28.

[51] Thiselton, *First Corinthians*, 399–400.

[52] The corresponding emphasis in 5:2,7,13b is the removal of the offender from the community, not his death.

article, "the spirit,"[53] some take a rather different view of Paul's instructions; the reference is not to the man's spirit but to the Holy Spirit. Collins, for example, argues that Paul "directs the community to excise the fleshly individual—so characterized by reason of his incestuous behavior—from its midst so that the community might live under the power of the Spirit and be preserved for the day of the Lord."[54] It is probably best, however, to see both individual and corporate emphases. Ciampa and Rosner, who hold to the view that "spirit" refers to the man, nevertheless emphasize the corporate element and link this passage to Paul's previous reference to the church as God's holy temple indwelt by the Spirit (3:16–17). In their view, 3:16–17 "provides the theological framework for understanding perhaps the most fundamental reason for the expulsion of the sinner in 5:1–13: his flesh must be 'destroyed' because he has defiled the holiness of God's temple, the church."[55] This corporate emphasis is further supported by Paul's statement in 5:6a, "Your boasting is not good," which forms an *inclusio* with 5:2, "And you are proud!"[56] Paul is no doubt appalled by the nature of the sin of the individual, but he is equally appalled at the church's state of arrogance in their toleration of the sin.

**5:6b–8** The focus of the argument shifts in 5:6b to the theological grounds for the church's action.[57] Paul explains his reasoning on the analogy of the Old Testament feast of Passover prefaced by the question, "Do you not know?"[58] The question assumes that Paul has already instructed them on such matters (5:9), but it also punctures their pride. The proverbial phrase, "A little yeast[59]

---

[53] Gk. τὸ πνεῦμα. The definite article can carry a possessive force, along with other meanings.

[54] Collins, *First Corinthians*, 213. Also J. A. Fitzmyer, *First Corinthians: A New Translation with Introduction and Commentary*, AB 32 (New Haven: Yale University Press, 2008), 239–40. Flesh also is used absolutely, "for the destruction of the flesh." Collins holds that "flesh" refers to the individual while "spirit" refers to the Holy Spirit. It is possible, however, that "flesh" refers to the fleshly orientation of the church (cf. 3:1–4). See K. P. Donfried, "Justification and Last Judgment in Paul," *Int* 30 (1976), 150–51; B. Campbell, "Flesh and Spirit in 1 Cor. 5:5: An Exercise in Rhetorical Criticism of the NT," *JETS* 36 (1993): 331–42.

[55] Ciampa and Rosner, *First Corinthians*, 210. See also A. Y. Collins, "The Function of 'Excommunication' in Paul," *HTR* 73 (1980): 263. Garland (*1 Corinthians*, 174–75) argues that Paul is concerned about both the individual and the church (cf. 2 Cor 2:5–11; 7:15–16). So also Thiselton (*First Corinthians*, 396–97), who argues that what is to be destroyed is a "fleshly" stance of self-sufficiency, both the self-glorying of the offender and the community.

[56] καύχημα and φυσιόω appear to be synonymous terms since they are also used together in 4:6–7 (so Fee, *First Corinthians*, 215).

[57] Ciampa and Rosner (*First Corinthians*, 212) suggest that the association of "cleansing the temple" with the observance of Passover may influence Paul's thought in 5:7–8 (see 2 Kgs 23:1–23; 2 Chr 29:5, 35; 30; 35:1–19; Ezra 6:13–22). Even in the New Testament cleansing the temple and celebrating Passover are connected (see Matt 21:12–13; Mark 11:15–18; Luke 19:45–47; John 2:13–22).

[58] This is the second occurrence of the question, "Don't you know?" Cf. 3:16–17.

[59] BDAG suggests that "leaven" is the preferable translation since yeast "popularly suggests a produce foreign to ancient baking practice."

works through the whole batch of dough" (see also 1 Cor 15:33; Gal 5:9), refers to the process of introducing fermented dough into a batch of unleavened dough in order to make the bread rise. If contaminated, however, the old leaven would infect the whole new batch of dough. Thus leaven came to symbolize the infectious power of evil (Matt 16:6). In context, what the Corinthians should have known was the contaminating influence of sin on the whole community. They should "get rid of the old yeast" in order to become what they already are, "a new batch without yeast" (5:7).[60] But what exactly is the "old yeast" in context? Is this yet another way of saying, "Expel the offender in order to guard the purity of the church," or is Paul referring more precisely to the church's boasting?[61] Both could be in view since both are causing significant harm to the church. Either way, Paul's reasoning is widely recognized as a core principle of his ethical instruction, commonly phrased as "become what you are."[62] In other words, the ethical imperative always flows from the indicative. Already they are a sanctified people (cf. 1:2; 6:11) by virtue of Christ's sacrifice.[63] On this basis they are to rid themselves of all corrupting influences. As celebrants of the festival of Passover, used here metaphorically of the Christian life, they are to observe it as "bread without yeast, the bread of sincerity and truth."

**5:9–11** In 5:9 Paul refers to a previous letter in which he instructed the Corinthians not to associate with "sexually immoral people."[64] He then clarifies his intent that he did not at all mean to disconnect from the immoral people of the world but rather with "anyone who calls himself a brother," who engages in profane behavior (5:10–11). The reference to the previous letter reinforces the question of 5:6b, "Don't you know?"[65]

[60] On the Jewish Passover ritual of cleaning out the old leaven, see Exod 12:15–19; 13:7; Deut 16:4. Note also how this is associated with the sacrifice of the Paschal lamb (Exod 12:6).

[61] So F. Grosheide, *Commentary on the First Epistle to the Corinthians*, NICNT (Grand Rapids: Eerdmans, 1953), 124.

[62] See discussion in Fee, *First Corinthians*, 214–17. As Fee (215) expresses it, "The death of Christ makes them new; yet they must get rid of the old in order to be new, precisely because in Christ they are already new!"

[63] This is the only place Paul refers to Christ as "our Passover Lamb."

[64] Here the Greek term is πόρνος, a cognate term to πορνεία used in 5:1.

[65] Is Paul correcting a previous misunderstanding or simply reminding them, with further clarification, what they already know? Most commentators assume that Paul's first letter was ambiguous. But is it plausible that the Corinthians do not associate with the immoral of the world yet they tolerate the most egregious of sins in their own community? The content of the letter suggests that they are not doing so well with "separation from the world." Ciampa and Rosner (*First Corinthians*, 216) comment, "The Corinthians had taken Paul to mean disassociation from all immoral people, both inside and outside the church, and, it seems, concluded that such teaching was too harsh and impractical; they had no intention of cutting off all ties with those outside the church." In my view, Paul merely expands on his previous instruction in order to clarify, not to clear up a misunderstanding. The NIV switches from past tense to present on the same verb in 5:9 ("I have written") and 5:11 ("Now I am writing you"), interpreting the second occurrence as an epistolary aorist, that is, writing in the present but from the viewpoint of the recipient. In both instances the

The Greek term translated by the NIV as "to associate" (also 5:11) is a double compound verb meaning "to mix up together."[66] The term occurs elsewhere only in 2 Thess 3:14 as a directive of dissociation.[67] The same idea is present in Titus 3:10–11. These texts raise important questions concerning how believers are to draw appropriate boundaries with respect to unbelievers "in the world," and to believers living in open rebellion. Paul is clear, for example, in this section, that dissociation from believers is required in certain situations. The same holds true with respect to unbelievers under certain circumstances, such as participating in the worship of idols (10:14–22). However, complete withdrawal from the world is impossible.[68] For this reason, believers need a good measure of wisdom.[69] Paul works out the believer's decision-making process in these matters in more detail in chaps. 8–10 on the question of food sacrificed to idols. Here, the point is simple; they should dissociate themselves from anyone who professes to be a Christian who openly flouts Christian standards,[70] but they should not disengage from the immoral people of the world. Contact with the world is essential to evangelism.[71]

In 5:11 Paul clarifies the nature of withdrawal from the professed believer who is immoral, "With such a man do not even eat." What may seem like a strange command to the modern reader was a more serious issue in the ancient world, where refusing to eat with someone broke all social ties. But what does

verb is in the aorist, ἔγραψα. I think the NASB has it right in 5:11, "But actually, I wrote to you . . ." In both instances (5:9 and 11) Paul refers to his previous letter. BDAG places 1 Cor 5:11 under the definition, "temporal marker with focus not so much on the present time as the situation pertains at a given moment, *now, as it is*."

[66] Gk. συναναμίγνυμι. Garland (*1 Corinthians*, 185) adds that, in the context of purity boundaries, the term means to set apart by virtue of strict moral standards.

[67] Paul follows in 2 Thess 3:15, "Yet do not regard him as an enemy, but warn him as a brother."

[68] Cf. Phil 2:14–16, "Do everything without complaining or arguing, so that you may become blameless and pure, children of God without fault in a crooked and depraved generation, in which you shine like stars in the universe as you hold out the word of life—in order that I may boast on the day of Christ that I did not run or labor for nothing."

[69] Morris (*1 Corinthians*, 89) comments, "When we reflect that Jesus ate with sinners and that Paul regards it as permissible to accept invitations to eat in heathen homes (10:27), the detailed application of this injunction is not easy. But the principle is plain. Where anyone claims to be Christian but leads a life that belies his profession, there is to be no such close fellowship as will countenance his sin."

[70] Paul lists five categories of people other than "the sexually immoral": the greedy, idolator, slanderer, drunkard, and thief (NIV, "greedy" and "swindlers," governed by one definite article, refer to the same thing). The sexual sinner is not the only one subject to church discipline. Garland (*1 Corinthians*, 189) notes how the sins listed fit the epistolary situation: the fornicator applies to the case of incest (5:1) and other passages (chaps. 6–7), the greedy and the swindler apply to the Christians suing in pagan court (6:1–11), idolatry is the focus of 8–10, the reviler causes dissensions (1:18–4:21), and the problem of drunkenness shows up at the Lord's supper in 11:21. See also P. Zaas, "Catalogues and Context: 1 Corinthians 5 and 6," *NTS* 34 (1988): 623–24. B. Rosner notes a connection with the vice list and sins connected to the command to expel the offender in Deuteronomy (*Paul, Scripture, and Ethics*, 68–70). See also also Ciampa and Rosner, *First Corinthians*, 217 for a chart laying out the parallels.

[71] See esp. 9:19–23.

Paul mean in this context, since the excluded professing believer presumably would be treated as an unbeliever and therefore as one to be won back to the Lord? Paul likely means exclusion from the Lord's Supper, not complete exclusion from private meals.[72] Fee thinks that Paul's concern is not that individual members disassociate from the incestuous man, but rather that he is excluded from the community as it gathers for worship and instruction.[73] How can the church strike a balance between narrow exclusivism and a community that welcomes sinners as a place for healing? Garland notes that the context "refers to a glaring sin that is very public and brings disgrace on the community. There is a limit beyond which patience, toleration, and charity toward another's sin ceases to be a virtue."[74] Fee suggests that Paul is speaking about persistent sins, not those who simply struggle with past sins.[75]

**5:12–13** Paul concludes with a final injunction to expel the wicked man from the community (5:13). In doing so, he contrasts the judgment of "insiders" and "outsiders."[76] Paul has no say in what unbelievers do, only believers. It is not the business of believers to judge the outsiders, but they must judge the insiders. In this context, however, the judgment has to do with the disciplinary action of the church and not to prophetic judgment of society.[77] The judgment of the incestuous man rests with the entire community, not only with the apostle Paul. Paul's final command, "Expel the wicked man from among you," picks up a recurring phrase in Deuteronomy,[78] although without the typical introductory formula, "It is written," perhaps because of the emotionally charged tenor of the instruction.[79] This final command is the capstone of Paul's argument (see 5:2,5,7) and is essential not only for the individual but also for the church. The emphasis on individual repentance and restoration is correct, but equally so, the church must exercise wise discipline in the preservation of her own purity. The effects of egregious, public sin on both the individual and the corporate body are profound.

[72] Ciampa and Rosner (*First Corinthians*, 218) note that the Lord's Supper and other fellowship meals are intended, but it is "less certain that the church as individuals is to refuse to eat with them . . . However, the case of the incestuous man may be more serious . . . and the words 'not even' point to private meals also." See also Titus 3:10, "Warn a divisive person once, and then warn him a second time. After that, have nothing to do with him."

[73] Fee, *First Corinthians*, 226.

[74] Garland, *1 Corinthians*, 190.

[75] Fee, *First Corinthians*, 224.

[76] On the designation, "outsiders," see Col 4:5; 1 Thess 4:12; and 1 Tim 3:7.

[77] Garland, *1 Corinthians*, 190.

[78] Deut 17:7,12; 19:19; 21:21; 22:21–22,24; 24:7.

[79] Ciampa and Rosner, *First Corinthians*, 220.

## 2. The Shame of the Righteous Taking Disputes Before the Unrighteous (6:1–11)

**[1]If any of you has a dispute with another, dare he take it before the ungodly for judgment instead of before the saints? [2]Do you not know that the saints will judge the world? And if you are to judge the world, are you not competent to judge trivial cases? [3]Do you not know that we will judge angels? How much more the things of this life! [4]Therefore, if you have disputes about such matters, appoint as judges even men of little account in the church! [5]I say this to shame you. Is it possible that there is nobody among you wise enough to judge a dispute between believers? [6]But instead, one brother goes to law against another—and this in front of unbelievers!**

**[7]The very fact that you have lawsuits among you means you have been completely defeated already. Why not rather be wronged? Why not rather be cheated? [8]Instead, you yourselves cheat and do wrong, and you do this to your brothers.**

**[9]Do you not know that the wicked will not inherit the kingdom of God? Do not be deceived: Neither the sexually immoral nor idolaters nor adulterers nor male prostitutes nor homosexual offenders [10] nor thieves nor the greedy nor drunkards nor slanderers nor swindlers will inherit the kingdom of God. [11]And that is what some of you were. But you were washed, you were sanctified, you were justified in the name of the Lord Jesus Christ and by the Spirit of our God.**

The topic shifts in 6:1 from the case of an incestuous man to another glaring problem in the Corinthian assembly, namely, litigation among believers in the secular civil courts.[80] The recurring theme of judgment between 5:1–13 and 6:1–11 has led some to argue that the wrongdoing in 6:1–11 is an extension of chap. 5, that the subject of disputes in the civil courts relates to some sexual impropriety.[81] But such a line of reasoning is unnecessary in order to establish a coherent line of reasoning between the two sections. Paul's remarks in 5:12–13 regarding judging those "inside" versus those "outside" provide the necessary link. Paul concludes his argument in chap. 5 with the admonition to render judgment against an "insider" by expelling the wicked person from

[80] The language of judgment pervades chaps. 5–6 with nine occurrences of the Greek word "to judge" (κρίνω) evenly distributed (see 1 Cor 5:3,12–13; 6:1–3; 6:6) Additionally, the term κριτήριον (NASB, "law court") appears in 6:2 and 6:4. The theme of the "unrighteous" pervades 6:1–9 (note the uses of ἄδικος or ἀδικέω in 6:1,7,8,9), which stands in contrast to their "righteous" status before God in 6:11 (δικαιόω).

[81] See J. H. Bernard, "The Connexion Between the Fifth and Sixth Chapters of 1 Cor," *ExpTim* 7 (1907): 433–43. More recently P. Richardson, "Judgment in Sexual Matters in 1 Corinthians 6:1–11," *NovT* 25 (1983): 37–58; R. A. Horsely, *1 Corinthians*, ANTC (Nashville: Abingdon, 1998), 86. Garland (*1 Corinthians*, 198–99) gives four reasons why this interpretation is unlikely: (1) Paul is citing cases of appalling moral failures in order to curb unwarranted Corinthian boasting and arrogance. The fact that 6:1–11 is sandwiched between cases of sexual immorality does not necessarily mean that the lawsuit in 6:1–11 has something to do with sexual immorality. (2) Paul's insistence in 6:7 that they should be willing to be wronged does not seem applicable to a case of adultery, let alone incest. (3) Paul would not dismiss incest as a minor dispute (6:2). Garland notes Winter's study on the different kinds of cases handled by the civil and criminal courts. See B. W. Winter, "Civil Litigation in Secular Corinth and the Church: The Forensic Background to 1 Cor 6:1–8," *NTS* 37 (1991): 561.

among them. Thus it follows that if believers are obligated to render judgments among themselves within the community then they also bear responsibility to settle other matters of dispute within the community before "the saints" instead of in the secular arena before the "unrighteous."[82] The Corinthians should expel the incestuous man, but they also are competent to settle other matters among themselves. Therefore, one believer taking another believer to court is yet another appalling moral collapse that disparages the church's witness before the world and demonstrates their failure to function properly as the people of God. As in 5:1–13, Paul has more to say about the failure of the church to settle disputes than he does about the actual offenders, and, as in previous sections of the letter, Paul constructs his argument within an eschatological framework (cf. 3:13–15; 4:1–13; 5:1–5).

In 6:2–4, Paul takes the notion of judgment a step further than he does in 5:1–13 in the assertion that believers will take part in the end-time judgment of the world and of angels. This does not stand in contradiction to what he has written in 5:12–13 regarding judging those outside the church. As Barrett points out, "The explanation is that 5:12 refers to a censorious kind of criticism practiced by church members in the present, whereas 6:2 refers to participation of the people of God in the judgment at the last day."[83] If believers will participate in something as weighty as the end-time judgment, then how is it that they cannot judge everyday matters pertaining to this life? Is there not one wise person among them to carry out the task (6:5)? Fee comments that "The whole scene fills Paul with indignation, so much so that there is scarcely any argument at all."[84] The most recent critical editions of the Greek New Testament punctuate 6:1–11 with no less than ten questions.[85] The question "Do you not know?" occurs three times in 6:1–11 and an additional three times in 6:12–20. The first word in Greek is "to dare,"[86] thus, with no connecting conjunction or particle to the preceding section, Paul abruptly moves to this topic with strong rebuke, "How dare you!"[87]

[82] So also Fee (*First Corinthians*, 228), who explains that Corinthian judgments "had to do first of all with the expulsion of the incestuous man; but it also has to do with another kind of 'judgment' that must take place within the Christian community, namely in matters of everyday life where one member has a grievance against another."

[83] Barrett, *First Corinthians*, 136.

[84] Fee, *First Corinthians*, 229. Fee notes that Paul alternates between statements of horror (6:1, 6), rhetorical quest ions (6:2–4,5b–6,7b), sarcasm (6:5), and threat (6:8–11).

[85] Whether 6:4 is an indicative or interrogative statement is debated. See discussion below.

[86] τολμάω. The term can also mean "to be bold" (see 2 Cor 10:2,12; 11:21; Phil 1:14).

[87] Thiselton (*First Corinthians*, 419–22) notes that the local situation in Corinth is a major factor in the reading of this passage since Paul is favorable to the role of civil authorities in rendering justice in Rom 13:1–7, which enjoins believers to obey them. He suggests that while the criminal courts of the Roman system would provide some relative justice, the local civil courts were another matter, often swayed and manipulated through the social networks of the powerful and influential leaving the poor and weak with no grounds for justice. See also A. C. Mitchell, "Rich and Poor in the Courts of Corinth: Litigiousness and Status in 1 Cor 6:1–11," *NTS* 39 (1993): 562–86; Winter,

Paul's argument in 6:1–11 is threefold. First, Paul expresses shock and outrage and reprimands them for behavior not fitting the people of God who will one day judge the world and angels and for taking matters of this life before the secular courts (6:1–6).[88] Second, Paul explains that the very presence of lawsuits among believers is a moral defeat for all involved. Nobody wins in this situation (6:7–8). Third, Paul issues a final reason for his rebuke accompanied by a strong warning (6:9–11). The "unjust" will not inherit the kingdom of God. On what basis should a believer take a matter before someone who has no inheritance in the kingdom of God? Furthermore, the Corinthian believers are no longer "unjust" because they have been "washed, sanctified, and justified." Again, the indicative of what they "are" lays the foundation of how they must behave.

**6:1** As noted above, the Greek verb translated "dare" occurs first in the sentence for emphasis. As in 5:1, Paul expresses shock and indignation over their behavior toward one another. They were unwilling to properly exercise judgment in the case of blatant immorality that would destroy the fabric of their existence as God's holy people, yet they resolved to settle grievances against one another in public courts before unbelievers. The NIV's "If any of you has a dispute with another" translates a Greek idiom for civil litigation.[89] We do not know if this is an isolated lawsuit or if this was a Corinthian practice.[90] Either way, the concern is their unrighteousness before God and the world. Their actions damaged their witness to the world and demonstrated a failure to exercise the wisdom of God, which is far greater than the wisdom of this world.

Paul's outrage has to do not with the fact of grievances but with the taking of a grievance before the "ungodly" and not before the "saints." Some translations render "ungodly" as "unrighteous." Barrett contends that this is an unfortunate translation, that Paul's use of the term is religious rather than a moral appraisal of the secular judges. In other words, the term simply designates the secular magistrates as "unbelievers."[91] They, unlike the Corinthians, have not been justified and are not rightly related to God in Christ. Paul did not intend to demean

"Civil Litigation in Secular Corinth and the Church: The Forensic Background to 1 Cor 6:1–8." Regarding Jewish practice, in Acts 18:12–18, when the Jews brought Paul before Gallio in Corinth, Gallio deferred the matter back to the Jews, "'But since it involves questions about words and names and your own law—settle the matter yourselves. I will not be a judge of such things.' So he had them ejected from the court" (Acts 18:15–16).

[88] This first unit is marked by an *inclusio* at 6:1 and 6:6, "before the unrighteous"/"before the unbelievers."

[89] Gk. πρᾶγμα ἔχων πρὸς τὸν ἕτερον. Literally, "Having a matter against another." BDAG, "Having a lawsuit with someone."

[90] Robertson and Plummer (*First Corinthians*, 110), noting the plural in 6:8, think that Paul has no isolated case in mind, unlike the situation in 5:1–13. Garland (*1 Corinthians*, 195), on the other hand thinks that, given the numbers in the church, it is probable that there was only one case.

[91] Barrett, *First Corinthians*, 135. Note the parallel in 6:6 where the term "unbelievers" (ἀπίστων) is used. Barrett prefers "non-Christians and Christians."

the court system as unjust.[92] Paul's choice may be explained by the eschatological framing of the argument. The "unrighteous," in contrast to the "saints," will not inherit the kingdom of God (6:11–12).[93] Garland thinks otherwise. He suggests that since Paul does not continue with the "outsider" language of 5:12–13, but rather calls them the "unjust," he does more than simply call them "unbelievers." "In the context, which refers to these persons serving as the judges in a dispute, this term would seem to offer a moral appraisal of them."[94] Paul's exhortation for the Corinthians to settle their disputes before the saints reflects his Jewish heritage, but his reasons will be new (6:2).[95]

**6:2–3** For the third time in the letter Paul asks, "Do you not know?" The first basic premise of his argument is that eschatological realities should determine present behavior. There is no elaboration on the phrase "the saints will judge the world," but the point is clear. If saints will be involved in the end-time judgment of the world and angels, then they are fully competent to handle matters pertaining to the affairs of this age.[96] In other words, Paul argues from the greater to the lesser.[97] Commentators routinely recognize Dan 7:22 as a possible background to the concept of saints judging the world.[98] Paul steps it up a notch in 6:3, once again asking, "Do you not know?" This time he includes the judgment of angels. The contrast is striking. If you will judge angels,[99] then how much more are you competent to judge matters pertaining to this life?[100]

---

[92] Robertson and Plummer (*First Corinthians*, 110) also note that the term does not necessarily impugn the justice of the Roman court system. The term simply reflects the world to which the judges belong.

[93] So Fee, *First Corinthians*, 232.

[94] Garland, *1 Corinthians*, 195–96. Garland (196) comments, "The judicial context and the meaning of the term in Rom 3:5 and 1 Cor 6:9 strongly suggest that Paul intends to deprecate the moral capacity and judicial fairness of these unbelievers before whom one Christian has brought another brother Christian to be judged." Garland notes as a parallel the "unjust" judge in Luke 18:2–6 who neither feared God nor respected persons.

[95] Fee, *First Corinthians*, 231.

[96] NIV, "Are you not competent to judge trivial cases?" NASB, "Are you not competent to constitute the smallest law courts?" Robertson and Plummer (*First Corinthians*, 112) suggest, "Are you unworthy of the smallest tribunals?"

[97] For the reverse argument, from the "lesser to the greater," see 9:11.

[98] See also Wisdom 3:7; 1 Enoch 1:9,38. In the New Testament see Matt 19:28; Luke 22:30; Rev 20:4.

[99] Paul does not elaborate on "judging the angels." For an argument for fallen angels, see P. M. Hoskins, "The Use of Biblical and Extrabiblical Parallels in the Interpretation of First Corinthians 6:2–3," *CBQ* 63 (2001): 287–97. Paul's purpose here is not doctrinal but rather to point out present inconsistencies. Garland (*1 Corinthians*, 203) comments, "It is probable that he wishes only to remind the Corinthians of their end-time destiny when they will be given dominion even over the angels. In that day, the current state of affairs will be radically reversed."

[100] The Greek μήτι γε strengthens the construction. BDAG, "not to mention, let alone." See also Robertson and Plummer, *First Corinthians*, 113.

**6:4–6** Whether we take the main verb in 6:4 as indicative or imperative[101] is a well-known interpretive crux. One can see the differences by comparing modern translations. The NIV, for example, takes it as an imperative: "Therefore, if you have disputes about such matters, appoint as judges even men of little account in the church!"[102] The meaning would be that the least esteemed among them are competent to settle their disputes. The phrase "men of little account" is based on the same term used in 1:28, translated as the "despised things,"[103] chosen by God in order to contradict the wisdom of the world. In the context of 6:1–11, with its eschatological overtones, it is just possible that Paul is playing on these ironies. God has chosen the "despised" all right, and those who are the least esteemed in the church are fully competent to handle matters pertaining to this life. Sometimes the greatest wisdom lies with those who are, from the world's point of view, the least powerful, influential, and educated. Kinman notes that while most modern commentators read as an indicative, most ancient commentators opted for the imperative. He sets forth grammatical, literary, and historical arguments for the imperatival translation.[104] This interpretation is followed most recently by Garland[105] and Ciampa and Rosner.[106]

The TNIV represents another possible reading of the sentence, which renders the verb as indicative and the sentence as a question, "Therefore, if you have disputes about such matters, do you ask for a ruling from those whose way of life is scorned in the church?"[107] In other words, following on the heels of the previous questions in 6:2–3, this is yet another probing question that would have the rhetorical effect of bringing them back to their senses. Paul asks, "Do you actually submit judgments before men who count for nothing in the church at all?" Fee is representative of those who believe this is the best way to read the text, noting that the two preceding eschatological arguments

---

[101] The second person plural form, καθίζετε, which occurs last in the sentence, can be either indicative or imperative.

[102] So also KJV.

[103] Gk. ἐξουθενέω. The term occurs elsewhere in Paul in Rom 14:3,10; 1 Cor 16:11; 2 Cor 10:10; Gal 4:14; 1 Thess 5:20.

[104] B. Kinman, "'Appoint the Despised as Judges!' (1 Corinthians 6:4)," *TynBul* 48 (1997): 345–54. Kinman argues that there is precedent in Paul's writings for the placement of the imperative as the last element in the sentence (citing Rom 12:14; 1 Cor 4:6; 7:21; 10:31; 11:33; 14:20; 16:1,13; Gal 5:1; Eph 5:11; Phil 4:4; Col 3:15; 1 Thess 5:22; 1 Tim 4:11; 5:22; 6:2; and Phlm 18). Furthermore, the Corinthian church could not "appoint" judges in secular courts, and the phrase "in the church" in all other instances in Paul carries a locative sense rather than instrumental, "by the church." Paul refers not to what has already transpired but what might hypothetically happen in the future. His solution is to "appoint those despised in the church as arbiters" (353). The social status of these members of the church would have stood in stark contrast to those typically involved in litigation (the wise and the influential and those of noble birth; 1:26).

[105] Garland, *1 Corinthians*, 205–7.

[106] Ciampa and Rosner, *First Corinthians*, 229–30.

[107] So also the critical editions of the Greek New Testament, RSV, NRSV, HCSB, NASB, and NET. Also NIV2011.

favor this view. This would not mean that Paul necessarily trivializes the pagan courts, but rather that "they are those people whose values and judgments the church has rejected by its adoption of totally different standards."[108] It is difficult to decide between the two views; both sides have good arguments. Robertson and Plummer counsel, "We must be content to leave the matter open."[109]

In 6:5, unlike 4:14 where he claimed his intent was to warn rather than shame, Paul says exactly the opposite, "I say this to shame you,"[110] followed by the added sarcasm, "Is it possible that there is nobody among you wise enough to judge a dispute between believers?"[111] Once again, the Corinthians' actions betray their claim to be truly wise. Paul's rebuke sharply undermines their boasting. The strong adversative in Greek sets 6:6 in stark contrast to the question of 6:5.[112] Instead of wisdom prevailing with at least one wise judge in the community, brother is being judged by brother before the unbelievers! It is bad to have disputes, but it is worse to go to law with a brother. Worst of all is the tragedy of doing this before the world.[113]

**6:7–8** In litigation, from a worldly point of view, one side wins and the other side loses. However, when one believer takes another believer to civil court over trivial matters, the guaranteed outcome is not only that nobody wins; even before the trial begins "you have been completely defeated already" (NIV).[114] The adverb translated "completely" is the same adverb translated "actually' in 5:1.[115] Robertson and Plummer take the adverb in the sense of "under any circumstance."[116] BDAG suggests as a possible translation of the phrase, "believe me, it's an utter disaster." The defeat is "the very fact that you have lawsuits among you," that one wise person in the church has not been able to adjudicate the matter (6:5). The parties involved (and the church) have failed to demonstrate the wisdom of God and have instead followed the course of the wisdom of the world. They have failed to live out the core principles of the gospel. The teaching of Jesus surely underlies Paul's ethics.[117] Paul asks, "Why not rather be wronged? Why not rather be cheated?" Instead, by having lawsuits among themselves they are the ones acting unjustly and defrauding

[108] Fee, *First Corinthians*, 235–36.

[109] Robertson and Plummer, *First Corinthians*, 114.

[110] See also 15:34.

[111] BDAG indicates that οὕτως in this context is equivalent to our colloquial, "Do you mean to tell me that there is not one person wise enough do settle a dispute between members?"

[112] Gk. ἀλλά.

[113] So ibid., 115.

[114] The Greek phrase is ἤδη μὲν [οὖν] ὅλως ἥττημα ὑμῖν ἐστιν.

[115] Gk. ὅλως.

[116] Ibid.

[117] Matt 18:15–17; cf. Rom 12:17; 1 Thess 5:15; 1 Pet 2:19–21. See Fee, *First Corinthians*, 241. Garland (*1 Corinthians*, 209–10) notes that while many appeal to the philosophical tradition, what Paul says here is the very core of the gospel.

their fellow believers.[118] What Paul says, in essence, is that, even if you have been wronged, you wrong others by taking them to court. It is far better to suffer wrong, to be cheated, than to tarnish the reputation of the gospel before the unbelieving world and to wrong another believer. How believers act in relation to other believers is a major emphasis in chaps. 8–14.[119]

**6:9–11** For the third time in his discussion of lawsuits Paul asks, "Do you not know?" What they should know in this instance is that "the wicked [or "wrongdoers" NIV2011] will not inherit the kingdom of God." Paul follows with a warning of deception and a vice list comparable to 5:10–11. First Corinthians 6:10 reiterates that those who are described by the list "will not inherit the kingdom of God." In 6:11 Paul reminds the Corinthians of what they used to be in contrast to what they now are by virtue of their conversion. But how do these three concluding verses relate to the subject of litigation among believers?

The most obvious function of 6:9–11 in Paul's argument is the continuing contrast between believer and unbeliever. Unbelievers will not inherit the kingdom. Believers, on the other hand, have been "washed," "sanctified," and "justified." But there is also a stern warning regarding deception (6:9).[120] That they bring their disputes before the unrighteous is shameful and unwise (6:1,5). Here, however, Paul raises the stakes even higher. To the previous vice list of six sins in 5:10–11 Paul adds four more.[121] The word translated "wicked" is the same word translated "ungodly" in 6:1.[122] The cognate verb occurs in 6:8,

---

[118] The Greek includes the emphatic conjunction plus the personal pronoun for emphasis, "*But you . . .*" (ἀλλὰ ὑμεῖς ἀδικεῖτε καὶ ἀποστερεῖτε).

[119] Fee (*First Corinthians*, 241) thinks that the use of the verb ἀποστερέω (to do wrong/defraud) indicates that the issue has to do with some sort of property or business dealings.

[120] Cf. 3:18, "Do not deceive yourselves. If any one of you thinks he is wise by the standards of this age, he should become a 'fool' so that he may become wise." The verb in 6:9 could be passive "Do not be deceived," or middle, "Do not deceive yourselves."

[121] The additional vices include three sexual sins (NIV, "adulterers, male prostitutes, homosexual offenders") and "thieves." Without question, the most discussed terms in recent times are the terms translated "male prostitutes" (μαλακός) and "homosexual offenders" (ἀρσενοκοίτης). The first term is used only here by Paul. It carries the meaning "soft" in its two occurrences in the Gospels (Matt 11:8; Luke 7:25). BDAG defines the occurrence in 1 Cor 6:9 as that "pertaining to being passive in a same-sex relationship, effeminate." The second term appears only here and in 1 Tim 1:10. Due to the rarity of the term, perhaps with no pre-history before Paul, the exact meaning is debated, but the word likely derives from the language of the LXX of Lev 18:22 and 20:13. NIV2011 translates both terms together with "nor men who have sex with men," with a note stating that the two Greek words "refer to the passive and active participants in homosexual acts." For a robust technical discussion on the contemporary homosexuality debate, see Thiselton, *First Corinthians*, 440–53. For a full book length discussion, see R. A. J. Gagnon, *The Bible and Homosexual Practice: Texts and Hermeneutics* (Nashville: Abingdon, 2001). See also D. O. Via and R. A. J. Gagnon, *Homosexuality and the Bible: Two Views* (Minneapolis: Fortress, 2003). The totality of the witness of Scripture on the issue of homosexuality is clear. Fee (*First Corinthians*, 244) comments, "For Paul's attitude toward homosexuality in general one need refer only to his own Jewish background with its abhorrence of such, plus his description of such activity (Rom 1:26–27)." Of course, there are other vices enumerated in 1 Cor 6:9–10 to which we must give equal attention.

[122] ἄδικος.

"acting unrighteously."[123] Thus, the wrongdoing of 6:8 takes a wider scope. By engaging in litigation, they themselves are acting unrighteously, just like those who will not inherit the kingdom. Their behavior is no different from the world. Instead of "becoming what they are" the Corinthians are "behaving like they were" (6:11). Paul's warning is not hypothetical but real. Those who persist in such behavior exclude themselves from the kingdom of God.[124] The kingdom of God consists of righteousness, joy, and peace in the Holy Spirit (Rom 14:17). Believers have been rescued from the dominion of darkness and brought into the kingdom of God's Son (Col 1:13).[125] The actions of believers should be worthy of those who belong to the kingdom (1 Thess 2:12).

While the function of 6:11 is to draw out the contrast between the Corinthians and the unrighteous who will not inherit the kingdom and to remind them of their status in Christ, in and of itself the statement is a remarkable testimony to the power of the gospel in conversion. Barrett comments, "Paul is not writing in merely literary or in imaginary terms, but addressing the greatest of miracles, a church of redeemed sinners, won from their old lifestyle by the power of God."[126] Similarly Morris: "The tremendous revolution brought about by the preaching of the gospel comes out in the quiet words, *And that is what some of you were*.[127] In Greek there is a threefold repetition of the strong adversative, "but,"[128] not captured in the NIV. This emphatic structure notes the contrast of their present condition and their past "and the consequent demand which their moral condition makes on them."[129] There is no theological significance in the sequence of the terms, "washed," "sanctified," and "justified" since similar terms appear in reverse order in 1:30.[130] The phrase, "You were washed," may include the imagery of baptism and its significance.[131] It seems that Paul is speaking of one event using three terms in order to convey his primary concern, namely, the transforming power and renewal of the gospel

---

123 ἀδικέω. HCSB, "You act unjustly."

124 Cf. Gal 5:21; Eph 5:5.

125 Note that Paul can speak both of the "kingdom of God" and the "kingdom of his Son."

126 Barrett, *First Corinthians*, 140–41.

127 Morris, *1 Corinthians*, 94.

128 Gk. ἀλλά. See NASB, "but you were washed, but you were sanctified, but you were justified in the name of the Lord Jesus Christ and in the Spirit of our God."

129 Robertson and Plummer, *First Corinthians*, 119.

130 "Righteousness" (δικαιοσύνη) and "holiness" (ἁγιασμός).

131 Barrett (*First Corinthians*, 141) thinks that Paul has baptism in mind since the formula "in the name of the Lord Jesus" is used, but "through the use of a non-technical word shows that it is the inward meaning rather than the outward circumstance of the rite that is important to Paul." Fee (*First Corinthians*, 246) agrees that is is possible but not certain that the term "washed" is an allusion to baptism. The verb itself is never used of baptism, but it is joined to it in Acts 22:16, the only other use of the term in the New Testament.

that occurs by the authority of Jesus and by the Spirit of God. Baptism most certainly depicts this reality.[132]

### 3. The Sanctity of the Body (6:12–20)

**[12]"Everything is permissible for me"—but not everything is beneficial. "Everything is permissible for me"—but I will not be mastered by anything. [13]"Food for the stomach and the stomach for food"—but God will destroy them both. The body is not meant for sexual immorality, but for the Lord, and the Lord for the body. [14]By his power God raised the Lord from the dead, and he will raise us also. [15]Do you not know that your bodies are members of Christ himself? Shall I then take the members of Christ and unite them with a prostitute? Never! [16]Do you not know that he who unites himself with a prostitute is one with her in body? For it is said, "The two will become one flesh." [17]But he who unites himself with the Lord is one with him in spirit.**

**[18]Flee from sexual immorality. All other sins a man commits are outside his body, but he who sins sexually sins against his own body. [19]Do you not know that your body is a temple of the Holy Spirit, who is in you, whom you have received from God? You are not your own; [20]you were bought at a price. Therefore honor God with your body.**

In this unit Paul returns to the topic of sexual immorality.[133] In 5:1–13 Paul addressed a case of incest. In 6:12–20 the main issue is prostitution (6:15–16). The command to flee sexual immorality in 6:18, however, is likely a summative command, taking into account the entire discussion from 5:1–6:20 with all forms of sexual immorality in view. In 7:2 the term *porneia* in the plural refers to the prevalence of immorality in Corinth.

The primary emphasis of 6:12–20 is stated succinctly in 6:13b, "The body is not meant for sexual immorality, but for the Lord, and the Lord for the body." As in the previous two sections (5:1–13; 6:1–11) Paul reminds them of things they know, or should know.[134] Here the warning against *porneia* is not cast in terms of exclusion from the kingdom of God, as in 6:9–10, but rather

---

[132] Regarding the trinitarian formulation of 6:11, Barrett (*First Corinthians*, 143) comments, "Trinitarian theology, at least in its New Testament form, did not arise out of speculation, but out of the fact that when Christians spoke of what God had done for them and in them they often found themselves obliged to use threefold language of this kind."

[133] The shift of topic from lawsuits (6:1–11) to prostitution (6:12–20) is abrupt. There is no linguistic connection (particle, conjunction) linking the two units. There is a thematic connection, however, with 5:1–13 and the mention of πορνεία in the vices lists of 5:10–11 and 6:9–10. The topic of πορνεία is relevant to the ensuing discussion in chap. 7 (see 7:2), along with the concept of "authority" (6:12; 7:4). Similarly, Thiselton (*First Corinthians*, 458) notes the common link of moral failures from 5:1–6:20. From a literary standpoint, 6:12–20 functions as a transition/hinge passage, relating significantly to what precedes and follows. See Collins (*First Corinthians*, 241–42) for an excellent literary analysis of the thematic connections between 6:12–20 and the letter as a whole.

[134] The question, "Do you not know?" occurs in 6:15,16,19. The question occurs a total of six times in chap. 6 alone.

rests on specific claims regarding the believer's body in relation to the Lord, culminating with the command to "honor God with your body" (6:20). Unlike 5:1–13 and 6:1–11, Paul levels no specific accusation against an individual or individuals in 6:12–20, leading some to question whether or not this passage addresses actual occurrences of Corinthians consorting with prostitutes.[135] If this is the case, then the argument would serve to establish a theological basis for further discussion on human sexuality in chap. 7.[136] However, even if Paul had no direct report of such aberrant behavior as he did in the case of incest and litigation, the tone of his argument framed as it is with the repeated question, "Do you not know?", demonstrates a very real and urgent concern.[137]

Another major interpretive issue of this passage has to do with the possibility that Paul is responding to Corinthian slogans. Many scholars see clear evidence in 6:12–20 of a two-way conversation between Paul and the Corinthians, meaning that some of the statements are possible expressions of Corinthian viewpoints. The ramifications for interpretation are significant since certain portions of the argument would be either Paul's assertion or the exact opposite, a Corinthian viewpoint that Paul seeks to correct or to qualify. Smith, in a recent article concerning the methodology of uncovering embedded slogans, defines a Corinthian slogan as "a motto [or similar expression that captures the spirit, purpose, or guiding principles] of a particular group or point of view at Corinth, or at least a motto that Paul was using to represent their position or attitudes."[138] Scholars debate the number of possible slogans, their source, what the slogan indicates concerning the belief structure of some in Corinth,

---

[135] See Robertson and Plummer, *First Corinthians*, 121; J. C. Hurd, *The Origin of 1 Corinthians* (New York: Seabury, 1965), 86, 90; B. Byrne, "Sinning Against One's Own Body: Paul's Understanding of the Sexual Relationship in 1 Corinthians 6:18," *CBQ* 45 (1983): 614–15.

[136] Collins (*First Corinthians*, 240) explains, "The issue of sexual intercourse with prostitutes was one that several of the philosophical moralists considered in their discussion of the relationship between law and morality. From this perspective it would appear that Paul chose a classic topos on the basis of which he could develop his discussion on sexuality with respect to the very issues the Corinthians had raised in their letter to him (7:1)."

[137] For a discussion of the possible historical scenarios that gave rise to Paul's instructions, see Ciampa and Rosner (*First Corinthians*, 246–49) who argue for the likelihood of temple prostitution as the background, to be distinguished from sacred prostitution, which bore ritual significance (condoned by the pagan priesthood and for the purpose of fertility). Temple prostitution involved the use of prostitutes associated with festive dinners on the temple precincts (cf. the association of feasting and immorality in Acts 15:20; Rev 2:14). Ciampa and Rosner conclude, "In the end it is not possible to be certain which type of prostitution Paul opposes in 1 Corinthians 6:12–20" but that "it was common in Jewish texts for idolatry and sexual immorality to be linked, not least because these two vices were considered to be the distinctive marks of the Gentiles" (249).

[138] J. E. Smith, "Slogans in 1 Corinthians," *BSac* 167 (2010): 82. Smith notes the more precise definition of Klein, Blomberg, and Hubbard, who describe slogans as Paul's quotations of "views held by some at Corinth that he wishes to dispute." See W. W. Klein, C. L. Blomberg, and R. L. Hubbard Jr., *Introduction to Biblical Interpretation*, 2nd ed. (Nashville: Thomas Nelson, 2003), 436.

and if it is possible through mirror-reading to determine the Corinthian theological error behind the supposed slogan.[139]

The structure of the passage supports the possibility of three slogans occurring at 6:12,13a, and 18b.[140] The first, "Everything is permissible for me,"[141] occurs twice in 6:12, each time qualified by strong contrast, "but not everything is beneficial" and "but I will not be mastered by anything." The second (lit.), "Foods for the belly and the belly for foods" (6:13a), may represent a distorted Corinthian view of the human body, to which Paul responds in 6:13b–18a. Some think the slogan includes the statement, "But God will destroy them both." The third purported slogan, "All other sins a man commits are outside his body," is less certain than the first two and more controversial. Either way, the interpretation of the statement is quite challenging. If not a slogan, then what does Paul mean by referring to sins committed "outside his body"? An increasingly popular view among the commentators is to identify this difficult verse as yet another instance of a Corinthian viewpoint related to the human body to which Paul responds in 6:18b. The parallel pattern of argumentation between 6:13–18a and 6:18b–20 supports this view. In each case a supposed slogan is followed by Paul's response, including the question, "Do you not know?", followed by a concluding command as follows:

Food for the stomach and the stomach for food. (slogan)
[But God will destroy them both]

(response)

The body is . . . meant . . . for the Lord . . . and the Lord for the body.
By his power God raised the Lord . . . and he will raise us also

Do you not know that your bodies are members of Christ himself?
Do you not know that he who joins himself to a prostitute is one with her in body?
But he who unites himself with the Lord is one with him in spirit.

Flee from sexual immorality (command)

All other sins a man commits are outside the body. (slogan)

(response)

But he who sins sexually sins against his own body.

Do you not know that
your body is a temple of the Holy Spirit
and
you are not your own; you were bought at a price.
Therefore, honor God with your body. (command)

[139] Garland (*1 Corinthians*, 219–22) is cautious regarding the possibility of accurately discerning Corinthian theological error through mirror-reading the text. In 6:12–20 Paul's emphasis falls on the gravity of the sin of *porneia*, and his argument provides a counter-cultural view of sexuality that lays the groundwork for arguments to follow.

[140] So also Thiselton, *First Corinthians*, 459.

[141] Other translations render, "All things are lawful for me" (so NASB, ESV).

In the end, one's view of the presence or absence of slogans does not obscure the clarity of Paul's teaching regarding the gravity of the sin of sexual immorality and the nature of the believer's body. The sanctity of the body is the key teaching of the passage as set forth through a number of positive affirmations: (1) The body is for the Lord and the Lord is for the body (6:13b). (2) The body is destined for resurrection through God's power (6:14). (3) The body is a member of Christ (6:15). (4) The one who is joined to the Lord is "one with him in spirit" (6:17). (5) The body is the temple of the Holy Spirit (6:19). (6) Christians must honor God with their bodies because they have been bought at a price (6:20). In sum, the theme of God's ownership of our bodies and the relational nature of embodied, physical existence, whereby we bring either shame or glory to God, dominates the passage. Throughout the argument Paul emphasizes both individual and corporate realities in his use of the term "body."[142] On the basis of Gen 2:24, Paul asserts that an individual joined to a prostitute constitutes "one body." Paul expands on the corporate identity of individual believers as members of Christ's body in chap. 12 (see esp. 12:12–14,27).

**6:12** We cannot know for certain the origin of the phrase, "Everything is permissible for me," or who was making the claim.[143] Even if a Corinthian slogan, the saying may have originated in Paul's own teaching regarding Christian freedom.[144] Either way Paul seems to affirm the pithy statement with two qualifications: "Not everything is beneficial" and "I will not be mastered by anything." Paul championed Christian freedom (Gal 5:1), but his view of freedom was always conditioned by the reality that

[142] The term σῶμα (body) occurs eight times in 6:12–20 and forty-six times in the letter. Scholars debate whether Paul uses the term holistically to denote the whole person or whether his emphasis in 6:12–20 is on the physical aspect of human life. On the holistic view see J. A. T. Robinson, *The Body: A Study in Pauline Theology* (London: SCM, 1966). In this view Paul uses anthropological terms such as "body" and "flesh" to refer to the whole person under different aspects. "Body," for example, is equated with "flesh" in 6:16. For a different perspective see R. H. Gundry, *Soma in Biblical Theology with Emphasis on Pauline Anthropology*, SNTSMS (Cambridge: Cambridge University Press, 1976). The body "is that part of man in and through which he performs concrete actions" (Gundry, 50). It is clear that Paul places great emphasis on embodied existence not only in this present passage but also in his discussion of the resurrection of the dead in chap. 15. If there is no resurrection of the dead, Paul argues, then those who have died have perished (15:18).

[143] Thiselton (*First Corinthians*, 460) states that, in spite of arguments to the contrary, "There can be no question that the initial clause of v. 12 represents a quotation used as a maxim by some or by many at Corinth." Barrett (*First Corinthians*, 144) thinks that the slogan was "the watchword of the gnostic party in Corinth. See also Bruce, *1 and 2 Corinthians*, 62; Conzelmann, *1 Corinthians*, 108–9. Fitzmyer (*First Corinthians*, 263) comments that it is difficult to know whether Paul is responding to a specific slogan (perhaps Stoic), but he knows that it is being bandied about in Corinth, which is sufficient reason for him to react to it.

[144] So Robertson and Plummer, *First Corinthians*, 121–22; Grosheide, *First Corinthians*, 144–45; Morris, *1 Corinthians*, 95; Fee, *First Corinthians*, 251–52; Thiselton, *First Corinthians*, 461. Dodd holds that 6:12 and 10:23 in their entirety are Paul's own words, though not a Corinthian slogan. See B. J. Dodd, "Paul's Paradigmatic 'I' and 1 Corinthians 6:12," *JSNT* 59 (1995): 39–58.

believers are "in Christ," under the Lord's authority, and exist in relation to others in community.[145] The word translated "beneficial" recurs in the repetition of the same phrase in 10:23 with reference to food sacrificed to idols and also in 12:7 with reference to the manifestations of the Spirit for the "common good" of all in the church.[146] Paul offers himself as the example of one who does what benefits others for the sake of the gospel (see 9:19–23; 10:31–33). The second qualification, "I will not be mastered by anything," indicates that one's actions in the name of so-called freedom can have the exact opposite effect of enslavement.[147] Fee suggests that the notion of being brought under the authority of another ties in to the issue raised in 6:15–16 and should be understood in light of 7:4. In 6:15–16 Paul refers specifically to being brought under the authority of the prostitute. Fee explains, "That is, by being joined to her in *porneia* the believer constitutes someone else, outside of Christ, as the unlawful lord over one's body."[148] In 7:4, husbands and wives each have "authority" over the body of their spouse in the lawful union of marriage. Robertson and Plummer suggest that the first qualification addresses the effect an action will have on others and the second addresses the effect it will have on oneself.[149] They further suggest that 6:12–13 forms a preface to the subject of *porneia* in order to show that it is not one of those things that may or may not be lawful according to circumstances. It is always outside the bounds of Christian liberty. "While many things are permissible and become wrong only if indulged to the extent that they are harmful to others or ourselves, fornication is not a legitimate use of the body. . . ."[150]

---

[145] Collins (*First Corinthians*, 241) notes, "The Corinthian slogan 'all things are lawful' (v. 12) is echoed in 10:23. The inclusio that is thus formed encompasses a multifaceted and complex development of thought in which Paul deals with the issue of human freedom." On the issue of one's rights in the context of freedom, see especially 8:9, 9:4–18.

[146] Gk. συμφέρω. The cognate adjective, σύμφορος, translated "good," occurs in 7:35 and 10:33.

[147] Cf. John 8:34, "Jesus replied, 'I tell you the truth, everyone who sins is a slave to sin.'"

[148] Fee, *First Corinthians*, 253.

[149] Robertson and Plummer, *First Corinthians*, 122.

[150] Ibid., 123. Garland (*1 Corinthians*, 227–28), following Dodd ("Paul's Paradigmatic 'I'), does not think that the phrase, "Everything is permissible for me" was a Corinthian slogan used theologically to justify certain behaviors: "It is more plausible that Paul cites a familiar notion about freedom found in the Corinthian culture and recasts it in Christian terms than that he parrots the arguments of sensualists in the church to repudiate them" (228). Garland thinks it unlikely that they could have so misconstrued Paul's teaching to proclaim such conduct permissible (cf. 5:9). Paul's response, however, is a "theological" response. We should not downplay the extent to which the church could misconstrue Paul's teaching. It is not hard to imagine, given the realities of first-century Greek culture, that Paul's teaching could become warped rather quickly, and thus the need for such lengthy and extensive communication with this church. In his letter to the Galatians, for example, Paul marveled at how quickly they turned from his original teaching and succumbed to legalism (Gal 1:6–7). Likewise, the Corinthians may have quickly adopted aberrant views of Christian freedom. See also the critique of Garland in J. Murphy-O'Connor, *Keys to First Corinthians: Revisiting the Major Issues* (Oxford: Oxford University Press, 2009), 24–26. In sum, there are

**6:13–14** The phrase, "food for the stomach and the stomach for food," if reflecting a Corinthian slogan/point of view, indicates a particular perspective of the human body that needs correcting in light of Jesus' resurrection and the destiny of the believer's body. It is commonly argued that the Corinthians believed that sexual activity was a mere bodily function like eating food, which led to the conclusion that normal bodily functions have no abiding significance and are therefore of no ultimate consequence. Thiselton contends that the slogan extends to the phrase, "but God will destroy them both."[151] This view surmises that the purpose of the slogan was to articulate a sense of distance between the deeds done in the body and a supposed "spiritual" level of life, a dualism foreign to Paul's thought. The logic that Paul employs in this section on the body receives fuller explication in 15:12–58.[152] Fee likewise thinks Paul's words indicate a very tight argument against the Corinthians' position about the human body.[153] Robertson and Plummer raise the possibility that the Corinthians have confused what Paul distinguishes, food and fornication (see Acts 15:23–29). Garland, who is far more cautious about Corinthian slogans, views the saying, "food for the stomach and the stomach for food," as a maxim that Paul cites in order to refer to the order of creation. Food is for the belly and will be destroyed, but the body is for the Lord but will not be destroyed.[154] The analogy simply demonstrates Christ's lordship over the believer's body[155] and the gravity of the sin of *porneia*. Paul argues that "they should live in ways congruent with who they are."[156] In the final analysis, therefore, it is possible, but not certain, that the Corinthians were correlating "the belly and food" and the "body and sex" in some way. Either way, if a correlation exists between the belly and food as long as earthly life lasts, there is no such correlation between the "body" and "fornication." The body was made in order to become a member of Christ who lived and died in order to redeem it. The body will not be destroyed but is destined for resurrection.[157] Jesus has as his purpose and destiny to dwell in and glorify the body (Rom 8:23) that is united to him

three options: (1) These are Paul's own words which the Corinthians have misconstrued. (2) This is a Corinthian slogan. (3) Paul cites a familiar notion within the culture, recasts in Christian terms, and adopts for his own purposes.

[151] A. C. Thiselton argues this in an earlier article ("Realised Eschatology at Corinth," *NTS* 24 [1978]: 510–26) and maintains this view in his more recent commentary (*First Corinthians*, 462). So also J. Murphy-O'Connor, "Corinthian Slogans in 1 Cor 6:12–20," *CBQ* 40 (1978): 391–96; Collins, *First Corinthians*, 245; Ciampa and Rosner, *First Corinthians*, 254.

[152] Thiselton, *First Corinthians*, 463. According to Thiselton, the "belly" (NIV, "stomach"; Gk. κοιλία) "stands as a kind of metonym for all things physical and transient."

[153] Fee, *First Corinthians*, 253.

[154] Garland, *1 Corinthians*, 230. So also V. P. Furnish, *The Theology of the First Letter to the Corinthians*, New Testament Theology (Cambridge: Cambridge University Press, 1999), 57–58.

[155] Cf. Rom 6:12–13,19; 12:1; Phil 1:20.

[156] Garland, *1 Corinthians*, 231.

[157] Robertson and Plummer, *First Corinthians*, 123.

through the Spirit (6:17).[158] Ciampa and Rosner comment that Paul was not dealing with an overrealized eschatology on this issue but rather "an underestimation of eschatology."[159] The fact that the body will be raised from the dead has enormous implications for present behavior. God will do away with food and the stomach, but God raised up Jesus and he will also raise believers by his power (cf. 15:43). The destiny of the body stands in direct contrast to the destiny of "food and the stomach." The latter will be destroyed, but the body will be raised from the dead. The body was not meant for dishonorable purposes but rather for God's glory (6:20). As the argument continues, Paul shows that there is the closest possible correlation between Christ and those who belong to him. What happens to Christ, happens to those incorporated into Christ (cf. Rom 6:4; 8:11; 1 Cor 15:20).

**6:15–17** Following the emphasis on resurrection in 6:14 and in response to the use of prostitutes, Paul constructs a two-part argument in support of the claim that "the body is for the Lord" (6:13). Each part of the argument is introduced by the question, "Do you not know?"[160] First, what they should know is that every believer is a member of Christ,[161] which is why sexual vice is so unthinkable for the Christian, even more so since the prostitute was often associated with the pagan temple.[162] From the basic premise that the believer is a member of Christ, Paul draws the inference in the form of a question, "Shall I then take the members of Christ and unite them with a prostitute? Never!"[163] Union with a harlot robs Christ of one of his members.[164] That a believer might join himself to a prostitute is unthinkable for Paul. Garland suggests that what Paul leaves unstated in the analogy is that the prostitute represents a different cosmic body. "The prostitute is not conceived of here as an individual person but as a confederate of evil, a member of the dark, death-dealing forces at war against Christ."[165]

---

[158] Ibid., 124.

[159] Ciampa and Rosner, *First Corinthians*, 255.

[160] Fee (*First Corinthians*, 257) suggests a chiasm: A—Their bodies are members of Christ; B—Therefore, they may not be members of a prostitute; B'—Joined to a prostitute, they become one body with her; A'—Joined to Christ they become one S/spirit with him. As in 6:3–4, the question, "Do you not know?", appears in successive verses.

[161] Gk. μέλος (member). The term occurs thirteen times in chap. 12 (12:12,14,18–20,22,25–27).

[162] So Morris, *1 Corinthians*, 97–98.

[163] The NIV translation, "Never!" in Greek is μὴ γένοιτο, an expression of strong disagreement, "May it never be!" The expression is common in Romans and Galatians (see Rom 3:4,6,31; 6:2,15; 7:7,13; 9:14; 11:1,11; Gal 2:17; 3:21; 6:14).

[164] So Robertson and Plummer, *First Corinthians*, 125.

[165] Garland, *1 Corinthians*, 233. Ciampa and Rosner (*First Corinthians*, 258) comment, "He does not have in mind the prostitute as an individual, but, opposite the corporate Christ, she appears as a symbol of that which is inimical to the sanctified status of God's people. Whether of the temple or secular variety, the prostitute here is a symbol of darkness and defilement. It is an argument from the incompatibility of two realms. Paul uses the same logic in 1 Corinthians 10:14–22 and 2 Corinthians 6:14–7:1. In both of these texts that which is opposed to God is named as the

Paul does not actually say that this sin severs all ties with Christ, but some think he implies it.[166]

The second stage of Paul's argument expands on 6:15 and implies that the nature of the sexual act was something known and accepted by the Corinthians based on the revelation of Scripture. Sexual union in and of itself is not incompatible with union with Christ (see 7:1–7), even in the case of the believer married to the unbeliever (7:12–16). Here Paul has in mind union with a prostitute.[167] The NIV translates the participle in 6:16 in the middle voice, "he who unites himself."[168] The basis of Paul's claim is Gen 2:24, "They will become one flesh."[169] In the sexual act two people become one, forming an enduring bond with one another. Paul makes the case in 7:4 that, in the marriage relationship, one's body belongs to the other. The Scriptural quote is introduced not by "it is written" but by a verb that could imply either "God says," or "it says,"[170] referring to Scripture.[171] By way of contrast, the one who joins himself to the Lord is one spirit with him. One might expect Paul to continue with "body" language, but the union between Christ and believers is of an altogether different kind than the union created by the sexual act, and this union can only be expressed in terms of the Spirit. Thus, we should probably see the NIV's "spirit" as a reference to the Holy Spirit's role in effecting union with Christ.[172] Grosheide notes that what is called into being by the sin of fornication is contrasted with what presently exists for members of the church. Paul refers to the glory of the church, and by doing so, he shows how great the sin

demonic. Here in chap. 6 the worry is not explicitly fellowship with the demonic, but rather the notion of contamination and uncleanness, a concern that is raised again in 1 Corinthians 7:14–15."

[166] Cf. B. N. Fisk, "*Porneuein* as Body Violation: The Unique Nature of Sexual Sin in 1 Corinthians 6.18," *NTS* 42 (1996): 554.

[167] So also Fee (*First Corinthians*, 259–60). The word translated "unite" (κολλάω) is often used in the LXX in a religious sense (see Deut 6:13; 10:20; 28:60; 1 Kgs 11:2; 2 Kgs 1:18; 3:3; 18:6). In Gen 2:24, the word is the compound προσκολλάω. This term, likewise, is used in a religious sense in the LXX (Deut 11:22, "If you carefully observe all these commands I am giving you to follow—to love the LORD your God, to walk in all his ways and to hold fast to him—").

[168] Gk. κολλώμενος. In this case a "gnomic present," referring to what is true in all circumstances. As often as and whenever a person has intercourse with a harlot, he becomes one flesh with her (so Grosheide, *First Corinthians*, 149). The participle could also be passive, "The one who is joined."

[169] See also Matt 19:5. Ciampa and Rosner (*First Corinthians*, 259) note that the Genesis text is used also in Mal 2:15–16 to prohibit divorce.

[170] Gk. φημί.

[171] Ciampa and Rosner (*First Corinthians*, 259–60) suggest that the function of the scriptural quotation serves not only to demonstrate the gravity of sex with a prostitute but also to draw attention to the "spiritual marriage" between the believer and Christ (see Rom 7:2–3; 1 Cor 7:32–35; 2 Cor 11:2; Eph 5:32).

[172] So Fee, *First Corinthians*, 260; Thiselton, *First Corinthians*, 469; Garland, *1 Corinthians*, 235; Ciampa and Rosner, *First Corinthians*, 261. On believers being "one spirit" with Christ see Rom 8:9–11; 1 Cor 15:44–45; 2 Cor 3:17. Note also the Spirit's role in chap. 12 in Paul's further development of the concept of the "body of Christ" (esp. 12:12–14).

of harlotry is and how imperative it is to hate this sin.[173] The language of Jas 4:4 captures Paul's sentiments: "You adulterous people, don't you know that friendship with the world is hatred toward God? Anyone who chooses to be a friend of the world becomes an enemy of God."

**6:18–20** In 6:18 Paul interjects the command, "Flee from sexual immorality." The command is paralleled in 10:14, "Flee from idolatry." Most commentators draw attention to the present tense of the imperative, which would carry the sense of habitually fleeing from this sin. It is also probable that the sin to be fled is much broader than the mention of prostitution in the immediate context.[174] There is no other response possible in light of the gravity of the sin and the propensity of humans to entrap themselves in it. Robertson and Plummer comment that the lack of grammatical connection to the previous statement marks the urgency of the situation.[175] The same command appears in Jewish literature, and it is often suggested that Paul may have in mind the story of Joseph's flight from Potiphar's wife in Gen 39.[176]

What follows the command to flee from immorality is the notoriously difficult phrase, "All other sins a man commits are outside the body," which, broadly speaking, is to be understood either as another Corinthian slogan to which Paul responds, or a further line of argument on why Christians should avoid sexual immorality. The word "other" is added for clarification in translation.[177] The Greek is unqualified, "Every sin which a man does is outside the body . . ." Nowhere else does Paul speak of sins "outside the body"[178] in contrast to a sin "against the body." What does Paul mean and to whose body does he refer? Is this the Christian's body, the body of anyone generally who commits this sin, or the body of Christ?[179] The view that this is another Corinthian slogan suggests that the statement is yet another Corinthian viewpoint concerning the nature of the physical body (cf. 6:13) that is untenable.[180] Paul

---

[173] Grosheide, *First Corinthians*, 150.

[174] So also Ciampa and Rosner (*First Corinthians*, 262). The command is "an apt concluding appeal to chaps. 5–6, the injunction is a blanket condemnation of all illicit sexual relations."

[175] Robertson and Plummer, *First Corinthians*, 127.

[176] *Testament of Reuben* 5.5, which contains the same phrase, also depends on the story of Joseph. See B. S. Rosner, "A Possible Quotation of Test. Reuben 5:5 in 1 Corinthians 6:18a," *JTS* 43 (1992): 123–27. For further warnings against immorality see esp. Prov 5:3 and 6:23–7:27. Ciampa and Rosner (*First Corinthians*, 263) note also that the *Testament of Reuben* mentions that Joseph "glorified God" (8.5) and that he was "one in whom is the Spirit of God" (41.38). Thus the *Testament of Reuben* may indicate a traditional interpretation of Gen 39 that influenced Paul.

[177] Matthew 12:31 is often pointed out as a parallel, "And so I tell you, every sin and blasphemy will be forgiven men, but the blasphemy against the Spirit will not be forgiven." The implication is "every *other* sin . . ."

[178] The phrase "out of the body" (ἐκτὸς τοῦ σώματος) occurs in 2 Cor 12:2.

[179] On the view that Paul refers to the corporate Body of Christ, see R. Kempthorne, "Incest and the Body of Christ: A Study of 1 Corinthians vi. 12–20," *NTS* 14 (1967): 568–74.

[180] Among the recent commentators who take this view, see Collins, Thiselton, and Fitzmyer. For a listing of the different positions taken on this prior to Collins, see Fisk, "*Porneuein*," 542–43.

responds to their erroneous view with the statement, "but he who sins sexually sins against his own body." Others are convinced that the entire verse is Paul's own formulation and what he means is that sexual sin is either more damaging than other sins or unique in kind, qualitatively different from other sins, that is, it is distinctive and worse than other sins in some way.[181] Both views have to contend with the meaning of "sinning against his own body." The context suggests that Paul has in mind the incompatibility of the "one body" constituted by the unlawful sexual union with the believer's union with Christ (6:15). Furthermore, the body is the "temple of the Holy Spirit" (6:19). Sexual immorality is a sin against Christ and a violation of the sanctity of the temple.[182]

The final two verses, therefore, further explain "sinning against the body." Already in 3:16–17 Paul has identified the Corinthian church corporately as the temple of God, the dwelling place of the Spirit. For this reason they are holy. In 6:19, the emphasis is on the believer's individual body, though incorporated into Christ's body. Paul's wording in 6:19–20 stresses that the Holy Spirit is a gift, "whom you have received from God" (cf. 4:7). It also stresses God's ownership of the temple: "You are not your own; you were bought at a price" (cf. 7:23). Thus, this unit concludes in similar fashion as the previous unit (6:11) by reminding the Corinthians of the realities of their salvation. Verses 19b–20a provide yet another metaphor depicting salvation as redemption from the slave market.[183] Klein sees a possible allusion to Hos 3:1–3 that describes Hosea's redemption of his wife out of her bondage back to a life of wholeness: "Similarly, in 1 Corinthians 6 the audience has been redeemed out of bondage to sin (including licentiousness) to a life in which sexual sin was unconscionable."[184] The final command to "honor God with your body" is the positive complement of the warning in 6:18 to "flee from immorality." In 8:1–11:1 Paul will take up another urgent issue in Corinth, namely, idolatry. His exhortation is the same: "Flee from idolatry" (10:14) and "do it all for the glory of God" (10:31).

### 4. Issues of Marriage and Singleness (7:1–40)

The phrase, "now for the matters you wrote about" (7:1) introduces a new topic and indicates Paul's response to matters raised by the Corinthians in a letter to him.[185] Although we cannot know for sure, the Corinthian letter to Paul may have been written in response to Paul's previous letter mentioned in 5:9. It is probable that Fortunatus, Stephanus, and Achaicus (16:8,17) delivered the letter from the Corinthians to Paul. There is a strong scholarly consensus that the

[181] Cf. Ibid.

[182] See also Byrne, "Sinning Against One's Own Body."

[183] Cf. 1:30, Christ is our "redemption."

[184] G. L. Klein, "Hosea 3:1–3—Background to 1 Cor 6:19b–20?," *CTR* 3 (1988): 374.

[185] For an overview of the various approaches to the issues raised in 1 Cor 7, see Thiselton, *First Corinthians*, 487–97.

recurring formula translated, "Now for,"[186] identifies matters raised by the Corinthians in their letter to Paul (see 7:25; 8:1; 12:1; 16:1; and 16:12). However, as noted in the introductory discussion of the letter's structure and main themes, not everything in the second half of the letter is a response to a Corinthian question since Paul refers again in 11:18 to what he has heard and there is no such introductory formula introducing the topic of head coverings (11:2–16) or the lengthy discussion of the resurrection (15:1–58). Mitchell has set forth arguments that there is no evidence that the formulaic expression, "Now about," functioned as an answering formula in the ancient world and that it may only indicate movement from one topic to another.[187] Even within chap. 7 each issue raised by Paul may not relate specifically to a Corinthian question. Winter, for example, suggests that 7:2–5 is Paul's response to their question but 7:6–24 is Paul's own argument.[188] Nevertheless, since Paul attaches the formula in 7:1 to the mention of what they wrote, it is highly probable that the other occurrences do, in fact, relate to their written correspondence. That Paul's response to their letter is mixed with his response to oral reports and other material only means that he has shaped the whole letter thematically. Chapter 7 logically follows the main emphases of the previous two chapters but especially the previous unit (6:12–20) in the mention of the two key terms *porneia* (7:2) and "body" (7:4).[189] The Corinthians' questions provide Paul an opportunity to address human sexuality positively, that is, how to honor God with the body (6:20).[190]

---

[186] Gk. περὶ δὲ. NASB, "Now concerning."

[187] M. M. Mitchell, "Concerning περὶ δὲ in 1 Corinthians," *NovT* 31 (1989): 229–56. Mitchell challenges three widespread assumptions in scholarship on 1 Corinthians, that (1) each περί δέ must introduce a topic contained in the Corinthians' letter, (2) Paul would only introduce a topic with this formula, and (3) Paul responds to the Corinthians according to the order of their letter. Mitchell claims that the περί δέ formula occurring in a wide variety of ancient Greek texts functions as a topic marker and does not, in itself, indicate a response to information received in a letter (232–33). "What we can say definitely is that each of the topics Paul introduces with the formula περί δέ (virgins, idol meat, spiritual things/people, the collection and Apollos) is readily known to both the Corinthians and Paul *from some element of their shared experience*." Mitchell concludes that the formula still "remains an important starting point for the investigation of the composition and rhetorical structure of the letter" (256).

[188] See B. W. Winter, "1 Corinthians 7:6–7: A Caveat and a Framework for 'The Sayings' in 7:8–24," *TynBul* 48 (1997): 57–65. Winter notes the repetition of "I say," in 7:6,8,10, and 12, each of which introduces various topics, such as issues of singleness and marriage in relation to widows and the unmarried (7:8–9), separation and reconciliation (7:9–10), and marriage and divorce for those married to unbelievers (7:11–16). Then, before addressing the next issue raised by the Corinthians in 7:25, Paul repeats a major emphasis of his own traditional teaching common to all churches, which addresses ethnic and social identity as the providential oversight of God (7:17–24). Just as the gifts of singleness or marriedness are given by God, Paul seems to imply the same for social and ethnic markers.

[189] Furthermore, the issue of authority in 7:4 has already been raised in 6:12 and the emphasis on believers "belonging to" Christ/God is conveyed again in the phrase "You were bought at a price" (7:23; cf. 6:20). The mention of Satan occurs for the second time in the letter (7:5; cf. 5:5).

[190] Ciampa and Rosner (*First Corinthians*, 266) give 7:1–40 the heading, "Affirmation of Sexual Purity: Glorify God with Your Bodies."

The content of chap. 7 has to do with issues of marriage and singleness, which may have had its roots in controversy within the church at Corinth or that may reflect Paul's own discernment of the needs of the community.[191] Commentators often rightly point out that in reading this section we must be mindful that Paul does not attempt a comprehensive discussion of marriage and related issues but rather responds theologically and pastorally to actual situations. We err on the assumption that Paul unloads his whole theology of marriage and singleness in chap. 7. On the other hand, however, it is also the case that Paul provides insight into matters not treated elsewhere in Scripture, such as the situation of a believer married to a nonbeliever (7:12–16).

As with other portions of the letter, identifying the overarching theme and the theology that informs Paul's discussion is an important interpretive step. The centerpiece of the chapter is 7:17–24, which sets forth the principle "remain as you are" (7:17,20,24), that governs the whole argument in 7:1–40 (see 7:2,8,10,11,12–16,26–27,37 and 40).[192] For the most part the structure of chap. 7 is straightforward. In 7:1–7 Paul advises married couples to maintain sexual relations. In 7:8–16 Paul continues to apply the core principle of "remain as you are" to various situations: to the unmarried, the married, and the believer married to the unbeliever. In 7:25–40 Paul addresses the issue of those contemplating marriage, whether never married or widowed.

### *(1) General Principles Concerning Marriage (7:1–7)*

**1Now for the matters you wrote about: It is good for a man not to marry. 2But since there is so much immorality, each man should have his own wife, and each woman her own husband. 3The husband should fulfill his marital duty to his wife, and likewise the wife to her husband. 4The wife's body does not belong to her alone but also to her husband. In the same way, the husband's body does not belong to him alone but also to his wife. 5Do not deprive each other except by mutual consent and for a time, so that you may devote yourselves to prayer. Then come together again so that Satan will not tempt you because of your lack of self-control. 6I say**

[191] Fee (*First Corinthians,* 269) thinks there was considerable pressure within the church to abstain from marriage altogether or to dissolve marriages. One of the intriguing aspects of 1 Cor 7 is the polarity of perspective on sexual matters in comparison with chaps. 5 and 6. How is it that 5:1–5 and 6:12–20 give the impression of a libertine faction in the Corinthian church whereas 7:1–7 seems to indicate exactly the opposite, an ascetic view advocating abstention from all sexual relations? Robertson and Plummer (*First Corinthians,* 132) comment, "Having in previous chapters warned the Corinthians against the danger of Gentile licentiousness, he here makes a stand against a spirit of Gentile asceticism." Garland (*1 Corinthians*, 251) notes, "Suffice it to say that an ascetic attitude toward sexuality was as much part of the intellectual landscape as was licentiousness, and it was attractive to many for a variety of reasons." Will Deming relates Paul's arguments closely to the "Stoic-Cynic marriage debate," which presupposed that marriage involved a man in weighty responsibilities. See W. Deming, *Paul on Marriage and Celibacy: the Hellenistic Background of 1 Corinthians 7*, 2nd ed. (Grand Rapids: Eerdmans, 2004).

[192] Commentators often note a chiastic arrangement of the chapter with 7:17–24 at the center. So C. L. Blomberg, who notes, "Paul's central point stresses that believers should not be in a hurry to change their marital status" (*1 Corinthians*, NIVAC [Grand Rapids: Zondervan, 1994], 132).

**this as a concession, not as a command. [7]I wish that all men were as I am. But each man has his own gift from God; one has this gift, another has that.**

The interpretation of 7:1–7 turns on how one understands the statement in 7:1b translated by the NIV, "It is good for a man not to marry." Other translations, such as the NASB render the Greek more literally, "It is good for a man not to touch a woman."[193] The more recent NIV2011 puts the sentence in quotation marks, more explicitly advocating the view that this is yet another Corinthian slogan: "It is good for a man not to have sexual relations with a woman."[194] Commentators concur that the sentence in and of itself is a euphemism for sexual relations. But what does it mean and to whom do we attribute the statement? Is this Paul's own personal view in response to a Corinthian question, or is the statement a Corinthian position (slogan) that receives Paul's limited approval with sharp qualifications to follow in 7:2–5? If the NIV (1984) translation is correct and these are Paul's own words, what could he possibly mean by affirming the goodness of the unmarried state? Does he mean acceptable, morally superior, or better (a comparative sense)? Only five verses earlier (6:16) Paul drew attention to the one-flesh relationship by appealing to Gen 2:24, which follows closely upon Gen 2:18 that expressly says, "It is not good for the man to be alone." Genesis 2 again comes into play in 11:2–16 as a key passage in Paul's discussion of husbands and wives and the glory of God (esp. 11:7–12). Paul explicitly affirms the marriage relationship in Eph 5:22–33 (cf. Col 3:18–19), which is analogous to the relationship of Christ and the church. In 7:12–16 Paul affirms the sanctity of the marriage of a believer to an unbeliever. Clearly Paul is not against marriage, but does he think that the unmarried state is better under certain conditions, or is he responding to and correcting some in Corinth who espoused celibacy, even within marriage, or could the phrase "to touch a woman" mean something else in the culture of Roman Corinth?

How one reads 7:1 affects the interpretation of 7:2, whether Paul is advising to "get married" or to maintain sexual relations within marriage "since there is so much immorality." In 7:3–5 Paul speaks directly to the issues of the conjugal obligations of husband and wife within marriage and self-control. In 7:6–7 Paul clarifies that his advice is a concession, not a commandment. But does the concession refer back to 7:5 and the consent to withdraw from sexual relations for a time of prayer? Does the concession refer to marriage in 7:1–2? Or does the concession point forward to 7:6–7, "I wish that all men were as I am." Or could the term translated "concession" mean something different altogether?[195]

[193] Gk. *καλὸν ἀνθρώπῳ γυναικὸς μὴ ἅπτεσθαι.*

[194] Similarly the HCSB, "It is good for a man not to have relations with a woman." The HCSB also puts it in quotation marks. Versions that do not place in quotation marks read as a teaching of Paul, but one might still understand the statement as reflecting a Corinthian point of view. Either way the reader is still left with discerning the meaning of the statement.

[195] Gk. *συγγνώμη*. The only occurrence of the term in the New Testament.

**7:1–2** There are two primary lines of interpretation of the claim in 7:1b that it is good for a man not to touch a woman and the command that follows in 7:2 that each man must have his own wife and each wife her own husband.[196] Some read 7:1b as Paul's own words reflecting his position on marriage generally in response to a Corinthian question regarding its advisability. The question may have had its roots in a dispute between libertine and ascetic elements in the church. In this reading, Paul agrees that to abstain from marriage altogether is good[197] but recognizes that the rampancy of immorality (7:2; cf. 5:1–5; 6:9–10,12–20) and the reality of the human condition requires concessions, so he encourages marriage. Robertson and Plummer clarify, "In a society so full of temptations, he advises marriage, not as the lesser of two evils, but as a necessary safeguard against evil. So far from marriage being wrong, as some Corinthians were thinking, it was for very many people a duty."[198] Support for the view that "good" (7:1b) is a Pauline term is its similar use in 7:8, "It is good for them to remain as I am," and 7:26, "Because of the present crisis, it is good for you to remain as you are."[199] It does not follow in this interpretation of 7:1–2 that the married state is not good, only that the unmarried state, as Paul preferred, is commendable. Morris, who thinks that the NIV translation of 7:1b is correct, "It is good for a man not to marry," explains that "Paul's view is that the unmarried are freer to serve God, since they are without the cares attendant on the married state (7:32ff)."[200] This view is often labeled the "traditional" view.

Critics of the traditional view point out that Paul himself, although celibate, was not an ascetic (Col 2:20–21; 1 Tim 4:3) and the idea that marriage might be thought of as a sin (7:28,36) can only express a Corinthian point of view. The term "good" could be a Corinthian term, much the same as "wisdom" in chaps. 1–3, that Paul uses with his own meaning.[201] As with the slogans in 6:12–20, Paul is responding to their perspective, not setting forth his own beliefs per se. He may agree with the Corinthian sentiment to a point, but he sharply qualifies their position (7:2–5). The phrase "not to touch a woman" indicates celibacy, but it does not signify "not to marry." In other words, some in Corinth espoused celibacy as an ideal, even within marriage. To the Corinthian catchphrase, "It is good for a man not to touch a woman," Paul responds, "Yes, but not within

[196] There are, of course, different nuances within the two views relating to how the interpreter reconstructs the historical setting. See below on Ciampa and Rosner's recent proposal for the meaning of 7:1b and the attendant historical reconstruction.

[197] Some interpreters think that the Greek term καλός has a comparative sense meaning "better" in this context. However, since Paul uses the comparative in 7:9 (κρείττων), it is unlikely that "good" has a comparative sense here. Note the "good"/"better" contrast in 7:8–9.

[198] Robertson and Plummer, *First Corinthians*, 133.

[199] Conzelmann, *1 Corinthians*, 115n10.

[200] Morris, *1 Corinthians*, 102. See also Grosheide, *First Corinthians*, 155; Conzelmann, *1 Corinthians*, 115.

[201] So Garland, *1 Corinthians*, 249.

marriage." Verse 1b is a slogan that expresses a viewpoint that Paul will accept only with certain modifications under certain conditions.[202] Thus, in 7:2, Paul does not advise to "get married," but rather he instructs the already married to maintain sexual relations within marriage and then elaborates in 7:3–5. The imperative of 7:5 reflects what is actually going on in Corinth; marriage partners are depriving one another from sexual relations. The verb "to have" in 7:2 means "to enjoy sexual possession of someone," as it does in 5:1. The verb can refer to the already married in certain contexts (7:12,13,29), but the sense of the term in 7:2 does not seem to indicate the meaning, "to acquire a wife." In this view, Paul strongly qualifies the Corinthian position of 7:1b. Celibacy is commendable for those who choose it, but it is not allowable in marriage. This gives due weight to the imperative verbs. Paul is not commanding marriage, but he is commanding that those who are married maintain their sexual relationship. Paul does not explicitly command, "Get married," as he does in 7:9. This view does not change the force of the causal phrase at the beginning of 7:2, "Since there is so much immorality," but it does give it a different focus.[203] Failure to maintain sexual relations among married couples increases the temptation to engage in illicit relationships. Thiselton notes an increasing consensus toward this view, both in commentaries and in specialist monographs.[204]

Against both the traditional interpretation and the new scholarly consensus, Ciampa and Rosner have recently articulated yet another perspective that revolves around a refined understanding of the euphemism in 7:1, "It is good for a man not to touch a woman."[205] In sum, their view holds, along with the consensus, that the statement is a Corinthian slogan, but, against the consensus,

---

[202] Thiselton, *First Corinthians*, 498.

[203] In Greek the term for "immorality" is plural, τὰς πορνείας. The NASB translates "because of immoralities." Some suggest that the plural is used to refer to specific cases of immorality mentioned in the immediate context (so Robertson and Plummer, *First Corinthians*, 132; Grosheide, *First Corinthians*, 155). Fee (*First Corinthians*, 278) thinks that the plural refers specifically to the cases of prostitution mentioned in 6:12–20, that it is even arguable that some husbands are being deprived of sexual relations and are going to the prostitutes. Thiselton (*First Corinthians*, 501) concurs that the use of the definite article does not refer to "fornication" generally but points to specific cases of immorality identified in 5:1–5; 6:9–10, and 6:12–20.

[204] Thiselton, *First Corinthians*, 498. For the articulation of this view in recent scholarship see Fee, *First Corinthians*, 274–77; Hays, *First Corinthians*, 113–14; Garland, *1 Corinthians*, 249–54. For a critique of the new "consensus view" and a partial defense of the traditional reading of 7:1–2, see C. C. Caragounis, "'Fornication' and 'Concession'?: Interpreting 1 Cor 7, 1–7," in *The Corinthian Correspondence,* ed. R. Bieringer (Leuven: University Press, 1996), 543–59. Caragounis especially challenges Fee's assumptions that "to touch a woman" cannot signify marriage and that "to have" never means to "acquire a wife." Paul addresses the entire church, not Corinthian ascetics. Furthermore, the term πορνεία in 7:2 is used metonymically of the desire for sex. What Paul means is, "but on account of the sexual urges let each man have his own wife" (551), an idea identical to 7:9. Caragounis rightly challenges some of Fee's linguistic assumptions but the consensus view still remains a viable interpretive option in context.

[205] R. Ciampa, "Revisiting the Euphemism in 1 Corinthians 7:1," *JSNT* 31 (2009): 325–38. For a more complete discussion, see Ciampa and Rosner, *First Corinthians*, 267–77.

the statement does not indicate a Corinthian commitment to celibacy[206] but a rejection of certain kinds of sexual activity, including sex with one's spouse motivated by pleasure or passion rather than for the sole purpose of procreation. This conclusion is based on a detailed study of twenty-five occurrences of the euphemism "to touch" in the ancient literature and discussions of sexual relations in Roman culture. Ciampa and Rosner clarify, "In a world where there was significant debate about whether pleasure and passion were acceptable motivations for sexual relations, or whether sexual relations should be engaged in solely for the purposes of procreation, it is quite remarkable that this particular euphemism is consistently used for sexual relations motivated by pleasure or passion rather than procreation (or reason or marital friendship, which would also have been acceptable motivations for some Stoics)."[207] Ciampa and Rosner suggest that the preferable translation of 7:1b would be, "It is good for a man not to use a woman for sexual gratification," or "It is good for a man not to have sex with a woman for the sake of pleasure." Paul would agree that certain kinds of sexual activity should be avoided, thus his limited agreement with their statement. He refutes, however, the view that married couples should avoid sex motivated by pleasure or passion, something idealized in the Scriptures in the Song of Solomon. Thus, in 7:2, Paul emphasizes both the need to avoid immorality and to meet the normal, appropriate needs of one's spouse.[208]

The solution to these exegetical options lies, to a large extent, in the historical context that is lost to us. We do not have the Corinthians' letter to Paul and so we are left to reconstruct the situation from the letter that we do have. On all accounts scholars agree that Paul is responding to a Corinthian viewpoint, even if the "slogan" of 7:1b is Paul's own words.[209] Whatever the historical circumstance in Corinth might have been, Paul brings them back to the biblical norm of God's design for sex within marriage. Whether the statement in 7:1b itself indicates an advocacy of celibacy among some in the Corinthian church or is indicative of a completely different situation as articulated by Ciampa and Rosner, Paul warns of "immoralities" and emphasizes the obligations of

---

[206] Ciampa and Rosner (*First Corinthians*, 268–69) make the case that the content of chaps. 5–7 and 10:6–8 indicate that celibacy was not the issue in Corinth. Chapter 7 in particular suggests that Paul is writing to "men and women who want to marry and/or have sex and that he is more inclined toward a fundamental commitment to celibacy than they are." Furthermore, they claim that it is best to understand their questions to Paul as a reaction to his warnings about immorality in his previous letter (5:9) and to the "present crisis" in Corinth (7:26) "in light of contemporary debates about the proper place and purposes of sex in Roman society" (271).

[207] Ciampa and Rosner, *First Corinthians*, 274.

[208] Ibid., 275. Thus, they agree with the consensus view of 7:2 that "to have" means "to have a sexual relationship with."

[209] Caragounis ("'Fornication' and 'Concession'?", 545–46), who insists that 7:1b cannot be a quotation but rather is Paul's own words, states that "it is not improbable—or rather, it is quite probable—that in their letter the Corinthians had given expression in the form of a question to some such idea as we find expressed in vs. 1b."

spouses within marriage.[210] In the end, as Ciampa and Rosner note, "Paul's discussion reflects the uniform biblical stance on sex. Fundamentally, in the Bible there are only two types of sex: sex within marriage and sexual immorality, *porneia*."[211]

**7:3–5** In 7:3–5 Paul continues the thought of 7:2 or, if the traditional view is correct, he elaborates on the duties of husband and wife in marriage. As in 7:2, Paul employs a third person imperative verb, which could be translated, "To the wife, the husband must render the debt that is due, and likewise, the wife to the husband." Some think that Exod 21:10–11 influences Paul's instructions.[212] Clearly, what he says here is an expansion on the one-flesh union (Gen 2:24) already mentioned in 6:16. Commentators also frequently note Paul's revolutionary stance regarding the mutuality of the relationship of husband and wife by ancient standards. Strikingly, the wife is mentioned first rather than the husband. Instead of the sexual relationship presented as only the wife's obligation to the husband, Paul first sets forth the husband's obligation to his wife. The term rendered "marital duty" speaks of this obligation and is used of financial debt in its other two New Testament occurrences.[213] Both husband and wife have sexual needs, and there are mutual obligations to meet those needs within marriage. Paul writes more completely about the Christian household in Eph 5:22–6:9.

The wife is mentioned first again in 7:4, but this time as one who does not have authority over her own body. This view would have been perfectly acceptable to nonbelievers. But what follows is again quite unconventional by ancient standards, that the wife also has authority over her husband's body. But such is the nature of the one-flesh relationship. There are not only mutual responsibilities but a mutual "belonging" to one another. The mention of the "body" recalls the discussion of the previous section (6:12–20).[214] Our bodies are members of Christ (6:15), thus the chief reason to flee immorality (6:16,18), yet bodies also belong to another in marriage. All believers have been "bought with a price" (6:20; again in 7:23), but for married couples there exists another level of ownership one to another.

Finally, in 7:5, Paul issues yet one more command, this time a negated present tense imperative, which could carry the force of, "Stop depriving one

---

[210] Ciampa and Rosner (*First Corinthians*, 277) point out that Paul's view that marriage is a way to avoid the danger of sexual immorality is consistent with the Old Testament and other Jewish literature (see Prov 5:15–20; *Testament of Levi* 9:9–10; Tobit 4:12).

[211] Ciampa and Rosner, *First Corinthians*, 277.

[212] So Garland, *First Corinthians*, 258; Ciampa and Rosner, *First Corinthians*, 279. Exod 21:10–11 reads, "If he marries another woman, he must not deprive the first one of her food, clothing and marital rights. 11 If he does not provide her with these three things, she is to go free, without any payment of money."

[213] Matt 18:32; Rom 13:7. Gk. ὀφειλή.

[214] Note also the reference to "authority" in 6:12.

another."[215] The verb "to deprive" is the same verb translated "to cheat" in 6:7–8 in the discussion of lawsuits. Whether or not the verb carries the sense of "fraud" in this context is uncertain; otherwise the next clause would indicate that "fraud" is acceptable if both consent! The meaning is simply, "Do not withhold obligations from one another unless there is agreement to set aside a time for spiritual purposes." Paul's allowance for the husband and wife to withdraw from sexual relations for a time for spiritual reasons is rooted in the Old Testament.[216] The withdrawal should only be for a time, however, when spouses should resume their normal physical relationship lest they be tempted to fulfill their God-given sexual desires in illicit ways. Paul advises a limited time of withdrawal from one another on the basis of the strength of human passions, that is, the lack of self-control (cf. 7:2,9). Paul does not hold a low view of marriage, that it is only a safety valve against the prevailing corruption of pagan culture, but he does hold a brutally honest and realistic view of the fact that humans are sexual beings. Paul is not against sex. He is against immorality (cf. 6:18).

**7:6–7** Most commentators agree that 7:6–7 belongs with 7:1–5, but there are differences of opinion on the function of the neuter demonstrative pronoun "this" in the phrase, "I say this." Does the pronoun point backward or forward? If backward, what exactly is the antecedent? Some argue that "this" refers all the way back to 7:2, or perhaps more broadly to 7:2–5, in which the concession is that some may marry, yet it is not commanded.[217] Others argue that the emphatic position of the pronoun in 7:6 refers immediately backward to the concession in 7:5b. In other words, Paul does not command that husband and wife may separate for a time but allows it only as a concession.[218] It seems unlikely that the pronoun *this* refers back to 7:2 or more broadly to 7:2–4, which consists of several commands. If pointing backward, the most likely option is 7:5, in which case the suspension of sexual relations for a limited time is the concession.[219]

---

[215] μὴ ἀποστερεῖτε. The Greek structure may indicate the cessation of an action in progress, but it can also be a general prohibition that is true all the time, "Make it your practice (habit) not to deprive one another." If the former is the case, then the issue in Corinth was abstinence within marriage (so Grosheide, *First Corinthians*, 157).

[216] Exod 19:15; Lev 15:18; 1 Sam 21:4–6; Eccl 3:5; Joel 2:16; Zech 12:12–14. Ciampa and Rosner (*First Corinthians*, 283) note a specific parallel in *Testament of Naphtali* 8:8, "there is a time for having intercourse with one's wife, and a time to abstain for the purpose of prayer."

[217] On this view see Morris, *1 Corinthians*, 104. See also Robertson and Plummer (*First Corinthians*, 135), who contend that the pronoun "this" covers "probably the whole of vv. 1–5."

[218] On this view see Barrett, *First Corinthians*, 157–58; Fee, *First Corinthians*, 283–84.

[219] The word for concession, συγγνώμη, appears only here in the New Testament. Caragounis ("'Fornication' or 'Concession'?," 554–58) thinks that we should consider other meanings of the term. He suggests that Paul may be apologizing for intruding on such sensitive matters as if to say, "I am saying this with your permission, not as a command!" Or, alternatively, in light of the near equivalence of γνώμη and συγγνώμη Paul is giving his considered opinion, which occurs repeatedly in chap. 7. Garland (*1 Corinthians*, 270), who thinks that the pronoun "this" in 7:6

Another view, argued recently by Winter and followed by Garland, takes the demonstrative "this" with what follows rather than with what precedes.[220] Winter proposes that the neuter demonstrative, when used with a verb of saying, as in 7:6, refers to a following subordinate clause and that its emphatic position in the sentence emphasizes the importance of the forward referent. In other words, the concession is found in 7:7a, "I wish that all men were as I am," which provides an overall conceptual framework for the discussion of the gifts of singleness and marriage in the subsequent sayings of 7:8–16. Paul links these gifts with his standard teaching in all the churches on other important issues of life such as the Christians' ethnicity and social status in 7:17–24.[221] In Winter's view, Paul takes up issues at his own initiative in 7:8–16.[222] In 7:25, he picks up the next issue raised by the Corinthians, marked by the second occurrence of the phrase "Now about."[223] If "this" points forward to 7:7, and if 7:1b represents a Corinthian position, then Paul gives limited agreement to the Corinthian viewpoint by expressing his own desire that all men were gifted in singleness. Either way one reads the referent of the pronoun "this," 7:7 seems to be parallel to 7:1, that is, Paul preferred singleness and affirmed its goodness.[224]

There are a couple of other issues of interest in Paul's remarks in 7:7. Clearly Paul was not married at the time of the writing of 1 Corinthians, but was he ever married (see below on 7:8)? Second, Paul refers to a "gift" that each one has from God. Does this refer to a special "gift" to resist sexual urges that he wished all had?[225] Or is Paul simply affirming his state of singleness as a gift from God, a state that allows full devotion to the service to Christ

points forward to 7:7 argues that "concession" in this context means "limited agreement" with the Corinthian slogan of 7:1b. Thiselton (*First Corinthians*, 510), argues that we cannot improve on the meaning "concession" and that 7:6 points back to 7:5b.

220 Winter, "1 Corinthians 7:6–7"; Garland, *1 Corinthians*, 267–70.

221 Winter, "1 Corinthians 7:6–7," 58. In Winter's view "gift" and "calling" (7:17–24) are synonymous terms (64). Winter notes numerous passages where the neuter demonstrative (τοῦτο) can be used as preparation for a subordinate clause with ὅτι (listing 24 occurrences in Paul; note esp. Rom 6:6 and 1 Cor 7:26). Sometimes the ὅτι is implied (1 Cor 7:29; Gal 3:17; Eph 4:17). Thus, Winter proposes, 1 Cor 7:6 could be preparation for the objective clause in 7:7. Furthermore, ὅτι is used with the demonstrative τοῦτο in Paul when the subsequent clause receives special emphasis (1 Cor 1:12; 15:50). Where the ὅτι is implied, the neuter demonstrative occupies the emphatic first position in the sentence (1 Cor 7:29; 2 Cor 9:6; Gal 3:17; Eph 4:17). Verbs of saying followed by an objective clause assume the ὅτι, as in 1 Cor 7:8,12. Winter assumes an adverbial function of the particle δέ in 1 Cor 7:7, meaning, "rather." This results in the following: "And this I am saying by way of concession and not command, [that] I wish rather all were as myself." Winter argues that τοῦτο cannot be the plurality of commands in 7:2–5 since it is singular, not plural.

222 Note the repetition of a verb of speaking, "I say" or "I command" (7:6,8,10,12).

223 Gk. περὶ δὲ. Winter (62) notes the near parallel between 7:6–7 and 7:25–26.

224 So Robertson and Plummer, *First Corinthians*, 136.

225 Barrett (*First Corinthians*, 158) argues that what Paul says in 7:7 is a wish capable of realization, approaching the force of a command. Paul wished that all had the same capacity as he for resistance to sexual urges.

(7:32–35)? That each one has his own gift from God implies that marriage, like singleness, is equally a gift.[226] The word for "gift" is the same word used for spiritual gifts in chaps. 12–14,[227] but the word does not always denote a spiritual empowerment.[228]

### *(2) Principles for Diverse Situations, Both Unmarried and Married (7:8–16)*

**8Now to the unmarried and the widows I say: It is good for them to stay unmar-
ried, as I am. 9But if they cannot control themselves, they should marry, for it is
better to marry than to burn with passion.**

**10To the married I give this command (not I, but the Lord): A wife must not
separate from her husband. 11But if she does, she must remain unmarried or else
be reconciled to her husband. And a husband must not divorce his wife.**

**12To the rest I say this (I, not the Lord): If any brother has a wife who is not
a believer and she is willing to live with him, he must not divorce her. 13And if a
woman has a husband who is not a believer and he is willing to live with her, she
must not divorce him. 14For the unbelieving husband has been sanctified through
his wife, and the unbelieving wife has been sanctified through her believing hus-
band. Otherwise your children would be unclean, but as it is, they are holy.**

**15But if the unbeliever leaves, let him do so. A believing man or woman is not
bound in such circumstances; God has called us to live in peace. 16How do you
know, wife, whether you will save your husband? Or, how do you know, husband,
whether you will save your wife?**

In this section Paul addresses diverse situations involving both the unmarried and the married. He advises the unmarried and the widows regarding marriage (7:8–9), reiterates Jesus' command forbidding divorce to the already married (7:10–11), and speaks to the issue of the believer married to an unbeliever (7:12–16). As noted above, this portion of chap. 7 either addresses further questions posed by the Corinthians, or it is Paul's own formulation based on what he knows of the needs of the community.

**7:8** The term "unmarried"[229] could, of itself, refer to the unmarried in general, whether never married, divorced, or single again due to the death of a spouse. Some think Paul has in mind especially widowers since the word is used in conjunction with the term "widows," who would also fall under the category of the "unmarried."[230] Fee holds this view and suggests the term

[226] See Robertson and Plummer, *First Corinthians*, 136. Fee (*First Corinthians*, 285) comments, "Sexual life in marriage is a gift of another kind." See also Thiselton, *First Corinthians*, 513.

[227] Gk. χάρισμα.

[228] Contra Barrett (*First Corinthians*, 158), who contends that there is no difference in meaning here from other gifts conferred by the Holy Spirit.

[229] Gk. ἄγαμος. The term occurs only in 1 Cor 7 in the New Testament and once in the LXX (4 Macc 16:9).

[230] Garland (*1 Corinthians*, 272) suggests that Paul may have focused attention on the widows since there were simply more widows than widowers and faced more serious economic challenges. "Paul offers them spiritual encouragement to remain unmarried."

"demarried" describes Paul's use of the term in chap. 7 since it is applied to the divorced woman in 7:11 and set in contrast to the virgins in 7:34. In his view Paul probably does not have in mind the "never married" since he addresses this group more specifically in 7:25–38. This understanding of the term gives a balanced symmetry to the chapter as a whole; 7:1–16 addresses those presently or formerly married, while 7:25–38 addresses those never married.[231] Fee contends that, although Greek has a term for "widower," its usage was rare and never occurs during the New Testament era. Furthermore, Paul deals with mutualities throughout this passage, and it would fit his pattern to set "widowers" and "widows" side by side.[232] Ciampa and Rosner find these arguments unconvincing, pointing out that evidence is lacking for assigning a specific meaning to the term such as "widower" or the like. The term is ambiguous and simply means "unmarried."[233]

If the term "unmarried" denotes a widower, some see in this passage a hint that Paul was once married since he advises to "remain as I am." That Paul would have been married at some point in his life would have been consistent with his Jewish heritage. The evidence is not conclusive, however, and ultimately we cannot know for sure.[234] It is clear that Paul was not married at the time of the writing of 1 Corinthians, and there is no trace of a wife or child anywhere in Acts or Paul's letters. It is best not to read beyond the evidence that we have and simply confess that we do not know.

There are formal similarities between 7:8 and 7:1 in Paul's use of the term "good." "It is good for them to remain as I am" parallels Paul's advice in 7:1, "It is good for a man not to touch a woman." As noted in the comments on 7:1, some feel that this parallel substantiates the claim that 7:1b is Paul's own opinion rather than a Corinthian slogan or sentiment.[235] The parallel is not decisive one way or the other since Paul could be using a Corinthian term to advance his argument. There are additional parallels between 7:2 and 7:9 that relate the sexual relationship within marriage to the realities of the human condition. In 7:2, husband and

[231] Although in the second half Paul does not exclude these other groups from his comments. 7:25 opens up with "now concerning the virgins," indicating a separate topic, but he includes references to those who are already married (7:27) and allows for the remarriage of widows (7:40).

[232] Fee, *First Corinthians*, 287–88. See also J. Moiser, "A Reassessment of Paul's View of Marriage with Reference to 1 Cor 7," *JSNT* 18 (1983): 108; Hays, *First Corinthians*, 118; Collins, *First Corinthians*, 263, 268. Moiser claims that Erasmus understood the term to mean "widowers."

[233] Ciampa and Rosner, *First Corinthians*, 287. Paul could just as easily be thinking of widows and their suitors. BDAG defines simply as "an unmarried man/woman." Thiselton (*First Corinthians*, 515) comments that the balance of writers adopt this view. Garland (*1 Corinthians*, 276) also questions the restricted meaning of "widowers" as evidenced by its semantic range in its few occurrences in 1 Cor 7.

[234] Morris (*1 Corinthians*, 104) thinks it unlikely that Paul was never married. So also Collins (*First Corinthians*, 260), who comments, "Had Paul been a rabbi of some sort it would have been virtually impossible for him not to have been married." Morris surmises that Paul was either a widower or that his wife had left him.

[235] So Conzelmann, *1 Corinthians*, 115.

wife are enjoined to continue sexual relations because of cases of immorality. Likewise in 7:9, the "unmarried" and "widows" are commanded to marry if they cannot exercise self-control (cf. 7:5). The first occurrence of the verb "to remain" (7:8) proves to be an important theme in the chapter as a whole.[236] In three of the occurrences of the verb Paul uses the imperative. In 7:11 the divorced woman "must remain" unmarried, and in 7:20,24, each person "must remain" in the calling in which they were called. Yet, Paul allows for latitude in the application of this core principle in his advice to the virgins (7:25–38) and to the widows who might consider remarriage (7:39–40).

**7:9** Paul's concession, "But if they cannot control themselves, they should marry," seems to imply that some were, in fact, not exercising self-control, that is, they were practicing immorality.[237] Fee suggests that, like the married men in 7:1–7, some of the widowers were actually going to prostitutes.[238] In contrast, Garland observes, "Since he does not censure them for this behavior, he apparently does not assume that they are guilty of sexual immorality. The clause 'if they are not exercising control' probably means that they have erotic desires and are struggling with them."[239] One would certainly expect a more stern response from Paul if some were practicing immorality in light of chaps. 5 and 6, unless the previous warnings are implied in his instructions here. Paul recommends marriage for those who cannot exercise self-control because "it is better to marry than to burn with passion."[240] Since the words "with passion" are not in the original Greek, Paul's words have been interpreted in two ways, either as referring to burning with sexual desire or as a reference to the flames of hell that is the destiny of those who practice immorality (cf. 6:9–10).[241] The former is more likely in context (cf. 7:2,5).[242]

---

[236] The term is used in 7:11,20,24,40.

[237] In Greek the sentence structure is a first-class conditional sentence in Greek, in which the "if" clause assumes reality for the sake of argument. A more literal rendering would be "If they are not controlling themselves."

[238] Fee, *First Corinthians*, 289. So also Barrett (*First Corinthians*, 161), who says that this phrase, in Greek, cannot be watered down to "If they find it difficult to . . ." Grosheide (*First Corinthians*, 161) says, "If they have not continence . . ." states a fact. See also Morris (*1 Corinthians*, 105); M. L. Barré, "To Marry or To Burn: πυροῦσθαι in 1 Cor 7:9," *CBQ* 36 (1974): 193–202.

[239] Garland, *1 Corinthians*, 273. Thiselton (*First Corinthians*, 518–19) similarly disagrees with the NIV translation, "If they cannot control themselves." "In 7:9 Paul envisages a couple for whom mutual love has become so powerful a force that it distracts them from 'everything for the sake of the gospel' when they are dominated by unfulfilled longing" (518). Thiselton suggests the translation, "If they do not have power over their passions," meaning "to devote themselves to more fundamental priorities" (519).

[240] The NIV's, "They should marry . . ." translates a third person imperative in Greek (γαμησάτωσαν). Depending on how one takes the imperative, a possible translation might be, "They must marry!"

[241] On the view that "to burn" refers to the flames of judgment see Bruce, *1 and 2 Corinthians*, 71; Barré, "To Marry or Burn."

[242] Paul uses the verb "to burn" metaphorically in 2 Cor 11:29 with reference to indignation when someone is made to stumble. In 1 Cor 7:9 the familiar association of burning with sexual

**7:10–11** There is a marked change of tone in 7:10. Instead of the previous, "I say," Paul is more assertive, "I give this command,"[243] since he reiterates the teaching of Jesus regarding divorce (Matt 19:1–10; Mark 10:2–12). A wife must not "separate" from her husband, and a husband must not "divorce" his wife. Paul further stipulates that if she does "separate" then she must remain unmarried or be reconciled to her husband. Here the group designated "the married" refers to a marriage between believers since Paul addresses the situation of the believer married to the unbeliever in the following verses (7:12–16). Jesus disallowed divorce, except in the case of sexual immorality (Matt 5:32; 19:9). Why Paul omitted the exception clause is a matter of speculation; perhaps it simply did not apply in this situation. We must keep in mind that Paul is responding to concrete circumstances and does not develop a comprehensive theology of divorce. In 7:10–11 he does not hint at the reason for the divorce, he only forbids it in light of Jesus' teaching. Apparently he envisions a separation/divorce for insufficient reasons, and on this basis does not permit remarriage. The only option following a separation/divorce is to remain unmarried or to be reconciled, which Paul also may have derived from Jesus' teaching that to divorce and marry another or to marry one who is divorced equals adultery (Matt 5:32). Collins argues that Paul's exhortation implies that "the woman is to remain unmarried in order that she be reconciled to her husband." In other words, remaining unmarried is essential for the possibility of reconciliation.[244] The verb "to reconcile" is a uniquely Pauline word in New Testament usage. In its other occurrences the term describes the reconciliation effected by the gospel.[245] Paul's insistence on reconciliation is a call to obey the demands of the gospel.[246]

In reiterating the Lord's command, why does Paul first address the wife? Some speculate the reason reflects the historical situation in Corinth that some of the women were seeking to absolve their marriages. Robertson and Plummer note, "The fact that he begins with the unusual case of a wife divorcing her husband indicates that such a thing had actually occurred or

---

passion would have been readily understood in context (so Garland, *1 Corinthians*, 274). Garland adds that what is distinctive about Paul's use of the metaphor "is his conviction that romantic passion necessitated marriage."

[243] Gk. παραγγέλλω. In both occurrences of the verb in 1 Corinthians (here and 11:17), the verb is associated with a tradition from the Lord (cf. 11:23–26). For other uses of the verb in Paul see 1 Thess 4:11; 2 Thess 3:4,6,10,12; 1 Tim 1:3; 4:11; 5:7; 6:13,17.

[244] Collins, *First Corinthians*, 269–70. So also Garland (*1 Corinthians*, 283). Collins bases this reading on Paul's Jewish tradition wherein a divorced woman who remarried and divorced again was forbidden to her former spouse (Deut 24:1–4). This may well be Paul's intention, but it is not how he expresses the situation grammatically, that she must remain unmarried "in order" to be reconciled.

[245] Rom 5:10; 2 Cor 5:18–20. See also Eph 2:16; Col 1:20,22, where the synonym ἀποκαταλλάσσω is used. The noun (καταλλαγή) is used in Rom 5:11; 11:15; 2 Cor 5:18–19.

[246] It is sometimes pointed out that Paul does not call for exclusion from the community if separation/divorce does occur. So Barrett, *First Corinthians*, 163; Hays, *First Corinthians*, 120.

was mentioned in the letter as likely to occur. Women may have raised the question."[247] Was there a sense of "liberation" among the female members of the church or a pro-celibacy faction that advocated the dissolution of marriages altogether? Were some seeking to escape sexual obligations through divorce? Paul's insistence that the woman remain unmarried implies that remarriage was a real possibility and seems to argue against such scenarios. Some may have been justifying the dissolution of one marriage only to find another spouse. The key point is that Paul restates the teaching of Jesus regarding divorce.[248]

Also of note is the use of different terms regarding the actions of the wife and the husband. The wife must not "separate" from her husband, but the husband must not "divorce" his wife.[249] Robertson and Plummer suggest the change is due to social custom. "The home is his [the husband's]: she [the wife] can leave it, but he sends her away from it." They note, however, that the term "separate" is used of divorce in the papyri.[250] Most likely, in Paul's use, the terms are generally interchangeable. In 7:13, for example, the believing wife is directed not to "divorce" her unbelieving husband. In 7:15, the verb "separate" is used generically, referring either to the unbelieving wife or to the unbelieving husband.[251] We err to read modern legal definitions of "separation" and "divorce" into the text.

**7:12–16** In 7:12–16, Paul addresses yet another category of married couples, those believers married to unbelievers.[252] Paul has no grounds to command anything to the unbeliever (5:12), yet he instructs the believer not to dissolve the marriage on the condition of the mutual consent of the unbeliever.[253] The words "I say, not the Lord," does not imply that Paul's instructions

---

[247] Robertson and Plummer, *First Corinthians*, 140. So also Collins, *First Corinthians*, 269. See also 7:39–40 where Paul specifies that "a woman is bound to her husband as long as he lives" without addressing the husband directly.

[248] Garland (*1 Corinthians*, 283) suggests that divorce among believers may not have been an issue at all in Corinth, but rather that in 7:10–11 Paul "only lays the foundation stone for his argument in what follows: the Lord forbids Christians to divorce."

[249] χωρίζω and ἀφίημι ("to leave, abandon").

[250] Robertson and Plummer, *First Corinthians*, 140.

[251] Cf. also Mark 10:9, "Therefore what God has joined together, let man not separate."

[252] Gk. τοῖς δὲ λοιποῖς ("but to the rest"). Moiser ("A Reassessment," 109) takes a minority view that the phrase "to the rest" does not refer to those that Paul has not yet addressed, but is connected directly to 7:10–11. "In vv. 10–11, Paul addresses Christians who abandon pagan partners, and he is able to quote Jesus in his support. In our present section (vv. 12–16), Paul addresses Christians abandoned by pagan partners: 'the rest' of those against whose marriage a question mark stands." It seems, however, that Paul is taking up yet a third category of which there is no direct teaching of Jesus, that is, those who are married to unbelievers in contrast to believers married to one another (7:10–11).

[253] Gk. συνευδοκέω. BDAG defines as "to join in approval, agree with, approve of, consent to, sympathize with." In Paul's letters the term occurs only here and in Rom 1:32 of those who approve of those who do things worthy of death.

lack authority,[254] or that he merely offers his opinion (cf. 7:25,40) since he provides a theological rationale for his directives (7:14). Rather, he is distinguishing his own words from the words of Jesus. Jesus had not spoken on this particular issue as he had spoken on the matter of divorce (7:10–11). Furthermore, Jesus' instructions regarding divorce were directed toward those within Israel. Paul's Gentile mission surely resulted in a different kind of situation for many believers. Sometimes whole households converted to Christ,[255] but such was not always the case. Apparently situations existed in Corinth where one spouse converted to Christianity and the other remained unevangelized.[256] This circumstance would have raised legitimate theological questions. Should the believer separate from the unbeliever in light of Paul's injunctions in his previous letter not to associate with the immoral (5:9–10)? Was it their Christian duty to dissolve the marriage and seek a believing spouse? Was marriage to a pagan somehow defiling based on the biblical teaching of the one-flesh union (6:16; cf. also Ezra 10:3,19)? If Paul is horrified by the prospect of a believer joined to a prostitute (6:15), what about the believer who is united in marriage to an unbeliever, who, like the prostitute, belongs to the realm of this world? Paul instructs that in a mixed marriage the Christian is not to initiate a divorce. Whether or not the marriage holds together hinges on the decision of the pagan partner (7:12–13).

With an explanatory "for"[257] Paul explains the reason for keeping the marriage of the believer to the unbeliever intact: "the unbelieving husband has been sanctified through his wife, and the unbelieving wife has been sanctified through her believing husband" (7:14). The word "sanctified" is the term Paul normally uses with reference to salvation, the setting apart of God's people unto himself (cf. 1:2; 6:11),[258] but in this context Paul's meaning is different since the pagan partner is designated an "unbeliever" and 7:16 clearly indicates the need of his or her "salvation." Fee speculates that by "sanctification" Paul implies that as long as the unbeliever remains in the marriage the potential for their salvation remains.[259] Most likely Paul's choice of the term "sanctified" addresses a concern that marriage to an unbeliever defiles the believing spouse in some way. As Thiselton states, "The key controlling principle lies in the

---

[254] See P. Richardson, "'I Say, Not the Lord': Person Opinion, Apostolic Authority, and the Development of Early Christian Halakah," *TynBul* 31 (1980): 65–86. Thiselton (*First Corinthians*, 526) translates "to the rest I say (not a saying of the Lord)."

[255] Acts 16:25–34.

[256] This text does not speak to the issue of a Christian marrying a non-Christian, which Paul clarifies in 7:39 when he allows remarriage for widows, but "only in the Lord." Thiselton (*First Corinthians*, 525) gives to 7:12–16 the heading, "Christians *Already* Married to Unbelievers" (italics mine).

[257] Gk. γάρ.

[258] Gk. ἁγιάζω. In the Greek sentence, the verb is in the perfect tense (cf. 1:2) and occurs first in the sentence for emphasis.

[259] Fee, *First Corinthians*, 300.

recognition of the nature of the anxiety which Paul seeks to allay."[260] Paul's logic goes in the exact opposite direction of his previous argument regarding defilement in the case of the incestuous man (5:6) and the defilement that results in union with a prostitute (6:15–17).[261] No such contamination exists in the marriage of the believer to the unbeliever. The union is lawful and holy according to God's established pattern for marriage. "Otherwise," Paul contends, "your children would be unclean, but as it is, they are holy."[262] Paul's argument parallels his argument in 5:10 where Paul clarifies that by forbidding association with immoral people he did not mean the immoral people of the world: "In that case you would have to leave this world."[263] In other words, Paul draws an inference from the view that marriage to an unbeliever somehow defiles the believer and the marriage. If this were the case, the children would be "unclean." But, as it stands, they are not unclean but holy. Thus, the principle of "holiness" widens to the children in the case of a mixed marriage, which is established on the scriptural principle that God's blessings are not confined to the immediate recipients but extend to others.[264] It is also possible that by the term "sanctified," in this context, Paul refers to the influence of the believer on the unbeliever. As Thiselton puts it, "The lifestyle of the Christian partner cannot but affect the ethos and to some extent the values and the lifestyle of the home, whether this be the husband or the wife."[265] Barrett suggests that mixed marriages, when one spouse is a believer, are essentially Christian marriages.[266]

Paul's instructions are tempered by the reality that marriages of believers to unbelievers may not hold together. So while Paul forbids the believer to initiate a divorce, he has no authority or control over the unbeliever, and so he counsels, "But if the unbeliever leaves, let him do so."[267] Interpreters do not agree, however, on the meaning of the statement that follows, "A believing man or woman is not bound in such circumstances." Many suppose the statement implies that the believer is no longer bound to the marriage commitment when

---

[260] Thiselton, *First Corinthians*, 528. Thiselton elaborates, "The believer asks Paul with genuine concern: if I have left behind the old life and become a new creation in Christ, does not my relation with my unbelieving, unrepentant spouse and my entire home atmosphere threaten to pollute and to corrode my purity as one who belongs to Christ?" See also Garland, *1 Corinthians*, 284. In context, the opposite of "holy" is "unclean" (7:14).

[261] So Hays, *First Corinthians*, 121. See also Rom 11:16.

[262] The cognate term ἅγιος is used (cf. 1:2).

[263] The Greek construction is the same, ἐπεὶ ἄρα, and occurs only in 5:10 and 7:14 in the New Testament.

[264] Morris, *1 Corinthians*, 107. Morris notes Gen 15:18; 17:7; 18:26; 1 Kgs 15:4; Isa 37:4.

[265] Thiselton, *First Corinthians*, 530.

[266] Barrett, *First Corinthians*, 166.

[267] D. B. Wallace (*Greek Grammar Beyond the Basics: An Exegetical Syntax of the New Testament* [Grand Rapids: Zondervan, 1996], 488–89) classifies the imperative χωριζέσθω in this instance as a permissive imperative, or "an imperative of resignation," that is, it is already an accomplished fact.

abandoned by the unbeliever and is free to remarry.[268] This reading of the text has given rise to what is known as the "Pauline privilege." This may well be the case, yet Paul does not speak directly to the issue of remarriage in 7:15.[269] We have to wonder if Paul might be saying something more, or perhaps even different. Paul disallows for remarriage in 7:11 in the case of the wife who leaves her husband (both believers). Paul specifies the freedom to remarry in 7:39 but only upon the death of one's spouse and only if the remarriage is a Christian marriage. The verb for "binding" in 7:15 is not the ordinary verb Paul uses for the "binding" character of marriage (7:27,39; Rom 7:2).[270] The term used in 7:15 means "to be enslaved," which could be somewhat synonymous with the normal term of "binding" if Paul's intention is to specify remarriage. In 7:17–24, however, Paul continues with the enslavement/freedom contrast (7:21–23) in support of the overarching principle "to remain as you are." Paul's meaning in 7:15 may be that the abandoned believer is not enslaved in their newfound circumstance and is free to serve the Lord without distraction (7:22,32–35). If the principle "remain as you are" holds, then Paul's trustworthy judgment would be to remain unmarried. However, if Paul views the abandoned believer in the same light as a widow or widower whose marriage has been dissolved by death, then while advocating singleness, he would allow for remarriage.[271]

There are different ways of understanding the next phrase, "God has called us to live in peace" (7:15b). The phrase may refer to the immediately preceding circumstance of separation and Paul advises the believer not to create further strife by contesting the divorce.[272] More likely, in using "calling" language Paul articulates a core principle for the believer that takes into account the whole of 7:12–16 and looks forward to the next section (7:17–24) where "calling" is a key term in a brief exposition of the guiding principle of the whole chapter, "to remain as you are." In other words, Paul is giving yet another reason for

---

[268] So Conzelmann, *1 Corinthians*, 123; Morris, *1 Corinthians*, 107; D. Instone-Brewer, *Divorce and Remarriage in the Bible: The Social and Literary Context* (Grand Rapids: Eerdmans, 2002), 202. So also Ciampa and Rosner (*First Corinthians*, 302–3), who suggest that Paul allows for remarriage in all cases of abandonment, "not merely than of being married to an unbeliever."

[269] Robertson and Plummer (*First Corinthians*, 143) contend all that "not bound" means is that the believer need not feel so bound by Christ's prohibition of divorce to be afraid to depart when the heathen partner insists on separation. See also Fee (*First Corinthians*, 303), who argues against the Pauline Privilege.

[270] Gk. δουλόω instead of δέω. Thiselton (*First Corinthians*, 534) translates, "the Christian husband or wife does not remain in slavery."

[271] So Bruce (*1 & 2 Corinthians*, 70), who comments that "It is conceivable that Paul speaks from personal experience." Garland (*First Corinthians*, 296) notes that Paul's primary goal in 7:12–16 is to argue against the dissolving of a marriage between believer and unbeliever for religious reasons and that he argues against changing one's status in 7:17–24. "But in 7:17–24, he also allows for an exception in the case of the slave obtaining freedom. In the same way, the one who has been divorced would be permitted to move from being married to being set free by divorce to being married again."

[272] Garland (*First Corinthians*, 291) thinks that this interpretation falters on the assumption that a spouse could contest a divorce under Roman law.

remaining in the marriage to the unbeliever. The concept of "peace" parallels to the concept of "reconciliation" in 7:11. If the believer was in a peaceful marriage when God called, then he/she should remain in that situation if the unbeliever is pleased to continue the marriage. In line with the emphasis of Paul's entire argument, the believer should not seek a change of status because of conversion. As Garland states, "He is barring them from causing unnecessary strife by divorcing on religious grounds unbelieving spouses who have consented to continue the marriage (7:12–13)."[273] The concepts of "reconciliation" and "peace" represent the heart of the gospel and are essential to decision-making.

The different ways of understanding Paul's concluding question in 7:16 regarding the salvation of the unbelieving spouse may be illustrated by comparing two modern translations. The more pessimistic reading is expressed by the NIV, "How do you know, wife, whether you will save your husband? Or, how do you know, husband, whether you will save your wife?" The meaning would be that it is uncertain whether a believer will succeed in the conversion of an unbelieving spouse if the marriage continues.[274] A more optimistic appraisal is that Paul advises the maintenance of the marriage for as long as possible in the hope for the conversion of the unbelieving spouse.[275] This view is conveyed by the NRSV translation, "Wife, for all you know, you might save your husband. Husband, for all you know, you might save your wife."[276] Supporting the more positive reading here is, first, the view that "God's call to peace" in 7:15b is reason to keep the marriage together and, second, Paul's evangelistic concern for the unbeliever in other passages in the letter (see 9:22–24; 10:23–33; 14:20–25).[277] Peter offers the same kind of optimism toward the conversion of the unbelieving spouse in 1 Pet 3:1–6. In sum, in 7:12–16 Paul argues against Christians initiating divorce from unbelievers on the basis of the sanctifying character of marriage and its evangelistic potential.

### *(3) The Guiding Principle for Decision-Making: Remain as You Are (7:17–24)*

**17Nevertheless, each one should retain the place in life that the Lord assigned to him and to which God has called him. This is the rule I lay down in all the**

---

[273] Garland, *1 Corinthians*, 292. So also Collins, *First Corinthians*, 267; Ciampa and Rosner, *First Corinthians*, 304. For Ciampa and Rosner, the New Testament usage of the word "peace," which entails reconciliation, is problematic for the first interpretation.

[274] So S. Kubo, "1 Corinthians 7:16: Optimistic or Pessimistic?," *NTS* 24 (1977): 539–44; Morris, *1 Corinthians*, 108.

[275] Barrett (*First Corinthians*, 167) notes that the Greek fathers interpreted 7:16 in a positive sense. Garland (*First Corinthians*, 294) points out that the question, "How do you know?" can be used in a sense of optimism and cites 2 Sam 12:22; Esth 4:14; Joel 2:14; and Jonah 3:9 among other texts.

[276] On "saving" the husband/wife, note Paul's similar statement in 9:22, "I have become all things to all men so that by all possible means I might save some."

[277] So also Collins, *First Corinthians*, 272.

**churches. [18]Was a man already circumcised when he was called? He should not become uncircumcised. Was a man uncircumcised when he was called? He should not be circumcised. [19]Circumcision is nothing and uncircumcision is nothing. Keeping God's commands is what counts. [20]Each one should remain in the situation which he was in when God called him. [21]Were you a slave when you were called? Don't let it trouble you—although if you can gain your freedom, do so. [22]For he who was a slave when he was called by the Lord is the Lord's freedman; similarly, he who was a free man when he was called is Christ's slave. [23]You were bought at a price; do not become slaves of men. [24]Brothers, each man, as responsible to God, should remain in the situation God called him to.**

As the structural center of the chapter, 7:17–24 is an integral component of Paul's response to the issues of marriage and singleness.[278] The phrase, "remain as you are," occurs three times in this section (7:17,20,24) and corresponds to the apostle's advice in other places in the chapter. In 7:8, for example, Paul expressed his opinion that it is good for the unmarried and widows to remain in their current state of singleness, a point restated in 7:40 with reference to widows. In 7:11, the wife who separates from her husband must remain in an unmarried state or be reconciled to her husband. Furthermore, in 7:12–16, Paul provides theological reasons and evangelistic incentive for believers married to unbelievers to remain in the marriage.

The mention of God's call to peace in 7:15b sets up the discussion of 7:17–24, where the verb "to call" occurs eight times and the noun "calling" occurs once.[279] Furthermore, the "enslavement" language of 7:15a ("a believing man or woman is not bound . . .") prepares the way for the illustration of slavery in relation to God's call in 7:20–23. The main point of 7:17–24 is that conversion, while altering moral and spiritual life, does not necessarily alter status in life.[280] Paul illustrates the principle by way of two leading identity markers in the ancient world: religious (circumcision/uncircumcision) and social (freedman/slave). Since Paul commands this in all the churches (7:17; see also 4:17; 14:33), the principle of remaining in God's calling is a central tenet of his theology of the Christian life rather than a response only to the local situation in Corinth.[281] What Paul says regarding circumcised/uncircumcised and slave/free applies in principle to decisions concerning marriage and remarriage. Social distinctions such as Jew/Gentile or slave/free have nothing to do with one's standing before God. In the same

[278] Among commentators 7:17–24 is widely noted as the structural center of the chapter providing the theological basis of the discussion in 7:1–40, much in the same way that 9:1–27 and 13:1–13 function in their respective units (8:1–11:1 and 12:1–14:40).

[279] Cf. the "calling" language in 1:2,9,24,26.

[280] C. Vaughan and T. D. Lea, *1 Corinthians*, Bible Study Commentary (Grand Rapids: Zondervan, 1983), 77. Morris (*1 Corinthians*, 108) notes that conversion means bringing what one is into the service of God. See also G. W. Dawes, "'But If You Can Gain Your Freedom' (1 Corinthians 7:17–24)," *CBQ* 52 (1990): 683.

[281] Hays (*First Corinthians*, 122–23) suggests that 1 Cor 7 is Paul's own explication of Gal 3:28.

way, whether one is married or celibate has nothing to do with one's standing before God. The only thing that truly matters is keeping the commands of God (7:19).[282] Furthermore, Paul stresses God's ownership of the believer in the phrase, "You were bought at a price" (7:23; cf. 6:20). God's ownership of the believer goes hand in hand with his calling of the believer. The Christian is God's slave, not a slave of men (7:23).

**7:17** The word, "nevertheless," in the NIV translates a Greek phrase that reflects a contrast with what precedes.[283] Barrett thinks the construction relates back to the believer married to the unbeliever and being "not bound" to the marriage if the unbeliever departs (7:15).[284] It might also relate to 7:16, that is, without the salvation of the wife or husband, one can still live out the Christian life as the assigned lot as given by God. If God's call came to one spouse, but not the other, the believing spouse is not to seek a change of marital status but should continue the marriage relationship if the unbeliever is pleased to oblige; the believing spouse can and should live out the calling of God in this circumstance. Thiselton comments that there are a number of ways to reflect a contrastive note in translation but the essential meaning of the construction is, "whatever has gone before, this is the principle . . ."[285] The construction introduces Paul's brief exposition of the core principle, "Remain as you are."

"Each one" is placed in an emphatic position and occurs twice. Paul has in mind God's assigned status to each individual Christian.[286] The point is that one's station in life is under the sovereign hand of God. Paul will make a similar point in chap. 12 regarding God's sovereign distribution of spiritual gifts to "each one" in the church (12:7). In context God's assignment and calling has to do with one's marital status at the time of conversion. If backward referring specifically to 7:12–16, then Paul has in mind the believer married to the unbeliever. More likely, Paul has in mind all of the situations addressed in chap. 7 to which the principle, "Remain as you are," applies. Blomberg observes, "The entire verse implies that in whatever state we are when we come to the Lord, we should function faithfully in that state without immediately seeking to change it."[287] The language of calling reminds the Corinthians yet again of

---

[282] Fee (*First Corinthians*, 309) asserts that Paul's concern is not that they retain their social setting, but that they recognize it as the proper one in which to live out God's call. Garland (*First Corinthians*, 300) points out that change of status is unnecessary in relation to God's call but not prohibited. Contemporary Christianity has witnessed its share of an emphasis on changing one's status in life as a key component of conversion. Paul's principle of "remain as you are" flies in the face of such thinking. It is not that Christians cannot do or should not do things to better themselves, but rather the notion that these kinds of things matter to God.

[283] εἰ μὴ, which BDAG defines as "If not," or "except (that)."

[284] Barrett (*First Corinthians*, 167) thinks Paul is contemplating the possibility of the separation of the believer and unbeliever in marriage.

[285] Thiselton, *First Corinthians*, 548. Thiselton renders as, "At all events."

[286] The term translated "assigned" is μερίζω, the same term used in 1:13, "Is Christ divided?" The meaning in 7:17 is "deal out, assign, apportion" (BDAG).

[287] Blomberg, *1 Corinthians*, 145.

the divine initiative in salvation that Paul emphasized repeatedly in chap. 1 (1:2,9,23,26). In 1:26–31 Paul reminded them of their status in life when God chose them. Paul uses the term calling "of the condition in which a man is when the converting call of God comes to him and summons him to the life of Christian faith and obedience."[288]

**7:18–20** Paul gives two examples that illustrate the principle of 7:17. The first has to do with religious distinctions: the circumcised and the uncircumcised.[289] If one was circumcised when converted, then he should not seek "uncircumcision."[290] Conversely, if one was not circumcised, then he should not seek circumcision. In other words, Gentiles are not to be compelled to take up Jewish identity and vice versa.[291] Circumcision is nothing and uncircumcision is nothing, that is, neither one has anything to do with one's standing before God. What matters is keeping God's commands.[292] One can only imagine how shocking and absurd Paul's words would have been to Jewish ears. As Fee comments, "It is hard for us to imagine the horror with which a fellow Jew would have responded. For not only did circumcision count, it counted for everything."[293] Circumcision marked Jews off as the people of God; it was a sign of the covenant (Gen 17:10–14). Any Jew would have equated circumcision with keeping God's commands, but Paul makes a distinction. In Paul's view it was possible to keep the commands of God in an uncircumcised state, or conversely, it was possible to be circumcised and not keep the commandments.[294] In the church, which is one body composed of both Jews and Gentiles, social distinctions are irrelevant (Gal 3:18; 5:6; 6:15).

---

[288] Barrett, *First Corinthians*, 168. See also Morris, *1 Corinthians*, 109.

[289] It is unlikely that circumcision and uncircumcision were contested issues in Corinth. Paul refers to this social identity as parallel illustrations to support his contention that the Corinthians should not seek a change in marital status. So Fee, *First Corinthians*, 311; Hays, *First Corinthians*, 122. Some think, however, that Paul's choice reflects an underlying historical situation in Corinth; see J. Moffatt, *The First Epistle of Paul to the Corinthians*, MNTC (New York: Hodder & Stoughton, 1938), 85; S. S. Bartchy, Μᾶλλον χρῆσαι*: First-Century Slavery and the Interpretation of 1 Corinthians 7*, SBLDS 11 (Missoula: Society of Biblical Literature, 1973), 130. While Jewish/Gentile controversies are not apparent in the letter as in Paul's letter to the Galatians, the issue of social status (slave/free), however, may have been a bigger deal (cf. 1:26; 9:15–18; 11:21–22; so Collins, *First Corinthians*, 280).

[290] The procedure of becoming "uncircumcised" was known as "epispasm" and was a means of Jewish males masking their Jewish identity in order to assimilate into the Greco-Roman culture. See R. G. Hall, "Epispasm: Circumcision in Reverse," *BibRev* 8 (1992): 52–57.

[291] Why would a Jew wish to hide circumcision? Bruce W. Winter (*Seek the Welfare of the City: Christians as Benefactors and Citizens*, First-Century Christians in the Graeco-Roman World [Grand Rapids: Eerdmans, 1994], 147–52) suggests that by doing so it would increase their status in society.

[292] For a recent and brief synopsis of the complexities involved in Paul's view of the law as it pertains to this text, see Ciampa and Rosner, *First Corinthians*, 312–16. In sum, with respect to the law, Paul sometimes engages in a polemical refutation, as in 7:19a, "Circumcision is nothing" (also 9:20, "I myself am not under the law"). Sometimes Paul offers radical replacement, as in 7:19b, to obey God's commands. Third, when Paul speaks positively of the Christian and the law, he says that they "fulfill" it (Rom 8:4; 13:8; Gal 5:14; 6:2).

[293] Fee, *First Corinthians*, 313.

[294] Barrett, *First Corinthians*, 169.

Paul does not elaborate on what he means by keeping God's commands. Fee suggests that Paul would perhaps make a distinction between keeping the commands of God and the "works of the law."[295] Hays thinks that Paul's statement presupposes that the law is to be read anew through a different hermeneutical lens, since Christ is the end of the law, a thought developed more fully in Rom 2:25–29; 8:1–4; 10:1–13; 13:8–10.[296] Ciampa and Rosner note the importance of the parallel texts in Gal 5:6 and 6:15 where the thing contrasted with circumcision is not a part of the law that remains but something that replaces the law entirely, "faith expressing itself through love" (Gal 5:6) and "a new creation" (Gal 6:15). In other words, "keeping God's commands" does not refer to the Mosaic law in this instance. Broadly speaking, we are safe in saying that Paul refers to God's will.[297] Ciampa and Rosner, following Garland, think that a more precise reference in context is the avoidance of sexual immorality. Quoting Garland, "Paul implies that the important distinction is not between those who are married and those who are celibate, but between those who avoid fornication and those who fall prey to it."[298] Verse 20 restates the principle of 7:17, although in a slightly different form. The noun "calling" is used with reference to one's station in life, the situation one was in when he was "called" by God.[299]

**7:21** The second illustration draws from the world of slavery and freedom.[300] The problem for interpretation is that commentators have read Paul's statement in exactly opposite ways. Is Paul saying, "Even if you can gain your freedom, make the most of your present condition instead"?[301] This would be in keeping with the principle of "remain as you are," that Paul articulates throughout the chapter. Or, is Paul saying, "If you can be made free, then make use of your new status. It is your relationship to the Lord that really matters"? Paul's allowance of exceptions throughout chap. 7 would substantiate this second approach. Fee argues, following Bartchy, that the positive makes more sense because the choice to remain in slavery once offered freedom did not exist.[302]

**7:22–24** By placing both the social status of the slave and the freedman in the context of one's status (calling) in Christ (7:22) and restating the principle

---

[295] Fee, *First Corinthians*, 313.

[296] Hays, *First Corinthians*, 124.

[297] Barrett, *First Corinthians*, 169.

[298] Garland, *1 Corinthians*, 299, 306. See Ciampa and Rosner, *First Corinthians*, 315.

[299] So also Barrett, *First Corinthians*, 169–70. See discussion on 1:26–31. The noun "calling" in 1:26 refers to the call to salvation in context. Thus, Paul uses the term with both meanings in 1 Corinthians (call to salvation and station in life). Barrett (170) comments that "A man is not called to a new occupation; his old occupation is given new significance."

[300] For a fairly recent survey of New Testament scholarship on the issue of slavery, see J. Byron, "Paul and the Background of Slavery: The *Status Quaestionis* in New Testament Scholarship," *CurBS* 3, no. 1 (2004): 116–39.

[301] So Barrett (*First Corinthians*, 170–71).

[302] Fee, *First Corinthians*, 317–18.

"you were bought at a price" (7:23; cf. 6:20), Paul underscores that all believers belong to the Lord and thus none should become "slaves of men." In 9:19 Paul will offer himself as an example of one who gives up his freedom for the sake of the gospel and will say the opposite: "Though I am free and belong to no man, I make myself a slave to everyone, to win as many as possible." In both cases Paul is speaking figuratively (spiritually) rather than of literal enslavement. In 7:24 Paul states yet a third time the guiding theological principle, "Remain as you are." Morris captures the gist of Paul's thought: "All of life is God's. We should serve God where we are until he calls elsewhere."[303] More specifically, in context, 7:17–24 functions "as an analogy in support of Paul's argument that the married should not abandon their marriages and that the unmarried should not necessarily be urgently seeking new partners."[304]

### *(4) Concerning the Virgins (7:25–40)*

**25Now about virgins: I have no command from the Lord, but I give a judgment as one who by the Lord's mercy is trustworthy. 26Because of the present crisis, I think that it is good for you to remain as you are. 27Are you married? Do not seek a divorce. Are you unmarried? Do not look for a wife. 28But if you do marry, you have not sinned; and if a virgin marries, she has not sinned. But those who marry will face many troubles in this life, and I want to spare you this.**

**29What I mean, brothers, is that the time is short. From now on those who have wives should live as if they had none; 30those who mourn, as if they did not; those who are happy, as if they were not; those who buy something, as if it were not theirs to keep; 31those who use the things of the world, as if not engrossed in them. For this world in its present form is passing away.**

**32I would like you to be free from concern. An unmarried man is concerned about the Lord's affairs—how he can please the Lord. 33But a married man is concerned about the affairs of this world—how he can please his wife—34and his interests are divided. An unmarried woman or virgin is concerned about the Lord's affairs: Her aim is to be devoted to the Lord in both body and spirit. But a married woman is concerned about the affairs of this world—how she can please her husband. 35I am saying this for your own good, not to restrict you, but that you may live in a right way in undivided devotion to the Lord.**

**36If anyone thinks he is acting improperly toward the virgin he is engaged to, and if she is getting along in years and he feels he ought to marry, he should do as he wants. He is not sinning. They should get married. 37But the man who has settled the matter in his own mind, who is under no compulsion but has control over his own will, and who has made up his mind not to marry the virgin—this man also does the right thing. 38So then, he who marries the virgin does right, but he who does not marry her does even better.**

**39A woman is bound to her husband as long as he lives. But if her husband dies, she is free to marry anyone she wishes, but he must belong to the Lord. 40In**

[303] Morris, *1 Corinthians*, 111.

[304] Hays, *First Corinthians*, 126.

**my judgment, she is happier if she stays as she is—and I think that I too have the Spirit of God.**

The second occurrence of the formulaic *peri de* in 7:25 (cf. 7:1), translated "Now about," signals a shift of topic, presumably indicating another issue raised by the Corinthians in their letter to Paul.[305] This section raises a number of interpretive questions. Who are "the virgins" mentioned in 7:28,34,36? What is the "present crisis" noted in 7:26? How does Paul's eschatological outlook condition his response (7:29–31)? Why does Paul mention widows again in 7:39–40 since he has already addressed this group in 7:8–9? One thing is clear; Paul is consistent in 7:25–40 in the application of the principle, "Remain as you are," that has served as his theological guidepost for the entire chapter.

The language Paul employs in this section parallels previous statements in the first half of the chapter. In 7:6 Paul advises according to concession and not according to commandment. He desires all men to be as himself, but recognizes each has his own gift (7:7). This follows with his opinion to the unmarried and widows, "It is good for them to remain as I am." Similarly, in 7:25–26, Paul states that he does not have a "command" from the Lord concerning the virgins, yet he gives his judgment as one who is trustworthy.[306] He then reiterates that it is "good to remain as you are." Even though the main topic throughout is "the virgins," Paul reiterates that a husband is not to seek to be loosed from his wife (7:27; cf. 7:10–11). Furthermore, he closes this section in parallel fashion to the opening by giving his judgment with the additional statement, "and I think that I too have the Spirit of God."[307] The language of the opening and closing suggests that, although Paul provides room for flexibility in decision-making, he is weighing in somewhat authoritatively against others in Corinth who would advise differently. Paul is clear in 7:25–40 that to marry in a situation where he thinks singleness is preferable is not sinful (7:28; cf. 7:9). Paul's reasons for his preference for the unmarried state relate to the "present crisis" and to the issue of serving the Lord without distraction.[308]

**7:25a** The term "virgins" occurs six times in 7:25–38 (7:25,28,34, 36–38).[309] The differences of opinion regarding the meaning of the word are

[305] The fact that Paul employs περὶ δὲ a second time may suggest that 7:8–16 is Paul's own expansion of the question posed in 7:1–7 rather than a response to issues specifically raised by the Corinthians. See Winter, "1 Corinthians 7:6–7."

[306] In 7:6 the Greek term for "concession" (συγγνώμη) is semantically close to the word in 7:25 for opinion (γνώμη). The term for "commandment" (ἐπιταγή) in 7:6,25 is the same.

[307] Thus 7:25 and 7:40 forms an *inclusio* built around the term γνώμη and Paul's qualification that he speaks as one entrusted and guided by God.

[308] Interestingly, Paul does not refer to the prevalence of sexual immorality as a reason for the virgin to marry, unless this is implied in 7:36; one who acts unbecomingly toward his virgin.

[309] Gk. παρθένος. Except for 7:25 all occurrences are in the singular. The only other occurrence in Paul is 2 Cor 11:2 where Paul applies it figuratively to the church, "I am jealous for you with a godly jealousy. I promised you to one husband, to Christ, so that I might present you as a pure virgin to him."

reflected in three modern translations of 7:36–38. First, the NASB translates all three occurrences of the term in 7:36–38 as "virgin daughter." This view holds that "virgins" refers to daughters of marriageable age and the indefinite pronoun "anyone" (7:36) is the father or the legal guardian, who faces the dilemma of whether or not to allow his daughter to marry. It is often claimed that this view was nearly the universal opinion of the church up to the twentieth century.[310] One of the crucial pieces of evidence for this view is the change of verbs in 7:38 to "given in marriage" from the usual "to marry."[311] This view assumes a certain cultural background where the daughter could not marry without permission of the father or legal guardian. The difficulty with this view is the absence of key terms like father, guardian, and daughter. Fee claims that there is no known evidence of a father-daughter relationship referred to in terms of her being "his virgin."[312] Furthermore, the word translated "to act improperly toward" in 7:36 translates a word that may carry sexual innuendos in certain contexts that would be inappropriate for a father-daughter relationship.[313] In order for this view to work, the NASB opts for a poorly attested textual variant in 7:36, "Let her marry," rather than the better attested, "Let them marry."[314]

A second view holds that in 7:25–38 Paul refers to "spiritual marriages." This view is represented by the NEB translation, "But if a man has a partner in celibacy and feels that he is not behaving properly towards her, if, that is, his instincts are too strong for him, and something must be done, he may do as he pleases; there is nothing wrong with it; let them marry." In other words, a couple, although married, lived together not as husband and wife but as brother and sister under a vow of celibacy in marriage, either because sex was viewed as sinful or celibacy was viewed as a superior spiritual state. The question for Paul had to do with whether or not they should, in fact, consummate the marriage. The verb translated "let them marry" would mean in this context "let them engage in sexual relations." The verb, however, does not mean "to

[310] Although see Thiselton (*First Corinthians*, 595), who questions the validity of this claim upon closer examination of the actual sources.

[311] γαμίζω rather than γαμέω. The latter is used throughout the chapter (7:9–10,28,33–34,36,39) but not in 7:38. The NIV does not see any distinction in the terms and translates the former (γαμίζω) as "marry" rather than "given in marriage." The NASB distinguishes the terms. All other New Testament occurrences of the term are translated "given in marriage" (see Matt 22:30; 24:38; Mark 12:25; Luke 17:27; 20:35). For Robertson and Plummer (*First Corinthians*, 159) the use of γαμίζω is decisive. "the Apostle is speaking of a father or guardian disposing of an unmarried daughter or ward." So also Morris, *1 Corinthians*, 117–19.

[312] Fee, *First Corinthians*, 326.

[313] So Blomberg, *1 Corinthians*, 153. The verb (ἀσχημονέω) appears again in 13:5, "It [love] is not rude." The verb appears only in these two instances in the New Testament. On the sexual connotations of the verb in the context of male/female relationships, see B. W. Winter, "Puberty or Passion? The Referent of ὑπέρακμος in 1 Corinthians 7:36," *TynBul* 49 (1998): 80.

[314] It is, of course, possible to imagine that the third person brings in the third party (the suitor) in the father-virgin daughter view. That is, the father permits the marriage to go forward, thus, "Let them marry."

consummate a marriage." Furthermore, Paul's instructions in 7:1–5 regarding married couples mitigates against this view.[315]

Finally, the view most widely held among recent commentators is that Paul is speaking to engaged couples in 7:25–38.[316] The term "virgin" may be shorthand for "betrothed virgin."[317] This view is conveyed by the NIV translation of 7:36, "If anyone thinks he is acting improperly toward the virgin he is engaged to, and if she is getting along in years and he feels he ought to marry, he should do as he wants. He is not sinning. They should get married." Similarly the NRSV translates, "If anyone thinks that he is not behaving properly toward his fiancée," and the ESV, "If anyone thinks that he is not behaving properly toward his betrothed." The ESV establishes this view as early as 7:25, "Now concerning the betrothed." Some translations of 7:36 do not interpret the term and simply translate as "virgin" (so the HCSB, "But if any man thinks he is acting improperly toward his virgin . . ."). While there are good arguments for both the "virgin daughter" view and the "engaged couple" view, neither view is without difficulties. The view taken here is that "virgins" refers to betrothed young women of marriageable age and that Paul directs his instructions primarily toward the men who took the lead in such matters.[318] The question before Paul is what those currently engaged should do about marriage in light of the "present crisis" (7:26).

**7:25b–26** Paul prefaces his judgment about the virgins by stating that he has no command from the Lord (cf. 7:10,12) but that he gives his judgment "as one who by the Lord's mercy is trustworthy." As Ciampa and Rosner point out, "Paul is not like a counselor in the modern sense of giving neutral help designed to help autonomous individuals come to their own decision." The term "mercy" refers to Paul's call to apostleship (2 Cor 4:1, cf. Gal 1:15–16). Earlier in the letter Paul referred to his stewardship of the mysteries of God and the requirement of trustworthiness (4:1–2).[319] As noted in the introduction to this section Paul ends this section with a parallel statement affirming the reliability of his instruction, "and I think that I too have the Spirit of God" (7:40). He clearly offers options and clarifies that there is no sin involved if they see

[315] This view assumes a particular historical reconstruction of the situation in Corinth. The idea of "spiritual marriage" did arise in the church in the second century but was vigorously opposed. For this view see Hurd, *The Origin of 1 Corinthians*, 169–78.

[316] Those who hold this view include Barrett, *First Corinthians*, 184; J. K. Elliott, "Paul's Teaching on Marriage in 1 Cor: Some Problems Considered," *NTS* 19 (1973): 219–25; Fee, *First Corinthians*, 326–27; Hays, *First Corinthians*, 126–27; Garland, *1 Corinthians*, 336–43; Ciampa and Rosner, *First Corinthians*, 355–63.

[317] Ciampa and Rosner (*First Corinthians*, 332) comment, "It may be that the Corinthians had referred to 'betrothed virgins in their letter to Paul and that he responds by referring to 'the virgins,' meaning 'the [betrothed] virgins you mentioned,' but that is speculation."

[318] So also Fee, *First Corinthians*, 327.

[319] Ciampa and Rosner, *First Corinthians*, 333–34.

things differently on whether or not to proceed with marriage, but they must not take Paul's advice lightly.

Paul's trustworthy opinion regarding "the virgins" is that it is good to "remain as you are"[320] "because of the present crisis" (7:26).[321] Some think the reference to the "present crisis" is to troubles preceding the second advent.[322] The term appears in Luke 21:23 with reference to the last days along with the statement, "How dreadful it will be in those days for pregnant women and nursing mothers!" Mark 13:17–20 speaks of the same thing and mentions a shortening of days (cf. 1 Cor 7:29). The eschatological language of 7:29–31 lends support to this view. Paul, however, does not use the term elsewhere in eschatological contexts,[323] unless he viewed present troubles in relation to the eschaton in some way. Others think that Paul has in view a more concrete historical situation, such as famine or persecution.[324] Furthermore, although the term "present" can mean "impending," giving credence to the eschatological view, in Pauline usage the participial form always refers to what is already present.[325] There is some pressing constraint on the believers at the time of Paul's writing, but we do not know what the distress entailed. Grosheide does not detect as eschatological reference at all, but rather suggests that Paul "has in view the distress which exists for every Christian at all times."[326] In context Paul speaks of "troubles in this life" (7:28), a shortened time (7:29a), and the world in its present form passing away (7:31). Hays, noting that the Greek term translated "crisis" occurs in 7:37 and again in 9:16, thinks that "present crisis (necessity)" in 7:26 is the urgent imperative of proclaiming the gospel and doing the work of the Lord in the short time that remains.[327] In recent scholarship, there is a tendency to take a both/and approach to the question of the "present crisis." Garland, for example, states, "It is most likely that he has in view a present crisis (perhaps the famine) interpreted as an end-time event."[328]

---

320 Barrett (*First Corinthians*, 174) detects the presence of another slogan in 7:26 (cf. 7:1).

321 The Greek term for "crisis" is ἀνάγκη. BDAG assigns 1 Cor 7:26 to the definition "a state of distress or trouble, distress, calamity, pressure." Other meanings include "necessity, pressure" or "compulsion by forcible means."

322 So Barrett, *First Corinthians*, 175.

323 See Rom 13:5; 1 Cor 7:37; 9:16; 2 Cor 6:4; 9:7; 12:10; 1 Thess 3:7; Phlm 14.

324 B. W. Winter, "Secular and Christian Responses to Corinthian Famines," *TynBul* 40 (1989): 86–106; B. Blue, "The House Church at Corinth and the Lord's Supper: Famine, Food Supply, and the Present Distress," *CTR* 5 (1993): 221–39.

325 The NRSV translates the Greek participle (ἐνεστῶσαν) as "impending," yet Paul always uses the perfect participle to refer to the present. In Rom 8:38 and 1 Cor 3:22 Paul uses the term to contrast what is present with the future. In Gal 1:4, the term is used to refer to this "present" evil age. The verb form does appear in eschatological contexts in two places in Paul. In 2 Thess 2:2, Paul warns of being unsettled because of some who claimed that the Day of the Lord "has already come," and in 2 Tim 3:1 Paul warns of the last days when difficult times "will come."

326 Grosheide, *First Corinthians*, 175.

327 Hays, *First Corinthians*, 129.

328 Garland, *1 Corinthians*, 324.

Similarly, Ciampa and Rosner propose, "Paul would probably have recognized that the present crisis in Corinth was like that of the End and might even have been a part of it; the present woes are typical, at least, of the parousia woes, if they are not in fact the first and outlying clouds spinning around the ultimate hurricane on the eschatological horizon."[329] However one understands the phrase, it is important to note that Paul's instructions are conditioned by some pressing constraint. There are presently unusually difficult circumstances in Corinth, and for the time being remaining single is, in his judgment, advisable. Otherwise, his judgment might differ.[330]

**7:27–28** In 7:27 Paul expands on the core principle, "remain as you are," mentioned in 7:26, speaking directly to the male, "Are you married? Do not seek a divorce. Are you unmarried? Do not look for a wife." The NIV follows the more traditional understanding of 7:27a, that Paul is speaking to the already married and is, for a second time, forbidding divorce. The Greek text reads literally, "Are you bound to a wife (woman)? Do not seek to be loosed (released)."[331] The more recent NIV2011 translation, however, renders 7:27 as follows: "Are you pledged to a woman? Do not seek to be released. Are you free from such a commitment? Do not look for a wife." This translation seeks to establish consistency in the view that Paul is speaking to engaged couples throughout 7:25–38. The evidence for this translation includes the following: (1) Paul has already restated the command of the Lord forbidding divorce in 7:10–11 and to do so again is unnecessarily redundant. Paul has in mind a separate group (the never married) throughout 7:25–38. (2) The term translated "divorce" (NIV) or "released/loosed" (NASB, HCSB) occurs only here in the New Testament and is a different term from the two terms used in 7:10–11 ("separate" and "leave").[332] (3) In 7:25 Paul states that he is addressing a situation where there is no command of the Lord. Yet, there is a command of the Lord regarding divorce (7:10–11).[333]

It is not certain, however, that we should abandon the traditional understanding of the verse. The term "bound" is the usual term Paul uses to denote the binding character of marriage (see 7:39; Rom 7:2). Furthermore, even though Paul addresses a different group the issue of marriage is still the question and

[329] Ciampa and Rosner, *First Corinthians*, 337. See also Thiselton (*First Corinthians*, 573) who states that the view that the present crisis represent a concrete historical circumstance is "by no means an alternative to an eschatological element" but rather that it only adds "a necessary circumstantial aspect to Paul's advice."

[330] Morris (*1 Corinthians*, 113) comments, "When high seas are raging it is no time for changing ships." Vaughn and Lea (*1 Corinthians*, 79) suggest that the reference to a "present crisis" means that we should not apply Paul's advice here to all Christians of every generation and place.

[331] δέδεσαι γυναικί, μὴ ζήτει λύσιν.

[332] In 7:10–11 the terms are χωρίζω and ἀφίημι. In 7:27 the term is λύσις.

[333] Among the recent commentators who advocate the view represented by the NIV2011, see Fee, *First Corinthians*, 332; Thiselton, *First Corinthians*, 576–77; Garland, *1 Corinthians*, 325–26; Ciampa and Rosner, *First Corinthians*, 338–40.

so emphasizing its binding character both at the beginning of the unit (7:27a) and at the end (7:39) does not entail redundancy.[334] It is clear from the context that the issue of which there is no command from the Lord is whether or not one should marry, not the binding character of marriage. Likewise, in 7:39–40 Paul juxtaposes a statement regarding the binding character of marriage, that a wife is bound to her husband as long as he lives, with a statement of his judgment that she is happier to remain unmarried should the husband die. The decision to marry or not to marry should always be made in the light of God's intention for the permanence of the marriage relationship. Finally, if 7:27a addresses the engaged couple, then Paul forthrightly says, "Do not seek to be released from your commitment." This seems to go against his advice in 7:36–38 that to remain unmarried is better. Thus, at face value the phrase "Do not seek to be loosed" seems to mean "Do not seek a divorce"; but in the second question, "Are you loosed from a wife?", the meaning is simply "Are you unmarried?" and does not necessarily mean "Are you divorced?"[335] The context clarifies that only the second command, "Do not look for a wife," has a measure of flexibility, that is, those who are unmarried may still choose marriage and not sin (7:28). The first command, "Do not seek a divorce," is a matter of the Lord's command, which Paul has already clarified in 7:10–11 and will state again in 7:39. Therefore, Paul's trustworthy judgment (7:26) in the light of present circumstances is that those who are unmarried should refrain from seeking marriage. However, there is no sin in the choice to marry, either for the man or for the betrothed virgin. Yet, Paul advises that with marriage comes many difficulties and he wants to spare them the added troubles of this life.[336] Since Paul does not specify the nature of the troubles, he may be referring to the same thing as the "present crisis" mentioned in 7:26. It is unlikely, in my view, that Paul is referring merely to the normal difficulties of marriage, which would be the case for all marriages of all times.

**7:29–31** To this point in the letter Paul's end-time outlook has proven to be a significant component of his instruction to the Corinthians.[337] Similarly, in 7:29–31, Paul puts the question of whether or not to marry, along with other activities that characterize the whole of life, into proper eschatological focus. The key to understanding the five paradoxical assertions of 7:29b–31a lies in the parallel statements that frame the unit: "the time is short" (7:29)[338] and "this

---

[334] Only two verses later Paul refers to those who are married, "From now on those who have wives should live as if they had none" (7:29).

[335] Thus the correctness of the NIV.

[336] The phrase is literally, "troubles in the flesh." There is no special theological significance to the term "flesh" in this context. It refers to the merely physical, earthly state in which marriage inevitably carries obligations (so Barrett, *First Corinthians*, 176).

[337] See 1:7–8; 2:6–9; 3:10–15; 4:1–5; 5:5; 6:1–3,9–10,14.

[338] The NIV translation, "What I mean, brothers, is that the time is short," suggests that Paul is now explaining the previous verses. The Greek phrase, however, introduces what follows. The construction is the same as in 15:50, "τοῦτο δέ φημι, ἀδελφοί."

world in its present form is passing away" (7:31). The language of 7:29b–31a cannot be pressed literally as if Paul advocates that those having wives should live literally as though not having a wife, and so forth. This would go against everything argued in 7:1–5,10–16. Rather, Paul uses such language with the objective to change the way the Corinthians view earthly things. Robertson and Plummer paraphrase Paul's intention as something like, "But though I counsel none to change their state, I do counsel all to change their attitude towards all earthly things."[339] As important as earthly concerns may be, believers should never allow such concerns to overshadow eternal realities.

Paul's eschatological aside begins with the statement, "The time is short." The NASB translates, "The time has been shortened." But what does Paul mean by it? In light of the parallel with 7:31, the "time" refers to the period of time that remains until the final consummation.[340] The "shortening" of time could refer to either the quantity of time left before the end or the character/quality of time that has been irrevocably altered by the event of the death and resurrection of Jesus, which signaled the dawning of the last days and brought the end into plain view.[341] Ciampa and Rosner are probably correct in suggesting that both quantity of time and quality of time are at work with more emphasis on the latter: "That is, Paul says that the remaining time is limited and that the fact that the End is coming affects the character and quality of the time we have left."[342] The word translated "short/shortened" appears in the New Testament only twice; here and in Acts 5:6.[343] The meaning in Acts is "to wrap or cover up" and is used with reference to those who gathered up the body of Ananias in preparation for burial. With reference to time the word takes up a different nuance. Robertson and Plummer suggest that the phrase in 7:29 literally means that time "has been drawn up together so as to be small in amount."[344] Others prefer to express the meaning as "the time is compressed."[345] As Fee explains, "The picture is that of one for whom the future was either nonexistent, as for most Greeks, or off in the vague distance; but the event of Christ has now compressed the time in such a way that the future has been brought forward so as to be clearly visible."[346] Paul's concern is not with the amount of time

---

[339] Robertson and Plummer, *First Corinthians*, 154. Similarly Fee (*First Corinthians*, 336), "he calls for a radically new understanding of their relationship to the world."

[340] The nuances of the Greek term καιρός are varied, including point in time, period of time, or a particular kind of time. See BDAG.

[341] So Fee, *First Corinthians*, 339.

[342] Ciampa and Rosner, *First Corinthians*, 344. Thiselton (*First Corinthians*, 579) clearly favors the latter; "time" is quality of time, not chronological duration. So also Garland, *1 Corinthians*, 328.

[343] Gk. συστέλλω.

[344] Robertson and Plummer, *First Corinthians*, 154.

[345] So Fee, *First Corinthians*, 339; Garland, *1 Corinthians*, 328; Ciampa and Rosner, *First Corinthians*, 344.

[346] Fee, *First Corinthians*, 339n14.

left "but with the radical new perspective the 'foreshortened future' gives one with regard to the present age."[347] The character of the present age alters the believer's relationship to the world and demands the reordering of priorities. Romans 13:11–14 provides expanded commentary on Paul's meaning in 1 Cor 7:29. Believers should "understand the time" and be vigilant "because our salvation is nearer now than when we first believed. The night is nearly over; the day is almost here. So let us put aside the deeds of darkness and put on the armor of light" (Rom 13:11–12). Similarly, in Eph 5:15–16 Paul admonishes to "be very careful how you live," and to make "the most of every opportunity because the days are evil."[348]

In 7:29b–31a Paul lists five examples that drive home the point that believers should live in light of the reality that the present structures of this world are passing away.[349] Even though marriage is by divine appointment, it is a temporary arrangement (Mark 12:19–25) that dissolves at death (Rom 7:2; 1 Cor 7:39). In context, even though Paul addresses "those who have wives," the focus of the exhortation is to those contemplating marriage, and he counsels that the decision to marry or not to marry should take into account eschatological realities. In the four additional examples, Paul touches on other areas of life that affect everyone, whether single or married. Paul is not oblivious to the ups and downs of life when he urges those who mourn to live as if they did not and those who are happy to live as if they were not.[350] In context, he is simply saying that sadness and joy are not decisive for the Christian; there is something of far greater significance. In the fourth and fifth examples Paul casts eschatological light on worldly possessions. Buying and selling is a part of life, but one's life does not consist in what he or she owns (Luke 12:15). As Garland states, "The mandate to buy presupposes that Paul does not intend for Christians to withdraw from the world (cf. 5:10). They may continue to do business, but they must watch lest they become consumed by their consuming."[351] James 4:13–17 warns of the same thing. To those who are overly preoccupied with plans to carry on business and make a profit James bluntly states, "Why, you do not even know what will happen tomorrow. What is your life? You are a mist that appears for a little while and then vanishes" (Jas 4:14). Paul's final example,

[347] Ibid., 339.

[348] The NIV's "making the most of every opportunity" is literally, "redeeming the time." The Greek term for "time" is καιρός. Such is the eschatological outlook of the New Testament. To take another example, consider Jas 5:7–9. The exhortation to patience until the Lord's return presumes a period of waiting, yet there is an urgency (imminence) regarding his return: "the Lord's coming is near" (5:8) and "The Judge is standing at the door!" (5:9)

[349] Signaled by the Greek τὸ λοιπόν (NIV, "from now on").

[350] See Rom 12:15; 2 Cor 2:4; Phil 1:18; 4:4.

[351] Garland, *1 Corinthians*, 330. Garland notes three Lucan parables that clarify Paul's warning: the parable of the rich fool (Luke 12:16–21), those shut out of the banquet who were distracted by marrying and buying (Luke 14:15–24), and those caught by surprise by the coming of the Son of Man because they were engaged too heavily in the things of this world (Luke 17:26–37).

"those who use the things of the world, as if not engrossed in them," employs a play on words in the Greek, reading literally, "those who make use of the world as not making full use."[352] The term "to make full use" appears again in 9:18 where Paul presents himself as an example of one who had full apostolic rights but did not make full use of those rights. The NIV nicely captures the essence of Paul's meaning in 7:31 by rendering the word "to be engrossed in." It is one thing to be engaged with the world, but the believer cannot afford to become entangled with the world.[353] Paul will return full force to the theme of disciplined Christian living for the cause of the gospel in 9:19–27.

Paul rounds out his eschatological parenthesis with the grounds for his exhortation and the main point of the paragraph, "For this world in its present form is passing away" (7:31b). By "form"[354] Paul refers to the structures of life just mentioned: marriage, sadness, joy, possessing, and making use of the things of the world.[355] Even though these things are fleeting, they do provide the content of this life. Paul is under no illusion that life's framework can be discarded altogether; people will marry, experience heartache and elation, and participate in the material aspects of this world. Paul's concern, as the next few verses demonstrate, is that believers live in order to please God. Those things done in the will of God and for his glory are the things that have lasting value.[356]

**7:32–35** If 7:29–31 expands on the "present crisis" (7:26), then 7:32–35 elaborates on "the troubles in this life" facing those who choose to marry.[357] The two sections are linked by the word "world," which concludes 7:29–31 and is a key term in 7:32–35.[358] If the world in its present form is passing away, then believers contemplating marriage need to give due consideration to the commitment of marriage in relation to pleasing the Lord and serving him without distraction. Thus, Paul gives yet another reason to those contemplating marriage to remain single, namely, that they may be free from concern and serve the Lord without distraction. Marriage entails many responsibilities equally for husband and wife as each seeks to please the other.[359] Such an arrangement inevitably leads to divided interests (7:34). Paul has no desire

---

[352] Gk. οἱ χρώμενοι τὸν κόσμον ὡς μὴ καταχρώμενοι.

[353] Ciampa and Rosner (*First Corinthians*, 348) comment, "Paul's stance toward the world is the opposite of that inspired by a denial of eschatology in 15:32b, where "full use" of the things of the world is encouraged: "If the dead are not raised, 'Let us eat and drink, for tomorrow we die.' "

[354] Gk. σχῆμα,

[355] So also Ciampa and Rosner, *First Corinthians*, 348.

[356] Serving others and doing all for the glory of God is a major theme in the next unit (8:1–11:1; see esp. 10:23–11:1). Cf. also Jas 4:13–17; 1 John 2:17.

[357] So Blomberg, *1 Corinthians*, 151–52.

[358] Occurring three times in four verses. "World" in this context does not carry negative connotations per se in the same way that "flesh" (NIV, "in this life") in 7:28 refers to mere earthly existence.

[359] Barrett (*First Corinthians*, 179) notes that, against the traditional reading 7:32 might mean, "The unmarried is anxious about the things of the Lord" in the sense of seeking to please the Lord through meritorious works. This interpretation assumes that there is a pro-celibacy party in Corinth

to restrict them, but he advises them in this way for their own good (7:35; cf. 7:28b). The word translated "good" means "advantageous"[360] and is cognate to the verb translated "beneficial"[361] in the slogan of 6:12, "Not everything is beneficial" (cf. also 10:23).[362] In 10:33 Paul writes similarly that he seeks to please others, not seeking his own advantage but the advantage of others.[363] The notion of what is best, beneficial, or advantageous is a critical element of Paul's decision-making and a key theme that runs through chap. 14. Paul wants the Corinthians to know that he has their best interests in view. He will clarify yet again in the following verses that it is no sin to choose marriage, yet apparently they have posed a question to him regarding marriage, and he is answering them as the Lord's trustworthy representative in the light of their present situation.

**7:36–38** The differences in the translation of 7:36–38, which represent the various views of this passage, has already been addressed in the comments on 7:25. I concur with the "engaged couple" view taken by most recent commentators and represented by the NIV translation (and by most English translations). The exegetical challenges presented by this paragraph are well-established and were touched on briefly in 7:25. In sum, the interpretive issues revolve essentially around the following questions: (1) Who is the "anyone" mentioned in 7:36? Does the pronoun refer to a man who is engaged or to a father/guardian of a virgin daughter or to someone in a "spiritual marriage"? (2) What does it mean "to act improperly toward his virgin?" Are there moral, legal, or social concerns involved? (3) Who is the virgin? Is the virgin the fiancee or the daughter or someone in a spiritual marriage? (4) What is the meaning of the Greek term translated "getting along in years," and who is the subject of the verb, which could either be male or female?[364] Does the word mean "past puberty/maturity," or is there a sexual overtone with the meaning, "If his passions are strong" (so NRSV)?[365] (5) What is the meaning of the phrase translated by the NIV, "and he feels he ought to marry," which reads literally, "And so it ought to be"?[366] (6) Why does Paul change to a verb in 7:38 that normally means "to be given in marriage," which seems to offer support to the "virgin daughter" view?[367]

---

promoting celibacy as a higher spiritual existence. Paul replies that one should not be anxious to please the Lord in this way.

[360] Gk. σύμφορος.

[361] Gk. συμφέρω.

[362] See also 12:7, "Now to each one the manifestation of the Spirit is given for the common good."

[363] In 10:33 the same term is used as in 7:35 (σύμφορος).

[364] The Greek verb makes no distinction.

[365] Gk. ὑπέρακμος.

[366] καὶ οὕτως ὀφείλει γίνεσθαι.

[367] From γαμέω in 7:36 to γαμίζω in 7:38.

Briefly, the consensus view, although not without difficulties, seems to provide the best reading of the evidence. In this interpretation, "anyone" is a man betrothed to a virgin (his fiancee). It is not certain, however, what Paul means by the following phrase rendered, "If he thinks he is acting improperly toward," since the nature of the "improper behavior" is not specified. Furthermore, as noted above, the phrase translated "If she is getting along in years" could also read "If his passions are strong" (so NRSV).[368] Paul's language is open to the interpretation that the decision to marry is related either to the pressures of sexual temptation (cf. 7:9)[369] or to social expectations.[370] Either way, there are two interrelated criteria for not getting married: (1) There must be a settled conviction regarding the right thing to do, and (2) there must be a determination if there is a necessity or compulsion to marry.[371] The phrase "to keep his own virgin" in 7:37 is problematic and may mean "not to marry" (NIV) or perhaps "to keep her as his betrothed" (ESV).[372] Either way, Paul commends that the man has "done the right thing" not to marry. Finally, it is commonly suggested that the change in verb in 7:38 does not necessarily indicate a causative action such as the NASB translation, "to give in marriage." The NIV translates simply, "to marry." Fee suggests that Paul may have used a different verb in 7:38 because of its transitive nuance, that is, the verb takes a direct object. All other occurrences of the other verb translated "to marry" in the chapter are intransitive (no direct object).[373] Thus, in line with the entire argument from 7:25 to this point, Paul advises the Corinthians to choose those things that are best in light of the present situation; yet marriage is not to be despised, and it is perfectly acceptable to proceed with marriage plans.

**7:39–40** Since Paul has already addressed "widows" in 7:8, he does not seem to be addressing them once again as a distinct group. Even though his instruction takes into account the widow and her freedom to remarry, it appears that Paul is still on the topic of the "betrothed virgins," reminding them that once married a wife is bound to her husband as long as he lives. In other words,

---

[368] The key term is ὑπέρακμος.

[369] So Winter, "Puberty or Passion?"; Garland, *1 Corinthians*, 340–41.

[370] So Collins (*First Corinthians*, 301) and, more recently, Ciampa and Rosner (*First Corinthians*, 357–58). Following Conzelmann (*1 Corinthians*, 135n38) and Thiselton (*First Corinthians*, 595), Ciampa and Rosner note that the church fathers all took the verb ἀσχημονέω in nonsexual ways. The only other occurrence of the verb in the New Testament is 1 Cor 13:5.

[371] Garland and Ciampa and Rosner both recognize these two criteria presented in an ABBA pattern in 7:37, but they read the evidence differently, the former opting for the "sexual temptation" view and the latter the "social custom" view. Ciampa and Rosner (362) explain, "The man's ability to decide and stand firm in his own heart (A, A') depends to a significant degree on whether or not some necessity or compulsion diminishes this ability to freely exercise his own will (B, B')."

[372] So also ibid., who suggest that the intent to keep her as his betrothed is temporary and remaining unmarried for the time being in light of the "present crisis" (7:26).

[373] Fee, *First Corinthians*, 355. So also Garland, *1 Corinthians*, 338. Fitzmyer (*First Corinthians*, 327) observes, however, that no one has been able to document such a meaning for γαμίζω apart from this occurrence.

Paul speaks to the issue of the permanence of marriage, both at the beginning and end of the unit (7:25–40; cf. 7:10–11), which is another strong consideration for decision-making for those contemplating marriage.[374] If the husband dies,[375] then the woman is free to marry whomever she wishes,[376] but "he must belong to the Lord." Paul's judgment, however, is that she will be happier if she remains single. Thus, this concluding paragraph draws the discussion of chap. 7 to a close by reiterating the permanence of the marriage bond and by stating the guiding principle of the chapter one final time, "to remain as you are." Paul's final comment, "and I think that I too have the Spirit of God" complements 7:25, "but I give a judgment as one who by the Lord's mercy is trustworthy." The mention of being guided by the Spirit may indicate that Paul is offering a counterpoint to others in Corinth who have advised otherwise under the auspices of "Spirit-inspired" advice. Already Paul has addressed "those who are spiritual" (2:6–3:4), and he will deal with them again full force in chaps. 12–14.

[374] See comments on 7:27.

[375] The word is literally "to sleep" (*κοιμάω*), which is a euphemism for death. For the use of *κοιμάω* elsewhere in Paul's letters see 1 Cor 11:30; 15:6,18,20,51; 1 Thess 4:13–15. Sometimes the term simply means "to sleep" in the literal sense (Matt 28:13; Luke 22:45; Acts 12:6). For the use of the term as a euphemism for death elsewhere in the New Testament, see Matt 27:52; John 11:11; Acts 7:60; 13:36.

[376] The "wish" of the woman to marry if she chooses is parallel to Paul's instructions to the man in 7:36, "he should do as he wants."

SECTION OUTLINE

IV. Christian Freedom, the Priority of Love, and the Peril of Idolatry (8:1–11:1)
1. The Priority of Love over Knowledge (8:1–13)
2. Paul's Apostolic Rights (9:1–12a)
3. Giving Up Rights for the Sake of the Gospel (9:12b–23)
4. Application and Transition: Run to Win! (9:24–27)
5. The Negative Example of Israel in the Wilderness (10:1–13)
6. Do Not Provoke the Lord to Jealousy—Flee Idolatry! (10:14–22)
7. Summary and Application: Do All for the Good of Others and the Glory of God (10:23–11:1)

## IV. CHRISTIAN FREEDOM, THE PRIORITY OF LOVE, AND THE PERIL OF IDOLATRY (8:1–11:1)

The formulaic "Now about"[1] in 8:1 introduces the next major topic of the letter, which extends to 11:1. The topic is food sacrificed to idols, but the real underlying issue is Christian freedom and the priority of love. The topic of idol food may appear to be rather irrelevant to Christians in the modern Western world, where there is virtually no concern for the history of food in terms of its religious significance. Cheung reminds us, however, that for some societies such concern remains a persistent problem.[2] In the ancient Greco-Roman world, the acknowledgment of pagan gods in various settings involved the eating of food that had been sacrificed to an idol. Furthermore, since remnants of the sacrifice were sold in the marketplace, the opportunities for eating such food were plentiful.

Like other portions of the letter, 8:1–11:1 raises complex literary and historical questions, which means that we have to do a bit of reading between the lines in order to understand the situation to which Paul responds. However, the core theological and ethical principles that guide Paul's thinking on this issue are crystal clear. Although Paul never quotes Deut 6 or Lev 19, the influence of these texts is apparent throughout the discussion.[3] Verse 3 speaks of one's love for God, and 8:4 clearly echoes the *Shema* (Deut 6:4), which follows with the command to love God with one's heart, soul, mind, and strength (Deut 6:5–6). The believer's exclusive allegiance to the

[1] The third occurrence of περὶ δὲ (cf. 7:1,25). A resumptive περὶ occurs in 8:4, following the brief digression of 8:1b–3.

[2] A. T. Cheung, *Idol Food in Corinth: Jewish Background and Pauline Legacy*, JSNTSup 176 (Sheffield: Sheffield Academic Press, 1999).

[3] Jesus established the "double-love command" as the sum of the law (see Matt 22:36–40 and par.).

one true God is especially apparent in Paul's strong denunciation of idolatry in 10:1–22. The principle of love for others also runs throughout the argument (8:1b,7–13; 9:19–23; 10:23–33). In Rom 13:8–10 and Gal 5:14 Paul quotes Lev 19:18, emphasizing that to love your neighbor as yourself is the sum of the law.

Before turning to an introduction of the issues raised by these chapters, it is helpful to consider the significant thematic links between 8:1–11:1 and other portions of the letter in order to highlight the theological and pastoral coherence of Paul's approach to a variety of issues that plagued the Corinthian church. First, we turn to the relationship of 8:1–11:1 to the immediately preceding section, 5:1–7:40. Already in 5:9–11, in the case of the toleration of the incestuous man, Paul clarified his previous letter's intent regarding his instruction not to associate with immoral people, including idolaters. His directive to refrain from eating with such people applied to professing Christians but not to unbelievers. Otherwise, believers would have to "leave the world" (5:10). At the same time, Paul scolded the church for taking up legal matters before the unbelievers (6:1–7), defrauding other believers (6:8), and he sternly cautioned that the unrighteous will not inherit the kingdom of God (6:9–10).[4] Similarly, in 8:1–11:1, Paul relates the issue of food sacrificed to idols to the believer's relationship to God, to other believers, and to the unbelieving world. Believers are free to eat whatever is sold in the marketplace and to accept invitations to dine with unbelievers (10:25–27), but Paul vigorously warns of the effect of idolatrous associations on others (8:7–13; 10:28–30) and the spiritual dangers of idolatry in relation to God (10:1–22).

There are further links between 8:1–11 and 6:12–20.[5] First, the dictum, "'Everything is permissible for me'—but not everything is beneficial" in 6:12 recurs in 10:23. In both instances the phrase is repeated a second time, although qualified differently. In 6:12 we read, "Everything is permissible'—but I will not be mastered by anything"; in 10:23, "Everything is permissible'—but not everything is constructive." The differences are due to the varying contexts in which the qualifications occur,[6] but the point to be made here is that Paul includes the phrase in his response to the twin issues of sexual immorality and idolatry, whether this expression represented a Corinthian slogan, a belief dominant in the culture, or a misapplication of Paul's own teaching. Second, both sections mention food in the context of a possible Corinthian slogan. In 6:13 we read, "Food for the stomach and the stomach for food," and in 8:8, "But food does not bring us near to God." Third, the command to flee immorality and glorify God in the body (6:18–20), finds

[4] Thus, Paul has already broached the topic of idolatry in 5:10 and 6:9–10.

[5] As noted earlier 6:12–20 functions in its immediate context as a "hinge" unit between 5:1–6:11 and 7:1–40.

[6] The word translated "constructive" in 10:23 is the word meaning "to edify/to build up," which is of particular concern in 8:1–11:1.

parallel expression in the command to flee idolatry and do all for the glory of God (10:14,31). Furthermore, there is a parallel between 6:20 and 7:23 that stands in paradoxical contrast to 9:19. In 6:20, we read, "You were bought at a price," followed by the command to "honor God in your body." Similarly, in 7:23 the statement, "You were bought at a price," follows with the command, "Do not become slaves of men." The preceding verse (7:22) frames the issue in terms of the believer's freedom in relation to God. The principle is simple enough to understand. Those called while in slavery are free in the Lord, and those called as freedmen are Christ's slaves. Believers belong to Christ, not to men. However, in 9:19 we read, "Though I am free and belong to no man, I make myself a slave to everyone, to win as many as possible." Such is the paradox of the Christian life. Believers are truly free, yet they belong to another (Christ) who gave himself for others. The meaning of "freedom" is of great concern to Paul, not only in 8:1–11:1, but also in other portions of the letter. Christian freedom is always conditioned and qualified by the reality that believers are "in Christ."

The content of 8:1–11:1 also stands in significant relationship to the first major section of the letter (1:18–4:21). Just as Paul's first major discourse on the wisdom of God concludes with the exhortation to imitate his manner of life in Christ (4:16–17), so also his discussion of food offered to idols concludes, "Imitate me, as I also imitate Christ" (11:1 HCSB). Furthermore, in both sections Paul advances the imitation theme by noting his own example and the example of other apostles as a way of life patterned by the cross (2:1–5; 4:6–13; 9:1–24). Paul was their father in the gospel (4:15), which is the criterion for all Christian conduct (9:19–23). Those who live according to the gospel seek the highest good of all people in order that as many as possible might be saved (9:22; 10:33). In both of these major sections a life patterned by the cross is the solution to the fundamental problem of pride that led to divisions (3:21; 4:6,17–21) and to the unloving actions of those with "knowledge" (8:1,7–13).[7]

Finally, the theological and ethical guidelines established in 8:1–11:1 cohere with Paul's instructions in what follows in the letter concerning the glory of God in worship (11:2–16), correctives regarding selfish behavior at the Lord's Supper (11:17–32), and the building up of the body of Christ in the exercise of spiritual gifts (12:1–14:40). The priority of love for others (8:7–13), the essence of which is to seek not one's own things but those of the other (10:24,33), finds full expression in chap. 13, the central section of Paul's discussion of spiritual gifts.[8]

[7] See also E. C. Still, "Divisions Over Leaders and Food Offered to Idols: The Parallel Thematic Structures of 1 Corinthians 4:6–21 and 8:1–11:1," *TynBul* 55.1 (2004): 17–41.

[8] So also A. C. Thiselton, "we urge that 11:2–16, 17– 34 and chs. 12–14 share with chs. 8–10 an exposition of the themes of love and respect for 'the other' in the light of biblical and shared

The exegetical challenges of 8:1–11:1 are numerous.[9] Since Paul links the expression "now about" in 7:1 to a previous correspondence, it is probable that the Corinthians also raised the issue of food sacrificed to idols in their letter to Paul. The phrase itself, "food sacrificed to idols" (NIV), translates one Greek word, which occurs fives times in 1 Corinthians (8:1,4,7,10; 10:19), but elsewhere in the New Testament only in Acts (15:29; 21:25) and Revelation (2:14,20).[10] In Acts 15 and 21, Luke writes of the decision of the Apostolic Council forbidding Gentile believers from eating food associated with idols, and in Rev 2 Jesus warns the churches of Pergamum and Thyatira of those who would lead believers to do the same. Paul's discussion of the issue is not as clear cut, involves a circuitous argument with what appears to be a long digression from 9:1–10:13, and raises a host of questions. Why did Paul respond at such length to the question? Did he implement the Apostolic Decree in Corinth, or was the situation in Corinth different from the concerns of Acts 15? Were the Corinthians in agreement on the matter of idol food over against Paul, or were they themselves divided over the issue, and did they appeal to their apostle to render a verdict between competing factions in the community? Why would those with "knowledge" (8:1) argue for the right to eat idol food? Was the motivation primarily theological (freedom to eat, "all things are lawful"), or did they want to eat idol food for social reasons and sought to justify their behavior theologically?[11] What is the relation of this passage to Rom 14 and 15 where Paul addresses the strong and the weak in the context of eating certain foods?[12]

There are three scenarios related to eating food sacrificed to idols in 8:1–11:1: (1) eating food sacrificed to an idol in the temple precincts (8:7–13; 10:1–22); (2) eating food purchased in the marketplace, which may or may not have been sacrificed to idols (10:23–27); and (3) eating food at the invitation

---

theological traditions" (*The First Epistle to the Corinthians: A Commentary on the Greek Text*, NIGTC [Grand Rapids: Eerdmans, 2000], 607).

[9] For a helpful review of the past thirty years of scholarship on 1 Corinthians 8:1–11:1, see W. Willis, "1 Corinthians 8–10: A Retrospective after Twenty-Five Years," *ResQ* 49 (2007): 103–12. Significant monographs in recent scholarship on 1 Cor 8:1–11:1 include W. Willis, *Idol Meat in Corinth: The Pauline Argument in 1 Corinthians 8 and 10* (Chico, CA: Scholars Press, 1985); Cheung, *Idol Food in Corinth*; J. F. M. Smit, *"About the Idol Offerings": Rhetoric, Social Context, and Theology of Paul's Discourse in 1 Corinthians 8:1–11:1,* CBET 27 (Leuven: Peeters, 2000); J. Fotopoulos, *Food Offered to Idols in Roman Corinth: A Social-Rhetorical Reconsideration of 1 Corinthians 8:1–11:1*, WUNT 151 (Tübingen: Mohr Siebeck, 2003).

[10] Gk. εἰδωλόθυτος. See also *Didache* 6.3.

[11] See the discussion on 5:1–13 (esp. 5:4) and the reasons for tolerating the incestuous man. There may be a significant socio-economic angle to the problem of idol food in addition to idolatry: the "knowledgeable" are the social elite while the "weak" are the socially disadvantaged (so R. B. Hays, *First Corinthians* [Louisville: John Knox, 1997], 137).

[12] Fotopoulos (*Food Offered to Idols*, 179) rightly notes that one of the main difficulties in the exegesis of 8:1–11:1 is isolating the contextual issues that led Paul to address the matter of eating food sacrificed to idols in Corinth.

of an unbeliever where some of the food served may have been previously sacrificed to an idol (10:28–31). The primary critical issue presented by these scenarios is consistency in Paul's thought. In 8:1–13, for example, Paul prohibits eating meat offered to idols on the basis of love for a brother who might stumble because of a weak conscience. Paul's language seems to suggest, in principle, that he agrees with those who have a certain knowledge about idols, God, and food. Idols are nothing in the world (8:4) since there is only one God (8:6), and food has nothing to do with one's relationship with God (8:8). Likewise, in 10:23–31, Paul appears to have no problem with food purchased in the marketplace of unknown history, but that may have been offered to idols, and he justifies this perspective from Ps 24:1, "The earth is the Lord's and everything in it" (10:26). Likewise, in the case of dining with an unbeliever Paul forbids eating only if someone discloses the history of the food (10:27–28). In these passages the guiding principle for Paul, it seems, is the effect eating has on another.

By way of contrast, 10:14–22 prohibits eating idol food in the temple of the idol because it is an act of idolatry. Furthermore, Paul warns of the incompatibility of eating at the Lord's table and the table of demons. To do the latter is to provoke the Lord to jealousy (10:22). So it appears that there are different reasons in 10:14–22 for not eating food offered to idols in comparison to 8:7–13.[13] How do we reconcile these perspectives? What is off limits for believers and what is allowable? Is the primary concern the location of the meal, whether in the idol's temple or another location such as one's private home? Or did Paul distinguish between the nature of the occasion for eating, whether overtly religious in purpose or merely an innocent social occasion, albeit in the temple of an idol?[14] And what are we to make of 8:10, where Paul clearly portrays a "knowledgable" Christian reclining in the temple of the idol? Is this

[13] So G. W. Dawes, "The Danger of Idolatry: First Corinthians 8:7–13," *CBQ* 58 (1996): 82. "At first sight, 1 Cor 8:7–13 would seem to imply that the eating of food offered to idols is itself a morally neutral act which should be avoided only because of the effect it may have on others. This position seems to be repeated in 10:23–11:1. Yet chap. 10 also contains a passionate denunciation of idolatry, and 10:14–22 suggests that eating food offered to idols is quite simply unacceptable."

[14] Willis (*1 Corinthians 8–10: A Retrospective*, 107–11) notes that while there is general consensus on the possible occasions for eating, there is less consensus on the nature of religious meals. The meals have been seen as clearly idolatrous, forming a worshipping community, eating with awareness of the presence of the patron deity, or primarily social gatherings. D. E. Garland suggests that we cannot suppose that there were meals on the temple grounds that could be divided into social purposes and religious purposes since religious and social life were inextricably bound together. "In the ancient world, people did not compartmentalize their religious, economic, and social lives, and it is anachronistic to think that they did" (*1 Corinthians*, BECNT [Grand Rapids: Baker, 2003], 349).

an actual idolatrous practice among some Corinthians,[15] permissible temple attendance,[16] an extreme example,[17] or only hypothetical?[18]

Whatever conclusions may be drawn regarding these questions, the overall thrust of Paul's theological and pastoral intention is crystal clear. Undoubtedly, Paul forbids all forms of idolatry and all idolatrous associations by virtue of the believer's allegiance to the one true God (8:2,6, and esp. 10:1–22).[19] In these chapters Paul disallows the eating of known idol food, including what is sold in the marketplace (10:28–29). Paul's stance against all forms of idolatry was uncompromising. In Athens, while waiting for Timothy and Silas, Luke records that Paul "was greatly distressed to see that the city was full of idols" (Acts 17:16). Injunctions against both idolatry and sexual immorality[20] would have been integral in Paul's missionary instruction during his eighteen-month stay in Corinth (Acts 18:9) since some believers in Corinth were former idolaters (6:9–11; 12:2), and like the converts in Thessalonica, their conversion entailed turning "to God from idols to serve the living and true God" (1 Thess 1:9). While it is true that Paul never mentions the Apostolic Decree (Acts 15:23–29) in his discussion, would he have been compelled to do so?

[15] So G. D. Fee, *The First Epistle to the Corinthians*, NICNT (Grand Rapids: Eerdmans, 1987), 357–63, 385–87. Fee argues that εἰδωλοθύτων ("food sacrificed to idols") refers to a form of idolatry prohibited by Paul. The Corinthians were at odds with Paul over this issue and had taken exception to his earlier prohibition. In Fee's view, the issue in 8:1–13 and 10:14–22 is the same, eating idol food in the pagan temple in the presence of the patron god. Only in 10:23–11:1 is marketplace food introduced. On this issue, Paul's answer is different. See also B. Witherington, *Conflict and Community in Corinth: A Socio-Rhetorical Commentary* (Grand Rapids: Eerdmans, 1994), 186–91; Hays, *First Corinthians*, 134–35.

[16] So B. N. Fisk, "Eating Meat Offered to Idols: Corinthian Behavior and Pauline Response in 1 Corinthians 8–10," *TrinJ* 10 (1989): 62.

[17] So A. Robertson and A. Plummer, *A Critical and Exegetical Commentary on the First Epistle of St. Paul to the Corinthians*, ICC, 2nd ed. (Edinburgh: T&T Clark, 1914), 171.

[18] So J. C. Hurd, *The Origin of 1 Corinthians* (New York: Seabury, 1965), 125. Garland (*1 Corinthians*, 353–62, 387–89) follows Hurd on this view and critiques what he labels a "traditional" reading of the passage at three key points: (1) This is not Paul's first word to the Corinthians on the issue of idol food. 1 Corinthians 8–10 represents an ongoing conversation between the Corinthians and Paul. (2) There is no internal dispute between the "strong" and the "weak." The issue in 1 Corinthians is not the same as the issue between the strong and the weak in Rom 14–15. In 1 Corinthians Paul's concern is not acting contrary to one's beliefs but the ever-present danger of idolatry. (3) Paul's problem with idol food is more than just the potential harm to the "weak" Christian.

[19] R. E. Ciampa and B. S. Rosner submit that Paul seems to wrestle with what they call *subjective* and *objective* idolatry. They explain, "By 'subjective idolatry' we mean an occasion when a person consciously participates in an activity that they consider idolatrous. Whether or not others judge it to be so may be beside the point. By 'objective idolatry' we have in mind people who do not consider themselves idolaters (they do not believe in idols or other gods) who participate in an activity that they consider innocent but which in fact is idolatrous" (*The First Letter to the Corinthians*, PNTC [Grand Rapids: Eerdmans, 2010], 369).

[20] These two sins are listed first in the vice list of 1 Cor 6:9. Paul reminds them that they know that those who practice such things will not inherit the kingdom of God.

Fotopoulos maintains that there was widespread prohibition of idol food and sexual immorality prior to and independent of the Apostolic Council.[21]

Obviously Paul's problem is not with food per se (10:25–26), but in addition to the dangers of idolatry associated with food sacrificed to idols, Paul's concern lies with those with "knowledge" who act without concern for and with dire consequence to fellow believers for whom Christ died (8:1–2,11–13). Paul advances a gospel-centered response that both answers their question and addresses the core problem of pride. As noted above, Paul concludes his response by exhorting the Corinthians to "imitate me, as I imitate Christ" (11:1), which parallels his approach to the problem of divisions in 1:10–4:21 (see 4:16–17). To "imitate Christ" entails a way of life conditioned by the cross in every respect, living out the message of the cross by extolling the exercise of love for others over asserting one's own rights. Imitating Christ means doing anything rather than hinder the gospel (9:12) and doing all things for the sake of the gospel (9:23). The gospel is the measure of true freedom. Paradoxically Paul states, "Although free, I have enslaved myself to all, in order that I might gain the more" (9:19). Paul's response to the Corinthians on the question of food sacrificed to idols is shaped by his vision to live for the glory of God and to give no reason for anyone to stumble, whether Jews or Greeks or the church of God, seeking the good of the many rather than seeking to please oneself (10:31–11:1).

### 1. The Priority of Love over Knowledge (8:1–13)

**[1]Now about food sacrificed to idols: We know that we all possess knowledge. Knowledge puffs up, but love builds up. [2]The man who thinks he knows something does not yet know as he ought to know. [3]But the man who loves God is known by God.**

---

[21] Fotopoulos, *Food Offered to Idols*, 183–87. See also Cheung, *Idol Food in Corinth*, 39–81. Cheung analyzes the prevailing attitudes toward idol food in early Judaism via the Old Testament and other Jewish writings. He concludes that "nothing in Paul's Jewish background would encourage Paul to condone eating idol food," and that "nothing in his encounter with the risen Christ or in his calling as an apostle to the Gentiles leads us to believe otherwise" (81). Scholarly assessment of the relation of Acts 15 to 1 Cor 8–10 naturally has to do with one's view of the historicity of Acts and/or Pauline chronology. For this reason many critical scholars simply see no relation between the two. Fotopoulos submits that scholarly judgments on this point are irrelevant since Paul would have forbidden idol food independently of the Council. C. L. Blomberg does not think Paul applied the directives of the Council in Corinth. "Paul apparently felt no need to apply it in Corinth, perhaps because he sensed it still made too many concessions to legalism in a context where its positive gains—paving the way for Jewish evangelism—were no longer major concerns" (*1 Corinthians*, NIVAC [Grand Rapids: Zondervan, 1994], 167). C. K. Barrett thinks that local Jews in Corinth were imposing the ban on the church (*A Commentary on the First Epistle to the Corinthians*, HNTC [New York: Harper & Row, 1968], 188). Robertson and Plummer (*First Corinthians*, 173–74) note that both in the case of sexual immorality and idolatry Paul's solution is ultimately in relation to Christ. Paul appeals to the Apostolic Decree in neither case because "the principles to which he appeals were far more cogent."

**[4]So then, about eating food sacrificed to idols: We know that an idol is nothing at all in the world and that there is no God but one. [5]For even if there are so-called gods, whether in heaven or on earth (as indeed there are many "gods" and many "lords"), [6]yet for us there is but one God, the Father, from whom all things came and for whom we live; and there is but one Lord, Jesus Christ, through whom all things came and through whom we live.**

**[7]But not everyone knows this. Some people are still so accustomed to idols that when they eat such food they think of it as having been sacrificed to an idol, and since their conscience is weak, it is defiled. [8]But food does not bring us near to God; we are no worse if we do not eat, and no better if we do.**

**[9]Be careful, however, that the exercise of your freedom does not become a stumbling block to the weak. [10]For if anyone with a weak conscience sees you who have this knowledge eating in an idol's temple, won't he be emboldened to eat what has been sacrificed to idols? [11]So this weak brother, for whom Christ died, is destroyed by your knowledge. [12]When you sin against your brothers in this way and wound their weak conscience, you sin against Christ. [13]Therefore, if what I eat causes my brother to fall into sin, I will never eat meat again, so that I will not cause him to fall.**

In 8:1–13 Paul identifies the source of the Corinthian problem (pride) and places the topic of food sacrificed to idols in its proper theological framework (love for God/love for neighbor). The chapter divides into three units (8:1–3,4–6,7–13). Each unit contains what many consider to be Corinthian beliefs or attitudes (slogans) to which Paul responds: "we all possess knowledge" (8:1), "an idol is nothing at all in the world and that there is no God but one" (8:4), and "food does not bring us near to God" (8:8).[22] Paul's opening assertion, "Knowledge puffs up, but love builds up" (8:1b), announces the main focus and sets the stage for the full discussion that follows through 11:1.[23] Already Paul has warned against boasting in men (3:21; 4:6). Here he warns of the sort of knowledge that puffs up to the detriment of another (8:10–11). Love, on the other hand, edifies, seeking not its own things but what is best for others (8:13;

[22] The exact number and content of the so-called slogans is an open question in scholarly debate (see discussion on 6:12–20 regarding Corinthian slogans). Some, for example, would designate the entire opening phrase in 8:1a, "We know that we all possess knowledge," as a Corinthian catchphrase, while others would consider the first two words, "We know," to be Paul's own way of identifying with his audience. Fotopoulos (*Food Offered to Idols*, 213–14) maintains that 8:6 is a confessional formula from the "strong" in Corinth, yet from Paul. D. Horrell points out that "disputes about the extent of Corinthian quotations here are perhaps less crucial for the interpretation of the passage than is sometimes assumed. For in 8:1,4,6, and 8 (where Corinthian quotations have been suggested) it does seem clear both that the opinions quoted are ones associated with the Corinthian 'strong' but also that they are opinions that Paul basically shares—even though he may qualify them sharply and differ as to their implications for conduct" ("Theological Principle or Christological Praxis? Pauline Ethics in 1 Corinthians 8:1–11:1," *JSNT* 67 [1997]: 86).

[23] The Greek word for "knowledge" (γνῶσις) occurs five times in this section alone (8:1,7,10–11). Additionally, the verb γινώσκω occurs four times (8:2–3) and οἶδα occurs twice (8:1,4). Paul expounds further on the permanence of love versus the limitations of knowledge in 1 Cor 13 (see esp. 13:2,8).

10:24). In 8:1–11:1 Paul calls on the Corinthians to practice the purest form of love that he himself pursued as epitomized by the death of Jesus (10:33–11:1). Thus, Christian "freedom" (9:1,18), properly understood, gives occasion to serve one another in love (Gal 5:13).[24] Before developing the implications of what it means to act in love for others, Paul addresses the issue of knowledge in relation to one's love for God (8:3–6), who alone deserves praise and worship. To sin against a fellow believer is to sin against Christ (8:11–12), whom Christians confess as the "one Lord" (8:6b). Thus, as noted in the introduction, the double love command (love God, love neighbor) is the theological formulation that drives Paul's argument.[25]

**8:1** According to Louw and Nida the word translated "food sacrificed to idols" is "a semantically complex word meaning literally 'that which has been sacrificed to an idol'."[26] Paul's statement in 8:13 suggests that he has in mind primarily "meat" offered to idols, but the NIV translation, along with most modern versions, assumes a more wide-ranging reference to "food," which seems substantiated by Paul's larger discussion that makes reference to drinking to demons (10:21), eating whatever is sold in the marketplace (10:25), and eating whatever is provided when invited to a meal (10:27).[27] Still, sociological approaches prefer the term "meat," which emphasizes that the problem in Corinth had to do with social stratification between the elite, who could afford meat in the first place and who were knowledgeable regarding the nonreality of idols, and the socially disadvantaged, who were deemed intellectually weak by their enlightened societal counterparts.[28]

As noted in the introduction, there are further debates regarding the meaning of the term in relation to the various contexts in which the eating might occur. Some, for example, think the term has a restricted meaning, referring only to the eating of sacrificial food in the presence of an idol or on the temple precincts.[29] Others call this into question, supposing that Paul has in mind

[24] C. Vaughan and T. D. Lea, *1 Corinthians*, Bible Study Commentary (Grand Rapids: Zondervan, 1983), 87.

[25] See also Ciampa and Rosner (*First Corinthians*, 370), who posit that the double love command undergirds Paul's argument from 8:1–14:40.

[26] Louw-Nida, 5.15. The term εἰδωλόθυτος does not occur in the literature prior to 1 Corinthians. It is a Jewish/Christian polemical term. A different term, preferred by pagans, appears in 10:28 (ἱερόθυτος).

[27] See Fotopoulos, *Food Offered to Idols*, 49–157, 208. In his survey of the pagan temples and cults in Roman Corinth, Fotopoulos notes that εἰδωλόθυτα consisted of a variety of food products, such as grain, fruit, fish, poultry, honey, etc.

[28] See discussion in Thiselton, *First Corinthians*, 607–9. See also G. Theissen, *The Social Setting of Pauline Christianity: Essays on Corinth*, trans. J. Schultz (Philadelphia: Fortress, 1982), 126–27.

[29] See Fee, *First Corinthians*, 482–85; B. Witherington, "Not So Idle Thoughts about Eidolothuton," *TynBul* 44.2 (1993): 237–54.

broader contexts from the outset.[30] This latter view presupposes that there were, in fact, social situations of permissible temple attendance where the eating of idol-food was, at least in principle, morally neutral. On the other hand, the very notion of something offered in sacrifice to an idol carries negative connotations, indicating that the term itself is not morally neutral.[31] As Ciampa and Rosner point out, "Paul's use of this term places the whole discussion in the context of Jewish and biblical concerns regarding idolatry and the historical role of avoiding such food out of loyalty to the God of Israel."[32]

Paul establishes common ground with the Corinthians in the affirmation, "We know that we all possess knowledge," which he immediately qualifies by setting up a contrast between knowledge that "puffs up" and love that "builds up." The specific knowledge to which Paul refers is indicated in 8:4, "We know that an idol is nothing at all in the world and that there is no God but one,"[33] another probable Corinthian assertion that relegated idols to the realm of nonreality in view of their knowledge that there is only one true God. Paul does not take issue with knowledge per se, only a particular application of knowledge that fuels arrogance.[34] In the letter opening Paul gives thanks to God for their enrichment in all knowledge (1:5). Paul affirms a "message of knowledge" as a gift of the Spirit (12:8) and the benefits of knowledge in the context of his discussion of prophecy (14:6). Furthermore, throughout the letter Paul reminds the Corinthians of what they "know." Repeatedly he poses the question, "Do you not know?" (see 3:16; 5:6; 6:2–3,15–16,19; 9:13,24). Paul affirms things they know (8:1,4; 15:58; 16:15), certain things he wants them to know (11:3), and things made known by the Spirit (2:6–16). So when Paul claims that "knowledge puffs up," in context he is speaking of the negative outcome of a specific claim regarding the reality of idols in relation to the one true God (8:4,6) and to a behavioral pattern that shows no regard for the welfare of others who lack certain "knowledge."[35] Paul certainly does not intend to separate "knowledge" and "love" since love is based in the knowledge of God and "informed and shaped by the pattern and example of Christ."[36]

---

[30] See especially Fisk's critique of Fee in Fisk, "Eating Meat Offered to Idols." For an overview of the complexities involved in the meaning of the term, see Thiselton, *First Corinthians*, 617–20.

[31] So Garland, *1 Corinthians*, 365.

[32] Ciampa and Rosner, *First Corinthians*, 373.

[33] In Greek, περί in 8:4 resumes the argument following the brief digression on love and knowledge in 8:2–3.

[34] Commentators often note the absence of the definite article with the first occurrence of the term "knowledge" and the presence of the article with the second occurrence in 8:1. The ESV explicitly identifies the phrase "All of us possess knowledge" as a Corinthian slogan and then translates the second instance of "knowledge" as "*this* knowledge puffs up," indicating that Paul has in mind a particular kind of knowledge.

[35] "Knowledge," in this context, may tend toward the meaning of "perception" (see 8:7).

[36] Horrell, "Theological Principle," 87. See the full discussion of 1 Cor 13. Cf. also 2 Cor 8:9.

**8:2–3** The brief digression in 8:2–3, playing off the polarity between knowledge and love in 8:1b, sets up yet another contrast between "the man who thinks he knows something" (8:2) and "the man who loves God" (8:3). Paul phrases the contrast with two conditional sentences, not conveyed in the NIV translation, in order to affirm the essential points he wants to make regarding knowledge and love.[37] Those who suppose they know something must recognize that knowledge is partial, a point developed further in 13:8–13. The limitations of human knowledge should promote humility rather than pride. What's more, Paul claims, if anyone loves God it is only so because they have been known by him. One might expect Paul to say, "If anyone loves God, this person has full and complete knowledge."[38] But the surprising turn of phrase establishes the proper relation between knowledge and love. The first principle of the Christian life is one's love for God. The important thing is not what one knows per se but by whom the person is known and the implications of that knowledge. To be known of God is to be in covenant with him.[39] This too promotes humility since God's elective purpose excludes all human boasting (1:26–31). The mention of one's love for God echoes the *Shema* (Deut 6:4–5), which is central to Paul's argument (8:4–6) regarding idolatry. Some Corinthians wrongly supposed that their touted knowledge granted certain freedoms without taking into account the theological implications of what it means to be Christian in the first place.

**8:4–6** Following the brief but important digression in 8:2–3, Paul picks up where he left off in 8:1a and provides the content of the knowledge claimed by some Corinthians: "We know that an idol is nothing at all in the world and that there is no God but one." The statement is likely a Corinthian position almost certainly derived from Paul's prior instruction in Corinth, yet his agreement with the "nothingness" of the so-called gods (8:5a) is not a denial of their presence in the world (8:5b),[40] nor of the existence of evil spiritual powers in the worship of false gods.[41] Paul's point is that over against the many gods and the many lords of the heathen world stands the Christian accla-

---

[37] The Greek text reads, "If anyone thinks that he knows anything, he does not yet know as it is necessary to know," and "If anyone loves God, this one has been known by him."

[38] Or something like 1 John 4:7, "Everyone who loves has been born of God and knows God."

[39] Paul uses the same language in Gal 4:9, "But now that you know God—or rather are known by God—. . ." and 2 Tim 2:19, "The Lord knows those who are his."

[40] Paul, in fact, concurs that "there are many 'gods' and many 'lords'" (8:5b). Similar statements regarding the "nothingness" of gods occur in Deut 32:21, "They made me jealous by what is no god and angered me with their worthless idols," and Isa 37:19, "They have thrown their gods into the fire and destroyed them, for they were no gods." This equates to the worthlessness of idols, not their nonreality. See also Hab 2:18 (NRSV), "What use is an idol once its maker has shaped it—a cast image, a teacher of lies? For its maker trusts in what has been made, though the product is only an idol that cannot speak!"

[41] Deut 32:17, "They sacrificed to demons, which are not God—gods they had not known, gods that recently appeared, gods your fathers did not fear." Similarly, Paul acknowledges the partnership of demons involved in idol sacrifices (see 10:19–21).

mation of one God and one Lord (8:6). Further the language of "gods" and "lords"[42] paves the way for 8:6, which takes up the terms "God" and "Lord" in a remarkable reformulation of the *Shema* of Deut 6:4,[43] already alluded to in 8:4b. Verse 6 explicitly brings Jesus into the definition of the one true God. Apart from the contextual reasons for the inclusion of 8:6 in Paul's argument concerning idolatry,[44] the verse in and of itself is of immense importance for Christian theology. The grammatical structure, precision, and conscious parallelism of the formulation, depicted as follows in the Nestle-Aland[28th] edition of the Greek New Testament, indicates its traditional character.

> But to us one God, the Father
>     from whom are all things and we unto him
>
> And one Lord, Jesus Christ
>     through whom are all things and we through him

Whether or not Paul is transmitting a pre-formed received tradition or whether he himself crafted the pithy statement, cannot be known for sure.[45] Either way, the assertion distinguishes between the one God, who is the Father, and the one Lord, who is Jesus Christ. The end result is a strong monotheism that incorporates Christ into the definition of God.[46] Moreover, there is an interplay between creation and new creation, which also plays a key role in Paul's argument. God the Father is the source and the goal of all things, "from whom all things came and for whom we live" (NIV2011; cf. 15:28). Jesus, the one Lord, is the agent of creation and the means by which believers exist in new creation, "through whom all things came and through whom we live."[47] The believer's allegiance to the one God and Lord rules out any idolatrous

---

[42] The terms "gods" and "lords" rarely occur together in the Old Testament (see Deut 10:17; Ps 136:2–3).

[43] Deut 6:4, the central Jewish confession, reads, "Hear, O Israel! The LORD is our God, the LORD is one!"

[44] Hays (*First Corinthians*, 140) notes, "Christian thought about this problem must start neither from an abstract doctrine of monotheism nor from a theoretical statement that 'gods' do not really exist: rather, Christian thought begins from a confession that binds us specifically to the one God of Israel and declares our personal allegiance to this one God. We exist 'for him,' not for our own purposes."

[45] A. Eriksson notes that commentaries written before the rise of form criticism treat 8:6 as a Pauline construction, whereas the majority of modern scholars are convinced it is a tradition Paul had already transmitted to the Christian in Corinth (*Traditions as Rhetorical Proof: Pauline Argumentation in 1 Corinthians*, ConBNT 29 [Stockholm: Almqvist & Wiksell International, 1998], 121).

[46] N. T. Wright coins the formulation a "christological monotheism" (*The Climax of the Covenant: Christ and the Law in Pauline Theology* [Minneapolis: Fortress, 1991], 129). Ciampa and Rosner (*First Corinthians*, 383) maintain that Paul reaffirms not only Jewish monotheism but also the "highest possible Christology imaginable." The "one God" formula occurs elsewhere in Paul in Rom 3:30; Gal 3:20; Eph 4:6; and 1 Tim 2:5.

[47] Other texts that affirm Jesus as the agent of creation include Col 1:16–17 and Heb 1:1–4. Cf. also Rom 11:36, which states of God, "from him and through him and to him are all things."

associations. Yet, at the same time, Paul affirms the goodness of God's creation, including food (10:26). New creation establishes new realities, binding the believer inextricably to Christ and to one another (6:15–20; 12:12–27).

**8:7–8** Whereas 8:2–6 takes up the question of knowledge regarding food sacrificed to idols in relation to the believer's acknowledgment of and love for the one God, the focus of 8:7–13 turns to the correlation between knowledge and one's love for others who belong to Christ. The statement in 8:7, "But not everyone knows this," seems quite shocking on the surface since it follows immediately from the central confession of one God and one Lord in 8:6. How can it be that some do not have knowledge of and adhere to such a fundamental confession (Rom 10:9; 1 Cor 12:3)? It is unlikely that Paul is claiming that some do not know that there is only one God. The pronoun "this"[48] refers to the whole argument and specifically to those who want to justify eating idol food because they possess knowledge that an idol is nothing in the world.[49] The multiple occurrences of the noun or verb form of the word "knowledge" throughout the passage indicates that Paul has in mind the whole context of 8:1–6. First Corinthians 8:7b clarifies the point further by introducing the "conscience" of the weak, who are the counterparts to "those with knowledge."[50] Some, who because of their pagan past are accustomed to idols, cannot eat known idol food with the strength of conviction that such eating is harmless. It is, in fact, not harmless, since their "weak" conscience is defiled by eating. For them there is no conviction that an idol is nothing in the world.

There are different ways to read 8:8, which may be another instance of a Corinthian slogan or a statement reflective of a Corinthian position. While it is possible to translate 8:8a, "Food will not bring us before (the judgment seat of) God,"[51] most translations follow the sense of the NIV reading, "Food does not bring us near to God." Even though there are differences in audience and context between 1 Cor 8 and Rom 14–15,[52] there are significant links between the two regarding Paul's view of food, namely, that no food in itself is unclean (Rom 14:14).[53] In principle, therefore, Paul would agree that food is

---

[48] That is inferred from the Greek definite article. There is no demonstrative pronoun "this" in the Greek text of 8:7.

[49] Horrell ("Theological Principle," 88) explains, "What he does perhaps mean is that not all possess this knowledge in a way that convinces them of the non-reality of idols and of the consequent acceptability of idol-food—in this sense they do not have the knowledge of the strong." Horrell further submits that the shift from 8:6 to 8:7 is key to the argument (89–90).

[50] The term translated "conscience" (συνείδησις) is a key component of Paul's argument, occurring eight times in 1 Cor 8–10 (8:7,10,12; 10:25,27–29). Elsewhere in the New Testament the word appears in Acts 23:1; 24:16; Rom 2:15; 9:1; 13:5; 1 Tim 1:5,19; 3:9; 4:2; 2 Tim 1:3; Titus 1:15; Heb 9:9,14; 10:2,22; 13:18; 1 Pet 2:19; 3:16,21.

[51] See also Thiselton, *First Corinthians*, 647.

[52] Food sacrificed to idols is not in question in Rom 14–15. Even so, Paul's argument in 1 Cor 8–10 clearly upholds the same principle that food per se is not unclean.

[53] Horrell ("Theological Principle," 89) thinks that since Paul expresses a view with which the strong in Corinth would agree, it is unnecessary and unconvincing to see the statement as another

neutral; yet, in context, Paul has in mind idol food, which in certain instances may not be eaten, not because of the food itself but because of the idolatrous associations.

**8:9–13** The eating in 8:7–13 has a specific context, which is clarified in 8:9, where Paul warns that the freedom of the knowledgeable might become a stumbling block to the weak. The word translated "freedom" in 8:9 by the NIV is a key term in chap. 9, where the word is translated "right."[54] Paul's language indicates that the "right" to eat any food, even in contexts of negative associations, is a Corinthian claim.[55] While some think that Paul accepts that a legitimate right is in question, this is not certain. Fotopoulos, for example, thinks that Paul does not in fact agree with the so-called strong at this point, but rather employs the word ironically in order to show the negative consequences of its use by them. In chap. 9 Paul speaks of giving up his legitimate rights for the sake of the gospel. It is mistaken to claim as a "right" the eating of sacrificial food that would cause a brother to stumble.[56]

In 8:10 Paul explains how the eating of idol food might become a stumbling block to those who are weak in conscience. The illustration, which switches from the plural pronoun in 8:9 to the singular in 8:10, portrays a believer with a weak conscience observing a knowledgeable brother reclining in an idol's temple.[57] Paul asks, "Won't he be emboldened to eat what has been sacrificed to idols?" The word translated "emboldened" is the same word translated "builds up" in 8:1.[58] Genuine love for others always builds up in the right way. But actions that flow from knowledge absent of love build up in the wrong way and can lead to catastrophic consequences.

The linguistic structure of 8:11 highlights the tragic result of the actions of the knowledgeable. The verb "to destroy" occurs first in the sentence for emphasis and the emphatic singular personal pronoun is used in the phrase "by *your* knowledge," carrying forward the illustration of 8:10. Furthermore, the one who is weak is none other than "the brother for whom Christ died." This leads to Paul's central point regarding the action of those with knowledge, which is not only a sin against a brother, who has been bought for a price

Corinthian quotation. Ciampa and Rosner (*First Corinthians*, 389) present another perspective. They think that Paul addresses specifically a suggestion by some Corinthians that, in fact, they are worse off socially if they do not eat idol food and better off it they do for the purpose of building relationships outside the church.

[54] Gk. ἐξουσία, in chap. 9 occurs at 9:4–6,12,18.

[55] Literally, "this right of yours."

[56] Fotopoulos, *Food Offered to Idols*, 218–24.

[57] This use of the first person pronoun is typical of the Greek diatribe, where the author takes on an imaginary opponent. Some think that Paul's example is only hypothetical, but it is likely to have some basis in reality.

[58] Gk. οἰκοδομέω.

(recall 6:20; 7:23), it is also a sin against Christ.[59] The actions of the one with knowledge in this situation are condemned in the strongest possible way.

In 8:13, Paul's argument comes full circle as he offers himself as an example of the correct way to respond to the issue of food sacrificed to idols. The example of Paul, as noted in the introduction, is a major component of this section, leading up to the concluding, "Follow my example, as I follow the example of Christ" (11:1). Love builds up (8:1), which means that love never acts to cause another believer to stumble (8:13). Paul has enumerated a string of negative consequences that result from the actions of those with knowledge: (1) Their actions defile and strike the conscience of the weak (8:7,12), (2) are a stumbling block to the weak (8:9), and (3) destroy those for whom Christ died and therefore constitute a sin against a brother and a sin against Christ. The word translated "therefore," which draws the first phase of Paul's argument to a close, is used in the New Testament only here and in 10:14, where Paul emphatically demands, "Therefore, my dear friends, flee from idolatry." Louw and Nida define the conjunction as a relatively emphatic marker of result.[60] This use of the rare conjunction, along with the Greek construction of emphatic negation, powerfully drives home Paul's point. The NIV translation, "I will never eat meat again" fails to capture the full force of Paul's rhetoric, which literally reads, "I will never eat meat again forever!"[61]

## 2. Paul's Apostolic Rights (9:1–12a)

**1Am I not free? Am I not an apostle? Have I not seen Jesus our Lord? Are you
not the result of my work in the Lord? 2Even though I may not be an apostle to
others, surely I am to you! For you are the seal of my apostleship in the Lord.**

**3This is my defense to those who sit in judgment on me. 4Don't we have the
right to food and drink? 5Don't we have the right to take a believing wife along
with us, as do the other apostles and the Lord's brothers and Cephas? 6Or is it
only I and Barnabas who must work for a living?**

**7Who serves as a soldier at his own expense? Who plants a vineyard and does
not eat of its grapes? Who tends a flock and does not drink of the milk? 8Do I say
this merely from a human point of view? Doesn't the Law say the same thing?
9For it is written in the Law of Moses: "Do not muzzle an ox while it is treading
out the grain." Is it about oxen that God is concerned? 10Surely he says this for us,
doesn't he? Yes, this was written for us, because when the plowman plows and the
thresher threshes, they ought to do so in the hope of sharing in the harvest. 11If we
have sown spiritual seed among you, is it too much if we reap a material harvest**

---

59 On sinning against Christ, see Matt 25:40–45; Acts 4:4–5. Robertson and Plummer (*First Corinthians*, 173–74) note, "In dealing with both the question of fornication and that of eating idol-meats, the Apostle brings the solution ultimately from our relation to Christ. Fornication is taking from Christ what is His property and giving it to a harlot. Reckless eating of idol-meats is an injury inflicted on Christ."

60 Louw-Nida, 89.47.

61 Gk. οὐ μὴ φάγω κρέα εἰς τὸν αἰῶνα.

**from you? 12If others have this right of support from you, shouldn't we have it all the more?**

First Corinthians 9 is integral to the argument of 8:1–11:1 as a whole. In this chapter Paul takes up the pivotal concept of "rights" mentioned in 8:9[62] and advances a compelling argument for the priority of the gospel as the framework for Christian decision making.[63] He accomplishes this by referring to his own perspective and practice concerning his "rights" as an example worthy of imitation (11:1). Paul relinquished his legitimate apostolic rights so that he would give no hindrance to the gospel of Christ (9:12,15,18; cf. 8:13),[64] Although free (9:1,19), he enslaved himself to all men and did all things for the sake of the gospel (9:19–23). How much more should the Corinthians give up any notion of a supposed right that harms others and violates their relation to Christ (8:9–13)?

The function of chap. 9 has been a matter of considerable debate. Some think that Paul not only sets forth an exemplary argument urging the Corinthians to imitate his manner of life as an apostle of Jesus Christ, but that he also responds to some in Corinth who question his apostolic authority and/or his unconventional behavior in refusing financial support.[65] That there was some tension between Paul and some in Corinth is tenable, yet Paul's primary purpose in chap. 9 seems not to be a defense of his apostleship per se since the legitimacy of his apostleship is the premise of the whole argument. If there were some in Corinth who questioned Paul's apostleship, he silences them immediately by reminding them that they themselves authenticate his apostleship in the Lord (9:2).[66]

---

[62] The Greek term "right" (ἐξουσία), translated "freedom" by the NIV in 8:9, occurs six times in chap. 9 (9:4–6,12,18). The NIV renders the term as "right" in all occurrences in chap. 9 with the exception of 9:6 where it is not translated at all, "Or is it only I and Barnabas who must work for a living?" A more literal translation of 9:6 is, "Or do only I and Barnabas not have a right not to work?" (ἢ μόνος ἐγὼ καὶ Βαρναβᾶς οὐκ ἔχομεν ἐξουσίαν μὴ ἐργάζεσθαι).

[63] In addition to the concept of "rights," the gospel (εὐαγγέλιον) is a key term in the chapter and becomes the main focus in 9:12c–23, which begins and ends with parallel statements: 9:12, ". . . we put up with anything rather than hinder the gospel of Christ"; 9:23, "I do all this for the sake of the gospel, that I may share in its blessings." See comments on structure below.

[64] While the focus of the chapter is on Paul's example, his argument takes into account other apostles (note the use of the plural "we" in 9:4–6,11–12).

[65] Fee (*First Corinthians*, 392–94) sees a dual purpose at work in chap. 9 with more emphasis on a "crisis of authority" that lies behind much of the letter and less emphasis on Paul setting forth his own practice as an example to follow. Fee gives 9:1–27 the heading, "Paul's Apostolic Defense." See also Barrett, *First Corinthians,* 199–202; F. F. Bruce, *1 and 2 Corinthians*, NCB (Grand Rapids: Eerdmans, 1971), 82–83; H. Conzelmann, *1 Corinthians: A Critical and Historical Commentary on the Bible,* Hermeneia, trans. J. Leitch (Philadelphia, Fortress, 1975), 153.

[66] The notion of chap. 9 as a full-blown apostolic defense has come under much scrutiny in recent scholarship (see Garland, *1 Corinthians*, 397–400). In addition to the rhetorical questions expecting an affirmative answer and the focus of the entire chapter on waiving rights, Garland notes that Paul actually did the opposite of what was expected of apostles, including abdicating the command of the Lord to "receive [his] living from the gospel" (9:14). The argument does not

One approach to the structure of chap. 9 is to divide it into two sections, 9:1–18 and 9:19–27,[67] which exhibit a parallel pattern of argumentation. Both sections begin with assertions of freedom. In 9:1, Paul establishes the fact of his freedom as apostle of Jesus Christ with the question, "Am I not free?", which assumes an affirmative "yes." In 9:18, Paul describes the self-imposed limits on his freedom. Although he is free, he enslaved himself to all in order to gain more. Both sections similarly emphasize the gospel as the reason for restricting legitimate freedoms (9:12c–18 and 9:23). In both sections Paul offers himself as one who exercises strenuous discipline in order to be an "approved" herald of the good news (9:15–18,26–27).[68] Thus Paul rigorously pursues the tensions between the freedoms enjoyed in the gospel and the demands of the gospel.

Another approach to the structure of Paul's argument is to divide it into three units. In 9:1–12a, Paul establishes his legitimate rights as an apostle. The unit begins and ends with an *inclusio* built around the reference to "others." Verse 2 establishes that Paul is indeed recognized as an apostle by the Corinthians, (lit.) "If to others I am not an apostle, indeed I am to you." Verses 11–12a conclude the first phase of the argument by asking two questions in the form of conditional sentences, "If we have sown spiritual seed among you, is it too much if we reap a material harvest from you? If others have this right of support from you, shouldn't we have it all the more?" The second unit, 9:12b–23, while continuing to establish the legitimate apostolic right to receive financial support from the church, coheres around the theme of giving up legitimate rights for the sake of the gospel. This unit also begins and ends with an *inclusio* built around the parallel statements of doing all things for the gospel (9:12c,23). The last unit, 9:24–27, is transitional, bringing the argument of Paul's example to a close while anticipating the exposition of Israel's negative example in the wilderness in chap. 10.

---

buttress his case if this is intended as a defense. Furthermore, there are no details of the opponents or of actual charges (see also M. Mitchell, *Paul and the Rhetoric of Reconciliation: An Exegetical Investigation of the Language and Composition of 1 Corinthians* [Louisville: WJK, 1991], 287). However, though 1 Cor 9 serves a paradigmatic purpose, this does not rule out entirely an apologetic motif. Horrell observes, "Certainly there are elements of defensiveness here in relation to Paul's apostleship (vv. 1–3) and perhaps also in relation to his refusal of financial support from the Corinthians. Yet in the argument of the passage as a whole it clearly serves as an example, spelling out for the strong the pattern of conduct that Paul calls them to imitate, and that he perceives as an imitation of Christ (11.1)" ("Theological Principle," 92). See also Thiselton, *First Corinthians*, 663.

[67] Some propose that the first two questions set up the argument of the chapter. The first question, "Am I not free?" anticipates 9:19–23, and the second question, "Am I not an apostle?" sets up 9:1c–18. See Garland, *1 Corinthians*, 403; Blomberg, *1 Corinthians*, 173.

[68] Note the switch to the first person singular in these texts. Both sections also employ the recurring question, "Do you not know?," in the argumentation (9:13,24).

**9:1–2** Chapter 9 opens with four rhetorical questions,[69] all of which expect an affirmative answer. That Paul was free and that he was an apostle of Jesus Christ should not have been in dispute in Corinth, as 9:2 makes clear. His apostolic credentials rested on the twin pillars of his personal witness of the resurrection of Jesus[70] and the existence of the Corinthian church, who were Paul's work and seal of apostleship in the Lord.[71] The very existence of the Corinthian church authenticated Paul's labor in ministry, although he gave all credit to God (3:7; 15:9). If Paul was not an apostle to others, surely he was an apostle to the Corinthians. The designation "apostle" indicates a special commission by Christ to proclaim the gospel, which is a major component of the overall argument of chap. 9 (9:12a–18,23). But, in relation to freedom, which is the main theme of the chapter, Paul sums up the essence of his apostolic ministry in 9:19: "Though I am free and belong to no man, I make myself a slave to everyone, to win as many as possible." The "freedom" mentioned in 9:1 and 9:19 relates to the "rights" of an apostle as outlined in 9:4–12a, which Paul relinquished in order to maximize the effectiveness of the gospel for the greatest number of people.

**9:3–6** The Greek word order suggests that the demonstrative pronoun "this" in 9:3 points forward rather than backward.[72] This suggests that Paul's defense has to do primarily not with the fact that he is an apostle but rather with objections that some might raise concerning his relinquishing of the rights of an apostle that others did not.[73] In other words, the rhetorical questions in 9:3–6 all expecting an affirmative "yes" anticipate questions that some might raise regarding Paul's self-imposed discipline.[74] Apostles had the right to daily

---

[69] The KJV reflects a textual variant that inverts the first two questions, reading "Am I not an apostle? Am I not free?" Paul's use of the first person singular provides a fluid transition from 8:13 to the rhetorical question in 9:1, "Am I not free?" So also Hays, *First Corinthians*, 149. Paul has already signaled his own commitments as an example in 8:13, "Therefore, if what I eat causes my brother to fall into sin, I will never eat meat again, so that I will not cause him to fall."

[70] On apostles as witnesses of the resurrection of Jesus, see Acts 1:21–22; 2:32; 3:15; 4:33; 22:14; and 26:16; also 1 Cor 15:8 and Gal 1:15.

[71] Note that Paul carefully qualifies the fact that the Corinthians are his work and seal of apostleship "in the Lord" (ἐν κυρίῳ). The "others" mentioned in 9:2 likely refers to those outside the scope of the Pauline churches (so also Garland, *1 Corinthians*, 405). Others might question Paul's apostleship, but there was no reason for any Corinthian to do so. Bruce (*1 & 2 Corinthians*, 83) notes that the first question "points the foundation of Paul's apostleship, the latter to its visible demonstration."

[72] In Greek, the demonstrative is last in the sentence, Ἡ ἐμὴ ἀπολογία τοῖς ἐμὲ ἀνακρίνουσίν ἐστιν αὕτη. Those who read chap. 9 as apostolic defense will tend to see 9:3 as pointing backward (so L. Morris, *1 Corinthians*, TNTC [Grand Rapids: Eerdmans, 1985], 130; Vaughan and Lea, *1 Corinthians*, 92–93; although see Fee, *First Corinthians*, 401). Ciampa and Rosner (*First Corinthians*, 400) report that the early Greek Fathers were divided on this issue.

[73] The key term "right" (Gk. ἐξουσία) occurs three times in 9:4–6. It is likely that Paul is responding to a Corinthian use of the term (cf. 8:9).

[74] Garland thinks that Paul utilizes a rhetorical figure of style (see *1 Corinthians*, 405–6, and the literature cited), that Paul raises questions himself that others might ask in a way that makes

provisions of food and drink. They had the right to take along a believing wife.[75] They also had the right to receive financial assistance from the churches. Some exercised these rights, such as the brothers of the Lord and Cephas,[76] who were married and who apparently journeyed with their wives with the expectation of support from the churches. But Barnabas and Paul did not exercise their right to refrain from working. This practice of self-support was often misunderstood (see 2 Cor 11:7–9; 12:13). Some would have expected Paul to conform to the pattern of traveling rhetoricians or philosophers of the day, not to mention that Paul explicitly says that other apostles did receive financial support. On occasion Paul accepted material provision (Phil 4:10–20), but his normal practice was to work at a trade in order not to be a burden to the churches (see 1 Thess 2:5–10; 2 Thess 3:7–9).[77]

**9:7–12a** Regarding the rights of apostles to receive material provisions, Paul appeals to common occurrences in everyday life (9:7,13), to the Scriptures (9:8–10), and ultimately to the Lord himself (9:14). Collectively these arguments heighten the effect of Paul's main point that he gave up his right for the sake of the gospel, something the Corinthians should imitate.

The analogies of the soldier, the field worker, and the shepherd (9:7) are easy enough to understand in and of themselves and would have been clear to Paul's readers. The simple point is that people expect to reap benefits from their labor. A soldier does not serve at his own expense. The one who plants a vineyard eats the produce from the harvest. Likewise, the shepherd drinks from the milk of his flock. In each case no one would object to the supply of daily provisions for those who labor accordingly.

Paul makes the same point in 9:8–10 yet with more authority since his appeal is to the law of Moses (Deut 25:4) rather than to common experience. The analogy itself is on par with the previous examples except that the one receiving the benefit for labor is the ox rather than a human being: "Do not muzzle an ox while it is treading out the grain." The example raises intriguing

---

the argument lively and interesting. In other words, Paul does not defend himself against actual charges but rather frames the discussion as a defense in line with the socio-rhetorical conventions of the day.

[75] Literally, "sister wives." Gk. ἀδελφὴν γυναῖκα.

[76] This is the third specific reference to Cephas in the letter (see 1:12 and 3:22). Cephas will be mentioned again in 15:5. These references may indicate that some in the church identified with Cephas in some way (see comments on 1:12).

[77] Although Paul's main point is to remind the Corinthians of his apostolic rights, which he renounced, what he says raises intriguing historical details. We know, for example, that other apostles were married and traveled with their wives, including Peter, unless the reference in 9:5 is to traveling female attendants, which is unlikely since the term "wife" is used. Furthermore, how were the brothers of the Lord involved in the missionary enterprise of church planting? Does the inclusion of Barnabas identify him as an apostle, or was the term "apostle" used in both a restricted sense and a broad sense in the New Testament (see Rom 16:7). On Barnabas as an apostle, see Acts 14:4,14. On Paul and Barnabas as co-workers in the gospel, see Acts 4:36–37; 9:26–28; 11:19–26; 15:36–41.

questions about Paul's appropriation of the Old Testament Scriptures since his claim is that the law says this "for us," referring to those who labor in ministry and who have the right to financial support. At first glance it seems that Paul is saying that God does not care about oxen,[78] but it is more likely that he is faithful to the original intent of the passage in Deuteronomy and employs a well-established method of interpretation of arguing from the lesser to the greater. In other words, if God cares about oxen, then he cares even more about humans.[79] The point is that Scripture is relevant to the question at hand and undergirds the principle that laborers work in hope of sharing in the harvest (9:10),[80] which leads to the logical conclusion that those who sow spiritual things have the expectation of reaping material benefit (9:11). This line of reasoning not only extends the sowing/reaping language appropriate to the agricultural example of the ox but employs once again the lesser/greater logic in reverse. If those who labor in ministry sow spiritual things (the greater), then should they not at least reap a material harvest (the lesser)? Furthermore, if others used this right of support from the Corinthians, even more so do Paul and Barnabas possess the same right (9:12a).

## 3. Giving Up Rights for the Sake of the Gospel (9:12b–23)

**But we did not use this right. On the contrary, we put up with anything rather than hinder the gospel of Christ. 13Don't you know that those who work in the temple get their food from the temple, and those who serve at the altar share in what is offered on the altar? 14In the same way, the Lord has commanded that those who preach the gospel should receive their living from the gospel.**

**15But I have not used any of these rights. And I am not writing this in the hope that you will do such things for me. I would rather die than have anyone deprive me of this boast. 16Yet when I preach the gospel, I cannot boast, for I am compelled to preach. Woe to me if I do not preach the gospel! 17If I preach voluntarily, I have a reward; if not voluntarily, I am simply discharging the trust committed to me. 18What then is my reward? Just this: that in preaching the gospel I may offer it free of charge, and so not make use of my rights in preaching it.**

**19Though I am free and belong to no man, I make myself a slave to everyone, to win as many as possible. 20To the Jews I became like a Jew, to win the Jews. To those under the law I became like one under the law (though I myself am not under the law), so as to win those under the law. 21To those not having the law I became like one not having the law (though I am not free from God's law but am under Christ's law), so as to win those not having the law. 22To the weak I became weak, to win the weak. I have become all things to all men so that by all possible means**

---

[78] So Barrett, *First Corinthians*, 205–6.

[79] Ciampa and Rosner (*First Corinthians*, 404–5) present the evidence that Deut 25:4 was, in fact, read this way.

[80] Hays (*First Corinthians*, 151) notes that the whole context of Deut 24–25 has to do with human justice and dignity, which indicates that the passage may have been figurative from the beginning. See also Morris, *1 Corinthians*, 132.

**I might save some. [23]I do all this for the sake of the gospel, that I may share in its blessings.**

**9:12b** Before offering two concluding reasons for the apostolic right to financial provision in 9:13–14, Paul interjects that he and Barnabas endure all things for the gospel rather than exercise their rights inherent in the gospel (9:12b).[81] This is the first use of the term "gospel" in chap. 9,[82] which occurs nine times in its noun or verb form in 9:12b–23, thus establishing these verses as a unit. The parallel statements of 9:12 and 9:23 regarding enduring/doing all things for the gospel succinctly capture the main theme of 8:1–11:1. On the one hand, the gospel brings glorious freedom in Christ for all believers, but on the other hand, the very nature of the gospel is radically others-centered and thereby restricts freedom and the use of so-called rights in relation to other believers. The key question for all Christian decision making is what brings glory to God and esteems the gospel in a manner that seeks to win as many as possible to Christ.

In addition to the numerous references to the gospel beginning in 9:12b, Paul mentions the giving up of apostolic rights for the cause of the gospel three times (9:12b,15,18). The first reference uses the plural "we," referring to both Paul and Barnabas. But in 9:15 and 9:18 Paul only refers to himself. The language of 9:15–18 conveys Paul's deep concern and gratitude for his apostolic role as a herald of the gospel. Paul follows the threefold assertion of the non-use of apostolic rights with the commitment, "Though I am free and belong to no man, I make myself a slave to everyone, to win as many as possible." Paul's resolve is that he does all things for the sake of the gospel, not only to win as many possible but also that he might become a fellow partaker of it (9:23).

**9:13–14** The final two arguments for the right of apostles to receive provision include the precedent of those who work and serve in the temple and the command of Jesus himself concerning those who proclaim the gospel. While it is possible that Paul's audience could have correlated his reference to the temple with the operation of the pagan temples in Corinth where those who offered meat to idols received a portion of the sacrifice for their own keeping, it is more likely that Paul's reference is to the temple practices described in the Old Testament. Paul may have two different groups in mind, making a distinction between the workers in the temple and those who actually offered sacrifices in the temple. But the point is simple. Both were sustained in daily provision by their service in the temple.[83] This goes a step further than the example of the ox taken from Deut 25:1 in relating material provision to sacred service as ordained by God.

---

[81] The strong adversative ἀλλά occurs twice. *But* we did not use this right, *but* we endure all things . . .

[82] The first occurrence in the letter is found at 4:15. The verb form appears in 1:17.

[83] See Lev 7:6–10,14,28–36.

The phrase "in the same way" in 9:14 supports the view that 9:13 refers to Israel's temple.[84] Just as the workers in the temple and those serving at the altar made their living from their service, so also should those who preach the gospel make their living from the gospel. Yet this is more than just an analogy. Just as Yahweh arranged for those in sacred temple service to make their living from the temple, so also Jesus commanded that those who preach the gospel live from the gospel. Thus, Paul concludes his argument with the most compelling reason of all to support those in ministry. The practice derives from Jesus himself.[85]

Paul's reference to a command of Jesus raises important questions. First, there is the question of source since there is no saying of Jesus that corresponds exactly to 9:14. Second, there is the question of Paul's obedience to Jesus' command. Did Paul set aside a directive of Jesus by refusing financial support for his apostolic ministry? Regarding source, the essence of 1 Cor 9:14 is found in the gospel tradition. In Matt 10:10, Jesus instructed his disciples to take no provisions for their journey, and in Luke 10:7 Jesus commented that the worker deserves his wages.[86] The implication of Jesus' teaching for his disciples is complete dependence on God for provision. The whole tenor of Paul's argument in 1 Cor 9 clarifies that he viewed financial provision as a right to forego for the sake of the gospel rather than an obligation of obedience to God. Paul's obligation was to preach the gospel. On this matter he had no choice (9:16–17). He did have a choice, however, regarding whether or not to receive pay, and for the sake of the gospel he offered it free of charge.[87]

**9:15** In this verse Paul expresses his renunciation of legitimate apostolic rights with great emotion. He no longer uses the first person plural, "we," as in 9:12, but reverts back to the first person singular and refers only to himself and his missionary practice. The use of the first person pronoun in Greek is emphatic, along with the verb translated "make use of," which is in the perfect tense.[88] Paul's conviction to give up his rights was a settled conviction, and he

[84] Ciampa and Rosner (*First Corinthians*, 413) suggest a syntactical parallelism between 9:13 and 9:14 that "highlights the relationship between preaching the gospel and serving in the temple or at the altar."

[85] Once again Paul's appeal shows that he was familiar with the teaching of Jesus and appealed to it when it served his purposes (cf. 7:10).

[86] The word for "wages" in Luke 10:7 is "reward" (Gk. μισθός).

[87] On occasion Paul received unsought gifts (see Phil 4:10–20). Paul's reason for adopting the *modus operandi* described in 1 Corinthians was so that he would not hinder the gospel, that he might win as many as possible, and that he might become a fellow partaker of the gospel. Commentators routinely point out the two different meanings of "gospel" in 9:14. On the one hand, the gospel is the content of the story of Jesus, his death, burial, and resurrection (cf. 15:1–4). But to "live from the gospel" implies that the word "gospel" can be used as shorthand for the missionary enterprise itself. Furthermore, in 9:23, Paul refers to the gospel as something that he seeks to become a fellow partaker of.

[88] In 9:12c, Paul uses the aorist, "We did not use this right." Here, in 9:15, the perfect adds more emphasis and brings the situation more vividly into the present.

wanted to be crystal clear that his intent in writing these things to the Corinthians was not in order to gain their financial support: "And I am not writing this in the hope that you will do such things for me." The NIV translation of 9:15c, "I would rather die than have anyone deprive me of this boast," fails to capture the broken grammatical construction in Greek. The phrase, "I would rather die," is incomplete and followed by the exclamation, "No one will empty my boasting!"[89] The construction expresses Paul's deep emotion and his ironclad commitment not to draw his living from the gospel. Garland points out the contrasting parallel between "living" from the gospel in 9:14 and Paul's statement in 9:15 that he had rather die. Garland posits that Paul is saying, "It is better for me to die than to live off the gospel."[90]

**9:16–18** Paul explains and elaborates on the concept of "boasting" raised in 9:15.[91] Whether or not he preaches the gospel has nothing to do with financial support but rather is wrapped up entirely in his apostolic calling. The gospel itself is grounds for boasting in the Lord (1:30–31), but in terms of preaching the gospel, like the prophets of old, Paul was under divine compulsion. He had no choice in the matter, expressed in Greek by two parallel conditional sentences: "If I preach, I have no reason to boast" and "Woe is me if I do not preach the gospel!"[92] In other words, there is no reason for boasting if Paul preaches because he is compelled to do so. If he does not preach the gospel then he faces "the ultimate calamity."[93] Paul did not preach the gospel willingly for a reward. If he had a choice in the matter and chose to do it willingly, then he might merit a reward.[94] Rather, Paul understood his calling as a

---

[89] The NET translates, "In fact, it would be better for me to die than—no one will deprive me of my reason for boasting!"

[90] Garland, *1 Corinthians*, 422. The emotion parallels Paul's affirmation that he will never eat meat again if it causes a brother to stumble (8:13). Garland mentions other instances of broken grammatical constructions in Paul (1 Cor 6:9; 15:1–2; Gal 2:3–5,6; 6:12; Phil 2:29).

[91] Normally, "boasting" carries negative connotations but not in this context. Commentators often note that "boasting" evokes a prophetic theme and that Paul viewed himself in line with the Old Testament prophets compelled to preach. Unlike Jeremiah, however, Paul's lament was not preaching since he understood that suffering was inherent in the gospel (see Garland, *1 Corinthians*, 424). On the notion of "necessity" or "constraint" evoking Paul's apostolic calling in terms of the experience of the OT prophets, see S. J. Hafemann, *Suffering and Ministry in the Spirit* (Grand Rapids: Eerdmans, 1990), 138–39.

[92] The NIV renders the first condition, "When I preach . . ." S. J. Kistemaker suggests a concessive translation, "Though I preach . . ." (*1 Corinthians*, New Testament Commentary [Grand Rapids: Baker, 1993], 304).

[93] So Ciampa and Rosner, *First Corinthians*, 416. Ciampa and Rosner note that in most instances in the prophets and the New Testament "woe" refers to the calamity of divine judgment (ibid., n99).

[94] Ciampa and Rosner explain, "While the previous verse contrasted the implications of preaching versus not preaching the gospel (making it clear that Paul has no choice but to preach the gospel), this one refers to two different conditions under which one might carry out such a task, as a free person who chooses to accept a given task, or as a slave who is given a task by the master and does not have the luxury of choosing his own projects. The former carries out his work *voluntarily*,

stewardship that required faithfulness (9:17; cf. 4:1–5).[95] This does not mean that Paul preached unwillingly, only that he wants to express in the clearest way possible the divine mandate that compelled him in ministry. His reward in preaching was to give up his rights inherent in the gospel and to preach without charge.

**9:19** Whereas 9:17 employs the metaphor of the household manager entrusted with the care of an estate, the image in 9:19 shifts to the slave who accommodates to his surroundings. In 9:17 Paul is the faithful steward compelled to preach. In 9:19–23 Paul enslaves himself to all so that he might make the greatest possible gains for the gospel. Paul's assertion of freedom in 9:19 not only plays off the idea of freely offering the gospel in 9:18 but also recalls the opening question of the chapter, "Am I not free?" In this instance Paul specifies freedom from all men,[96] which in context may refer to his financial independence that released him from any obligation to wealthy patrons.[97] Yet, for Paul, the very nature of the gospel obliged him to all men in other ways in order to gain as many as possible for the gospel. To this end Paul enslaved himself to all, and in this way he imitated Christ, who came to serve and to give his life for others (Mark 10:45; Phil 2:5–8). Paul's stewardship of the gospel (9:17) embodied the essence of the gospel by entailing a complete inversion of the world's values whereby the slave occupies a position of considerable influence.[98] Just as God's folly, the cross, is the power of God unto salvation (1:18) so also is Paul's enslavement to different classes of men the best possible means for gaining others for Christ.[99]

---

while the task is imposed on the latter. The former is entitled to a reward for what he does, while the latter is not. Paul falls under the latter category, not the former" (ibid., 418).

[95] Gk. *οἰκονομία* (cf. Eph 3:2,9; Col 1:25; 1 Tim 1:4) is cognate to the term *οἰκονόμος* in 4:1, "those entrusted with."

[96] The NIV clarifies the intent of the Greek with the translation, "Though I am free and belong to no man." It is possible to read *πάντων* as "all things" since the gender of the Greek adjective could be neuter. The context, however, clarifies that people are in view. The Greek literally reads, "Though I am free from all, to all I enslaved myself" (Ἐλεύθερος γὰρ ὢν ἐκ πάντων πᾶσιν ἐμαυτὸν ἐδούλωσα). In Greek, the word for "free" is emphatic, occurring first in the sentence. Paul's assertion of freedom from all men in 9:19 parallels his command to the Corinthians in 7:15, "Do not become slaves of men."

[97] The concept of freedom is, of course, wide ranging. In the very next verse Paul affirms that he himself is not under law. In 9:19, however, Paul seems to have in mind something other than liberation from the Mosaic law.

[98] So Ciampa and Rosner, *First Corinthians*, 422. "His ultimate concern for the gospel and utter lack of concern for the social prejudices of others could hardly be stated more bluntly than to say that for the sake of the gospel he, though free, willingly became slave of all."

[99] The word "gain" (Gk. *κερδαίνω*) is a key word in this passage, occurring five times in 9:19–23. The term occurs in Paul only here and in Phil 3:8, "I count all things rubbish that I might gain Christ." The term is used of gaining one's brother in Matt 18:15, and of wives winning their husbands without a word in 1 Pet 3:1. The word also carries the sense of profiting financially (Matt 25:16–22; Jas 4:13), which raises the prospect of financial overtones in Paul's usage here. In other words, the only profit that Paul hoped to gain in the preaching of the gospel was to win as many as possible for the gospel.

**9:20–22** Paul describes his missionary life among various classes of people in explanation of what he means by the previous statement of making himself a slave to all in order to win as many as possible. Although Paul is clear regarding the essence of his missional strategy, his lack of elaboration on the particulars leaves us either to speculate or to look to other places in Paul's letters or the missionary narratives in Acts in order to fill out the details. Paul mentions four groups: the Jews, those under the law, those without law, and the weak. The first two groups may be one and the same, that is, the Jews are further described as "those under the law." Or it may be that the term "Jews" refers to one's national identity while "those under the law" takes into account Gentile proselytes who came under the Mosaic law by conversion to Judaism. Supporting the view that Paul only has three groups in mind is the conceptual parallel in 10:32 where Paul concludes his argument with the exhortation, "Do not cause anyone to stumble, whether Jews, Greeks, or the church of God."

The fact that Paul, a self-described Hebrew of the Hebrews (2 Cor 11:22; Phil 3:8), affirmed that he became *like* a Jew is quite astonishing.[100] This, along with the parenthetical explanation, "though I myself am not under the law," provides considerable insight into Paul's break from his religious past. Barrett comments that "Paul's Judaism was no longer of his very being."[101] That believers are not under law but under grace was a key tenet of Paul's teaching (see esp. Rom 6:14–15; 10:4; Gal 3:23; 4:4–5,21; 5:18). Paul does not elaborate concerning how he became like Jews and those under the law, but the Lukan narratives in Acts reference Paul's occasional accommodation to Jewish practice in order to open doors of evangelism (Acts 16:1–3; 21:23–26). Garland suggests that the best commentary on Paul's becoming as a Jew and one under the law is found in 2 Cor 11:24, where Paul describes his submission to synagogue discipline five times. In other words, Paul submitted to the discipline of the community in order to maintain connections and to keep open opportunities for preaching in the synagogue.[102]

Likewise, Paul related to the Gentiles as "those not having the law," which does not mean freedom from God's law. Rather, he is under Christ's law, which entailed obedience to God in a completely different way, that is, he was lawful with reference to Christ.[103] Paul does not elaborate further about his identification

[100] Barrett (*First Corinthians*, 211) thinks that the use of the definite article with Jews, since it is rare in Paul, points to a definite occasion. This may be overreading the use of the article.

[101] Barrett, *First Corinthians*, 211. Ciampa and Rosner (*First Corinthians*, 426) comment that even though Paul was a Jew in terms of ethnicity and heritage, he would not consider himself a Jew in that he defined his relationship with God in terms of the Mosaic covenant.

[102] Garland, *1 Corinthians*, 430.

[103] The Greek phrase ἔννομος Χριστοῦ occurs only here in the New Testament. The word ἔννομος occurs elsewhere in the New Testament only in Acts 19:39 in the phrase, "in lawful assembly." ἔννομος stands in contrast to ἄνομος, "without law." BDAG offers the following translation of 1 Cor 9:21, "Subject to the jurisdiction of Christ as opposed to Mosaic jurisdiction." The verse can be rendered, "I identified with one outside Mosaic jurisdiction with those outside it; not, of course,

with Gentiles in order to win them to Christ. At the very least we know that Paul vigorously opposed any effort to impose Jewish legal requirements, such as circumcision, as a component of conversion to Christ (Acts 15; Galatians). Garland suggests that Paul is speaking theologically about living under grace, a relationship with God based on faith in Christ apart from the law, instead of referencing the abandonment of Jewish practices. In other words, he became like a Gentile by giving up any reliance on heritage or the law for salvation.[104] It is not certain, however, that we can derive this "theological" sense from the context. Paul seems to be referring to his missionary practice in some way.

Paul's reference to the weak breaks the grammatical symmetry with the preceding examples. He does not say "I became as weak," but rather "I became weak." Paul may have excluded the word "*as/like*" as a stylistic variation. In the context of the overall argument of 8:1–11:1, the "weak" are those who were in danger of being destroyed by those with knowledge (8:7–13). If we assume the same identification in 9:22, then the weak in this instance are believers, rather than unbelievers. To gain them would be to save a brother from destruction. It is possible that Paul may have intended something different, however, in light of the prominence of the theme of "weakness" in the letter as a whole. The term "weak" describes the character of the gospel and Paul's ministry. In 1:25, the weakness of God is stronger than men. In 1:27, God has chosen the weak things of the world to shame the strong. In 2:3, Paul writes that he came to them preaching in weakness. In Rom 5:6 the term is used theologically of believers before conversion to Christ: ". . . when we were still powerless [weak], Christ died for the ungodly." If Paul used the term in this sense in 1 Cor 9:22, then the reference is to unbelievers and the symmetry with the previous examples is preserved, or "the weak" is not a third group at all but rather refers to both unconverted Jews and Greeks.[105] The immediate argument, however, associates "weakness" with believers rather than unbelievers (8:11–12). The gospel shapes our conduct with reference to both believers and unbelievers.

The summative statement, "I have become all things to all men so that by all possible means I might save some" (9:22b), must be interpreted in context, which means that the reference is to the preceding categories, which are as broad as possible, taking into account both Jews and Gentiles. To become all things to all people does not entail the abandonment of lawfulness toward God, nor does it abandon faithfulness to the essential content or character of

being outside God's jurisdiction, but inside Christ's." Louw-Nida define ἔννομος as, "pertaining to being under obligation imposed by law; subject to law, under law," and render 9:2, "but subject to the law of Christ." Most translations render the phrase as "under the law of Christ." On the "law of Christ" see also Rom 8:2; Gal 6:2. The phrase may refer to the norm or principle of Christ in reference to sacrificial living for others (so Hays, *First Corinthians*, 154). Thiselton (*First Corinthians*, 704) comments, "Christians stand under the direction of the gospel as that which witnesses to Christ in a broader and more comprehensive sense (Galatians 6:2)."

[104] Garland, *1 Corinthians*, 431–32.

[105] For this line of reasoning see ibid., 433–34.

the gospel, which is especially taken up in the category of the "weak." It is noteworthy that Paul switches to the perfect tense, "I have become," when the previous examples use the aorist, "I became." "I have become" expresses more of the settled conviction/manner of life that Paul had taken up for the cause of winning the most people possible to Christ.

**9:23** With one final use of the word "all," which has dominated 9:19–23, Paul declares that everything he does is for the sake of the gospel. In the final analysis it is the gospel that determines conduct. Also noteworthy is the repetition of the word translated "to become."[106] In 9:20–22a Paul rehearsed how he "became" toward different groups of people, and in 9:22b, in a switch to the perfect tense, he expressed that he "has become" all things to all people. Now, in 9:23, he says, "I do all things for the gospel that I might become a fellow partaker of it" (NASB). This final use of "become" is missed in the NIV translation, "that I might share in its blessings," which may be understood in different ways. The key term is the word translated "share."[107] There are those who think the passage is eschatological.[108] Ciampa and Rosner point out that a number of translations render the result clause as "that I might share in its blessings" (ESV, NRSV, NIV, TNIV, NLT), but the more literal "so that I might be a participant in it" is supported by the NET, NASB, and KJV. They suggest the meaning is best understood in light of other references in Phil 1:5–7, that is, financial resources for the effective spread of the gospel.[109] Garland thinks that Paul means partnership in an active sense, namely, participation in the gospel enterprise of winning others (2 Cor 8:23; Phil 1:5; Phlm 17).[110] Thiselton offers yet another perspective: "In our view (with Collins) the issue is neither that of bringing benefits to others (NJB), nor that of sharing in these benefits as a missionary-pastor (NRSV, NIV, REB, Fee). To stand alongside the Jew, the Gentile, the socially dependent and vulnerable, or to live and act in solidarity with every kind of person in every kind of situation is to have a share in the nature of the gospel, i.e., to instantiate what the gospel is and how it operates."[111]

[106] Gk. γίνομαι.

[107] Gk. συγκοινωνός (cf. Rom 11:17; Phil 1:7; Rev 1:9). BDAG defines as a participant, or a partner; Louw-Nida (57.10), "one who shares jointly with someone else in a possession or relationship, with emphasis on that which is in common—'sharer, partner, one who shares in.' ἵνα συγκοινωνὸς αὐτοῦ γένωμαι, 'in order that I might become one who shares in it' (that is, '. . . in the gospel')."

[108] Barrett (*First Corinthians*, 216) does not think that Paul means a partner with the gospel nor does he mean one who shares in the work of the gospel. "His word means participation in (the benefits of) the Gospel; and his participation is not guaranteed." This "eschatological" interpretation is thought to fit with Paul's statement in the following passage, 9:25–27, that he runs in such as way so that he is not disqualified at the end (so Fee, *First Corinthians*, 432; Robertson and Plummer, *First Corinthians*, 193, "i.e. not lose his share in the salvation which he tries to bring to others").

[109] Ciampa and Rosner, *First Corinthians*, 432.

[110] Garland, *1 Corinthians*, 437.

[111] Thiselton, *First Corinthians*, 707.

### 4. Application and Transition: Run to Win! (9:24–27)

**[24]Do you not know that in a race all the runners run, but only one gets the prize? Run in such a way as to get the prize. [25]Everyone who competes in the games goes into strict training. They do it to get a crown that will not last; but we do it to get a crown that will last forever. [26]Therefore I do not run like a man running aimlessly; I do not fight like a man beating the air. [27]No, I beat my body and make it my slave so that after I have preached to others, I myself will not be disqualified for the prize.**

It seems best to regard this unit as transitional, functioning both as the conclusion of Paul's self-exemplary argument, which began in 9:1, and also as an introduction to chap. 10, which brings the discussion back to the main topic of food sacrificed to idols by way of the negative example of Israel in the wilderness following their exodus from Egypt.[112] In relation to the previous unit, the emphasis on gaining more for the gospel, becoming all things to all men to save some, and doing all things for the gospel in order to become a fellow-partaker of it (9:19–23) is exemplified in the athlete who exercises self-control in all things in order to receive the prize (9:24–27). Three components of 9:24–27 specifically relate to the preceding argument. First, Paul's self-reference to preaching to others continues the dominant theme of preaching the gospel in 9:14–23. Second, the notion of bringing the body into subjection (slavery) parallels the notion of being enslaved to all men (9:19). And third, the phrase "lest I myself might become disqualified" in 9:27 parallels the statement in 9:23, "that I might become a partaker of the gospel."[113] This all sets the stage for what follows in the strong warning against idolatry via the example of Israel (10:1–22). The Corinthians, too, should exercise proper restraint lest they also find themselves unapproved before God. That the illustration in 9:24–27 extends beyond Paul to the Corinthians is evident in his explicit exhortation to the Corinthians to "run in such a way as to get the prize" (9:24). The whole point of the overall argument of 8:1–11:1 is for the Corinthians to imitate Paul, who imitates Christ (11:1).

The athletic metaphor was widespread among philosophers in the ancient world[114] and would have been especially relevant to Paul's audience since Corinth hosted the biennial Isthmian games, which was second only to the famed Olympic games. Here Paul employs both the image of the runner and the boxer. Paul found athletic metaphors useful on a number of occasions in his letters.[115] We should exercise caution, however, in overinterpreting any given

---

[112] On the transitional nature of the passage, see Mitchell, *Rhetoric of Reconciliation*, 239n297.

[113] On the parallel between 9:23 and 9:27, see also Conzelmann, *1 Corinthians*, 162.

[114] On the image of the athletic games in pagan moral philosophy, see V. C. Pfitzner, *Paul and the Agon Motif: Traditional Athletic Imagery in the Pauline Literature* (Leiden: Brill, 1967), 23–37. The games would have occurred in Corinth in AD 49 and again in 51.

[115] See Phil 2:16; 3:13–14; 1 Thess 2:2; 1 Tim 1:18; 4:7; 2 Tim 2:5; 4:7; 1 Cor 15:32.

metaphor by seeking to apply every detail of the analogy to the Christian life. In this present example it would be absurd to suggest that only one believer receives the prize out of all those who enter the race. Here Paul's primary point has to do with *how* one runs the race.[116] In Paul's example only one receives the prize, but obviously he is urging all believers to run like the well-trained athlete who exercises self-control in all things in order to achieve a greater goal. The analogy also effectively accentuates the contrast between the victor's wreath, which is of only temporal value, and the believer's crown of permanent worth. In context, the overall argument has to do with putting others before self in order to maximize one's effectiveness for the gospel, which requires rigorous self-discipline. Specifically, in context, Paul is concerned with abstaining from sacrificial meals tainted by idolatry, which brings the judgment of God, as Israel's history illustrates (10:1–22).

One of the major interpretive issues in 9:24–27 is Paul's statement regarding "disqualification," or more accurately, being "unapproved."[117] The NIV picks up on the mention of the "prize" in the metaphor in 9:24 and translates 9:27 as disqualification for the prize, but the text reads literally, "Having preached to others I myself might not become unapproved." What does Paul intend by this statement in relation to the athletic metaphor and in the context of the overall argument of 8:1–11:1? Does Paul fear that he might be rejected from the contest altogether if he fails to run a disciplined race, that is, the ultimate outcome might be the loss of eschatological salvation?[118] Or does the notion of being "unapproved" have more to do with Paul's role as an effective herald of the gospel and the Lord's final verdict on one entrusted with a stewardship?

Paul does not elaborate on the prize itself, yet he does refer to the reception of an imperishable crown (NIV, "a crown that will last forever"). Obviously this points to something of enduring value, but what the crown is, in this context, Paul does not say. On two occasions Paul applies the crown image to other believers (Phil 4:1; 1 Thess 2:19), and once he refers to a crown of righteousness that the Lord awards to all who long for his appearing (2 Tim 4:8). Other New Testament passages refer to a crown of life and a crown of glory (Jas 1:12; 1 Pet 5:4; Rev 2:10). The only other place that Paul refers to the "prize" is Phil 3:14, which Paul specifies as the upward call of God in Christ Jesus.[119]

The meaning of "unapproved" is contextually determined and depends on what is being tested. The immediate context has to do with subordinating

[116] Note the repetition, "Run in this way" (9:24), "I, therefore, run in this way" (9:27).

[117] Gk. ἀδόκιμος. The term appears seven times in Paul (Rom 1:28; 2 Cor 13:5–7; 2 Tim 3:8; and Titus 1:16) and once in Heb 6:8.

[118] Some commentators think so. So Barrett (*First Corinthians*, 218), "His conversion, his baptism, his call to apostleship, his service in the Gospel, do not guarantee his eternal salvation." Garland (*1 Corinthians*, 445) thinks the good crown to be won is salvation but states, "Paul is engaged in moral exhortation and not discoursing on the security of the believer."

[119] NIV, "for which God has called me heavenward in Christ Jesus."

everything to the gospel. To infer that "disqualification" in this context means the ultimate loss of salvation is to push the analogy a bit far.[120] An important consideration in this regard is what Paul has said already regarding the "testing" of the Day of the Lord (3:5–17), which will show the quality of one's works.[121] The end result is the loss of reward, but the individual himself is saved yet only as through fire (3:15). This is followed by the dire warning that God will destroy those who destroy the temple of God (3:17). Destruction, albeit severe, does not necessarily entail eternal damnation. Likewise, in 4:1–5 Paul reminds the Corinthians that he himself is not capable of rendering a final verdict concerning his own ministry and motives. Rather, it is the Lord who brings to light the secrets of darkness and reveals the desires of men's hearts. God alone bestows praise on his servants. It seems reasonable, therefore, to conclude that the primary intent of the term "disqualified/unapproved" in this context has more to do with God's final verdict on his people for which there will be both reward and loss. In terms of ultimate salvation Paul has the highest expectation for the Corinthian believers. We should recall the beginning of the letter where Paul addresses them as "those set apart in Christ Jesus" (1:2). His introductory prayer expressed confidence that God in his faithfulness would confirm them to the end blameless on the Day of the Lord (1:8–9).[122] This reading of 9:27 in no way mitigates the severity of Paul's warnings regarding God's judgment. There are ample warnings in Paul and in the rest of the New Testament to dispel any notions of false security.[123] It is certainly the case that there are many in the church who profess faith in Christ but who do not possess genuine faith.[124]

### 5. The Negative Example of Israel in the Wilderness (10:1–13)

**[1]For I do not want you to be ignorant of the fact, brothers, that our forefathers were all under the cloud and that they all passed through the sea. [2]They were all baptized into Moses in the cloud and in the sea. [3]They all ate the same spiritual food [4] and drank the same spiritual drink; for they drank from the spiritual rock**

[120] So also Thiselton, *First Corinthians*, 716–17. Paul certainly makes the point earlier in the letter that those who practice idolatry, as well as other vices, will not inherit the kingdom of God (1 Cor 6:9–11). Paul also presumes that genuine faith will persevere (cf. 15:2).

[121] In 3:13, ". . . the fire will test the quality of each man's work." The verb translated "test" is δοκιμάζω. The notion of "testing" or being "approved" in 3:13 is similar to Paul's expression of being "unapproved" in 9:27.

[122] See also Rom 8:31–39; Phil 1:3–6.

[123] For "proving/testing" language in Paul, see also 2 Cor 13:3–5. In terms of the language and the notion of human striving in 1 Cor 9:24–27, compare the striking parallels in Phil 3:7–21; Paul speaks of counting all things as loss and "gaining" Christ, pressing on for the prize of the upward call of God in Christ (3:14). Yet Paul clearly does not have in mind a works righteousness or human striving as a means of securing an eternal inheritance. Righteousness comes by faith (Phil 3:9). In Phil 3:17, as in 1 Cor 11:1, Paul urges others to follow his example. See also 2 Tim 2:5; 4:6–8.

[124] Matt 7:21–27; Jas 2:14–26; 1 John 2:3–5.

**that accompanied them, and that rock was Christ. [5]Nevertheless, God was not pleased with most of them; their bodies were scattered over the desert.**

**[6]Now these things occurred as examples to keep us from setting our hearts on evil things as they did. [7]Do not be idolaters, as some of them were; as it is written: "The people sat down to eat and drink and got up to indulge in pagan revelry." [8]We should not commit sexual immorality, as some of them did—and in one day twenty-three thousand of them died. [9]We should not test the Lord, as some of them did—and were killed by snakes. [10]And do not grumble, as some of them did—and were killed by the destroying angel.**

**[11]These things happened to them as examples and were written down as warnings for us, on whom the fulfillment of the ages has come. [12]So, if you think you are standing firm, be careful that you don't fall! [13]No temptation has seized you except what is common to man. And God is faithful; he will not let you be tempted beyond what you can bear. But when you are tempted, he will also provide a way out so that you can stand up under it.**

In order to underscore the peril of standing before God unapproved, Paul finds Israel's negative example of disobedience in the wilderness following the exodus from Egypt to be particularly relevant and instructive to the Corinthian situation.[125] The catchword "all," which occurs five times in 10:1–4, picks up on the reference to "all" who run the race in 9:24.[126] Just as the athletic metaphor draws attention to the self-restraint required of all competitors under the consequence of disqualification, so also the story of Israel's sojourn demonstrates that of "all" who identified with their spiritual leader Moses in their deliverance from Egypt, God was displeased with "most" of them (10:5). Of all the original Israelites redeemed from Egypt by God's power, only Joshua and Caleb entered the Promised Land.[127] Paul's point is that one's identification with the people of God coupled with extraordinary spiritual experiences does not preclude the possibility of spiritual disaster. In spite of God's perpetual presence and provision, Israel committed serious sins and perished in the wilderness.

Paul rehearses the facts of Israel's disobedience because these things serve to warn all who crave the same kinds of evil, including idolatry (10:7), sexual

---

[125] As with the previous unit, 9:24–27, one must not push the analogies in 10:1–22 beyond Paul's primary intent, which is to warn the Corinthians in the strongest possible way of the dangers of idolatry by way of the example of Israel.

[126] In addition to the repetition of "all," 10:1 links to 9:27 in the use of the Greek conjunction γάρ. Some think that the structure and argumentation of 10:1–13 suggests a prior composition reworked by Paul or others for the present context. See discussion in W. A. Meeks, "'And Rose Up to Play': Midrash and Paraenesis in 1 Cor 10:1–22," *JSNT* 16 (1982): 64–78. See also G. D. Collier, "'That We Might Not Crave Evil': The Structure and Argument of 1 Corinthians 10:1–13," *JSNT* 55 (1994): 55–75.

[127] Num 26:65; 32:11–12. That Moses himself was excluded from entering the land demonstrates the absurdity of pushing the analogy too far. Paul's pattern of argument couples strong warning (10:1–12) with strong encouragement (10:13).

immorality (10:8), testing Christ (10:9), and grumbling (10:10).[128] The argument presupposes familiarity with the story and symbols associated with the exodus, such as the cloud that guided the Israelites by day and night, the deliverance from the Egyptians at the Red Sea, and the miraculous provision of manna and quail from heaven and of water from the rock.[129] Paul's argument also introduces new elements, however, including Israel's baptism into Moses (10:2), the designation of the food and drink and rock as "spiritual" (10:3–4), and the identification of the rock as Christ (10:4), suggesting the use of typology whereby persons, institutions, or events in the Old Testament prefigure New Testament realities.[130] Although the passage draws from a combination of Old Testament texts, the only explicit quotation is Exod 32:6 (10:7b).[131] This intersection between the Old Testament narratives and the gospel speaks volumes regarding the content of Paul's missionary instruction during his eighteen-month stay in Corinth, the continuity of the Scriptures, and the use of the Old Testament for the church.[132]

First Corinthians 10:1–13 divides into three units. First, in 10:1–5 Paul recounts God's redemption and provision for "all" Israel, who, in the end, displeased God and incurred God's judgment. For this reason the Corinthians must heed the example of the Israelites so that they would not crave the same

[128] The purpose of the record of these events is captured in the *inclusio* occurring at 10:6 and 10:11. "Now these things occurred as examples to keep us from setting our hearts on evil things as they did" (10:6) and "These things happened to them as examples and were written down as warnings for us. . . ." (10:11). See also Rom 15:4.

[129] Exod 12–14 narrates the Passover, the exodus from Egypt, and God's deliverance of Israel from the Egyptians in the sea. For the account of the water-giving rock, see Exod 17:1–7 and Num 20:1–16.

[130] On the use of typology in Scripture, see L. Goppelt, *Typos: The Typological Interpretation of the Old Testament in the New* (Grand Rapids: Eerdmans, 1982); R. M. Davidson, *Typology in Scripture: A Study of Hermeneutical Typos Structures* (Berrien Springs, MI: Andrews University Press, 1981); E. E. Ellis, *The Old Testament in Early Christianity* (Grand Rapids: Baker, 1991). For a brief recent survey, see D. J. Treier, "Typology," *Dictionary for Theological Interpretation of the Bible*, 823–27. The Greek word, τύπος (10:6) can mean "type" in the sense of a prefiguring or pattern of a greater reality (cf. τυπικῶς, 10:11). Typology normally involves correspondence and escalation whereby the Old Testament type finds its ultimate anti-type in the New Testament reality. For example, Paul uses the term in Rom 5:14 of "Adam, who was a pattern of the one to come" (i.e., Jesus). More often, however, Paul uses the term with the simple meaning of "example," as in Phil 3:17; 1 Thess 1:7; 2 Thess 3:9; 1 Tim 4:12; Titus 2:7.

[131] In addition to Exod 32:6, see also Exod 13:21–22; 14:13–31; Num 11:4–34; 20:1–13; 21:16–20; 25:1–9; and Deut 32 (also Pss 75; 105; 106). On the use of the Old Testament in this passage see Collier, "That We Might Not Crave Evil." Collier argues that this section has significant connections with Num 11 as the main text, of which Exod 32:6 is a summary. For the view that Exod 32:6 is the main text, see Ciampa and Rosner, *First Corinthians*, 456.

[132] See Thiselton, *First Corinthians*, 718–19. Some suppose that Paul addresses a "magical" view of baptism and the Lord's Supper, as if this somehow guaranteed their final salvation (so Morris, *1 Corinthians*, 138; Fee, *First Corinthians*, 443). But, as Ciampa and Rosner (*First Corinthians*, 448–49) point out, the problem with this view is that those with "knowledge" did not think they were guilty of idolatry.

forms of evil and fall under God's judgment (10:6–11). Third, the concluding exhortation and warning stresses both human frailty and God's faithfulness to provide the path of escape to those who encounter common temptations (10:12–13).

**10:1–2** The phrase, "For I do not want you to be ignorant," like the question in 9:24, "Do you not know," amplifies the importance of what follows.[133] Paul strengthens his appeal to the Corinthians through the use of familial language in addressing them as "brothers" and by using the phrase "our forefathers" in referring to the ancient Israelites. The continuity of God's actions toward his people in the Old Testament and the church is a major assumption of the overall argument.[134]

The cloud and the sea were both powerful reminders of Israel's deliverance through Moses, Yahweh's appointed deliverer. In the exodus narrative the cloud was more than a mere symbol of Yahweh's continual presence and leadership; Yahweh himself went before his people "in a pillar of cloud to guide them on their way" (Exod 13:21–22). At the Red Sea the cloud moved around behind Israel in order to separate them from the Egyptians (Exod 14:19–20). Other passages parallel Paul's description of Israel as "under the cloud" (see Exod 14:24; Num 14:14; Ps 105:39).

The phrase "baptism into Moses" is uniquely Pauline since, as far as we know, there is nothing in Jewish literature that antedates the phrase. Paul's intent is clear, however, which is to establish the parallel between the experience of ancient Israel in her salvation from the Egyptians and the believer's deliverance from the bondage of sin symbolized in Christian baptism (Rom 6:3; Gal 3:27; see also 1 Cor 1:14; 12:13; Acts 8:16; 19:5). Just as Israel identified with Moses in the events of the exodus, so too believers identify with their deliverer, Christ, in the new and greater exodus.[135] The phrase "baptism into Moses," lays the groundwork for Paul's main point, namely, that Israel's identification with God's divinely appointed leader and her participation in

[133] For the use of the phrase elsewhere in Paul, see Rom 1:13; 11:25; 1 Cor 12:1; 2 Cor 1:8; 1 Thess 4:13. Thiselton (*First Corinthians*, 723) notes that the phrase is a broadly standard formula in first-century Graeco-Roman letters or treatises.

[134] It is possible, of course, that in using the phrase "our fathers" Paul is speaking only of himself and fellow Jews or possibly quoting an existing interpretive tradition, but nothing in the context suggests this restriction. Paul regarded both Jew and Gentile converts as sharing a common ancestry (cf. Rom 4:11, Abraham is the "father of all who believe"). The Corinthians stood in continuity with God's actions in the past. See Robertson and Plummer, *First Corinthians*, 199; Barrett, *First Corinthians*, 220; Garland, *1 Corinthians*, 448; Fee, *First Corinthians*, 444; Thiselton, *First Corinthians*, 724.

[135] Garland (*1 Corinthians*, 450) suggests a move backward by Paul; as the latter Redeemer (Christ), so also the first redeemer (Moses). Barrett (*First Corinthians*, 220–21) prefers the textual variant, which occurs in the middle voice, "they baptized themselves into Moses." Cf. Exod 14:31, "And when the Israelites saw the great power the LORD displayed against the Egyptians, the people feared the LORD and put their trust in him and in Moses his servant." Peter draws a parallel between baptism and the flood (1 Pet 3:20–21).

the deliverance of the exodus did not prevent most of them from perishing in the wilderness. God's blessings flow to those who are obedient, not merely to those who identify with Christ in baptism.[136]

**10:3–4** God's provision of food and drink in the wilderness yields further correspondences between the Corinthians and Israel and is especially linked to Israel's apostasy to idols mentioned in 10:7b, where the key words "eat" and "drink" occur in the quote of Exod 32:6. This not only brings us back to the main theme of "food offered to idols" raised in chap. 8; it also sets up the stark contrast between the mutually exclusive activities of eating and drinking unto the Lord (the Lord's Supper) and eating and drinking in the presence of idols, which Paul takes up explicitly in 10:14–22.

In 10:3–4, Paul calls the food, the drink, and the rock "spiritual,"[137] which, in context likely refers to the divine character of the gift; that is, they were of supernatural origin over against the natural order of things,[138] or it may refer to the divine presence since Paul adds that "the rock was Christ." This latter claim remarkably recasts the Old Testament story in relation to the Corinthian church by indicating Christ's presence to bless and punish the ancient Israelites. Paul's choice of imperfect verb tense is required by the description of the rock as that which "followed" them,[139] which emphasizes both the continual provision of water and the perpetual presence of Christ among the Israelites. The assertion of the presence of Christ in the wilderness as the source of Israel's provision in the wilderness is of immense Christological significance,[140] but it also elevates the argument to a new level.[141] Whereas the "baptism in

---

[136] Robertson and Plummer (*First Corinthians*, 200) note that baptism is a sign of allegiance and trust. The phrase "baptism into Moses" implies that union with Moses, God's anointed leader, was the salvation of the Israelites. Likewise, union with Christ was the salvation of the Corinthians. Thiselton (*First Corinthians*, 724) explains, "The significance of baptized in relation to Moses is not least to identify the participating nature of their status and experience. Baptism signifies being bound up with the one in whose name, or in whose sphere of influence, a person is baptized, so that in Paul Christian baptism signifies above all else identification with Christ, especially with Christ's saving death and resurrection (Rom 6:3–11). For a recent study on the issue of believer's baptism, see Thomas R. Schreiner and Shawn D. Wright, eds., *Believer's Baptism: Sign of the New Covenant in Christ*, NAC Studies in Bible and Theology (Nashville: B&H, 2006).

[137] Gk. πνευματικός. The term has already been used as a key term in 1 Cor 2:13,15, and 3:1. Other occurrences in 1 Corinthians include 9:11; 12:1; 14:1,37; 15:44–46 (elsewhere in the New Testament only in 1 Pet 2:5). Barrett (*First Corinthians*, 222) notes that the word "spiritual" in Paul is employed to denote a thing or person that is the bearer or agent of the Holy Spirit (cf. 9:1; 12:1; 14:1; 15:44,46; Rom 1:11; 7:14; 15:27).

[138] Ps 78:24

[139] Literally, "for they were drinking from a spiritual following rock" (ἔπινον γὰρ ἐκ πνευματικῆς ἀκολουθούσης πέτρας). The NIV does not capture the switch in verb tense, from aorist (they drank) to the imperfect (they were drinking).

[140] Cf. 1 Cor 8:6.

[141] Hays (*First Corinthians*, 160) comments, "To make the correspondence complete, Paul goes so far as to suggest that Christ was present with Israel in their wanderings: the rock from which they drank 'was Christ' (v. 4). Thus, in every respect Israel enjoyed the grace and the presence of God."

Moses" naturally corresponds to the believer's "baptism into Christ," here Paul makes the case for the actual presence of Christ among the Israelites (10:9). So also Christ is continually present among the Corinthians as signified in the drinking of the cup and the breaking of the bread (see 10:14–22; 11:27–31). Blomberg's comments are helpful: "New Testament writers regularly use the Old Testament in 'creative ways.' One of the most common is to see Christ at work where the Old Testament speaks only of God. But once one believes that Christ formed part of the Godhead from all eternity past, this equation becomes natural, particularly in contexts where God provides salvation for his people, which was precisely the heart of Jesus' first-century mission. Paul regularly responds to and revises common Jewish interpretive methods and traditions."[142] This brings the negative example of Israel powerfully into the present. The same God/Christ who meted out judgment on Israel will do the same to the Corinthians who follow in their steps.

How does Paul arrive at the conclusion that the rock was Christ and that it (he) followed Israel on their journey? Some suppose that Paul draws from a Jewish exegetical tradition that sought to explain the appearance of the well at both the beginning and the end of Israel's journey (Exod 17:6; Num 20:11).[143] This interpretation was facilitated by the ambiguity of Num 21:16–20.[144] It is apparent that, while Paul's point of reference may be the literal rock, just as there was literal food to eat and literal water to drink, the designation of all three as "spiritual" suggests Paul has moved from the literal rock to another point, namely, that of Christ as the source of Israel's support during the wilderness wanderings.[145] There was a spiritual rock that followed them, and that rock was Christ. From Christ they continually received their provisions. Garland explains, "When Paul says, 'The rock was Christ,' he is not thinking of a material rock or of a transportable well, "but of the divine source of the water that journeyed with them. He understands the replenishing rock in a spiritual sense, not a physical sense."[146]

---

[142] Blomberg, *1 Corinthians*, 196. On spiritual food and drink, see Exod 16:1–36; Ps 78:23–29; on the water from the rock, see Exod 17:1–17; Num 20:2–13; and Ps 78:15–16.

[143] So Garland, *1 Corinthians*, 455–58. See also P. E. Enns, "The 'Moveable Well' in 1 Cor 10:4: An Extrabiblical Tradition in an Apostolic Text," *BBR* 6 (1996): 23–38.

[144] So Ciampa and Rosner (*First Corinthians*, 450), who note that Jewish tradition held that God gave the well itself: "The understanding that the well/rock traveled with Israel was based on an interpretation that Paul and other Jewish interpreters evidently inherited from their fathers."

[145] So Robertson and Plummer, *First Corinthians*, 201.

[146] Garland, *1 Corinthians*, 457. Garland suggests a number of Old Testament images evoked by the Rock: (1) a title for God in Deut 32, (2) stability and permanence, (3) reminder of God's miraculous provision; his saving and redeeming work. Hays (*First Corinthians*, 161) sees Deut 32, which repeatedly identifies Yahweh with the title, "Rock," as central to Paul's thinking (see Deut 32:4,15,18,30,31; also 12:15; Ps 18:2). Hays proposes that "Paul is reading Israel's story through the lens of the church's experience and discovering figurations of God's grace."

**10:5** "Nevertheless" translates a strong adversative in Greek,[147] which sets 10:5 in sharp contrast with the blessings and privileges of "all" Israel described in 10:1–4. In spite of divine deliverance, protection, and provision, God was not pleased with most of them. Paul often refers to God's pleasure when speaking of salvation in Christ,[148] but here Paul announces that God was not pleased with the Israelites, which resulted in the scattering[149] of their bodies over the desert. The reference to "most" of Israel anticipates the large number of those who fell under God's judgment (10:6–11), although it is clear that "some," rather than "all" committed these sins.[150]

As noted above, one should exercise due caution in pressing the correspondence to Israel's judgment to indicate a loss of salvation/regeneration. The warnings, however, are real, and God's judgment is severe, as Paul will demonstrate in 10:6–11. In the Old Testament context, the judgment is consistent loss of blessing and loss of physical life. We should not immediately assume that God's judgment meted out against sin implies the loss of eternal salvation, nor should we assume that every single Israelite who left Egypt was "saved" in the New Testament sense of the word. Such speculation misses Paul's point. When it comes to ultimate salvation, Paul is rather optimistic regarding the Corinthians' standing on the Day of the Lord (cf. 1:4–9). However, those who hold a false sense of security while flirting glibly with idols and associated sins should heed the warning. In context, the punishment for sin is death. In 11:30 we read that many of the Corinthians are sick and some have died as a result of their behavior at the Lord's table.

**10:6** The use of an *inclusio* at 10:6 and 10:11 marks off 10:6–11 as a unit and clarifies that "these things" in 10:6 refers to what follows rather than what precedes.[151] This lends support to the translation of the Greek term *typos* as "example" rather than "type."[152] This is not to say that typology is

[147] ἀλλά.

[148] See 1 Cor 1:21; Gal 1:15; Col 1:19; on the use of the noun εὐδοκία, see Eph 1:5,9; Phil 2:13.

[149] The Greek term, καταστρώννυμι, occurs only here in the New Testament. The word appears in Num 14:16 (LXX). The word means "to spread out," which in context offers the image of being slaughtered (so BDAG).

[150] The fourfold repetition of τινες (10:7–10) is parallel to the fivefold repetition of πάντες (10:1–4).

[151] The *inclusio* is marked by five parallel terms in 10:6–7 and 10:11 (10:6–7, ταῦτα δὲ, τύποι, κἀκεῖνοι, γέγραπται; 10:11, ταῦτα δὲ, τυπικῶς, ἐκείνοις, ἐγράφη). Collier ("That We Might Not Crave Evil," 60–63) suggests a formal chiasm based on parallels between the alternation of present imperatives and hortatory subjunctives as follows: 10:7, Present Imperative (γίνεσθε), "Do not become idolators"; 10:8, Hortatory Subjunctive (πορνεύωμεν), "Let us not commit sexual immorality"; 10:9, Hortatory Subjunctive (ἐκπειράζωμεν), "Let us not test Christ"; 10:10, Present Imperative (γογγύζετε), "Do not grumble." Collier also notes the progressively strong language: cause of their downfall (10:7); they fell (10:8); they were being destroyed by the serpents (10:9), and they were destroyed by the angel of destruction (10:10).

[152] So also Robertson and Plummer, *First Corinthians*, 203. In other words, "these things" points to the negative example of Israel's disobedience (10:6b–10) rather than to the symbols in 10:1–4. Paul rehearses Israel's negative example of disobedience with the intention of correcting

not at work in the passage in the correspondences that Paul makes between Israel and the church (10:1–4). It does, however, seem to point to a mixture of analogy and typology. In other words Paul's point is that Israel is a negative example to be shunned rather than a prophetic type of the Corinthians. Furthermore, Paul's application is local and narrow, referring only to the Corinthians, rather than to the whole church. The negative example of Israel applies to all believers and to all churches. Some will fall under judgment but others, who heed the warning, will be spared. Fee thinks there is a typological sense to Israel and its sacraments but an analogical sense to the events used as warning examples: "As typology, the passage breaks down precisely at the point of warning."[153]

These events occurred, Paul says, "to keep us from setting our hearts on evil things as they did." Collier suggests that Paul's choice of language indicates a conscious allusion to Num 11:4–34, where the notion of craving begins and ends the passage.[154] What follows in 10:7–10 are four instances of Israel's corporate sin that resulted from the basic sin of craving evil. Commentators often note that there is more to the four admonitions in 10:7–10 than a conventional listing of evil practices but rather a pulling together of a number of Old Testament texts that apply directly to the Corinthian situation.[155] All of the examples tie into the theme of eating and drinking that reverberates through chaps. 8–10.[156]

**10:7** Idolatry, the key issue in the discussion of meat sacrificed to idols in chaps. 8–10 (cf. 10:14), heads the list of evil cravings that the Corinthians must avoid at all costs. The citation of Exod 32:6b[157] locates Paul's warning historically in one of Israel's most appalling acts of apostasy in the worship

and preventing Corinthian disobedience. Overall the argument of 8:1–11:1 leads to the admonition to imitate Paul's positive example, "Imitate me, as I imitate Christ" (11:1). For Paul's use of the term τύπος to refer to his own example, see Phil 3:17; 1 Thess 1:7; 2 Thess 3:9.

[153] Fee, *First Corinthians*, 452. Ciampa and Rosner (*First Corinthians* 454) concur that the passage seems to fall "somewhat short of what typology is usually understood to entail (a correspondence between the past and the future which has been designed by God). Paul clearly establishes a typological relationship between Israel and Christian experience in 10:1–4. It could be argued, however, that in 10:5–11 he does not point to a divinely established pattern but rather to patterns which the Corinthians must avoid fulfilling." Furthermore, "the basic understanding that the church's experience would correspond to patterns found already in Israel's experience seems to be required of Paul's argument. The pattern would not require that believers experience destruction similar to that of the Israelites, but that behavior similar to that of the Israelites would result in a judgment that was also similar to theirs."

[154] See Collier, "That We Might Not Crave Evil." The NIV's "setting our hearts on" (10:6b) translates ἐπιθυμητής ("to desire/crave"), which occurs in Num 11:4 and 11:34 with reference to Israel's craving after meat in the wilderness. On the connection to Num 11, see also Hays, *First Corinthians*, 162; Barrett, *First Corinthians*, 224.

[155] Fee, *First Corinthians*, 451; Garland, *1 Corinthians*, 460.

[156] Hays, *First Corinthians*, 163.

[157] An exact citation of the LXX.

of the golden calf as Moses was receiving the law on Mount Sinai.[158] Aaron complied with Israel's demand for "gods who will go before us," fashioned the Israelites gold into the form of a calf, and shamelessly associated the idol with Yahweh (Exod 32:1–5). Paul chooses the portion of the narrative that focuses on eating and drinking in the presence of the idol since this most closely associates Israel's action to the Corinthian context. The reference to eating and drinking stands in sharp contrast to Israel's eating "spiritual" food and drinking "spiritual" drink mentioned in 10:3–4, thus all the more highlighting the egregious nature of the sin. Psalm 106:21 sums it up well: "They forgot the God who saved them."

The account in Exodus further describes the "pagan revelry" as singing, shouting, and dancing (Exod 32:17–19), but it may have also included sexual debauchery.[159] There is a natural association between idolatry and sexual immorality, and Paul explicitly takes up the latter in the next verse. In each of the subsequent examples of Israel's sin (10:8–10) Paul mentions the punishment meted out by God. In 10:7 Paul omits the punishment of three thousand deaths and a subsequent plague that occurred as a result of Israel's idolatry. Koet, however, suggests that Paul actually includes the punishment by fusing together elements of Exod 32 and Num 11 in the case of sexual immorality described in the next verse.[160]

**10:8** Paul's second exhortation, "We should not commit sexual immorality, as some of them did," unlike the previous warning, is followed by a description of the subsequent punishment, which was twenty-three thousand deaths in one day. Although Paul does not quote the Old Testament, the number of deaths ties the example to the account of Israel's harlotry with the Moabite women and their idolatrous worship of the Baal of Peor recorded in Num 25:1–9.[161] What may be implicit in the first example of the golden calf is explicit here, namely, the close association of sexual immorality and idolatry. The first two examples of Israel's craving of evil things clearly link two of the major emphases of the letter in the warnings against sexual immorality and idolatry (6:18; 10:14). Garland suggests that although the primary reference in 10:8 is

[158] On the golden calf episode, see also Deut 9:8–16,18–21; Judg 2:17; 1 Kgs 12:28; Neh 9:16–18; Ps 106:19–23; Acts 7:39–43.

[159] The NIV's "pagan revelry" translates the Greek, παίζειν, "to play." The term may carry sexual overtones (Gen 26:8; 39:17) but not always (Gen 21:9; Judg 16:25). Louw-Nida (50.8) comment, "The specific reference of παίζω in 1 Cor 10:7 is probably to dancing, but some scholars interpret παίζω in this context as a euphemism for sex." Garland (*1 Corinthians*, 461) posits that Paul's quotation of this portion of Scripture underscores the point that both feasting and playing were aspects of idolatry. Paul chooses not to quote the portions of the narrative that mention the actual worship of the idol (Exod 32:6a,31c). Thiselton (*First Corinthians*, 734–35) notes how the description in Exodus of Israel's behavior stands in contrast to the restraint and sober self-control demanded of God's covenant people (cf. 9:24–27).

[160] B. J. Koet, "The Old Testament Background to 1 Cor 10,7–8," in *The Corinthian Correspondence*, BETL 75, ed. R. Bieringer (Leuven: University Press, 1996), 607–15.

[161] The word for "gods" in Num 25:2 (LXX) is idols (εἰδώλων).

to literal acts of immorality, there is also a strong metaphorical sense in the abandoning of God for the idol (cf. Rev 2:14,21).[162]

Paul mentions twenty-three thousand who fell (died) in one day, whereas Numbers records an additional thousand who died under God's judgment. The actual solution to the problem of the missing thousand should not divert our attention from the focus of the passage.[163] Both Paul and the Old Testament passage report round numbers, and Paul adds that twenty-three thousand died in one day, a detail not recorded in Numbers. It is possible that Paul drew on an exegetical tradition, as in 10:1–5, which offered further details of the story. Paul's exegetical and intertextual moves in the use of the Old Testament Scriptures can be quite complex.[164] Koet suggests that Paul modeled his wording after Exod 32:28, which records three thousand deaths in one day, and integrated an approximation of twenty-thousand from Num 25. By doing so he connects the punishment in Num 25 with the punishment in Exod 32.[165]

**10:9** The third sin mentioned is that of testing Christ. The NIV renders 10:9 as, "test the Lord," but the more difficult reading adopted by the Nestle-Aland Greek text and followed by many English translations is "test Christ."[166] That Israel's sin could be regarded as against Christ is a natural inference from the identification of Christ as the following-rock in 10:4, the source of Israel's provision, and the previous acknowledgment of Jesus as the one Lord in 8:6. The Old Testament passage is Num 21:4–9, possibly used in conjunction with other texts that refer to Israel's repeated offense of putting God to the test (Exod 17:2–7; Deut 6:16; Ps 78:18; 95:8–11).[167] Numbers 21 records that the people grew impatient and complained bitterly against God and Moses: "Why have you brought us up out of Egypt to die in the desert? There is no bread! There is no water! And we detest this miserable food!" (21:5). Once again the contextual link between the Corinthian situation and the example of Israel is apparent in the mention of food and drink. The Israelites detested God's provision, desiring instead the food from Egypt. In response the Lord sent venomous snakes among the people and many perished. The NIV translation of 10:9b, "—and were killed by snakes," does not adequately capture the force

[162] Garland, *1 Corinthians*, 461–62.

[163] It is far too simplistic a solution to assert that Paul merely had a lapse of memory at this point.

[164] For example, the basic premise of Collier's study ("That We Might Not Crave Evil") is that 1 Cor 10:6 evokes Num 11 of which Exod 32:6 is a summary.

[165] Koet, "Old Testament Background," 611–13. Noted also by Garland, *1 Corinthians*, 462–63. There is not enough evidence to know whether or not this is the actual solution to the problem, but it remains a possibility.

[166] Representative English translations that adopt "Christ" as the correct reading include KJV, NRSV, ESV, HCSB, NET, NIV2011.

[167] The verb "to test" is ἐκπειράζω, appearing four times in the New Testament; here and in Matt 4:7; Luke 4:12; 10:25; cf. Deut 6:16; Ps 77:18 (LXX). The usual verb "to test/tempt" is πειράζω. The reference to Israel's sin of "testing Christ" anticipates 10:21–22, provoking God to jealousy.

of the imperfect tense verb that is a bit more graphic and descriptive of the process of being destroyed.[168] By going to the idol's temple the Corinthians were testing Christ just as the Israelites tested Christ in the wilderness and placed themselves under God's judgment.

**10:10** Hays notes that the fourth and final warning "is the most difficult to connect to a specific OT text and also the most difficult to relate to any known behavior of the Corinthians."[169] Paul may have in mind Israel's bitter complaint recorded in Num 14 against Moses and Aaron and ultimately Yahweh. The Israelites expressed regret for leaving Egypt (14:1–4), demonstrating their unbelief (14:11). Although Moses' intercession saved the Israelites from imminent judgment (14:12–19), only Joshua and Caleb would enter the promised land due to Israel's disobedience and contempt for Yahweh (14:22–23). The Lord referred to Israel as a "wicked congregation" that grumbled against him (14:26–27). God declared that the dead bodies of those who grumbled against the Lord would fall in the wilderness, and of those twenty years old and upward, only Joshua and Caleb would enter the promised land (14:28–30). The spies who brought back a report that caused the people to grumble died from a plague (14:36–38). The Num 14 passage includes key connections with 1 Cor 10:5–10, including grumbling, testing the Lord, and dead bodies falling in the wilderness. As Hays points out, if this is the correct background text, then Paul concludes with an example that is comprehensive in scope, implicating virtually the entire nation in judgment.[170]

There are, of course, other possible textual connections, such as Num 16, which records Israel's complaint against Moses for the punishment of Korah.[171] The mention of the "destroying angel" in 1 Cor 10:10 is found neither in Num 14 or 16.[172] Nevertheless, the implication is that the same instrument of death unleashed against the Egyptians struck those who, although delivered by the angel, experienced wrath in their disobedience.[173] It may be that Paul has no specific Old Testament text in mind, but rather his admonition in 1 Cor 10:10 is a general and summary statement of the numerous references to grumbling in the exodus narrative.[174] Some think that Paul singles out

---

[168] Gk. ἀπώλλυντο. So Thiselton, *First Corinthians*, 741.

[169] Hays, *First Corinthians*, 165.

[170] Ibid.

[171] Collier ("That We Might Not Crave Evil") suggests Num 11 is in view. Garland (*1 Corinthians*, 464) notes a number of connections between 1 Cor 10 and Ps 105 (LXX), which is a summary of Israel's wilderness experience.

[172] The phrase "destroying angel" (NIV) is literally, "the Destroyer" (so HCSB, ESV). The reference may be to the angel who carries out the divine sentence (see Exod 12:23, LXX). See also Heb 11:28. R. F. Collins suggests that the Destroyer was the avenging Lord (Num 14:15–16; cf. Exod 16:3) (*First Corinthians*, SP [Collegeville, MN: Liturgical Press, 1999], 372).

[173] Garland (*1 Corinthians*, 464) comments, "If the destroying angel who killed the firstborn in Egypt (Exod. 12:23) is in view, it reveals a terrifying mystery that God's instrument to liberate the people can return, in boomerang fashion, to strike them dead for their disobedience."

[174] So Thiselton, *First Corinthians*, 742; Ciampa and Rosner, *First Corinthians*, 463.

grumbling because the Corinthians have been murmuring against him.[175] This view assumes a particular historical reconstruction underlying the letter, and it is plausible since the other three examples seem to cohere closely with the Corinthian situation.[176] On the other hand, grumbling/complaining was one of the most persistent of Israel's sins and is a common human response to testing.

**10:11** This verse makes essentially the same point as 10:6, that God's judgments on Israel serve as a warning to all believers. "These things"[177] refers to God's judgment on the Israelites in the exodus for their idolatry, sexual immorality, testing Christ, and grumbling.[178] These events were written down for a purpose, namely, for our instruction/admonition.[179] The Old Testament Scriptures are more than mere historical record; the situations of the Old Testament are analogous to situations in the New. Scripture transcends the local historical situation and is always relevant to God's people.

The word translated "as examples" (*typikos*) by the NIV occurs only here in the New Testament but derives its meaning from the parallel term *typos* in 10:6. The meaning invested in the term in 10:6 determines the sense of the word in 10:11.[180] As noted in our comments on 10:6, Paul can use the term *typos* to refer to an Old Testament type with a New Testament counterpart, or he can use the term to refer to a model or example. Translations opt for the latter in this case. This does not mean, however, that typology plays no role in the passage. Whatever view one takes of Paul's "typological" approach to the Scriptures, the essential point is clear. The things that happened to Israel served a purpose for us, namely, that we should not lust after evil things as they lusted.

The phrase "on whom the fulfillment [lit. "ends"] of the ages has come," is found only here in the New Testament. The phrase is unique in the use of the two plurals ("the ends" and "the ages").[181] The eschatological emphasis

---

[175] Robertson and Plummer, *First Corinthians*, 206; Fee, *First Corinthians*, 457.

[176] Hays (*First Corinthians*, 165) points out, "There is not enough information given in the text to make a confident decision about whether Paul's final illustration is specifically related to the controversies at Corinth or whether it is simply a general homiletical remark based on the wilderness narratives."

[177] Forms an *inclusio* with 10:6. Fee (*First Corinthians*, 458) identifies "these things" as a parallel conclusion.

[178] The imperfect verb is used, συνέβαινεν, which Robertson and Plummer (*First Corinthians*, 207) classify as an iterative imperfect (they happened one by one).

[179] Gk. νουθεσία, used only by Paul in the New Testament (Eph 6:4; Titus 3:10; see 1 Cor 4:4 for the verb form).

[180] Fee (*First Corinthians*, 458n41) notes that the word does *not* mean "typologically." Thiselton (*First Corinthians*, 746) comments, "Paul, however, does not say in this verse that the events of the wilderness happened *typikos* to us, but these things happened in succession (continuous imperfect) to them in the mode (adverb) of their formative models."

[181] If a Hebraic idiom that uses the plural where English uses the singular, the meaning would be "the end of the age" or "the last days." The phrase may describe the overlapping of the two ages of Jewish apocalyptic thought, i.e., the close of one age coinciding with the beginning of the new (so Thiselton, *First Corinthians*, 743–44). Witherington (*Conflict and Community*, 223), however, suggests that "Paul is likely not referring to the overlap of the old and new ages. Probably Paul

is obvious, but Paul does not explain precisely what he means. The end itself has not yet arrived, as 15:20–28 makes clear, but in some sense the "end (s) of the age (s)" has arrived.[182] Robertson and Plummer suggest that the phrase could mean something like believers, who stand at the end of the ages, reap the benefits of the experience of prior ages, or it could mean that the end of the ages has now reached us, which means that we are now in the final age.[183] Fee thinks that it is this eschatological dimension that constitutes the "typological" element in that the whole Old Testament has been pointing to the eschatological fulfillment in God's new people.[184] The phrase may function rhetorically to heighten the warning along the lines of a "lesser to the greater" argument. If the wilderness generation experienced God's judgment, then how much more the Corinthians.[185]

**10:12** Paul concludes with a strong, summative warning against self-confidence that captures the overarching intent of this section and paves the way for the imperative in 10:14, "Flee from idolatry!"[186] In context, the phrase "the one who thinks he stands"[187] targets "those with knowledge" mentioned in 8:10.[188] Paul began this section with, "I do not want you to be ignorant" (10:1). In the course of his argument Paul has shown how "those with knowledge" have become "puffed up" (8:1) and may not be truly knowledgeable at all. The one who loves God (8:3) has been known by him, and love for God is shown by shunning idolatry. Paul has persuasively made his case that those who "know" and who think they stand may lack the most essential knowledge of all concerning the ways of God. In context, the meaning of "fall" is to die (10:8), which had already occurred in Corinth over abuses of the Lord's

---

believed that the goals to which history has been pressing had in his day begun to be realized since Christ had died and risen."

[182] The verb used is in the perfect tense (κατήντηκεν, "to arrive, to attain"; BDAG, "to reach a condition or goal). Cf. 1 Cor 14:26; Eph 4:13; Phil 3:11.

[183] On the first view Robertson and Plummer (*First Corinthians*, 207–8) comment, "Such an interpretation comes as a fitting conclusion to a passage in which the Corinthians are exhorted to take the experience of the Israelites as lessons for themselves."

[184] Fee, *First Corinthians*, 459.

[185] Garland (*1 Corinthians*, 465) comments, "If the wilderness generation met such a horrifying end by spurning a concealed Christ who nurtured them throughout their journey, how much more the Corinthians will be condemned if they spurn the revealed Christ." God has not become more lax in punishing transgression with the shift of the ages.

[186] 10:12 begins with the conjunction ὥστε (therefore) expressing inference.

[187] The phrase "He who thinks" or "If anyone thinks" recurs throughout the letter (see 3:18; 11:16; 14:37). The phrase itself carries a tone of warning.

[188] Note the parallel phrase in 8:2, "If anyone thinks he knows anything, he has not yet known as it is necessary to know." Cf. also the parallel to 8:9, "Be careful" (both 8:9 and 10:12 use an imperative form of βλέπω, "Take heed!"). Both 8:2 and 10:12 use perfect tense infinitives (ἐγνωκέναι and ἑστάναι). Both phrases in 8:2 and 10:12 strike at the self-assured. Garland (*First Corinthians*, 466) notes the sense of covenant security conveyed in the expression "to stand." Fee (*First Corinthians*, 459) suggests that "the one who thinks he stands" points back to 10:1–4.

Supper (11:27–30). "Falling" may also be synonymous with standing before God "unapproved" (9:27). Both certainly entail God's judgment.

**10:13** The final verse of this unit, in contrast to the strong warning of 10:12, offers encouragement for those who seek refuge in the faithfulness of God. From a literary point of view 10:13 is a self-contained, proverbial statement, perhaps inserted as a summary of 10:1–12 and providing a bridge to 10:14. Robertson and Plummer suggest 10:12–13 provides two admonitions; one to the self-confident who think they have no need to be watchful and the other to the despondent, who think it useless to struggle with temptation.[189] Paul does not specify the nature of the temptation, a term that can refer either to an external trial (testing) or to the internal allurement of sin.[190] As a stand-alone verse the meaning and applications could be wide-ranging, but in context Paul has in mind the allurement of idolatry and associated sins enumerated in 10:6–10, the "craving for evil" that Israel demonstrated in the desert.[191] Such temptations are "common to man," that is, they are not extraordinary trials but the kinds of things experienced by all believers. Garland thinks that what may be in view is external testing in the sense of persecution against those who excluded themselves from the idolatrous feasts.[192]

The phrase "God is faithful" is found also in the letter's opening, where Paul expressed confidence in the Corinthian's final outcome, that God would confirm them blameless in the Day of the Lord.[193] Here Paul relates the phrase to the fact that God will not allow believers to encounter a temptation that they are unable to bear. Not all of the Israelites succumbed to the wilderness temptations, only "some" of them did.[194] The clear implication is that God is faithful to provide the way of escape for his people in a time of temptation.[195] Sinful though we still are, God's grace is sufficient in every case. The very next verse, 10:14, specifies the way of escape for the situation at hand, "Flee from idolatry!" The path of escape is often a path we are unwilling to take.[196]

---

[189] Robertson and Plummer, *First Corinthians*, 208. So also Thiselton (*First Corinthians*, 749); 10:13 constitutes a warning to the "knowledgeable" in Corinth and comfort to those who are weak in conscience.

[190] Gk. πειρασμός. See Jas 1:2–15 where the term seems to carry both nuances of external trial (1:2–4,12) and an internal allurement to sin (1:13–15).

[191] So also Thiselton, *First Corinthians*, 747.

[192] Garland, *1 Corinthians*, 467. The verb "to overtake" occurs in other contexts of persecution (see 2 Tim 3:12; 1 Pet 2:19).

[193] For other references to God's faithfulness in Paul, see 2 Cor 1:18; 1 Thess 5:24; 2 Thess 3:3; 2 Tim 2:13.

[194] Cf. Num 14:20–30 and the Lord's commendation of Caleb and Joshua.

[195] Robertson and Plummer (*First Corinthians*, 209) draw attention to the use of the definite article in the phase "the way of escape." It is the necessary way of escape, the one suitable for such difficulty.

[196] Cf. Gal 5:13, "You, my brothers, were called to be free. But do not use your freedom to indulge the sinful nature; rather, serve one another in love."

### 6. Do Not Provoke the Lord to Jealousy—Flee Idolatry! (10:14–22)

**[14]Therefore, my dear friends, flee from idolatry. [15]I speak to sensible people; judge for yourselves what I say. [16]Is not the cup of thanksgiving for which we give thanks a participation in the blood of Christ? And is not the bread that we break a participation in the body of Christ? [17]Because there is one loaf, we, who are many, are one body, for we all partake of the one loaf.**

**[18]Consider the people of Israel: Do not those who eat the sacrifices participate in the altar? [19]Do I mean then that a sacrifice offered to an idol is anything, or that an idol is anything? [20]No, but the sacrifices of pagans are offered to demons, not to God, and I do not want you to be participants with demons. [21]You cannot drink the cup of the Lord and the cup of demons too; you cannot have a part in both the Lord's table and the table of demons. [22]Are we trying to arouse the Lord's jealousy? Are we stronger than he?**

Although the implications regarding Israel's negative example in the wilderness should be apparent, Paul spells it out in no uncertain terms with the command to flee from idolatry.[197] Paul appeals to their reason as "sensible people"[198] (10:15) and through a series of rhetorical questions makes a final climactic argument by comparing the two incompatible activities of participation in the Lord's Supper and participation in pagan feasts. This section (10:14–22) and the next (10:23–11:1) bring the discussion of meat sacrificed to idols to conclusion in summarizing fashion.[199]

The emphatic conjunction translated, "therefore," denotes the vital connection of the command in 10:14 to the preceding warnings. The same conjunction occurs also in 8:13 where Paul concluded that he would never eat meat again if food caused his brother to stumble.[200] Whereas 8:13 draws a strong inference regarding meat sacrificed to idols in relation to one's love for others, the command to flee idolatry in 10:14 sets forth the only acceptable response of those bound in covenant with the one true God (cf. 8:3–6), who is faithful to protect and preserve his people in the day of temptation (10:13). Christians must have no part in idolatry, which embodies all that is the opposite of one's love for the one true God.[201] The injunction to take flight from idolatry is heightened by way of analogy to the Lord's Supper, which signifies the believer's participation in Christ and demonstrates the complete incompatibility between God

---

[197] Fotopoulos (*Food Offered to Idols*, 233) calls this Paul's "central refutation of the Corinthian's idol-food consumption constituting idolatry." See also Cheung, *Idol Food in Corinth*, 146.

[198] Gk. φρόνιμος. BDAG defines as "pertaining to understanding associated with insight and wisdom; sensible, thoughtful, prudent, wise. Paul used the term in a sarcastic, negative sense in 4:10. See also Rom 12:16; 2 Cor 11:19.

[199] This section shows that idolatry is the key issue throughout (so Collins, *First Corinthians*, 378–79; Garland, *1 Corinthians*, 474; Ciampa and Rosner, *First Corinthians*, 470).

[200] Gk. διόπερ. 8:13 and 10:14 are the only occurrences of the conjunction in the New Testament.

[201] Cf. Jas 4:4, "You adulterous people, don't you know that friendship with the world is hatred toward God? Anyone who chooses to be a friend of the world becomes an enemy of God."

and the idols of the world, between the false worship of idols in which the participants fellowship with demons, and the worship of the one true God in the celebration of the covenant meal.

The command to flee idolatry parallels Paul's previous command to flee sexual immorality (6:18). Furthermore, there are significant parallels between Paul's argument regarding the believer's body in 6:12–20 and his warning against idolatry (10:14–22), followed by the summarizing conclusion (10:23–31).[202] The dangers of sexual immorality and idolatry, associated sins rooted in the Corinthian's pagan past, perpetuated under a misguided understanding of grace captured by the maxim "Everything is permissible for me" (6:12; 10:23). In both instances Paul reminds the Corinthians of their exclusive relationship to Christ. Just as Paul demonstrates the utter incompatibility of a believer, who is a member of Christ, being joined to a prostitute (see esp. 6:15–20), so also he reminds the Corinthians that their participation in the Lord's Supper is mutually exclusive of their attendance and participation at pagan feasts that constitute idolatry (10:16–21). Both sections conclude with the exhortation to bring glory to God (6:20; 10:31).

This passage, together with 11:23–29, provides significant insight into the theology of the Lord's Supper.[203] The main point of 10:14–22 is that participation in pagan meals constitutes idolatry and results in disastrous consequences for believers. First Corinthians 11:23–29 indicates that the abuse of the Lord's Supper itself has already led to the death of some Corinthians. God's judgment had already fallen on some of them. Those who participate in the Lord's Supper must not do so in an unworthy manner lest they too incur God's wrath. In 10:14–22 the Lord's Supper is brought in only as part of the argument against attendance at pagan feasts. Nevertheless, the analogy and what Paul has to say is significant for our theology and understanding of the meal.

**10:14–15** Paul's injunction to the Corinthians to flee from idolatry is strengthened both by the address "my dear friends" (10:14) and by Paul's sincere appeal to them to judge the matter for themselves (10:15).[204] Similarly in 4:14, in concluding his lengthy argument regarding human wisdom, Paul warned the Corinthians as his "beloved children." Such language expresses deep affection and concern for their spiritual well being. Some think that Paul's appeal to their discernment may have a touch of irony since the same term was

---

[202] See Fee, *First Corinthians*, 463; Garland, *1 Corinthians*, 474.

[203] Ciampa and Rosner (*1 Corinthians*, 469) call attention to the neglect of 10:15–22 in the church and its rich theology of the Lord's Supper: "It complements and fills out the material in chap. 11 by explaining that the Supper entails participation in the blood and body of Christ, that the single loaf speaks to the heart of the unity that must mark the life of the church, and that the meal serves to renew the exclusive covenant with God established in Christ, and that its abuse constitutes a foolish and dangerous challenge to the God who is present in its celebration."

[204] The term is φρόνιμος rather than σοφός (see 4:10).

used in 4:10 with this sense.[205] But this seems unlikely in this context since it occurs in conjunction with the address "my dear friends." Collins suggests that instead of rhetorical irony Paul's appeal is better understood as a rhetorical move to gain favor with the audience.[206] Paul writes to them in this manner because the Corinthians prided themselves in their knowledge and had intimated as much to Paul in their letter to him. Paul wants "to show them how sensible his position is based on their experience of the Lord's Supper."[207] The use of the present imperative may indicate the perpetual nature of the temptation to idolatry (cf. also 6:18). The Corinthians must make it their habit to continually flee occasions that would implicate them in idolatry.[208] The close connection between 10:14 and 10:13 may indicate that the only escape from idolatry is to flee.[209] Idolatry is a very real and present danger for the Corinthians, who find themselves in a situation directly analogous to the ancient Israelites.

**10:16–17** Paul's appeal to them to judge for themselves the rightness of his firm position regarding idolatry takes the form of six rhetorical questions (10:16–22). The first two questions (10:16) bring the Lord's Supper into the argument by way of analogy in order to draw out the implications for his main concern regarding their participation in idols feasts, which is idolatry.[210] Paul's intent, therefore, is not to set forth a full statement of the theology of the Supper, yet what he does say is no small contribution to our understanding of the meaning and function of the meal in the early church, particularly when read in conjunction with 11:23–29 where Paul refers to the traditions derived from Jesus that he received and passed on to the Corinthians.

The first two questions refer to the "cup of blessing" and the "breaking of bread," both of which constitute "participation" in the blood and the body of Christ. The term "participation" translates the Greek term often rendered

---

[205] Barrett (*First Corinthians*, 321) says that "sensible men" has a touch of irony to it in connection with those who claim "to know" (so also Witherington, *Conflict and Community*, 224; Fotopoulos, *Food Offered to Idols*, 234). Robertson and Plummer (*First Corinthians*, 211), however, suggest that Paul intends no sarcasm in the use of "wise/sensible." Paul appeals to their good sense and is part of his persuasive argument. So also Fee, *First Corinthians*, 463–64; Collins, *First Corinthians*, 379; Garland, *1 Corinthians*, 475; Ciampa and Rosner, *First Corinthians*, 470–71.

[206] A *captatio benevolentiae.* Collins, *First Corinthians, 377.*

[207] Fee, *First Corinthians*, 464. Ciampa and Rosner (*First Corinthians*, 471) agree that Paul appeals to the Corinthians' own self-perception as wise people. The implication is that if they are wise and sensible then they will recognize the soundness of Paul's thinking. Furthermore, Paul's appeal to their wisdom reinforces the traditional opposition that underlies the relationship between wisdom (chaps. 1–4) and idolatry (chaps. 8–10). Those who lack wisdom lapse into the worship of idols (cf. Rom 1:21–23).

[208] Cf. 1 John 5:21, "Keep yourselves from idols."

[209] Robertson and Plummer (*First Corinthians*, 211) comment, "They must not try how near they can go, but how far they can fly."

[210] So Fee, *First Corinthians*, 465; Garland, *1 Corinthians*, 476.

"fellowship"[211] and recalls the letter's opening where Paul reminded the Corinthians of their call to "fellowship/partnership" with God's Son (1:9). What Paul means by the term in this context is one of the chief interpretive issues of the passage and has generated considerable debate. Paul does not indicate how participation occurs, only that it does occur. The clear implication from what follows is the exclusivity of the Lord's Supper to all other sacral meals, which involve incompatible spiritual realities. Those with "knowledge" in Corinth failed to comprehend the hostile spiritual powers present in pagan corporate gatherings. The Lord's Supper, on the other hand, signifies the corporate solidarity of the redeemed with their Redeemer. It is this solidarity that forbids all other incompatible unions.[212] This line of reasoning directly addresses one of the fundamental assertions of those with "knowledge" in Corinth regarding the reality of idols in the light of the basic Christian confession that there is only one God (10:19; 8:4–6).

What is the nature of the believer's participation in the blood and body of Christ and what is its meaning in the context of corporate worship? Does the term "participation" denote the divine aspect of our common worship, or does the term refer more to the relational aspect of partnership with others in the meal? In other words, is Paul expressing that believers enter into communion with the Lord in the celebration of the Lord's Supper, or does one enter into partnership with others who partake in the meal? Or could there be an element of both?[213] That the phrases "blood of Christ" and "body of Christ" do not have a material sense here is confirmed in 11:24–25, where Paul draws on Jesus' own interpretation of the cup as "the new covenant in my blood."[214] Both the "blood" and the "body" in this instance refer to the death of Jesus (11:24b), which ratified the new covenant. At the same time Paul refers to the "many" who are one "body," that is, the church, a concept developed further in

---

[211] Gk. κοινωνία.

[212] Fee, *First Corinthians*, 469.

[213] As Fee (*First Corinthians*, 466) explains, "The problem has to do with whether Paul's point—or emphasis—is that in sacred meals one has *koinonia* with the deity (in the Christian's case, with Christ himself), or with fellow participants in the meal as they worship the deity by sacrifice and by eating in his/her honor. Most likely the solution lies somewhere in between. The linguistic and literary evidence indicates that *koinonia* has to do with the worshipers themselves; but the basis and focus of their worship were the deity, who in most cases was considered to be present among them." See the discussion in Ciampa and Rosner, *First Corinthians*, 473. Thiselton translates "communal participation" and likens the Lord's Supper to Israel's recital of the Passover *Seder*, which actively involved those who participated in the ritual—they were "there," so to speak, in the events (*First Corinthians: A Shorter Exegetical and Pastoral Commentary* [Grand Rapids: Eerdmans, 2006], 158).

[214] Hays (*First Corinthians*, 167–68) notes that the language has nothing to do with mysteriously ingesting Christ. Hays further suggests Deut 14:22–26 as a probable background for 10:18 in reference to the provisions of tithes and offerings. The notion of a mystical union was foreign to the Old Testament. Rather the meal was eaten in the presence of the Lord. For a comprehensive analysis of these issues, see Willis, *Idol Meat in Corinth*.

12:12–27 (esp. 12:27, "You are the body of Christ").[215] The context, language, and full argument, including chap. 12, does not allow for a sacramental understanding as though the wine and the bread were actually the Lord himself.[216] On the other hand, it is also mistaken to assert that the Lord's Supper is *merely* symbolic.[217]

**10:18** As in the previous section (10:1–13), Paul develops his point with reference to Israel, but there is an interpretive question regarding the meaning of the phrase translated by the NIV, "Consider the people of Israel." The Greek literally reads, "Consider Israel according to the flesh."[218] Most translations, as the NIV, render the phrase as "the people of Israel" or "the nation of Israel," apparently adopting the view that Paul refers to the nation of Israel as distinct from Christians, the Israel of God (Gal 3:29; 6:16; Phil 3:3); that is, the church is Israel after the Spirit as opposed to Israel after the flesh.[219] Others think, however, that Paul has in mind Israel's negative example in light of the preceding argument of 10:6–13. In this view the phrase "Israel according to the flesh" refers to Israel in the wilderness who succumbed to idolatry and immorality.[220] When the Israelites partook of idolatrous sacrifices, they participated in the altar and what the altar represented. Those who ate the food of the sacrifice entered into a partnership with all that the altar stood for. This would be true either way, if the reference is to sanctioned sacrifices in the Old Testament or if the reference were to Israel's participation in pagan sacrifices.

---

[215] On sharing in the benefits of his blood and body given for us as participants in the New Covenant, see Fee, *First Corinthians*, 468; Vaughan and Lea, *1 Corinthians*, 104.

[216] So Fee (*First Corinthians*, 467), "Neither the language and grammar nor the example of Israel nor the examples from the pagan meals allow such a meaning. The 'fellowship,' therefore was most likely a celebration of their common life in Christ, based on the new covenant in his blood that had previously bound them together in union with Christ by his Spirit." Fee points out that the early church understood Jesus to be present by the Spirit in their gatherings (5:3–5). Barrett (*First Corinthians*, 233–34) suggests that "the body of Christ" refers to the church and the Corinthians themselves are the unleavened loaves. Paul's argument is analogous to 5:7–8.

[217] So J. MacArthur. The Lord's Supper "is a profound celebration of common spiritual experience" (*1 Corinthians* [Chicago: Moody Press, 1984], 237).

[218] Gk. βλέπετε τὸν Ἰσραὴλ κατὰ σάρκα.

[219] Vaughan and Lea, *1 Corinthians*, 104. More recently, Ciampa and Rosner, *First Corinthians*, 477–78. Paul makes a distinction between the Judaism that found its identity in the Jerusalem cult and believers who considered themselves the true heirs of Israel (Rom 2:28–29; Gal 4:25–26). This is a variation of the distinction in the Old Testament and ancient Judaism between the faithful remnant and unqualified citizens of Israel. Paul points to cultic practices of the Judaism of his day based on Old Testament teaching.

[220] The phrase κατὰ σάρκα occurs elsewhere in Paul in 1 Cor 1:26; Rom 1:3; 4:1; 8:4,12,13; 9:3,5; 2 Cor 1:17; 5:16; 10:2; 11:18; Gal 4:23,29; 5:17; Eph 6:5; Col 3:22. Garland (*First Corinthians*, 479) is representative of those who think the phrase carries a negative connotation in this context, "Paul has in view Israel's idolatrous sacrifices that resulted in their miserable downfall in the wilderness, and he refers to an altar dedicated to an idol, not the altar in the temple." Collins (*First Corinthians*, 380) thinks the term refers to Israel as it actually existed (10:5), and given the experience of some during the wandering through the desert (10:6–11) some negativity may be implied.

**10:19–21** The next two rhetorical questions indicate a movement toward conclusion, a summarizing of the argument, and link back to the beginning of the whole discussion in 8:4–8. What is Paul's final answer to "those with knowledge" who claim that food sacrificed to idols is nothing and that an idol is nothing? Is Paul, in fact, claiming that idol food is contaminated and should not be consumed and that there really are other gods? Paul himself poses the question, "Do I mean then that a sacrifice offered to an idol is anything, or that an idol is anything?" The contrasting conjunction in 10:20 indicates that Paul's answer to the question is, "No."[221] The rhetorical question and its implied "no" is consistent with what Paul has already said in 8:4–8 and anticipates his further advice in 10:25 to eat whatever is sold in the marketplace. Food does not become spiritually contaminated in the idol sacrifice. The idol itself is also nothing, as the Old Testament affirms. There is only one God and one Lord (8:6). On the other hand, however, Paul interjects something not considered by the "knowledgeable" in Corinth, namely, the reality of demons, who are present and involved in the pagan sacrifices.[222] In others words, the issue is not the food but rather association with spiritual powers opposed to God. Those who sacrifice at the pagan altar do not sacrifice to God, and Paul does not want them to become partners with demons, which is the stark antithesis to the participation that occurs in the Lord's Supper (10:16). To eat and drink at the table of the Lord rules out eating and drinking at the table of demons.

The subject of the verb "to sacrifice" in 10:20 is ambiguous. The NIV reads, "but the sacrifices of the pagans are offered to demons." While this statement is a true assertion, the Greek leaves the question open, reading only "what things they sacrifice, they sacrifice to demons and not to God." It is possible that the "they" refers to Israel's participation in the pagan sacrifices (see Deut 32). Some ancient manuscripts include the subject, "the Gentiles," as a clarification, but this may or may not be Paul's intent.[223]

---

[221] Gk. ἀλλά. The NIV translation, "No," is not in the text but is supplied as the meaning of the contrast (so also other English translations: NASB, ESV, HCSB).

[222] For a discussion of "demons" in ancient Jewish literature, see Ciampa and Rosner, *First Corinthians*, 481. Garland (*1 Corinthians*, 480) comments, "Paul's argument assumes that although idols are only dumb objects made from inanimate material, they still represent a reality, if only a value system, that directly competes with God. Though the deities worshiped by idolaters are unreal, the intention of the worshipers to have communion with them and the fellowship created by joining in their feasts are very real and very dangerous. Idols have no significance, but actions do . . . they represent something demonic."

[223] Thiselton (*First Corinthians*, 774–75) thinks that Paul has in mind Israel's failure (so also Garland, *First Corinthians*, 480). Ciampa and Rosner (*First Corinthians*, 481) comment, "While Paul is clearly thinking of Israel's failure in the past, it seems fair to say that the sacrifices referred to in Deuteronomy 32:17 and 1 Corinthians 10:20 are pagan sacrifices. Paul does not suggest that the Corinthians (like the Israelites) were themselves tempted to (consciously or intentionally) offer sacrifices to pagan gods, but he does indicate that by knowingly partaking in meals where sacrificial food was consumed they were still to be considered participants in the sacrifices themselves establishing the relevance of his argument in vv. 16–18 to his use of Deuteronomy 32:17."

**10:22** The final two rhetorical questions cap Paul's argument to flee from idolatry. To engage in any form of idolatry is to provoke the supremely powerful Lord to jealousy.[224] The background text is the Song of Moses in Deut 32, which recounts Israel's unfaithfulness to God through sacrificing to demons (32:17) and arousing the Lord's jealous anger.[225] The "strength" of God mention in 10:22 may draw from the epithet "Rock" as a title for God throughout Deut 32. The comparative "stronger" recalls Paul's assertion that the "weakness of God is stronger than men" (1:25) and God's choice of the weak things of the world to nullify the "strong things" (1:27). Is the reference to God's strength a subtle reference to the so-called "strong" (i.e., "knowledgeable") in Corinth?[226]

## 7. Summary and Application: Do All for the Good of Others and to the Glory of God (10:23–11:1)

**23"Everything is permissible"—but not everything is beneficial. "Everything is permissible"—but not everything is constructive. 24Nobody should seek his own good, but the good of others.**

**25Eat anything sold in the meat market without raising questions of conscience,**
**26for, "The earth is the Lord's, and everything in it."**

**27If some unbeliever invites you to a meal and you want to go, eat whatever is put before you without raising questions of conscience. 28But if anyone says to you, "This has been offered in sacrifice," then do not eat it, both for the sake of the man who told you and for conscience' sake—29the other man's conscience, I mean, not yours. For why should my freedom be judged by another's conscience? 30If I take part in the meal with thankfulness, why am I denounced because of something I thank God for?**

**31So whether you eat or drink or whatever you do, do it all for the glory of God.**
**32Do not cause anyone to stumble, whether Jews, Greeks or the church of God—**
**33even as I try to please everybody in every way. For I am not seeking my own good but the good of many, so that they may be saved. 1Follow my example, as I follow the example of Christ.**

The proverbial catch-phrase (slogan) in 10:23, repeated and qualified twice, followed by a summarizing principle of seeking the good of others (10:24), signals that Paul is bringing the discussion of food sacrificed to idols that began in 8:1 to a close.[227] Paul exemplifies his own instructions to the Corinthians and affirms that he himself seeks not his own good "but the good of the many

[224] On God's jealousy in relation to idols, see Exod 20:5; 34:14; Deut 5:9; 6:14–15; Josh 24:19–20; 1 Kgs 14:22; Ezek 8:3; Ps 78:58–64; Zeph 1:14,18; Nah 1:2.

[225] The only other reference to demons in the LXX is Ps 106:37. Paul's only other reference to "demons" (δαιμονίων) is 1 Tim 4:1.

[226] Barrett, *First Corinthians*, 238.

[227] This is especially evident in the second qualification of the slogan, "but not everything is constructive." The term "constructive" translates οἰκοδομέω, the same term used in 8:1, "Love builds up."

so that they may be saved" (10:33), which summarizes everything argued in 8:1–11:1.[228] In conducting themselves in this manner believers model their lives after the pattern of Christ's sacrifice for others and bring glory to God (10:33–11:1). This section, however, is more than a summing up of the argument of food sacrificed to idols; it is very strategic and important thematically, relating as much to what follows as to what precedes. The principles of living out the Christian life with reference to others and doing all for the glory of God are themes that resonate throughout chaps. 11–14.

In 10:25–30 Paul spells out the implementation of the principle of living for the good of the others by means of two real-life scenarios in the Corinthian social context, namely, purchasing meat in the Corinthian marketplace and accepting dinner invitations from unbelievers. The Corinthians must not suppose that Paul demands complete withdrawal from unbelievers (cf. 5:9–10), which would undercut basic principles of evangelism (9:19–23). To "follow my example as I follow the example of Christ" (11:1) entails seeking "the good of the many, so that they may be saved" (10:33). The concluding command to "follow my example" (11:1) parallels the same exhortation that concluded the lengthy exposition regarding the wisdom of God (4:16–17). As noted in the introduction to this section, although Paul does not quote the double command of love for God and others, it is the overarching theological principle that guides his discussion for Christian decision making.[229]

**10:23–24** The phrase, "Everything is permissible, but not everything is beneficial," first appeared in 6:12 in the context of Paul's discussion regarding the believer's body and the perils of sexual immorality. As noted in the discussion of 6:12, the phrase reflects either a Corinthian slogan or an attitude that possibly had roots in Paul's own instruction regarding Christian liberty. If, however, this perspective actually derived from Paul, the Corinthians have both misunderstood and misapplied the principle.[230] At the very least the qualification in each instance is Paul's own rebuttal or correction of a misguided ethic. The resurfacing of the phrase, "Everything is permissible," in 10:23 shows that the Corinthian problems relating to idolatry derived from the same wrong-headed perspective as the problems related to sexual immorality in 6:12–20. The first restatement of the slogan in 10:23 reproduces the first part

---

[228] The verb συμφέρω ("beneficial) in 10:23 (cf. 6:12) parallels the noun σύμφορος ("good") in 10:33.

[229] Structurally, Fee (*First Corinthians*, 478) views the whole of 10:23–33 as a chiasmus alternating between Paul's two concerns of personal freedom and the benefit of others. A—(23–24) The criterion: the good of others; B—(25–27) Personal freedom with regard to food; C—(28–29a) The criterion illustrated: freedom curtailed for the sake of another; B'—(29b–30) Personal freedom defended; A'—(31–33) The criterion generalized: that all might be saved.

[230] Garland (*1 Corinthians* 489) does not think that "All things are lawful" derived from Paul's standard teaching. "Paul has problems with this credo because it feeds the conviction that one's personal understanding of what is permitted becomes the only measuring rod of what is right and the only thing of interest."

of 6:12 except for the phrase "to me." However, the second restatement of 6:12, "Everything is permissible for me, but I will not be mastered by anything," changes in 10:23 to "Everything is permissible, but not everything is constructive." The change reflects the primary focus of the 10:23–11:1, which is doing all things for the edification of one another.[231]

The "building" language first appeared in 1 Cor 3 with reference to Christian leaders building on the church's one foundation, Jesus Christ (3:10–15).[232] Paul warned workers in the church that "each one should be careful how he builds" (3:10). The discussion of food sacrificed to idols began with the overarching statement that "knowledge puffs up, but love builds up" (8:1). In 8:9–10 Paul warned that one who is weak in conscience would be "built up" in the wrong way if he observed one with "knowledge" eating in the idol's temple. The notion of "building up" the church, which entails the edification of the individual members of the body is a major emphasis in Paul's discussion of spiritual gifts in chaps. 12–14.[233]

In 10:24 Paul clarifies and defines what he means by the qualification, "not everything is constructive" (10:23); "Nobody should seek his own good, but the good of others." This, no doubt, was a standard component of Paul's teaching and is found throughout his letters.[234] Paul has already given an expanded statement of the principle in 8:7–13 and 9:19–23. The "others" that Paul has in mind in this context is wide-ranging and encompasses both believers and unbelievers (see esp. 9:19–23; 10:32). The notion of "the other" occurs again in 10:29 and anticipates the summative command to follow Paul's example as he follows the example of Christ (11:1).

**10:25–26** The first example that Paul offers of the outworking of the principle of seeking the good of others that also impinges on the question of Christian freedom in relation to food sacrificed to idols has to do with food sold in the marketplace.[235] The illustration assumes that the history of the food would be known by some but not by others and that not all food sold in the marketplace would necessarily have been previously associated with idolatry.[236]

---

[231] Ciampa and Rosner (*First Corinthians*, 485) offer that whereas chap. 6 had the well-being of self primarily in mind, in 10:23 the well-being of others is more in focus. Collins (*First Corinthians*, 386) observes that in one instance the phrase justifies sexual immorality and in the other a radical individualism.

[232] The term ἐποικοδομέω occurs four times in 3:10–15. The term rendered "constructive" by the NIV in 10:24 translates the Greek οἰκοδομέω (also 8:1).

[233] οἰκοδομέω occurs in 14:4 and 14:17.

[234] See also Rom 14:7; 15:2–3; 1 Cor 13:5; 2 Cor 12:14; Gal 5:1–2; Phil 2:1–7,20. Fee (*First Corinthians*, 479) notes that this formula "is so basic to his understanding of Christian ethics that it probably had long been a part of the instructions he gave to his churches . . . For Paul the death of Christ, in which he gave himself 'for us,' is not only God's offer of pardon for sinners, but also the only proper model of discipleship."

[235] The Greek, μάκελλον, occurs only here in the New Testament.

[236] On this issue see Fotopoulos, *Food Offered to Idols*, 141. Cf. also Cheung (*Idol Food in Corinth*, 154–55n230), who interprets a comment of Tertullian to indicate that nonsacrificial meat

Otherwise there would be no point in asking questions in order to determine the food's history. Paul advises the Corinthians to, "Eat anything that is sold in the meat market without raising questions of conscience,"[237] which affirms that he had no issue with food per se. His rationale for freely purchasing and consuming anything in the market is based on Scripture. Psalm 24:1, quoted almost verbatim from the LXX without the common introductory formula, "It is written," affirms that the earth and everything in it belongs to the Lord (cf. 8:4–6). Nothing is unclean in and of itself. Food is food and belongs to the one true God.[238]

It is not immediately clear whose conscience Paul's refers to in 10:25. Does he refer to the conscience of the one asking or the conscience of another? In the second example it is the conscience of another (10:29). The whole section resonates with concern for "the other," and so it is likely that Paul has in view "others" in the first illustration as well. But who is asking the question in the first place? Are the interrogators "those with knowledge" or the so-called "weak"? If Paul primarily addresses the weak in this section, then they are the ones instructed not to ask questions in the marketplace or at the home of unbelievers, in which case Paul encourages the weak to take up a more wide-ranging perspective on Christian freedom. Paul, however, could easily specify that he is addressing the weak but does not. It is perhaps best to see Paul's instructions as wide-ranging, including all believers, setting forth a general principle for all, whether weak or strong, that takes into account Christian liberty but also appropriately understands the bedrock principle of living out one's Christian life with "the other" in view.

In the first example Paul does not qualify the Christian's freedom to eat anything, as he does in the second example by suggesting a scenario where someone raises an issue about the history of the food sold in the marketplace. Presumably the same principle applies to the marketplace as to a private meal, but in the latter case it is far more likely that someone would raise an issue about idol food. What is clear in the first example is that believers should not inquire about the food's history in the buying process. The principle that emerges from both examples is that freedom is restricted in any situation that hints of the participation in or condoning of idolatry. The principle of seeking

---

was available in the marketplace. There are competing theories on the availability of meat to the poor. Collins (*First Corinthians*, 383) notes that meat would have been available to those of limited financial means after the games or other civic events. See also J. Murphy-O'Connor, *St. Paul's Corinth: Texts and Archaeology* (Glazier: Wilmington, 1983), 32.

[237] Morris (*1 Corinthians*, 146) notes that the stance to not ask questions stands in sharp contrast to a typical Jewish approach. Barrett (*First Corinthians*, 146) quips that nowhere is Paul more un-Jewish. Garland (*1 Corinthians*, 490) counters that it is more accurate to say that nowhere is Paul more un-Pharisaic.

[238] Cf. also Mark 7:14–23; Rom 14:13–15. The context of Rom 14 is different, but the theological principle is the same. In the Old Testament see Pss 50:12; 89:11 (noted by Garland, *1 Corinthians*, 490).

"the good of others" (10:24) requires a decision-making process guided by the perceptions of others in relation to their spiritual well-being.[239]

**10:27–29a** The second example imagines an unbeliever inviting a believer to dinner. Such invitations would have been common in the ancient world as a means of social and political networking and advancement.[240] Paul does not specify where the meal occurs, whether in a public facility or in a private home. His instructions in 8:7–13 rule out that the location is in one of the dining rooms of the pagan temple. For the believer, dining with an unbeliever would present a situation of intimate interaction with the pagan world, even if the primary function was social. As in the previous example Paul advises to go and eat without raising questions, which might have been quite surprising to the Corinthians, who already had misunderstood Paul on the issue of relating to unbelievers (5:9–10).[241] We may assume that the reason for Paul's advice is the same here as his reasons for freely buying and eating marketplace food, namely, the earth and everything in it belongs to the Lord (Ps 24:1). In this section's example, however, he introduces a scenario that illustrates the main point of this section, that of seeking the good of others (10:24,29a,33).[242] If someone points out that the food has been offered in sacrifice, the situation changes, and the believer must refrain from eating because of the conscience of "the other" who provided the information (10:29a).[243]

Paul does not specify whether the informant is a believer or an unbeliever but speaks generally, "If someone says." Some suppose that since an unbeliever issued the dinner invitation and the reference to the sacrificial food

---

[239] Regarding the use of Ps 24:1, Ciampa and Rosner (*First Corinthians*, 489) comment, "Paul's citation of Psalm 24:1 is consistent with the prevalent Jewish understanding of its relevance for the way God's people approach the food that he graciously provides. Paul is thoroughly Jewish and biblical in his understanding that creation is good and that the food we receive has been provided for us by God and should be received with thanksgiving (1 Cor 10:30) and with the understanding that food, like everything else in creation, exists to fulfill the purpose God has in mind for it, namely, his glory (1 Cor 10:31)."

[240] P. Gooch, *Dangerous Food: 1 Corinthians 8–10 in Its Context* (Waterloo, ON: Wilfrid Laurier University Press, 1993), 27–46; Cheung, *Idol Food in Corinth*, 27–38.

[241] Commentators often point out the apparent parallel with Exod 34:15 that instructs the Israelites to avoid invitations of pagan neighbors in order to avoid eating their pagan sacrifices. Paul is consistent in forbidding eating anything of known idolatrous associations. On the interaction of believers with unbelievers in 1 Corinthians see 6:6; 7:12–15; 14:22–24. Collins (*First Corinthians*, 383) points out that the unbelievers who might invite a believer to dinner could even be the Christian's in-laws (cf. 7:12–15).

[242] 10:29a is essentially a restatement of 10:24 in the juxtaposition of "the things of oneself" and the "the things of the other. In Greek, compare 10:24, τὸ ἑαυτοῦ ἀλλὰ τὸ τοῦ ἑτέρου and 10:29a, τὴν ἑαυτοῦ ἀλλὰ τὴν τοῦ ἑτέρου.

[243] 10:27 is a first-class conditional sentence, "If anyone of the unbelievers invites you." 10:28 employs a third-class (present-general) condition, "If anyone says to you." Robertson and Plummer (*First Corinthians*, 221) suggest the change is perhaps intentional. The first-class condition is likely; the second is only hypothetical, that someone would inform of the food's history.

is a different word than the pejorative term used throughout Paul's discussion,[244] the "someone" is, in fact, an unbeliever, perhaps even the host who speaks out of courtesy to the believer's convictions.[245] There is not enough information given to know why the informant makes known the food's history, whether it is a courtesy to the known believer present at the meal or a subtle test of the Christian's convictions regarding things associated with idols. Paul simply does not say since the motives of the informant are irrelevant.

Others think that the informant may be a weak brother since the language of "conscience" is used as in 8:7–13. The different term used for the food might be out of respect for the host. But how would a fellow believer know the history of the food? In the end, the identity of the "someone" does not matter. In either case, whether an unbeliever or a weak believer is the informant, the believer who receives the information must not eat out of love for the spiritual well being of others. Food matters when it matters to someone else, whether to a fellow Christian or to an unbeliever.[246] Garland proposes that a believer's willing consumption of idol food would compromise their confession of the one true God, confirm the unbeliever's idolatrous convictions, and would disable the basic Christian censure of pagan gods as false gods that embody something demonic.[247]

**10:29b–30** An explanatory "for" introduces two questions in the first person; "For why should *my* freedom be judged by another man's conscience?" "If *I* partake in the meal with thankfulness, why am *I* denounced because of something *I* thank God for?"[248] How should we understand the questions in context? Is Paul speaking of himself in self-defense of his own practice of eating against his critics? Is he reverting to the style of Greek diatribe in anticipation of the objections of the knowledgeable Christians regarding limitations on their freedom? Does Paul address the "weak" Christian, urging a more wide-ranging view of Christian liberty for the sake of the "strong"? The best alternative is that these two questions pick up the discussion from 10:27 following the brief parenthesis of 10:28–29a where someone raises the issue of the character of the food. In other words, Paul returns to the thought of 10:27 in order to

[244] The term in 10:28 is ἱερόθυτος, indicating food sacrificed at the temple, devoted to a god, not εἰδωλόθυτος (8:1,4,7,10), which is polemical and identifies the food as sacrificed to an idol.

[245] Cheung (*Idol Food in Corinth*, 158n240) notes that this is commonplace in the Asian context.

[246] See Garland, *1 Corinthians*, 496.

[247] Ibid., 497.

[248] The two questions are connected thematically to the argument as a whole. The mention of being judged by the conscience of another in the first question links not only to the parallel phrases in 10:25 and 10:27 to "ask no questions for conscience sake" but also to the discussion of how behavior impacts the conscience of another in 8:7–13. The mention of "freedom" relates back to 9:1 and 9:19 and Paul's lengthy discussion of the giving up of his rights for the good of the many, a theme that is explicit in this section (10:23–11:1; see especially 10:29–33). In the second question, the notion of "partaking" recalls the language of 10:21, "partaking of the table of the Lord and of demons."

explain why it is permissible to eat anything served at the unbeliever's house.[249] Ciampa and Rosner propose that Paul is simply explaining what he has just said, that is, he is thinking of a particular view of individualizing freedom that leads one to think their own attitude is all that matters concerning the issue of food offered to idols: "Freedom and thankfulness are not the keys to ethical discernment."[250]

**10:31–11:1** Three commands sum up Paul's instructions regarding the issue of Christian liberty and food sacrificed to idols: (1) Do all to the glory of God (10:31), (2) do not cause anyone to stumble (10:32), and (3) follow my example as I follow the example of Christ. These verses essentially restate Paul's agenda of doing all things for the gospel (9:19–23). God is glorified in the progress of the gospel. God is glorified among his people in their relations to one another and in their efforts to win unbelievers to Christ.

The first command to do all for God's glory mentions "eating" and "drinking" because this has been the focal point of the entire discussion. It is by eating and drinking that believers interact with each other (Lord's Supper) and in the same way should avoid all entanglements with idolatry. Eating and drinking in the ancient world was the locus of relational interaction where dominant worldviews collided. Paul has articulated a very careful gospel-centered decision-making ethic that can be summed up in the maxim, "Do it all for the glory of God." The second command reiterates that believers should not cause anyone to stumble (cf. 8:9),[251] whether Jews, Greeks, or the church of God, which is the most wide-ranging outlook possible. Bringing glory to God has to do with the progress of the gospel among believers and unbelievers. All things boil down to the imitation of Paul who imitates Christ, and Paul imitates Christ by not seeking the things of himself but what is for the benefit of others that they might be saved (10:33–11:1; cf. 10:24). Ultimately the paradigm of "Christ crucified" (1:23; 2:2) is the guiding principle for Christian decision-making and behavior. The glory of God, in this context, is not an individual pursuit per se but is rather an ambition lived out in relation to others, both believers and unbelievers. Building up one another and living among unbelievers with the goal of their salvation is the pursuit of the glory of God.

[249] So Bruce, *1 and 2 Corinthians*, 100. "Paul associates himself with the man who is disposed to accept his pagan neighbor's invitation: he says, in effect, 'If I were disposed to accept such an invitation, I would eat whatever is set before me without raising any question on the ground of conscience, for to what purpose is my liberty judged by another conscience?'"

[250] Ciampa and Rosner, *First Corinthians*, 494.

[251] Cf. Phil 1:10.

## SECTION OUTLINE

V. The Church Gathered for Worship (11:2–14:40)
   1. Husbands and Wives and the Glory of God (11:2–16)
   2. Disorder and Divisions at the Lord's Table (11:17–34)
      (1) Paul's Sharp Rebuke for Their Behavior at the So-Called Lord's Supper (11:17–22)
      (2) The Received Tradition of the Lord's Supper (11:23–26)
      (3) Eating and Drinking the Lord's Supper Unworthily (11:27–34)
   3. The Manifestation of the Spirit for the Common Good (12:1–31)
      (1) Confession of Jesus as Lord by the Spirit (12:1–3)
      (2) The Distribution of Gifts by the One and the Same Spirit (12:4–11)
      (3) One Body, Many Members (12:12–31)
   4. Controlling Principle of Love (13:1–13)
      (1) Love: The More Excellent Way (13:1–3)
      (2) What Love Does and Does Not Do (13:4–7)
      (3) Love's Permanence (13:8–13)
   5. Do All Things for the Edification of the Church (14:1–40)
      (1) The Case for Prophecy over Uninterpreted Tongues (14:1–5)
      (2) The Vital Link between Intelligibility and Edification (14:6–19)
      (3) The Negative Effect of Tongues on Unbelievers (14:20–25)
      (4) Do All Things Decently and in Order (14:26–40)

## V. THE CHURCH GATHERED FOR WORSHIP (11:2–14:40)

In chaps. 11–14 Paul turns to matters relating to the gathering of the Corinthians in assembly for worship. Specifically, he addresses proper attire for men (husbands) and women (wives) in relation to prayer and prophecy (11:2–16), the problem of divisions in the observance of the Lord's Supper (11:17–34), and the proper exercise of spiritual gifts (12–14).[1] In a letter replete with correction and warning, this section opens surprisingly with Paul praising the Corinthians for keeping the traditions he passed on to them (11:2), although he immediately gives further instruction regarding head coverings in worship (11:3–16). By way of contrast, in 11:17–34 Paul contends that he cannot praise them regarding their behavior at the Lord's Supper (11:17–22) and reminds them of the received tradition of the Supper and its significance for the life of the church (11:23–34). Chapters 12–14 continue the theme of the church

[1] So C. L. Blomberg, *1 Corinthians*, NIVAC (Grand Rapids: Zondervan, 1994), 207.

gathered in corporate worship and constitute the most lengthy discussion of spiritual gifts in the New Testament. Each of the units that make up this section (11:2–16; 11:17–34; and 12:1–14:40) addresses in some way the underlying problem of divisions among the Corinthians, from contention arising over head coverings (11:16) to splits between the rich and the poor in the celebration of the Lord Supper (11:17–22) to the overarching purpose of unity achieved by the Holy Spirit (see esp. 12:4–31).

The strong emphasis on unity in these chapters recalls the letter's opening exhortation (1:10–17), but equally significant is the theological content and continuity of argument with the letter as a whole.[2] In the previous section, 8:1–11:1, Paul countered misguided notions of individual rights and freedom rooted in pride (8:1) by emphasizing the priority of love for others embodied in the gospel and exhorting the Corinthians to follow his example as he followed the example of Christ (8:7–13; 9:19–23; and 10:31–11:1). In 1:10–4:21 Paul identified pride as the chief culprit of the personality factions that demonstrated adherence to worldly wisdom rather than the wisdom of cross. Paul's solution to the problems addressed in both 1:10–4:21 and 8:1–11 is the same: "become imitators of me" (4:16–17; 11:1). In response to the catch-phrase (slogan) "everything is permissible to me," Paul qualified that not everything is beneficial or constructive (10:23; see also 6:12) and summarized his argument by calling the Corinthians to imitate his example of seeking the good of the many (10:33–11:1). The same overarching concerns dominate chaps. 11–14. In 11:2–16 Paul's primary concern is that the Corinthians glorify God and avoid bringing shame on others in the corporate practice of prayer and prophecy. In 11:22, Paul rebukes the Corinthians for despising the church of God and shaming the poor. And in the lengthy discussion of spiritual gifts, which are given for the common good of all (12:7), Paul's chief concern is the upbuilding/edification of the church.[3]

### 1. Husbands and Wives and the Glory of God (11:2–16)

**2I praise you for remembering me in everything and for holding to the teachings, just as I passed them on to you.**

**3Now I want you to realize that the head of every man is Christ, and the head of
the woman is man, and the head of Christ is God. 4Every man who prays or proph-
esies with his head covered dishonors his head. 5And every woman who prays or
prophesies with her head uncovered dishonors her head—it is just as though her
head were shaved. 6If a woman does not cover her head, she should have her hair**

[2] So also A. C. Thiselton, *The First Epistle to the Corinthians: A Commentary on the Greek Text*, NIGTC (Grand Rapids: Eerdmans, 2000), 799. Thiselton notes the "fundamental continuity between the arguments and themes of 8:1–11:1 and the application of these very same themes to issues concerning public or corporate worship in 11:2–14:40."

[3] The verb συμφέρω (NIV, "beneficial") in 10:23 appears again in 12:7 (NIV, "common good"). The noun σύμφορος is used in 10:33 (NIV, "good"). See also 6:12; 7:35.

**cut off; and if it is a disgrace for a woman to have her hair cut or shaved off, she should cover her head. [7]A man ought not to cover his head, since he is the image and glory of God; but the woman is the glory of man. [8]For man did not come from woman, but woman from man; [9]neither was man created for woman, but woman for man. [10]For this reason, and because of the angels, the woman ought to have a sign of authority on her head.**

**[11]In the Lord, however, woman is not independent of man, nor is man independent of woman. [12]For as woman came from man, so also man is born of woman. But everything comes from God. [13]Judge for yourselves: Is it proper for a woman to pray to God with her head uncovered? [14]Does not the very nature of things teach you that if a man has long hair, it is a disgrace to him, [15]but that if a woman has long hair, it is her glory? For long hair is given to her as a covering. [16]If anyone wants to be contentious about this, we have no other practice—nor do the churches of God.**

Commentators routinely recognize 11:2–16 as one of the most difficult passages in the New Testament. At the outset it is helpful to emphasize what is clear in the passage, namely, that each believer should behave in worship in a manner that brings glory and honor to their respective head (11:4–10). This fundamental concern relates directly to the main emphasis of the previous section regarding food sacrificed to idols summed up in 10:23–11:1 as seeking the good of others in the ultimate pursuit of the glory of God. In 11:2–16 Paul submits that a man (husband) ought not to cover his head since he is the image and glory of God (11:7a), and conversely, a woman (wife) should cover her head when praying and prophesying because she reflects the glory of man (11:7b). Thus, in keeping with the emphasis of the preceding section (8:1–11:1), Paul's main concern in 11:2–16 is the edification of others to the glory of God.[4]

Interpretive challenges begin with the commendation in 11:2, "I praise you," which immediately precedes the correction that follows in 11:3–16 and stands in contrast to Paul's scolding in 11:17,22, "I do not praise you." In 11:3 we encounter the contested Greek term translated "head," which Paul uses both literally and metaphorically, that is, to one's anatomical head and to one's spiritual head.[5] Anyone familiar with the history of interpretation knows that scholars debate at length the precise nuance of the metaphorical sense, whether the term denotes "authority over," "source," or "that which is the foremost/at the top." Furthermore, the Greek terms translated "man" and "woman" often mean "husband" and "wife" when occurring together,[6] which suggests that Paul has

[4] Cf. J. M. Gundry-Volf, "Gender and Creation in 1 Corinthians 11:2–16: A Study in Paul's Theological Method," in *Evangelium, Schriftauslegung, Kirche* (Gottingen: Vandenhoeck & Ruprecht, 1997), 157: "Man and woman are both the *glory of another* and therefore have an obligation not to cause shame to their heads." R. E. Ciampa and B. S. Rosner assert that an equally important emphasis is *whose* glory each one reflects (*The First Letter to the Corinthians*, PNTC [Grand Rapids: Eerdmans, 2010], 524–25).

[5] Gk. κεφαλή.

[6] The Greek terms are ἀνήρ and γυνή, which the NRSV translates "husband" and "wife" in 11:3 but as "man"/"woman" in the rest of the passage. Blomberg (*1 Corinthians*, 209) notes that in

in mind primarily the husband/wife relationship in the context of public worship.[7] The interpretive difficulties compound with the shame/dishonor/glory language (11:4–6) in relation to one's covered or uncovered head and with obscure phraseology such as "because of the angels" (11:10) as the reason the woman should "have a sign of authority on her head." The nature of the head covering is also disputed. Does Paul refer to a customary veil worn by women in public worship in keeping with the traditions of all the churches (11:16)? Or does he refer instead to hairstyles, as some think the context demands (11:14–15)?

For the modern reader one of the more pressing issues has to do with the contemporary application of the passage. To what extent are Paul's instructions culture-bound to the first century and to what extent is the passage binding for all believers regardless of historical location in place and time? On the one hand, there are numerous elements of the passage that are of a universal, timeless character. The relational hierarchy that frames Paul's whole discussion and sets the relation of man (husband) and woman (wife) alongside the relation of man to Christ and Christ to God is not a cultural argument but an argument grounded in the nature of God and his creation. Likewise, Paul's assertion that the woman "ought to have authority upon her head" (11:10) follows 11:7–9, which draws from the Genesis creation narrative. Furthermore, Paul appeals to what nature (custom) teaches regarding these matters (11:14–15) and concludes with, "We have no other practice—nor do the churches of God" (11:16). On the other hand, there is the explicit assumption of shame that Paul attaches to the covered and uncovered head. Both the man and the woman bring shame on their "head"[8] by behaving in a certain way. Since Paul equates the uncovered head of the woman with the shaved head, an object of shame (11:5–6), he relates his instruction to what is conveyed in the local cultural context by the covered and uncovered head. Paul's concern was the violation of a bedrock theological principle (11:3) that the lack of a head covering on the woman conveyed in Roman Corinth.[9] Paul's ultimate concern in the passage, which

every other place in Paul where the terms are paired the reference is to husband and wife with the possible exception of 1 Tim 2:8–15. Winter submits that the very notion of a veil "would automatically indicate to the Corinthians that the females under discussion in this passage were married." B. W. Winter, *After Paul Left Corinth: The Influence of Secular Ethics and Social Change* (Grand Rapids: Eerdmans, 2001), 127.

[7] D. E. Garland argues for the generic "man" and "woman," since women other than wives could pray and prophesy (*1 Corinthians*, BECNT [Grand Rapids: Baker, 2003], 514).

[8] This could be literal, "Brings shame on himself/herself," or metaphorical, that is, a man (husband) with covered head brings shame on Christ, and the woman (wife) with uncovered head brings shame on the man (husband).

[9] This is the traditional reading of the passage. So Winter (*After Paul Left Corinth*, 121), "Husbands and wives veiled or unveiled themselves in certain situations in Corinthian society." See also J. Delobel, "1 Cor 11:2–16: Towards a Coherent Explanation," in *L'Apôtre Paul: personnalité, style et conception due ministère*, BETL 73, ed. A. Vanhoye (Leuven: Peeters, 1986), 369–89. The primary theme of the passage is the shame attached to a woman who prays or prophesies with an

is timeless and applicable to a broad range of situations, relates to doing all things for the glory of God, which, as the previous passage emphasized, entails imitating Christ by doing all things for the good of another (10:31–11:1).

The underlying assumptions and the main emphases of the passage help keep us on track. Paul does not dispute that both men and women pray and prophesy in the public assembly of believers. The gift of prophecy is not gender specific. Paul will make the point in 12:11 that all gifts are sovereignly bestowed by the Holy Spirit. Gender distinctions, however, are important in the exercise of the gifts in light of the relational hierarchy inherent in the created order (11:3,7–10). The main point of 11:2–16 has to do with the practice of prayer and prophecy in the Corinthian context in a manner consistent with God's creation design, which, in turn, brings glory to the "other" and ultimately to God. In a parallel passage, 14:33b–36, Paul instructs women to be silent in church, as he does all prophets in certain situations (14:30; see comments on 14:34–36).[10]

Structurally, the passage begins and ends with an appeal to what is customary and acceptable (11:2,13–16). The principle of headship in 11:3 is balanced by the principle of interdependence between the man and the woman in 11:11–12. The middle portion, 11:4–10, describes behavior in worship that is shameful to one's respective head and sets forth the obligations of both men

uncovered head in a worship setting. So A. C. Perriman, "The Head of a Woman: The Meaning of *Kephalē* in 1 Cor 11:3," *JTS* 45 (1994): 621. Garland (*1 Corinthians*, 506–11) observes that the structure of the passage confirms that Paul's main concern is "exclusively with the Corinthians' women's behavior" (506). "Paul oscillates back and forth with statements about men and women, but this pattern is broken in 11:13 with a statement about women" (507). 11:13 is the crux of the whole argument, "Judge for yourselves: Is it proper for a woman to pray to God with her head uncovered?" So also Delobel (379–80). The issue is sexual propriety, and Paul is concerned about the woman's appearance in public worship in an honor and shame society. Winter (*After Paul Left Corinth*, 121) counters, however, "It is surprising that this passage was, and continues to be, regarded as a discussion about 'the veiling of women'. Paul clearly begins with the veiling of men (11:4), and returns to the problem some three verses later." For a recent analysis of some of the hermeneutical issues involved in the application of theological principle to culture, see B. L. Merkle, "Paul's Arguments from Creation in 1 Corinthians 11:8–9 and 1 Timothy 2:13–14: An Apparent Inconsistency Answered," *JETS* 49 (2006): 527–48. Merkle contends that the primary issue in 11:2–16 is gender distinction, which is blurred when women fail to wear appropriate attire. Paul's argument from creation (11:8–9) substantiates the point that "man is the image and glory of God and woman is the glory of man" (11:7) and relates only indirectly to the issue of head coverings (11:4–6).

[10] Garland (*1 Corinthians*, 510) notes the following parallels that constitute an *inclusio* between 11:2–16 and 14:33b–36: (1) "The churches of God" (11:6) parallels churches of the saints (14:33b). (2) 11:7–12 alludes to the Genesis account and 14:34 appeals to what the law says. (3) Both 11:6 and 14:35 refer to shameful behavior. L. Johnson submits that 11:2–16 describes the charismatic gifts of prayer and prophecy while 14:34–36 suggests the context of teaching, an activity associated with males in Judaism. It is particularly the manner of performance that upsets Paul (*The Writings of the New Testament: An Interpretation*, rev. ed. [Minneapolis: Fortress, 1999], 307).

and women in order to avoid such behavior. The nature of Paul's argument yields the following chiastic pattern.[11]

- A Praise for Holding to Traditions (11:2)
  - B Principle of Headship (11:3)
    - C Shaming One's Head (11:4–6)
    - C' Obligations of Men (Husbands) and Women (Wives) (11:7–10)
  - B' Principle of Interdependence (11:11–12)
- A' Appeal to Nature (Custom) (11:13–16)

**11:2** We cannot know with certainty what prompted Paul's unexpected praise in 11:2, but perhaps the prior exhortation in 11:1, "Follow my example," brought to Paul's mind that the Corinthians followed certain traditions, even if in need of further instruction. It is also possible that Paul simply recognizes a claim made by the Corinthians in their letter to him that they were holding to established traditions,[12] or that he offers a complimentary introduction that precedes criticism,[13] much in the same way that the introductory thanksgiving (1:4–9) preceded the exhortation regarding divisions (1:10–17).[14] In a similar way, following commendation, Paul strikes a corrective tone in 11:3, "Now I want you to realize,"[15] and concludes in 11:16 with the disclaimer "If anyone wants to be contentious about this, we have no other practice—nor do the churches of God." The commendation of 11:3 stands in contrast to 11:17–22, where Paul expresses the exact opposite, "I do not praise you," which has to do not with the tradition itself, the Lord's Supper, but with their unacceptable behavior in the practice of the tradition.[16]

Paul does not specify what traditions he has in mind in his commendation in 11:2. In 11:23–26 he refers to the tradition of the Lord's Supper and in

---

[11] See Garland (*1 Corinthians*, 511) for a different and more elaborate chiastic arrangement.

[12] J. C. Hurd suggests that Paul quotes back a claim of the Corinthians with a touch of irony (*The Origin of 1 Corinthians* [New York: Seabury, 1965], 182–83). Even though the περὶ δὲ ("now about") formula does not occur here, some think that the Corinthians expressed their intention to follow Paul but sought further advice [so R. B. Hays, *First Corinthians* (Louisville: John Knox, 1997), 182–83].

[13] Some think Paul's statement is rhetorical, securing the goodwill of the hearers (so M. M. Mitchell, *Paul and the Rhetoric of Reconciliation: An Exegetical Investigation of the Language and Composition of 1 Corinthians* [Louisville: WJK, 1991], 260). 11:2–3 conforms somewhat to the "yes, but" pattern followed elsewhere in the letter (cf. 7:1; 8:1; 12:1–3). Ciampa and Rosner (*First Corinthians*, 505) note that "praise" language is consonant with the theme of glory or honor (see 1 Chr 16:27; Eph 1:6,12,14; Phil 1:11; 1 Pet 1:7).

[14] There are differences, however, between the two passages. In 1:4–9, the focus is solely on God's gracious work among the Corinthians. There is no commendation of the church per se. In 11:2, however, Paul commends them for holding to traditions.

[15] The verb translated "realize" by the NIV is οἶδα, "to know," which recalls other instances in 1 Corinthians where Paul points out their failure to act according to what should have been clearly known (see esp. 3:16; 5:6; 6:2–3,9,15–16; 9:13,24. Cf. also 10:1,20; 12:1; 14:5,19,35).

[16] The pattern of a positive/negative parallel assertion appears earlier in the letter; compare 4:14, "I am not writing this to shame you, but to warn you," with 6:5, "I say this to shame you!" There are things in Corinth that are praiseworthy (11:2) and things that are not praiseworthy (11:17–22).

15:1–11 to the received tradition of the gospel. The immediate context of 11:3 has to do with the roles of men (husbands) and women (wives) in the gathered assembly. Regarding all three traditions Paul offers further instruction and/or correction regarding their present behavior.[17] The traditions were not Paul's own but rather those handed down to him (11:23; 15:1–3).[18] What Paul says in 11:2–16 is not merely his opinion but represents traditional teaching practiced by all the churches (11:16).

**11:3** The phrase "Now I want you to realize" introduces a statement of principle regarding the issue of headship, which their behavior contradicts and thus detracts from the glory of God in worship. The principle is that "the head of every man is Christ, and the head of the woman is man, and the head of Christ is God." Since Paul begins with man's relation to Christ and ends with Christ's relation to God, we should distinguish between Paul's main intention and the underlying assumptions of the passage. In other words, Paul's primary intent is not to establish a chain of hierarchy of authority and submission,[19] but the principle of authority and submission is assumed and integral to the argument. The nature of Paul's argument dictates the order man-Christ, woman-man, Christ-God. Ciampa and Rosner explain, "Paul is interested especially in the way men and women fit into a broader hierarchical framework. That explains why he begins not with God or Christ but with the identification of the head of every man and goes next to the head of the woman and why he does not name the head first but introduces the man and then his head, then woman and then her head."[20] The pattern of Paul's argument indicates that the chief concern in Corinth had to do with women praying and prophesying with their heads uncovered (11:13), but the pattern of argument also assumes a divinely prescribed descending hierarchy in the created order. The word order in Greek emphasizes the word "head."[21] Without question, the most debated issue in this verse is the metaphorical sense intended in the use of the term. A secondary issue is whether the terms "man" and "woman" carry a more restricted contextual meaning of "husband" and "wife."[22]

---

[17] In 11:17–24, Paul censures their behavior at the Lord's Supper. In 1 Cor 15 Paul admonishes those who are saying, "There is no resurrection from the dead" (15:12). In 11:2–16 Paul's tone is corrective throughout.

[18] See also Rom 6:17; 2 Thess 2:15; 3:6.

[19] So Garland, *1 Corinthians*, 508.

[20] Ciampa and Rosner, *First Corinthians*, 506–7. So also Blomberg, *1 Corinthians*, 209. ". . . since the problem in Corinth involved men and women (but not Christ) dishonoring their heads, it is natural that he should refer to the heads of the man and of the woman first. The rationale for placing Christ's relationship to God last is most likely to draw attention to it as an analogy for the relationship between men, women, and their heads (the same sequence in v. 12)." The clear hierarchy is God, Christ, man, woman. We should also distinguish between the notions of "hierarchy" and "equality," which is especially evident in the God/Christ pair.

[21] Gk. κεφαλή.

[22] As translated by the NRSV. So also Winter, *After Paul Left Corinth*, 127. "The very mention of the word 'veil' by Paul would automatically indicate to the Corinthians that the females under

The most widely attested meaning of the Greek term translated "head" is one's physical, anatomical head.[23] The term can also denote the whole person symbolically,[24] but the chief interpretive question in 11:3 has to do with the metaphorical sense as it denotes the relationship between man/Christ, woman/man, and Christ/God.[25] The traditional, most widely held view until recent times maintains that the term in this context indicates a hierarchy that entails authoritative leadership, that is, the man (husband) as the head of the woman (wife) occupies a position of superior relational authority that corresponds to the principle of subordination within the Godhead. The woman (wife) is equal in essence but subordinate to the man (husband) in function and role.[26] In the contemporary debate Grudem and Fitzmyer rigorously defend this position against others as the correct understanding of Paul's usage of the term here.[27] In Pauline usage, the word occurs once in Romans and seven times in Ephesians and Colossians.[28] "Head" is often used in conjunction with "body" in designating Christ's supreme position in relation to the church (Eph 1:22; 4:15; 5:23; Col 1:18; 2:19). In Col 2:10, Christ is the "head over every power and authority." In Eph 5:23, the relation of the husband to his wife is set in direct correlation to the relation of Christ to the church.

The traditional understanding has been challenged by those who propose the alternate meaning of "source" or "origin" for the Greek term, *kephalē*, that is, the "head" is the one through whom others exist.[29] Contextual support for this meaning, it is claimed, is found in 11:8, "For man did not come from the woman, but woman from the man."[30] A number of notable scholars hold this

discussion in this passage were married." So also Ciampa and Rosner, *First Corinthians*, 508. For the more generic "man/woman" see Garland, *1 Corinthians*, 514.

[23] In Grudem's analysis of 2,336 uses of the term, over 2,000 denote the actual physical head. W. A. Grudem, "Does *Kephalē* (Head) Mean 'Source' or 'Authority over' in Greek Literature? A Survey of 2,336 Examples," *TrinJ* 6 (1985): 38–59.

[24] This use is possible in 11:4b–5. To "shame one's head" would mean to bring shame on oneself. This figurative sense occurs in Rom 12:20, "If your enemy is hungry, feed him; if he is thirsty, give him something to drink. In doing this you will heap burning coals on his head."

[25] Thiselton (*First Corinthians*, 812) observes, "The history of claims about the meaning of κεφαλή is immense and daunting." Thiselton comments further that more than one patristic commentator notes the highly open-textured and multivalent force of the term.

[26] So C. Vaughan and T. D. Lea, *1 Corinthians*, Bible Study Commentary (Grand Rapids: Zondervan, 1983), 111–12.

[27] See Grudem, "Does *Kephalē* Mean 'Source' or 'Authority Over'?"; id., "The Meaning of *Kephalē* ("Head"): A Response to Recent Studies," *TrinJ* 11 (1990): 3–72; J. A. Fitzmyer, "Another Look at *Kephalē* in 1 Corinthians 11:3," *NTS* 35 (1989): 503–11; Id., *First Corinthians: A New Translation with Introduction and Commentary*, AB (New Haven: Yale University Press, 2008), 409–10.

[28] Rom 12:20; Eph 1:22; 4:15; 5:23; Col 1:18; 2:10,19.

[29] Scholars who hold his view often refer to the study of S. Bedale, "The Meaning of *Kephalē* in the Pauline Epistles," *JTS* 5 (1954): 211–15. Bedale, however, did not deny the sense of authority in 11:3.

[30] So L. Morris, "Paul is saying that the woman derives her being from man (Gen 2:21–22), as man does from Christ and Christ from God" (*1 Corinthians*, TNTC [Grand Rapids: Eerdmans, 1985], 149).

view.[31] Although those who hold this view still maintain an orthodox doctrine of the relation of the Son to the Father, that both are equal in essence, one might argue that the "source" view opens the door to a view that holds that God the Son is less than God the Father.[32] Furthermore, the figurative meaning of "source" has been rigorously contested.[33]

A third view has gained wider acceptance in recent years, namely, that both "authority over" and "source" are not entirely satisfactory meanings in numerous occurrences of the term *kephalē*. Rather the term means something along the lines of "that which is most prominent, foremost, uppermost, preeminent."[34] In other words, to be the "head" is to occupy a prominent position in relation to a group or individual. This may result in or entail leadership, but it is not the basic denotation of the term. Garland thinks that this understanding of the term bolsters the notion that Paul's primary intent is "not to assert the supremacy of man and the subordination of the woman."[35] Ciampa and Rosner counter, however, that the Old Testament patriarchal background informs Paul's understanding of the relationship between husband and wife and that even if Paul used the term in the sense of "the more prominent partner" or "one through whom the other exists," "his language and the flow of the argument seems to reflect an assumed hierarchy through which glory and shame flow upward from those with lower status to those above them."[36] It is important to note that all three views (whether authoritative leadership, source, or that which is most prominent) are consistent with the broader biblical and theological framework that woman is functionally subordinate to man.

**11:4–6** The theological principle of headship lays the foundation for Paul's explanation of the uncovered and covered head in 11:4–6. Paul recognizes the

---

[31] C. K. Barrett, *A Commentary on the First Epistle to the Corinthians*, HNTC (New York: Harper & Row, 1968), 248; F. F. Bruce, *1 & 2 Corinthians*, NCB (Grand Rapids: Eerdmans, 1971), 103; Morris, *1 Corinthians*, 149; G. D. Fee, *The First Epistle to the Corinthians*, NICNT (Grand Rapids: Eerdmans, 1987), 502–5.

[32] Garland (*1 Corinthians*, 516) cautions, "Although the idea of source may fit the account of the woman's creation from the man's rib, it does not fit God as the source of Christ and opens the door to a subordinationist Christology."

[33] See P. Cotterell and M. Turner, *Linguistics and Biblical Interpretation* (Downers Grove: InterVarsity, 1989), 141–45; Grudem, "The Meaning of *Kephalē*." Perriman ("The Head of a Woman") claims that the meaning "source" is entirely absent (or suspect) in the LXX. Fitzmyer (*First Corinthians*, 409–10) claims that there is no instance of κεφαλή meaning "source" of individual persons.

[34] Perriman, "The Head of a Woman," 621. Perriman states, "The point seems to be . . . that the behavior of the woman reflects upon the man who as her head is representative of her, the prominent partner in the relationship, or that the woman's status and value is summed up in the man." Among recent commentators this view is followed by Garland (*1 Corinthians*, 516) and Thiselton (*First Corinthians*, 816–18). Thiselton refers to this as *synecdoche*, that is, a representative use of the term κεφαλή, a figure of speech whereby a part represents the whole.

[35] Garland, *1 Corinthians*, 516.

[36] Ciampa and Rosner, *First Corinthians*, 509. See also Grudem, "The Meaning of *Kephalē*," 37–39.

principle of headship in 11:3 because what one does with their anatomical head in worship has implications of either honor or shame for one's respective spiritual head. Paul's immediate concern in this passage is not with the different roles of husbands and wives in worship since both are portrayed as praying and prophesying, but rather with the behavioral ramifications of wives worshipping with an uncovered head (see also 14:33b–36).[37] Both the Old and New Testament recognize women prophets.[38] In Acts 2:14–21 Peter announces at Pentecost the fulfillment of Joel 2:28, which includes the prediction that "your sons and your daughters shall prophesy." Paul's concern in 11:2–16 is not the fact that women are prophesying in Corinth but rather the manner of their praying and prophesying. In the parallel passage, 14:33b–36, which occurs in the context of doing all things unto edification and in an orderly manner (14:26,40), Paul instructs the wives to remain silent in certain situations and to learn from their husbands at home.[39]

The translation, "with his head covered," in the Greek reads literally, "down from the head having."[40] Scholars debate whether or not this phrase refers to a customary head covering, such as a veil that comes down over the face or to hairstyles. The "head covering" view is the traditional view. The "hairstyle" view is more recent and is based in part on Paul's concluding remarks on hair in 11:14–16. Those who hold the traditional view posit that Paul appeals to hairstyles and nature only by way of analogy.[41] In a recent article Massey briefly rehearses and assesses the history and argument of the hairstyle view and mounts a rigorous linguistic defense of the traditional view.[42] If hairstyle

[37] Neither is the leadership structure of the church in view in 11:2–16. Paul addresses only the exercise of prayer and prophecy. Neither does Paul define prophecy in 11:2–16, which is identified as one of the spiritual gifts in 12:10 (see also 12:28–31).

[38] Exodus 15:20; Judg 4:4; 2 Kgs 22:14; 2 Chr 34:22; Neh 6:14; Isa 8:3; Luke 2:36; Acts 21:7.

[39] 14:35, like 11:4–6, raises the motif of "shame" as the reason for a restriction on wives in certain situations (see comments on 14:33b–36). As with much of the letter, we simply lack sufficient information to reconstruct the complete historical situation. The perspective taken here is that 11:2–16 and 14:33b–36 are complementary rather than contradictory and that neither are non-Pauline interpolations as it is sometimes proposed.

[40] Gk. κατὰ κεφαλῆς ἔχων.

[41] See R. Oster, "When Men Wore Veils to Worship: The Historical Context of 1 Corinthians 11.4," *NTS* 34 (1988), 485–88.

[42] P. T. Massey, "The Meaning of κατακαλύπτω and κατὰ κεφαλῆς ἔχων in 1 Corinthians 11.2–16," *NTS* 53 (2007): 502–23. Massey traces the hairstyle view to the seminal article by S. Lösch, "Christliche Frauen in Corinth (1 Cor 11.2–16): Ein neuer Lösungsversuch," *TQ* 127 (1947): 216–61. More influential, however, is the 1965 dissertation by Abel Isaksson and a subsequent 1972 article by James Hurley. See A. Isaksson, *Marriage and Ministry in the New Temple: A Study with Special Reference to Mt. 19.13–12 [sic] and 1 Cor. 11.3–16*, ASNU 24 (Lund: Gleerup, 2002); J. B. Hurley, "Did Paul Require Veils or the Silence of Women: A Consideration of 1 Cor 11:2–16 and 14:33b–36," *WTJ* 35 (1973): 190–220. Massey surveys the literary history of ἀκατακάλυπτος (uncovered) and κατακαλύπτω (to cover) and concludes that ἀκατακάλυπτος consistently means "uncovered" and, when used in conjunction with κεφαλή, "it describes the socially significant behavior of having one's head uncovered or unveiled. When this adjective describes the head of a married woman, it indicates immodest dress that has the potential to shame or embarrass her husband (522).

is the issue, then the central problem might relate either to blurred gender distinctions or disorderly worship with possible pagan associations. There is no compelling reason, however, to abandon the traditional view and that Paul's chief concern is the shame that wives bring on their husbands by the lack of proper attire.

The dishonor that one brings to his/her head could refer to shaming oneself (cf. Rom 12:20), but in light of the principle of headship established in 11:3, it is more likely that Paul refers to one's metaphorical head, so that the meaning is that the husband who prays covered dishonors Christ, his spiritual head. Likewise, the wife who prays uncovered dishonors her husband, her spiritual head. The explanation for why the husband should cover his head is that "he is the image and glory of God" (11:7). Since the covered male head was normal ritual behavior in the ancient Roman world for one offering ritual sacrifice, some suppose that Christian tradition established a unique practice in contrast to pagan devotion.[43] Collins likewise asserts that there seems to be a clash of customs that is the real issue in 11:2–16 since men prayed with heads covered in Roman and Jewish practice but prayed uncovered in traditional Greek custom.[44] There are no clues in 11:2–16 regarding why the women (wives) might remove the traditional marriage veil. Ciampa and Rosner note the linguistic parallels of 11:2–16 and 2 Cor 3:13–16, which may provide a background clue concerning why the men should be unveiled in worship and why women might have attempted the same practice.[45] It is possible that the house-church setting blurred the distinction between private and public gatherings, but Winter points out that the crux of the issue had to do with "those who were deliberately removing their veils while praying and prophesying."[46] Paul equates the

---

Furthermore, there is no corroborating text for the theory that ἀκατακάλυπτος means "with unbound hair" or "with hair hanging loose." Likewise, "the verb κατακαλύπτω, from Homer to Athenaeus (a period stretching approximately 1,000 years), means 'to veil' or 'cover the head' in texts describing dress and physical appearance. When the verb without the alpha privative is applied to a Greek male, it describes the socially significant act of covering the head and indicates a state of shame" (523).

[43] See D. W. J. Gill, "The Importance of Roman Portraiture for Head-Coverings in 1 Corinthians 11:2–16," *TynBul* 41 (1990): 245–60; Winter, *After Paul Left Corinth*, 121–23. Garland (*1 Corinthians*, 517) explains, "Because of the clear association of this practice with pagan devotion, pulling the toga over the physical head in Christian worship would shame the spiritual head of the man, Christ." Garland notes, however, that Paul presents a hypothetical case in 11:4–6 as he argues from how shameful it would be for a man to pray or prophesy as one arrayed for pagan devotion to make the case that it is no less shameful for a woman to do the same uncovered. Winter does not think the example is hypothetical and that Paul is equally concerned about "veiled men."

[44] R. F. Collins, *First Corinthians*, SP (Collegeville, MN: Liturgical Press, 1999), 401. Collins, however, adopts the view that hairstyles is the issue, not head coverings and submits that gender distinction is a chief concern. Collins (392) gives the following heading for 11:2–16, "Let Men Be Men and Women Be Women."

[45] Ciampa and Rosner, *First Corinthians*, 513–20.

[46] Winter, *After Paul Left Corinth*, 128. Winter comments further, "Paul equated not wearing a veil with the social stigma of a publicly exposed punished adulteress reduced to the status of a prostitute."

unveiled wife in Corinthian culture "as though her head were shaved" (11:4) and follows in 11:5–6 with "If a woman does not cover her head, she should have her hair cut off; and if it is a disgrace for a woman to have her hair cut or shaved off, she should cover her head." Whatever historical background informs the "shaved head," Paul clearly indicates that it was a sign of disgrace, which he equates with a women presenting herself unveiled.

**11:7–10** This section, which is parallel to and extends the argument of 11:4–6, is framed by an *inclusio* concerning the obligations of husbands and wives respectively (11:7 and 10).[47] The language of "glory" in 11:7–10 stands in contrast to the language of shame in 11:4–6 and, like 11:3, provides the theological basis for Paul's explanation in 11:4–6 of why husbands should pray and prophesy with uncovered head and wives should pray and prophesy with covered head.[48] Both the husband and the wife are the "glory" of another. The husband is obligated not to cover his head because he is the image and glory of God and to do so would obscure the glory of God in worship.[49] Things are different, however, for the wife, who is the "glory" of her husband (11:7b) and who, in her origins, was created from and for her husband (11:8–9).

As in 11:3, Paul's argument derives from the larger biblical framework involving the husband's relation to God and the wife's relation to her husband according to the creation narratives of Gen 1:26–27 and 2:18–23. Simply put, men and women have distinct origins and were created for unique purposes. The Genesis account affirms that the woman was from the man and that she was created for him. In stating that men are the image and glory of God, Paul's point is not that women were not also created in the image of God. As the argument shows, Paul's concern is that both the man and the woman are the glory of another. Genesis 1:27 affirms that all humans bear the image of their maker (cf. 1 Cor 15:49).[50] The veiling of the woman has to do with the fact that she is man's "glory." The purpose of the veil, then, is that people should not gaze on that which is man's glory in worship since the focus is on God's glory. Ciampa and Rosner assert that the dress code for Paul was not merely a symbolic expression of gender distinction to be maintained for the sake of respect for the created order but "understood to be essential to avoiding the infiltration of anything that might distract a worshiper's attention away from the glory of God."[51]

---

[47] The verb ὀφείλω (is obligated to) occurs at the beginning and end of the unit (11:7,10).

[48] 11:7 begins with the explanatory conjunction, γάρ.

[49] On glory and shame language see Ciampa and Rosner, *First Corinthians*, 528–29. Cf. Ps 8:3–5, "When I consider your heavens, the work of your fingers, the moon and the stars, which you have set in place, what is man that you are mindful of him, the son of man that you care for him? You made him a little lower than the heavenly beings and crowned him with glory and honor."

[50] Gen 1:27 affirms that God created man in his image, both male and female. Paul's point seems to be that only man is the direct creation of God since woman is "from the man" (Gen 2:18–23).

[51] Ibid.

For the reasons stated in 11:7–9, and "because of the angels," Paul claims, "the woman ought to have a sign of authority on her head." The NIV translation supplies the word "sign." Other translations, such as the NASB, use the word "symbol."[52] The more recent NIV2011 omits sign and translates more accurately, "a woman ought to have authority over her own head."[53] The close linguistic parallel with 11:4 suggests that "to have authority upon her head" is another way of referring to the head covering.[54] Every other occurrence of the three-word construction translated "to have authority upon" in the New Testament carries the meaning "to have authority (or control) over."[55] The meaning, in this context, is not that the woman has a newfound authority to do something that she was previously forbidden to do in worship, such as to pray and prophesy,[56] but rather that she should exercise control over her own head by keeping it covered in the recognition that she stands in a particular relation to her husband in the light of creation.[57] Both husbands and wives are to bring glory rather than shame to their "head." Verses 2–16 are not about rights but about obligations.

Paul's additional reason for women exercising control over their head, "because of the angels," has been subject to a number of explanations in the history of interpretation.[58] Few modern commentators follow the view of Tertullian that the reference is to the woman's vulnerability to fallen angels in light of a common Jewish understanding of the identity of the "sons of God" in Gen 6:1–4.[59] Edwards proposes that the phrase "because of the angels"

[52] So also HCSB and ESV.

[53] Similarly the KJV, "For this cause ought the woman to have power on her head."

[54] Both 11:4 and 11:10 employ the verb "to have" with the noun "head" but with two different prepositions "down from/or down upon" and "upon" (11:4, κατὰ κεφαλῆς ἔχων and 11:10, ἐξουσίαν ἔχειν ἐπὶ τῆς κεφαλῆς). The natural flow of thought and the further parallelism between 11:7 and 11:10 regarding one's obligations indicates that both expressions refer to the covered head. Men "ought" to have their heads covered being the image and glory of God. Women "ought" to have authority upon the head (head covering). So also Massey, "The Meaning of κατακαλύπτω and κατὰ κεφαλῆς ἔχων," 522.

[55] So Blomberg, *1 Corinthians*, 212. See Matt 9:6; Rev 11:6; 14:18; 16:9; 20:6 and similar constructions in Luke 19:17 and 1 Cor 7:37. See also J. Murphy-O'Connor, "1 Corinthians 11:2–16 Once Again," *CBQ* 50 (1988): 271. Cf. also the language of obligation and authority in 7:1–5. Husbands and wives have obligations one to another.

[56] So M. Hooker, "Authority on Her Head: An Examination of 1 Cor. xi.10," *NTS* 10 (1966): 410–16; Bruce, *1 and 2 Corinthians*, 106; Barrett, *First Corinthians*, 255.

[57] J. D. BeDuhn, "'Because of the Angels': Unveiling Paul's Anthropology in 1 Corinthians 11," *JBL* 118 (1999): 303–4; Garland, *1 Corinthians*, 525; Ciampa and Rosner, *First Corinthians*, 532.

[58] Garland (*1 Corinthians*, 526) comments, "He must assume that the Corinthians can fill in the blanks about what this cryptic reference means from some shared, prior knowledge—either from their own theological speculation about angels or from something he has taught them. Modern readers are left in the dark as a result, and none of the explanations is without problems." Fitzmyer (*First Corinthians*, 417–19) lists seven different interpretations.

[59] Tertullian, *On the Veiling of Virgins*, 7.2. For the Jewish sources that interpreted "sons of God" in Gen 6:2 in this fashion Ciampa and Rosner (*First Corinthians*, 529) list Philo, *On Giants*,

refers to imitating the angels, who cover their faces in God's presence as in Isa 6:2.[60] The most fruitful interpretation links Paul's reference to the angels to the context of worship and to the motifs of glory and creation raised in 11:7–9. As Thiselton observes, "Among the Jewish traditions which find their way into the New Testament, those in which angels are perceived as 'guardians of order' as well as 'participants in the church's praise to God' provide the best clue to Paul's meaning."[61] Ciampa and Rosner explain, "By wearing her veil during public worship the woman signals her own status as created by God even while covering up any trace of human glory in the presence of God and his angelic court."[62]

**11:11–12** In 11:11–12 Paul offers an important qualification of his argument to this point by clarifying that "in the Lord" the man and the woman are fundamentally interdependent on one another.[63] Verse 12 explains, "For as woman came from man, so also man is born of woman."[64] In 11:8–9 Paul appealed to the creation of the first man and the first woman as an important principle for the behavior of husbands and wives in worship. In 11:11–12, Paul asserts that since the creation of the first man and the first woman, who was fashioned from the man, man has been dependent on the woman for his existence through birth. Paul's statement mirrors rabbinic tradition that distinguished between the creation of Adam and Eve and the rest of humanity.[65] In the overall structure of the passage, 11:11–12 is parallel to 11:3, which means

---

16–18; Josephus, *Antiquities*, 1.73; *1 Enoch* 6–19; 21; 86–88; 106:13–15, et al. A. Robertson and A. Plummer submit that the fallen angels view is "somewhat childish" and that the use of the definite article with "angels" stands against this view since the articular "the angels" always refers to good angels (*A Critical and Exegetical Commentary on the First Epistle of St. Paul to the Corinthians*, ICC, 2nd ed. [Edinburgh: T&T Clark, 1914], 233).

[60] T. C. Edwards, *A Commentary on the First Epistle to the Corinthians*, 2nd ed. (London: Hodder & Stoughton, 1885), 278. Robertson and Plummer (*First Corinthians*, 233–34) do not take this view but think that it is worth consideration.

[61] Thiselton, *First Corinthians*, 841.

[62] Ciampa and Rosner, *First Corinthians*, 533. Ciampa and Rosner (530) note the death of Herod Agrippa I by an angel in Acts 12:23 for accepting praise rather than giving glory to God. This passage "presupposes an understanding of a great angelic zeal for the protection of God's glory." On the possible connection with Ps 8 see J. P. Heil, *The Rhetorical Role of Scripture in 1 Corinthians*, Studies in Biblical Literature 15 (Atlanta: Society of Biblical Literature, 2005), 183–84. Additional recent commentators who follow the view that Paul's reference is to good angels present in worship include Collins, *First Corinthians*, 412; Garland, *1 Corinthians*, 526–29; Fitzmyer, *First Corinthians*, 418–19. Fitzmyer thinks that evidence from Qumran that speaks of angels present at gatherings of the Essene community bolsters this interpretation (see 1QSa 2:3–9; 1QM 7:4–6). Fitzmyer (418) also notes Ps 138:1 (LXX), "before angels I shall sing your praise."

[63] The Greek sentence begins with the conjunction πλήν, which BDAG defines as a "marker of something that is contrastingly added for consideration). Paul uses the same conjunction in Eph 5:33 in qualifying his instructions for wives to be submissive to their husbands, "However, each one of you must also love his wife as he loves himself."

[64] The sentence begins with the explanatory conjunction γάρ.

[65] So Ciampa and Rosner, *First Corinthians*, 534. Ciampa and Rosner note *Genesis Rabbah* 8:9, "In the past Adam was created from dust and Eve was created from Adam; but henceforth it

that the principle of headship is balanced by the principle of interdependence. Neither rules out the other; both are valid principles in the light of creation. Paul is not retreating from his prior argument, only recognizing the balance inherent in creation. Just as God is at the top of the hierarchy in 11:3, in 11:12 Paul concludes, "But everything comes from God" (see 3:21–23; 8:6; 15:28). The meaning of the prepositional phrase "in the Lord" in 11:11 may refer also to creation and stand parallel to "all things are from God" in 11:12.[66] Thiselton translates the Greek "as those in the Lord" in the sense of "among the Lord's people." He explains, "Paul almost certainly means to say that gender differentiation is decreed in creation, expressed in societal convention, and not abrogated in the order of the gospel." In other words, Paul applies a third point of reference to his argument and stresses that "in the gospel differentiation is determined more explicitly by a principle of mutuality and reciprocity."[67]

**11:13–16** As in his argument regarding the dangers of idolatry (10:15), Paul asks the Corinthians to judge the matter for themselves, that is, he wants them to think carefully and critically about his present argument with the confidence that they will reach the same conclusion in light of the theological principles articulated thus far. He is not leaving the matter of head coverings up to them to rule one way or another. There is no other custom practiced by the churches (11:16). For wives to remain covered while praying to God is the only proper thing to do. Commentators sometimes point out that in Paul the verb "to pray" normally has no direct object, suggesting that the addition of the words "to God" may serve to reinforce the serious nature of worship as a reflection of God's created order.[68]

In 11:14–15, by way of analogy to what nature teaches regarding the length of men's and women's hair, Paul adds yet another argument to his arsenal for the propriety of head coverings.[69] The NIV translation, "the nature of things," translates only one Greek word rendered by other translations simply as "nature."[70] Thiselton lists four views and key proponents of each in the history of interpretation:[71] by "nature" Paul means (1) an intuitive or inborn sense of what is fitting, right, or seemly (Bengel, Meyer); (2) the ways humans are

---

shall be 'in our image, after our likeness' [Gen. 1:26]; neither man without woman nor woman without man, and neither of them without Shekinah." Cf. also 1 Esdras 4:14–17.

[66] So Ciampa and Rosner, *First Corinthians*, 535. Ciampa and Rosner propose an instrumental understanding of the phrase, "by/through the Lord," which "would correspond perfectly to the Jewish exegetical tradition about the Lord's role in the formation of every human being." See also Delobel, "1 Cor 11:2–16," 384.

[67] Thiselton, *First Corinthians*, 842.

[68] So Robertson and Plummer, *First Corinthians*, 234; Heil, *Rhetorical Role of Scripture*, 186; Ciampa and Rosner, *First Corinthians*, 538.

[69] In Greek, an intensive construction is used, "Does not *nature itself* teach . . .? (ἡ φύσις αὐτὴ).

[70] So NASB, HCSB: "Does not even nature itself teach you . . ." Gk. φύσις. The term appears elsewhere in Rom 1:26; 2:14,27; 11:21,24; Gal 2:15; 4:8; Eph 2:3; Jas 3:7; 2 Pet 1:4.

[71] Thiselton, *First Corinthians*, 844–46.

constituted as men and women (de Wett); (3) the physical reality of how the world is ordered (Osiander, Hofius); and (4) the customs of a given society (Chrysostom, Calvin). BDAG classifies this verse under the definition "the regular or established order of things, nature." A number of recent commentators adopt the fourth view, that Paul is speaking of what is customary in a given society. Fee explains, "for Paul it is a question of propriety and of 'custom' (vv. 13, 16), which carries with it 'disgrace' or 'glory' (vv. 14–15). Hence, this is an appeal to the 'way things are' (NIV, 'the nature of things'), to the 'natural feeling' that they shared together as part of their contemporary culture. In other words, Paul's appeal in this unit is to what is 'proper' and 'customary.'"[72] Ciampa and Rosner leave the matter open by commenting, "Paul is suggesting that the pattern established by nature or human custom provided a clue that women's heads should be covered."[73] Paul's use of the intensive construction ("nature itself) and his prior appeal to the created order in 11:7–10 suggests that mere human convention is not Paul's meaning here. Heil's comments are on track: "For Paul this natural order of things is based on the scriptural order of God's creation."[74] Paul, however, is not stipulating hair length for men and women but making a general observation about what is typical in the service of his argument about head coverings.

Paul concludes his discussion of the head covering with a warning about contentiousness and a final argument for the use of head coverings in worship. The phrase "If anyone thinks . . ." (NIV, "If anyone wants") occurs now for the third time in the letters (cf. 3:18b; 8:2), which may suggest that Paul is still addressing "those with knowledge" in Corinth who perhaps were members of the church of high social status. Paul reminds those who might be contentious[75] over this matter that there is no other custom[76] practiced by the churches. Bruce notes that Paul's comments in 14:36 imply a "tendency on the part of the Corinthian church to be a law unto itself, without reference to Christian procedure elsewhere."[77]

## 2. Disorder and Divisions at the Lord's Table (11:17–34)

In 11:17–34 Paul responds to a report of divisions among the Corinthians in their observance of the Lord's Supper that ran along socio-economic lines.

[72] Fee, *First Corinthians*, 527. See also Thiselton, *First Corinthians*, 846; Garland, *1 Corinthians*, 530–31.

[73] Ciampa and Rosner, *First Corinthians*, 539.

[74] Heil, *Rhetorical Role of Scripture*, 186n27. Cf. esp. Paul's use of the term in Rom 1:26.

[75] Gk. φιλόνειϰος. The only occurrence in the New Testament. BDAG defines, "quarrelsome, contentious." Mitchell (*Rhetoric of Reconciliation*, 262n418) emphasizes "that the contentiousness of which Paul writes is not that of the Corinthians against his teaching, but the Corinthians against one another." Paul's overall concern is for the unity of the church.

[76] Gk. συνήθεια (cf. 8:7, "those accustomed to idols").

[77] Bruce, *1 & 2 Corinthians*, 108.

This is the third time in the letter that Paul specifically relates his instructions to oral reports (cf. 1:10–17; 5:1–13).[78] As noted in the introduction to 11:2–14:40, Paul responds to this issue here in the letter for thematic reasons that have to do with concerns regarding the assembled congregation.[79] Paul's assertion that he has no praise for them (11:17,22) stands in stark contrast to the praise offered in 11:2 for holding fast to cherished traditions. As in 11:2, Paul recounts a tradition he delivered to them, the Lord's Supper (11:23–25),[80] but he cannot praise them in light of their behavior that completely contradicted the purpose of the meal (11:18–22), which proclaims Jesus' death for others (11:26). As in 11:2–16 Paul's instructions continue to address issues of honor and shame. In 11:2–16 the core issue was bringing shame rather than glory to one's respective spiritual head. In 11:17–22 the issue is behavior that brings shame on the poor.[81] Paul cannot praise them for behavior that does not imitate Christ (11:1). Since their gatherings did not contribute to the mutual edification of the body, Paul scolds that their "meetings do more harm than good" (11:17). Their factious behavior, which discriminated against the poor, was the very opposite of the essence of the meaning of the meal, the very antithesis of love for one another.[82] Such behavior shows contempt for the church of God (11:22). Paul's response falls into three parts: (1) He sharply denounces their abuse of others at what they call the Lord's meal (11:17–22), (2) he recounts the received tradition of the Lord's Supper (11:23–26), and (3) he instructs the Corinthians to eat the supper in a worthy manner by properly discerning the Lord's body (11:27–34).[83]

### *(1) Paul's Sharp Rebuke for Their Behavior at the So-Called Lord's Supper (11:17–22)*

**[17]In the following directives I have no praise for you, for your meetings do more harm than good. [18]In the first place, I hear that when you come together as a church, there are divisions among you, and to some extent I believe it. [19]No doubt there have to be differences among you to show which of you have God's approval. [20]When you come together, it is not the Lord's Supper you eat, [21]for as you eat, each of you goes ahead without waiting for anybody else. One remains hungry, another gets drunk. [22]Don't you have homes to eat and drink in? Or do**

[78] Fee (*First Corinthians*, 531) notes that this is the one certain instance in chaps. 7–16 that is not a response to the Corinthian's letter.

[79] A key term that gives cohesion to 11:17–34 is the verb συνέρχομαι, "to come together," which occurs five times (11:17,18,20,33,34).

[80] The term "to deliver/hand down" (Gk. παραδίδωμι) occurs in 11:2 and 11:23.

[81] The term "shame" (Gk. καταισχύνω) in 11:4–5 recurs in 11:22 along with the accusation of "despising" the church of God. On the relation of 11:17–34 to the dominant themes and concerns of 8:1–11:1, see Thiselton, *First Corinthians*, 850.

[82] Cf. Jas 2:1–13 on showing favoritism in the gathered assembly.

[83] The structure of 11:17–34 is an A B A' chiastic pattern. Paul's recitation of the tradition is framed by his confrontation of their unacceptable behavior.

**you despise the church of God and humiliate those who have nothing? What shall I say to you? Shall I praise you for this? Certainly not!**

**11:17–18** The title I have given to this unit takes its cue from 11:20, "When you come together, it is not the Lord's Supper you eat." The Corinthians may have called their fellowship meals "the Lord's Supper," but Paul could not praise them since their gatherings failed to demonstrate the most basic understanding of the significance of the meal.[84] The report of divisions (11:18) recalls the report from Chloe's household mentioned at the beginning of the letter (cf. 1:10–17). Here Paul adds, "and to some extent I believe it" (NIV), a phrase that is capable of different interpretations. Some think the statement has a rhetorical force, meaning something like, "I can't believe it!", as an indirect way of expressing shock and disbelief at the report.[85] Others suggest that Paul expresses judicious pastoral caution by avoiding unnecessary confrontation and overly hasty speech. Thiselton thinks the REB translation has it right, "I believe there is some truth in it."[86] It is clear, however, from the passage that Paul believes the report.

Although the word translated "divisions" in 11:18 is the same as the word used in 1:10, it is difficult to know if the two situations were related. The first mention of divisions in 1:10–17 clearly had to do with personality factions expressed in the slogans, "I am of Paul," "I am of Apollos," etc. In 11:17–22 the divisions are clearly sociological in nature, centered on the rich and the poor. For this reason some think it unlikely that the "divisions" here reflect the same situation as in 1:10–12.[87] Thiselton points out, however, that the possible role of the host-patron may call into question the contention that the splits described in 11:17–22 are different in kind from the splits in 1:10–12.[88]

**11:19** Fee refers to 11:19 as "a theological aside" and "one of the true puzzles in the letter."[89] On the surface the statement, "No doubt there have to be differences among you to show which of you have God's approval," seems to interject a surprising change of perspective in light of the prior rebuke for divisions (both in 11:18 and in 1:10–17). Paul suddenly appears to assume that divisions are necessary and inevitable, which serve to distinguish the true and

---

[84] An *inclusio* brackets the unit; Paul begins and ends with the statement that he cannot praise them (11:17,22).

[85] So Hays, *First Corinthians*, 195.

[86] Thiselton, *First Corinthians*, 858. Robertson and Plummer (*First Corinthians*, 239) suggest that Paul is reluctant to believe the worst.

[87] Morris, *1 Corinthians*, 155–56; Fee, *First Corinthians*, 537.

[88] Thiselton, *First Corinthians*, 850. "Just as in 1:10–12, the groupings caused splits by generating an ethos which came to give the peer group or subgroup more prominence than the 'one' Body (cf. 10:16, 17) of the whole church, so the dynamics of the celebrations of the Lord's Supper in house groups in all probability generated the same spirit of focusing on a patron or host to a group rather than exclusively on Christ." See also B. W. Winter, "The Lord's Supper at Corinth: An Alternative Reconstruction," *RTR* 37 (1978): 73–82.

[89] Fee, *First Corinthians*, 537–38.

the false in the church. The NIV translation "differences" is rendered "factions" in other translations (so NASB). Although it is not the same word as the word for divisions in 11:18, it is probably synonymous.[90]

There are three different views regarding Paul's meaning. Some think Paul's statement reflects his "already, but not yet" eschatological perspective, inserted here in anticipation of the emphasis on judgment in 11:28–32. In keeping with the teaching of Jesus, Paul expected "divisions" to accompany the end that separate the true believers from the false. God is working out his own purposes, and this separation of the true and the false is part of the divine testing process at work in their midst.[91] Hays explains that apocalyptic texts often warn that times of trial will bring out the true colors of those who profess faith (cf. Matt 4:14–20; 13:9–13). Those who are the "approved" will stand the test, while those who are not will fall away or separate themselves from the community (1 John 2:9). Paul acknowledges the inevitability of splits in the community. "By placing the fact of the community's divisions in an apocalyptic context, he emphasizes the gravity of the situation."[92]

Others, however, perceive irony in Paul's remark since the conjunction "for" follows as the explanation for why Paul cannot praise them. In this view, it is misleading to label 11:19 as a digression or a "theological aside," a description of a preliminary separation of the false and the true in anticipation of final judgment since Paul does not apply the same line of reasoning in 1:10–17. Rather than asserting the eschatological necessity of factions in the church, Paul's expression is to be understood as bitter irony. In this view, the "approved" are the dignitaries who are culpable for allowing divisions between the rich and the poor. Horsely suggests the following translation of 11:19, "For of course there must be 'discrimination' among you so that it will become clear who among you are 'the distinguished ones.'"[93]

A third view takes 11:19 as yet another Corinthian utterance/slogan. Thiselton, also noting the use of "for" as an explanation for the abuses described in 11:20–21, suggests that this may be an allusion to a saying in an

---

[90] Gk. αἵρεσις, which occurs in Paul only here and in Gal 5:20 as one of the works of the flesh. The word is used in Acts to refer to different sects to which a person might choose to belong (Acts 5:17; 15:5; 24:5,14; 26:5; 28:22). The word carries the sense of "heresies" in 2 Pet 2:1.

[91] Ibid., 538–39.

[92] Hays, *First Corinthians*, 195. See also D. G. Horrell, *The Social Ethos of the Corinthian Correspondence: Interests and Ideology from 1 Corinthians to 1 Clement* (Edinburgh: T&T Clark, 1996), 150–51.

[93] R. Horsely, *1 Corinthians*, ANTC (Nashville: Abingdon, 1998), 159. So also Garland, *1 Corinthians*, 538–39. "The splits at the Lord's Supper are imposed by prideful, insensitive humans seeking to differentiate the top-drawer members from the common rabble." The divisions between the rich and the poor reveal a church that has not taken to heart the message of the cross. Garland notes the study by R. Alastair Campbell and thinks Campbell's proposed translation makes the best sense of the historical context: "For there actually has to be discrimination in your meetings, so that, if you please, the elite may stand out from the rest." See R. A. Campbell, "Does Paul Acquiesce in Divisions at the Lord's Supper?" *NovT* 33 (1991): 70.

eschatological context, but it is not Paul who has taken up the axiom; it is the strong in Corinth, who had already anticipated criticism about their divisiveness. Thiselton translates, "For 'dissensions are unavoidable,' it is claimed among you, in order that those who are tried and true among you may be visibly revealed."[94] Thiselton provides a more concise summary of his view in his shorter exegetical commentary, "It seems most probable that the phrase expresses an excuse or pretext made by householders in Corinth for the way in which the Lord's Supper was conducted, for it is likely that complaints had been made by the poor about the outrageous effects described in vv. 20–22, and corroborated in v. 33."[95]

**11:20–22** In 11:20–22 Paul draws out the implications of the preceding verses (11:17–19).[96] When the church gathered together, what occurred could not in any way be called the "Lord's Supper"[97] with integrity. Instead, their behavior was a travesty of love and the epitome of self-indulgence. Paul paints a stark contrast between the hungry poor and the drunken rich. The actions of the "haves" showcased contempt for the church of God and brought shame on the "have nots." They were in clear violation of the principle of doing all things for the good of others and the glory of God (recall 10:23–33). This was no occasion for praise.

### *(2) The Received Tradition of the Lord's Supper (11:23–26)*

**[23]For I received from the Lord what I also passed on to you: The Lord Jesus,
on the night he was betrayed, took bread, [24]and when he had given thanks, he
broke it and said, "This is my body, which is for you; do this in remembrance of
me." [25]In the same way, after supper he took the cup, saying, "This cup is the new
covenant in my blood; do this, whenever you drink it, in remembrance of me."
[26]For whenever you eat this bread and drink this cup, you proclaim the Lord's
death until he comes.**

The tradition of the Lord's Supper, which originated with the Lord himself, stands in sharp contrast to the Corinthians' present behavior. Paul cites the tradition by way of illustration with the intent to remedy their appalling actions toward one another. He does not introduce anything new about the Supper nor does he seek to correct their theology of the meal.[98] The tradition itself is theologically rich and of central importance to the life and worship of the church.[99] Already in 5:7 Paul has identified Christ as the sacrificed "Passover lamb" in connection

[94] Thiselton, *First Corinthians*, 848.

[95] A. C. Thiselton, *First Corinthians : A Shorter Exegetical and Pastoral Commentary* (Grand Rapids: Eerdmans, 2006), 181.

[96] The NIV does not translate the inferential coordinating conjunction οὖν ("therefore").

[97] The use of the adjective κυριακός ("Lord's") occurs only here and in Rev 1:10 in the New Testament.

[98] So Garland, *1 Corinthians*, 544–45.

[99] For a recent collection of essays on the theological, historical, and practical issues concerning the Lord's Supper, see T. R. Schreiner and M. R. Crawford, eds., *The Lord's Supper: Remem-*

with the injunctions to remove the incestuous man from the church. The problem in Corinth was that they failed to embrace and apply the theology of the tradition in their relations to one another in the reenactment of the meal.[100] Their actions toward one another demonstrated a profound lack of commitment to the fundamental meaning of the meal, namely, Christ's atoning sacrifice for others. As noted above in the comments on 11:17–22, it is for this reason that Paul stated, "When you come together, it is not the Lord's Supper you eat" (11:20).

**11:23** The language of "receiving" and "passing on" is stock language for the transmission of traditions.[101] Paul's reminder that what he passed on to them originated "from the Lord" reinforces not only the authority of the tradition but also Paul's role as the mediator of the tradition in the founding of the church at Corinth. Paul's statement that he received the tradition "from the Lord" implies the original source of the tradition not necessarily direct revelation.[102] The first disciples received the tradition of the Lord's Supper directly from the Lord and faithfully passed it on to others. Paul's rendition of the received tradition is closest to Luke's account (Luke 22:17–20; cf. also Matt 26:26–28; Mark 14:22–24). The unique Lukan elements that appear in 1 Cor 11:23–26 include the command to "do this in remembrance of me" in connection with the bread, the statement that Jesus' body is "for you," and the association of the cup with the new covenant.[103]

Paul locates the tradition historically "on the night he was betrayed," that is, Jesus' last meal with his disciples before his crucifixion.[104] The word "betrayed" translates the same word in the first half of the verse rendered "passed on" with reference to the handing down of traditions.[105] The meaning in 11:23b is that Jesus was "handed over" unto death. This may, of course, refer specifically to Judas' betrayal of Jesus,[106] but since the verb is used repeatedly in the gospels in connection with betrayal unto death,

*bering and Proclaiming Christ Until He Comes*, NAC Studies in Bible and Theology (Nashville: B&H, 2010).

[100] 11:23–26 is introduced by the explanatory conjunction γάρ, which connects directly to the preceding unit. Paul will explain why he cannot praise them for their behavior.

[101] Cf. 11:2; 15:1–3. The Greek verbs are παραλαμβάνω (to receive) and παραδίδωμι (to pass on).

[102] Robertson and Plummer (*First Corinthians*, 242) note that if Paul intended to say that he received the tradition through direct communication with the Lord then we should probably expect the preposition παρά instead of ἀπό. Cf. Gal 1:12; 1 Thess 2:13; 4:1; 2 Thess 3:6. The source of communication is what is important, not the mode. See also O. Hofius, "The Lord's Supper and the Lord's Supper Tradition: Reflections on 1 Corinthians 11:23b–25," in *One Loaf, One Cup: Ecumenical Studies of 1 Cor 11 and Other Eucharistic Texts*, New Gospel Studies, ed. B. F. Meyer (Macon, GA: Mercer University Press), 76n3.

[103] On the relationship of this passage to the gospel traditions see I. H. Marshall, *Last Supper and Lord's Supper* (Grand Rapids: Eerdmans, 1981); J. Jeremias, *The Eucharistic Words of Jesus* (London: SCM, 1966).

[104] Since scholars generally concede that 1 Corinthians was written before the Gospels, 11:23–26 is the earliest written account of the Lord's Supper tradition.

[105] Gk. παραδίδωμι.

[106] So Fee, *First Corinthians*, 549n26.

Paul's reference may be more wide-ranging.[107] Robertson and Plummer, for example, note the imperfect tense of the verb and comment, "The delivery to His enemies had already begun and was going on at the very time when the Lord instituted the Eucharist. Moreover, to translate 'was betrayed' confines the meaning to the action of Judas; whereas the Father's surrender of the Son is included, and perhaps is chiefly meant, and the Son's self-sacrifice may also be included."[108] Paul's word choice may echo the LXX of Isa 53:6 ("The Lord gave him up for our sins") and 53:12 ("he was delivered because of their iniquities").[109]

**11:24–25** Paul describes four components of the celebration, including thanksgiving, the eating of the bread, the meal itself, and the drinking of the cup.[110] The Passover celebration was explicitly tied to God's redemption of his people, which all the more heightened the association of the bread with Jesus' body, "which is for you." Already Paul has referred to Christ as our redemption (1:30) and "our Passover lamb" (5:7), and twice he has reminded the Corinthians that they were "bought at a price" (6:20; 7:23). In the same way the saying "This is my body, which is for you" focuses on Jesus' sacrifice for others. The controversy in the history of the church regarding these words is well established.[111] The word "is" can have various identifications and in this context means to signify or represent.[112] The bread signifies the body of Jesus, and the cup represents the new covenant ratified by the shedding of blood.[113] Both the bread and the cup denote sacrifice. Commentators often note that Exod 24:8 and Jer 31:31 provide the scriptural background to Jesus' statement, "This cup is the new covenant in my blood."[114]

---

[107] So Ciampa and Rosner (*First Corinthians*, 549n167), who note the following passages (Matt 10:21; 17:22–23; 20:18–19; 24:9; 26:2; 27:26; Mark 9:31; 10:33; 13:12; 15:15; Luke 18:32–33; 21:16; 24:7,20; John 19:16).

[108] Robertson and Plummer, *First Corinthians*, 243. The Greek verb (παρεδίδετο) could be passive, "was being delivered," or middle, "was delivering himself."

[109] So Ciampa and Rosner (*First Corinthians*, 545). Garland (*1 Corinthians*, 545) concurs that the translation "handed over" retains a measure of ambiguity that allows for a broader understanding. "God's hand (Rom. 4:25; 8:32; cf. Isa. 53:6–12 LXX) and Jesus' willing submission (Gal. 2:20; Eph. 5:2,25) are ultimately behind Christ's being delivered up."

[110] On the order of the meal see Hofius, "The Lord's Supper," 80–88; A. Eriksson, *Traditions as Rhetorical Proof: Pauline Argumentation in 1 Corinthians*, ConBNT 29 (Stockholm: Almqvist & Wiksell International, 1998), 176. For a different view see Jeremias, *The Eucharistic Words of Jesus*, 121.

[111] That is, whether or not the bread actually becomes the body of Jesus or whether it is symbolic.

[112] Morris (*1 Corinthians*, 158) mentions John 8:12; 10:9; and 1 Cor 10:4 as examples of different identifications for the verb "is."

[113] On references to the blood of Christ in Paul outside of 1 Corinthians in connection with redemption, see Rom 3:25; 5:9; Eph 1:7; 2:13; Col 1:20.

[114] So Barrett, *First Corinthians*, 268; Garland, *1 Corinthians*, 547; Ciampa and Rosner, *First Corinthians*, 552.

To take the view that Jesus' words regarding the bread and the cup are representative does not and should not reduce the Lord's Supper to mere symbolism. The Supper is a rich and meaningful symbol that involves actual realities. Already Paul has established that partaking of the cup and the bread is to participate in the body and blood of Christ (10:16). Furthermore, there is the explicit identification of believers as "one body" (10:17; recall 6:15), which is developed further in 12:12–27 and serves an important role in the warning of 11:27–34 regarding eating and drinking "in an unworthy manner" (11:27) by failing to properly discern the Lord's "body" (11:29). Clearly there is also a memorial character to the meal, captured in the repetition, "Do this in remembrance of me" (11:24–25).[115] Passover itself was a memorial (Exod 12:14), recalling the Israelites redemption from Egypt. The Lord's Supper, by way of contrast, is a memorial to Christ himself, who redeemed his people from the bondage of sin. Additionally, when believers gather to celebrate the Lord's Supper, the Lord himself is living and present in the celebration of the meal as the participants look forward to his coming again (11:26).

**11:26** The conjunction "for" indicates that 11:26 explains the memorial character of the meal, that it is a proclamation of the Lord's death until he comes.[116] The proclamation may refer to both speaking and doing,[117] but in context, Paul's emphasis probably falls on the latter, that is, on the manner of their observance of the meal, which failed to proclaim the meaning and significance of Jesus' death for others.[118] Garland explains, "'Eating' and 'drinking' are mentioned five times in 11:26–29, and this is what Paul wishes to emphasize more than the verbal repetition of the story of the Lord's death. It is not what is said during or after the meal that concerns him, but what is said in the action of eating and drinking . . . He believes that their actions in their meal do not proclaim the Lord's death, which is why he says that their meal is not the Lord's Supper (11:20)."[119] The phrase "the death of the Lord" is placed first in the Greek main clause for emphasis. In their behavior at the Lord's Supper

---

[115] Whereas the Gospel traditions connect the saying, "Do this in remembrance of me," with the bread, Paul links the saying with both the bread and the cup.

[116] The eschatological character of the meal derives also from the Gospel tradition (Matt 26:29; Luke 22:17).

[117] Barrett (*First Corinthians*, 270) comments, "That is, when Christians held a common meal they recalled aloud the event on which their existence was based. This recalling (which closely resembles the narration of the exodus from Egypt in the Jewish Passover) must have had some narrative content, and the fact helps to explain the relative continuity and fixed form of the Passion Narrative in the gospels."

[118] So Hays (*First Corinthians*, 199–200). "The proclamation of the Lord's death occurs not just in preaching that accompanies the meal; rather, the community's sharing in the broken bread and the outpoured wine is itself an act of proclamation, an enacted parable that figures forth the death of Jesus 'for us.'" Furthermore, "The problem is not that they are failing to say the right words but that their enactment of the word is deficient: their self-serving actions obscure the meaning of the Supper so thoroughly that it no longer points to Christ's death."

[119] Garland, *1 Corinthians*, 548–49.

they were not imitating Christ (11:1); and as the next unit indicates, in their unworthy observance of the meal, the Corinthians were eating and drinking judgment on themselves (11:29b).

### *(3) Eating and Drinking the Lord's Supper Unworthily (11:27–34)*

**[27]Therefore, whoever eats the bread or drinks the cup of the Lord in an unworthy manner will be guilty of sinning against the body and blood of the Lord. [28]A man ought to examine himself before he eats of the bread and drinks of the cup. [29]For anyone who eats and drinks without recognizing the body of the Lord eats and drinks judgment on himself. [30]That is why many among you are weak and sick, and a number of you have fallen asleep. [31]But if we judged ourselves, we would not come under judgment. [32]When we are judged by the Lord, we are being disciplined so that we will not be condemned with the world.**

**[33]So then, my brothers, when you come together to eat, wait for each other. [34]If anyone is hungry, he should eat at home, so that when you meet together it may not result in judgment.**

**And when I come I will give further directions.**

In 11:27–34 Paul draws out the implications of the tradition of the Lord's Supper as instituted by Jesus and its meaning in light of the Corinthians' present behavior. Eating the Supper "unworthily" is the controlling theme of the whole unit, which is replete with judgment language.[120] As Thiselton observes, "Paul's primary point is that attitude and conduct should fit the message and solemnity of what is proclaimed."[121] There are two subunits, each introduced by the same Greek conjunction.[122] In 11:27–32 Paul calls on those who partake of the Lord's Supper to prove themselves lest they eat and drink unto judgment by failing to "rightly judge/discern/recognize" the body (11:27–29). Judgment has, in fact, already fallen on some (11:30), not final condemnation, but rather the discipline of the Lord (11:31–32). In 11:33–34, Paul concludes the whole discussion that began in 11:17 by instructing them to observe the meal correctly "so that when you meet together it may not result in judgment."

**11:27–30** In context, to eat the bread and to drink the cup of the Lord "in an unworthy manner"[123] is to be understood in light of Paul's sharp rebuke for

---

[120] English translations fail to capture the play on words in the use of "judgment" language in 11:29–34. The Greek terms along with the NIV translation include κρίμα (11:29,34, "judgment"), διακρίνω (11:29,31, "to recognize," "to judge"), κρίνω (11:31b,32a, "to come under judgment," "when we are judged" [participle]), κατακρίνω (11:32, "to be condemned"). In addition to the judgment terms, Paul warns of being guilty (ἔνοχος) of the body and the blood of the Lord and urges that a man ought to "examine/prove" (δοκιμάζω) himself before eating the Lord's Supper.

[121] Thiselton, *First Corinthians*, 889.

[122] Gk. ὥστε, a marker of result, captured by the NIV, "Therefore" (11:27) and, "So then" (11:33).

[123] The NIV's "in an unworthy manner" translates one Greek word, ἀναξίως, which occurs only here in the New Testament. Paul uses the opposite term, ἀξίως ("in a worthy manner), five times to speak of actions that are proper and fitting for God's people (Rom 16:2; Eph 4:1; Phil 1:27; Col 1:10; 1 Thess 2:12; cf. also 3 John 1:6).

their behavior that humiliated the poorer members of the church (11:17–22). To shame others and to show contempt for the church of God (11:22) is to be guilty of the body and the blood of the Lord, which means to be liable for the death of Jesus by profaning what the meal stands for.[124] To partake in an unworthy manner is to sin against Christ.[125] Ciampa and Rosner suggest that the statement, "to sin against the body and the blood of the Lord," encompasses two ideas, namely, sinning against those who constitute the body and the blood of the Lord by virtue of their participation in the meal and sinning against the new covenant that the Supper represents thereby sinning against Christ who established the new covenant.[126] "To worship Christ in a way that shows disrespect toward those who have been 'united with the Lord,' have become 'one with him in spirit' (6:17), and who share or participate in his body and blood (10:16) is to sin not just against them but also against the covenant reaffirmed in the meal, against the Lord of the meal and of those brothers and sisters in Christ."[127] Paul has already stated in 8:12 that to sin against one's brother is to sin against Christ.

In light of the stern warning of 11:27 Paul calls for a rigorous self-examination as essential preparation for the observance of the meal. In context, Paul does not have in mind mere self-introspection as this verse is often understood. As Fee put it, "Rather, it stands in contrast to the 'divine examination' to which unworthy participation will lead."[128] Paul's perspective is communal. To examine oneself is "to examine one's compliance with the covenant as reflected in their ways of relating to other members of the community."[129] Thiselton translates, "A person should examine his or her own genuineness."[130] The verb "to examine" (11:28)[131] is cognate to the noun designating the ones who "have God's approval" (11:19).[132] If Paul is referring ironically to the social dignitaries in 11:19, then in 11:28 he may be engaging in a wordplay

[124] So Fee, *First Corinthians*, 561; Garland, *1 Corinthians*, 550.

[125] Thiselton (*First Corinthians*, 888–90) reviews the lexicographical evidence for ἔνοχος (NIV, "guilty") and likewise prefers the notion of "liability" and translates "to be held accountable." He explains, "The syntax therefore implies not a sacrilege against the elements of the Lord's Supper but answerability or being held accountable for the sin against Christ of claiming identification with him while using the celebration of the meal as an occasion for social enjoyment or status enhancement without regard to sharing in what the Lord's Supper proclaims."

[126] Ciampa and Rosner, *First Corinthians*, 554–55.

[127] Ibid., 555. Garland (*1 Corinthians*, 550) explains Paul's logic as follows: "The Lord's Supper proclaims the Lord's death. Those whose behavior at the Lord's Supper does not conform to what that death entails effectively shift sides. They leave the Lord's side and align themselves with the rulers of this present age who crucified the Lord (1 Cor. 2:8; cf. Heb. 6:5). This explains how they make themselves so vulnerable to God's judgment."

[128] Fee, *First Corinthians*, 561.

[129] Ciampa and Rosner, *First Corinthians*, 555.

[130] Thiselton, *First Corinthians*, 891.

[131] Gk. δοκιμάζω. BDAG defines, "to make a critical examination of something to determine genuineness, put to the test, examine."

[132] Gk. δόκιμος.

by calling on the self-assured "approved ones" to "prove" themselves, that is, to undergo a rigorous self-examination with the intent to eat and drink in keeping with the genuine character of the meal.[133] Garland explains, "Those who may imagine themselves to be the dignitaries and want to make sure that others recognize their higher status should check their pride at the door. They must examine themselves at this meal in light of Christ's sacrifice for all."[134] Earlier in the letter, employing the athletic metaphor, Paul reported that he disciplined himself lest having preached to others he himself might become "unapproved."[135]

In 11:29 Paul states the reason for self-examination.[136] To eat and to drink disingenuously is to eat and drink judgment to oneself. But what does Paul mean by the phrase "without recognizing the body of the Lord"? The Greek word translated "to recognize" by the NIV is the same word translated "to judge" in 11:31.[137] BDAG references both 1 Cor 11:29 and 11:31 under the definition, "to evaluate by paying careful attention to, evaluate, judge," but includes "to recognize" with 11:29, which is picked up by the NIV.[138] The HCSB follows suit but leaves off the modifier "of the Lord," which is not in the Greek text, and renders, "For whoever eats and drinks without recognizing the body . . ." The NIV2011 translates, "without discerning the body of Christ." Morris is among those who think that failure to "recognize" or "discern the body of the Lord" means to fail to distinguish the Lord's Supper from other meals.[139] Others think that the "body" is shorthand for both "the body and the blood" and that Paul's meaning is that one eats and drinks judgment to himself by not properly evaluating what the elements of the meal represent, namely, the death of Christ for them. In other words, to properly discern or recognize the meaning of the death of Christ, which the Supper proclaims (11:26), "impinges transformatively on believers' attitudes and behavior toward others."[140] Yet a

---

[133] In Greek the text reads, "But a man must examine (test, prove) himself and in this way (οὕτως) he must eat from the bread and he must drink from the cup. In other words, the participants in the Lord's Supper are to eat and drink in the way indicated, "by examining themselves to confirm that their understanding, attitude, and conduct are genuine in sharing in all that the body and blood of Christ proclaims, both in redemptive and in social terms" (Thiselton, *First Corinthians*, 891). 11:28 contains three imperative verbs: "to examine," "to eat," and "to drink."

[134] Garland, *1 Corinthians*, 551.

[135] Gk. ἀδόκιμος.

[136] 11:29 begins with an explanatory γάρ.

[137] Gk. διακρίνω. In 1 Corinthians the term appears also in 4:7; 6:5; and 14:29.

[138] BDAG also includes other nuances: (1) to differentiate by separating, separate, arrange; (2) to conclude that there is a difference, make a distinction, differentiate; (3) to render a legal decision, judge, decide.

[139] Morris, *1 Corinthians*, 161. Garland (*1 Corinthians*, 552) notes that this view goes back to Justin and Augustine and is reflected in some modern commentators (Godet, Weiss, Leitzmann, and Hering).

[140] Thiselton, *First Corinthians*, 893. Thiselton explains further, "The Lord's Supper, by underlining participation in, and identification with, the cruciform Christ, thereby generates the social transformation, which is Paul's second concern. Nevertheless, he never leaves behind the

third view, defended ardently by Fee, is that Paul's absolute use of "the body," without the genitive qualifier "of the Lord," is not shorthand for "the body and the blood" but rather has in view the church as the body of Christ. The parallel is not 11:27 but rather 10:16–17 "where Paul singled out the bread alone for interpretation and emphatically declared that their all partaking of the 'one loaf' was evidence that they themselves were therefore 'one body.'"[141] The whole point of 11:17–34 "is to correct a considerable abuse of the church as it is visibly portrayed at the Lord's Supper."[142] The problem was that they were despising the church of God by their actions (11:22).

Because of their actions, God's judgment on them had already begun. "That is why many among you are weak and sick, and a number of you have fallen asleep" (11:30). The punishment that came on the Israelites of old (10:4–11) had already taken effect among many of the Corinthians.[143] Ciampa and Rosner point out that it "should not be assumed that the sick or dying were particularly guilty of the sin, but, like most plagues of divine judgment in the Old Testament, the plague could fall indiscriminately on the community as a whole (e.g., Exod 32:35; Num 8:19; 11:33; Deut 32:24; Josh 22:17)."[144] There was no possibility of repentance for those who were guilty and had already died, but the church as a whole could heed the warning and make necessary corrections.

**11:31–32** Paul writes not only to warn but also to rectify their behavior. The statement, "But if we judged ourselves, we would not come under judgment" is parallel to the call for self-examination in 11:28.[145] The verb in the conditional clause "if we judged" is the same verb translated "to recognize" in 11:29.[146] The verb is in the imperfect tense, indicating a continuous, habitual practice, "If we were judging/evaluating/discerning ourselves . . ." The Corinthians were not doing this and were therefore currently experiencing divine judgment. The meaning of "judging ourselves" takes its cue from the meaning of the term in 11:29. On the view that 11:29 refers to the body of Christ, Fee

proclamation of the cross (1:18–25) as the ground of identity transformation, and it is of the very essence of the Lord's Supper (and of baptism) to keep this anchorage in grace and in the cross in sharp focus." So also Garland (*1 Corinthians*, 553), "A proper understanding of what these elements represent should change the Corinthians' attitude and behavior toward others."

[141] Fee, *First Corinthians*, 564.

[142] Ibid. Similarly Ciampa and Rosner (*First Corinthians*, 555), "To examine oneself means to examine one's compliance with the covenant as reflected in their ways of relating to other members of the community and to discern the body of Christ must include recognizing that those other members of the community represent Christ himself (since they have also been united with him) and must be treated as people for whom Christ chose to give up his life and to shed his blood."

[143] The word translated "many" is ἱκανός. BDAG references 1 Cor 11:30 under the definition, "in relatively large numbers, many, quite a few." The word can also mean "sufficient in degree, sufficient, adequate, large enough."

[144] Ciampa and Rosner, *First Corinthians*, 556.

[145] So also Robertson and Plummer, *First Corinthians*, 254.

[146] Gk. διακρίνω.

explains, "Their 'examination' of themselves is to take the form of 'discerning' the body."[147] On the view that the word in question simply means "to judge rightly," the outcome is the same, namely, that the way to avoid God's judgment is to observe the Lord's Supper in a worthy manner. Even in judgment, however, Paul clarifies that to be judged by the Lord is to be disciplined[148] by him in order that "we will not be condemned with the world."[149] In other words, final judgment is not in view but rather a temporal punishment for disciplinary purposes.[150]

**11:33–34** In Paul's concluding remarks on the Lord's Supper he uses the verb "to come together" for the fifth time in this unit (11:17–18,20,33–34). This unit began with the assertion that their gathering together was not for the better but for the worse and gave evidence of divisions among them. Paul now concludes by instructing them to "wait for each other." Fee argues that in contexts of hospitality the meaning is "to receive," and that "Paul here is urging the wealthy to demonstrate normal Christian hospitality (cf. Rom. 12:13). They are to 'welcome' or 'receive' one another when they come together to eat."[151] Thiselton thinks, however, that the lexicographical evidence is not strong for this meaning and prefers "wait for (one another)." The verb is typically not used in the sense of receiving another person but rather of receiving something from someone. While it is certainly true that the poorer members were not to be overlooked, the situation in Corinth "was largely an outcome of the more privileged guests arriving at an earlier time and reclining in the triclinium."[152] Winter, on the other hand, offers further support for Fee's position that in the social context of a dinner, the verb means "to welcome."[153] The more recent NIV2011 avoids both "to wait for" and "to receive/welcome" and translates "you should all eat together." Clearly the emphasis is on eating in community, and the important point is that in 11:33–34 Paul offers a corrective to his sharp rebuke in 11:20–22. The advice to "eat at home" in 11:34 is parallel to the question in 11:22, "Don't you have homes to eat and drink in?" Paul's advice has to do with the focus and purpose of the meal, which is not to fill their stomachs but rather to proclaim the Lord's death.[154] To focus solely on eating with disrespect for others turns the gathering into an occasion for God's judgment, as it had already become. Paul warns them so that their gatherings might be an

---

[147] Fee, *First Corinthians*, 556.

[148] Gk. παιδεύω, "to instruct, discipline." In Paul's letters see 2 Cor 6:9; 1 Tim 1:20; 2 Tim 2:25; Titus 2:12.

[149] Two different terms are used: κρίνω (to judge) and the more intensive κατακρίνω (to condemn).

[150] Cf. Heb 12:4–10.

[151] Ibid., 568. The Greek verb is ἐκδέχομαι.

[152] Thiselton, *First Corinthians*, 899. Also Ciampa and Rosner, *First Corinthians*, 558.

[153] Winter, *After Paul Left Corinth*, 151–52. Followed by Garland, *1 Corinthians*, 555.

[154] So ibid.

occasion for profound blessing as they genuinely participate in the body and the blood of the Lord (cf. 10:16–17).

Since Paul does not elaborate on his concluding words, "And when I come I will give further directions," we cannot be sure of his reference. Perhaps there are further issues concerning the Lord's Supper that he feels can only be addressed in person. Or perhaps the reference is to other issues. We simply do not know.

### 3. The Manifestation of the Spirit for the Common Good (12:1–31)

The phrase "Now about spiritual gifts" signals the next major topic of the letter (12:1–14:40) albeit within the framework of the topic of public worship that began in 11:2. The NIV supplies the word "gifts" since the Greek has only the adjective "spiritual" in the plural, which could mean either "spiritual things" or "spiritual persons," depending on the gender of the word.[155] The HCSB omits the word "gifts" and translates more broadly, "About matters of the Spirit."[156] The more specific discussion of gifts begins in 12:4.[157] In light of the larger discussion of chaps. 12–14, it does not appear that the Corinthians posed a general question about "spiritual gifts" per se but rather that the issue had more to do with manifestations of inspired speech by local prophets or those deemed "spiritual persons." This is confirmed by Paul's conclusion in 14:37, which forms an *inclusio* with 12:1, "If anybody thinks he is a prophet or spiritually gifted, let him acknowledge that what I am writing to you is the Lord's command."[158] The phrase "spiritually gifted" translates the same word rendered "spiritual gifts" in 12:1, yet it is clearly masculine in 14:37 and means "spiritual person."[159] Thus, Paul begins and concludes the discussion with reference to "spiritual persons." In other words, in these chapters the primary concern is what it means to be "spiritual" in the context of public

[155] In Greek τῶν πνευματικῶν may be either neuter or masculine in the genitive plural. The same ambiguity between the neuter and the masculine exists in 1 Cor 2:13.

[156] Most English translations render τῶν πνευματικῶν in 12:1 as "spiritual gifts."

[157] The Greek term for gift, χάρισμα, occurs five times in chap. 12 (12:4,9,28,30–31), all in the plural, "gifts." The modifying adjective "spiritual" (πνευματικὸν) occurs with "gift" only in Rom 1:11 in the New Testament, "I long to see you so that I may impart to you some spiritual gift to make you strong." All of the occurrences of χάρισμα in the New Testament include the following additional passages Rom 5:15–16; 6:23; 11:29; 12:6; 1 Cor 1:7; 7:7; 2 Cor 1:11; 1 Tim 4:14; 2 Tim 1:6; 1 Pet 4:10.

[158] The *inclusio* is formed by two key terms. The opening in 12:1, "Now about spiritual (persons)" (περὶ δὲ τῶν πνευματικῶν) follows with "I do not want you to be ignorant" (οὐ θέλω ὑμᾶς ἀγνοεῖν). Similarly, in 14:37, Paul follows the statement regarding one who thinks he is a prophet or spiritual (πνευματικός) with, "If he ignores this, he himself will be ignored" (14:38). The verb translated "to ignore" in 14:38 is ἀγνοέω, the same verb in 12:1.

[159] Gk. πνευματικός (so the NET translation, "If anyone considers himself a prophet or spiritual person . . .).

worship.[160] Paul is not necessarily sorting out Corinthian confusion over spiritual gifts in general, but in order to address the issue of what true spirituality entails, he broadens the discussion considerably in order to clarify the role of the Spirit among all believers.[161] Therefore, before making the case for intelligible prophecy over against unintelligible tongues so that the church might be edified (14:1–40), Paul reminds the Corinthians that it is only by the Holy Spirit that believers confess Jesus as Lord in the first place (12:1–3), that all believers are gifted individually by the Spirit for the common good (12:4–31), and that love, the more excellent way, is the only proper context for the exercise of the gifts (13:1–13).[162]

As with the previous sections, Paul's discussion of things pertaining to the Spirit at this juncture in the letter is thematic. Thiselton is on target in his observation that "too many writers treat 12:1–14:40 as if it were simply an ad hoc response to questions about spiritual gifts (or spiritual persons) rather than an address to this topic within the broader theological framework of 11:2–14:40 in deliberate continuity with 8:1–11:1, and indeed ultimately with 1:1–4:21."[163] The theological underpinnings of 8:1–11:1 and 12:1–14:40 are, in fact, the same, both emphasizing the primacy of edifying love (8:1–13; 9:19–23; 10:23–33; 12:7; 13:1–13; 14:1–25) as integral to glorifying God.[164]

In 12:1–14:40 Paul continues to respond to matters concerning the church assembled for worship (11:2–34).[165] Since, however, Paul begins his discussion by reminding the Corinthians of their pagan, idolatrous past (12:2), the discussion of the Spirit's role in the church's worship connects thematically, by way of contrast, with the prior discussion of food sacrificed to idols (8:1–11:1), which had to do ultimately with the perils of idolatry (see esp. 10:14–22). Furthermore, 8:1–11:1 and 12:1–14:40 exhibit a similar pattern of argumentation, each structured around a central unit that expands on the guiding theological

---

[160] The issue of what it means to be "spiritual" has already been broached in 2:6–3:4.

[161] Fee (*First Corinthians*, 570–72) thinks the key problem in Corinth was the abuse of the gift of tongues and begins his analysis with chap. 14 since, in his view, the whole argument aims at the specific correctives in chap. 14. Fee submits that Paul's emphasis on the diversity of the gifts in the unity of the one Spirit is best understood in their singular enthusiasm for tongues.

[162] Morris (*1 Corinthians*, 163) considers Paul's discussion as "epoch-making": "In contrast to the usual idea, he was clear that the Holy Spirit comes not only on a few outstanding people, but on all believers (Rom 8:9,14). And the presence of the Spirit is to be seen characteristically in what he calls the 'fruit of the Spirit,' qualities like love, joy, peace, and so on (Gal 5:22–23), not ecstatic behavior. Here he begins by showing that it is the Lordship of Christ that is the touchstone. If the exercise of 'spiritual gifts' does not make for the Lordship of Christ, they are not from God."

[163] Thiselton, *First Corinthians*, 900.

[164] The concise statement of 8:1b sets the stage for Paul's argument for the whole of 8:1–14:40, "Knowledge puffs up, but love builds up." Paul's concern is for what is "beneficial," a term used in the slogans of 6:12 and 10:23 (Gk. συμφέρω). The adjective form (σύμφορος) appears in 10:33, "For I am not seeking my own *good* but the good of the many . . ." The same adjective recurs in 12:7, "Now to each one the manifestation of the Spirit is given for the *common good*" (emphasis added).

[165] The key term in 11:17–34, συνέρχομαι ("to come together"), appears in 14:23 and 14:26.

principle of "love for others" as the necessary demand of the gospel. In chap. 9, for example, Paul offers himself as an exemplar of giving up so-called rights as the benchmark for decision-making regarding idol food. Self-sacrifice is the essence of imitating Christ (11:1). Similarly, in chap. 13, Paul redirects the Corinthians' focus from their apparent infatuation with certain spiritual endowments to the more excellent way of love.[166]

Thiselton's observation, noted above, that 12:1–14:40 ultimately stands in deliberate continuity with 1:10–4:21 deserves further comment. The most apparent thematic link is Paul's mention of his preaching as a demonstration of the Spirit (2:5), which paves the way for his exposition of the wisdom of God as "hidden" from those who belong to this age but now revealed "to us" through the Spirit (2:6–10). The Spirit makes known the wisdom of God and reveals those things freely given by God (2:12). Man in his natural state is not able to receive the things of the Spirit of God (2:14). Only the "spiritual person" is able to properly judge all things (2:15). This revelatory role of the Spirit is Paul's first matter of emphasis in 12:1–3. No one who confesses that Jesus is Lord does so except by the Spirit (12:3). Furthermore, as noted above, the key term "spiritual (person)" opens and closes the discussion (12:1; 14:37)[167] that identifies a central issue in Corinth, namely, what it means to be "spiritual."[168] Furthermore, in connection with the identification of the church as the dwelling place of the Spirit (3:16–17), Paul employs the language and imagery of "building up" the church in relation to church leaders and God's wisdom (see esp. 3:4–15). The church as God's "building"[169] and wisely "building upon"[170] the foundation of Jesus Christ anticipates the strong emphasis on "edification" in chap. 14.[171]

---

166 Garland (*1 Corinthians*, 559) submits that there are two controlling concerns in 8:1–11:1 and 12:1–14:40: (1) the need to build up the fellow-Christian (8:7–11; 10:23; 14:1b–19) and (2) the missionary effect of the Christian conduct on unbelievers (10:23–33; 14:20–25).

167 In 1 Corinthians the adjective πνευματικός occurs fifteen times (2:13,15; 3:1; 9:11; 10:3–4; 12:1; 14:1,37; 15:44, 46). There are only nine other occurrences in the remainder of the Pauline corpus.

168 So Fee, *First Corinthians*, 573; Garland, *1 Corinthians*, 558. Fee comments that the Corinthian understanding of what it means to be "spiritual" is decidedly different from Paul's view. In 1 Cor 3:1–4 Paul reports that he is not able to speak to them as "spiritual" because of their jealousy and strife.

169 Gk. οἰκοδομή (3:9).

170 Gk. ἐποικοδομέω (3:10,12,14).

171 Gk. οἰκοδομέω (14:4,17; see also 8:1,10; 10:23) and οἰκοδομή (14:3,5,12,26; the same term used in 3:9). There are other references to the Spirit beyond the first major unit (1:10–4:21), including the "spirit" language of 5:3–5 in the judgment of the incestuous man, the reference to justification by the Spirit (6:11), the joining of believers to the Lord "as one spirit" (6:17), and the believer's body as the temple of the Holy Spirit (6:20). There is also the interesting parallel between 7:40, "and I think that I too have the Spirit of God" and 14:37, "If anybody thinks he is a prophet or spiritually gifted, let him acknowledge that what I am writing to you is the Lord's command." Apparently there were those in Corinth claiming to speak by the authority of the Spirit of God who offered interpretations of the Christian life different from Paul, thus challenging his authority.

### *(1) Confession of Jesus as Lord by the Spirit (12:1–3)*

**[1]Now about spiritual gifts, brothers, I do not want you to be ignorant. [2]You know that when you were pagans, somehow or other you were influenced and led astray to mute idols. [3]Therefore I tell you that no one who is speaking by the Spirit of God says, "Jesus be cursed," and no one can say, "Jesus is Lord," except by the Holy Spirit.**

These opening verses introduce the topic and lay the foundation for the discussion of things related to the Spirit. Since the Corinthian question most likely had to do with inspired speech in the gathered assembly, Paul opens the discussion with an emphasis on speech. No one speaking by the Spirit curses Jesus and no one says, "Jesus is Lord," except by the Spirit. This bedrock confession of all believers, which is the touchstone of all things "spiritual," stands in contrast with the pagan experience of being led astray by mute idols. As noted above, the reference to idols recalls the prior discussion of food sacrificed to idols (8:1–11:1).[172]

**12:1** As noted in the introduction to this section, the NIV translation "Now about spiritual gifts" is capable of other interpretations, such as "spiritual things/manifestations," "spiritual persons," or even "things that come from the Spirit." Although I opt for the view that the primary reference is to "spiritual persons," which may garner support in the reference to those who speak by the Spirit in 12:3, in the end there may not be a great deal of difference between "spiritual gifts" and "spiritual persons." In other words, Paul is thinking of spiritual people who exercise spiritual gifts.[173] Evidence for understanding the adjective "spiritual" as neuter, thus "spiritual things/gifts," is found in the clear use of the neuter in 14:1, which the NIV translates "eagerly desire spiritual gifts." The phrase could, however, be translated "eagerly desire the things of the Spirit," which includes the gifts, but gifts may not be the primary issue. The parallel between 12:31 and 14:1 ("eagerly desire the greater gifts" and "eagerly desire spiritual things") indicates the close relationship between the two. Since the word "gift" occurs five times in chap. 12,[174] it is possibly synonymous with "spiritual" in the present context.

Another approach to the ambiguity is that Paul is picking up on the Corinthians' use of the term "spiritual" yet filling it with his own meaning. Garland,

[172] The phrase, "I do not want you to be ignorant," occurs also in 10:1 with reference to Israel's past follies with respect to idolatry.

[173] Robertson and Plummer (*First Corinthians*, 259) take the view that the adjective is neuter, "spiritual things," but agree that the difference between "spiritual things" and "spiritual persons" is not significant. See also Barrett, *First Corinthians*, 278; Fee, *First Corinthians*, 576; Thiselton, *First Corinthians*, 910. Ciampa and Rosner (*First Corinthians*, 562) concur that Paul is dealing with issues broader than spiritual gifts in these opening verses. "Paul probably has in mind the difference between acting under the power of God's Spirit and acting under the influence of other spiritual powers (cf. Eph 6:12)."

[174] Gk. χάρισμα (12:4,9,28,30–31).

for example, prefers the translation "spiritual ones" since this captures the rhetorical setting and the flow of the argument as Paul announces the topic from the Corinthian point of view. Furthermore, this matches the reference to the "spiritual person" at the end of the discussion in 14:37, where Paul refers to the Corinthian outlook. In other words, "Paul cites the Corinthians' question about the 'spiritual ones' in the announcement of the topic and then seeks to correct their misconceptions."[175] Garland contends that the Corinthians restricted its use to denote those who gave evidence of the spiritual gifts prized by them. Paul, on the other hand, broadens the meaning to include all spiritual gifts. Paul uses their language, as in 7:1, but he does not necessarily give it the same meaning as they do.[176] Thiselton agrees and adds that while *pneumatikos* (whether in reference to persons or gifts) is the preferred Corinthian term, Paul decisively changes it to the Greek word *charismata*, 'freely given gifts, given without merit and without strings.'"[177] In the end, I favor the "spiritual person" view as the right translation and reflective of a Corinthian viewpoint that Paul corrects, especially in light of the prior use of the term in 2:6–3:4.[178]

**12:2** The grammatical challenges of this verse are well known, but the gist of what Paul intends is clear; that is, in conjunction with the following verse he contrasts the Corinthians' pagan past with their present experience of the Spirit, who enables the confession "Jesus is Lord."[179] In terms of historical context, a conventional reading of 12:3 understands Paul to refer to past experiences of ecstasy in pagan religions. In this view Paul would be warning that what happened in the past can occur again, but that ecstasy resulting in "inspired" speech is not a criterion for the working of the Holy Spirit. Others think that this reading of the text is not supported by context and grammar. Grudem claims that to read "being led astray"[180] as referring to ecstatic experience "finds no support at all in the other uses of the word."[181] Instead,

[175] Garland, *1 Corinthians*, 563.

[176] For Garland's full discussion see ibid., 561–64.

[177] Thiselton, *Shorter Commentary*, 192.

[178] The phrase "I do not want you to be ignorant" repeats the same phrase in 10:1, and may carry with it a measure of sarcasm or rebuke, namely, that Paul has to instruct those who perceive themselves to be "spiritual," that is, truly wise or knowledgable (so Blomberg, *1 Corinthians*, 243). On Paul's use of the phrase see also Rom 1:13; 11:25; 2 Cor 1:8; 1 Thess 4:13. Certainly, the endowments of the Spirit had not made the possessors morally better; in some cases the opposite was true; they had become puffed up, looking down on others (Robertson and Plummer, *First Corinthians*, 259).

[179] Morris (*1 Corinthians*, 163–64) calls this verse "ungrammatical." One solution suggests a scribal omission. Instead of ὅτε (when) we should read ποτέ (once, formerly), so that the text reads, "You know that formerly you were Gentiles, carried away . . ." Another solution, followed by most English translations, including the NIV, supplies an additional "you were" with the participle "led astray" at the end of the sentence (so Robertson and Plummer, *First Corinthians*, 259).

[180] Gk. ἀπαγόμενοι, a participle form of ἀπάγω.

[181] W. A. Grudem, *The Gift of Prophecy in 1 Corinthians* (Lanham, MD: University Press of America, 1982), 163–64.

Paul simply means "that they were under strong compulsion to attend idol temples."[182] Garland concurs, "If the verbs hint at some kind of compulsion, it need not arise from some demonic influence, but could just as well come from social pressure to participate in idol festivals."[183] Grammatically, the preposition used with "the mute idols" implies movement toward something, "to the idols," rather than being led "by them."[184] Paul merely describes their pagan past rather than insinuate that they have allowed their former pagan worship to influence their present Christian worship.[185]

**12:3** It is clear enough that one who is genuinely led by the Holy Spirit confesses, "Jesus is Lord," but Paul's prior statement that "no one who is speaking by the Spirit of God says, 'Jesus be cursed,'" has proven to be quite elusive and engendered a number of explanations.[186] Obviously, anyone cursing Jesus is not being led by the Holy Spirit, but what historical setting could possibly explain such utterance? Morris suggests that atonement theology is a possible explanation in the context of ecstatic worship, "It is not beyond the bounds of possibility that some excitable and imperfectly instructed Corinthian had distorted the thought in an ecstatic utterance."[187] Few have followed Cullmann's suggestion that both confessions reflect a setting of persecution since there is no evidence for such persecution in Corinth.[188] Fee thinks that Paul presents a purely hypothetical scenario that serves to remind the Corinthians that not all so-called inspired utterances are utterances of the Spirit.[189]

More recently, Winter has proposed yet another view that Thiselton endorses in his *Shorter Commentary* as a strong hypothesis.[190] Winter's view is based on inscriptional evidence for the fairly widespread practice of religious curse pronouncements in the Graeco-Roman world.[191] The evidence shows that religious curses were used in various areas of life, including sports, politics, love, and business. Winter suggests that in the verbless Greek phrase Jesus is subject,

---

[182] Ibid., 164.

[183] Garland, *1 Corinthians*, 565.

[184] Gk. πρός.

[185] See Garland's full discussion (*1 Corinthians*, 564–66). In support of this view and for a discussion of idol festivals, see T. Paige, "1 Corinthians 12:2: A Pagan Pompe?" *JSNT* 44 (1991): 57–65. Cf. also Collins, *First Corinthians*, 447.

[186] Thiselton (*First Corinthians*, 918–24) lists twelve different interpretations. In his follow-up *Shorter Commentary* (193) he takes up Winter's new proposal (see below) as a strong hypothesis.

[187] Morris, *1 Corinthians*, 165. That such an utterance occurred during ecstatic worship has been a popular suggestion. See also J. D. G. Dunn, *Jesus and the Spirit* (London: SCM, 1975), 234.

[188] O. Cullmann, *The Christology of the New Testament*, 2nd ed. (London: SCM, 1963), 218–20.

[189] See Fee, *First Corinthians*, 581.

[190] Thiselton, *Shorter Commentary*, 193.

[191] Winter, *After Paul Left Corinth*, 167. Winter notes that twenty-seven curse tablets have been unearthed in Corinth in recent years as a possible background understanding for 1 Cor 12:3a. Winter further notes that over one thousand examples have come to light of the widespread pagan practice of cursing others.

thus his novel translation, "Jesus grant a curse."[192] In this way, by asking Jesus to disadvantage someone for whatever reason, the Corinthians were acting like their pagan neighbors, as they had done in other areas (see 5:1–13; 6:1–11). "It suggests that like their successors in late Roman Corinth and Coptic Egypt they invoked the second person of the Godhead Jesus to curse others for the purpose of punishing or disadvantaging rivals. They appeared to have behaved no better than their pagan counterparts or subsequent generations in Corinth or Coptic Egypt."[193] Winter contends that this proposal fits the immediate context: "in some way 12:2 epitomizes popular pagan activity while the beginning of the next verse establishes the aspect of paganism to which he refers."[194] This interpretation also fits the broader discussion of 12:4–14:40, where Paul argues for the edification of the church in love. No one who is a truly spiritual person would seek to disadvantage another. As intriguing as this proposal may be, the grammatical parallelism of the two confessions seems to argue against it. In other words, the parallel to "Jesus (is) cursed" is "Jesus (is) Lord." The Greek sentence structure is the same for both.[195]

In the final analysis Garland may be correct in his assertion that all attempts to explain why believers would say, "Jesus is cursed," are dead ends and that Paul merely describes three religious experiences in these introductory verses: the pagan being led astray to dumb idols, the Jew who declares Jesus anathema, and the Christian who confesses Jesus as Lord.[196] The pronouncement, "Jesus is accursed," alludes to an appraisal of Jesus Christ by unbelieving Jews and contrasts with the indicative statement, "Jesus is Lord."[197] In terms of the discourse function of 12:1–3, Paul's point is simple. All who confess Jesus as Lord are led by the Spirit and qualify as spiritual ones. Paul "wants to affirm at the start that all of the members of the body of Christ are spiritual."[198] The key point is that the Lordship of Christ is not a human discovery. The confession "Jesus is Lord" is made with full meaning and understanding only at the prompting of the Spirit. Anyone can "say" the words "Jesus is Lord," but what Paul has in mind here is speaking with full conviction and complete personal allegiance.[199]

---

[192] Ibid., 175. Winter contends that there is every justification for translating the sentence this way in the light of the evidence of curse inscriptions that occur with no verb.

[193] Ibid., 178.

[194] Ibid., 174.

[195] Ἀνάθεμα Ἰησοῦς and Κύριος Ἰησοῦς.

[196] Garland, *1 Corinthians*, 568–71. Also C. H. Talbert, *Reading Corinthians: A Literary and Theological Commentary on 1 and 2 Corinthians* (New York: Crossroad, 1987), 81–82.

[197] See also Robertson and Plummer, *First Corinthians*, 261.

[198] Garland, *1 Corinthians*, 572.

[199] Cf. Phil 2:5–11 where Paul anticipates everyone's future confession that Jesus is Lord.

### *(2) The Distribution of Gifts by the One and the Same Spirit (12:4–11)*

**[4]There are different kinds of gifts, but the same Spirit. [5]There are different kinds of service, but the same Lord. [6]There are different kinds of working, but the same God works all of them in all men.**

**[7]Now to each one the manifestation of the Spirit is given for the common good. [8]To one there is given through the Spirit the message of wisdom, to another the message of knowledge by means of the same Spirit, [9]to another faith by the same Spirit, to another gifts of healing by that one Spirit, [10]to another miraculous powers, to another prophecy, to another distinguishing between spirits, to another speaking in different kinds of tongues, and to still another the interpretation of tongues. [11]All these are the work of one and the same Spirit, and he gives them to each one, just as he determines.**

Having established in 12:1–3 that all believers are "spiritual" by virtue of the basic Christian confession "Jesus is Lord," which is uttered in sincerity only by the Holy Spirit, Paul now describes different kinds of gifts distributed to each believer by the one and the same Spirit. The sixfold repetition of the word "same," along with the emphasis on diversity, indicates Paul's main emphasis in 12:4–11. Not all have the same gift or the same assignment in the body of Christ, yet all gifts, ministries, and empowerments derive from the same Spirit/Lord/God (12:4–6). The very notion of unity in diversity is grounded in the very nature of the one, triune God. The emphasis on God as a trinity in 12:4–6 parallels 12:1–3, which refers to the Spirit of *God*, *Jesus* as Lord, and the Holy *Spirit*.[200] Furthermore, Paul's language about God parallels his language about the Spirit. In 12:4 it is the same God who works all things in all, but in 12:11 it is the one and the same Spirit who works "all things" and distributes the gifts "as he wills." In 12:8, God places the members in the body "as he wills." The implications for the doctrine of God are hard to miss. The essence of Paul's argument in 12:4–11 is stated concisely in 12:7, "Now to each one the manifestation of the Spirit is given for the common good."

**12:4–6** The word translated "different kinds" occurs only here in the New Testament.[201] The NIV translation emphasizes varieties of gifts,[202] but the word can also mean "distributions" or "allotments," which places more emphasis on the sovereign work of the Spirit. Paul's argument in 12:4–11 supports both ideas. In favor of "varieties/different kinds" is the theme of unity and diversity that governs the passage. The different gifts proceed from the one and the same Spirit/Lord/God.[203] In favor of "allotments/distributions" is the use

---

[200] Cf. also the strong trinitarian focus of 2:6–16.

[201] Gk. διαίρεσις.

[202] So also NASB, "There are varieties of gifts."

[203] So Fee, *First Corinthians*, 586.

of the cognate verb "to apportion" in 12:11,[204] meaning that the Spirit "allots" or "apportions" the gifts as he chooses.[205]

Although the work of the Spirit in the church is clearly the main topic and "gifts" play a significant role in the discussion, Paul's language is more encompassing than "gifts" and includes the other divine persons of the Godhead. Thus, in addition to the "gifts" of the same Spirit, Paul speaks of the "services/ministries" of the same Lord and the "workings" of the same God.[206] We probably miss Paul's point if we try to distinguish between the terms or to even suggest that each person of the Godhead does different things.[207] Paul's language is fluid and the "manifestation" of the Spirit for the common good in 12:7 probably encompasses all the categories of 12:4–6. The more important theological point is that the rich variety of the allotted gifts reflects the very nature of God himself and that it is the "same" Spirit/God/Lord who distributes the gifts, workings, and services in the church.[208] Paul intends to broaden the Corinthians' understanding of what it means to be "spiritual." We, too, would fare well to include a more wide-ranging terminology in our contemporary discussions of spiritual gifts with a more rigorous trinitarian focus that includes not only the person of the Holy Spirit but also the Lordship of Christ (12:3) and God who works all in all (cf. 8:6; 15:28).

**12:7–11** I concur with Fee's observation that 12:7 is the thesis statement for the entire chapter, "Now to each one the manifestation of the Spirit is given for the common good."[209] First Corinthians 12:8–10 develops the idea that "to each one is given," and 12:12–26 develops the idea "for the common good."[210] As noted in the introductory comments, the purpose of the gifts "for the common good" links Paul's discussion to his prior discussion of food sacrificed to idols and the guiding theological principle of behavior that aims for the benefit and edification of others.[211] Morris correctly observes, "Spiritual gifts are always given to be used, and to be used in such a way as to edify the whole

---

[204] Gk. διαιρέω.

[205] BDAG favors this interpretation. Barrett (*First Corinthians*, 283) prefers to translate 12:4, "There are distributions of gifts." Garland (*1 Corinthians*, 575) notes that most interpreters go with "allotments" or "distributions" in 12:4–6 because of the cognate verb in 12:11.

[206] The Greek terms, all in the plural, are χαρισμάτων (gifts), διακονιῶν (services/ministries), and ἐνεργημάτων (workings, operations).

[207] E.g., the Spirit gives the gifts, service is unto the Lord, and God effects everything. In 12:10 a manifestation of the Spirit is "workings of powers," and in 12:11 the Spirit "works all things." Thus "to work"/"workings" is used in reference to both God and the Spirit.

[208] Paul argues similarly in 11:2–16 that the relationship of husbands and wives reflects the relation of God to Christ and is grounded in the created order.

[209] In Greek, an objective genitive, that is, the Spirit is manifest/made known/disclosed.

[210] Fee, *First Corinthians*, 588; Garland, *1 Corinthians*, 577.

[211] See 10:23–24,31–33 and the use of the verb συμφέρω (to benefit) and σύμφορος (good). In 12:7, the "common good" is the participle form of the verb συμφέρω.

body of believers, not some individual possessor of a gift. A schismatic individualism contradicts the purpose of the gifts."[212]

The manifestation of the Spirit is given not only for the common good but also to "each one," which Paul takes up in 12:8–11. Different lists appear elsewhere (see 12:18; 13:1–3; Rom 12:6–8; Eph 4:11–12). The only gift occurring in all lists is the gift of prophecy, which means that the lists in 1 Cor 12:8–11,28 are not comprehensive, only sufficiently representative of all the gifts. In the letter's introduction Paul thanked God that they did not lack any spiritual gift (1:7). If by this statement Paul infers that the Corinthians had the full complement of gifts, then the list here must be only representative of those gifts operative in the church at Corinth. Paul's purpose, in this context, is not to list all the gifts, nor to define the gifts. The nature of the gifts would have been sufficiently clear to the Corinthians. Paul's concern lies elsewhere, namely, to emphasize that the manifestation of the Spirit "to each one" is "the work of one and the same Spirit" (12:11). Paul's aim is not to establish a hierarchy of gifts but to insist that all gifts come from the same source and are thus given to achieve a unified purpose.[213] In 12:8–11 Paul lists nine gifts as a manifestation of the Spirit: (1) a word of wisdom, (2) a word of knowledge, (3) faith, (4) gifts of healings, (5) working of powers, (6) prophecies, (7) distinguishing of spirits, (8) kinds of tongues and (9) the interpretation of tongues.[214] Five of the nine gifts listed involve speech.

In listing the gifts as the manifestation of the Spirit "to each one," Paul uses two different Greek words, both translated "to another."[215] Following the introductory "to one" is given a word of wisdom, the following pattern ensues: to another (*allos*) a word of knowledge, to another (*heteros*) faith, then four occurrences of *allos* (gifts of healings, workings of powers, prophecy, discerning of spirits), followed by *heteros* (kinds of tongues) and *allos* (interpretation of tongues). It is difficult to know if the reason for the vacillation is merely stylistic or if Paul intends to divide the gifts into different classes. Robertson and Plummer suspect the latter is the case,[216] but since the vacillation between *allos* and *heteros* is not uniform, and *heteros* occurs roughly at the beginning and the end, it is not certain how the distinction would clearly demarcate differ-

[212] Morris, *1 Corinthians*, 166–67.

[213] Barrett, *First Corinthians*, 286; Garland, *1 Corinthians*, 580–81.

[214] On the nature of the gifts Robertson and Plummer (*First Corinthians*, 257) comment, "The phenomena which are described, or sometimes only alluded to, were to a large extent abnormal and transitory. They were not part of the regular development of the Christian Church. Even in Chrysostom's time there was so much ignorance about them as to cause perplexity."

[215] Gk. ἄλλος and ἕτερος. The predominant word is ἄλλος. ἕτερος occurs twice, with "faith" (12:9) and "tongues" (12:10).

[216] Robertson and Plummer, *First Corinthians*, 265. Garland (*1 Corinthians*, 574) suggests three divisions: two speech gifts (word of wisdom and word of knowledge), a sampling of five gifts, and then two more speech gifts (tongues and the interpretation of tongues). The gift of prophecy, however, another speech gift, is among the sampling of five gifts.

ent classes of gifts. It seems more likely that the reason may be stylistic since Paul varies his language concerning the Spirit as well. For example, the word of wisdom is given "through the Spirit," the word of knowledge "according to the same Spirit," and faith "by the same Spirit."[217] If there is any sort of classification of gifts intended, it would seem that there are four groups: (1) word of wisdom and word of knowledge, both speech gifts; (2) faith, gifts of healing, and miraculous powers; (3) prophecy and distinguishing between spirits, and (4) tongues and the interpretation of tongues.

The first two manifestations of the Spirit, a word of wisdom and knowledge, held particular importance for the Corinthian congregation. The distinction between the two is not clear, but both were problems for the Corinthians and both were speech gifts. A "word of wisdom" is the exact opposite of the phrase "wisdom of word" in 1:17, which denoted clever human speech that emptied the cross of Christ. In 12:8 the phrase "word of wisdom" denotes a gift of speech that proceeds from genuine wisdom as a special endowment of the Spirit. Since Paul distinguishes a "word of wisdom" given to one and a "word of knowledge" given to another, the implication is that Paul speaks of a special measure of wisdom and knowledge that is not the possession of all believers, but rather a particular manifestation of the Spirit to certain individuals for the benefit of the whole. In 1:5 Paul pairs "speech" (word) and "knowledge" in commenting on the Corinthians' enrichment in these graces, but "knowledge" takes up an especially negative tone in chap. 8 (8:1,7,10–11). In 12:8, "word" and "knowledge" are combined, thus a "word of knowledge."

The gift of faith is to be distinguished from faith as a possession of all believers that brings one into relationship with God (12:3). Paul must have in mind a particular kind of faith that believes God for extraordinary things, or a faith that guides the church through exceptional circumstances (1 Cor 13:1–3). If Paul has intentionally categorized the gifts, then there may be some relationship between the gift of faith and gifts of healings and miraculous powers that immediately follow. Since Paul does not elaborate on "healings" and "miraculous powers," both in the plural, we are left with a certain amount of ambiguity regarding the particular manifestation of these gifts. The translation "miraculous powers" probably conveys something to the contemporary reader that is foreign to Paul's meaning here. In Greek the phrase is the "workings of powers."[218] In 12:6 Paul writes of the different kinds of "workings" but the same God who "works" all things in all. "Power" was a key term in Paul's argument in 1:17–4:21. The message of Christ crucified is the "power" of God (1:18,24), Paul's preaching was a demonstration of the Spirit and "power" (2:4–5), and the kingdom of God does not consist in mere speech but

---

[217] Different Greek prepositions occur with each phrase: *διὰ τοῦ πνεύματος*, *κατὰ τὸ αὐτὸ πνεῦμα*, and *ἐν τῷ αὐτῷ πνεύματι*.

[218] Gk. *ἐνεργήματα δυνάμεων*.

in "power" (4:19–20). Paul uses similar language regarding the Spirit and the working of power in Gal 3:5. Whatever historical manifestation these "miraculous powers" (NIV) might have taken, the end result of such gifts would have been the edification of the church as a whole and the confirmation of one's faith in God rather than in the wisdom of men (cf. 2:4–5).

Of the remaining gifts listed in 12:10 (prophecy, distinguishing between spirits, speaking in different kinds of tongues, and the interpretation of tongues) Paul devotes the bulk of his argument in chap. 14 to the gift of tongues and the interpretation of tongues in relation to prophecy, describing how each gift functions and the value of each for the edification of the church, which is the primary point (12:7).[219] Prophecy edifies but uninterpreted tongues do not (14:1–5). Defining prophecy and tongues has turned out to be quite the challenge in scholarship.[220] Grudem thinks that Paul defines prophecy rather broadly and that its function "could include any kind of speech activity that would be helpful to the hearers."[221] Fee asserts that Paul's description of prophecy indicates "spontaneous, Spirit-inspired, intelligible messages, orally delivered in the gathered assembly, intended for the edification or encouragement of the people."[222] Thiselton questions, however, whether or not all manifestations of prophecy reflect this pattern, and submits that prophecy does not necessarily exclude teaching and doctrine (14:3,31). Prophecy, in Thiselton's view, is the near equivalent of pastoral preaching.[223] After a lengthy survey of options he defines prophecy as a gift of the Spirit that "combines pastoral insight into the needs of persons, communities, and situations with the ability to address these with a God-given utterance or longer discourse (whether unprompted or prepared with judgment, decision, and rational reflection) leading to challenge or comfort, judgment, or consolation, but ultimately building up the addressees."[224] Schreiner defines prophecy more simply as "communicating revelations from

[219] "Discerning" of spirits may be related to prophecy in a way similar to the relation between interpretation of tongues and tongues (cf. 14:29). So also Ciampa and Rosner, *First Corinthians*, 581–82.

[220] On the nature of the gift of prophecy the literature is vast. For representative studies see E. E. Ellis, *Prophecy and Hermeneutic in Early Christianity* (Grand Rapids: Eerdmans, 1978); Grudem, *Gift of Prophecy*; D. E. Aune, *Prophecy in Early Christianity and the Ancient Mediterranean World* (Grand Rapids: Eerdmans, 1983); C. Forbes, *Prophecy and Inspired Speech in Early Christianity and Its Hellenistic Environment*, WUNT 75 (Tübingen: Mohr, 1995). First Corinthians 12–14 provide the best clues to Paul's own understanding of prophecy, although the data is limited since the argument has to do with the contrast between prophecy and tongues. The word "prophecy" (προφητεία) occurs elsewhere in Paul in Rom 12:6; 1 Thess 5:20; 1 Tim 1:18; 4:14. The verb form "to prophesy" (προφητεύω) occurs only in 1 Corinthians (11:4–5; 13:9; 14:1,3–5,24,31,39). On Paul's reference to "prophets" outside of 1 Corinthians (12:28–29; 14:29,32,37), see especially Eph 2:20; 3:5; 4:11.

[221] Grudem, *Gift of Prophecy*, 229.

[222] Fee, *First Corinthians*, 595.

[223] Thiselton, *First Corinthians*, 956–65. So also Garland, *1 Corinthians*, 582–83.

[224] Thiselton, *First Corinthians*, 964.

God in a spontaneous utterance."[225] Commentators often note the spontaneous nature of prophecy based on Paul's description in 14:29–33,[226] but Schreiner stresses the revelatory nature of the gift as well in light of 14:6,30 and a few examples in Acts where Luke reports that prophets received spontaneous revelations from God (Acts 11:28; 13:1–3; 21:10–11). Against Grudem, Schreiner contends that the New Testament prophets, like the apostles, spoke the word of the Lord accurately without error.[227] Similarly, Ciampa and Rosner comment, "At the very end of chap. 14 Paul seems to indicate that the argument he has just completed is to be understood as a prophetic message, carrying the authority of Christ himself, and that such an understanding will be confirmed by any true prophets that the Corinthians have in their midst (14:37)."[228] Paul claims that what he writes "is the Lord's command." In the end, defining the nature of prophecy (and tongues) is not Paul's primary task. Rather, his concern is for the edification of the church, which is the purpose of all the gifts.

Regarding tongues, the key question in scholarship has been the nature of the gift. Forbes sets forth five established views and the support for each:[229] (1) Tongues is the miraculous ability to speak unlearned human languages; (2) tongues is the miraculous ability to speak heavenly or angelic languages; (3) the gift of tongues is some combination of the two; (4) tongues is something analogous to but not identical with speech, that is, speaking in tongues is language-like but unstructured and inarticulate yet capable of conveying meaning; and (5) Paul conceived of tongues as a peculiar dialect of prayer dominated by archaic and foreign terms.[230]

The basic meaning of the word translated "tongue"[231] is "language."[232] Whether referring to a known human language or something else as described above, the biblical data suggests that a tongue is nonetheless a language, capable of either being understood immediately by the hearers (Acts 2:4–11) or capable of interpretation (1 Cor 12:10; 14:5,13). Paul insists that tongues must be interpreted in order for edification to occur (14:13–19,28). The gift of

---

[225] T. R. Schreiner, *Paul, Apostle of God's Glory in Christ: A Pauline Theology* (Downers Grove: InterVarsity, 2001), 360.

[226] Note esp. 14:30, "And if a revelation comes to someone who is sitting down, the first speaker should stop."

[227] Ibid., 361–63. Schreiner contends that the evaluation of prophecies (14:29; also 1 Thess 5:19–22) in the New Testament "is no different from the Old Testament standard because the legitimacy of the prophet was discerned by the accuracy of the prophecies (Deut 18:20–22)," *Paul*, 363.

[228] Ciampa and Rosner, *First Corinthians*, 581.

[229] Forbes, *Prophecy and Inspired Speech*, 57–72. See also the survey in Thiselton, *First Corinthians*, 970–88.

[230] As an example Forbes (*Prophecy and Inspired Speech*, 58) suggests that this view would "perhaps make glossolalia an extreme first century equivalent of praying in 'King James English.'"

[231] Gk. *γλῶσσα*.

[232] The HCSB translation renders *γλῶσσα* as "language" throughout; e.g. in 12:10, "to another, different kinds of languages, to another, interpretation of languages."

tongues occurs in all of the gift lists in 1 Corinthians but is mentioned nowhere else in the other Pauline letters. This does not necessarily imply that the gift was not present in other churches, but it does suggest that it was a problem in Corinth.

The gift of tongues is mentioned in three places in the book of Acts. In Acts 2:4–11, the apostles spoke in tongues under the inspiration of the Holy Spirit (2:4), declaring the wonders of God (2:11), and were understood by those present in their native languages (dialects). Clearly the gift of tongues at Pentecost was inspired speech exalting God in known human languages.[233] In Acts 10:44–48 Gentiles also spoke in tongues exalting God, "For they heard them speaking in tongues and praising God" (Acts 10:46). The gift was recognized by Jewish believers as the same gift of Pentecost, "Then Peter said, 'Can anyone keep these people from being baptized with water? They have received the Holy Spirit just as we have'" (Acts 10:46b–47). In Acts 19:1–7, the gift of tongues accompanied the reception of the Spirit of the disciples of John the Baptist, but the content of the tongues in Acts 19 is left unstated.[234]

In 1 Corinthians Paul recognizes tongues as a gift of the Spirit (12:10).[235] Paul is clear that not all speak in tongues (12:30) and that prophecy is preferable to uninterpreted tongues since only intelligible speech edifies the church (14:1–40). Like other gifts, tongues is a manifestation of the Spirit given for the common good, that is, for the benefit of the church (12:7). Although given to individuals, the gift of tongues, like all the gifts, is corporate in focus and function. In chap. 14, the most extensive discussion of tongues in the New Testament, Paul makes the following statements concerning the nature of the gift. (1) The one who speaks in a tongue (language) speaks to God and not to men. No one understands since he speaks mysteries "in spirit," which means either "in (with) his spirit" or "in (by) the Spirit" (14:2).[236] (2) The one who speaks in a tongue edifies himself, but the one who prophesies edifies the church (14:4). The context suggests that we should understand Paul to be saying that

[233] It is sometimes suggested that the gift was a gift of hearing in Acts 2 rather than speaking since emphasis falls on what was heard: "each one heard them speaking in his own language" (2:6); "Then how is it that each of us hears them in his own native language?" (2:8); "we hear them declaring the wonders of God in our own tongues!" (2:11). This view, however, is doubtful since tongues is a speech gift.

[234] Tongues is mentioned also in Mark 16:17 but with no further information about the nature of the gift, only "they will speak in new tongues."

[235] Paul's argument does not presume that the Corinthians were practicing a counterfeit gift of tongues, only an inadequate expression of the gift when uninterpreted. Paul concludes the argument, "Therefore, my brothers, be eager to prophesy, and do not forbid speaking in tongues" (14:39).

[236] Cf. the difference between the NIV, "with his spirit," and the HCSB, "in the Spirit." In Acts we may also possibly conceive of tongues as speech to God, that is, "declaring the wonders of God" (2:11) and "praising God" (10:46). The difference, however, is that the hearers understood what was being said in Acts. In 1 Corinthians, "no one understands" (14:2). The implication is that no one (but God) understands.

the one who speaks in an "uninterpreted" tongue edifies only himself since no one else understands what is being said (14:2). In other words, if someone speaks an unknown language and there is no interpretation of the language for the benefit of others, then only the tongues-speaker is edified. It is a mistake, in my view, to read Paul's statement in 14:4 in isolation of the context as a stand alone commendation of private tongues-speaking for personal edification. Not only does this contradict the corporate function of the gift (12:7); it is counter to Paul's consistent emphasis from 8:1–14:40 on the edification of others (see esp. 14:1–5,12,17,26).[237] (3) Although Paul recognizes the legitimacy of the gift of tongues (14:5,39), he contends that apart from interpretation it is of no value to the church (14:1–19) and especially detrimental to unbelievers (14:20–25). (4) Tongues may be expressed in prayer and song in the corporate worship setting if accompanied by interpretation (14:13–19).[238]

### *(3) One Body, Many Members (12:12–31)*

**12The body is a unit, though it is made up of many parts; and though all its**
**parts are many, they form one body. So it is with Christ. 13For we were all baptized**
**by one Spirit into one body—whether Jews or Greeks, slave or free—and we were all given the one Spirit to drink.**

**14Now the body is not made up of one part but of many. 15If the foot should**
**say, "Because I am not a hand, I do not belong to the body," it would not for that**
**reason cease to be part of the body. 16And if the ear should say, "Because I am not**
**an eye, I do not belong to the body," it would not for that reason cease to be part of**
**the body. 17If the whole body were an eye, where would the sense of hearing be? If**
**the whole body were an ear, where would the sense of smell be? 18But in fact God**
**has arranged the parts in the body, every one of them, just as he wanted them to**
**be. 19If they were all one part, where would the body be? 20As it is, there are many**
**parts, but one body.**

**21The eye cannot say to the hand, "I don't need you!" And the head cannot say**
**to the feet, "I don't need you!" 22On the contrary, those parts of the body that seem**
**to be weaker are indispensable, 23and the parts that we think are less honorable**
**we treat with special honor. And the parts that are unpresentable are treated with**
**special modesty, 24while our presentable parts need no special treatment. But God**
**has combined the members of the body and has given greater honor to the parts**
**that lacked it, 25so that there should be no division in the body, but that its parts**
**should have equal concern for each other. 26If one part suffers, every part suffers**
**with it; if one part is honored, every part rejoices with it.**

**27Now you are the body of Christ, and each one of you is a part of it. 28And in**
**the church God has appointed first of all apostles, second prophets, third teachers, then workers of miracles, also those having gifts of healing, those able to help others, those with gifts of administration, and those speaking in different kinds**
**of tongues. 29Are all apostles? Are all prophets? Are all teachers? Do all work**

237 See the full discussion on 14:1–5.

238 Note the mention of both prophecy and prayer in 11:4–5 as expressions of speech in the corporate setting.

**miracles? 30Do all have gifts of healing? Do all speak in tongues? Do all interpret?**
**31But eagerly desire the greater gifts.**
**And now I will show you the most excellent way.**

The remainder of chap. 12 expands on the unity and diversity theme of 12:4–11 under the concept of the church as the one body of Christ composed of many members. The fourfold repetition of the motif of "the one and the many" drives home the point emphatically (12:12,14,20,27).[239] Furthermore, the emphasis on the one Spirit in 12:12–14 and the repetition of God's sovereign arrangement of the body (12:18,28) ties this section explicitly to the concluding statement in 12:11, "All these are the work of one and the same Spirit, and he gives them to each one, just as he determines."[240] Structurally, this section divides into three units (12:12–14,15–27,28–31).[241]

The first unit (12:12–14) introduces the main theme of one body with many parts as analogous to the church, which consists of all believers who have been immersed in one Spirit into the body of Christ. There is only one Spirit and one body, yet the one body has many members. To state it another way, the body is *one*, yet the body is not *one member*. That Paul intends an analogy of church to the human body is clear (12:12,14–27),[242] but that he also asserts more than analogy is equally clear. In other words, there is both analogy and ontological reality involved in Paul's argument; that is, the analogy of the body is an apt

239 12:12, "The body is a unit, though it is made up of many parts; and though all its parts are many, they form one body. 12:14, "Now the body is not made up of one part but of many." 12:20, "As it is, there are many parts, but one body." 12:27, "Now you are the body of Christ, and each one of you is a part of it." Thus, 12:12–27 develops the concept of "oneness" that concluded 12:4–11, "All these are the work of one and the same Spirit" (12:11).

240 Thus, just as Paul speaks of God as "the one who works all things in all" (12:6) and the Spirit "who works all things" (12:11), he also speaks of the Spirit who distributes "as he wills" (12:11) and God who arranges the body "as he pleases" (12:18).

241 Garland (*1 Corinthians*, 589) proposes a four-part argument arranged in a chiasm: A—12:12–14, The body as one but with many members; B—12:15–20, Inescapable diversity of members within the body; B'—12:21–26, Inescapable interdependence of members of the body; A'—12:27–31, Differing functions within the body. Taking into account the previous unit, another possible chiastic arrangement might be: A—12:4–11, The sovereign distribution of the gifts by the one Spirit; B—The constitution of the one body by the one Spirit; B'—12:15–27, One body, many members; A'—12:28–31—God's sovereign arrangement of the body.

242 Mitchell (*Rhetoric of Reconciliation*, 157) notes that New Testament scholars have long acknowledged "that the metaphor of the body for the society or state was extremely common in ancient political literature, and must have influenced Paul's Christian formulation of it in 1 Cor 12." For Mitchell's full discussion see 157–64, 268–69. Collins (*First Corinthians*, 460) points out, however, that Paul's use of the metaphor was different from the classical topos; "Paul attributes the diversity of the various members of the body and the order among them to God rather than to nature," and "Paul used the metaphor to urge all members to utilize their gifts for the common good (12:7; cf. Rom 12:3–8) rather than to urge the subordination of some members to others for the good of the whole. He employed the image to advocate the interdependence of all bodily members (vv. 21,25–26)." Commentators routinely cite the speech of Menenius Agrippa as one of the best known examples of the use of the body image to exhort the Roman populace to stop their revolt against the state and to submit to the aristocracy (see Livy, *History of Rome*, 2.32.7–33.1).

metaphor of the reality that the church is the body of Christ constituted by the Spirit (12:27). Believers are immersed by/in one Spirit into one body (12:13). Believers are, in fact, the body of Christ (12:27). This is not Paul's first use of "body" language in the letter to describe the corporate realities of believers in relation to Christ, to other believers, and to others. In his discussion of sexual immorality in 6:12–20, Paul predicated his argument on the fact that the believer's body is a member of Christ and joining one's body to a prostitute constitutes "one body" that is wholly incompatible for those who are "one spirit" with the Lord (6:15–17). In the same chapter Paul exhorted the Corinthians to glorify God in their bodies since their bodies were a temple of the Holy Spirit and belonged to God (6:19–20). In the exhortation to flee idolatry (10:14–22) Paul reminded them of their participation in the body and the blood of Christ in the Lord's meal (10:16) and of the fact that "we who are many are one body" (10:17). Similarly Paul warned those who were mistreating other believers at the Lord's Supper that they were guilty of the body and the blood of the Lord (11:27) and that such behavior incurs judgment to oneself for not properly discerning the body (11:29).[243] None of these passages in chaps. 6; 10; and 11 employ body language as analogy but rather speak of actualities.[244]

The second unit, 12:15–27, comprised of two paragraphs (12:15–20,21–27) each employing the classical rhetorical device of personification ("If the foot should say," "If the hand should say," etc.), takes up the analogy of the body in order to underscore the main theme of the unity of the one body with many members while at the same time making a number of complementary points. In both paragraphs Paul emphasizes God's wise and sovereign arrangement of the body. God has arranged the body as he pleased (12:18), and he has combined the parts of the body for the purpose of unity and mutual concern of members of the body for one another (12:25). Both units end with parallel conclusions that restate the basic premise of 12:12–14: 12:20, "As it is, there are many

[243] For other texts that use "body" language in Paul, see Rom 6:6,12; 7:4,24; 8:10–13,23. Paul's language in Rom 12:4–6 is especially close to the language of 1 Cor 12:12–14, "Just as each of us has one body with many members, and these members do not all have the same function, so in Christ we who are many form one body, and each member belongs to all the others."

[244] Barrett (*First Corinthians*, 287–92) argues that Christ is eternally distinct from the church, that he rules over it as Lord of the church. Paul is not saying that the church is a body, which is Christ, but rather that the church is a body that belongs to Christ (genitive of possession). Fee (*First Corinthians*, 602n13) thinks that Paul's use of the body is "metaphor, pure and simple, whose point is not the nature of the church per se but the need for it to experience its proper diversity in unity." See also Garland, *1 Corinthians*, 593. It may be that analogy is the primary point in this context, and the body metaphor might function only as analogy if not for Paul's prior "body" language in 1 Corinthians (cf. also Eph 5:25–32, where following the quote of Gen 2:24, "the two will become one flesh," Paul asserts, "This is a profound mystery—but I am talking about Christ and the church"). Ciampa and Rosner (*First Corinthians*, 590–91) note that 12:13 "points to a theological justification (rather than a merely pragmatic one) for the use of the body analogy, and suggests that the comparison is a proper one due to real ontological parallels between the nature of the human body and the nature of the church."

parts, but one body," and 12:27, "Now you are the body of Christ, and each one of you is a part of it."[245] A proper understanding of both paragraphs proceeds not only upon the self-evident applications derived from the body imagery but also in light of the fact that Paul has the Corinthian church in mind.[246]

The last unit (12:28–31) reprises 12:4–11, calling attention yet again to God's sovereign arrangement of the body, which is explicitly identified as the church (12:28; cf. 12:18,24).[247] In a surprising twist, this last unit introduces the idea of priority ("And in the church God has appointed first of all apostles, second prophets, third teachers," etc.), and concludes with the exhortation to "eagerly desire the greater gifts." The notion of what is "greater" or "more beneficial" prepares the way for the emphasis on the priority of love in chap. 13.

**12:12–14** These verses continue the thought of 12:4–11 under the notion of "oneness," as seen in the six occurrences of the word "one" in 12:12–14. Just as the previous unit stressed both the concept of "sameness" (the same Spirit, Lord, and God, 12:4–6) and diversity in the distribution of gifts (12:7–11), 12:12–14 emphasizes the "one" body that has many members. Unity and diversity are equally emphasized. The unit itself is a chiasm with parallel statements at 12:12 and 12:14: the body is "one" but it has many members, yet all the members constitute only "one" body. The repetition reinforces the essential point of the metaphor.[248] It is commonly noted that "Christ" in 12:12 is shorthand for the church as the body of Christ in light of the parallelism with 12:27, "You are the body of Christ."[249] Since this is the case, Christ may be said to be a body with many members.[250] Already Paul has argued in 6:15 that believers are "members of Christ."

---

[245] In my view 12:27 is transitional, belonging both to what precedes and follows.

[246] Ciampa and Rosner (*First Corinthians*, 589) submit that 12:15–20 approaches the subject from the perspective of those who perceive themselves to be inferior, while 12:21–26 approaches the subject from the perspective of those who perceive themselves to be superior, contra Fee (*First Corinthians*, 610–11) who thinks that Paul's point in 12:15–20 is "not the inferiority of one to another but the need for all members; otherwise some function of the body would be missing." Ciampa and Rosner (*First Corinthians*, 599) counter, "But he (Fee) has no explanation for why one body part would say something like what is attributed to the foot or the ear. He simply observes that those statements (of the foot and ear) are 'obviously absurd.' This seems to unnecessarily divorce this text from its context and to dismiss a logical inference. The ear feels that it would be part of the body if it were an eye and the foot feels the same about the hand." Paul's statements demonstrate that he is concerned with the way things are: each member of the body is essential, each has its own function, and each has been assigned its place by God.

[247] The only occurrence of the term ἐκκλησία in the chapter.

[248] The NIV translates the Greek conjunction καί as "though." Fee (*First Corinthians*, 600–601) thinks this is incorrect. Paul's concern is not that the body is one even though it has many members but rather "that *even though the body is one*, it does not consist of one member but many, thus arguing for their need for diversity, since they are in fact one body." See NIV2011.

[249] Fee, *First Corinthians*, 603; Garland, *1 Corinthians*, 590; Ciampa and Rosner, *First Corinthians*, 590.

[250] Vaughan and Lea, *1 Corinthians*, 130.

The mention of baptism "in/by" the Spirit in 12:13 follows closely on the heels of 12:12. The explanatory "for"[251] indicates how it is that the Corinthian believers have become one body.[252] It is possible to read the prepositional phrase "into one body" in terms of the result or goal of the immersion in the Spirit, that is, believers were baptized in one Spirit so as to become one body.[253]

The NIV translation "by one Spirit" indicates agency and could imply that the Spirit is the baptizer. However, as Fee points out, nowhere in the New Testament does this dative with "baptize" imply agency and that the Spirit does the baptizing. Rather, the phrase is locative, expressing the element in which they were all immersed. "In one Spirit" denotes the sphere of the action, not the agency.[254] The parallel phrase "all were made to drink of one Spirit" describes the same experience under a different figure.[255] The baptism here should not be equated with water baptism, although water baptism depicts what Paul describes. Paul's emphasis on baptism into one body in one Spirit strongly emphasizes the unity of the body.[256] The phrase baptize in/by the Spirit occurs seven times in the New Testament. All of the other six uses refer to John the Baptist's prophecy that Jesus would baptize with or in the Holy Spirit (Matt 3:11; Mark 1:8; Luke 3:16; John 1:33; Acts 1:5; 11:16). Blomberg contends that Acts 1:5 clarifies that this was fulfilled at Pentecost. Paul has in mind an initiation experience that immerses one in the realm of the Spirit, which is the experience of all believers (cf. Rom 8:9).[257]

**12:15–20** In 12:15–20 Paul makes three self-evident observations about the individual members of the body.[258] First, each member of the body is equally a part of the body. The rhetorical device of personification ("If the foot should say . . . ," "If the ear should say . . .") allows Paul to portray more vividly the envy that one Corinthian believer might have for another or the sense of being an "outsider" instead of an integral part of the church. Just because

---

[251] Gk. γάρ.

[252] Paul includes himself in the formula, "*We all* were baptized . . ."

[253] Barrett, *First Corinthians*, 288. So also Fee, *First Corinthians*, 605–6; Garland, *1 Corinthians*, 592.

[254] Fee, *First Corinthians*, 605–6. So also Vaughan and Lea, *1 Corinthians*, 130–31. D. B. Wallace (*Greek Grammar Beyond the Basics: An Exegetical Syntax of the New Testament* [Grand Rapids: Zondervan, 1996], 374) argues for an instrumental dative, "by one Spirit," but in the sense that the Holy Spirit is the instrument Christ uses to baptize.

[255] So also Fee, *First Corinthians*, 604–5. Garland (*1 Corinthians*, 591) notes that "Whatever the specifics of Paul's analogy, the point is that the Spirit saturates the church body and that all Christians are imbued with the same Spirit." Paul's point is clear, namely, "that every Christian has been made part of one body and immersed in (or by) the Spirit."

[256] Recall Paul's opening argument for unity in 1:10–17 and the absurdity of being baptized in the name of anyone other than Christ (1:13b–16).

[257] Blomberg, *1 Corinthians*, 252.

[258] English translations punctuate 12:15 as a statement whereas the Greek New Testament punctuates as a rhetorical question (so KJV, "Is it therefore not of the body?"). The difference is not significant to the meaning of the verse.

the foot is not a hand or an ear is not an eye does not mean that either is any less a member of the body (12:15–16). There is no insignificant, unimportant, or inconsequential member of the body. Garland explains, "The failure of one little valve can shut down the whole bodily system. The implication is that there is no unimportant gift or person in the body of Christ."[259]

Second, each part of the body has its own unique function. The logic of 12:17 is intuitive and simple. "If the whole body were an eye, where would the sense of hearing be? If the whole body were an ear, where would the sense of smell be?" The corollary point is that there is no such thing as a body that is only one part, expressed in the question of 12:19, "If they were all one part, where would the body be?" In other words, if the whole body were only one part, then not only are other vital functions missing, there is no body at all, only a body part. Garland suggests that the "application may or not have been obvious to the Corinthians. A church full of only glossolalists would be no less freakish."[260]

Third, the one body of many parts is by God's sovereign design (12:18). "The hypothesis and the analogy is over and done with: now for realities as God has arranged them."[261] Paul is careful to stress that God placed "each one" of the members in the body "just as he wanted them to be."[262] Each member of the body has its own function according to God's design. The emphasis on "each one" and the placement of the members in the body according to God's pleasure builds up the main point of 12:4–11 that describes the manifestation of the Spirit "to each one" (12:7), the distribution of gifts "to one" and "to another" (12:8–10), and the allotment of gifts of the Spirit "just as he determines" (12:11). This third point is perhaps Paul's chief point, since he not only restates the essence of 12:4–11 but will do so again in 12:24 and 12:28.[263] Paul concludes the first part of his elaboration on the body with a reprise of the essential point of 12:12–14, "If they were all one part, where would the body be? As it is, there are many parts, but one body" (12:19–20).

**12:21–27** In 12:21–27 the personification of body parts continues in order to make a different point. Here the main consideration is the need that members of the body have for one another with an emphasis on the weaker, less honorable, and unpresentable members of the body. The shameful treatment of the poor at the Lord's Supper by the more distinguished and honorable members of

---

[259] Garland, *1 Corinthians*, 594.

[260] Ibid., 595.

[261] Thiselton, *First Corinthians*, 1003. 12:18 translates the Greek νυνὶ δὲ, "But in fact." BDAG places 1 Cor 12:18 under the definition, "introducing the real situation after an unreal conditional clause or sentence *but, as a matter of fact*."

[262] Gk. "Just as he pleased."

[263] Thiselton (*First Corinthians*, 1004) is on target in his comment, "To try to rank some gifts as 'more essential' than others, let alone as necessary marks of advanced status to which all should aspire, is to offer a blasphemous challenge to God's freedom to choose whatever is his good will for his people both collectively and individually."

the church (11:17–34; esp. 11:22) is undoubtedly in the background and aptly illustrates the necessity of this particular application of the body image.

In 12:21–27 Paul makes four key assertions. First, the members of the body need one another (12:21), "The eye cannot say to the hand, 'I don't need you!' And the head cannot say to the feet, 'I don't need you!'" Paul changes the image from the previous paragraph a bit by having one of the sensory organs (eye) speak to one of the external limbs (hand) and replaces the ear with the head that speaks to the feet. Most commentators suggest that the new pairings reflect the hierarchical attitudes of some Corinthians. The head and the eye are obvious metaphors for the supposed higher status members of the church who viewed themselves to be of greater value than others.[264]

Second, the weaker members are indispensable (12:22).[265] The verse opens with a strong adversative statement, "On the contrary."[266] In other words, in stark contrast to the attitude that one body part has no need of the other, what only appears to be weaker is actually all the more essential.[267] Furthermore, the body parts we deem less honorable we treat with greater honor and the unpresentable parts we treat with modesty (12:23).[268] The language of weakness, honor, and shame brings to mind some of the major emphases of the letter. In explaining Christ crucified as God's wisdom, Paul reminded the Corinthians that God's weakness is stronger than men (1:25) and God's choice of the weak things of the world shames the strong (1:27). Paul's ironic rebuke of the Corinthians' arrogance by comparing their self-exaltation to the suffering of the apostles in 4:10 employs the weak/strong and honor/dishonor motif, "We are weak, but you are strong!" Paul warned those with knowledge to watch their so-called freedom lest their liberty causes their weaker brother

[264] So Fee, *First Corinthians*, 612; Thiselton, *First Corinthians*, 1005; Garland, *1 Corinthians*, 595; Ciampa and Rosner, *First Corinthians*, 602.

[265] Gk. ἀναγκαῖος, "necessary."

[266] Gk. ἀλλὰ πολλῷ μᾶλλον. BDAG, under the entry for μᾶλλον, refers to this text and suggests the meaning, "they are even more necessary." Thiselton (*First Corinthians*, 1006) suggests that ἀλλὰ carries full adversative force here and means, "even more to the point."

[267] Blomberg (*1 Corinthians*, 246) notes, "The true value of a particular body part is often inversely proportional to its outward appearance. Paul's fundamental concern is that the gifts and/or people the Corinthians are demeaning should be affirmed, while those they are overly exalting should be put in more balanced perspective." Ciampa and Rosner (*First Corinthians*, 604) offer the following example: "One could imagine a comparison between a car's oil drain plug and its electronic ignition system. One is as low-tech (and unimpressive) as could be, while the other is highly sophisticated. But a car won't last long without its oil drain plug no matter how impressive its ignition system!"

[268] Commentators concur that in speaking of what is unpresentable Paul refers to the sexual organs. There is a lexical opposition in Greek that is lost in the NIV rendering, "the parts that are unpresentable are treated with special modesty." The NASB translates, "our less presentable members become much more presentable." So also the HCSB, "our unpresentable parts have a better presentation." Garland (*First Corinthians*, 596) comments, "Genitalia appear to be honorless, are regarded as 'unpresentable,' and are shown a special modesty. Their function is not public, and they are kept hidden, but they are essential to the body's survival."

to stumble (8:9–10). Paul explicitly identified with the weak: "To the weak I became weak, to win the weak" (9:22). In chap. 11 the notion of shame and honor is a major motif in Paul's discussion of the head covering (11:2–16) and the Lord's Supper (11:17–22). All of this suggests that in 12:22–23 Paul's analogies and word-choices concerning the body parts are carefully chosen.

Third, and relatedly, God gives greater honor to the members that lack it according to his design (12:24b). God has combined, or "mixed together," the members of the body for this very purpose.[269] This is essentially a restatement of 12:18, that God put the members in the body as he pleased. Here, however, Paul adds a clarifying purpose statement concerning the divine blending of the body: "so that there should be no division in the body, but that its parts should have equal concern for each other" (12:25).[270] Collins notes that the compound purpose clause emphasizes what it means for there to be no division in the body. "In place of division there should exist mutual concern of the members for one another."[271] The unity of the church is one of the primary themes of the letter.

Fourth, what affects one member of the body affects all members of the body. Thus, not only is the one body many members, one member of the body affects the whole: "If one part suffers, every part suffers with it; if one part is honored, every part rejoices with it" (12:26). Everyone can relate to the pain that reverberates throughout the body when one small member is compromised. On the positive side, "If one part is honored, every part rejoices with it."[272] The implication is that a profound solidarity exists between the members of the body.[273] Like the previous paragraph (12:15–20) Paul concludes 12:21–27 with a summarizing statement, which states in no uncertain terms that they are the body he is talking about, "Now you are the body of Christ, and each one of you is a part of it."

**12:28–31** For the fourth time in the span of seventeen verses Paul mentions the sovereign action of either the Spirit or God in the distribution of gifts to believers and the arrangement/composition of the church, Christ's body (12:11,18,24b).[274] This last unit essentially reprises the main emphasis of 12:4–11 yet with some additional elements. As in 12:8–10, Paul mentions prophets, those who work miracles (powers), those with gifts of healing, those speaking in tongues, and those interpreting tongues. But to this list he adds apostles, teachers, those who help others, and those with gifts of

[269] Gk. συγκεράννυμι. BDAG defines, "to bring about a blend by mixing various items, blend, unite; to effect a harmonious unit, compose."

[270] The word for "division" (σχίσμα) is the same word used in 1:10 and 11:18.

[271] Collins, *First Corinthians*, 465. Collins notes that the word for concern (μεριμνάω) is the same term used in 7:32–34 that speaks of the concern that spouses have for one another.

[272] Cf. 2 Cor 11:29; Rom 12:15.

[273] So Ciampa and Rosner, *First Corinthians*, 608.

[274] 12:28, "God has appointed . . ." employs the same verb as 12:18, "God has arranged. . . ." Gk. τίθημι."

administration. There are two unique aspects of this second list that are worth noting. The first is the ranking of apostles, prophets, and teachers as first, second, and third. The other distinctive feature is the reference to both persons and gifts. In 12:8–10 the focus is on the gifts of the Spirit given to each believer: "to one is given a message of wisdom, to another the message of knowledge," etc. In 12:28–30, on the other hand, there is a combination of the mention of gifts and persons who exercise certain gifts or hold certain offices within the church. The first four, for example, includes apostles, prophets, teachers, and workers of miracles. The list then shifts to those who "have" certain gifts, "those who have gifts of healing," etc.[275] The focus, of course, is on God's sovereign appointment of both persons and gifts in the church, and as the rhetorical questions of 12:29–31 indicate, not all hold the same office and not all exercise the same gift, which has been the point all along. But Paul almost certainly intends to make a distinction between offices and gifts.[276] The designation "first, second, and third" may not imply so much rank of importance, which would seem to counter what Paul has just argued about the arrangement of the body (12:15–27), as it does a "chronological priority."[277] Ephesians 2:20, for example, refers to the "foundation of the apostles and prophets," and the same order appears in Eph 4:11: "It was he who gave some to be apostles, some to be prophets," which is followed by evangelists, pastors, and teachers. Bruce, however, thinks that the explicit enumeration of apostles, prophets, and teachers "mark these out as exercising, in Paul's estimation, the three most important ministries."[278] Perhaps it is best to hold the idea of rank and interdependence in healthy tension since we find the same principles at work in Paul's argument regarding headship in 11:2–16 (cf. esp. 11:3,7–12). If Paul does intend to convey rank by the enumeration in 12:28, one should keep in mind his assessment of apostleship in 4:9, "For it seems to me that God has put us apostles on display at the end of the procession, like men condemned to die in the arena. We have been made a spectacle to the whole universe, to angels as well as to men." Apostles are the epitome of those who live out the way of the cross and put others before self.

The "apostles" were a select group, including Paul, the Twelve, and others commissioned by Christ.[279] The word "apostle" designates one officially commissioned to preach the gospel.[280] Apostles were eyewitnesses of the resurrection (see 1 Cor 9:1–2; 15:5–9), which confines this unique group to the

[275] The word "gifts" (χάρισμα) occurs in 12:28 and 30, both with reference to gifts of healing.

[276] Thiselton (*First Corinthians*, 1013) calls 12:28 "an exegetical and lexicographical minefield."

[277] Blomberg, *1 Corinthians*, 247.

[278] Bruce, *1 and 2 Corinthians*, 122.

[279] The term "apostle" (ἀπόστολος) is used of Titus (2 Cor 8:23), Epaphroditus (Phil 2:25), James (Gal 1:19), and Andronicus and Junia (Rom 16:7).

[280] Cf. 1 Cor 1:17, "For Christ did not send me to baptize, but to preach the gospel."

first century. Some think that prophets, like the apostles, were also a select group; they were those who spoke under the immediate inspiration of the Spirit and were instruments of divine revelation.[281] Others take a more broadened view of the gift of prophecy (see discussion on 12:10). Should we distinguish between the gift of prophecy and the office of the prophet? In other words, if all prophets have the gift of prophecy, does this necessarily mean that all who prophesy are de facto prophets?

The office of teacher follows naturally in sequence from the listing of apostles and prophets and would seem to imply that teachers are those who expound on divine truth already revealed. Acts 13:1 makes reference to both prophets and teachers in the church at Antioch. However one interprets Paul's ranking and listing of offices/gifts, it is clear that all do not hold the same office or exercise the same gift. All the questions in 12:29–30 expect the rhetorical, "No." All are not apostles, prophets, or teachers. All do not work miracles, have gifts of healing, speak in tongues, or interpret tongues. All of these things come by divine appointment.

The concluding command in 12:31 to earnestly desire the greater gifts is not a contradiction to the principle of the divine arrangement and endowment of the church. To desire what is "greater" likely means to desire what is the most beneficial for the church. In context, Paul has in mind prophecy over against uninterpreted tongues (14:1–40). To desire the "greater" gifts is simply a different way of stating what the overall argument makes clear, namely, that all things should be done for the edification of the whole. In every way, individual members of the body should seek the welfare of others. To seek what is more useful is an exhortation to the church to recognize the value and the place of every gifted believer. There is, however, an even more excellent way (12:31b), which Paul expounds in 13:1–13.

### 4. Controlling Principle of Love (13:1–13)

First Corinthians 13 is clearly one of the best known chapters in the New Testament, although commonly read in isolation from its biblical, theological, and literary context. The chapter certainly possesses a "stand-alone" quality, and one can profit much from it apart from chaps. 12 and 14.[282] But in order to fully and correctly appreciate its content, Paul's words must be read in light of the full argument of the letter. Rhetorically, 1 Cor 13 is a digression, not in the sense of leaving the discussion in order to develop a different topic or

---

[281] Vaughan and Lea (*1 Corinthians*, 132), for example, state, "After the New Testament writings came into general circulation, the need for apostles and prophets ceased, and with the cessation of the need the offices ceased also."

[282] Morris aptly notes that 1 Cor 13 is a "passage of singular beauty and power" (*1 Corinthians*, 176), and that the "commentator cannot finish writing on this chapter without a sense that soiled and clumsy hands have touched a thing of exquisite beauty and holiness" (186).

theme but a digression that is central to the argument, much in the same way that 7:17–24 and 9:1–10:22 function in their respective contexts. Paul urges the Corinthians to "eagerly desire the greater gifts" (12:31a) and to "eagerly desire spiritual gifts" (14:1b), but not apart from love (13:1–13).[283] Even though God and Christ are not mentioned specifically in the chapter, God's love in Christ is the fundamental defining reality for Paul's understanding of love.[284] Indeed, the character of love as described in 13:4–7 shows that this chapter is not only central to the present argument; in many ways it is crucial to the letter as a whole.

Structurally, 1 Cor 13 divides into three sections: Verses 1–3 expound the absolute necessity and primacy of love, vv. 4–7 describe the nature or character of love, and vv. 8–13 establish the permanence of love.[285] Paul's exposition of love is particularly suited to the Corinthian context. The chapter begins by establishing the preeminence of love in relation to spiritual gifts (tongues, prophecy, knowledge, and faith) and exceptional sacrifice (13:1–3). Paul then provides a definition of love, not in terms of mere abstract qualities but in terms of what love does (13:4–7).[286] The chapter concludes by showing that whereas prophecy, tongues, and knowledge will cease, love never fails (13:8–13). Love as the "greatest" of the faith/hope/love triad resonates with the exhortation of 12:31a to earnestly desire the "greatest" gifts.

Love, biblically defined, is the obvious theme of the passage. The word for love in 13:1–13 is the predominant word for love in the New Testament.[287] It is not the word itself that necessarily carries special meaning but rather the contexts in which the word occurs.[288] Paul is careful in this passage to delineate what love is and what love is not (13:4–7) in a way particularly suited to the Corinthian context (see below). Jesus singled out love for God and love for one's neighbor as the two great commandments, a summary of the law (Matt 22:36–40). As already noted, the double love command provides the

283 The parallel between 12:31a and 14:1 is widely acknowledged. So Robertson and Plummer, *First Corinthians*, 285; Fee, *First Corinthians*, 626; Collins, *First Corinthians*, 471; B. Witherington, *Conflict and Community: A Socio-Rhetorical Commentary* (Grand Rapids: Eerdmans, 1994), 264.

284 So Garland, *1 Corinthians*, 606.

285 These three divisions are widely recognized by commentators. An attractive alternative is to include the negated verb "never fails" with the other verbal descriptors of love so that the structure is 13:1–3,4–8a,8b–13 (so Fitzmyer, *First Corinthians*, 488–89).

286 Love is defined by verbs rather than nouns.

287 Gk. ἀγάπη, occurs 116 times in the New Testament. The verb form, ἀγαπάω, occurs 143 times. By way of contrast, the noun φιλία (friendship) occurs only once (Jas 4:4) and the verb (φιλέω) 25 times.

288 So Ciampa and Rosner (*First Corinthians*, 619), "The word did not come with a tremendous amount of pre-established content, which is why the New Testament texts dedicate so much space to explaining exactly what love means and requires of believers." There are well-known examples of the use of ἀγαπάω with negative overtones, such as Amnon's love for Tamar (LXX 2 Sam 13:1–4) and Demas who loved this present world and deserted Paul (2 Tim 4:10).

theological framework for Paul's discussion of food sacrificed to idols (8:1–11:1).[289] In the letter's conclusion Paul urges, "Do everything in love" (16:14) and warns, "If anyone does not love the Lord—a curse be on him" (16:22). Paul concludes the letter with the affirmation, "My love to all of you in Christ Jesus" (16:24).

There is no real consensus regarding the genre of 1 Cor 13, whether we should understand the passage as a hymn or a poem or a form of exalted prose.[290] Sigountos argues that 1 Cor 13 fits the pattern of an encomium, a literary discourse dedicated to a person or to a thing (virtue), which suggests that Paul penned a praise to love.[291] Fee claims that this chapter is primarily ethical instruction, as 14:1 makes clear.[292] Most recent commentators take a both/and approach; that is, formally 1 Corinthians is praise (encomium) but functionally it is exhortation. As Thiselton explains, "If this chapter is to be viewed as a rhetorical encomium with a patterned rhetorical format or structure, Paul is using it for his own ends as well as for Corinth."[293] While it is true that the passage functions primarily as exhortation, it is the rhetorical components of metaphor, hyperbole, comparison, heightening, and climax that render the exhortation powerful. Witherington dubs 1 Cor 13 an "epedeictic showpiece."[294]

It is impossible to know if Paul composed this chapter separately over a period of time or if he borrowed from previous material. Questions of independence and origin are ultimately irrelevant since the passage is so thoroughly shaped with Corinthian problems in mind.[295] The content strongly suggests that Paul composed 13:1–13 extemporaneously for the Corinthian situation.[296]

---

[289] Representative passages pertaining to the theme of love in the New Testament include Rom 5:5; 8:31–39; 13:8–10; 2 Cor 13:11–13; Gal 5:14; 1 Thess 1:4; Jas 2:8–13; 1 John 3:1; 4:7–12. On the faith, hope, and love triad see Gal 5:5–6; Eph 4:2–5; Col 1:4–5; 1 Thess 1:3; 5:8; 1 Pet 1:3–8; Heb 6:10–12.

[290] Barrett (*First Corinthians*, 299) notes how Rom 8, which is moral exhortation, climaxes with a description of love (Rom 8:31–39; cf. also Paul's rhetorical climax in 1 Cor 3:18–23; 15:50–58).

[291] J. G. Sigountos, "The Genre of 1 Corinthians 13," *NTS* 40 (1994): 246–60. Sigountos (246) notes eleven different proposed genres for 1 Cor 13. See also Mitchell, *Rhetoric of Reconciliation*, 271–73; J. F. M. Smit, "Two Puzzles: 1 Corinthians 12.31 and 13.3: A Rhetorical Solution," *NTS* 39 (1993): 246–64.

[292] Fee, *First Corinthians*, 627.

[293] Thiselton, *First Corinthians*, 1029. So also Fitzmyer, *First Corinthians*, 487. Garland (*First Corinthians*, 607) notes also the element of rebuke, "In praising love, Paul indicts the church for its lack of love, which he judges to lie at the bottom of the Corinthians' problems, and the recognition of which is to be the beginning of their solution."

[294] Witherington, *Conflict and Community*, 264. "Epedeictic" refers to rhetorical speech (or writing) that praises or blames.

[295] So Fee, *First Corinthians*, 626.

[296] See Mitchell, *Rhetoric of Reconciliation*, 274n500. This is not to say, of course, that Paul could not have modeled the chapter after some sort of comparable preexisting literary piece or incorporated ideas from other sources or written over a period of time and inserted into the letter. Such speculation cannot be proven or disproven. Mitchell argues, "It is possible that 13:4–7 goes back to some originally separate composition, but even this section's point-by-point correspon-

The things that Paul says love is not (13:4–7) are exactly the things the Corinthians are doing! Love does not envy, yet envy and strife are present (3:3). Love is not arrogant or puffed up, yet the Corinthians are boasting in men (4:6), puffed up in spite of egregious sin (4:18; 5:1), and reveling in their knowledge (8:1). Love does not act shamefully or rejoice in unrighteousness, yet the Corinthians have tolerated an incestuous man (5:1–13), taken one another to court (6:1–11), and failed to honor the sanctity of the human body (6:12–20). Love does not seek the things of oneself, which forms a key part of Paul's argument in chaps. 8–10 regarding food sacrificed to idols. Both the necessity and permanence of love (13:1–3,8–13) are demonstrated in comparison with gifts that are especially important to the Corinthians and the focal point of Paul's argument in chaps. 12 and 14 (tongues, knowledge, and prophecy).[297]

One final literary feature worth noting is the shift from the second person plural at the end of chap. 12 to the first person singular in 13:1–3. Is this yet another instance of "Paul's self-presentation as a personal example to illustrate his teaching,"[298] as in 9:1–27? Collins submits, "The structural parallelism of chs. 12–14 with chs. 8–10 confirms the autobiographical and self-referential character of the first subunit of Paul's digression (13:1–3)."[299] Paul employs the singular "I" in 13:1–3 to show hypothetically that even if he possessed and exercised gifts in the most extraordinary way, he is nothing apart from love.[300]

### *(1) Love: The More Excellent Way (13:1–3)*

**1If I speak in the tongues of men and of angels, but have not love, I am only a resounding gong or a clanging cymbal. 2If I have the gift of prophecy and can fathom all mysteries and all knowledge, and if I have a faith that can move mountains, but have not love, I am nothing. 3If I give all I possess to the poor and surrender my body to the flames, but have not love, I gain nothing.**

The first unit, 13:1–3, opens with three parallel conditional clauses[301] and a threefold assertion that apart from love spiritual gifts amount to nothing. Paul affirms that though he could speak with languages, both human and divine, possess prophetic powers, fathom all mysteries and knowledge, have mountain-moving faith, benevolently give to the poor, and give his body in sacrifice, he is nothing if he does not have love. Whereas the gift of tongues and the interpretation of tongues occur last in the previous list of gifts, here

---

dence with Paul's argument against factionalism and for unity throughout the letter casts doubt on this hypothesis."

[297] See also ibid., 168–71; Witherington, *Conflict and Community*, 265.

[298] Garland, *1 Corinthians*, 609.

[299] Collins, *First Corinthians*, 472. See also C. R. Holladay, "1 Corinthians 13: Paul as Apostolic Paradigm," in *Greeks, Romans, and Christians: Essays in Honor of A. J. Malherbe,* ed. D. Balch et al. (Minneapolis: Fortress, 1990), 80–98.

[300] Paul employs both second person plural and first person singular verbs in 13:9–12.

[301] 13:2 and 13:3 both have compound conditions.

tongues occurs first. The reason may be linked to Paul's rhetorical strategy, a progression from the lesser to the greater (cf. 12:31, "eagerly desire the greater gifts). Tongues is mentioned first here because it is the least beneficial when uninterpreted. The repetition of the phrase "but have not love" elevates love above all gifts as "the most excellent way" (12:31b).

**13:1** Paul begins by hypothetically claiming that if he could speak with the tongues of men and of angels he is nothing if he does not have love. While it is possible that the phrase "tongues of men" refers to human eloquence[302] and "tongues of angels" refers to the gift of tongues, it is more likely in context that Paul refers only to the spiritual gift of tongues (languages) and heightens the rhetorical impact by referring to "tongues of angels" by way of hyperbole. This is not to say that there is no such thing as a "heavenly tongue," or to deny that the Corinthians themselves may have thought of the gift of tongues in this way. The point of Paul's statement is not to establish different kinds of tongues[303] but rather to emphasize that the gift, if exercised apart from love, is meaningless noise.[304]

The ambiguity of Paul's reference to the "resounding gong" or "clanging cymbal" has resulted in a number of possible interpretations. However, even if the reference is somewhat ambiguous, the essential meaning of the hypothetical example is clear. The term translated "gong" by the NIV was used of various kinds of metals but mainly bronze or brass. Based on a few references in Greco-Roman literature, Harris and Klein suggest that Paul refers to the acoustic vase used in the theaters in order to project and amplify sound.[305] Portier-Young has recently challenged this interpretation by suggesting that both the resounding brass (gong) and the clanging cymbal describe the same thing. The clanging cymbal simply clarifies what is intended by the resounding gong. In the biblical tradition the cymbal was never played solo but always in conjunction with other instruments. By using the metaphor Paul is urging the tongues-speakers to use their gifts for the edification of the church.[306] Still others suggest that Paul intends comparison instead of disjunction so that the

---

[302] Cf. the emphasis in chaps. 1–4 on human rhetoric as antithetical to the wisdom of the cross (1:17–18; 2:1–5).

[303] So Barrett (*First Corinthians*, 299–300); Collins (*First Corinthians*, 475), "Paul begins his digression on love with a reference to ordinary speech and speaking in tongues."

[304] The structure of the passage supports the view that Paul refers to angelic languages as hyperbole for the sake of argument, Ἐὰν ταῖς γλώσσαις τῶν ἀνθρώπων λαλῶ καὶ τῶν ἀγγέλων. The phrase "and of angels" is separated from "of men" by the verb, "I speak." The sense of the Greek is, "If I speak with the tongues of men, *and even of angels* . . ." See J. H. Petzer, "Contextual Evidence in Favor of καυχήσομαι in 1 Corinthians 13:3," *NTS* 35 (1989): 239; Sigountos, "The Genre of 1 Corinthians 13," 252–53.

[305] W. V. Harris, "'Sounding Brass' and Hellenistic Technology: Ancient Acoustical Device Clarifies Paul's Well-Known Metaphor," *Biblical Archaeological Review* 8 (1982): 38–41; W. M. Klein, "Noisy Gong or Acoustic Vase: a Note on 1 Corinthians 13:1," *NTS* 32 (1986): 286–89.

[306] A. Portier-Young, "Tongues and Cymbals: Contextualizing 1 Corinthians 13:1," *BTB* 35 (2005): 99–105.

text should read, "I have become as sounding brass rather than a resounding cymbal."[307] Some see in the mention of the "clanging cymbal" a reference to pagan worship.[308]

**13:2** From tongues Paul moves on to prophecy, knowledge, and faith. Knowing all mysteries may be a separate gift from prophecy, but it could also be coordinate with it.[309] In others words, prophecy includes insight into the mysteries of God. Paul, of course, does not know all mysteries nor does he possess all knowledge (13:9). He clearly exaggerates to make a point and presents a hypothetical scenario. Paul did have the gift of prophecy, he did have insight into the mysteries disclosed in the gospel, and he did possess great faith, even to the point of effecting miracles (Acts 14:3; 16:16–24; 19:11; 28:3–6; Rom 15:19; 2 Cor 12:12). In 14:6 Paul hypothetically describes himself as bringing teaching, revelation, knowledge, and prophecy to the Corinthians in assembly (cf. 14:37–38). In his mission to Corinth Paul announced the "mystery of God" (2:1). He, along with other apostles and gifted prophets (teachers), taught God's hidden wisdom (2:7) and were stewards (administrators) of the mysteries of God (4:1). Even in the letter itself, Paul makes known a "mystery" regarding the transformation of believer's mortal bodies (15:51; see also Rom 11:25; 16:25; 2 Thess 2:7). The reference to a faith that could remove mountains, an idiom for great faith, resonates with the teaching of Jesus and may be derived from it (see Matt 17:19–20; 21:21; Mark 1:22–24; Luke 17:6). Even though Paul possessed these gifts, the repetition of the word "all" functions as hyperbole to make a point.[310] Paul is saying that even if he possessed these gifts in perfection, without love he would be nothing.

**13:3** In the third and final hypothetical example Paul asserts that even the ultimate in self-sacrifice profits nothing apart from love. The giving away of one's possessions, even the offering of one's very life apart from love ultimately profits nothing. This verse contains one of the most difficult textual variants in the New Testament. The NIV reads, "and surrender my body to the flames" (cf. NASB, "surrender my body to be burned"). The more recent NIV2011 (cf. also the NRSV, HCSB) follows the editors of the Greek New

[307] So Collins, *First Corinthians*, 475.

[308] Barrett (*First Corinthians*, 300) thinks the reference is to more than a meaningless phenomenon, "It is mere paganism." See also Fee, *First Corinthians*, 632.

[309] Ciampa and Rosner (*First Corinthians*, 632) hold that Paul "describes a prophetic gift that subsumes all mysteries and all knowledge within it." This means Paul only describes two gifts in 13:2, prophecy and faith. They suggest further, "The reference to 'knowing all mysteries' evokes the portrayal of Daniel in Daniel 2 and 4, especially in 4:9 in Theodotion's version, where because 'the Holy Spirit of God' is in him 'no mystery is too hard for him.'" Fee (*First Corinthians*, 632–33) notes the conjoining of "mysteries and knowledge" in Jewish apocalyptic literature (Dan 2:19–23; *1 Enoch* 41:1; 52:2; 61:5; 63:3; 68:5; 71:4).

[310] The NIV misses the repetition of "all" in the Greek by omitting the third occurrence with faith; "all mysteries, all knowledge, and all faith," which carries over into 13:3, "And if I give all I possess . . ."

Testament and adopts a variant reading, "and give over my body to hardship, that I may boast." The Greek terms for "burn" and "boast" are very close in the Greek.[311] Many agree that "boast" is the more likely reading, although there are significant detractors.[312]

If "boasting" is the correct reading, what does Paul mean, especially in a letter where boasting is one of the key problems in Corinth? Although Paul often refers to boasting disparagingly, he also uses the term on occasion with reference to his ministry (2 Cor 8:24; Phil 2:16; 1 Thess 2:19; also Rom 5:2–3; 1 Cor 1:29–31; 9:15; 2 Cor 2:14). Fee, who is a proponent of this interpretation, suggests that in 13:3 "this final item is most likely a genuine reflection on his own ministry, in which he is referring to the kinds of bodily sufferings of which he 'boasts' in 2 Cor 11:23–29 and 12:10, which also help to bring about his greater 'boast,' their salvation."[313]

Another intriguing aspect of this passage is the mention of giving possessions and giving oneself, either in martyrdom or for the cause of the gospel, alongside the spiritual gifts of tongues, prophecy, knowledge, and faith. Does Paul consider extreme sacrifice to be a gift of the Spirit? Ciampa and Rosner think so, "The context makes clear that the actions mentioned here are understood to reflect the practice of spiritual gifts . . . not as clear whether or not they are embodiments of one or two of the gifts mentioned in 12:8–10 or 12:28–30."[314] Whether or not 13:3 should be understood as a "gift" in the traditional sense, I would submit that such actions are most certainly a "manifestation of the Spirit." We may sometimes think too narrowly in restricting a "spiritual gift" to something possessed.

### *(2) What Love Does and Does Not Do (13:4–7)*

**4Love is patient, love is kind. It does not envy, it does not boast, it is not proud.**
**5It is not rude, it is not self-seeking, it is not easily angered, it keeps no record of**
**wrongs. 6Love does not delight in evil but rejoices with the truth. 7It always pro-**
**tects, always trusts, always hopes, always perseveres.**

---

311 Gk. καυχήσωμαι, "I might boast," versus καυθήσομαι or καυθήσωμαι, "I might be burned."

312 For the view that "boast" is the correct reading, see Fee, *First Corinthians*, 634–35; Petzer, "Contextual Evidence"; Ciampa and Rosner, *First Corinthians*, 633–34. For those who submit that "burn" is the correct reading, see Sigountos, "The Genre of 1 Corinthians 13," 254; Collins, *First Corinthians*, 476–77; Garland, *1 Corinthians*, 615. Even though "burning" was not a form of martyrdom until the Neronian persecution, one of the key arguments against this view, Paul's reference may be an allusion to Dan 3. Sigountos submits that the statement, "I may be burned," fits contextually with the hyperbole of 13:1–3. The reading preferred by the NIV1984 is not out of the question.

313 Fee, *First Corinthians*, 635.

314 Ciampa and Rosner, *First Corinthians*, 634. Garland (*First Corinthians*, 614) also seems to connect martyrdom with the gifts. Fee (*First Corinthians*, 633), however, thinks that these are not gifts but rather an enlargement of Paul's perspective beyond the gifts.

In 13:4–7 Paul personifies love in order to describe what love does and does not do, delineating its nature or character by means of sixteen verbs with love as the subject.[315] While it is probably incorrect to say that love in its biblical sense has no emotional or affectionate element,[316] Paul's concern here is on the visible manifestations of love within the Corinthian community. The first two verbs offer a positive appraisal of love (love is patient and kind) followed by eight negated verbs indicating what love does not do. The last negated verb, "Love does not rejoice in unrighteousness," is balanced by another positive, "but rejoices with the truth." The unit concludes with a fourfold positive crescendo (love endures, believes, hopes and perseveres all things/always) that paves the way for the emphasis on the permanence of love in 13:8–13.[317] There is a consensus among commentators and specialist studies that Paul's description of what love does not do unmistakably addresses the Corinthian context and thus functions to point out their lack of love.[318]

**13:4a** The first two qualities of love, to exercise patience and to show kindness, form a complementary pair. The cognate nouns often occur together in Paul's writings (Rom 2:4; 2 Cor 6:6; Gal 5:22; Col 3:12).[319] Patience is the more passive idea and, coupled with kindness, indicates a relational quality. In other words, the patience and kindness Paul has in mind is lived out in community in relation to others. The only other use of the verb form "to be patient" in Paul's letters occurs in 1 Thess 5:14, "And we urge you, brothers, warn those who are idle, encourage the timid, help the weak, be patient with everyone." As divine attributes, God's patience and kindness lead men to repentance (Rom

[315] The sixteenth verb is "love never fails" (13:8a), which forms a bridge between love's acts and love's permanence (13:8b–13).

[316] Ciampa and Rosner (*First Corinthians*, 639) note that the view that love is not a feeling is widespread in New Testament interpretation is "based on a misunderstanding of emotion. While love is not just a feeling, it is not less than or other than a feeling. The cognitive approach regards emotion as a indicator of what we believe and value and as such is an integral part of our reason and ethics." Ciampa and Rosner draw from M. Elliot's study, *Faithful Feelings: Emotion in the New Testament* (Leicester: InterVarsity Press, 2005).

[317] Commentators often note the chiastic arrangement of Paul's description of love (positive, negative, positive).

[318] Sigountos ("The Genre of 1 Corinthians 13," 256–57) offers a typical appraisal of 13:4–7: "The negative verbs describe behaviour that love would prevent. Yet, those behaviours occur in Corinth, suggesting that love is something they lack. Since virtually every behavioural problem at Corinth is mentioned in vv. 4–7, Paul seems to say that the real problem is their lack of love, for love does not behave in the way they do. The section becomes quite ironic, because while Paul is praising love, he is at the very same time blaming the Corinthians. . . . Paul can quickly move from praise to blame, for in rhetorical practice they are two sides of the same coin. On this basis we can expect all of the negative verbs to have some reference to the Corinthian situation." So also Garland (*First Corinthians*, 617, "Rather than being a hymn glorifying how wonderful love is, this text becomes a subtle commentary on what is rotten in Corinth." Collins (*First Corinthians*, 479) notes that much of what Paul says in 13:4–7 is paralleled in Rom 12:9–21.

[319] Gk. μακροθυμία and χρηστότης. The verb form "to be kind" (χρηστεύομαι) occurs only in 1 Cor 13:4 in the New Testament.

2:4). In Eph 5:1–2, the command to "be imitators of God," and to "live a life of love just as Christ loved us" is preceded by the command "Be kind and compassionate to one another, forgiving each other, just as in Christ God forgave you" (Eph 4:32). In Eph 4:1–2, Paul urges believers to walk worthy of their calling, which entails humility, gentleness, and patience, and bearing with one another in love. Paul commended his ministry to the Corinthians as a ministry characterized by patience and kindness (2 Cor 6:6). Patience and kindness are both listed as a fruit of the Spirit in Gal 5:22, and Col 3:12 commands that believers clothe themselves with patience and kindness, among other things.

**13:4b–6** Since Paul's description of love includes eight negated verbs, his primary concern is with the Corinthians' behavior, which demonstrates a lack of love. The first assertion that "love does not envy" recalls the jealous and strife of 3:3 where Paul accused them of fleshly behavior and walking according to mere men.[320] "To be jealous" for something can have a positive connotation, as in 12:31, to "eagerly desire" the greater gifts.[321] But here the connotation is clearly negative. Love does not envy what another has; it does not pit one leader against another or one group against another. The problem of jealousy and quarreling underlies other portions of the letter, such as the lawsuits of 6:1–8 and the social divisions between the rich and the poor in the celebration of the Lord's Supper in 11:17–22.

The second assertion, "love does not boast,"[322] employs a rare verb used only here in the New Testament and may be somewhat synonymous with the following negated verb "is not proud,"[323] which is a key term in the letter (4:6,18; 5:2; and 8:1). Taken together these designations of what love does not do recalls Paul's sharp criticisms of the Corinthians' arrogance (1:29–31; 3:21; 4:6,18; 5:2). To be inflated with pride and to brag is the very opposite of what love does, which is to "build up" (8:1). To the first term, BDAG assigns the meaning "to heap praise on oneself, to behave as a braggart." Sigountos notes that its use outside the New Testament connotes ostentatious bragging.[324] Garland suggests that Paul possibly alludes to rhetorically sophisticated speech (recall chaps. 1–4).[325]

The fourth item, "is not rude," also translates a rare term. The verb occurs only here and in 7:36, where Paul describes the improper actions of a man toward his fiancee or of the father toward his virgin daughter, depending on how one interprets 7:25–38.[326] The cognate word group normally connotes

[320] The verb ζηλόω (13:4) is cognate to the noun ζῆλος (3:3).

[321] The same verb as in 13:4, ζηλόω.

[322] Gk. περπερεύομαι.

[323] Gk. φυσιόω.

[324] Sigountos, "The Genre of 1 Corinthians 13," 257. See also Collins, *First Corinthians*, 480.

[325] Garland, *1 Corinthians*, 618.

[326] Gk. ἀσχημονέω. The cognate adjective ἀσχήμων occurs in 12:23.

shameful behavior, often with sexual overtones,[327] and can mean to act in defiance of social and moral standards.[328] Cognate nouns occur in Rom 1:27 of shameful male homosexual relations, in Jude 13 of the shame of false teachers, and in Eph 5:4 of behavior inappropriate for God's people.[329] There are, of course, numerous places in 1 Corinthians where shameful behavior has been of great concern. There has been no shame over the behavior of the incestuous man (5:1–13)[330] or in taking one another to court (6:1–8),[331] and the theme of shame is prominent in Paul's discussion of their behavioral patterns related to head coverings (11:2–16) and the treatment of the poor at the Lord's meal (11:17–34).[332]

The next item, "is not self-seeking," is a phrase virtually identical in Greek to the exhortation of 10:24, "let no one seek the things of himself," which is balanced with "but the things of another," and Paul's description of his pattern of life in 10:33 as not seeking his own good but the good of the many. This characteristic of love provides a direct link to the previous discussion of food sacrificed to idols and the hermeneutic of love that guides Paul's response.

The next term, translated by the NIV "not easily angered," is another rare term, used elsewhere only in Acts 17:16 of Paul's great distress when he saw the city of Athens given over to idols.[333] In the passive voice the term means "to become irritated or angry."[334] Fee submits, "With this verb Paul begins to move beyond the immediate situation in Corinth, at least as it is reflected in the present letter."[335] Hays concurs that both this term and the next, "keeps no record of wrongs," are harder to relate to specific portions of the letter, but "they are probably to be seen in contrast to the rivalry and dissensions in the Corinthian church."[336] Collins points out that the term is used of God in the LXX at Deut 1:34; Hos 8:5; and Zech 10:3. The term "suggests that the one who has love does not succumb to any sort of irate self-justification." Furthermore, "Noting the use of the verb in the LXX, some commentators suggest that Paul may have had in mind a kind of anger that leads to murmuring against God (cf. Num 14:11;

[327] Sigountos ("The Genre of 1 Corinthians 13," 257–58) notes that Paul's use of the noun and adjective all have some kind of sexual overtone and sees here a likely reference to 6:12–20 and Corinthians visiting prostitutes.

[328] Louw-Nida (88.149) define the word-group, "to act in defiance of social and moral standards, with resulting disgrace, embarrassment, and shame."

[329] Gk. ἀσχημοσύνη (Rom 1:27); αἰσχύνη (Jude 13); αἰσχρότης (Eph 5:4).

[330] 5:2, "And you are proud! Shouldn't you rather have been filled with grief and have put out of your fellowship the man who did this?"

[331] Note especially 6:5, "I say this to your shame."

[332] The related term καταισχύνω occurs in 11:4–6 and 11:22.

[333] Gk. παροξύνω.

[334] So BDAG.

[335] Fee, *First Corinthians*, 638.

[336] Hays, *First Corinthians*, 227. So also Sigountos, "The Genre of 1 Corinthians 13," 258. Sigountos suggests a likely reference to schisms of chaps. 1–4 and possibly to 11:17–34; the provocation would be the humiliation of the poor in the assembly (11:22).

16:30; 20:24; Deut 9:7,8; 31:20; Ps 9:25). If so, this negative qualification might evoke the exodus experience exploited by Paul in 10:1–13."[337]

That love "keeps no record of wrongs" is literally "it does not reckon, calculate the bad/evil."[338] While the phrase could mean, "Does not contemplate evil," the meaning in context more likely has to do with holding wrongs against someone else.[339] Barrett suggests the meaning, "Does not put down evil to one's account."[340] Collins renders as "does not calculate evil" and comments, "Following on the mention of being carried away in anger it may be a subtle reminder that vengeance belongs only to the Lord alone (cf. Rom 2:19 with its citation of Deut 32:35; 1 Thess 4:6 with its allusion to Ps 94:1)."[341] Most commentators take note of Paul's distinctive theological use of the term "to reckon" in other contexts to refer to God not counting sins against us (Rom 4:1–12; 2 Cor 5:19; Gal 3:6).[342] Just as demonstrating patience and showing kindness to others imitates God's love for us in Christ (see above on 13:4), so also "to keep no record of wrongs" reflects the character of God. Sigountos suggests that Paul has in mind the revenge of the lawsuits in 6:1–11.[343]

The final descriptor of what loves does not do is set forth in 13:6a, "Love does not delight in evil," with a positive counterpart, "but rejoices with the truth" (13:6b). Although the noun "evil"[344] does not occur elsewhere in 1 Corinthians, the cognate adjective "unrighteous" and the verb "to harm/wrong" are key terms in 6:1–11, which means that Paul may still have in mind their wrongful behavior in taking one another to court.[345] BDAG places 1 Cor 13:6 under the definition, "the quality of injustice, unrighteousness, wickedness, injustice."[346] In context, the primary emphasis of 13:6 seems to be that love does not rejoice in behaving unjustly toward others but instead embraces God's way of righteousness in relation to others, that is, love "rejoices with the truth." Hays also connects 13:6 with 6:1–11 and explains, "Given the juxtaposition

---

[337] Collins, *First Corinthians*, 481.

[338] Gk. οὐ λογίζεται τὸ κακόν. BDAG, "Love keeps no score of wrongs."

[339] Ciampa and Rosner, *First Corinthians*, 647. Also Fee (*First Corinthians*, 639), who notes Zech 8:17 and the similar language used there, suggesting a meaning like "love does not devise evil against someone else." Fee thinks, however, that Paul's use in 1 Cor 13:5 more likely refers to that done to one by another person. Paul's claims that love "keeps no record of wrongs" reflects the Jesus tradition at this point, "Father, forgive them" (Luke 23:34). The next quality of love, "does not rejoice in unrighteousness," would be redundant if 13:5 means "does not contemplate/think upon evil."

[340] Barrett, *First Corinthians*, 305.

[341] Collins, *First Corinthians*, 481.

[342] Gk. λογίζομαι.

[343] Sigountos, "The Genre of 1 Corinthians 13," 258. So also Garland (*1 Corinthians*, 619), "Paul embodies the attitude found in 2 Corinthians 2:5–11."

[344] Gk. ἀδικία.

[345] Gk. ἄδικος (unrighteous; 6:1,9); ἀδικέω (to harm, wrong; 6:7–8). Garland (*First Corinthians*, 619) thinks that 13:6 refers to 6:1–11. Paul may also have in mind the case of the incestuous man (5:1–13) and the Corinthians' boasting in spite of such egregious sin (cf. Rom 1:32).

[346] The language of 1 Cor 13:6 is very close to the idea expressed in 2 Thess 2:12 concerning those who refuse the truth but "delight in wickedness."

with 'wrongdoing,' the term 'truth' here surely has a moral sense, as it does in the Johannine tradition (e.g., John 3:21; 1 John 3:18). Thus, to rejoice in the truth would mean, among other things, to embrace God's way of righteous living—a pointed contrast to the Corinthians' present conduct as Paul sees it."[347]

**13:7** With this verse Paul reverts back to positive assertions about what love "always" does; it always protects, trusts, hopes, and perseveres (NIV). The NIV translation takes the Greek adjective, "all things," and renders as an adverb, "always."[348] Other translations, such as the HCSB, render the verse, "It bears all things, believes all things, hopes all things, endures all things." With the switch to the positive side of things, Paul closes out the unit on his definition of love. The two middle statements, love believes and hopes, anticipate the concluding triad of "faith, hope, and love" in 13:13. Fee suggests that the middle two qualities focus on the future (believes and hopes) while the outer two (bears and endures) focus on the present.[349] Thiselton endorses the REB precedent for translating 13:7 with a series of negations in order to protect Paul's meaning and to capture the rhetorical force. Thiselton translates, "Love never tires of support, never loses faith, never exhausts hope, never gives up."[350]

The NIV translation of the first verb, "always protects," is possible,[351] although it carries a different nuance in other Pauline uses. The only other occurrence of the word in 1 Corinthians is 9:12 where Paul refers to himself and other apostles who endure all things in order not to give any offense to the gospel. The verb also appears in 1 Thess 3:1–5 with reference to enduring difficult circumstances. The notion of putting up with all things, doing all things for the cause of the gospel, which is so prominent in chap. 9, concords with the qualities of love expressed in 13:4a–6. Fee concurs that in context "the meaning is probably not to conceal or to hide something, but rather to endure all things for the cause of the Gospel, recalling 9:12."[352] This "suggests again that Paul may be pointing to himself as a model of the kind of love that should mark the Corinthian church."[353]

To always believe and to always hope carries the idea of never losing faith and never losing hope. The enduring character of love is the main theme of the concluding unit, 13:8–13. To believe and to hope always (all things) may express optimism for the future, but there may also be a present element. As

[347] Hays, *First Corinthians*, 227. This is not to deny that Paul also has in mind the "content" of truth. So BDAG, "Truth expresses itself in virtues like righteousness and holiness, Eph 4:24. Hence it is contrasted with ἀδικία (cf. Rom 1:18; 2:8)."

[348] BDAG, "in all respects, in every way, altogether."

[349] Fee, *First Corinthians*, 639–40.

[350] Thiselton, *First Corinthians*, 1056–57. Thiselton claims that the translation "all things" invites misunderstandings of Paul and Christianity.

[351] Gk. στέγω.

[352] Fee, *First Corinthians*, 640. So also Hays, *First Corinthians*, 228; Garland, *1 Corinthians*, 620.

[353] Ciampa and Rosner, *First Corinthians*, 649.

Garland explains, "Paul also uses hope language to express optimism about his churches. As the relationship with Corinth gets rockier, Paul keeps firing off letters to the Corinthians because he does not believe that they are a hopeless case. He is confident in God that they will reform."[354] Paul expresses such hope in the letter's opening (1:4–9). Paul is confident of the eschatological future because "God is faithful" (1:9). To believe all things certainly does not entail, in this context, to "believe the best about everybody or everything."[355] Love is far more discerning as 13:6 has already made clear: "Love does not delight in evil but rejoices with the truth."

### *(3) Love's Permanence (13:8–13)*

**8Love never fails. But where there are prophecies, they will cease; where there are tongues, they will be stilled; where there is knowledge, it will pass away. 9For we know in part and we prophesy in part, 10but when perfection comes, the imperfect disappears. 11When I was a child, I talked like a child, I thought like a child, I reasoned like a child. When I became a man, I put childish ways behind me. 12Now we see but a poor reflection as in a mirror; then we shall see face to face. Now I know in part; then I shall know fully, even as I am fully known.**

**13And now these three remain: faith, hope and love. But the greatest of these is love.**

Once again Paul contrasts the prized spiritual gifts in Corinth (prophecy, tongues, and knowledge) and love (cf. 13:1–3) but now with a different emphasis.[356] The phrase "Love never fails" (13:8a) forms a bridge between the acts of love (13:4–7) and the emphasis on love's enduring character (13:8–13).[357] The adverb translated "never" is Paul's only use of the term in his letters and is a bit more emphatic than simple negation.[358] There is never a time when love as described in 13:4–7 fails.[359] Fee notes that love, which is for now and forever, "must dictate how the gifts function in the present life of the church."[360]

---

[354] Garland, *1 Corinthians*, 620.

[355] So Barrett, *First Corinthians*, 305.

[356] Both units, however, reflect on the value of the gifts in comparison to love. Collins (*First Corinthians*, 484) notes the striking series of contrasts (permanence/transitoriness, partial/full reality, infancy/adulthood, oblique/direct vision) that underscore the eschatological character of love.

[357] The abiding character of love is emphasized by repetition, "Love endures" (13:7), "never fails" (13:8a), "remains" (13:13), and by way of contrast with things that pass away and cease (13:8b–10). So also Fee, *First Corinthians*, 643.

[358] Gk. οὐδέποτε.

[359] Paul's language about the never-failing character of love is comparable to his discussion of the Spirit in Gal 5:16–26. Those led by the Spirit are "not under the law" (5:18) and "there is no law" (5:23) against the fruit of the Spirit. The word translated "fail" in 1 Cor 13:8a is πίπτω, used in 1 Cor at 10:8 of Israel "falling" in the wilderness and in the admonition of 10:12 to those who think they stand lest they "fall." Ciampa and Rosner (*First Corinthians*, 652–53) suggest that Paul's use of this particular verb reflects eschatological connotations associated with its use in 10:12, "having to do with failing to pass the ultimate judgment and enter into its reward, being judged and failing to 'make the cut.'"

[360] Fee, *First Corinthians*, 642.

**13:8–10** Following the introduction "Love never fails," Paul compares never-failing love with the temporal gifts of prophecy, tongues, and knowledge. These three gifts are not the only gifts that will cease, but rather represent all gifts and are chosen because of their relevance to the Corinthian context. Prophecy is Paul's preferred gift (14:1–40), while tongues and knowledge are Corinthian favorites. All three will cease since they are partial and incomplete.[361] Robertson and Plummer suggest that the repeated "whether" is depreciatory and "suggests indifference to the gifts of which the use was at best temporary."[362] Ciampa and Rosner counter, "More likely it suggests indifference with respect to which particular gift a person might have."[363] Either way, prophecies will cease, tongues will be stilled, and knowledge will pass away (13:8b). The remainder of the unit (13:9–12) focuses on the incomplete character of knowledge and prophecy along with two illustrations that distinguish the present age and the age to come in order to emphasize the eschatological character of love, which remains forever (13:13).[364]

"Will cease" and "will pass away" (13:8) translate the same verb in Greek, which regularly has eschatological connotations.[365] The verb appears four times in this unit alone, "When perfection comes, the imperfect *disappears* (13:10), and "When I became a man I *put* childish ways *behind me*" (13:11). The same verb appears several times in the letter. In 1:28, Paul refers to the lowly and despised things of the world that God has chosen in order "*to nullify* to nothing the things that are." Similarly, in 2:6, Paul describes the rulers of this age as those "*who are coming to nothing*."[366] Yet again in 6:13, Paul indicates that God will *destroy* both the stomach and food in the resurrection, and in 15:24–26 Paul declares that in the end, the Son will hand the kingdom over to the Father after he has *destroyed* all dominion, authority, power, and death. Paul's use of the word in 1 Corinthians clearly indicates that the word refers "to those things that do not survive the transition from this age into the fullness of the age to come."[367] Paul stresses not only the temporal character of knowledge and prophecy but also its limited scope in the present age. Both prophecy and knowledge are presently incomplete, and in the age to come both gifts are no longer necessary: "I shall know fully, even as I am fully known" (13:12).

---

[361] Fitzmyer (*First Corinthians*, 497) observes, "That Paul is serious about this cessation of prophecy can be seen from the skepticism he has already expressed about it in 1 Thess 5:19–22."

[362] Robertson and Plummer, *First Corinthians*, 296. So also Fitzmyer, *First Corinthians*, 497.

[363] Ciampa and Rosner, *First Corinthians*, 653.

[364] Collins (*First Corinthians*, 486) comments that the fourfold "to pass away" stresses the temporary character of the gifts whereas the fourfold "in part" underscores their limited character.

[365] Gk. καταργέω.

[366] An attributive participle of the same verb, τῶν καταργουμένων.

[367] Ciampa and Rosner, *First Corinthians*, 653–54. The Pauline uses of καταργέω outside of 1 Corinthians include Rom 3:3,31; 4:14; 6:6; 7:2,6; 2 Cor 3:7,11,13–14; Gal 3:17; 5:4,11; Eph 2:15; 2 Thess 2:8; 2 Tim 1:10.

The verb used of tongues, "they will *be stilled*," is a different verb.[368] Scholars debate the significance of Paul's word-choice. Is the variation between the verb used of prophecy and knowledge and the verb used of tongues purely stylistic?[369] Is the verb "to be stilled/to cease" in the middle voice with the meaning that tongues will cease in and of themselves, or is the verb deponent, which means that the verb is middle in form but active in meaning and simply means, "will cease"?[370] In the end, debates over the significance of the verb are secondary to Paul's overarching concern, which is to stress the temporal and partial character of the gifts in order to elevate the prominence of love (14:1). Furthermore, if Paul mentions only prophecy, knowledge, and tongues as representative gifts, then he is not commenting on when any of the gifts cease per se; he is only saying that everything "partial," which is true of all the gifts, will disappear when the perfect comes. Whether or not any gifts have ceased already is a matter of God's choice (12:11,18,28).

The coming of "perfection," literally, "the perfect thing,"[371] undoubtedly refers to the consummation of all things, which is clarified by the language of 13:12, seeing "face to face" and "knowing fully even as I am fully known." But why does Paul refer to the eschaton in this way rather than more directly as "the revelation of our Lord Jesus Christ" (1:7 NASB) or "till the Lord comes" (4:1–5)? The answer lies in the argument itself, where "perfect" is

---

[368] Gk. παύω. In Paul's letter the verb occurs also Eph 1:16 and Col 1:9. Elsewhere in the New Testament see Luke 5:4; 8:24; 11:1; Acts 5:42; 6:13; 13:10; 20:1,31; 21:32; Heb 10:2; 1 Pet 3:10; 4:1.

[369] So Fee, *First Corinthians*, 643n17; D. A. Carson, *Showing the Spirit: A Theological Exposition of 1 Corinthians 12–14* (Grand Rapids: Baker, 1987), 66–67; Garland, *1 Corinthians*, 622n13; Ciampa and Rosner, *First Corinthians*, 655.

[370] The implication would be that tongues cease of their own accord prior to the cessation of prophecy and knowledge. So S. D. Toussaint, "1 Corinthians Thirteen and the Tongues Question," *BSac* 120 (1963): 311–16. D. B. Wallace rehearses the possibility that Paul distinguishes between the situation with tongues and that of prophecy and knowledge and that Paul does not speak of the end of tongues in connection with the coming of perfection (13:10), only prophecy and knowledge. More importantly, Wallace challenges the dominant opinion among New Testament scholars that παύω (to cease) in the future is deponent. "In sum, the deponent view is based on some faulty assumptions as to the labeling of παύσονται as deponent, the parallel in Luke 8:24, and even the meaning of deponency. Paul seems to be making a point that is more than stylistic in his shift of verbs" (*Greek Grammar Beyond the Basics*, 422–23; quote is from p. 423). Ciampa and Rosner (*First Corinthians*, 655) counter that Wallace's argument "reflects a failure to synthesize the information provided by both grammar and context." The "for" in 13:9 explains why the things affirmed in 13:8 are so, that is, they explain why and when all three, which are merely representative examples, will come to an end. "There is nothing about the middle voice to suggest that tongues would stop or come to an end at any point in time other than that which is clarified in the following verses—at the final consummation." Wallace (423) admits, "This verse does not specifically address *when* tongues would cease, although it is giving a *terminus ad quem*: when the perfect comes." In Wallace's view the "perfect" is not the closing of the canon (423n44). Fee (*First Corinthians*, 643–44) thinks the view that the middle voice has independent significance "misses Paul's concern rather widely. The change of verbs is purely rhetorical; to make it otherwise is to elevate to significance something in which Paul shows no interest at all."

[371] A neuter substantival adjective in Greek, τὸ τέλειον.

both the logical opposite of "partial/incomplete"[372] and the logical opposite of the "infant/child" language in the illustration that follows in 13:11. In the other two occurrences in the letter, "perfect" or "mature" is set in contrast to "infant." By using the term "perfect/mature," Paul is probably picking up on the Corinthians' language and self-understanding in order to add rhetorical force to his argument. In 2:6–3:4, for example, the message of wisdom spoken to the mature (2:6) is set in contrast to Paul's claim that he could only speak to them as mere infants in Christ (3:1). The Corinthians considered themselves to be mature, wise, and spiritual. Paul pointed out that their behavior indicated otherwise. The mature/infant contrast appears again in 14:20, "Brothers, stop thinking like children. In regard to evil be infants, but in your thinking be adults."[373] The whole argument of 12:1–14:40 has to do with what it means to be "spiritual" (12:1; 14:37). In 2:6–3:4, "mature" and "spiritual" are virtually synonymous terms. The use of the term "perfect" in 13:10 allows Paul to highlight not only the partial nature of the gifts; it allows him to underscore the permanence of love that "never fails" (13:8a) and occupies first place among the gifts that last forever (13:13). In other words, if the Corinthians want to truly lay hold of the "perfection" of the future in the here and now, then they must pursue love, for it has genuine abiding value. To say it another way, "the perfect" is the consummation of all things of which love holds a prominent place. When perfection arrives, love will be present but the gifts will not. The true indicator of maturity/spirituality is love, not the exercise of the temporal gifts.

**13:11–12** The two illustrations of 13:11–12 both distinguish the present age from the age to come. The first illustration is that of a child maturing into adulthood and putting away childish things. The second illustration contrasts looking into a mirror with seeing God face to face. As noted above, Paul's concern is twofold, namely, to clarify that the gifts are temporal but also to affirm the eschatological character of love that remains forever (13:13). The link between the "child" and the "perfect" is strengthened not only by the pairing of these two words elsewhere in the letter but also by the use of the verb translated "to put behind," which is the same verb translated "disappears" in 13:10.[374] Paul is not equating the gifts of the Spirit with childishness, but he is perhaps scolding the Corinthians for their childish behavior in the practice of the gifts (cf. 14:20). Already Paul has inferred blame on the Corinthians in his description of what love does and does not do (13:4–7).

The metaphor of the mirror enjoyed widespread use in the ancient world and was particularly relevant to Corinth where bronze mirrors were manufactured.

---

[372] The contrast is conveyed by the repetition of the neuter definite article, literally, "When *the* perfect comes, *the* partial will be done away."

[373] In 14:20 the verb form "to be infants" is used, νηπιάζω.

[374] Gk. καταργέω.

Although looking into a mirror could carry different connotations,[375] the use of the metaphor in context points to the indirectness of one's vision, to partial and incomplete knowledge. Seeing in a mirror is contrasted with seeing "face to face" and having full knowledge. The phrase "poor reflection" renders a phrase occurring only here in the New Testament,[376] but scholars concur that the reference is to Num 12:6–8, which contrasts Moses' prophetic experience with other prophets. Other prophets received revelation through visions and dreams (Num 12:6), but the Lord spoke to Moses face to face (Num 12:8). Ciampa and Rosner submit that Paul's allusion to Num 12:8 "is consistent with other early Jewish interpretations in understanding that in the age to come all God's people would have an experience similar to that which distinguished Moses from the other prophets. We already see the Lord as through a mirror (imperfectly) and know him as well as that experience allows (cf. 2 Cor 3:18), but the day is coming when we will see him as Moses did, face to face, an experience of knowing him fully as we are already fully known by him."[377]

**13:13** The words "and now"[378] may carry temporal or logical force. If the sense of the construction is primarily temporal then Paul is referring to the experience of faith, hope, and love in the present life of the church. Even though love is forever, Paul ends his argument by emphasizing that love is for the present as well. In this reading, love is the greatest because only love carries into the future. Faith and hope are strictly for this present age.[379] If, however, the sense of the words "and now" is logical, this opens the door for a different understanding.[380] In other words, "now" refers to the conclusion of

---

[375] Garland (*First Corinthians*, 624) mentions two other associations of the mirror in ancient literature, that of seeing with clarity (Philo spoke of mirrors producing clear reflections) and as a metaphor for self-knowledge through which one catches glimpses of one's true character. Fee (*First Corinthians*, 648) comments, "More likely the emphasis is not on the quality of seeing that one experiences looking into a mirror—that would surely have been an affront to them—but to the indirect nature of looking into a mirror as opposed to seeing someone face to face."

[376] Gk. ἐν αἰνίγματι. BDAG defines as "that which requires special acumen to understand because it is expressed in puzzling fashion, riddle" and "indirect mode of communication." Occurrences in the LXX include Num 12:8; Deut 28:37; 1 Kgs 10:1; 2 Chr 9:1; Prov 1:6; Wis 8:8; Sir 39:3; 47:15; Dan 8:23.

[377] Ciampa and Rosner, *First Corinthians*, 659. See also M. Fishbane, "Through the Looking Glass: Reflections on Ezek 43:3, Num 12:8, and 1 Cor 13:8," *HAR* 10 (1986): 74. The verb translated "fully known" is the compound verb ἐπιγινώσκω, which Fitzmyer (*First Corinthians*, 500) submits does at times have the connotation of "know fully, deeply" instead of simply "to know" (γινώσκω). See Luke 24:16,31; Acts 12:14; Rom 1:32; 2 Cor 6:9.

[378] Gk. νυνὶ δὲ.

[379] That faith and hope are future would seem to contradict passages such as Rom 8:24, "For in this hope we were saved. But hope that is seen is no hope at all. Who hopes for what he already has?" and 2 Cor 5:7, "We live by faith, not by sight." Fee (*First Corinthians*, 649–51) defends this view. See also Collins (*First Corinthians*, 487), "Now is the present moment. Faith, hope, and love are the abiding realities of the present moment of salvation."

[380] BDAG assigns this meaning to 1 Cor 13:13, that is, νυνί is a "temporal marker with focus on a prevailing situation, with the idea of time weakened or entirely absent, as the situation is."

the argument, and the present tense verb "to remain" connotes something present that continues in the future. Already, Paul has included faith and hope in his definition of love (13:7, "always trusts, always hopes"), and the main thrust of the passage is the permanence of love over against the temporary spiritual gifts. In the age to come the people of God will continue to exercise faith in the sense of reliance on and trust in God, and they will continue to hope in the sense of expressing confidence in him. Paul does not say why love is the greatest. Perhaps it is because love is more than faith and hope (13:4–7) or that love is the very essence of God's character: 1 John 4:16, "And so we know and rely on the love God has for us. God is love. Whoever lives in love lives in God, and God in him."[381] There is nothing greater than to love God and to love one's neighbor as oneself (Matt 22:36–40).

### 5. Do All Things for the Edification of the Church (14:1–40)

The topic of chap. 14 is the edification of the church, which cannot occur apart from the practice of love. The noun translated "edification"[382] occurs four times in this chapter (14:3,5,12,25), and the cognate verb "to build up,"[383] which occurred previously in the letter at 8:1,10 and 10:23, appears three times (14:4 [2x]; 14:17). Paul expounds on the theme of edifying love primarily in the context of the gifts of prophecy, tongues, and the interpretation of tongues.[384] All three gifts were listed in 12:7–11 as sovereign distributions of the Holy Spirit for the common good. In chap. 14 Paul explains how these gifts work together for the good of the church gathered together for worship. Paul's focus throughout on the necessity of intelligibility and order in Christian worship recalls the prior discussion of prophecy and prayer (11:2–16) and the Lord's Supper (11:17–34). Worship reflects the character of God who is "not a God of disorder but of peace" (14:33a).[385] For this reason "everything should be done in a fitting and orderly way" (14:40). Paul goes to great lengths to remind them that when the gifts operate in love, the well-being of the whole church

[381] A number of commentators take the "eschatological" view of 13:13. See Robertson and Plummer, *First Corinthians*, 300; Barrett, *First Corinthians*, 308–10; Ciampa and Rosner, *First Corinthians*, 664. Garland (*First Corinthians*, 626) comments, "If Paul is saying that faith, hope, and love abide only in the present epoch, then the contrast that he has set up between their duration and that of tongues, prophecy, and knowledge has been wiped away."

[382] Gk. οἰκοδομή.

[383] Gk. οἰκοδομέω.

[384] Other manifestations of the Spirit are mentioned (14:6,26), but the bulk of the argument has to do with prophecy, tongues, and interpretation of tongues (intelligibility). The verb to prophesy occurs in 14:1,3,4,5,24,31,39; "prophecy" in 14:6 and 22; and "prophet" in 14:29,32,37. The word "tongue" or "tongues" occurs fifteen times in the chapter (14:2,4–6,9,13–14,18–19,22–23,26–27,39).

[385] The theme of "shame" recurs in 14:33–36 as well (cf. 11:4–6,22).

is the primary concern.[386] Paul addresses these issues authoritatively and prophetically: "If anyone thinks that he is a prophet or spiritual, let him know that what I have written to you is the command of the Lord" (14:37).[387] Chapter 14 makes frequent use of the present imperative.[388]

Paul's intent is not to eliminate the gift of tongues from use among the Corinthians. He does not call into question the legitimacy of the gift, nor does he say that they cannot or should not exercise the gift. There is no suggestion that the Corinthians were practicing a counterfeit gift of tongues. Tongues and the interpretation of tongues are listed as one of the manifestations of the Spirit for the common good (12:7–10). Paul does establish clear guidelines for the use of tongues in the church, which must include interpretation (14:13,26–28). Paul writes that he has no problem if all speak in tongues (14:5), claims that he himself speaks in tongues (14:18), and expressly commands, "Do not forbid speaking in tongues" (14:39). However, Paul qualifies each positive statement regarding the gift of tongues with a corresponding assessment of prophecy, demonstrating that prophecy is the preferred gift. Paul preferred prophecy over uninterpreted tongues (14:5), had rather speak five intelligible words in church in order to instruct others than ten thousand words in a tongue (14:18), and while not forbidding them to speak in tongues, exhorts that they "be eager to prophesy" (14:39).[389] Paul's focus on corporate worship and careful attention to rhetorical elements, such as comparison, contrast, exaggeration, and irony, should control the interpretation of this chapter.[390] Chapter 14 is part of the larger concern expressed throughout the letter of living for "the other."

Chapter 14 divides into four sections. In 14:1–5 Paul explains why prophecy is preferable to uninterpreted tongues. In 14:6–19, Paul illustrates the link between intelligibility and edification. If intelligibility is absolutely essential to the edification of the church, then tongues must be interpreted. The contrast between prophecy and tongues continues in 14:20–25 with reference to Isa 28:11 in order to illustrate the effect of prophecy and tongues on unbelievers. Only intelligible communication brings one from a state of unbelief to

---

[386] Thiselton (*First Corinthians*, 1074) suggests that 14:1–25 relates to concerns about love while 14:26–40 reflects concerns about differentiation and order (cf. 12:4–31). There must be respect for others but also differentiation and order, which characterize the activity of God himself.

[387] In other words, Paul's written instructions carry weight and authority over those in Corinth who deem themselves to be a "prophet" or a "spiritual person."

[388] Occurring twenty-one times in the chapter (14:1,12–13,20,26–30,34–35,37,39–40).

[389] The chapter opens and closes with parallel statements regarding Paul's preference for prophecy (14:1,39).

[390] Statements such as, "I would like every one of you to speak in tongues" (14:5), " I thank God that I speak in tongues more than all of you" (14:18), and the notion of everybody either speaking in tongues or prophesying (14:23–25) clearly employ hyperbole to make a point (cf. 12:29–30, "Are all apostles? Are all prophets? Are all teachers? Do all work miracles? Do all have gifts of healing? Do all speak in tongues? Do all interpret?"). The three texts all employ comparison/contrast as well. Cf. 1:14, "I am thankful that I did not baptize any of you except Crispus and Gaius. . . ."

faith. Finally, Paul concludes the argument by setting forth guidelines for their assemblies in order to promote peace, decency, and order (14:26–40).[391]

### *(1) The Case for Prophecy over Uninterpreted Tongues (14:1–5)*

**[1]Follow the way of love and eagerly desire spiritual gifts, especially the gift of prophecy. [2]For anyone who speaks in a tongue does not speak to men but to God. Indeed, no one understands him; he utters mysteries with his spirit. [3]But everyone who prophesies speaks to men for their strengthening, encouragement and comfort. [4]He who speaks in a tongue edifies himself, but he who prophesies edifies the church. [5]I would like every one of you to speak in tongues, but I would rather have you prophesy. He who prophesies is greater than one who speaks in tongues, unless he interprets, so that the church may be edified.**

Verses 1–5 open and close with parallel statements regarding prophecy as preferable to uninterpreted tongues.[392] Paul does not prefer prophecy over tongues because he possesses one gift but not the other. Paul has and exercises both gifts. Rather, his preference for prophecy over uninterpreted tongues is very simple. Prophecy edifies the church. Uninterpreted tongues do not. Paul makes the point by contrasting prophecy and tongues (14:2–4) and concludes that the one who prophesies is greater than the one who speaks in tongues, unless there is interpretation (14:5).[393] Paul's concern is for the edification of the church.

**14:1** If love is the most excellent way (12:31b), and if there is no profit in the exercise of the gifts and extraordinary sacrifice apart from love (13:1–3), and if love never fails (13:8–13), and if love is the greatest in relation to faith and hope (13:13), then the command to "pursue love" in 14:1 naturally follows, linking the discussion of tongues and prophecy with the previous two chapters.[394] Paul implores the Corinthians to pursue love as described in 13:4–7. He also exhorts that they eagerly desire spiritual gifts but with a preference for prophecy. That Paul resumes the argument from 12:31b in 14:1–5 is clear from the use of the verb "to eagerly desire" in 14:1 and the comparative adjective "greater" in 14:5.[395] As in 12:31b, by "greater" Paul means more beneficial. The term "greater" in 13:13 sets love apart from faith and hope and all of

---

[391] Thiselton's (*First Corinthians*, 1146) observation concerning 14:1–40 has merit: "It is far more important to read ch. 14 in the light of the earlier chapters and of chs. 12–13 than to impose upon it a lens forged out of modern controversies surrounding charismatic renewal and theologies of church order as 'ecclesiologies.' Paul insists on 'order' not as self-contained 'doctrine of the church,' but because the church must reflect the nature of God and respect for 'the other.'"

[392] In the Greek the statements are identical, a feature not captured by the NIV translation; μᾶλλον δὲ ἵνα προφητεύητε, "but rather that you may prophesy" (14:1,5).

[393] Greater in the sense of more beneficial (cf. 12:31a). The role of the prophet is second only to that of the apostle, at least in the sense of chronological priority (see on 12:28).

[394] The pursuit of love has, in fact, been the central theme of Paul's argument since 8:1 in his introduction to the topic of food sacrificed to idols with the statement, "Love builds up."

[395] Gk. ζηλοῦτε and μείζων.

the gifts. Thus, 14:1 opens by setting forth priorities: pursue love and eagerly desire spiritual gifts with a preference for prophecy.[396]

The object of the verb "eagerly desire" is "spiritual things"[397] rather than the "greater gifts"[398] of 12:31a. This means that Paul is either drawing a direct parallel to 12:31a and means "spiritual gifts" in 14:1 or that he is returning "to the Spirit-language with which he opened his discourse in 12:1, rather than continuing with the grace-gift language he took up in 12:4 and used in 12:9,28,30,31."[399] The grace-gift language[400] of chap. 12 disappears altogether in chap. 14 suggesting that Paul may be once again picking up on the Corinthians' understanding of the term "spiritual" in 14:1 (cf. 12:1) and referring primarily to gifts of inspired speech, which is the focus of 14:1–40.[401] While it is difficult to know how restrictive or how broad Paul's use of "Spirit-language" is in 14:1,[402] it is clear that those who pursue love will eagerly desire the manifestations of the Spirit and seek the edification of the church.

The verb "to pursue"[403] may be a bit stronger than the verb "to eagerly desire."[404] While Paul can readily affirm that they are eager for spiritual things (14:12), he cannot say the same regarding love. They should excel in both; that is, they should lovingly desire the manifestations of the Spirit for the good of the church. Paul frequently uses the verb "to pursue" to refer to persecution but he also uses the verb metaphorically of spiritual effort in some contexts, as in 1 Cor 14:1.[405] Both senses of the term occur in Rom 12:13–14, to "pursue/practice" hospitality in contrast to blessing those who "persecute"

[396] Although Paul does not use the language of one's "rights" as he does in chaps. 8–9, the same principle applies. If one has the gift of tongues, the gift is only to be exercised in building up others. Otherwise, the tongues-speaker should be silent. Thiselton (*Shorter Commentary*, 237) notes, "If the criterion for evaluating gifts, therefore, is love for others (v. 1), prophetic speech is clearly the more important."

[397] Gk. τὰ πνευματικά, clearly neuter in this instance.

[398] Gk. τὰ χαρίσματα τὰ μείζονα.

[399] Garland, *1 Corinthians*, 632.

[400] Gk. χάρισμα.

[401] So Fee, *First Corinthians*, 632; Thiselton, *First Corinthians*, 1083.

[402] Ciampa and Rosner (*First Corinthians*, 670) argue for a less-restrictive use of τὰ πνευματικά, "If Paul's reference to 'the gifts of the Spirit' in 12:1 was a case of employing the preferred language of the Corinthians themselves, and their view of spiritual gifts was restricted to tongues and prophecy (or other speech gifts), by the time Paul finished 12:4–11 the Corinthians should have understood that in Paul's own view many gifts were given and distributed by the Spirit, including many that were not speech gifts. The term used in 12:1 is understood to apply to all of the gifts mentioned in that chapter. The Corinthians would not be expected to apply a more restricted sense at the beginning of this chapter." That Paul himself would not limit τὰ πνευματικά to gifts of perception, speech, or interpretation is clear from 12:4–31. The Corinthians, however, likely held the speech gifts in high esteem and attached status to them. Note especially Paul's mention of "the prophet" and the "spiritual person" in 14:37.

[403] Gk. διώκω.

[404] Gk. ζηλόω.

[405] All occurrences of the term in Paul include Rom 9:30–31; 12:13–14; 14:19; 1 Cor 4:12;

you. Romans 14:19 parallels 1 Cor 14:1, "To *make every effort* to do what leads to peace and to mutual edification." In Phil 3:12–14 Paul uses the term of *pressing on* toward the heavenly prize. Paul urged the Thessalonians to pursue what is good for others (1 Thess 5:15), and he enjoined Timothy to "pursue righteousness" (1 Tim 6:11; 2 Tim 2:22).

**14:2–4** In 14:2–4 Paul explains why the Corinthians should prefer prophecy over uninterpreted tongues by contrasting the two gifts.[406] First, the person who speaks in a tongue does not speak to men but to God. In context, we should understand Paul to mean that he who speaks in an "uninterpreted" tongue speaks only to God.[407] In other words, God is the only one who understands what is being said. No one else understands because the speaker "utters mysteries with his spirit."[408] Paul's intent in 14:2 is not to define tongues per se, or prophecy, but rather to describe the effect of uninterpreted tongues and prophecy in relation to the edification of the church.[409] In contrast to uninterpreted tongues, the one who prophesies "speaks to men for their strengthening, encouragement and comfort" (14:3).

The second contrast follows from the first. The one who speaks in a tongue edifies himself, while the one who prophesies edifies the church (14:4). That prophecy edifies the church is easy enough to understand,[410] but the assertion that the one who speaks in tongues edifies himself "remains acutely controversial."[411] Is Paul's claim to be taken at face value, or is he using the verb "to edify" in a negative sense in this context?[412] The broader argument

---

14:1; 15:9; 2 Cor 4:9; Gal 1:13,23; 4:29; 5:11; 6:12; Phil 3:6,12,14; 1 Thess 5:15; 1 Tim 6:11; 2 Tim 2:22; 3:12.

[406] 14:2 begins with an explanatory γάρ.

[407] That "uninterpreted" tongues is the issue is clarified by 14:5, "unless he interprets."

[408] It is also possible to render, "He speaks mysteries in the Spirit" (so HCSB, ESV). Support for "spirit" is found in 14:14, "For if I pray in a tongue, my spirit prays." Normally, in Paul, the term "mystery" refers to truths previously unknown now disclosed in the gospel (cf. 2:1,7; 4:1; 15:51). If "mysteries" carries this meaning in this context, then Paul is saying that truths revealed by the Spirit remain hidden since no one understands. Garland (*First Corinthians*, 633) suggests that mysteries are revelatory only if interpreted. But does "mystery" carry this restricted meaning in this context?

[409] Thiselton (*Shorter Commentary*, 236) offers that 14:2 gives one of the clearest and concise definitions of tongues in the New Testament. The nature of the gift, however, remains the subject of intense debate. Ciampa and Rosner (*First Corinthians*, 671) concur with Thiselton that tongues is a language expressed in prayer and praise, but they do not agree that it is not a human language.

[410] Paul's description is best understood as a primary function of prophecy rather than a definition. Ciampa and Rosner (*First Corinthians*, 672) note how the three words describing the function of prophecy (strengthening, encouragement and comfort) "show that prophetic ministry flows out of a deep concern for others." Furthermore, "It is interesting to note that much Old Testament prophecy hardly would have been described as comforting, since much of it was dedicated to condemning disobedience and apostasy" (673).

[411] Thiselton, *First Corinthians*, 1095.

[412] There is precedent for a negative sense of the verb "to edify" in 8:10, "For if anyone with a weak conscience sees you who have this knowledge eating in an idol's temple, won't he be emboldened to eat what has been sacrificed to idols?" The word for "emboldened" is the same word

suggests that Paul is not commending the use of tongues as a means of self-edification, which would not only counter the recurring emphasis on "others";[413] it would contradict the purpose of spiritual gifts, which are given for the common good (12:7). Paul is not expressing contempt for tongues in 14:4 but rather stating a fact concerning uninterpreted tongues as he does in 14:2. It is the reality that no one but God understands uninterpreted tongues and that no one is edified except the speaker that meets with Paul's disapproval. Paul's argument allows that tongues may be expressed in prayer and praise to God in corporate worship, but he also insists that intelligibility is essential to edification when so expressed (14:13–17), which raises doubts about incomprehensible private tongues as a means of self-edification. If intelligibility is essential to edification corporately (14:6–19), why would unintelligibility be acceptable privately if Paul is conceding that the one who speaks in tongues edifies himself in a positive sense? In other words, if uninterpreted tongues cannot edify the church, then how can tongues edify the individual privately apart from comprehension? Or to state the question in reverse, if unintelligible tongues can edify the individual why not also the whole church? The notion of incomprehensible tongues as private, edifying prayer runs counter to Paul's argument as a whole and to the corporate purpose and function of spiritual gifts.[414]

**14:5** This verse closes out the introductory paragraph with Paul's affirmation of the gift of tongues but his preference for prophecy. The phrase, "I

---

translated "edifies" in 14:4 (οἰκοδομέω). Thiselton seeks to hold the positive and negative meanings in tension, that tongues can be uplifting in private but in public there is a negative side effect when there is no interpretation. He comments, however, "Whether or not the individual is edified, Paul attacks a concern for the individual in contrast to the wider whole of the church community" (ibid.). The negative effect of uninterpreted tongues comes into sharp focus in 14:20–25 with reference to the unbeliever. If Paul can infer that "tongues," a gift of the Spirit, is a sign of judgment to unbelievers when uninterpreted then he can also infer that the "edification" of the self is also a negative situation, particularly in contrast to prophecy that edifies the whole.

[413] E.g., 8:1, "Love builds up"; 8:13, "Therefore, if what I eat causes my brother to fall into sin, I will never eat meat again, so that I will not cause him to fall"; 9:22, "I have become all things to all men so that by all possible means I might save some"; 10:24, "Nobody should seek his own good, but the good of others"; 10:33, "For I am not seeking my own good but the good of many"; 11:4–5a, "Every man who prays or prophesies with his head covered dishonors his head. And every woman who prays or prophesies with her head uncovered dishonors her head"; 11:33, "So then, my brothers, when you come together to eat, wait for each other"; 13:5, Love "is not self-seeking"; 14:12, "try to excel in gifts that build up the church"; 14:17, "You may be giving thanks well enough, but the other man is not edified"; 14:19, "But in the church I would rather speak five intelligible words to instruct others . . ."; 14:26, "All of these must be done for the strengthening of the church"; 14:31, "For you can all prophesy in turn so that everyone may be instructed and encouraged"; 14:40, "But everything should be done in a fitting and orderly way."

[414] Contra Fee (*First Corinthians*, 669), who argues that what is said in 14:2–4 and intimated in 14:15 is "that the one who speaks in tongues is edified by his or her communion with God through the Spirit, without the need of perceptual understanding." Although Fee contends that self-edification is not self-centeredness, he concedes that "Paul's present concern is not with private devotion but with public worship" (657). Fitzmyer (*First Corinthians*, 511) contends that 14:4 is derogatory, that it is vain "to see in such speech some 'benefit,' if only to the individual."

would like every one of you to speak in tongues," is disputed. Already in 12:30 Paul has made clear that not everyone has the gift of tongues. Does Paul mean that he allows tongues (a mere concession) or that he "wants" tongues?[415] It is sometimes suggested that Paul alludes to Moses' wish in Num 11:29 "that all the LORD's people were prophets and that the LORD would put his Spirit on them!"[416] Paul, like Moses, rejects "the individualism and elitism of any exclusive bestowal of the Spirit."[417] To be sure, Paul would reject individualism and elitism, but it is not certain that Paul has this Old Testament text in mind; nor is it certain that it would serve his argument well, that is, if Paul is saying that he wishes the Holy Spirit to come on all in full measure, he would not link the bestowal to one gift.[418] In context Paul simply clarifies that he does not discount the gifts of tongues if interpreted, "so that the church may be edified." The one who interprets may be the tongues-speaker (14:13)[419] or someone else (14:26–27).[420] The vital link between intelligibility and edification is a point Paul develops at length in the next unit (14:6–19).

### *(2) The Vital Link between Intelligibility and Edification (14:6–19)*

**6Now, brothers, if I come to you and speak in tongues, what good will I be
to you, unless I bring you some revelation or knowledge or prophecy or word of
instruction? 7Even in the case of lifeless things that make sounds, such as the flute
or harp, how will anyone know what tune is being played unless there is a distinc-
tion in the notes? 8Again, if the trumpet does not sound a clear call, who will get
ready for battle? 9So it is with you. Unless you speak intelligible words with your
tongue, how will anyone know what you are saying? You will just be speaking into
the air. 10Undoubtedly there are all sorts of languages in the world, yet none of
them is without meaning. 11If then I do not grasp the meaning of what someone is
saying, I am a foreigner to the speaker, and he is a foreigner to me. 12So it is with
you. Since you are eager to have spiritual gifts, try to excel in gifts that build up
the church.**

**13For this reason anyone who speaks in a tongue should pray that he may inter-
pret what he says. 14For if I pray in a tongue, my spirit prays, but my mind is
unfruitful. 15So what shall I do? I will pray with my spirit, but I will also pray**

[415] Note the different translations of 14:5. ESV, "I want you all to speak in tongues." HCSB, "I wish all of you spoke in other languages." NASB, "Now I wish you all spoke in tongues." NRSV, "Now I would like all of you to speak in tongues." Thiselton (*First Corinthians*, 1097–98) translates, "I take pleasure in all of you speaking in tongues."

[416] S. J. Kistemaker, *1 Corinthians*, New Testament Commentary (Grand Rapids: Baker, 1993), 481–83.

[417] Thiselton, *First Corinthians*, 1097. See also Garland, *1 Corinthians*, 634–35.

[418] Fitzmyer (*First Corinthians*, 512) considers the connection to Num 11:29 "simply far-fetched," since "that episode involves a different kind of 'prophecy,' and it has nothing to do with speaking in tongues—or with Paul's wish."

[419] So Hays, *First Corinthians*, 236; Garland, *1 Corinthians*, 635; Ciampa and Rosner, *First Corinthians*, 676.

[420] If two or three speak in a tongue, only one should interpret according to Paul's regulation of tongues in public worship.

**with my mind; I will sing with my spirit, but I will also sing with my mind. [16]If you are praising God with your spirit, how can one who finds himself among those who do not understand say "Amen" to your thanksgiving, since he does not know what you are saying? [17]You may be giving thanks well enough, but the other man is not edified.**

**[18]I thank God that I speak in tongues more than all of you. [19]But in the church I would rather speak five intelligible words to instruct others than ten thousand words in a tongue.**

Having made the case for prophecy over uninterpreted tongues by comparing the two gifts, Paul now elaborates on the vital link between intelligibility and edification. He begins by using himself as the first point of illustration, asking what good he would be to them apart from intelligible speech.[421] Three analogies follow. First, in the case of musical instruments, Paul asks, "How will anyone know what tune is being played unless there is a distinction in the notes?" The corollary illustration of the military trumpet poses the same dilemma: "Again, if the trumpet does not sound a clear call, who will get ready for battle?" In the third illustration Paul observes broadly that all sounds (languages) in the world have meaning and exist to be distinguished and understood.[422] In sum, in 14:6–12 Paul argues that the preacher must speak intelligibly in order for the message to be understood, instruments produce meaningful music by making a distinction of sounds, the military trumpet issues commands through an intelligible signal, and a foreigner can only be understood if there is a common language. Paul concludes the analogies with the second explicit exhortation in the chapter to "seek the edification of the church" (14:12; cf. 14:5). In 14:13–19, Paul infers from the illustrations that the interpretation of tongues is essential to the edification of others.

**14:6** The words, "Now, brothers," marks the new unit of thought. The rhetorical question, "What good will I be to you . . . ?" recalls Paul's statement in 13:3 that he gains nothing from extraordinary sacrifice apart from love.[423] Paul hypothetically imagines that if he came to them speaking in tongues there would be no benefit because there would be no understanding. The Corinthians would only profit if he ministered to them by revelation, prophecy, knowledge, or teaching, all modes of intelligible speech. The phrase, "If I come to you," echoes Paul's earlier statement in the letter of how he actually did come to them in his initial ministry in Corinth (2:1–5).[424] He proclaimed the "mystery" of God (2:1), but it was a clear, simple message of Christ crucified (2:2) and a powerful demonstration of the Spirit (2:5). The wisdom that Paul and others

[421] Paul refers to himself in 14:6,11,15,18–19 and makes direct application to the Corinthians in 14:9,12,16–17.

[422] Robertson and Plummer (*First Corinthians*, 308–9) detect intentional progression in the analogies/illustrations. "If the military trumpet is more potent than pipe or lyre still more expressive is the human tongue" (309).

[423] The same verb is used in 13:3 and 14:6 (ὠφελέω), a nuance missed in translation.

[424] So also Hays, *First Corinthians*, 237. Cf. also 4:18–19,21; 16:2,5.

imparted "among the mature" was a wisdom that had been hidden in mystery before the ages (2:6–7) but now revealed by God through his Spirit (2:10). Paul conveyed "spiritual" words that were discerned by "spiritual people" (2:12–13). Furthermore, Paul speaks to them in this letter clearly, sometimes boldly (5:1–13) and prophetically (14:37). By way of contrast Paul now imagines that if he came to them speaking in unintelligible tongues there would be no benefit whatsoever. Intelligible content is essential to communication and thus edification.

Verse 6 includes yet another list of spiritual gifts. In addition to prophecy and knowledge, which have already been mentioned in the previous two chapters (12:8–10; 13:2,8), Paul adds "revelation" and "teaching."[425] The common element in all four is intelligibility, which is why Paul singles them out. Hays thinks the list of gifts other than prophecy in 14:6 "suggests that the term 'prophecy' should be read throughout chap. 14 as synecdoche for all forms of intelligible speech gifts that edify the church."[426] In other words, the real issue is intelligibility, and prophecy is the representative gift.[427] Whether Paul intends to draw fine distinctions between the four gifts listed here is difficult to discern.[428] It has been suggested that revelation and knowledge are ways of perceiving truth, while prophecy and teaching are modes of conveying truth.[429] Teaching is listed alongside revelation in 14:26, but revelation is associated with prophecy in 14:30,[430] and prophecy and knowledge are linked in 13:1–2,8. God's appointment of prophets and teachers in 12:28 corresponds to the association of the gifts of prophecy and teaching in 14:6. Since prophecy is linked with teaching, Ciampa and Rosner wonder if Paul clearly distinguishes between the two or whether "he sometimes thinks of them as interrelated gifts or ministries, perhaps ones that have to do with the communication of (different kinds of) knowledge." Along with Fee they conclude, "Usage weighs against thinking that Paul uses the four words as technical terms."[431] It is clear that these gifts edify the church because they are intelligible. Paul would add "tongues" to the list if accompanied by the gift of interpretation, in which case the church would receive edification (14:13,26–27).

**14:7–9** The first two analogies of musical instruments recalls the comparison of the tongues of men and angels to the resounding gong and clanging

---

[425] "Teaching" probably corresponds to the office of "teacher" mentioned in 12:28. Other occurrences of "teaching" (διδαχή) in Paul include Rom 6:17; 16:17; 2 Tim 4:2; Titus 1:9.

[426] Ibid.

[427] So Fee, *First Corinthians*, 662.

[428] So Barrett, *First Corinthians*, 317.

[429] See H. Conzelmann, *1 Corinthians: A Critical and Historical Commentary on the Bible*, Hermeneia, trans. J. Leitch (Philadelphia: Fortress, 1975), 235n20; Grudem, *Gift of Prophecy*, 138–39.

[430] In 14:30, the passive verb form is used, ἀποκαλυφθῇ, "But if something *has been revealed*" (HCSB). Cf. also 2:6–16, esp. 2:10, on the revelation of the hidden things of God by the Spirit.

[431] Ciampa and Rosner, *First Corinthians*, 679; Fee, *First Corinthians*, 663.

cymbal (13:1). The analogies are self-evident and easy to understand. Even lifeless instruments such as the flute or harp and the military trumpet distinguish their sounds in order to communicate intelligibly. No one can appreciate or know what is being played on the flute or the harp apart from a distinction of notes. Likewise the military trumpet must give a distinct, coherent signal in order to call men to battle. Hays points out Paul's use of military metaphors elsewhere to describe the calling of Christians (Rom 6:12–14; 2 Cor 10:3–6; Phil 1:27–30; 1 Thess 5:8; cf. Eph 6:10–20; 2 Tim 4:7) and thinks that the metaphor in 14:8 "suggests that public speech in the Christian assembly should awaken members of the church to action in the cosmic conflict in which the church is engaged."[432]

With the phrase "So it is with you" (14:9), Paul aims the analogies directly at the Corinthians. The word "tongue" is used to refer to the human instrument of speech, not to the spiritual gift of "tongues," in the question, "Unless you speak intelligible words with your tongue, how will anyone know what you are saying?" Just as musical instruments and the military trumpet offer distinct sounds for their respective purposes, so also the Corinthians should use the human tongue to convey distinct sounds. Otherwise, they will be speaking "into the air," that is, to no one and to no effect.[433]

**14:10–12** Paul's third analogy, all sorts of languages ("sounds") in the world, was especially relevant to Corinth with its two harbors positioning the city as a major crossroads to the world.[434] The citizens of Corinth would have been all too familiar with the alienation and frustration caused by the blend of different languages and different cultures in a major urban setting. Such alienation and frustration, however, should never characterize the assembly of believers. By means of a wordplay Paul asserts that of all the different kinds of sounds in the world none are "without sound,"[435] that is, without meaning. If someone speaks and the hearers cannot understand what is being said, then meaningful communication cannot occur. The odd phrase in 14:11, literally, "Therefore, if I do not know the power of the voice . . . ,"[436] may hark back

[432] Hays, *First Corinthians*, 236. On the trumpet imagery in Paul see also 1 Cor 15:52 and 1 Thess 4:16.

[433] Cf. Paul's use of the athletic metaphor in 9:26, "I box, not as one beating the air."

[434] As Collins (*First Corinthians*, 497) explains, "In Paul's day the city was a provincial capital, under the influence of Hellenistic culture and Roman politics. It was located on the intersection of two major trade routes, one going north and south, the other going east and west. The presence of various sanctuaries in the city underscores the influence of a wide range of cultures on metropolitan Corinth. Transient merchants, some of whom may have had to winter in Corinth (cf. 16:6), exposed the city's population to a variety of languages. The Greek and Latin tongues would have been known to various segments of the population."

[435] The word used for "language" in 14:10 is not γλῶσσα (tongue) but φωνή (sound). That Paul uses a different word for language here does not mean that "tongues" are not human languages. The lexical choice of "sound" may be rhetorical wordplay or may link with the preceding analogies of the sounds of musical instruments.

[436] Gk. ἐὰν οὖν μὴ εἰδῶ τὴν δύναμιν τῆς φωνῆς.

to Paul's previous use of the word "power" in his opening argument regarding speech and wisdom. Paul's clear speech about the cross was a demonstration of the Spirit's power (2:5; cf. 1:18), and he challenged the puffed-up in Corinth, wanting to know "not only how these arrogant people are talking, but what power they have" (4:19). In order for language to be powerful, that is, effective, language has to be understood. Unintelligible communication is absolutely detrimental to genuine community and renders brothers and sisters in Christ as foreigners to one another.[437] Thus, the situation with uninterpreted tongues is far more severe than just the lack of edification; unintelligible tongues erects barriers of alienation.[438] God is a God of relationship, order, peace, and intention.

The phrase, "Thus also you" (14:12; cf. 14:9, "so it is with you"), signals the second application to the Corinthians, "Since you are eager to have spiritual gifts, try to excel in gifts that build up the church." The phrase translated "eager to have spiritual gifts" in the NIV is a more ambiguous phrase in Greek, reading literally "since you are eager for spirits."[439] The term translated "eager" is the noun form of the verb used at 12:31, "eagerly desire the greater gifts," and 14:1, "eagerly desire spiritual gifts." The NIV translation "spiritual gifts" in 14:12 takes the view that the term is simply shorthand for the gifts of the Spirit. In 14:14–15 Paul refers to praying and singing in his spirit and in 14:32 to the spirits of the prophets. Fee suggests that it may be Paul's way of speaking of the Spirit working through their human spirit, but he thinks it is more specific and refers to their desire for one particular manifestation of the Spirit, speaking in tongues.[440] The odd phraseology has led some to suggest that the phrase is a form of mild rebuke.[441] Whatever the precise meaning of the phrase, Paul recognizes their zeal and has no problem with it as long as they seek the edification of the church.[442]

---

[437] Mitchell (*Rhetorical of Reconciliation*, 172) notes that common language is essential for unity. The Greek term for "foreigner" is βάρβαρος, which refers to a non-Greek speaking person. The word is onomatopoetic, that is, the pronunciation sounds like the meaning with the repetition of *bar-bar* indicative of senseless repetition. Ciampa and Rosner (*First Corinthians*, 683) suggest that Paul's reference to the "foreigner" anticipates the use of Isa 28:11–12 in the next unit, 14:20–25.

[438] So Hays, *First Corinthians*, 237; Garland, *1 Corinthians*, 637; Ciampa and Rosner, *First Corinthians*, 684.

[439] Gk. ἐπεὶ ζηλωταί ἐστε πνευμάτων. The term "spirits" is not the same term as "spiritual person or thing" (12:1; 14:1) nor is it the word for "gifts" (12:4,9,28,30–31).

[440] Fee, *First Corinthians*, 666. So also Witherington (*Conflict and Community*, 283), "Each of you is eager about your own spirit speaking in tongues by the moving of the Holy Spirit." Thiselton (*First Corinthians*, 1107) suggests "powers of the Spirit."

[441] Robertson and Plummer, *First Corinthians*, 311. But cf. 2 Cor 8:7, "But just as you excel in everything—in faith, in speech, in knowledge, in complete earnestness and in your love for us—see that you also excel in this grace of giving."

[442] The phrase "try to excel" translates the Greek ζητέω, "to seek" (cf. similar uses of the verb in 10:24,33; 13:5).

**14:13** "For this reason" signals Paul's conclusion based on the argument for intelligibility in 14:6–12.[443] The logical inference of the preceding analogies is that since intelligibility is essential to the edification of the church, the one who speaks in a tongue "should pray that he may interpret what he says" (cf. 14:5).[444] Paul will insist on interpretation yet again in 14:26–27 as an essential component of order in public worship. Grosheide wants to distinguish interpretation in this verse from the "gift of interpretation" (12:10): "This is not the same as praying for the charisma of interpretation, for then the Corinthians might think that it would be proper to pray for a charisma."[445] Ciampa and Rosner, on the other hand, suggest that this is the clearest indication in the letter of what Paul means by striving for the greater gifts (12:31). "Part of striving for them, apparently, is praying that God would grant them to you."[446] There is no reason to doubt that Paul has the gift of interpretation in mind. His command to the one who speaks in tongues to pray for interpretation complements the command in the preceding verse to seek the edification of the church (14:12). Paul's statement indicates that the one speaking in a tongue and the one interpreting is the same person.[447] Verses 26–27, on the other hand, present a scenario where someone else might have the gift of interpretation and provide intelligibility to the tongue. The verb "to pray" is in the imperative mood that is often rendered idiomatically in English as "should pray."[448] This often fails to capture the force of the imperative, which could be rendered, "must pray." Paul says that it must be done, otherwise edification cannot occur, which is critical to the exercise of spiritual gifts in the church. Paul consistently has in mind the welfare of the community.

**14:14–15** The reason interpretation is essential for the one who speaks in a tongue is that speaking in a tongue apart from the mind is unfruitful. There is no spiritual benefit for either the speaker or the hearer, and in such speaking the church is not edified (14:5,12). As in 14:6, Paul shifts to the first person and uses himself as the example, "For if I pray in a tongue, my spirit prays, but my mind is unfruitful." The description of tongues as a form of communion with God in prayer parallels the description of tongues in 14:2 as speaking to God and not to men. However, Paul is describing prayer in the context of public

---

[443] Gk. διό, a strong inferential conjunction, indicating the close relationship with 14:6–12.

[444] Fee (*First Corinthians*, 668) thinks that we might expect Paul to say that the one who speaks in tongues should seek rather to prophesy, but Paul does not say this because intelligibility is the primary concern, not prophecy.

[445] F. W. Grosheide, *Commentary on the First Epistle to the Corinthians*, NICNT (Grand Rapids: Eerdmans, 1953), 324.

[446] Ciampa and Rosner, *First Corinthians*, 688.

[447] Thiselton (*First Corinthians*, 1108) notes that all main English versions ascribe the interpreting to the one who prays in tongues (see AV, KJV, NRSV, REB, NJB, NIV, ESV, NASB, HCSB). The NIV2011 translates as a plural, "one who speaks in a tongue should pray that they may interpret what they say."

[448] Gk. προσευχέσθω.

worship, indicating that all prayer in the gathered assembly, although directed toward God, has an edifying effect on others and must be intelligible for edification to take place. In other words intelligible prayers are directed primarily to God, and others who hear the prayer, though not the direct recipient of the speech, are nonetheless edified.

One of the key interpretive issues in 14:14 has to do with the conjunction "for" in the phrase "For if I pray in a tongue." Its certainty in the textual tradition is somewhat in doubt as indicated by the brackets in the critical Greek texts.[449] If original then it introduces an explanation for 14:13, that is, why the one who speaks in a tongue must pray that he may interpret. Some think that the meaning of 14:13–14 is that the tongues-speaker should pray for the gift of interpretation for his own benefit.[450] This is doubtful since the context is public worship and Paul's concern is for the edification of the church, as the illustration in 14:16–17 clarifies in the shift to the second person plural "you." However, in using himself as the example in 14:15 and by asserting that "my mind" is unfruitful if only "my spirit" prays, the illustration itself suggests that there is no benefit to the speaker as well if there is no corresponding interpretation. Thus, as a corollary to what Paul says regarding the necessity of intelligibility for the sake of the community, the argument also requires that meaningful prayer is intelligible prayer, even if in private.[451]

The "spirit" in 14:14–15 refers to Paul's spirit as clarified by the possessive pronoun *my* and the parallel expression *my* mind.[452] Barrett suggests three possible meanings of the phrase "my spirit prays": (1) Paul refers to a part of his

---

[449] Nestle-Aland 28th. ἐὰν [γὰρ] προσεύχωμαι γλώσσῃ.

[450] So Grosheide, *First Corinthians*, 325–26.

[451] V. Verbrugge explains, "But since he does not understand with his mind the words he is using, there is no personal benefit or fruit to him (and, of course, were it done in public the prayer would have equally no value for those listening to him). Who wants to listen to a lengthy prayer that sounds like gibberish? What benefit is this either to the pray-er or to those listening in?" ("1 Corinthians" in *The Expositor's Bible Commentary: Galatians–Romans*, ed. T. Longman and D. E. Garland, rev. ed. [Grand Rapids: Zondervan, 2008], 381). Fitzmyer (*First Corinthians*, 516) asserts that Paul concedes that tongues-speaking might be a form of prayer but that in such utterances the mind is unproductive, "not reaping a spiritual benefit for the speaker or building up the community. . . . The ideal prayer to God is that uttered by all human faculties working together." Even though Paul's discussion focuses solely on the public worship setting, many think that Paul's argument implies that the use of tongues in private (apparently without interpretation) is acceptable (14:18–19,28). His argument, however, establishes a necessary correlation between intelligibility and edification. Paul does not say, "If anyone wants to speak in tongues apart from interpretation, then do so at home," as he advises regarding other issues of concern (11:22; 14:35). Morris (*1 Corinthians*, 190) comments, "The Christian life is considerably more than a mental exercise, but anyone whose mind is unfruitful is not being true to his Christian calling."

[452] For representative uses of Paul's use of "spirit" with the personal pronoun, see Rom 1:9 (whom I serve in my spirit); Rom 8:16 (the Spirit testifies with our spirit that we are children of God); 2 Cor 2:13 (no rest for my spirit); 2 Cor 7:13 (his spirit [Titus] has been refreshed). There is also a pattern of the use of "spirit" with the personal pronoun in Paul's concluding benedictions, "The grace of Jesus be with your spirit" (Gal 6:18; Phil 4:23; 2 Tim 4:22; Phlm 25).

psychological make-up, a nonrational part of his being that is the counterpart of his mind. (2) Paul refers to his gift as given by the Spirit (14:12) or refers to the spiritual agency that induces inspired speech. (3) "My Spirit" is the Holy Spirit given *to me*. Barrett thinks that the second option is correct.[453] Fee suggests that Paul's intent can be expressed as "my S/spirit prays."[454] Thiselton counters, however, that to merge *spirit* as a noncognitive or spiritual human capacity with *Spirit* as the Holy Spirit of God creates "disastrous confusion."[455] Paul "probably refers to the human capacity or disposition that stands in contrast to human apprehension."[456] Fitzmyer thinks it is far from certain that the spirit is the faculty by which one is in communion with the deity and that Paul cannot mean that his "spirit" is the superior part of his person since the contrast implies that the "mind" is superior.[457]

Paul's exposition of wisdom and the Spirit in 2:6–16 is particularly relevant to the discussion concerning the relationship of the Spirit to the mind. The hidden things of God have been revealed through the Spirit (2:6). The reception of the Spirit is for the purpose of knowing what has been freely given by God (2:12). Furthermore, Paul refers to "words taught by the Spirit" (2:13) and having the "mind of Christ" (2:16). Thiselton explains that being spiritual "occurs when the Holy Spirit controls both the spirit and the mind. If only the mind is active, everything remains at a theoretical level; if only the heart is active, the door lies open to self-deception and credulity. If both are open to the Holy Spirit, the result can build up the community and bear the fruit (v. 14a) of love for the other."[458]

---

[453] Barrett, *First Corinthians*, 320. Barrett explains, "Paul's language lacks clarity and precision here because he is compressing into a few words the thoughts (1) that it is the Holy Spirit of God is at work, inspiring Christian worship and prayer; (2) that the work of the Spirit is crystallized into a specific gift; (3) this gift is given in such personal terms to *me* that I can speak of it as *mine*—in short as *my spirit,* which, being what it is, operates through appropriate psychological channels independently of *my mind.*"

[454] Fee, *First Corinthians*, 670. "The most viable solution to this ambiguity is that by the language 'my spirit prays' Paul means his own spirit is praying as the Holy Spirit gives the utterance. Hence, 'my S/spirit prays.'"

[455] Thiselton, *First Corinthians*, 1112–13. Thiselton explains, "First, Pauline specialists generally agree that Platonic or Idealist notions of the human spirit as a point of 'divine contact' are alien to Paul and plainly alien to the explicit thrust of 1 Cor 2:10–12. Second, to read this into 14:15 is to fall into the very trap to which the Corinthians and many today fall prey, namely, of associating the operation of the Holy Spirit more closely with noncognitive 'spontaneous' phenomena than with a self-critical reflection upon the word of God as that which addresses the understanding and thereby transforms the heart (cf. 14:23–25)." So also Fitzmyer (*First Corinthians*, 515–16), "Fee only confuses matters by interpreting 'my spirit' as 'my S/spirit' because Paul's phrase would then imply that the Holy Spirit could be 'mine' in some way."

[456] Thiselton (*First Corinthians*, 1114) translates, "the depths of our being."

[457] Fitzmyer, *First Corinthians*, 516. "Paul's contrast of pneuma and *nous* implies that the *nous* is superior to *pneuma,* which is rather the inward immaterial faculty of a human being that wills and reacts emotionally to things about them and that is open to the influence of the divine Spirit; it thus differs from the *nous* that makes rational judgments about such things and enables a human being to communicate consciously with God (in prayer and song)."

[458] Thiselton, *First Corinthians*, 1113.

If it is the case that praying in a tongue is unfruitful apart from understanding, Paul asks, "So what shall I do?" His conclusion is simple; he will do both, "I will pray with my spirit, but I will also pray with my mind." To this he adds singing with his spirit and his mind, which suggests that singing praise to God as communal prayer was also part of the worship experience of the early church.[459]

**14:16–17** In 14:16 Paul continues the illustration of someone speaking in tongues but shifts to the second person plural and uses the Corinthians as the example rather than himself. The phrase "If you are praising God with your spirit"[460] is consistent with Paul's prior assertions of tongues as speaking to God (14:2), praying (14:14), and singing (14:15) when the church is gathered together. It is not clear, however, what Paul means by the phrase translated the "one who finds himself among those who do not understand." The difficulty lies in the Greek phrase, "the one who occupies the place of,"[461] and the designation, "one who does not understand."[462] The NIV rendering is an interpretation, which is necessary for translation.[463] The word translated "one who does not understand" occurs only five times in the New Testament. The only occurrence outside of Paul's letters is Acts 4:13, where Peter and John are cast as "unschooled" men. Paul refers to himself as an "untrained" speaker in 2 Cor 11:6; that is, he was not a professional rhetorician (cf. 1:17; 2:1–5). The word occurs again in 14:23–24 in conjunction with the unbelievers. The entry in BDAG claims those described by the term "are neither similar to the unbelievers nor are they full-fledged Christians, but stand between the two groups, probably as prospects for membership." It is doubtful, however, that the word carries such a technical meaning in this context since Paul envisions the response "Amen" if only what was being said could be understood.[464] More likely, the phrase "to occupy the place" is metaphorical and does not

---

[459] So Collins, *First Corinthians*, 502.

[460] Lit., "blessing God" (Gk. εὐλογέω; cf. Eph 1:3).

[461] Gk. ὁ ἀναπληρῶν τὸν τόπον.

[462] That translates the Greek word ἰδιώτης.

[463] NASB, "The one who fills the place of the ungifted." ESV, NRSV, "Anyone in the position of an outsider." HCSB, "The uninformed person." NET, "Someone without the gift." NIV2011, "someone else, who is now put in the position of an inquirer."

[464] The word "amen" occurs frequently in the New Testament at the end of a doxology. For Pauline usage see Rom 1:25; 9:5; 11:36; 15:33; 16:27; 1 Cor 14:16; 2 Cor 1:20; Gal 1:5; 6:18; Eph 3:21; Phil 4:20; 1 Thess 3:13; 1 Tim 1:17; 6:16; 2 Tim 4:18. For references other than Paul see Heb 13:21,25; 1 Pet 4:11; 5:11; Jude 25; Rev 1:6, 7:12. Concerning the Old Testament background of the term, Thiselton (*First Corinthians*, 1115–16) comments, "The use of the liturgical term here to signify endorsement or solemn assent to the praise or prayer of another occurs in Num 5:22; Deut 27:15; 1 Chr 16:36; Neh 5:13; 8:6, and our verse reflects the appropriation of this use in the earliest Christian churches." BDAG defines as "strong affirmation of what is stated, an expression of faith, a liturgical formula at the end of the liturgy, spoken by the congregation."

refer to a literal place in the assembly occupied by those interested in Christianity[465] but rather to those who assume the role of a social outsider since they are alienated by the unintelligible speech (cf. 14:11). Garland explains that the phrase is "open-ended and refers to all those who find themselves in the role of the novice when someone prays in a tongue. In this case, it describes all members of the community who do not understand what is said."[466] This is the view conveyed in the NIV translation. That Paul is referring to a believer seems also to be confirmed by 14:17, "You may be giving thanks well enough, but the other man is not edified." Edifying others consistently refers to the edification of other believers in Paul's argument.[467] The main point, of course, is that edification is possible only in response to intelligible speech.

**14:18–19** Continuing with the theme of thanksgiving (14:16) Paul declares, "I thank God that I speak in tongues more than all of you," yet followed by the qualification, "But in the church I would rather speak five intelligible words to instruct others than ten thousand words in a tongue." Clearly Paul's statement is hyperbolic, for how could he know that he speaks in tongues more (quantitatively) than others? Thiselton suggests that Paul refers to his speaking in tongues qualitatively rather than quantitatively, that is, the meaning is not to the frequency of his speaking in tongues but rather to the giftedness he has in this area. He translates, "I am more gifted in tongues than any of you."[468] Paul's own experience with the gift of tongues gives him quite a bit of leverage in making his main point, which is to insist on intelligible speech in the assembly of believers.[469] In church, Paul desires to speak five words "with my mind" (cf. 14:13) to instruct others rather than ten thousand words in a tongue.[470] His "desire" to speak five intelligible words contrasts with his desire that they all speak in tongues mentioned in 14:5.[471] In both places the

[465] So Robertson and Plummer (*First Corinthians*, 313), "it is unlikely that at this early period, when the Christians in each town met for common worship in private houses, there was a portion of the room set apart for the ἰδιῶται or that these were laymen as distinct from officials. No clearly marked distinctions had as yet been drawn between ministers and laity."

[466] Garland, *1 Corinthians*, 641. So also Ciampa and Rosner, *First Corinthians*, 692. Another nuance to the meaning of ἰδιώτης in this context might be "those without experience or acquaintance with the gift of speaking in tongues" (so Fitzmyer, *First Corinthians*; cf. also Grosheide, *First Corinthians*, 327; Thiselton, *First Corinthians*, 1115). Hays (*First Corinthians*, 238) takes the view that ἰδιώτης is synonymous with "unbeliever" in 14:20–25. "Whoever they are, the present context requires that they be people who are not yet committed worshipers of the one God of Israel."

[467] So Fee, *First Corinthians*, 673. Ciampa and Rosner (*First Corinthians*, 693) rightly point out, "By this point in Paul's argument, that all those others are not edified is clearly understood as an indictment (8:1; 10:23; 14:3,4,5,12)."

[468] Thiselton, *First Corinthians*, 1117. Following the REB. The point at issue turns on giftedness in contrast to the "one who does not know" in 14:16.

[469] 14:19 begins with the strong contrastive conjunction ἀλλά.

[470] The verb "to instruct" (κατηχέω) is rarely used by Paul (elsewhere only in Rom 2:18; Gal 6:6).

[471] The same verb is used in both places (θέλω).

positive appraisal of tongues is qualified in favor of edification or instruction. Both the number five and ten thousand are symbolic; five meaning "a few" and ten thousand meaning "countless."[472]

### *(3) The Negative Effect of Tongues on Unbelievers (14:20–25)*

**[20]Brothers, stop thinking like children. In regard to evil be infants, but in your thinking be adults. [21]In the Law it is written:**

> **"Through men of strange tongues**
> **and through the lips of foreigners**
> **I will speak to this people,**
> **but even then they will not listen to me,"**

**says the Lord.**

**[22]Tongues, then, are a sign, not for believers but for unbelievers; prophecy, however, is for believers, not for unbelievers. [23]So if the whole church comes together and everyone speaks in tongues, and some who do not understand or some unbelievers come in, will they not say that you are out of your mind? [24]But if an unbeliever or someone who does not understand comes in while everybody is prophesying, he will be convinced by all that he is a sinner and will be judged by all, [25]and the secrets of his heart will be laid bare. So he will fall down and worship God, exclaiming, "God is really among you!"**

To this point Paul's argument for prophecy over uninterpreted tongues has addressed believers.[473] Repeatedly, Paul has emphasized the purpose of the gifts to edify the church by contrasting prophecy and uninterpreted tongues. The one who prophesies is greater than the one who speaks in tongues, unless there is interpretation, so that the church might receive edification (14:5). In their eagerness for the things of the Spirit, the Corinthians should "try to excel in gifts that build up the church" (14:12). The one who speaks in a tongue must interpret (14:13), otherwise the mind is unfruitful (14:14) and others are not edified (14:16–17). Again, in 14:26, Paul will insist that all things must be done toward edification. However, before setting forth specific guidelines for the public assembly of believers (14:26–40), Paul addresses the impact

[472] Many think that in 14:18–19 Paul implicitly distinguishes between uninterpreted tongues in public worship and uninterpreted tongues in private devotion (so Fee, *First Corinthians*, 675). This fails to take into account the clear implication of Paul's argument concerning the correlation between edification and intelligibility. Fitzmyer (*First Corinthians*, 518) reads 14:17 and following as irony, "as Paul's argument develops in the next few verses, his words in this verse continue the irony begun in v. 17. It will continue in v. 21, as he quotes the OT in the same way and applies that to himself. The ironic sense of 'I thank God' is matched by Paul's use of the same expression in 1:14, where he shows the absurdity of people siding with him as a preacher who baptized some of them. Hence, it is stretching a point to say that Paul is merely seeking common ground here with the Corinthians whom he is trying to correct and that he considers speaking in tongues to be 'a wonderful and treasured gift, part of the complete spectrum of Christian experience' (quoting K. Stendahl, "Glossolalia—The New Testament Evidence," in *Paul Among Jews and Gentiles* [London: SCM, 1977], 113)."

[473] Unless the term ἰδιώτης in 14:6 refers to an unbeliever.

of the Corinthians' present behavior on unbelievers (14:20–25). Believers are mentioned by way of contrast (14:22), and "those who do not understand" are mentioned alongside unbelievers (see discussion on 14:16); but the primary focus is on the negative effect of tongues on those outside the community.[474]

Paul's concern for unbelievers was a chief component of his apostolic calling (1:17–25).[475] In 9:19–23 he expresses his commitment to become all things to all people in order that he might by all means save some. In his discussion of food sacrificed to idols, Paul considers the social situation of unbelievers inviting believers to a meal (10:27–30) and articulates the principle of doing all things for the glory of God, which entails seeking not what is good for oneself but what is for "the good of many, so that they may be saved" (10:31–33). Paul's focus on unbelievers in his discussion of prophecy and tongues is, therefore, not surprising. The attention given to unbelievers in 14:20–25 expands considerably the church's perspective on spiritual gifts and worship. It is not the case that the church gathers to worship with no regard for the outsider. On the contrary, the church brings glory to God by making God known to unbelievers. The presence of unbelievers in the gathered assembly of believers provides yet one more reason why prophecy is preferable to uninterpreted tongues. Only prophecy can bring about conviction and conversion resulting in the worship of the one true God.[476]

The difficulty of this paragraph lies not in understanding Paul's chief point, which is clearly conveyed in the illustrations of 14:23–25, but rather in the details of how he gets there in his use of the Scriptures (Isa 28:11–12; 45:13; cf. Zech 8:13) and the claim that tongues constitute a "sign" for unbelievers and prophecy for believers.[477] The illustrations seem to move in the opposite direction from the claim of 14:22, that is, unbelievers and "some who do not understand" think that tongues-speakers are mad while prophecy brings about conversion. How, then, are tongues a sign to those who conclude, "You are out of your mind!"? And how is prophecy a sign to believers when the illustration in 14:24 relates prophecy to the unbeliever's declaration, "God is really among you!"? In other words, how do the hypothetical situations of 14:23–25 fit with

---

[474] Thiselton (*First Corinthians*, 1118) calls 14:20–25 the "corroboration and reinforcement of the cumulative argument."

[475] Collins (*First Corinthians*, 506) observes, "Although it was a community set apart, the church did not exist in isolation from nonbelievers (cf. 1:18–25; 5:1; 6:1–11; 7:12–16; 8–10; 10:27; 12:2). Legal structures, social situations, and even marriage created a situation in which Christians interacted with non-Christians."

[476] Ciampa and Rosner (*1 Corinthians*, 696) call attention to the echo of Isa 45:13 in 1 Cor 14:25, which has to do with the Gentiles glorifying God.

[477] The difficulties of the passage are widely acknowledged by commentators and specialist studies. Thiselton (*First Corinthians*, 1122) notes that 14:22 "is acknowledged to be one of the most difficult verses in our epistle." Kistemaker (*1 Corinthians*, 500) concurs that 14:20–25 is "problematic for every interpreter."

the claim of 14:22, and how does Paul derive the claim in 14:22 from the appeal to Scripture in 14:21?

The structure of the passage is straightforward. The passage opens in 14:20 with the familiar address "Brothers," followed by an exhortation to be mature in understanding. Paul then introduces a portion of Isa 28:11–12 with the formula "It is written," but his free rendering conforms neither to the LXX or the MT.[478] The inference Paul derives from the quotation is that tongues are a sign to unbelievers but prophecy [is a sign] to believers (14:22).[479] Two illustrations ensue (14:23–25) in order to show that only prophecy brings about conviction, makes known the secrets of the heart, engenders the worship of God, and prompts the declaration, "God is really among you!" The acknowledgment of God's presence echoes Isa 45:14. Paul opens and closes his argument with the weight of the authority of Scripture.[480]

The interpretation of 14:20–25 hinges not only on Paul's use of the Old Testament, the meaning of the key term "sign," and its place in the argument of chap. 14 and, more broadly, the full argument of chaps. 12–14; but also in relation to Paul's first treatment of issues relating to the Spirit in 2:6–3:4. The connection of 14:20–25 with 2:6–3:4 is signaled by the introductory verse 14:20, where for the third time in the letter Paul employs language contrasting infancy or childhood and maturity. The most recent use of infant/adult imagery occurred in connection with tongues, prophecy, and knowledge and the coming of "perfection" (see discussion on 13:8–11).[481] But equally, if not more significant, is Paul's use of the same image and language in 2:6–3:4. Specifically, Paul's exhortation to be adults in 14:20 recalls the language of 2:6.[482] The argument of 2:6–3:4 suggests that "mature" was a Corinthian term, perhaps synonymous with the term "spiritual," which also figures prominently in 2:13–3:4 and in the present argument (12:1; 14:1,37). The Corinthians viewed themselves as mature, spiritual, and wise. Paul counters that their behavior indicates otherwise; they are "infants" in Christ (3:1). Their strife and jealousy demonstrate more than just a lack of maturity, they are behaving like mere men (3:2–4). Paul's rebuke in 14:20 parallels his rebuke of their fleshly behavior in 3:2–4. The Corinthians are thinking and behaving like infants with respect to

[478] This is Paul's first appeal to the Scriptures in the argument of 12:1–14:40. The introductory formula "It is written" appeared last in 10:7.

[479] The term "sign" appears only in connection with tongues, but translations supply "sign" with prophecy also because of the apparent parallelism.

[480] The same pattern appears in 2:9–16. In 2:9, a free citation from Isaiah is introduced by the formula "It is written," followed by an echo of Isa 40:13 in 2:16.

[481] Thiselton (*First Corinthians*, 1119) comments, "Nowhere does Paul state more clearly than in v. 20 that the way in which speaking in tongues is used at Corinth ministers to childish love of display or thoughtless self-centeredness. It is utterly pointless to seek to disengage references to childishness in ch. 13 from issues about tongues when the connection here is transparent and explicit."

[482] In both 14:20 and 2:6 Paul uses the word τέλειος ("mature").

the gift of tongues. Paul is not saying that the gift of tongues itself is infantile, only that their perspective on the gift and their use of it in the public assembly betrays a lack of maturity. The gift of tongues is a gift of the Spirit, but they are not exercising the gift for the "common good" (12:7). Furthermore, their use of uninterpreted tongues in the assembly not only fails to edify believers; it repels the unbeliever. Only intelligible speech edifies believers and holds out hope for the conversion of unbelievers.[483]

**14:20** The opening verse of the paragraph clarifies Paul's intent to admonish and correct the Corinthians. Although Paul begins his address with "Brothers," he writes to them in a fatherly admonitory tone as he did in 4:14–21.[484] Paul uses the verb "to be an infant/child"[485] rather than the noun "infant" (cf. 3:1; 13:11) and in a positive sense, "In regard to evil be infants." In other words, infantile behavior is a good thing with respect to wickedness, but such deportment is not a good thing with respect to "thinking."[486] Barrett comments, "It is time the Corinthians learn to adjust their scale of values and to make mature Christian judgments."[487] The force of the Greek imperative in this context is captured by the NIV: "Stop thinking like children."[488] The implication is that they should cease what is in progress. The admonition against infantile/childlike behavior anticipates Paul's use of the Old Testament to follow in 14:21. Ciampa and Rosner suggest, "Paul's appeal to the Corinthians to reason as

---

[483] Note also Paul's use of the term "mind" (Gk. νοῦς) in 2:16, "We have the mind of Christ," and in the immediate context of 14:20–25 (4x in 14:14–19). Furthermore, just as the spiritual person "examines/judges" spiritual things (2:14), the exercise of the spiritual gift of prophecy "examines/judges" the heart (14:24). The verb is ἀνακρίνω in both instances (cf. also 4:1–5).

[484] Collins, *First Corinthians*, 505. So also Ciampa and Rosner (*First Corinthians*, 696), who note that the term "brothers" prepares for the "chiding which they are about to receive for their childish thinking (and behavior). The rest of the verse is clearly intended to shock the Corinthians since those Paul had in mind evidently thought of themselves as being extraordinarily wise and spiritually advanced."

[485] Gk. νηπιάζω.

[486] Thiselton (*First Corinthians*, 1119) claims that a survey of the lexicographical evidences shows that the term translated "children" (Gk. παιδία) denotes a young infant only days old, or a newborn. Thiselton prefers the translation "wickedness" instead of "evil." "The difference of translation seriously affects the meaning of an important maxim. To be innocent in matters of *evil* may imply remaining aloof from seeking to understand the evil forces which contend against the good. However, to be innocent of wickedness entails rejecting knowledge of devious strategies which may promote one's own evil purposes, including here perhaps a hint that even religious contexts can offer subtle temptations to manipulate them on behalf of self-interests in ways which ultimately may come to be *wicked*." The term "thinking" (φρήν) occurs only here in the New Testament, although the cognate verb is used in 13:11 (φρονέω), "I thought like a child." The term is plentiful, however, in the LXX, and is probably somewhat synonymous with Paul's use of the term "mind" (14:15–16). Paul not only wants them to speak clearly and maturely, he knows that in order to do this they must think this way.

[487] Barrett, *First Corinthians*, 322.

[488] Present imperative, νηπιάζετε.

adults rather than children may echo Isaiah's encounter with childish people who thought they were too wise to hear his message."[489]

**14:21** The formula "It is written" introduces Isa 28:11 into the argument. Even though the text is from the Prophets, Paul refers to what is written "in the Law," indicating a broadened sense of the term "law" in this context. In 9:9 he specified the "law of Moses" when referring to Deuteronomy.[490] Paul will refer again to what the "law says" in 14:34, but there is no citation of a specific text. This is the only place in his letters that Paul does not link the formula, "It is written," to what precedes with a conjunction.[491] This does not mean that the scriptural citation is disconnected altogether from 14:20 but implies that Paul is not drawing support from the Old Testament for the preceding command to "become mature" but rather to establish the claim that follows in 14:22, namely, that tongues are a sign to unbelievers rather than believers, which is amplified by the illustrations in 14:23–25.[492] Bracketing the Isaiah text by "It is written" and "the Lord says" heightens the authority of the citation.

The citation approximates a portion of Isa 28:11–12, departing from both the LXX and the MT. The differences between the text as it stands in 1 Cor 14:21 and the Old Testament texts as we have them may be set forth as follows. First, Paul inverts "strange tongues" (lit., "other tongues") and "lips of foreigners" ("other lips") from the LXX and MT word order. The MT speaks of a "stammering lip" and the LXX of "contemptuous words" whereas Paul refers to "*other* tongues" and "*other* lips."[493] The LXX/MT reference to "another/

---

[489] Ciampa and Rosner, *First Corinthians*, 697. So also Thiselton (*First Corinthians*, 1121), "The two contexts match well. Those who are 'wise' and 'gifted' in their own eyes dismiss the plain message as 'childish,' when in reality it is the supposedly wise who think and act like children. The disdain of plain speech comes home with a vengeance: if they want something other than intelligible speech, they can have it; however, it will serve as an uncomfortable judgment, for it will place many of God's own people for whom they ought to care in the position of *aliens and outsiders*."

[490] On the use of "law" in a more broadened sense to refer to the Scriptures outside of the Pentateuch, see Matt 5:18; Luke 10:26; 16:17; John 7:49; 10:34; 12:34; 15:25. In Paul see Rom 3:19. Fitzmyer (*First Corinthians*, 519) claims that Isa 28:11 is itself a rewriting of Deut 28:49.

[491] On Paul's other uses of "It is written" followed by a scriptural citation in 1 Corinthians see 1:19,31; 2:9; 3:19; 9:9; 10:7; 15:45. Paul normally uses the conjunction *καθώς* or *γάρ* with *γέγραπται* ("just as it is written" or "for it is written").

[492] 14:22 is the key statement in Paul's argument, the link between the quotation and the two hypothetical cases. So J. F. M. Smit, "Tongues and Prophecy: Deciphering 1 Cor 14, 22," *Bib* 75 (1994): 180. "A clear perception of this verse is essential for the coherence of this entire paragraph. . . . Because of its central position we are able to approach v. 22 from two sides. On the one hand we can start from the quotation of Scripture and, from there, try to define the exact meaning of v. 22a, a conclusion derived from the quotation. On the other hand we can reason back from the two examples and, in the light of these illustrations, define what the assertions of v. 22 have to say. "

[493] Fee (*First Corinthians*, 680) comments that the "others" are now the Corinthians whose "tongues" have an adverse effect on unbelievers. Thiselton (*First Corinthians*, 1122) suggests that Paul is faithful to the force of Isa 28:11 but that he also engages in wordplay with the repetitive use of "other" as both an adjective and as a compound. This resonates with the wordplay in the

alien tongue" is singular, whereas Paul has the plural.[494] Second, in Paul's citation the verb *to speak* is first person singular, "I will speak." In the MT it is "he will speak" (the Lord) but in the LXX, "They will speak" (i.e., the Assyrians). The "I" in Paul's citation refers to the Lord as clarified by the addition of "says the Lord" at the end of the verse. Third, Paul omits a portion of Isa 28:12[495] since this does not directly apply to the Corinthian situation. Fourth, Paul changes "they would not hear" to "and even so they will not obey."[496] Again he employs the future tense.[497] "And even so" makes the text more pointed. The unusual form of God's communication to Israel did not result in obedience. Garland suggests that in context this means that "other tongues" will be useless in causing unbelievers to respond to the Lord.[498]

What are we to make of Paul's rendering of the Isaianic text? Thiselton explains, "The technical issues assume due proportion only in the light of understanding how Paul superimposes the parallel situations of Corinth and Isaiah 28 onto one another with the effect that the genuine force of OT scripture speaks creatively to a new situation."[499] In other words, Paul "is simultaneously quoting and applying a passage."[500] In Isaiah the people unwilling to listen to the Lord's speech in clear language would have to listen unwillingly through invaders speaking Assyrian. By taking over some of the words of Isa 28:11–12, Paul's formulation depicts God addressing the Corinthian Christians. Of particular note is the change to the first person and Paul's addition of "Says the Lord," which "makes God utter this statement through the prophet to the Corinthians."[501] Paul's choice of text is apparently due to the reference to God speaking in "another tongue" in order to communicate to his people. The message, however, was a message of judgment to Israel, not salvation. Having refused to hear the simple message, God spoke judgment in unintelligible languages.[502] Paul's point is that uninterpreted tongues in public worship is

letter between disdain for the "other" and concern for the "other" (cf. 4:6; 6:1; 14:17 [disdain] and 10:24,29 [concern].

[494] Paul uses a compound term for "other tongues" (ἑτερογλώσσοις).

[495] The MT reads, "This is rest; give rest to the weary; and this is repose." The LXX, "This is rest to him that is hungry, and this is the calamity."

[496] Paul uses a compound verb for hearing, εἰσακούω, meaning "to obey."

[497] Thiselton (*First Corinthians*, 1122) comments, "The future tense embraces the consequences which will follow if people persist in their love of the esoteric or unusual at the expense of the welfare of 'the other,' for whom Christ died (cf. 8:6–13)."

[498] Garland, *1 Corinthians*, 647.

[499] Thiselton, *First Corinthians*, 1120–21. See also Collins, *First Corinthians*, 507–8; Ciampa and Rosner, *First Corinthians*, 699.

[500] Thiselton, *First Corinthians*, 1122.

[501] Fitzmyer, *First Corinthians*, 520.

[502] Collins (*First Corinthians*, 505) notes, "In both its biblical setting and its use by Paul Isa 28:11–12 is an oracle of judgment. Speaking to the people in a foreign tongue will not lead them to fidelity, says the Lord. The speech may come from the Lord but it does not build up the people as God's own people. In Isaiah these words were addressed to the ruling classes in Jerusalem. In Paul they are addressed to glossolalists that pride themselves in the gift that is theirs." In the

inappropriate because it places many of God's own people in the situation of feeling like foreigners in a foreign land and will not bring the message of the gospel of Christ home to unbelievers.[503]

**14:22** This brings us to Paul's central claim in the argument, which sets forth a parallel contrast between believers and unbelievers in relation to the gifts of tongues and prophecy. The inference Paul draws from Isa 28:11–12 is that tongues are a sign to unbelievers and prophecy is a sign to believers.[504] The meaning of 14:22 hinges both on the quotation from Isa 28 and the illustrations that follow in 14:23–25. The consensus among recent commentaries and specialist studies is that unintelligible tongues leave unbelievers in a state of unbelief, and therefore judgment, while prophecy is able to bring unbelievers to faith.[505] In other words, Paul uses the term "sign" negatively in relation to tongues; that is, tongues are a sign of judgment, shutting up the unbeliever in his unbelief.[506] Prophecy, on the other hand, brings about conversion and in this sense is a positive sign of God's presence among believers. In a sense the "sign" relates to judgment in both cases, that is, tongues confirm unbelievers in their unbelief while prophecy "judges" the secrets of the heart and leads to conversion.[507] "Sign" is both negative and positive in this context, depending on what the "sign" indicates.[508] "Paul invites the Corinthians to evaluate the

---

Old Testament context Isaiah refers to a simple message for infants, those weaned from the breast (28:9–10; cf. 14:20).

[503] Thiselton, *First Corinthians*, 1121–22. Garland (*First Corinthians*, 648) concurs and explains, "This reading makes good sense of what follows. When God speaks intelligibly, it is to reveal. When God speaks unintelligibly, it is to judge. In the Corinthian context, speaking in 'other tongues' will fail to convey any meaningful message or bring repentance, just as it failed to do in Isaiah's day. The citation from Isaiah makes clear that tongues are not a saving sign but a sign of retribution. They do not stimulate belief but instead seal unbelief. In jeering at the simple message of the cross, the unbelievers in the Corinthian setting are like Isaiah's nemeses. They find the message of Christ crucified to be utter foolishness. Nevertheless, this simple message is the only message that will bring about their repentance."

[504] The conjunction ὥστε introduces 14:22. When introducing an independent clause, the conjunction means "therefore," or "for this reason" (BDAG). BDAG notes this usage and meaning also in 1 Cor 3:7; 7:38; and 11:27.

[505] Thiselton (*First Corinthians*, 1122–23) notes that this understanding is the ancient solution proposed by Bengel (*Gnomon Novi Testamenti* [London: MacMillan, 1855], 659), "Prophecy makes believers of unbelievers; the one speaking in tongues leaves the unbeliever to himself."

[506] The word "sign" does not occur in the Old Testament context. Ciampa and Rosner (*First Corinthians*, 702) comment, "It may well have been the Corinthians who introduced the language of 'sign,' suggesting that tongues were a sign given by God to believers which should be prominent in Christian worship. Paul's citation of Isaiah 28 seems intended to counter such a view."

[507] Barrett (*First Corinthians*, 324) notes the "judgment" connection but states a different perspective, "the connection appears to be that prophecy acts upon the Corinthian believers in the same way that tongues act upon 'outsiders'. The Corinthians tend to shut their ears to prophecy because they gain more satisfaction from listening to tongues than from hearing their faults exposed and their duties pointed out in plain rational language. Thus they incur judgement (cf. xi. 34)."

[508] So J. P. M. Sweet, "A Sign for Unbelievers: Paul's Attitude to Glossolalia," *NTS* 13 (1966): 244–45; W. A. Grudem, "1 Corinthians 14.20–25: Prophecy and Tongues as Signs of God's

respective *effects* of tongues and prophecy: what signal does each convey?"[509] Thiselton explains that Paul has just stated in 14:21 that the experience of being surrounded by the "tongues" of the Assyrians in Isaiah served as a sign of judgment for unbelief. Since tongues serve as a sign for unbelievers, Christian believers should not have such a "sign" marking their community worship. On the other hand, prophetic speech has the effect of nurturing people of faith and bringing unbelievers to faith. Unbelievers do not produce prophetic speech. Whereas prophetic speech characterizes the believing church at worship, uninterpreted tongues constitute negative signs generating barriers and alienation inappropriate for believers.[510]

There are other perspectives on this difficult passage. Johanson proposes that 14:22a is a rhetorical question posed by some in Corinth and the illustrations in 14:23–25 constitute Paul's swift rebuttal. Johanson contends that the term "sign" can only carry a positive connotation in 14:22a if we attribute the words to someone other than Paul.[511] Verbrugge adopts this view and offers the following translation of 14:22 as a rhetorical question posed by the Corinthians rather than a statement by Paul: "So, then, are tongues a sign not for believers but for unbelievers, and prophecy a sign not for unbelievers but for believers?"[512] Paul's answer to the question would be, "No!" In other words, some in Corinth presumed that the gift of tongues was a sign of the presence of God and had value for the unbeliever over against prophecy that was only for believers. Paul counters that only prophecy will lead unbelievers to proclaim, "God is really among you!"[513]

---

Attitude," *WTJ* 41 (1979): 381–96; Fee, *First Corinthians*, 683; Garland, *1 Corinthians*, 650; Thiselton, *First Corinthians*, 1123.

[509] Thiselton, *First Corinthians*, 1123. See also K. O. Sandnes, "Prophecy—a Sign for Believers (1 Cor 14, 20–25)," *Bib* 77 (1996): 1–15.

[510] Thiselton, *First Corinthians*, 1123. In addition to these points, we have to remember also that Paul is answering a question concerning "spiritual persons/things" (12:1). The nature of Paul's argument suggests that the speech gift of tongues was viewed by some in Corinth as a sure sign of God's presence. Paul counters this by affirming that the opposite is true according to Scripture when the tongues are unintelligible. Prophecy is the representative gift of intelligible speech that not only edifies the church but also brings about conversion and the worship of the one true God. Paul does not mention the interpretation of tongues in this passage as he does in every other section of the argument.

[511] B. C. Johanson, "Tongues, A Sign for Unbelievers," *NTS* 25 (1979): 180–203.

[512] Verbrugge, "1 Corinthians," 383.

[513] Garland (*First Corinthians*, 649) objects to this interpretation since there are no signals that Paul is citing a Corinthian position and this view fails to take into account the conjunction οὖν in 14:23, "which serves to point out the consequences of the statement in 14:22 rather than to contradict it." Verbrugge ("1 Corinthians," 383–84) notes, however, that ὥστε can introduce a rhetorical question (cf. Gal 4:12), that οὖν can have a mild adversative connotation (Rom 10:14; cf. also John 9:18; Acts 23:21; 25:4; 28:5; Rev 3:3), and 14:23 is without doubt a rhetorical question. In 14:23 "Paul is citing the consequence of their mistaken thinking, using *oun* as a mild adversative to what seems obvious to him." Verbrugge (384) offers the following paraphrase, "But [you should know that] if the entire church comes together and everyone is speaking in tongues and some new believers or unbelievers join you in worship, will they not think they are in a madhouse?"

Drawing from the theory of argumentation from the classical handbooks of rhetoric, and assuming a certain historical setting where ecstatic utterances were widely practiced by unbelievers, Smit proposes an entirely different understanding of 14:22.[514] According to Smit, the rhetorical handbooks distinguish between "signs" and "refutation."[515] Signs are ambiguous and may be explained in more than one way. Refutations, on the other hand, are irrefutable proofs, a feature that distinguishes this kind of proof from the ambiguous sign that is easily misunderstood.[516] This information, Smit claims, explains Paul's descriptions of both tongues (a sign) and prophecy (a refutation). Paul depicts tongues as a sign "which inexpert outsiders do not interpret as a gift from God, but as a *mania* coming from the idols. Prophesying, however, he depicts as a 'refutation,' which irresistibly reveals the truth to critical hearers and unmistakably confronts them with God, who addresses them through the believers."[517] Paul's intention in the hypothetical examples of 14:23–25, which he exaggerates to make a point, is to show the perspective of ordinary people. Their verdict, "you are mad," evokes "the entire range of religious and ecstatic phenomena familiar to the ancient world."[518] In other words, according to Smit, Paul argues that ordinary Christians cannot distinguish the tongues of believers from the ecstatic utterances of the unbelievers. The inevitable conclusion would be, when confronted with tongues, that they are dealing with unbelievers "seized" by *mania*. Prophecy, on the other hand, is a "refutation" that convinces of the truth.[519]

On this reading of the evidence Smit proposes a different translation. First, he assumes that the believer/unbeliever contrast does not refer to the audience that the glossolalists and prophets address in 14:22. This is reserved for the illustrations in 14:23–25. The verb "to be" plus the dative indicates "belonging to" or "to be meant for, to be proper to." In other words, outsiders have the perception that tongues-speakers belong to the unbelievers, but they know for certain that the prophets are believers. Smit proposes the following translation: "The tongues are proper not to the believers but to the unbelievers; the prophecy, however, is proper not to the unbelievers but to the believers."[520] Since tongues are regarded as a sign of recognition, "Paul declares, somewhat circumstantially, that in the eyes of ordinary people ecstatic speaking is a

[514] Smit, "Tongues and Prophecy."

[515] Smit connects "refutation" with the term ἐλέγχω in 14:24 (NIV, "to convince").

[516] Ibid., 180–82.

[517] Ibid., 182.

[518] Ibid., 183. It doesn't matter, according to Smit, if the "layperson" is a believer or unbeliever; they are relative outsiders, ordinary people who are unfamiliar with the charismata.

[519] Ibid., 184.

[520] Ibid., 185. So also Collins (*First Corinthians*, 506), "These non-Christians may not have been unfamiliar with people speaking in tongues (cf. 12:2). Tongues are not proper to believers; they are known to unbelievers. Prophecy was, on the other hand, a gift that is given to believers. At least in the sense in which Paul understands prophecy it is unknown among nonbelievers."

phenomenon belonging so obviously to the unbelievers that they are recognisable by it."[521] Ecstatic speakers characteristically belong to the religious life of the Hellenistic pagan environment. "The thesis is simple: faced with ecstatic speakers the ordinary observer does not think of believers, but of unbelievers."[522]

There are weaknesses in Smit's view. First, he considers the original context and meaning of the source of Paul's quote (Isa 28:11–12) entirely irrelevant. "For Paul the text refers exclusively to the ecstatic speaking in his own day, occurring outside as well as inside the church-community."[523] It is not Paul's pattern, however, to divorce his use of the Old Testament from its historical context. Second, Smit assumes that 12:1–3 refers to the former pagan experiences of the Corinthians: "Notwithstanding their conversion the enthusiastic utterances unabatedly continue and give the impression that nothing has changed. One would think they are still heathen. Paul resumes this idea in 1 Cor 14:20–25 and expands on it."[524] This seems to overlook the fact that there was a genuine gift of tongues and interpretation of tongues distinguishable from the ecstatic utterances of the pagan world. We may also question Smit's assertion of the "explicitly individual character of the gift."[525] Paul's argument assumes otherwise. The gift of tongues repeatedly appears in the argument alongside the companion gift of interpretation. Paul allows for tongues in public and sets forth appropriate guidelines for its use including interpretation (14:26–27).[526]

**14:23** The illustrations of 14:23–25 explain the claim of 14:22 that tongues are a sign to unbelievers and prophecy to believers.[527] The consensus position, as noted above, is that tongues are a negative sign of judgment keeping the outsider in a state of unbelief.[528] Paul hypothetically imagines the

[521] Smit, "Tongues and Prophecy," 185.

[522] Ibid., 187.

[523] Ibid., 186.

[524] Ibid., 188.

[525] Ibid., 186.

[526] So also Garland (*First Corinthians*, 650), "Smit's conclusion that they leave the impression that they are still heathen by continuing these enthusiastic utterances in Christian worship directly contradicts Paul's perspective on tongues. Paul understands tongues to be a gift of the Spirit, not an unfortunate spiritual residue from the Corinthians' pagan past, and he assures them that he speaks in tongues more than all of them. His own tongue-speaking experience is certainly not a pagan vestige." In addition to Smit, S. J. Chester also challenges the consensus view and argues that the exclamation *μαίνεσθε* is a positive response of the unbeliever meaning, "You are inspired!" Tongues are a positive sign to the unbeliever of divine activity yet inadequate since they fail to communicate the gospel and lead to conversion ("Divine Madness? Speaking in Tongues in 1 Corinthians 14.23," *JSNT* 27 [2005]: 417–46).

[527] 14:23 begins with the inferential conjunction, *οὖν* (NIV, "So . . .).

[528] Since Paul refers to both "those who do not understand" (*ἰδιῶται*) and "unbelievers" (*ἄπιστοι*), this view normally distinguishes the term *ἰδιώτης* in 14:23–24 from its use in 14:16. In other words, while 14:16 refers to making believers feel like an outsider, here Paul actually refers to the outsider. There are not two groups in view, the "unskilled believer" and the "unbeliever" but rather one group. As Fee (*First Corinthians*, 685) puts it, "the visiting 'unbeliever' is also 'untutored' in the faith." So also Barrett, *First Corinthians*, 324; Garland, *1 Corinthians*, 651. Ciampa

whole church coming together in one place and all present either speaking in tongues or prophesying.[529] This does not suggest that all can speak in tongues or that all can prophesy (see 12:29–30).[530] Paul exaggerates to make his point. If everyone spoke in tongues and unbelievers entered the assembly, they would immediately conclude, "You are out of your mind!" This is a step beyond Paul's statement in 14:6 that if he came to them speaking in tongues there would be no benefit. Here, the conclusion is that those speaking are insane.[531] Ultimately Paul's concern is for the conversion of the unbeliever, as the next two verses clarify.[532]

**14:24–25** The second hypothetical example demonstrates the value of prophecy over tongues in relation to the unbeliever, which is the chief point of the paragraph. In the example the unbeliever is not repelled by prophecy as he is with tongues, but rather he is convicted and judged by all who prophesy. The power of prophetic speech to discern the secrets of the heart recalls Paul's description of the day of judgment when the Lord will "bring to light what is hidden in darkness and will expose the motives of men's hearts" (4:5).[533] Paul's shift to the singular, "a certain unbeliever,"[534] personalizes the application. Unintelligible tongues speak to no one in particular, but prophecy has a different, individual effect. The NIV translation, "He will be convinced that he is a sinner," is the translation of one verb in Greek.[535] In this

---

and Rosner (*First Corinthians*, 704) explain that in 14:23–24 the word "is not referring to those who have been made to feel and respond like mere pre-Christian God-fearers or inquirers (by being exposed to unintelligible tongues in their own church), but to actual inquirers, people who have shown some interest in the Christian faith but who have not yet taken the step of expressing a clear faith commitment and joining the church through baptism."

[529] On the term "to come together" (συνέρχομαι), see 1 Cor 11:17–18,20,33–34. The term occurs again in 14:26.

[530] Contra Fee (*First Corinthians*, 683), who thinks that although hypothetical 14:23–25 presents reasonable scenarios. "This means that Paul's point in 12:29–30, as we noted there, was to discourage 'all' from doing so; he did not mean that only a few could be so gifted (cf. v. 5). The same is true of prophecy." Collins' (*First Corinthians*, 509) perspective is more judicious: "That all would be speaking in tongues flies in the face of both the Pauline principle that the Spirit distributes to individuals such gifts as he wills (12:4–11) and the analogy of the body (12:12–26). That all would be speaking in tongues points to the 'desirability' of this particular gift in the Corinthians' popular estimation."

[531] The verb translated "you are out of your mind" is μαίνομαι. Thiselton (*First Corinthians*, 1126) translates, "you are raving and out of your mind." The verb occurs in the New Testament elsewhere in John 10:20; Acts 12:15; 26:24–25. Both Jesus (John 10:10) and Paul (Acts 26:24–25) were accused of being insane. The term in 1 Cor 14:23 could refer to the frenzy associated with the pagan cults (so Fee, *First Corinthians*, 685; Chester, "Divine Madness?") but Paul's argument does not require it (so Thiselton, *First Corinthians*, 1127; Garland, *First Corinthians*, 652).

[532] Cf. 9:20–23; 10:27–30.

[533] In both passages, 14:25 and 4:1–5, the key verb is ἀνακρίνω.

[534] Gk. τις ἄπιστος.

[535] Gk. ἐλέγχω. The term appears seventeen times in the New Testament (Matt 18:15; Luke 3:19; John 3:20; 8:46; 16:8; 1 Cor 14:24; Eph 5:11,13; 1 Tim 5:20; 2 Tim 4:2; Titus 1:9,13; 2:15; Heb 12:5; Jas 2:9; Jude 1:15; Rev 3:19).

particular instance, since 14:25 describes conversion, the content of prophecy must include the gospel. Paul is not saying that the one prophesying knows the secrets of the unbeliever,[536] but rather that the unbeliever becomes keenly aware of his alienation from God.[537] The metaphor of "falling down" depicts worship.[538] Prophecy not only brings about conviction and discernment of the things of the heart, but it is capable of bringing about the wholesale change of one's perspective. Instead of proclaiming, "You are out of your mind!," the visitor proclaims "God really is among you!," an echo of Isa 45:14.[539] In the Old Testament context the reference is to God's presence among Israel, but here Paul applies the passage to the predominantly Gentile Corinthian church. Paul's argument opens and closes with Scripture, both texts drawn from the prophet Isaiah, and demonstrates that prophecy has not only a superior function for the believing church but a far superior function for the unbelievers who might be present when the church gathers for worship.[540]

### *(4) Do All Things Decently and in Order (14:26–40)*

**26What then shall we say, brothers? When you come together, everyone has a hymn, or a word of instruction, a revelation, a tongue or an interpretation. All of these must be done for the strengthening of the church. 27If anyone speaks in a tongue, two—or at the most three—should speak, one at a time, and someone must interpret. 28If there is no interpreter, the speaker should keep quiet in the church and speak to himself and God.**

**29Two or three prophets should speak, and the others should weigh carefully what is said. 30And if a revelation comes to someone who is sitting down, the first speaker should stop. 31For you can all prophesy in turn so that everyone may be instructed and encouraged. 32The spirits of prophets are subject to the control of prophets. 33For God is not a God of disorder but of peace.**

**As in all the congregations of the saints, 34women should remain silent in the churches. They are not allowed to speak, but must be in submission, as the Law says. 35If they want to inquire about something, they should ask their own husbands at home; for it is disgraceful for a woman to speak in the church.**

**36Did the word of God originate with you? Or are you the only people it has reached? 37If anybody thinks he is a prophet or spiritually gifted, let him**

---

536 So Hays (*First Corinthians*, 239), "We should think of something more like the argument of Romans 1–3, a discourse in which all human pretensions to righteousness are stripped away by the proclaimed message of the severity and kindness of God. Paul envisions that unbelievers who encounter this sort of unparalleled truth-telling in the form of Spirit-inspired utterance will be cut to the heart (cf. Acts 2:37) and brought to 'bow down before God and worship him' (1 Cor. 14:25)."

537 Cf. Heb 4:12.

538 See Gen 17:3; Rev 7:11; 11:16. In the New Testament the verb "to fall" (πίπτω) frequently occurs in contexts of worship (see Matt 2:11; 4:9; 18:26; Acts 10:25; Rev 4:10; 5:14; 7:11; 11:16; 19:4,10a; 22:8)

539 Fee (*First Corinthians*, 687) calls 14:25 a "conscious reflection" of Isa 45:14. Hays (*First Corinthians*, 239) mentions Isa 49:23; 60:10–16; Zech 8:22–23.

540 The term "judged" (ἀνακρίνω) in 14:24 is a key term in the letter (see 2:14–15; 4:3–4; 9:3; 10:25,27).

**acknowledge that what I am writing to you is the Lord's command. [38]If he ignores this, he himself will be ignored.**

**[39]Therefore, my brothers, be eager to prophesy, and do not forbid speaking in tongues. [40]But everything should be done in a fitting and orderly way.**

The concluding unit of this chapter, 14:26–40, is marked off by an *inclusio* regarding how "all things must be done" (14:26,40). All things must be done "for the strengthening of the church" (14:26) and all things must be done "in a fitting and orderly way" (14:40).[541] The two commands complement one another. The church is strengthened (edified) only when everything is done in the right way and in an orderly fashion. Order in worship imitates Christ by taking others into account and brings glory to God, who is the God of peace rather than disorder (14:33; cf. 10:31–11:1). Paul's instructions are theologically grounded.[542]

To this point in the argument Paul has made a strong case for intelligibility as essential to edification. Intelligibility alone, however, is not enough. There must also be consideration for the edification of the church as a whole. In 14:26–40 Paul sets forth clear guidelines for all speech when the church gathers so that all might be edified. Fourteen imperative verbs occur in the span of fifteen verses.[543] Garland explains that Paul's pattern of argumentation in 14:26–40 is to set forth a rule, followed by a condition, then an explanation.[544] Three criteria govern the passage: all things must be done for edification, there should be limitations on all speech in the assembly, and nothing must be done that is shameful.[545]

**14:26** The phrase "What shall I say then?" is the same Greek phrase translated "What shall I do?" in 14:15.[546] In both instances, the question signals a conclusion, but in 14:26 the question indicates a more comprehensive focus, taking into account the whole of chap. 14. Repeatedly Paul has emphasized and made the case for the exercise of prophecy and intelligible tongues for

---

[541] In Greek, the parallel is even more apparent in the repetition of πάντα (all things) and the imperative γινέσθω (must be done). πάντα πρὸς οἰκοδομὴν γινέσθω (14:26) and πάντα δὲ εὐσχημόνως καὶ κατὰ τάξιν γινέσθω (14:40).

[542] Collins (*First Corinthians*, 512), "Cacophony is to be excluded because God is not a God of disorder and confusion. Upbuilding the community is necessary because God is a God of peace. The God of the covenant wills the well-being of his people."

[543] Twelve are third person imperative verbs. The remaining two are second person imperatives, "be eager to prophesy" and "do not forbid to speak in tongues" (14:39).

[544] Garland (*First Corinthians*, 655), "In developing his argumentation, Paul states an overarching principle in 14:26. He then gives a rule regarding tongues, followed by a condition (14:27–28). In 14:29–33, he follows the same pattern of giving a rule followed by a condition regarding prophets but adds an explanation in 14:31–33a. In 14:33b–36, he follows this pattern regarding the conduct of wives: rule (14:33b–34a), condition (14:35a), explanation (14:34b,35b), with a double rhetorical question added in 14:36 to underline the point."

[545] Ibid.

[546] Gk. τί οὖν ἐστιν.

the edification of the church (14:6,12,17).[547] Now he will set forth criteria for the exercise of all gifts unto edification. Guidelines do not preclude spontaneity, but even sudden impulses are subject to the principle of peace and order (14:30–33).

"All things" refers specifically to vocal gifts: psalm, teaching, revelation, tongues, and interpretation (of tongues).[548] Although Paul does not mention prophecy in 14:26, it is probably implied in relation to the gift of revelation in anticipation of the specific guidelines for prophecy set forth in 14:29–32.[549] Paul devotes more attention to the ordering of prophetic speech than he does to the gift of tongues. Robertson and Plummer wonder if the gift of prophecy was "so despised in Corinth that those who possessed it did not come forward?"[550] The list in 14:26 does not match exactly any previous list, although it overlaps somewhat with the list in 14:6. The list is not merely ad hoc but rather focuses on representative speech gifts.[551] Paul does not list all things that might be done when the church gathers for worship, but all things that are done must be done for edification.

The verb "to come together,"[552] a recurring term since 11:17,[553] reminds that Paul's focus is on the corporate gathering of the church for worship.[554] The use of the term "each one" recalls earlier statements, such as the manifestation of the Spirit given "to each one" (12:7–11) and God placing "each" member in the body just as he pleased (12:18). Thus, just as Paul emphasized the "one" and the "many" in 12:12–27, there is the juxtaposition of the corporate "you" (plural) and "each one" (singular) in 14:26. We should not press Paul's point to mean that every single individual in the church gathering has one of the five gifts listed here (cf. 12:7–10). Paul presents a hypothetical scenario. The meaning is "one has this-another has that."[555]

For the second time Paul mentions a "hymn" in the chapter. Does this suggest that some are especially gifted by the Spirit in singing? Surely "hymnody was an important feature of early Christian worship"[556] (cf. Col 3:16; Eph 5:19). In 14:15 singing is closely associated with speaking in tongues, although

---

[547] Thiselton (*First Corinthians*, 1133) notes that the purpose of building up the community "has cumulatively become a refrain or axiom in 14:3,5,12,26." See also the use of the verb "to edify" in 8:1,10; 10:23; 14:4,17.

[548] Thus the NIV translation of *πάντα* as "All of these."

[549] So also Collins (*First Corinthians*, 513), "As Paul speaks of prophecy he appears to identify revelation and teaching (vv. 26,30,31) as forms of prophecy even though prophecy and teaching are presented as seemingly different gifts in 12:28–29."

[550] Robertson and Plummer, *First Corinthians*, 320.

[551] With the exception of "revelation," which is conveyed through speech (14:29–30).

[552] Gk. *συνέρχομαι*.

[553] 11:17–18,20,33–34; 14:23,26.

[554] Some suggest that the gathering Paul describes in 14:26 occurs after the Lord's Supper (so Collins, *First Corinthians*, 518; Garland, *First Corinthians*, 657).

[555] So Conzelmann, *1 Corinthians*, 244.

[556] Garland, *1 Corinthians*, 658.

Paul insists on singing with understanding. Paul does not seem to have this same association in mind here. The text does not say whether the hymn is spontaneous or previously prepared, but there is no reason to rule out either possibility as long as it is done for the edification of all. The same would apply to all the gifts, although presumably some gifts would more likely entail previously planned material, such as teaching.[557]

**14:27–28** Having established the general principle in 14:26 that all things must be done for edification, Paul sets forth guidelines for both tongues and prophecy (14:27–33). Both require regulation. Tongues must be interpreted, and prophecy must be evaluated. Both must occur in an orderly manner so that all might be edified. Paul only describes tongues as a condition ("If anyone speaks in a tongue") since it is not certain that an interpreter would always be present. On the other hand, Paul appears to assume that prophecy or a comparable gift of intelligible speech, such as teaching, normally occurred when the church gathered.

Paul first addresses tongues and the interpretation of tongues. If anyone has a tongue (14:26) and is prompted to speak in the assembly (14:27), whether spontaneously or otherwise, he directs that only two should normally do so, at the most three, and only one at a time. This regulation prevents the hypothetical scenario described in 14:23, which may have actually been occurring in Corinth. Since intelligibility is necessary for edification, there must be an interpretation of the tongue (14:27b). Already Paul has stressed the need for interpretation and explained why interpretation is necessary (14:5,6–19). In the previous references to interpretation, it appears that the one who speaks in tongues is also the one who interprets (14:5,13), but here Paul's guidelines suggest that someone other than the speaker might have the corresponding gift of interpretation and would interpret the speech.[558] It is even possible that one person interpreted all tongues-speaking. Either way, it is clear that if there is no interpretation, that is, if the one who speaks is unable to interpret the meaning of the tongue for others or if there is no one present who is gifted in interpretation, then the speaker must be silent in church. In this case he must speak only to himself and to God (cf. 14:2). Paul describes a controlled situation, which rules out any notion of tongues as ecstatic, uncontrollable speech.[559] Ciampa and Rosner observe, "The fact that the person feels enabled (by the Spirit,

[557] Ciampa and Rosner (*First Corinthians*, 710) comment, "Spontaneity or the lack thereof does not seem to play any significant part in Paul's discussion of these gifts. That each one *has* one of those things seems to suggest that they bring them to the gathering rather than that they receive them during the meeting." See also Thiselton, *First Corinthians*, 1134–35.

[558] So Fitzmyer, *First Corinthians*, 525; Ciampa and Rosner, *First Corinthians*, 711–12. Some argue that here Paul also indicates that one of the tongues-speakers is also an interpreter (so Collins, *First Corinthians*, 518; Thiselton, *First Corinthians*, 1137–38).

[559] So Garland, *1 Corinthians*, 660. "Paul lists 'self-control' as one of the fruits of the Spirit (Gal. 5:23). If tongues are of the Holy Spirit, then one should be able to hold one's peace to maintain order in the worship so that things do not get out of hand."

presumably) to speak in tongues during the service does not mean that God has authorized them to speak out to the congregation. The exercise of the gifts of the Spirit entails a mysterious relationship between the Spirit's enabling and human will and abilities. The fact that the gift is given by the Spirit does not mean that it can be used in places, times, and manners that are inappropriate and that would grieve the Spirit."[560]

The phrase "to be silent" in church recalls Paul's previous desire to speak five intelligible words "in church" rather than ten thousand words in an unknown tongue (14:19). Some think this presupposes that the appropriate venue for speaking in tongues apart from interpretation is privately at home, much in the same way that Paul advises to eat and drink at home (11:22) and instructs wives to ask questions of their husbands at home (14:35) rather than to speak shamefully "in church."[561] Paul is not as specific, however, regarding tongues. He does not mention doing this at home but only that that speaker must be silent in church and speak to himself and to God. The gift of tongues and the interpretation of tongues are corporate gifts distributed by the Spirit for the common good (12:7–11). Furthermore, Paul argues that edification cannot occur apart from comprehension (14:13–17). It is unlikely that Paul means, "Let him speak to himself and to God without comprehension."

**14:29–33a** Paul regulates prophetic speech similarly to tongues by instructing two or three prophets to speak and others to judge, although as Thiselton observes, "Virtually all commentators note Paul's change of tone. There is no reluctance about 'at most' three, but a positive and unqualified encouragement to speak."[562] The weighing of prophecies parallels the interpretation of tongues,[563] and the regulation further indicates that prophecy requires more than intelligibility in order to edify the church. All can learn and all can be encouraged only if there is order, one by one (14:31).[564] More than one prophesying at the same time would only create confusion.[565] In keeping with the principle that edification gives preference to others, Paul orders that a prophet must be silent if a revelation comes to another (14:30). This does not give license for one prophet to interrupt another, which would violate the

[560] Ciampa and Rosner, *First Corinthians*, 713.

[561] So Ciampa and Rosner (*First Corinthians*, 713), "The distinction between the contexts of church and home helps us understand what Paul has in mind by the final clause of this verse." See also Thiselton, *First Corinthians*, 1139. Robertson and Plummer (*First Corinthians*, 328) suggest that the two datives in 14:28 should be translated differently, "to God" but "for himself." "Paul does not suggest that prayer in a tongue is self-addressed delusion. It is genuine prayer, addressed to God, though only the speaker can participate in it."

[562] Thiselton, *First Corinthians*, 1140.

[563] Ciampa and Rosner (*First Corinthians*, 714) refer to the discernment of prophecy as the "exercise of the companion gift."

[564] Paul's point is not that all can prophesy, but that all who do prophesy can do so one by one (so Thiselton, *First Corinthians*, 1143).

[565] Fitzmyer (*First Corinthians*, 526) notes a parallel in 1 QS 6:10–13 (*Manual of Discipline*), which stipulates that no one should talk during the discourse of another.

principle of order and peace that governs the argument. Rather, it indicates that the one speaking should be keenly aware of the purpose and function of prophetic speech and keenly aware that others are gifted in this area.[566] A worship service is not a one-man show. Control and order is just as much a function of the Spirit as the prophetic utterance itself.[567]

The reference to "the others," who "should weigh carefully what is said" (14:29b), indicates an overriding principle of submission that governs the gathering of the church for worship, which is spelled out further in 14:32, "the spirits of the prophets are subject to the control of prophets." "The others" may refer to other prophets or to those especially equipped by the Spirit with the gift of discernment (12:10).[568] There are other passages in the New Testament, however, that suggest whole church involvement in the weighing of prophetic speech (see Acts 17:11; 1 Thess 5:19–21; 1 John 4:1). Since Paul invites other prophets and spiritual persons to evaluate his own teaching in 14:37, Ciampa and Rosner suggest that "those recognized with the gift of prophecy would be the most common contributors of prophetic messages and those with the gifts of prophecy or discerning spirits would be the most frequent contributors of evaluations or weighing of those prophecies, but others would also be free to prophesy or to 'weigh-in' on the prophecies of others."[569]

Paul does not specify exactly what the others must discern and by what criteria it is measured, but we can assume that such genuine prophetic speech resonated with the Scriptures and with the gospel as given through the apostles.[570] Garland helpfully suggests that we can infer seven norms for gauging prophetic

[566] Garland (*First Corinthians*, 660) comments, "In offering these guidelines, Paul may not be concerned simply to promote good 'order.' He also may wish to check any selfish monopoly of prophecy by those who may esteem themselves as belonging to a select circle of prophets (12:28; 14:37; Rom. 12:6) and who are used to taking center stage during the worship."

[567] Robertson and Plummer (*First Corinthians*, 323) note that God "cannot be a promoter of tumult, and therefore cannot inspire two people to speak simultaneously to the same audience. The fact of His inspiring a second speaker is proof that the first can stop and ought to do so."

[568] "To weigh carefully" translates the Greek verb διακρίνω. In 12:10 the word for "discerning" spirits is the cognate noun διάκρισις. In 12:10, the "discerning of spirits" immediately follows prophecy just as the interpretation of tongues follows tongues in the list of gifts. Paul does not say that "all might discern," but rather "the others," indicating a known group.

[569] Ciampa and Rosner, *First Corinthians*, 715. Garland (*First Corinthians*, 663) argues vigorously that Paul intends the prophet's message to be examined by all and not by a special circle of prophets alone since Paul assigns the task to the whole church in 1 Thess 5:20–21 (cf. also 1 Cor 2:12–16). So also Barrett, *First Corinthians*, 328; Forbes, *Prophecy and Inspired Speech*, 264–69; Hays, *First Corinthians*, 242.

[570] Thiselton (*First Corinthians*, 1140) suggests that the others are to distinguish between truly God-given speech and "speech which is merely self-generated rhetoric reflecting the speaker's disguised self-interests, self-deceptions, or errors, albeit under the guise of supposed 'prophecy.'" By weighing carefully what is said, "The authentic is to be sifted from the inauthentic or spurious, in the light of the OT scriptures, the gospel of Christ, the traditions of all the churches, and critical reflections. Nowhere does Paul hint that preaching or 'prophecy' achieves a privileged status which places them above critical reflection in the light of the gospel, the Spirit, and the scriptures."

speech based on what Paul says in the letter: "(1) Does what is said accord with the tradition of Jesus (7:10; 9:14; 11:23; 12:3; 15:3; cf. 2 Thess. 2:15–3:6) and with the preaching of Christ crucified (1 Cor. 1:18–25)? (2) Does it accord with the Scripture as it is properly interpreted through Christ (1:19,31; 4:6)? (3) Does it accord with what their apostle [Paul] has handed on to them and taught them (2:1–5; 7:25; 11:2; 15:3)? (4) Does it accord with sacrificial love for others (13:1–13; 8:1)? (5) Does it promote the community's good (14:3–5,12,17,26; cf. 12:7)? (6) Does it not cause another Christian to stumble in the faith (8:7–13)? (7) Does it lead outsiders to come to faith by reproving, convicting, and convincing them that God is present in their midst (14:20–25)?"[571] That everyone receives instruction and is encouraged (14:31) suggests that the gift of prophecy is similar to the gift of teaching.[572]

The phrase "The spirits of the prophets are subject to the control of prophets" (14:32)[573] seems to be parallel to the others who "weigh carefully what is said" (14:29). The language of "spirits" recalls not only the discerning of spirits (12:10) but also the language of 14:12, where the plural likely refers to the manifold working of the Holy Spirit. The NIV leaves untranslated the Greek conjunction "and" that may join this phrase to the preceding purpose clause, which is subordinate to the main clause, "For you can all prophesy in turn." In other words, by prophesying in order and deferring to other prophets, the spirits of the prophets are under the control of the prophets. Garland suggests that "the spirits of prophets" refers to the impulses of the Spirit at work in the prophets: "The urge to prophesy is subject to the prophet. The impulse to speak may still be present, but the speaker can restrain those impulses and must yield the floor to another."[574] The reason for order and control is given in 14:33a, "For God is not a God of disorder but of peace."[575] In 2 Cor 12:20 Paul expresses fear that when he comes to them "there may be quarreling, jealousy, outbursts of anger, factions, slander, gossip, arrogance and disorder."[576] Paul wants their behavior to reflect the character of God. Disorderly, self-centered worship fails to glorify the God of order and peace.[577]

---

[571] Garland, *1 Corinthians*, 664. Collins (*First Corinthians*, 519) notes that distinguishing true prophets from the false and authentic utterance from inauthentic is rooted in the biblical tradition (Deut 18:22).

[572] So Collins, *First Corinthians*, 519; Ciampa and Rosner, *First Corinthians*, 716.

[573] Robertson and Plummer (*First Corinthians*, 323) note the "proverb like statement."

[574] Garland, *1 Corinthians*, 661. So also Collins, *First Corinthians*, 519–20.

[575] 14:33 begins with an explanatory γάρ.

[576] The same word for "disorder" used in 14:33, Gk. ἀκαταστασία. James writes, "For where you have envy and selfish ambition, there you find disorder and every evil practice" (Jas 3:16).

[577] On God as the "God of peace" see Phil 4:4–9. Collins (*First Corinthians*, 520) observes that the mention of the God of peace "appears as a significant element in Paul's final benediction (Rom 15:33; 2 Cor 13:11; Gal 6:16; Phil 4:9; 1 Thess 5:23), but there is no such blessing in 1 Corinthians." Thiselton (*First Corinthians*, 1145) comments that "order in the nature of the God who acts coherently, faithfully, and without self-contradiction should be reflected in the lifestyle and worship of the people of God."

**14:33b** Commentators do not agree on the placement of the clause "As in all the congregations of the saints." Does the phrase belong with the previous statement concerning God's ordered nature so that Paul means, "God is not the author of disorder but of peace as [he is] in all the congregations of the saints"? Or does it belong with what follows, introducing Paul's instructions regarding women (wives) speaking in church, as in the NIV, "As in all the congregations of the saints, women should remain silent in the churches"? Since the phrase "in the churches" occurs twice,[578] it would seem redundant to take the two statements together unless the meaning is something like, "As in all the churches of the saints the women must be silent in the assemblies." In other words Paul appeals to the common practice of the churches for guidance on the behavior of women (wives) when the church gathers together.[579] That Paul has in mind "wives" instead of women is clarified in 14:35.

A case can be made for both views. Most recently, Ciampa and Rosner contend for the view that Paul intends to say, "As in all the gatherings of the saints, God is to be worshiped as the God of order and peace." They note that this was the view of Chrysostom, who supplied the verb "to teach" in order to clarify that Paul means, "As [I teach] in all the churches." The manuscript tradition lends some support for this view since some of the textual witnesses displace 14:34–35 rather than 14:33b–35 or 14:33b–36. Furthermore, the close parallel between 14:33b and 14:40 suggests that both statements serve the similar function of summarizing the theological basis for the teaching in each respective unit. In other words, that God is worshipped as the God of order and peace in all the churches (14:33) parallels the statement that "everything should be done in a fitting and orderly way" (14:40).[580] Barrett similarly argues that 14:33b concludes the unit on the prophets, which is then picked up again at 14:36, "with perhaps the suggestion that there are Christian assemblies elsewhere from whose example the Corinthians might learn a lesson; they are not to think of themselves as the beginning or the end of the Gospel, nor are they the whole people of God."[581]

In spite of the apparent redundancy of the phrase "in the churches," it is still possible that the phrase in question goes with what follows. The alleged redundancy does not involve identical phrases. 14:33b reads, "in the churches (assemblies) of the saints," while 14:34 reads only "in the churches (assemblies)." As noted above, the NIV translates the word for "church" differently

[578] The NIV renders the same Greek word (ἐκκλησίαις) "in the congregations" in 14:33b but as "in the churches" in 14:34a.

[579] Regarding Paul's appeal to the practice of other churches, see 4:17 and 11:16.

[580] Ciampa and Rosner, *First Corinthians*, 717. Ciampa and Rosner suggest further that the point of 14:40 "may be understood as the bridge between the two parts of this verse such that the thought is that *God is not a God of disorder but of peace*, [therefore everything should be done in a fitting and orderly way] *as in all the congregations of the Lord's people*."

[581] Barrett, *First Corinthians*, 329. Cf. also Robertson and Plummer, *First Corinthians*, 324.

in order to capture Paul's possible meaning: "As in all the congregations of the saints, women should remain silent in the churches." Collins, who argues for this view, offers the intriguing possibility that the phrase "the congregations of the saints" refers to Jewish gatherings rather than Christian gatherings.[582] In 16:1 the term "saints" is associated with the Jerusalem church, but since the phrase "churches of the saints" occurs only here in Paul, there is not enough evidence to substantiate this view.[583] In 4:18 Paul begins a new sentence with the same particle that introduces the clause of 14:33b,[584] but this is the only other place in the letter that he does so (cf. also Col 2:6).

**14:34–35** These two verses have generated no small amount of discussion and debate. The crux of the issue is how to reconcile what appears to be an absolute prohibition of women speaking in church in 14:34–35 with the presumption that both men and women prophesy in 11:4–6.[585] Linguistic and conceptual ties between 14:34–35 and the surrounding literary context abound, lending strong support to the authenticity of the text as we have it.[586] First, in keeping with the main emphasis of the unit as a whole, namely, that all things "must be done for the strengthening of the church" (14:26) and "everything should be done in a fitting and orderly way" (14:40), Paul calls for the silence of three groups: one who speaks in a tongue without an interpretation (14:28), one who prophesies when a revelation comes to another (14:29–30), and wives who should ask questions of their husbands at home (14:34–35).[587] Second, the principle of submission applies equally to the prophets and the wives. Just as "the spirits of prophets are subject to the control of prophets," so also wives "must be in submission, as the Law says."[588] Submission language is prominent in the next chapter as Paul explains the Son's relation to the Father in the

---

[582] Collins, *First Corinthians*, 520. Collins even entertains the idea "that the groups of saints to whom reference is being made are not Christian gatherings, but Jewish synagogues, where women were not permitted to speak." This is unlikely since the term "saints" uniformly refers to believers in Paul's letters.

[583] Garland (*First Corinthians*, 669) thinks "it is remotely possible that Paul had in mind Jewish churches, since the saints are connected to the Jerusalem church in 16:1 (cf. Rom 15:25–26,31; 2 Cor 8:4; 9:1)."

[584] Gk. ὡς.

[585] Garland (*First Corinthians*, 665) succinctly states the issue, "The demand that women are to keep silent in the churches comes as a surprise in this letter. If tongues and prophecy are spiritual gifts, and if each individual is allotted gifts as the Spirit chooses (12:11)—presumably without regard to gender, social status, or race—why should women with these gifts be silent in the assembly? Does Paul countermand Joel's prophecy that the Spirit will be poured out on both men and women so that they will prophesy (Joel 2:28; Acts 2:18; cf. 21:9)?"

[586] See discussion below on those who argue that 14:34–35 is a non-Pauline interpolation.

[587] In my view, Paul specifically addresses wives in 14:34–35. The Greek γυνή usually has this connotation when used in conjunction with ἀνήρ (14:35). The point to be made here is that Paul also silences men under certain conditions. The issue is not so much who is speaking as to what kind of speaking is taking place and to what extent the speech edifies the church.

[588] Gk. ὑποτάσσω (14:32,34).

summing up of all things (15:27–28).[589] Paul is especially concerned that worship reflects the ordered nature of God (cf. 11:3; 14:33a). Third, Paul's appeal to the law in 14:34 parallels his appeal to the law in 14:21. In 14:34 Paul does not cite a text but the correlation of this passage with 11:2–16, and the theme of shameful behavior suggests the Genesis creation narratives as a probable background.[590] Fourth, the desire for the wives to learn (14:35) parallels the restriction placed on prophecy so that "all might learn" (14:31).[591]

Scholarship has carved out three basic approaches to 14:34–35. First, in spite of the connections to the literary context mentioned above, some claim that 14:34–35 was not original with Paul but was added at a later time. Hays boldly claims, "Paul never told women to be silent in churches: this order is the work of a subsequent Christian generation."[592] For those who hold this position, 1 Cor 14:34–35 does not inform Pauline theology since Paul did not write it. Second, others believe the text is authentic and belongs in its canonical location but with the caveat that these verses represent a Corinthian point of view, that is, 14:34–35 is an extended quotation or a representative viewpoint of some in Corinth, which Paul dismisses in 14:36. This view also rescues Paul from what some consider to be a contradiction to his prior statement in 11:4–6 that women prophesy. The third view holds that the text is authentic and written by Paul. The precise meaning of Paul's instructions is debated among those who hold this view. The issue is the relationship between 1 Cor 14:34–35; 11:2–16; and 1 Tim 2:11–15. Each approach deserves further elaboration.

Garland lists more than twenty scholars who argue that 14:34–35 (sometimes including v. 36) is a non-Pauline interpolation.[593] Among these scholars, Fee brings to the interpretive task his expertise in textual criticism. The alleged evidence for the interpolation view is twofold. As Fee states, "Although these two verses are found in all known manuscripts, either here or at the end of the chapter, the two text-critical criteria of transcriptional and intrinsic probability combine to cast considerable doubt on their authenticity."[594] On the matter of transcriptional probability Fee contends that "Bengel's first principle must

---

[589] ὑποτάσσω occurs six times in 15:27–28 (cf. also 16:16).

[590] Gk. αἰσχρός (11:6; 14:35).

[591] The same Greek verb in both instances, μανθάνω.

[592] Hays, *First Corinthians*, 248. Hays recognizes, "Nonetheless, the passage remains in our Bibles, even if we think it is an interpolation. Furthermore, passages such as 1 Timothy 2:11–15 reinforce the same teaching." According to Hays, this view constrains "a more nuanced view of authority and diversity in the canon." The "unresolved discussion in the early church about the appropriate role of women as public witnesses to the gospel . . . has left its marks in the divided teaching of our canonical New Testament." Hays submits that New Testament texts that seek to silence women should be overridden by "Paul's vision of Christian worship in which the gifts of the Spirit are given to all members of the church, men and women alike, for the building up of the community" (249). This view assumes, of course, that we are dealing with two different and incompatible visions rather than one coherent vision that can be explained contextually.

[593] Garland, *1 Corinthians*, 665n17.

[594] Fee, *First Corinthians*, 699. Transcriptional probability has to do with what a copyist is

rule: That form of the text is more likely the original that best explains the emergence of the others."[595] Since 14:34–35 occur after 14:40 in some manuscripts Fee concludes that the best explanation of the evidence is that these verses were not original but were a very early marginal gloss subsequently placed in two different locations. Textual displacements of this kind do not occur elsewhere in the New Testament,[596] and, Fee claims, "no *adequate* reason can be found for such a displacement."[597] Regarding intrinsic probability Fee claims that 14:34–35 interrupts the flow of thought, has little to do with the present argument regarding the gifts of the Spirit, and presents an absolute injunction to silence unlike the silencing of those who speak in tongues or prophesy (14:28–30). Furthermore, Fee claims that 14:34–35 stands in contradiction to 11:2–16, which assumes that women prophesy, and that the language of these two verses in some instances is foreign to Paul.[598]

Carson provides a point-by-point critique of Fee's argument.[599] In sum, Fee's application of Bengel's principle is not convincing. A gloss would have to be introduced extraordinarily early in order to make its way into every extant manuscript. Glosses of substantial size seek to clarify or to explain a text rather than introduce difficulties into the text.[600] Furthermore, it would only take one copyist to introduce a transposition that seems to alleviate the breaking up of what appears to be a cohesive unit of thought.[601] Appeals to intrinsic probability are equally weak. While Fee appeals to Bengel's first principle of textual criticism, he omits the principle that the most difficult reading is to be preferred. Furthermore, Carson points out that Fee's concern for the alleged contradiction between 11:2–16 and 14:34–35 points the way to another criterion of adequate interpretation, that is, how two passages, although on the surface different, can stand consistently within the same letter each within its

most likely to have done while intrinsic probability assesses the likelihood of what the author (Paul) is most likely to have written.

[595] Ibid.

[596] With the exception of John 7:53–8:11, which Fee acknowledges.

[597] Ibid., 700.

[598] Ibid., 701–8. For example, Fee (707) thinks that the phrase "as the Law says" presents real problems for Pauline authorship since elsewhere Paul always cites a text (9:8; 14:21). Another example would be Paul's use of submission language in 14:34 where he does not indicate the submissive relationship as he does elsewhere, e.g., the spirits of the prophets as subject to the prophets (14:32), the Son's submission to the Father (15:27–28), and submission to those who dedicate themselves to the Lord (16:15–16). See also Rom 13:1; Eph 5:21,24; Col 3:18; Titus 2:5,9; 3:1. But how much weight do such arguments actually carry? In Rom 13:1 the object of submission is "the governing authorities," but in 13:5 there is no object for the verb. The language of Titus 2:5, "be subject to your own husbands," is similar to 1 Cor 14:35, "asking your own husbands."

[599] D. A. Carson, "Silent in the Churches: on the Role of Women in 1 Corinthians 14:33b–35," in *Recovering Biblical Manhood and Womanhood: a Response to Evangelical Feminism*, ed. J. Piper and W. Grudem (Wheaton: Crossway, 1991), 140–53.

[600] Ibid., 142. E.g., John 5:4; Acts 8:37; and 1 John 5:7b–8.

[601] Ibid., 143. Carson concedes that the position after 14:33 seems to break the flow of argument.

own context. Fee's concern for Paul's unqualified prohibition of women speaking in 14:34–35 may be qualified in the larger unit and not necessarily as a part of the syntactical unit in question.[602] All in all, the evidence weighs in favor of the authenticity of the text. Furthermore, one faces a serious canonical issue by removing a text that appears in every extant manuscript.[603]

Since the textual tradition strongly favors the authenticity of 14:34–35, another solution that allegedly solves the tension between these verses and 11:2–16 is the view that 14:34–35 represents a Corinthian point of view that Paul rejects in 14:36 by means of two rhetorical questions, "Did the word of God originate with you? Or are you the only people it has reached?" Odell-Scott is widely associated with this view.[604] Among the recent commentators this view has been adopted by Collins, Fitzmyer, and Verbrugge. As Collins explains, Paul's rhetorical rejoinder in 14:36 "challenges those who would limit Christian women's right to speak."[605] Collins follows Odell-Scott's suggestion that the masculine pronoun "you" refers to males, to those men who object to women speaking in the assembly. "Bluntly and forcefully he asks them, 'Do you presume to have an exclusive claim on the word of God?'"[606] This argument rests on the evidence of Corinthian slogans used elsewhere in the letter and the alleged force of the Greek particle translated "or" that introduces both rhetorical questions.[607]

There are weaknesses with this view. First, 14:34–35 does not fit the pattern of other possible slogans in 1 Corinthians, which are usually more succinct and to which Paul more clearly responds. In 6:12, for example, the phrase "all things are lawful, but not all things are beneficial," not only has a proverbial structure that raises the possibility that Paul is either picking up on their viewpoint or correcting a misconception of his own teaching, but the phrase is repeated again in 10:23. In 7:1, when Paul writes, "It is good for a man not to

---

[602] Ibid., 144. 1 John 3:9 is a case in point, "No one who is born of God will continue to sin, because God's seed remains in him; he cannot go on sinning, because he has been born of God." Carson notes that "responsible exegesis must not only fit it into the flow of 1 John 3 but also take note of 1 John 1:6,8,10, where all pretensions to sinless perfection are specifically denied."

[603] So Garland (*First Corinthians*, 666), "Treating 14:34–35 as a later addition to the text may expunge a difficult passage, but it does not erase the fact that no ancient manuscript lacks it, which raises a canonical issue. What status does a text have that may not be original but is represented in every extant manuscript?" For two more recent studies that take on the issues and reach different conclusions, see P. B. Payne, "Fuldensis, Sigla for Variants in Vaticanus, and 1 Cor 14:34–35," *NTS* 41 (1995): 240–62; C. Niccum, "The Voice of the Manuscripts on the Silence of Women: The External Evidence for 1 Cor 14:34–35," *NTS* 43 (1997): 242–55. The earliest manuscripts, including the important $P^{46}$, have the text in its canonical location, after 14:33.

[604] D. W. Odell-Scott, "Let the Women Speak in Church: An Egalitarian Interpretation of 1 Cor 14:33b–36," *BTB* (1983): 90–93; D. W. Odell-Scott, "In Defence of an Egalitarian Interpretation of 1 Cor 14:34–6.," *BTB* 17 (1987): 100–103.

[605] Collins, *First Corinthians*, 522.

[606] Ibid.

[607] Gk. ἤ, translated only in the second question by the NIV.

touch a woman," this is preceded by, "Now concerning the things about which you wrote." In 15:12, with reference to the resurrection, Paul writes, "How can some of you say that there is no resurrection of the dead?" There is no indication in 14:34–35 that Paul is quoting what others are saying in Corinth, and the alleged quotation is much longer, with two subordinate clauses. Second, the notion that 14:36 refers to males only because of the use of the masculine pronoun in Greek is not decisive. The masculine gender is the default gender when both males and females are addressed. The reference is to the entire church. Third, as Ciampa and Rosner point out, 14:36 would seem to be an insufficient response if Paul was countering a viewpoint in Corinth expressed in 14:34–35. "One would expect Paul to give more space to his own position than to that which he opposes, as would be the case if vv. 34–35 were a quotation from the Corinthians."[608]

This leaves us with the third main option, that Paul wrote it. But what did he mean by it? Paul either prohibited women from all forms of speech in the assembly, or he prohibited a certain kind of speech as indicated by the context; either tongues, prophecy, participation in the weighing of prophecies, or asking questions in a socially unacceptable manner. The interpretation of 14:34–35 among those who view the text as an authentic Pauline statement rather than a Corinthian viewpoint moves in different directions depending on one's reading of the immediate context and the larger discourse, particularly in relation to 11:2–16. Robertson and Plummer, for example, suggest that 11:5 may be hypothetical and that 14:34–35 forbids women from teaching (1 Tim 2:12), a rule taken over from the synagogue and applied to the church.[609] Others have proposed that 11:2–16 has in mind more informal gatherings while 14:34–35 has to do with the public gatherings of the church, but this suggestion has not been widely accepted.[610] There are more plausible ways to resolve the tension.

Most agree that Paul's directives are contextually nuanced in 14:34–35 so that he does not intend to prohibit women's speech absolutely, but rather calls for the constraint of certain kinds of speaking in order to maintain the integrity of the husband/wife relationship and/or the peace and order of the church gathered for worship.[611] As with many passages in 1 Corinthians there is a

[608] Ciampa and Rosner, *First Corinthians*, 720. Hays (*First Corinthians*, 248) labels this view "far-fetched in the extreme." Blomberg (*First Corinthians*, 280) adds that unlike previous slogans these verses "do not represent the libertine wing of the church," nor does the letter support that there was a significant Judaizing element in the church, which this interpretation requires.

[609] Robertson and Plummer, *First Corinthians*, 325.

[610] Carson ("Silent in the Churches," 145–46) gives a number of reasons that this view is implausible. (1) Paul thinks of prophecy as a revelation from God delivered to believers in the context of the church. (2) The distinction between house-groups and church would not have been as finely nuanced to first-century Christians. (3) 11:16 indicates a church setting. (4) 11:17–34 clearly indicates public worship.

[611] Witherington (*Conflict and Community*, 276) comments, "Paul requires respect, submission, and silence of any listener when any prophet is speaking (vv. 28–32), and his dealing with

context of historical situation known to the author and to the addressees that is not immediately apparent to us.[612] One of the more popular interpretations is that Paul forbids women from the oral weighing of prophecies as indicated by the context of the preceding verses, 14:29–32.[613] In this view women may participate in prophesying properly attired, as indicated in chap. 11, but "they may not participate in the oral weighing of such prophecies."[614] Paul's appeal to the law is an appeal to the creation narratives of Gen 1–2 as in 1 Cor 11:8–9 and 1 Tim 2:13. Carson contends that "Paul understands from this creation order that woman is to be subject to man—or at least that wife is to be subject to husband. In the context of the Corinthian weighing of prophecies, such submission could not be preserved if the wives participated: the first husband who uttered a prophecy would precipitate the problem."[615] Carson goes on to assert "that Paul refused to permit any woman to enjoy a church-recognized teaching authority over men (1 Tim 2:11ff), and the careful weighing of prophecies falls under that magisterial function."[616] Verses 33b–36 further refine the immediately preceding verses regarding the discernment of prophecies. Structurally, 14:30–33a expands on "two or three prophets should speak" (14:29a), and 14:33b–36 places constraints on the evaluation of prophecies (14:29b). This view sees no problem with Paul allowing prophecy on the one hand and forbidding the weighing of prophecy on the other hand since, in this view, prophecy is a broad category and it does not carry the same weight of authority of the Old Testament writing prophets. The prophecy that Paul speaks of here was in need of evaluation (14:29) and was inferior to the truth presented by Paul (14:37–38).[617]

This basic approach finds support among recent commentators. Thiselton states, "We must therefore firmly keep in view that since 11:5 makes it clear that Paul approves of women using prophetic speech their silence may allude either to stopping speaking or more probably to the possibility of sitting in judgment over prophetic speech which may come from their husbands, i.e., sifting prophetic speech, or to a constant intervention of questions (cf. v. 35) under the guise of sifting what has been said."[618] Thiselton further suggests that Paul's reasons relate to the broader culture in a positive sense, that he

some women who are asking questions (vv. 34f.) is a specific implementation of principles already applied in general to everyone. One must assume that he singles these women out for comment because he had heard that some of them were notable violators of these principles. Throughout the chapter Paul is correcting abuses, and his words must be read in that context."

[612] So Thiselton, *First Corinthians*, 1147.

[613] So Carson, "Silent in the Churches," 151–52. See also M. E. Thrall, *1 & 2 Corinthians* (Cambridge: Cambridge University Press, 1965), 101–2; Grudem, *Gift of Prophecy*, 245–55.

[614] Carson, "Silent in the Churches," 151.

[615] Ibid., 152.

[616] Ibid.

[617] Ibid., 152–53.

[618] Thiselton, *First Corinthians*, 1152.

is deeply concerned to avoid any confusion between the emerging churches and marginal Graeco-Roman cults wherein women exercised more prominent roles than in synagogues that formed the Jewish roots of the churches.[619] Thiselton envisions a situation wherein wives were interrogating the prophets, which "would become especially sensitive and problematic if wives were cross-examining their husbands about the speech and conduct which supported or undermined the authenticity of a claim to utter a prophetic message, and would readily introduce Paul's allusion to reserving questions of a certain kind for home."[620] Similarly, Garland explains, "In the context, it is likely that Paul imagines a wife joining in the process of weighing what is being said during the congregational scrutiny of prophecy (14:29). They either raise questions or contradict their husbands or other senior male relatives. By doing so, they compromise their husband's authority over them and appear to undermine the good order of the household."[621] Thiselton and Garland articulate different views on the language of submission. Thiselton translates 14:34, "Let them keep to their ordered place," and comments, "The Pentateuch (the Law) declares the ordered character of creation and human life and the regulative character (especially Leviticus, Deuteronomy, Numbers) of boundaries or differentiations."[622] Garland, on the other hand, suggests that the verb "to submit" is most appropriate to the husband-wife relationship."[623]

Although there is a growing consensus among evangelical commentators that Paul has in mind the oral weighing of prophecies in 14:34–35, this view is not without its critics. Forbes comments, "Though it is possible that, in the context, the inquiries to which Paul is referring are actively a part of the evaluation of prophecy, the text does not require or naturally suggest that interpretation."[624] Ciampa and Rosner agree and contend that there is no clear support for the view that Paul was prohibiting women from speaking in tongues, prophesying, or participating in the weighing of prophecies. Paul addresses two situations, tongues and prophecy, but the third situation of women speaking in assembly is not directly related to the overarching theme of tongues and prophecy that governs the chapter but rather to the theme of maintaining decency and order

[619] Ibid., 1157. "Paul expresses his missionary or evangelistic concern in his allusions to what unbelievers will make of tongues (14:23) and his hopes for their conversion under sober prophetic communication (14:24,25). In 9:19–23 he has stated that he himself is willing to undergo voluntary restraint and control, even of that to which he has a 'right,' if it enhances his attempts to win others for Christ. Controlled speech reflects the traditions of the Bible, the synagogue, and the early churches. Perhaps this is why he uses the rabbinic formulations concerning whether permission exists and what the law indicates."

[620] Ibid., 1158.

[621] Garland, *1 Corinthians*, 668.

[622] Thiselton, *First Corinthians*, 1153.

[623] Garland, *1 Corinthians*, 667–69. Cf. Eph 5:21–24; Col 3:18; 1 Tim 2:11–15; Titus 2:5; 1 Pet 3:1–6.

[624] Forbes, *Prophecy and Inspired Speech*, 274. See 272–77 for full discussion.

and peace in the gathered assembly. In other words, Paul's concern is not with the wives' speech per se or with their participation in the evaluation of prophecy but with behavior that would be offensive to their husbands. The reference to submission would be understood in Paul's world as a reference to the wife's submission to her husband. While asking one's husband questions or calling into question their prophecies would bring shame, Ciampa and Rosner think it is more likely that women were asking questions of other men during the church meeting that would have brought shame on her husband.[625] Thus, the improper questions were not necessarily related to the weighing of prophecies but other kinds of disruptive questions that would have been considered shameful. The clearest hint of what was occurring is found in 14:35, that is, the desire for the wives to learn and asking their husbands at home.

In sum, four observations are in order regarding these difficult verses. (1) The weight of the textual evidence and the surrounding literary context strongly support the authenticity of the text as we have it. (2) As with much of the letter, there is a historical context of situation known to both the author and the reader that informs the key terms "to be silent" and "to speak." What was crystal clear to them is not quite as clear to us. Since the command to be silent is not absolute in the case of both prophecy and tongues, it is not absolute with respect to the wives. Silence, in this context, means "to refrain from asking questions" (14:35).[626] (3) Tongues, prophecy, and the weighing of prophecies are all in the immediate context, but the overall theme of doing all things unto edification in an orderly way, which reflects the character of the God of peace and order, is sufficient reason for Paul to address a third, somewhat unrelated situation. (4) Even though cultural context is important and probably explains a lot, especially concerning behavior that brings social shame, theological considerations are also in view. In other words, Paul disallowed certain kinds of speech and called for submission "as the Law says."[627] Paul's concern is for the integrity of all relationships for the good of the church to the glory of God.

---

[625] Ciampa and Rosner, *First Corinthians*, 722–27. For others who critique the "weighing of prophecies" view, see J. Greenbury, "1 Corinthians 14:34–35: Evaluation of Prophecy Revisited," *JETS* 51 (2008): 721–31; E. Hiu, *Regulations Concerning Tongues and Prophecy in 1 Corinthians 14:26–40: Relevance Beyond the Corinthian Church*, LNTS 406 (London: T&T Clark, 2010), 147–50.

[626] So Ciampa and Rosner (*First Corinthians*, 725), "We should assume that unless there was a clear reference in the Corinthians' letter to Paul to a particular kind of women's speech in worship that was creating a problem in the church, the Corinthians would have found Paul's statement that women are not permitted 'to speak in church' just as unclear as modern readers. Although it is stated without qualification, it clearly cannot be understood in any absolute manner."

[627] Blomberg (*First Corinthians*, 287) helpfully points out that "Paul gives the same threefold rationale for his commands in 14:33b–35 as he did for honoring one's head in 11:2–16. These include cultural disgrace (v. 35), the universal practice of the churches in Paul's day (v. 33b), and an appeal to creation order (v. 34). As in chap. 11, the specific injunction is supported by situation-specific arguments, while the broader principle of submission is supported by an appeal to a timeless mandate."

**14:36–38** In a similar fashion to 12:29–30, Paul moves toward his conclusion with two rhetorical questions that introduce a stinging rebuke against those independently minded Corinthians who apparently had no problem in countering the established practice of the churches.[628] The rhetorical questions combine with 14:37–38 for a direct confrontation between Paul and those who deem themselves to be a "prophet" or a "spiritual person." This reference to the "spiritual person" (14:37) recalls the opening of Paul's discussion at 12:1–3 and confirms that this has been the primary issue all along. From the beginning of the letter Paul has emphasized at various points that the Corinthians are not an end unto themselves but exist as only one of many other churches.[629] The word of God did not originate with them,[630] and they were not the gospel's only destination (14:36).[631] Paul will remind them in the very next chapter that neither did the gospel originate with him. Paul received the gospel (15:3), and his preaching conformed to the uniform apostolic proclamation of the gospel (15:11).

The phrase "If anybody thinks" appears now for the third time in the letter. The phrase occurs in three of the major argumentative sections of the letter as a rebuke to those who consider themselves to be wise (3:18), knowledgeable (8:2), and spiritual (14:37). Fee suggests that in each case "Paul is zeroing in on the Corinthians' perspective as to their own spirituality."[632] In 4:18–21 Paul promised to come to them in order to find out what kind of power the arrogant people in Corinth actually possess, and in 11:34 he mentioned yet again that he will come to them and give further directions. Here, in 14:37, "Paul now brings in the full power of his apostolic authority in a remarkable way."[633] What he writes to them is the Lord's command.[634] The severity of Paul's rebuke in 14:37 carries forward in 14:38. The NIV reads, "If he ignores this, he himself will be ignored."[635] In effect, Paul is saying that the truly spiritual person will recognize that his instructions are indeed the Lord's command,[636] but scholars disagree regarding the severity of the rebuke. Barrett, for example, thinks

---

[628] Ciampa and Rosner (*First Corinthians*, 731) also see in this verse "a rebuke directed against those prophets who tended to monopolize the church's time, refusing to be silent long enough for others to have their own opportunities to speak to the congregation."

[629] See 1:2; 4:17; 11:16.

[630] Barrett (*First Corinthians*, 333), "The Corinthians will be well advised to have an eye to general Christian practice; they do not have a monopoly of the Gospel, or of its interpretation." The "Word of God" here probably means the gospel.

[631] Cf. Rom 15:19.

[632] Fee, *First Corinthians*, 711.

[633] Ciampa and Rosner, *First Corinthians*, 732.

[634] Since 14:37–40 forms an *inclusio* with 12:1–3, Paul's statement, "that what I am writing to you is the Lord's command" takes into account the whole of chaps. 12–14. Cf. also 7:40.

[635] That 14:38 carries forward the rebuke is signaled by the parallel condition, "If anyone" (Gk. εἰ τις).

[636] 14:37–38 forms an *inclusio* with 12:1–3 in the repetition of the key terms πνευματικός and ἀγνοέω.

"Paul means that he does not recognize the man in question as inspired in his opinion, not that he does not recognize him as a Christian. There is nothing here to suggest excommunication, nor is it necessary to suppose that the man is not recognized, known, by God."[637] Others think the rebuke is far more serious. If the one who thinks he is "spiritual" ignores Paul's command from the Lord, then that person will be ignored by God.[638] Paul is speaking of God's judgment.[639]

**14:39–40** With these verses Paul summarizes and closes the long exposition regarding "spiritual persons/things" that began in 12:1. In conclusion Paul reiterates his preference for prophecy[640] and advises that they should not forbid tongues since it is a gift of the Spirit, as long as interpretation is provided so that all might be edified. The concluding statement, "But everything should be done in a fitting and orderly way," closes out the unit that began with the similar statement in 14:26, "All of these must be done for the strengthening of the church."[641]

---

[637] Barrett, *First Corinthians*, 334.

[638] BDAG translates, "anyone who disregards (it), is disregarded (by God). So Collins (*First Corinthians*, 523), "Paul's use of this sentence of holy law provides a strong reinforcement of the idea evoked in v. 37. If anyone does not acknowledge the command of the Lord that person will not be acknowledged by the Lord." So also Fee, *First Corinthians*, 712; Hays, *First Corinthians*, 244; Kistemaker, *1 Corinthians*, 516; Garland, *1 Corinthians*, 674; Fitzmyer, *First Corinthians*, 537.

[639] Modern commentators and translations opt for the indicative verb, but earlier manuscripts have the imperative, "Let him be ignored/ignorant." So KJV, "But if any man be ignorant, let him be ignorant." Robertson and Plummer (*First Corinthians*, 327) think the alternative reading is correct, "His ignorance does not alter facts, and he must be left in his unedifying condition." They recognized the variant, and suggest that if ἀγνοεῖται is the correct reading, the meaning is "I do not care to dispute with him."

[640] The verb "to be eager" (ζηλόω) is the same verb translated "eagerly desire" in 12:31 and 14:1.

[641] "Orderly" translates a prepositional phrase κατὰ τάξιν "according to order." The noun "order" occurs only here and in Col 2:5 in Paul's letters. Thiselton (*First Corinthians*, 1168) comments, "The prepositional phrase κατὰ τάξιν is a metaphor drawn from a military universe of discourse. The cognate noun τάγμα means that which is ordered, especially in literal terms of a body of troops drawn up in ordered ranks."

## SECTION OUTLINE

VI. The Resurrection of the Dead (15:1–58)
1. The Centrality of the Resurrection to the Gospel (15:1–11)
2. The Consequences of No Resurrection, Part 1 (15:12–19)
3. The Defeat of Death So That God Might Be All in All (15:20–28)
4. The Consequences of No Resurrection, Part 2 (15:29–34)
5. The Nature of the Resurrection Body (15:35–49)
6. The Necessity of Transformation and Death's Final Defeat (15:50–58)

# VI. THE RESURRECTION OF THE DEAD (15:1–58)

Chapter 15 takes up the last comprehensive subject of the letter, which also happens to be the most in-depth discussion of bodily resurrection in Scripture. The resurrection of believers from the dead signals the consummation of all things when the Son hands the kingdom over to the Father (15:24) and death is finally destroyed (15:26) so that "God may be all in all" (15:28). Eschatology is a vital component of Christian theology, casting not only a clear vision of things to come in God's ultimate intention for his creation but also speaking profoundly to the priorities of this present life (15:58).[1]

At first glance the shift of topic from things pertaining to the Spirit (12:1–14:40) to the resurrection of the dead seems abrupt, but Paul must address another serious matter among the Corinthians; namely, some are saying, "There is no resurrection of the dead" (15:12). From a thematic perspective the discussion of resurrection naturally occurs toward the end of the letter. In the immediate context, however, Paul also expands on the premise of 14:36 that the word of God did not originate with the Corinthians. Paul too proclaimed a received gospel uniformly attested by apostolic witnesses (15:1–11). The word of God originated with neither Paul nor the Corinthians.[2] Chapters 14 and 15 also link thematically in the use of verbs related to knowledge or the lack of it.[3] The previous section opened and closed with statements regarding ignorance.[4]

[1] R. E. Ciampa and B. S. Rosner comment, "Our life in this world matters, in part, because it turns out to be not merely a waiting room in which we pass our time until being invited into the rest of the building where we will really live. Our life in this world establishes the starting chapters for a story that will continue and flourish in radically new ways (and not merely begin for the first time) upon the resurrection of the dead" (*The First Letter to the Corinthians*, PNTC [Grand Rapids: Eerdmans, 2010], 738).

[2] Cf. 1:17, "Christ sent me to preach the gospel. . . ."

[3] Gk. γνωρίζω (to make known), ἀγνοέω (to be ignorant).

[4] 12:1, "I do not want you to be ignorant," and 14:38, "If he ignores this, he himself will be ignored."

Paul begins the topic of resurrection with the declaration, "I make known to you," in the same way he began his discussion of the Spirit in 12:3, "Therefore I tell you."[5] Thus, the opening statements of the last two major topics of the letter continue to address "the knowers" in Corinth who were undoubtedly a source of many, if not most, of the problems in the church.[6] Others note an even broader thematic connection of 1 Cor 15 to the letter as a whole that entails a movement from thc subject of fleeing idolatry (chaps. 8–10) to the worship of the living and true God (chaps. 11–14) to the resurrection of the dead and the final installation of the kingdom (chap. 15).[7] Both the first and last major discourses of the letter center on different aspects of the gospel. Whereas the first major discourse (1:17–4:21) focuses primarily on Christ crucified (esp. 1:17–2:9), the last major discussion centers on Christ risen from the dead.[8]

Paul's exposition of the resurrection in 15:1–58 brings into sharp focus the eschatological perspective that pervades the letter from beginning to end.[9] In the letter opening Paul expressed confidence that God would confirm the Corinthian believers blameless in the Day of the Lord Jesus Christ (1:8). He further affirmed that God is in the process of abolishing the "things that are" (1:28) and bringing the rulers of this age to nothing (2:6–9). Believers, especially teachers, should live in the light of the Day of the Lord when God will test the quality of workmanship by fire (3:12–15) and reveal the secrets of the heart (4:1–5). In 5:1–13, Paul called for the church to discipline the incestuous man so that his spirit might be saved on the Day of the Lord. In chap. 6, Paul mentioned saints judging the world and angels (6:1–3), inheriting the kingdom of God (6:9–11), and the raising of believers' bodies from the dead as one reason to flee sexual immorality (6:14). In his instructions regarding marriage

[5] Both phrases use the same Greek verb, γνωρίζω. G. D. Fee notes two themes from the preceding argument of 14:33–38: (1) this is common ground of *all* who believe in and preach Christ, and (2) his own apostolic ministry is the source of their life in Christ (*The First Epistle to the Corinthians*, NICNT [Grand Rapids: Eerdmans, 1987], 714).

[6] Cf. also the use of ἀγνοέω in 10:1, "For I do not want you to be ignorant . . ." R. F. Collins notes the view that 1 Cor 15 may be a prophetic utterance with intertextual links to the discussion of prophecy in chap. 14. "As an instance of prophetic utterance it consists of the interpretation of the apostolic kerygma (vv. 3b–8) in the light of a revelation (vv. 50–58). Its use of illustrative Scripture and its critique of a so-called prophetic utterance (v. 12b) confirms its being an instance of prophetic utterance" (*First Corinthians*, SP [Collegeville, MN: Liturgical Press, 1999], 525). See T. W. Gillespie, *The First Theologians: A Study in Early Christian Prophecy* (Grand Rapids: Eerdmans, 1994), 235.

[7] So Ciampa and Rosner, *First Corinthians*, 737, following N. T. Wright, *The Resurrection of the Son of God* (Minneapolis: Fortress, 2003), 735.

[8] Although both sections include the death and resurrection of Jesus as components of the gospel; e.g., 1:17 presumes a risen Lord (cf. also 2:8, "Lord of glory") and 15:3 specifies that "Christ died for our sins according to the Scriptures." Collins (*First Corinthians*, 527) suggests that Paul's use of the title "Christ," which is used without the name Jesus or the title "Lord," is striking in chap. 15 and emphasizes both death and resurrection.

[9] See also J. A. Fitzmyer, *First Corinthians: A New Translation with Introduction and Commentary*, AB 32 (New Haven: Yale University Press, 2008), 540.

and singleness Paul stressed that the form of this world is passing away (7:31). Regarding food sacrificed to idols Paul recounted that all things must be done for the sake of the gospel (9:19–23) as believers strive toward the imperishable crown (9:24–27). In 11:27, he reminded the Corinthians that the Lord's Supper proclaims the death of Jesus until he comes again. In the discussion of things pertaining to the Spirit, Paul explained the permanence of love and that the gifts are rendered useless "when the perfect comes" (13:10). Chapter 15, although comprehensive in scope (15:20–28), especially picks up and elaborates on the mention of bodily resurrection in 6:14, "By his power God raised the Lord from the dead [cf. 15:1–11,20–23], and he will raise us also [15:20–23,35–57]."[10]

The problem Paul addresses in chap. 15 is not disclosed until 15:12b in the question, "How can some of you say that there is no resurrection of the dead?" Since there is no formulaic "now concerning" introducing the topic of resurrection as with the discussion of marriage (7:1), food sacrificed to idols (8:1), and things pertaining to the Spirit (12:1), the problem of some denying the resurrection most likely came to Paul's attention by way of oral report.[11] The phrasing of the question and the nature of Paul's argument suggests that the problem in Corinth was not an outright denial of Jesus' resurrection but rather a denial of resurrection generally,[12] which probably derived from the prevailing Greek philosophical worldview that held to the immortality of the soul rather than the resurrection of a dead body.[13] The crux of the problem for

[10] Ciampa and Rosner (*First Corinthians*, 737) note the emphasis on the "body" in the letter. "In one sense all of chaps. 5–15 have to do with the body in one way or another. While chaps. 5–7 focus primarily on the body's sexual purity (or lack thereof), and chaps. 8–11 focus on eating and drinking, in chaps. 12–14 the body serves as a metaphor for the healthy functioning of a church and its worship. While chaps. 5–14 deal with the sanctification of the individual and corporate bodies of believers in this 'time-between-the-times,' chap. 15 looks forward to and relates all of that earlier material about what it means to be God's holy people in this present age to God's ultimate plans for the complete transformation of our bodies (=ourselves) and of our world and the final glorification of God in and through his creation."

[11] Fitzmyer (*First Corinthians*, 540) opines that this topic is the "most serious problem that he addresses in this letter, and the instruction that he will give about this eschatological topic is the most important in the whole letter."

[12] Although Collins (*First Corinthians*, 526) thinks that we cannot rule out the possibility that some may have denied Jesus' resurrection since "Paul devotes as much attention as he does to the appearances of the risen Christ."

[13] Fee (*First Corinthians*, 715) lists four other approaches on the question of who denied the resurrection and why: (1) The deniers were Jewish opponents who had a Sadducean theology. (2) Some had adopted Gnostic views. (3) The "some" were forerunners of the over-realized eschatology advocated later by Hymenaeus and Philetus in Ephesus (2 Tim 2:17–18), who argued that the resurrection has already occurred in a spiritual sense. (4) In their sacramental union with Christ they believed they had received present immortality, and what they denied was the possibility of death itself. Fee thinks that after Paul's departure from Corinth a false theology took hold that was rooted in a radical emphasis on the spirit to the exclusion of the significance of the body and expressed in a spiritualized eschatology, two matters that climax "in their pneumatic behavior (chs. 12–14) and their denial of a resurrection of the dead (chap. 15)" (715n6).

the Greek mindset is expressed in the two questions of 15:35, "How are the dead raised? With what kind of body will they come?"[14] Paul responds to the resurrection deniers by showing that to deny resurrection generally is to deny Jesus' resurrection implicitly (15:13,16) and that a denial of resurrection not only flies in the face of the apostolic gospel (15:1–11), but to deny resurrection is to deny Jesus' full humanity (15:13,16,21).[15] The theological and practical (15:29–34) consequences are far-reaching (15:12–19,29–34). To deny resurrection is to call into question God's sovereignty and transformative power (15:20–28,35–57).

Chapter 15 divides into six distinct units (15:1–11,12–19,20–28,29–34,35–49,50–58) that make up three major movements. The chapter opens by establishing the resurrection as central to the gospel uniformly preached by apostolic witnesses and others (15:1–11). Paul does not attempt to prove the resurrection of Jesus, although there is apologetic value in the enumeration of eyewitnesses who affirmed the resurrection as historical reality. Rather, Paul establishes the premise that Christ's resurrection is central to the gospel that was preached from the very beginning. There was unwavering apostolic testimony to the resurrection of Jesus, the man, from the dead. The second movement, 15:12–34, probes the theological, practical, and ethical dilemmas if there is no resurrection of the dead and works out the positive ramifications of the fact of Jesus' resurrection.[16] The third movement, 15:35–58, takes up the question of the resurrection body and concludes with a climactic exhortation to prosper in the work of the Lord.

## 1. The Centrality of the Resurrection to the Gospel (15:1–11)

**[1]Now, brothers, I want to remind you of the gospel I preached to you, which you
received and on which you have taken your stand. [2]By this gospel you are saved, if
you hold firmly to the word I preached to you. Otherwise, you have believed in vain.**

**[3]For what I received I passed on to you as of first importance: that Christ died
for our sins according to the Scriptures, [4]that he was buried, that he was raised on
the third day according to the Scriptures, [5]and that he appeared to Peter, and then
to the Twelve. [6]After that, he appeared to more than five hundred of the brothers**

[14] So D. E. Garland, *1 Corinthians*, BECNT (Grand Rapids: Baker, 2003), 678. So also Ciampa and Rosner (*First Corinthians*, 739–40), who also note that, whatever the background, the notion of resurrection was firmly rooted in Paul's Jewish heritage. Some Old Testament texts employ resurrection language (Ezek 37:1–34), and at least two texts affirm a bodily resurrection (Isa 26:19; Dan 12:1–3). "Jewish intertestamental writings from almost every quarter include resurrection as central to their beliefs" (740). From the outset Paul will argue that Jesus was raised from the dead "according to the Scriptures."

[15] The gospel embraces both the full deity of Christ (12:3, "Jesus is Lord") and the full humanity of Christ (15:3–4, "Christ died, was buried, and was raised").

[16] 15:12–34 is arranged chiastically in three parts: 15:12–19,20–28,29–34. The first and third address the question "What if there is no resurrection?" The center portion, 15:20–28, counters that indeed Christ has been raised from the dead and works out the implications.

**at the same time, most of whom are still living, though some have fallen asleep.**
**[7]Then he appeared to James, then to all the apostles, [8]and last of all he appeared**
**to me also, as to one abnormally born.**
**[9]For I am the least of the apostles and do not even deserve to be called an**
**apostle, because I persecuted the church of God. [10]But by the grace of God I am**
**what I am, and his grace to me was not without effect. No, I worked harder than**
**all of them—yet not I, but the grace of God that was with me. [11]Whether, then, it**
**was I or they, this is what we preach, and this is what you believed.**

The first unit opens and closes with parallel statements concerning the gospel that Paul preached and the Corinthians believed (15:1–2,11). In light of what follows in 15:12–19, Paul's major premise is that the resurrection of Christ, which is central to the gospel, proves that the resurrection of the dead is possible.[17] The concise, formulaic presentation of the components of the gospel in 15:1–5 suggests traditional, creedal material uniformly proclaimed by apostolic witnesses.[18] It is possible that the formulation is Paul's own, or that he expanded on an existing creed to include a larger circle of witnesses beyond Peter and the Twelve (15:6–8). Either way, there are four components of the gospel listed, each introduced by the same conjunction in Greek.[19] Paul delivered to the Corinthians what he received, namely, *that* Christ died for our sins according to the Scriptures, *that* he was buried, *that* he was raised the third day according to the Scriptures, and *that* he appeared to others. Paul expands considerably on the fourth component of the gospel in order to demonstrate a constant chain of witnesses to the resurrection of Christ beginning with Peter and the Twelve and culminating with his own personal encounter with the risen Lord. Paul mentions some resurrection appearances that are not recorded elsewhere in the New Testament, such as Jesus' appearance to five hundred people on one occasion and his appearance to James (15:6–7).

**15:1–2** Paul's opening statement, "I want to remind you of the gospel I preached to you,"[20] probably serves as a mild rebuke to those who considered themselves to be knowledgeable and spiritual (12:1–3; 14:37).[21] The statement is also a bit surprising since the whole letter has been about the gospel, focusing especially on the death of Jesus and its significance for Christian behavior.[22] In chap. 15, however, Paul focuses on the resurrection of Jesus

[17] Since 15:1–11 predates the Gospels, this passage is considered to be one of the earliest written accounts attesting to the resurrection of Jesus (cf. also 1 Thess 1:10; Rom 4:25; 6:3–4).

[18] It is, of course, possible that this particular formulation is Paul's own, but Paul's argument is that the elements of the content of the gospel were uniformly affirmed by all.

[19] Gk. ὅτι.

[20] Gk. γνωρίζω, "I make known to you."

[21] So also L. Morris, *1 Corinthians*, TNTC (Grand Rapids: Eerdmans, 1985), 200; Fee, *First Corinthians*, 719; Fitzmyer, *First Corinthians*, 544. A. C. Thiselton translates "I want to restore your full knowledge" and notes the key role played by the theme of ignorance and knowledge in the chapter (see 15:34,36,51,58) (*The First Epistle to the Corinthians: A Commentary on the Greek Text*, NIGTC [Grand Rapids: Eerdmans, 2000], 1183).

[22] Cf., 1:17–25; 1:30; 2:1–5; 4:16–17; 5:7–8; 6:11,20; 7:23; 8:11; 9:19–23; 11:23–26.

and the implications for believers, a different but equally significant aspect of the gospel. In introducing the topic, Paul reminds them yet again of his role in bringing the gospel to them.[23] He refers to the gospel not only as that which he preached and they received, but also as that "on which you have taken your stand" and "through which you are being saved."[24] Paul's description of the gospel consists of four verbs: two aorists (I preached, you believed), one perfect (in which you stand), and one present (through which you are being saved). The present continuous "are being saved"[25] parallels Paul's description of believers in 1:18 as "those who are being saved."

The syntax of 15:2b is a bit awkward but "can be clarified when it is recognized that Paul correlates his preaching of the gospel with their response."[26] Paul mentions for a second time his prior preaching, which is modified by a prepositional phrase meaning "with what word,"[27] so that the Greek reads, "with what word I preached to you, if you hold [to it], unless you believed in vain." The phrase "with what word" denotes either the substance of the gospel[28] or the form of Paul's speech ("what form of words"), that is, the reasoning that he used in proclaiming the gospel.[29]

The more significant interpretive question is the meaning of the conditional sentence, "If you hold firmly . . . otherwise, you believed in vain." There is nothing unusual about the exhortation to hold firmly to the gospel (cf. 16:13, "Stand firm in the faith."). In 11:2 Paul used the same verb to praise the Corinthians for holding to his teachings.[30] Failure to hold firmly to the gospel is to "believe in vain." In other words, Paul warns them not to deviate from the gospel they received. But what does it mean to believe "in vain" in context? BDAG lists 1 Cor 15:2 under the meaning, "pertaining to being without careful thought, without due consideration, in a haphazard manner."[31] Thiselton adopts this meaning, arguing that "in vain" is not the best translation. Rather, the phrase refers to the lack of a coherent grasp of the gospel.

---

[23] Cf., 2:1–5; 4:14–15; 9:1–2.

[24] In Greek, four relative clauses modify "gospel" (Gk. εὐαγγέλιον).

[25] C. K. Barrett takes as a futuristic present (*A Commentary on the First Epistle to the Corinthians*, HNTC [New York: Harper & Row, 1968], 336). Others recognize a future element, so A. Robertson and A. Plummer, *A Critical and Exegetical Commentary on the First Epistle of St. Paul to the Corinthians*, ICC, 2nd ed. (Edinburgh: T&T Clark, 1914), 331; Fee, *First Corinthians*, 720; Thiselton, *First Corinthians*, 1185. Certainly a future element is implied, but the present is well-chosen. Morris (*1 Corinthians*, 200) comments, "We do not exhaust the meaning of salvation by our experience when we first believe. Salvation goes on from strength to strength and from glory to glory."

[26] Garland, *1 Corinthians*, 682.

[27] Gk. τίνι λόγῳ.

[28] So Thiselton, *First Corinthians*, 1185; Garland, *1 Corinthians*, 682.

[29] So Barrett, *First Corinthians*, 336; Fitzmyer, *First Corinthians*, 545.

[30] Gk. κατέχω. BDAG, "to adhere firmly to traditions, convictions, or beliefs, hold to, hold fast."

[31] Gk. εἰκῇ. See also Gal 3:4; 4:11.

Thiselton explains, "Here Paul envisages the possibility of such a superficial or confused appropriation of the gospel in which no coherent grasp of its logical or practical entailments for eschatology or for practical discipleship had been reached. Incoherent belief is different from believing in vain."[32] Garland agrees that the phrase highlights the Corinthians' confusion but adds, "We cannot exclude the possibility that Paul also has in mind the ultimate outcome of such a truncated faith (cf. Rom 13:4; Gal 3:4; 4:11), since it has an impact on their salvation."[33] Since the word translated "vain" also denotes that to which there is no result or pertaining to being without purpose,[34] the phrase highlights an important emphasis in the chapter as a whole. In 15:10, for example, Paul claims that God's grace toward him was not "without effect." If, however, Christ has not been raised from the dead, then both preaching and faith are useless (15:14). Paul concludes the chapter with the exhortation to remain steadfast in the Lord's work "because you know that your labor in the Lord is not in vain" (15:58).[35] In other words, "believing in vain," in context, has to do with the implications of denying the resurrection. If there is no resurrection, then neither has Christ been raised, and to deny Christ's resurrection is to deny the gospel. Apart from resurrection there is no hope. Believers remain under the power of sin and death (15:12–19).[36]

**15:3–4** In four succinct statements Paul recounts what he received and handed down to the Corinthians as a matter "of first importance," namely, "that Christ died for our sins according to the Scriptures, that he was buried, that he was raised on the third day according to the Scriptures, and that he appeared" to select witnesses. The first and the third statements recount the facts of Jesus' death and resurrection, both qualified by the phrase "according to the Scriptures." The second and fourth assertions reinforce their preceding statements, that is, the burial of Jesus solidified the reality of his death and Christ's appearances to others established the veracity of his resurrection.

The language of handing down and receiving has long been recognized as technical vocabulary drawn from Paul's Jewish heritage related to the reception and transmission of traditions. The formulation itself bears the marks of a traditional confessional statement.[37] Already Paul has used this language with

---

[32] Thiselton, *First Corinthians*, 1186. See also Robertson and Plummer, *First Corinthians*, 332.

[33] Garland, *1 Corinthians*, 683.

[34] Definitions also listed in BDAG for εἰκῇ.

[35] The Greek κενός (vain) occurs in each instance (15:10,14,58). Cf. also 15:17, "Your faith is futile (μάταιος)."

[36] So also Fee, *First Corinthians*, 721. 15:2 anticipates the argument of 15:14–19. "If they do not hold fast to the gospel, that is, if their current position as to 'no resurrection' is correct, then Christ did not rise, which in turn means that they did indeed believe in vain. If they are right, everything is a lie, and they cease to exist as believers altogether."

[37] The key terms are παραλαμβάνω (to receive) and παραδίδωμι (to hand down). See the discussion in H. Conzelmann, *1 Corinthians: A Critical and Historical Commentary on the Bible*, Hermeneia, trans. J. Leitch (Philadelphia: Fortress, 1975), 251–54. First Corinthians 15 contains

reference to head coverings and the Lord's Supper in chap. 11. In 11:2 Paul praised the Corinthians for "holding to the teachings just as I passed them on to you," and in 11:23 he recounted that he passed on to them what he received from the Lord.[38] In Gal 1:12 Paul uses the same language of reception, yet claims that he received the gospel by a direct revelation. There is a difference, however, between the traditional formulation of core beliefs, that is, the historical facts, and the significance of those facts.[39] In Galatians, Paul establishes both his independence and continuity with the other apostles. In 1 Cor 15:1–11, Paul's primary concern is to establish the uniformity of apostolic witness to the gospel. In both 1 Corinthians and Galatians Paul affirms that there is only one gospel on which all the apostles agree.[40] Concerning the longstanding issue of "revelation" versus "tradition" in Paul's experience, Ciampa and Rosner explain, "While the basic gospel message was received by revelation from the Lord, the formulation he used in preaching the gospel included elements that had been passed on to him by those who were Christians before him, perhaps including the fact that Christ died for our sins and that it was according to the Scriptures, that his resurrection took place on the third day and that that was also according to the Scriptures, and the information about the witnesses to Christ's resurrection."[41]

The phrase "Christ died for our sins" expresses a central tenet of the Christian faith.[42] Galatians 1:4 expresses the same thought in stating that Jesus "gave himself for our sins." Elsewhere in 1 Corinthians Paul has interpreted Christ's death as a death for others: "Christ, our Passover lamb, has been

---

the longest of the traditional formulas cited by Paul (cf. also 1 Thess 1:10; 4:14; 5:10). See J. N. D. Kelly, *Early Christian Creeds* (London: Longmans, 1950), 16–29. Paul himself may have put the traditional material in its present literary form, but the content represented the core of earliest Christian beliefs.

[38] Both passages employ the same Greek terms, παραδίδωμι (11:2, 23) and παραλαμβάνω (11:23).

[39] So Robertson and Plummer, *First Corinthians*, 333. The facts were received. The significance of the facts were revealed. So also Garland (*First Corinthians*, 684), "Paul asserts in Gal. 1:11–12 that he came to understand the theological ramifications of Christ's death and resurrection through a revelation from Christ and did not receive it from another's interpretation, which his limited contact with the other apostles proves (Gal 1:15–2:21)."

[40] There are significant correspondences between 1 Cor 15 and Gal 1: (1) Both passages employ the same formula, "I make known to you the gospel" (1 Cor 15:1; Gal 1:11). (2) Both passages refer to Paul's preaching of the gospel (15:1–2, "which I preached to you"; Gal 1:11, "the gospel which was preached by me'). (3) Both refer to Paul's reception of the gospel (1 Co 15:3, "which I received"; Gal 1:12, "I did not receive it from man). (4) Both passages refers to three individuals: Peter, James, and Paul. (5) Both refer to Paul's pre-conversion persecution of the church (1 Cor 15:9–10; Gal 1:13–14). (6) Both passages employ a birth metaphor (1 Cor 15:8–10; Gal 1:15). See also G. W. E. Nickelsburg, "An ἔκτρωμα, though Appointed from the Womb: Paul's Apostolic Self-Description in 1 Corinthians 15 and Galatians 1," *HTR* 79 (1986): 200–203.

[41] So Ciampa and Rosner, *First Corinthians*, 745.

[42] The exact phrase appears nowhere else in Paul's letters, along with other phrases such as "he was buried" and "on the third day." On the significance of Jesus' death in Paul's other letters, see Rom 5:6–8; 8:32; 2 Cor 5:14–15; Eph 5:2; Titus 2:14.

sacrificed" (5:7), "you were bought at a price" (6:20; 7:23), and the "weak brother, for whom Christ died" (8:11). The significance of Jesus' death for others originated with the Lord himself, who presided over the Last Supper with his disciples and said, "This is my body, which is for you" (11:23–24). That the death of Christ for our sins was "according to the Scriptures" appeals broadly to the witness of the Old Testament rather than to a specific passage. Like the phrase "Christ died for our sins," the exact words "according to the Scriptures" occur only in 15:3–4 in Paul's letters.[43] Although we cannot be certain, Paul may have in mind Isa 53.[44] However, as Garland explains, "The allusions to the psalms of the righteous sufferer in Mark's passion narrative reveal how Christians found scriptural antecedents and associations with Jesus' death in a broad range of Scripture."[45]

Jesus' burial correlates with his death and serves the argument regarding resurrection. Romans 6:4 also employs burial and resurrection language with reference to believer's baptism, "We were buried with him through baptism into death, in order that just as Christ was raised from the dead through the glory of the Father, thus also we should walk in newness of life." Concerning Jesus' burial, Thiselton explains that the role played by the phrase "he was buried" in the traditional formula "is to assert the double reality of the genuine death and authentic resurrection of Jesus Christ. The history of subsequent debate vindicates the importance of this clause."[46] Death and burial combine to emphasize the finality and the reality of his death.

The second appeal to the Scriptures in 15:4b may refer only to the resurrection of Jesus and not to the "third day" since the Old Testament never explicitly specifies that Jesus would be raised on the third day.[47] Paul is probably referring to the totality of Scripture rather than to a single passage or a collection of passages.[48] The phrase calls "attention to Christ's death as something that has happened in God's plan for the salvation of humanity."[49] Jesus himself interpreted his death and resurrection in terms of the Scriptures (Luke 24:25–

[43] But cf. Rom 1:2, "the gospel of God . . . promised . . . through his prophets in the Holy Scriptures." See also Matt 21:42; Mark 12:42; Luke 24:32. In Rom 15:4 Paul refers to the hope and encouragement of the Scriptures.

[44] Fee (*First Corinthians*, 724) links Paul's statement to Isa 53 in the use of the plural "sins," which is rarely used by Paul.

[45] Garland, *1 Corinthians*, 685.

[46] Thiselton, *First Corinthians*, 1193.

[47] There are, however, several candidates for metaphorical or typological references. Texts such as Jonah 1:7 and Hos 3:2 are often suggested as possibilities. In addition to these two, C. L. Blomberg mentions a number of texts that suggest a typological significance of "the third day": Gen 42:18; Exod 19:16; Josh 2:22; Ezra 8:32; Esth 5:1 (*1 Corinthians*, NIVAC [Grand Rapids: Zondervan, 1994], 296). Garland (*First Corinthians*, 687) adds Gen 22:4, Exod 19:11; Josh 3:2.

[48] Such as Pss 16:8–11 and 110:1 (cf. Acts 2:24–31); 56:13; 116:8. Cf. also Isa 53:11a: "After the suffering of his soul, he will see the light [of life] and be satisfied." Ciampa and Rosner (*First Corinthians*, 747) note the use of Pss 110 and 8 in 1 Cor 15:24–28.

[49] Fitzmyer, *First Corinthians*, 546. Thiselton (*First Corinthians*, 1195) suggests that the

27,44–46). The reference to the third day probably made its way into the creed simply because this was the day of the discovery of the empty tomb and the beginning of resurrection appearances.[50]

**15:5–7** Paul expands on the fourth element of the traditional creed by listing witnesses to Christ's resurrection in what appears to be a chronological order: Peter (the first apostolic witness at the tomb), then the Twelve (as a collective group), then five hundred at one time, then James, (presumably the Lord's brother, although not stated), then all the apostles, then Paul, who was the last of all.[51] Paul's mention that most of the five hundred were alive at the time of his writing implies a known group rather than five hundred anonymous witnesses. Paul's list corresponds roughly to the Gospel accounts of resurrection appearances, although he does not mention Jesus' first appearance to the women. The list is therefore not exhaustive, and there is overlap within the enumeration of witnesses since Peter was also one of the Twelve, a technical term designating the band of Jesus' disciples. Paul's present concern is to demonstrate a chain of eyewitness testimony culminating with his own experience of the risen Lord. Aside from the appearance to more than five hundred at one time, Paul seems especially interested in the apostolic witnesses since his primary emphasis is the uniformity of apostolic proclamation of the resurrection as a component of the gospel. Christ did not appear to apostles only, but all who were apostles were eyewitnesses of the resurrection (9:1–2). The appearance to more than five hundred on one occasion would be unknown to us if Paul had not mentioned the event here. The occasion may have been the Great Commission (Matt 28:16),[52] which was delivered to the eleven remaining disciples (twelve minus Judas) in the presence of others, but we cannot know for sure. The mention that some of five hundred "have fallen asleep," that is, have died, prepares the way for the argument that dead believers will be raised (15:18,20,51).[53]

---

phrase relates to the theme of promise and God's faithfulness to vindicate the Messiah, a climatic fulfillment of "God's promised eschatological act of sovereignty and vindication in grace."

[50] So Fee, *First Corinthians*, 726; Thiselton, *First Corinthians*, 1196; Garland, *1 Corinthians*, 686. For New Testament occurrences of the phrase "the third day" with reference to Jesus' resurrection, see Matt 16:21; 17:23; 20:19; Luke 9:22; 18:33; 24:7,21,46; Acts 10:40. In Matt 27:64 the chief priests and the Pharisees ask Pilate to secure Jesus' tomb "until the third day." Cf. also John 2:19–22.

[51] The Greek conjunction ὅτι introduces this fourth component of the gospel, suggesting that the appearances of Jesus were part of the traditional confessional formula. Collins (*First Corinthians*, 531–32) notes that the verb "to appear" occurs in the LXX of the appearances of God (Gen 12:7; 26:24; 35:9; 48:3; Exod 6:3; 1 Kgs 3:5; 9:2; 2 Chr 1:7; 3:1; 7:12) and the manifestation of God's glory (Exod 16:10; Lev 9:23; Num 14:10; 16:19; 17:7; 20:6) and suggests, "Given the Septuagint's tendency to use this expression of the manifestation of God during the great eras of Israel's salvation (the patriarchs, the exodus, David and Solomon), the use of this verb form in the credal formula indicates that the appearance of Jesus inaugurates a new era of salvation."

[52] So Robertson and Plummer, *First Corinthians*, 337.

[53] So Garland (*First Corinthians*, 690), "Their deaths are nothing alarming. Death precedes resurrection, and using the figure of sleep for death implies that it is not a permanent condition but one of waiting."

The James in 15:7 is surely the Lord's brother, the leader of the Jerusalem church, although Paul only mentions his name without further designation. As with the five hundred we know nothing of this appearance to James outside of this passage. By referring to Peter and James by name, Paul links his gospel with the Jewish mission as he does in Gal 1–2. It is not clear who would have been included in the third group designated "all the apostles," but it presumably extends beyond the Twelve mentioned in 15:5. Although the term "apostle" was used of persons beyond the Twelve (Acts 14:14; 1 Cor 9:5–6; Gal 1:17–19),[54] "the apostles" were a restricted group of eyewitnesses to the resurrection, as 15:7 confirms.[55]

**15:8** Finally, Jesus appeared to Paul "last of all" and "as to one abnormally born." The first phrase, "last of all," bears a temporal meaning in light of Paul's chronological listing of witnesses. It does not mean that Paul was "the least significant," since this is stated in the next verse, "I am the least of the apostles."[56] Rather, the phrase probably indicates "the closure with Paul of the apostolic circle."[57] The most challenging exegetical question in 15:8 is Paul's self-reference, "as to one abnormally born." The word translated "abnormally born" occurs only here in the New Testament.[58] In the LXX the word has the meaning of a stillborn child,[59] but what Paul intends by the word is debated. Did the term originate with others as an insulting epithet against Paul, or is this Paul's own way of describing his conversion and apostolic calling?

Paul may intend a temporal point of comparison in light of Christ's appearance to him "last of all" (15:8a). Unlike the Twelve, who participated in the ministry of Jesus, Paul's call to apostleship came suddenly and unexpectedly. Whereas the other apostles experienced a more gradual and normal process, Paul's experience was swift and abnormal. Robertson and Plummer hold this view and think the term in question indicates Paul's "intense feeling respecting

[54] Cf. also Rom 16:7, a debated text. Regarding Andronicus and Junias compare the NIV, "They are outstanding among the apostles," and the ESV, "They are well known to the apostles." The NIV translation of Gal 1:19 is likewise ambiguous regarding James, "I saw none of the other apostles—only James, the Lord's brother." Cf. HCSB, "But I didn't see any of the other apostles except James, the Lord's brother." James is probably mentioned separately in 1 Cor 15:7 because of his prominence as the leader of the Jerusalem church. Cf. Robertson and Plummer (*First Corinthians*, 338), who argue that the wording of 15:7 (to James then to all the apostles) "does not imply that James was an Apostle."

[55] So Thiselton (*First Corinthians*, 1208), "Even if Paul uses apostles regularly in a wider sense than the Twelve, as foundational witnesses there is also a limit or boundary to those who are designated by this term." Fee (*First Corinthians*, 731–32) suggests that this probably refers to a tradition similar to that recorded in Acts 1:6–11. See also Garland, *1 Corinthians*, 690; Ciampa and Rosner, *First Corinthians*, 750.

[56] Contra Collins, *First Corinthians*, 539; Fitzmyer, *First Corinthians*, 552.

[57] Thiselton, *First Corinthians*, 1210. See P. R. Jones, "1 Corinthians 15:8: Paul the Last Apostle," *TynBul* 36 (1985): 3–34.

[58] Gk. ἔκτρωμα. NASB, "to one untimely born."

[59] Num 12:12; Job 3:16; Eccl 6:3.

the errors of his career previous to his conversion."[60] There are other possible explanations of the phrase. The NEB translation, "though this birth of mine was monstrous," suggests that Paul's self-reference is to his dreadful persecution of the church mentioned in 15:9. Others suppose the word may have originated with Paul's opponents. Barrett speculates, "The word may even have been used not only of Paul's supposed deficiencies as a Christian and apostle, but also with reference to his bodily characteristics."[61] Fee submits that the term describes Paul from the Corinthians' point of view, but "what they see as weakness and therefore as evidence of a lesser standing, he sees as the true evidence that his apostleship is from the Lord."[62] Ciampa and Rosner adopt one of the suggested definitions in BDAG, "birth beyond term," and suggest that the word denotes something late and abnormal. Christ's "appearance to Paul was later than that of others and came only after a period of opposition on Paul's part. It may conjure up the image of Paul as a grotesque infant whose birth experience was far from what might normally be expected."[63] Nickelsburg develops the idea of the incomplete and unformed nature of a stillborn fetus in light of the parallels between 1 Cor 15:8–9 and Gal 1:15.[64] In spite of Paul's persecution of the church (1 Cor 15:9), which contradicted the purpose for which he was appointed in the womb (Gal 1:15), "God revealed the risen Christ to him and made him what he was intended to be from the womb."[65] In other words, when Christ appeared to him the promise of his appointment from the womb was yet unfulfilled and unrealized. This negative aspect is the focus of 15:9. The self-designation "least of the apostles" and "not worthy to be called an apostle" are consonant with the metaphor of one deficient, embryonic, and unrealized. In Nickelburg's view the issue is "Paul's appointment as an apostle and his initial opposition to that appointment through his persecution of the church."[66] The simplest contextual explanation is that Paul employs the metaphor of the stillborn child in order to highlight the grace and the power of God. As an unbeliever and persecutor of the church, Paul was in a deplorable condition of spiritual death. The image of a stillborn child is an especially powerful image in an argument for resurrection. The next two verses highlight the undeserved grace of God, "who chooses to give life and new creation to those reckoned as dead."[67]

---

[60] Robertson and Plummer, *First Corinthians*, 339.

[61] Barrett, *First Corinthians*, 344.

[62] Fee, *First Corinthians*, 733.

[63] Ciampa and Rosner, *First Corinthians*, 751.

[64] Nickelsburg, "An ἔκτρωμα." Nickelsburg (202–3) points out that both 1 Cor 15:8–9 and Gal 1:15 make reference to Isa 49.

[65] Ibid., 204.

[66] Ibid.

[67] Thiselton, *First Corinthians*, 1208. So also Garland, *1 Corinthians*, 693; Fitzmyer, *First Corinthians*, 552. The theme of giving life to the dead is consonant with the emphasis on resurrection in chap. 15.

**15:9–10** These two verses explain the image of the stillborn child.[68] The language is very personal as seen in the repetition of the first person singular verb "I am" and the use of the first person pronouns translated "I" and "to me" and "with me."[69] Paul confesses, "*I am* the least of the apostles," and "*I am* not worthy to be called an apostle,"[70] but by God's grace, "*I am* what *I am*!"[71] Paul speaks of God's grace "*to me*" and "*with me*," emphasizing God's grace against the backdrop of his former way of life in Judaism and the astounding circumstances of his conversion and call.[72] Paul's autobiographical statements about his conversion describe God's gracious call (Gal 1:15), the righteousness that comes only by faith (Phil 3:6–9), and God's mercy as a pattern for all who will believe on Jesus Christ for eternal life (1 Tim 1:13–16).[73]

In 3:10 Paul referred to his work of church planting among the Corinthians as "according to the grace of God given to me." In a possible reflection on Isaiah's complaint, "I have labored to no purpose" (Isa 49:4),[74] Paul expresses confidence that God's grace toward him was not in vain: "No, I worked harder than all of them—yet not I, but the grace of God that was with me" (15:10).[75] Paul often refers to the work of the Lord as labor,[76] and here he "reminds us that difficulty and cost in Christian work, far from suggesting an absence of God's grace, presupposes the gift of such grace."[77] As noted in the comments on 15:1–2, the theme of "vanity," which is prominent in chap. 15, is to be understood in the context of resurrection. Paul will remind the Corinthians in 15:14 that both preaching and faith are vain if Christ has not been raised from the dead, and he concludes the chapter on a high note assuring the Corinthians that the promise of the future resurrection of all believers gives confidence "that your labor in the Lord is not in vain."[78]

---

[68] 15:9 begins with an explanatory *γάρ*.

[69] The Greek verb εἰμί (I am) occurs four times, and forms of the Greek ἐγώ (I) occur four times in 15:9–10.

[70] "Worthy" translates ἱκανός, which also means "sufficient" or "able." Cf. 2 Cor 3:5, "Not that we are competent in ourselves to claim anything for ourselves, but our competence comes from God."

[71] Cf. Eph 3:8 where Paul refers to himself as "less than the least of all God's people." The term "least" in 15:9 does not refer to his rank within the apostolate (2 Cor 11:5; Gal 2:11).

[72] For Luke's account of Paul's preconversion state, see Acts 9:1–5; 22:7–8; 26:14–15.

[73] Cf. also Rom 1:5; 12:3–6; 15:15–19; 1 Cor 3:10; Gal 2:7–9.

[74] Nickelsburg, "An ἔκτρωμα," 202–3. So also Fitzmyer, *First Corinthians*, 553.

[75] Collins (*First Corinthians*, 539) understands the phrase "I worked harder than all of them," as "rhetorical hyperbole employed to underscore his own apostolic endeavor." Cf., 14:18, "I speak in tongues more than all of you." Cf. Paul's admonition in 15:58 "to abound in the work of the Lord" and 2 Cor 11:23, "I have worked much harder." It is just possible that Paul is referring to his physical labor as a means to support his own ministry without burdening the churches.

[76] For the use of the verb "to labor" (κοπιάω), see Rom 16:6,12; 1 Cor 15:10; 16:16; Gal 4:11; Phil 2:16; Col 1:29; 1 Thess 5:12; 1 Tim 4:10; 5:17; 2 Tim 2:6. For the use of the noun (κόπος), see 1 Cor 3:8; 15:58; 1 Thess 1:3; 2:9; 3:5.

[77] Thiselton, *First Corinthians*, 1212.

[78] On "laboring in vain" see also Phil 2:16 and 1 Thess 3:5. Cf. also 2 Cor 6:1; Gal 2:2; 1 Thess 2:1.

**15:11** In 15:1–2 Paul recalled what he preached to the Corinthians, but in light of the enumeration of witnesses in 15:5–10, he now shifts to the first person plural and refers to what all witnesses of the resurrection preach as a matter of common practice, "this is what *we* preach, and this is what you believed." There is only one true gospel, whoever may preach it. All gospel preaching proclaims the resurrection of Christ as a core component; otherwise, there is no gospel. To believe any other gospel is to "believe in vain" (15:2). Once again Paul emphasizes "that their current behavior and theology are out of step with those of the other churches (cf. 1:2; 4:17; 7:17; 11:16; 14:33)."[79] The summary statement of 15:11 closes out the prologue to chap. 15 and paves the way for Paul's confrontation of some who were saying, "There is no resurrection of the dead."

## 2. The Consequences of No Resurrection, Part 1 (15:12–19)

**[12]But if it is preached that Christ has been raised from the dead, how can some of you say that there is no resurrection of the dead? [13]If there is no resurrection of the dead, then not even Christ has been raised. [14]And if Christ has not been raised, our preaching is useless and so is your faith. [15]More than that, we are then found to be false witnesses about God, for we have testified about God that he raised Christ from the dead. But he did not raise him if in fact the dead are not raised. [16]For if the dead are not raised, then Christ has not been raised either. [17]And if Christ has not been raised, your faith is futile; you are still in your sins. [18]Then those also who have fallen asleep in Christ are lost. [19]If only for this life we have hope in Christ, we are to be pitied more than all men.**

The function of 15:1–11 in Paul's argument becomes clear as the rest of the chapter unfolds. Having established the resurrection of Christ as essential to the gospel, preached uniformly by the apostles, and believed universally by the churches, Paul now confronts the problem of some in Corinth who were denying the resurrection of the dead. The argument unfolds in two parts (15:12–34,35–58). The first part deals with the question of resurrection generally and divides into three units (15:12–19,20–28,29–34). In 15:12–19 Paul takes up the position of those who deny the resurrection. He argues that to deny the resurrection of the dead generally is to deny the resurrection of Christ specifically, which has disastrous theological consequences. The whole structure of Christian preaching and belief collapses. In 15:29–34, Paul develops further the implications of the "no resurrection" position as it relates to their current practice and to the life of the apostles. Thus, 15:12–19 and 15:29–34 are parallel units[80] that stand on either side of the central unit, 15:20–28. This literary arrangement of the argument, with 15:20–28 at the center, emphasizes

[79] Fee, *First Corinthians*, 736.

[80] Clearly indicated by the repetition of the conditional clause "If the dead are not raised" in 15:13,15,17,29,32.

the fact and the implications of Christ's resurrection. The resurrection of Christ irreversibly set in motion certain events, namely, the future bodily resurrection of all believers, who will be raised at his coming (15:20–23), and the end, when Christ delivers the kingdom to the Father (15:24a) and all enemies are destroyed (15:24b–25), including death (15:26), so that God may be all in all (15:28). Thus, in sum, "Paul's concern is to demonstrate from their commonly held position—the resurrection of Christ—both the absurdity of their present position (vv. 12–19) and the splendor of his (20–28). And in case that is not fully heard, there are always practical absurdities of both their and his daily lives if there is no resurrection of the dead (29–34)."[81]

Verses 12–19 consist of an introductory statement (15:12), followed by two parallel units (15:13–15,16–18) and a conclusion (15:19). The two parallel units both begin with the claim, "If there is no resurrection of the dead, then not even has Christ been raised" (15:13,16). Three consequences follow from each parallel statement. Each consequence has to do with preaching or faith, the two focal points of the opening section (cf. 15:1–2,11).[82] The consequences in 15:15 and 15:17–18 follow from the two overarching consequences stated in 15:14, "our preaching is useless and so is your faith."[83] The conclusion is also stated as a condition, "If only for this life we have hope in Christ, we are to be pitied more than all men" (15:19; cf. 4:6–13). The theological implications of Paul's argument regarding the person of Christ and the destiny of the dead are substantial. Simply stated, the resurrection of the dead is linked inextricably to Christ's resurrection and his full humanity (15:13; cf. also 15:21), and, apart from Christ's resurrection, there is no hope of eternal life (15:18).

**15:12** Since the uniform preaching of the apostles affirms the resurrection, Paul expresses shock that some among the Corinthians were saying that there is no resurrection of the dead.[84] Based on the content of Paul's argument in 15:35–49, it appears that the problem for some in Corinth was not postmortem existence per se, but rather the bodily nature of resurrection.[85] It is possible

---

[81] Ibid., 738.

[82] There are significant thematic connections between 15:12–19 and the prior section, which shows that 15:1–11 relates specifically to the claim of "no resurrection." The connections include: (1) the death of Jesus for our sins (15:3) but apart from resurrection, "you are still in your sins" (15:17); (2) the uniform testimony of apostolic witnesses (15:5–8) yet apart from resurrection, "we are false witnesses of God" (15:15); (3) the death of some since the resurrection (15:6) although apart from resurrection, "those who have died have perished" (15:18). Thus the connections include preaching, belief, atonement, apostolic testimony, and the fate of dead believers.

[83] The word for "preaching" is κήρυγμα, used also 1:21 and 2:4. Denial of resurrection empties "preaching" of its content. Faith in an empty message is itself futile.

[84] Cf. Gal 1:6; 3:1.

[85] So Robertson and Plummer, *First Corinthians*, 329. Garland (*First Corinthians*, 700) explains, "The Corinthians apparently believed in an afterlife but retained the dualistic anthropology that was the legacy of their Hellenistic environment. According to this view, humans are composed of two inharmonious parts, body and soul, that are of unequal value. At death, the mortal body is shed like a snake's skin, and the immortal soul continues in a purely spiritual existence." See

that those who denied the resurrection were a minority of the socially upper-class, who would have been prone to such philosophical leanings.[86] Some in Corinth had already died (11:30), and Paul's reference to those who "baptize for the dead" (15:29) indicates some measure of concern in Corinth for those who had died.[87] Paul faced a different pastoral problem in Corinth, however, than the one he encountered in Thessalonica, where the church expressed great concern for dead believers and Paul wrote to reassure them by explaining that the dead in Christ will rise first (1 Thess 4:13–18). In Corinth, the problem was denial of the resurrection altogether, and Paul endeavors to demonstrate the ruinous implications of such belief. In addressing the problem in Corinth Paul does not refer to any particular person, nor does he call for the severity of discipline as he did in the case of the incestuous man (5:1–13). Paul refers only to those who were saying something in error and who failed to reckon with the implications of their erroneous thinking.[88] Garland explains, "Paul is not countering opponents in this section, as so many assume, but dealing with the Corinthians as students who need further instruction. His tone and style are didactic throughout."[89]

**15:13–14** Paul's premise, "If there is no resurrection of the dead, then not even Christ has been raised," indicates that the deniers of resurrection in Corinth did not contest the resurrection of Christ. They may have conceded that the resurrection of Jesus was a unique occurrence and unrelated to the rest of humanity.[90] Yet the major premise of Paul's logic is that to deny the resurrection of the dead generally excludes even the resurrection of Jesus.[91]

Paul draws two inferences from the premise that Christ has not been raised, which is the case "if there is no resurrection from the dead," namely, that both

Thiselton (*First Corinthians*, 1216) for a discussion and a list of useful surveys on the background question. Also Fitzmyer, *First Corinthians*, 560–62.

[86] Hays (*First Corinthians*, 259) imagines that in Corinth there might have been "those who knew enough philosophy to distance themselves from the apocalyptic worldview of Paul, whom they may have viewed as an unsophisticated, literalist Jewish preacher." See also Thiselton, *First Corinthians*, 1217. It is impossible to know who the "some" were or if they were related in any way to the factions mentioned in 1:11–12.

[87] Cf. also the reference in 15:6 to some of the eyewitnesses of the resurrection of Jesus who had already died.

[88] So Robertson and Plummer, *First Corinthians*, 347; F. W. Grosheide, *Commentary on the First Epistle to the Corinthians*, NICNT (Grand Rapids: Eerdmans, 1953), 356.

[89] Garland, *1 Corinthians*, 696.

[90] So Robertson and Plummer, *First Corinthians*, 346. Thiselton (*First Corinthians*, 1214) comments on Paul's logic, "If the universal principle has no currency, a particular instance of it has no currency either." Robertson and Plummer (347–48), followed by Fee (*First Corinthians*, 741) submit that Paul's argument is not merely logical but also causal. Fee explains, "Paul already has in mind the causal connection between Christ's resurrection and that of believers. That is, to deny the resurrection of the dead is to deny the resurrection of the one who makes any and all resurrections possible."

[91] In the next unit, 15:20–28, the logic is that Christ's resurrection guarantees the resurrection of all believers (15:20).

preaching and faith are vain. The word for "vain" is the same word used in 15:10 where Paul affirmed that God's grace toward him was not in vain. In 15:14, the word "vain" occurs in the first or emphatic position, "Vain is our preaching and vain is your faith!" The implications for preaching are spelled out further in 15:15–16, and implications for faith are given in 15:17–18.[92] "A whole theology is at stake."[93]

**15:15** The position of "no resurrection" not only empties preaching of its content, it implies something very troublesome about the eyewitness testimony. Again, Paul's working premise is that Christ's resurrection did not happen if the dead are not raised (cf. 15:13). If this is true, then the witnesses enumerated in 15:5–8 are false witnesses, including Paul.[94] Collins observes, "The juridical language ups the ante of Paul's rhetoric. If Christ has not been raised, Paul's preaching is perjured testimony with regard to God."[95] The apostles were not mere preachers of ethical ideals; they were men who testified to something they saw and experienced. If the resurrection did not happen, then all the apostles were liars, and nothing else they said (or wrote) can be trusted. Robertson and Plummer note that "the alternative possibility, that he and the other Apostles were honest, but deluded witnesses, does not occur to him at all. The modern theory, that those who believed that they had seen the Risen Lord were victims of an hallucination, is wholly absent from his thought, even as a possibility."[96] In 1 Thess 2:4–6 Paul calls God as witness to the integrity of the apostles who were entrusted with the gospel (cf. also 1 Cor 4:1–5).[97]

**15:16–18** Paul draws further inferences regarding the vanity of faith apart from resurrection (15:14b): faith is futile, believers are still in their sins, and the dead in Christ have perished. Although the word for "futile"[98] may be somewhat synonymous with "vain" in 15:14, some make a distinction. "Vain" in 15:14b has the idea of lacking in reality or content, while "futile" means wanting in result, fruitless, to no effect.[99] The second and third consequences derive from the first; that is, if Christ has not been raised from the dead, faith has not resulted in the forgiveness of sins, which means that believers remain under the tyranny of sin and death and those who have already died have perished.[100] If

---

[92] So Collins, *First Corinthians*, 544.

[93] Thiselton, *First Corinthians*, 1219.

[94] To bear false testimony is a violation of God's commandments (Exod 20:16; Matt 19:18; Mark 10:19; Luke 18:20).

[95] Collins, *First Corinthians*, 544.

[96] Robertson and Plummer, *First Corinthians*, 349.

[97] Fee (*First Corinthians*, 743) takes 15:16 with the preceding statement and suggests that the repetition of the premise, "If the dead are not raised, then Christ has not been raised" (15:13,15,16), implicates those denying the resurrection as those who are truly the false witnesses against God.

[98] Gk. μάταιος.

[99] So Robertson and Plummer, *First Corinthians*, 349; Thiselton, *First Corinthians*, 1219–20.

[100] The NIV translates the Greek ἀπόλλυμι, "are lost," but the idea is much stronger, "to be destroyed." Cf. the use of the word elsewhere in 1 Corinthians (1:18–19; 8:11; 10:9–10). On the relationship of resurrection to justification, see Rom 4:24. Cf. also Rom 5:10; 6:10.

there is no resurrection of the dead then the claim that the message of the cross is the power of God to those who are being saved is false (1:18). The statement, "you are still in your sins," confirms "that without the resurrection of Christ, Christ's death alone has no atoning, redemptive, or liberating effect in relation to human sin."[101] The gospel preached by the apostles affirms Christ's death for our sins (15:3) and his resurrection on the third day (15:4), but if the latter did not happened, then there is no reason to suppose that the former is valid.[102] If one continues in sin as the result of faith in a dead Christ, then death retains its victory (15:54–56).[103] Fee observes, "The reason for quoting the creed in full in vv. 3–5 now comes into sharper focus. The denial of their future, that they are destined for resurrection on the basis of Christ's resurrection, has the net effect of a denial of their past, that they have received forgiveness of sins on the basis of Christ's death."[104]

**15:19** Paul concludes his explanation of the consequences if Christ has not been raised from the dead with an assessment of the present state of things: "If only for this life we have hope in Christ, we are to be pitied more than all men."[105] Paul's point is not that there are no present benefits to the Christian life here and now, but rather that "the complex and fulfilling life of the Christian community has integrity only if it is premised on the truth and ordered towards the ultimate fulfillment of God's promises."[106] The richness of Christian existence is predicated on eschatological hope and confidence in a righteous judgment to come.[107] Paul's perspective is to be understood in the light of his present sufferings (4:9–13; cf. also Rom 8:18; 2 Cor 4:7–16; 6:3–10; 11:23–29) and the disastrous chain of consequences enumerated in 15:12–18.

### 3. The Defeat of Death So That God Might Be All in All (15:20–28)

**[20]But Christ has indeed been raised from the dead, the firstfruits of those who have fallen asleep. [21]For since death came through a man, the resurrection of the dead comes also through a man. [22]For as in Adam all die, so in Christ all will be made alive. [23]But each in his own turn: Christ, the firstfruits; then, when he comes, those who belong to him. [24]Then the end will come, when he hands over**

[101] Thiselton, *First Corinthians*, 1220. On the phrase "in your sins" cf. John 8:21–24; Eph 2:1–5; Col 2:13.

[102] Robertson and Plummer (*First Corinthians*, 350) prefer this interpretation but offer another possible meaning, namely, that if Christ had not been raised they would still be in a state of wickedness (cf. 6:11)

[103] So Barrett, *First Corinthians*, 349.

[104] Fee, *First Corinthians*, 743.

[105] The word "only" in 15:19 occurs at the end of the protasis of the conditional clause and modifies the whole clause (so Barrett, *First Corinthians*, 349–50; Garland, *First Corinthians*, 702–3). Paul portrays someone who has placed their hope solely in Christ in this life (Thiselton, *First Corinthians*, 1221).

[106] R. B. Hays, *First Corinthians* (Louisville: John Knox, 1997), 262.

[107] Cf. Phil 3:10–11; Col 1:27; Jas 1:12; 2:5.

**the kingdom to God the Father after he has destroyed all dominion, authority and power. [25]For he must reign until he has put all his enemies under his feet. [26]The last enemy to be destroyed is death. [27]For he "has put everything under his feet." Now when it says that "everything" has been put under him, it is clear that this does not include God himself, who put everything under Christ. [28]When he has done this, then the Son himself will be made subject to him who put everything under him, so that God may be all in all.**

The triumphant declaration in 15:20 that Christ has been raised from the dead and is the firstfruits of those who have fallen asleep follows closely upon the hypothetical scenario of 15:18 concerning those who have fallen asleep in Christ with no hope of resurrection and, in effect, reverses the logic of the calamitous consequences that flow from the assertion that the dead are not raised (15:14–18). Those who have fallen asleep in Christ have not perished. Faith and preaching are not vain, and the death of Christ truly liberates his people from the penalty of sin.

Paul is not done with the implications that ensue from the premise that there is no resurrection of the dead. He will pick up the question again in 15:29–34, but first, in 15:20–28, he expounds on the ramifications derived from the fact that Christ has been raised from the dead in what is truly one of the high points of the letter.[108] In a brief but sweeping apocalyptic narrative Paul compares the first man, Adam, who implicated humanity in death, to the eschatological man, Jesus Christ, who grants eternal life by virtue of his resurrection to all who belong to him. Christ's resurrection set in motion a sequence of events, including the future resurrection of all believers at his coming (15:23) and "the end" (15:24), when Christ delivers the kingdom to the Father and when all rule and authority and power are destroyed, including the last enemy, death. When all things have been subjected to the Father, including the Son, God will be all in all (15:28).[109]

The units on either side of 15:20–28 take up the question, "What if there were not resurrection?" We should not fail, however, to ask the same question of 15:20–28. In other words, there are further calamitous consequences implied if the assertions of 15:20–28 are false. All enemies must be subdued and death must be overthrown as a principle of God's sovereignty over the hostile powers of the cosmos. If there is no resurrection of the dead, then ultimately God is not sovereign.[110]

---

[108] Rhetorically, 15:20–28 is a digression, much in the same way as 9:1–27 and 13:1–13, not in the sense of moving off topic but rather a digression in order to emphasize the main point more forcefully.

[109] Fitzmyer (*First Corinthians*, 568) comments, "Paul's theological argument in this paragraph is both typological (vv. 21–23) and apocalyptic vv. 24–28)." Paul will pick up the Adam/Christ contrast again in 15:45–49 (cf. also Rom 5:12–21) and build to a triumphant declaration of the believer's victory in Christ (15:50–58).

[110] So also Fee, *First Corinthians*, 746–47.

Verses 20–28 divide into two units (15:20–23,24–28). The passage opens with a reaffirmation of Christ's resurrection and the claim that he is the firstfruits of those who have fallen asleep (15:20), followed by an explanation of death and resurrection by way of a typological contrast between Adam and Christ (15:21–22). Paul then repeats that Christ is the firstfruits in order to clarify the order of resurrection. Christ and those who belong to him are each raised "in his own turn" (15:23).[111] Christ has already been raised from the dead, and the resurrection of believers will occur at the Lord's coming. The second unit takes its cue from the word "the end."[112] Paul describes the end as the time when Christ delivers the kingdom to the Father and abolishes all rule, authority, and power, including death (15:24b–26). The destruction of all enemies is necessary "so that God may be all in all" (15:27–28). Paul finds scriptural warrant for God's sovereignty over his creation in Pss 8 and 110:1.

**15:20** The declaration, "Christ has indeed been raised from the dead," is the hallmark of Christian faith and flies in the face of those who were saying, "There is no resurrection of the dead."[113] Hays refers to 15:20 as a "ringing affirmation" wherein "Paul moves from illusion to reality."[114] Robertson and Plummer describe the transition from 15:19 to 15:20 as Paul's "joyful outburst."[115] Collins notes the "strong declarative statement in contrast to the beginning conditional sentences in 15:12,29."[116] Following the affirmation that Christ has been raised from the dead, Paul describes Christ as "the firstfruits of those who have fallen asleep" (NIV). The metaphor of sleep refers to dead believers and occurs four times in chap. 15. Paul employs the expression of eyewitnesses of the resurrection who had already died at the time of Paul's writing (15:6) and hypothetically of dead believers who have perished if there is no resurrection (15:18). Death, however, is not the lot of all believers. In 15:51, Paul declares, "We will not all sleep."[117]

The concept of firstfruits[118] is rooted in the Old Testament. In Lev 23:9–14 the term describes a consecrated portion of the harvest offered to God in sacrifice.

---

[111] 15:20–23 is thus bracketed by an *inclusio* that provides the leitmotif of the unit, the "firstfruits" (so Collins, *First Corinthians*, 547).

[112] NIV, "Then the end will come." Gk. εἶτα τὸ τέλος (lit., "then the end).

[113] But . . . indeed, translates the Greek, νυνὶ δὲ. BDAG lists 1 Cor 15:20 under the definition "introducing the real situation after an unreal conditional clause or sentence; but, as a matter of fact" (cf. other places in Paul where νυνὶ δὲ introduces profound contrasts: Rom 3:21; 6:22; 7:6; 1 Cor 12:18; 13:13; Eph 2:13; Col 1:22).

[114] Hays, *First Corinthians*, 262. All of the "if" clauses of 15:12–19 are counter-factual.

[115] Robertson and Plummer, *First Corinthians*, 351.

[116] Collins, *First Corinthians*, 547.

[117] For other uses of the metaphor in Paul, see 1 Cor 7:39; 11:30; 1 Thess 4:13–15.

[118] Gk. ἀπαρχή. In the New Testament the term appears in Rom 8:23; 11:16; 16:5; 1 Cor 15:20, 23; 16:15; 2 Thess 2:13; Jas 1:18; Rev 14:4. It is predominantly a Pauline term, occurring elsewhere only in Jas 1:18 and Rev 14:4. In the LXX, see Exod 22:28; 23:19; 25:2–3; 35:5; 36:6; 39:1; Lev 2:12; 22:12; 23:10; Num 5:9; 15:20–21; 18:8,11–12,29–30,32; 31:29; Deut 12:6,11,17; 18:4; 26:2,10; 33:21; 1 Sam 2:29; 10:4; 2 Sam 1:21; 2 Chr 31:5,10,12,14; Ezra 8:25; Neh 10:38,

Commentators generally note that the cultic nuance of a consecrated or choice portion is absent here. The emphasis falls more on the temporal sequence and the representative aspect; that is, Christ is the first to be raised from the dead and representative of more resurrection bodies to come.[119] The metaphor of firstfruits functions similarly to the metaphor of a downpayment or a pledge (2 Cor 1:22; 5:5; Eph 1:14) and to the concept of the "firstborn" (Rom 8:29). Thiselton helpfully summarizes the three emphases of the term "firstfruits": "(1) prior temporality; (2) representation of the same quality or character; and (3) promise or pledge of more of the same kind to come."[120] The designation of Christ as "firstfruits" anticipates the fuller argument of 15:35–49.

**15:21–22** An explanatory "for" introduces an elaboration on the metaphor of firstfruits in terms of an Adam/Christ typology. Verse 21 sets forth a verbless parallelism: "For since through man [came] death, also through man [came] resurrection from the dead." Verse 22, introduced by another "for," explains further, "For as in Adam all die, so in Christ all will be made alive." Paul employs the Adam/Christ typology again in 15:45–49 and in Rom 5:12–20.[121] The specific designation of Adam as a "type" does not appear in 1 Cor 15, though it is implied. The word "type" is used of Adam in Rom 5:14, "Adam is a type of the one to come."[122] There are similarities and differences between Paul's use of the typology in 1 Corinthians and Romans. The typology is more developed in Rom 5 in the context of Paul's exposition of justification by faith with the added focus on sin as the cause of death (5:12). Just as sin and death entered the world through the one man, Adam, so also the gift of grace abounded to many through the one man, Jesus Christ (Rom 5:15). Just as Adam's disobedience implicated humanity in sin and death, so also Christ's obedience resulted in the free gift of eternal life for many (Rom 5:18–19). The far-reaching consequences of Adam's sin are counter-balanced by the far-reaching consequences of Christ's act of obedience.[123]

In 1 Cor 15:21–22 there is no mention of sin, only that which is pertinent to Paul's immediate concern, namely, death and resurrection through

---

40; 12:44; 13:5; Jdt 11:13; Tob 1:6; Pss 77:51; 104:36; Sir 7:31; 35:7; 45:20; Song 15:3; Ezek 20:31,40; 44:30; 45:1,6–7,13,16; 48:8–10,12,18,20–21; Mal 3:8.

[119] See the discussion in Garland, *1 Corinthians*, 705. Paul uses the term to refer to the first and representative part (Rom 8:23; 11:16) and of the first converts of a region (Rom 16:5; 1 Cor 16:15).

[120] Thiselton, *First Corinthians*, 1224.

[121] Some see an Adam typology at work also in Phil 2:6–11 (so Collins, *First Corinthians*, 551).

[122] Gk. τύπος.

[123] On the comparison of Rom 5 and 1 Cor 15, Thiselton (*First Corinthians*, 1227–28) notes, "The parallel between Rom 5:12–16 and 1 Cor 15:21–22 is close, but whereas the former stresses the 'how much more' of divine grace (Rom 5:15), our passage stresses the pledge of new creation as the promise of the resurrection of the dead on the basis of being in Christ, also, however, by divine grace." Ciampa and Rosner (*First Corinthians*, 763) observe that in 15:21–22 "Paul is presenting the most concise form of the story of redemption imaginable."

a man.[124] The repetition, "through a man," used of both Adam and Christ, emphasizes Christ's humanity. In Rom 5, resurrection is not mentioned, but implied, "so that, just as sin reigned in death, so also grace might reign through righteousness to bring eternal life through Jesus Christ our Lord" (Rom 5:21). Romans 5:12–20 and 1 Cor 15:21–22,45–49 are complementary texts and, when read together, present a more complete picture, but each emphasizes what is necessary to the argument in each respective context. First Corinthians 15:22 elaborates further on each respective man, Adam and Christ, and introduces the notion of corporate solidarity, that is, those who are "in Adam" and those who are "in Christ." Adam and Christ are representative human beings.[125] All "in Adam" die (present tense). All "in Christ" will be made alive (future tense). Thiselton explains that "the argument that humanity is, simply as a brute fact, bound up in the solidarities, vulnerabilities, and consequences of the life and destiny of Adam finds its saving parallel in the gospel assurance that the new humanity is bound up in the solidarities, atoning work, and resurrection victory and promise of Christ as the 'last' (i.e., eschatological) Adam (see 15:45)."[126] Those who are in Christ still die, but they will come to life in the future, which is the pertinent point of Paul's whole argument. The timing of the believer's resurrection is clarified in the next verse in the phrase, "at his coming."

It should be obvious from the context that the word "all" is qualified respectively by "in Adam" and "in Christ." In other words, "all" who are in Adam die. "All" who are in Christ will be made alive. Since Paul's focus rests solely on the resurrection of believers, it is possible that the "all" is absolute in both instances, that is, both occurrences of "all" refer to believers only. If referring to believers only, the statement would mean that just as all believers die by virtue of their union with Adam, so also all believers will be made alive by virtue of their union with Christ. It is true, of course, that all people (believers and unbelievers) are "in Adam," and this is likely Paul's meaning here.[127] Paul clearly does not advocate the resurrection of all people to eternal life (1 Cor 1:18;

[124] Although "sin" is still prominent in the context (15:3, "Christ died for our sins"; 15:17, apart from resurrection "you are still in your sins"; 15:56, "the sting of death is sin"). Furthermore, the reign of Christ that destroys the hostile powers, including death (15:24–28), overturns the reign of sin and death brought about by Adam (Rom 5:14–21).

[125] So F. F. Bruce, "Paul now draws an analogy between two uniquely representative men: Adam, head of the old creation, in whom all die, and Christ, head of the new creation, 'the first-born from the dead' (Col 1:18; cf. Rev 1:8) in whom all are to be made alive in resurrection" (*1 & 2 Corinthians*, NCB [Grand Rapids: Eerdmans, 1971], 145).

[126] Thiselton, *First Corinthians*, 1225.

[127] Regarding the statement "all will be made alive," Robertson and Plummer (*First Corinthians*, 353) ponder, "The meaning may be that all will be raised, will be quickened, which is not the same as saying that all will be saved" (cf. Dan 12:2).

5:13; 6:9–10). The following verse clarifies that those who will be made alive are "those who belong to him [Christ]," not all human beings (15:23).[128]

**15:23** The first subunit closes out with another mention of Christ as the firstfruits and elaborates further on the resurrection of believers. Military imagery dominates the rest of this unit.[129] Paul mentions two "orders," Christ, who has already been raised from the dead, and those who belong to Christ at his coming. While some have argued for a third order of resurrection (i.e., the resurrection of the wicked) from the term "the end" in 15:24, most conclude that this is not germane to Paul's present argument.[130] The resurrection of all the dead, both righteous and wicked, is affirmed in the Old and New Testaments (see Dan 12:2; John 5:29; Rev 20). Some will be raised to everlasting life; others will be raised to everlasting condemnation. Here, however, Paul's concern lies only with the resurrection of believers, not unbelievers.[131] The time of the resurrection of believers is the "coming" of Christ, a word that means presence and that was used in some contexts in the ancient world in a technical sense to denote the coming of a political figure of high office, such as the visit of an emperor to a province.[132] In the New Testament the term takes on the technical meaning of the second coming of Christ in certain contexts (1 Thess 2:19; 3:13; 4:15; 5:23; 2 Thess 2:1).[133] Paul clarifies in 1 Thess 4:13–18 that the dead in Christ will rise first, followed by the transformation of those who are alive at the time of his coming, a point developed further in 15:51–52.

**15:24–28** Following the resurrection of all believers, the end arrives.[134] Paul's language is compact and precise and does not specify the time interval

---

[128] "To be made alive" (ζῳοποιέω) is another term denoting resurrection in this context. The word itself can mean "to keep alive" or "to make alive" (BDAG). In 1 Cor 15, however, the meaning entails complete transformation (15:35–49). Concerning the uniqueness of Jesus' resurrection, Robertson and Plummer (*First Corinthians*, 353) comment, "Others had been raised from the dead before He was; He had raised some Himself. But only to die again. None of those who had been restored to life remained forever alive, for death had not yet been conquered."

[129] So Hays, *First Corinthians*, 264. The military imagery is signaled by the Greek, τάγμα, which denotes order or rank, translated "turn" by the NIV. The picture is one of the hostile powers being subdued and finally destroyed, including the dreadful last enemy, death.

[130] For a full discussion see Thiselton, *First Corinthians*, 1230–31; Garland, *1 Corinthians*, 709.

[131] Even though Paul's focus is on the death and resurrection of believers and he does not address directly the resurrection of the wicked, the narrative of 15:20–28 is wide-ranging, taking into account the whole of God's judgment and redemption of his creation. All humans are implicated in the statement, "in Adam all die."

[132] Gk. παρουσία. BDAG, "On the one hand the word served as a sacred expression for the coming of a hidden divinity, who makes his presence felt by a revelation of his power, or whose presence is celebrated in the cult. On the other hand, παρουσία became the official term for a visit of a person of high rank, especially of kings and emperors visiting a province."

[133] The term does not always refer to Christ's coming. In 16:17 the word is used of the arrival of Stephanas, Fortunatus, and Achaicus. Cf. also 2 Cor 7:6–7; 10:10; Phil 1:26; 2:12. In 2 Thess 2:8 the word refers to the "coming" of the lawless one.

[134] Stated concisely in Greek with no verb, εἶτα τὸ τέλος, "then the end."

between the resurrection of those who belong to Christ and the end. Since a rather long interval exists between the resurrection of Christ and the resurrection of his followers, it is possible that another lengthy interval exists between the resurrection of believers and the final consummation, including the millennial reign of Christ mentioned in Rev 20:5–6. Paul does not reveal his full understanding of end-time events in the span of only two verses! As noted in the comments on 15:20–23, Paul does not mention the resurrection of unbelievers. Neither does he mention the resurrection of some believers immediately following the resurrection of Jesus (Matt 28:52). Paul is fully aware of other events attendant to the last days (see esp. 2 Thess 2:1–11). While some argue for an "interval" (millennium), others think Paul speaks of a more immediate consummation.[135] First Corinthians 15:20–28 is not decisive on this matter.[136] Paul's immediate concern in this passage is not to establish precise time intervals but to show how Christ's resurrection set in motion a sequence of events that will culminate with the complete overthrow of all hostile powers opposed to God, including death, which entails the subjection of all things to God the Father. Two temporal clauses clarify what happens in the end; the Son hands over the kingdom to God the Father and he destroys all dominion, authority, and power (15:24).[137] There is a strong scholarly consensus that the second use of the personal pronoun "he" in 15:24 refers to Christ,[138] although the use of Pss 110:1 and 8:6 in the subsequent verses favor "God."[139] If the timing of the end is ambiguous in this passage, what will occur in the end is not.

Paul's Christological reading of Pss 110:1 and 8:6 (15:25–27) explains that Christ must reign until all enemies are vanquished.[140] Paul does not specify when Christ begins his reign, only the necessity of his reign that brings to an end the reign of sin and death introduced by the first man, Adam (Rom

---

[135] For the millenarian perspective, see L. J. Kreitzer, *Jesus and God in Paul's Eschatology*, JSNT 19 (Sheffield: JSOT Press, 1987), 134–45. For the view of an immediate consummation at the coming of Christ (amillennial), see Barrett, *First Corinthians*, 356–57; C. E. Hill, "Paul's Understanding of Christ's Kingdom in 1 Corinthians 15:20–28," *NovT* 30 (1988): 573–89; Garland, *1 Corinthians*, 710; Ciampa and Rosner, *First Corinthians*, 766.

[136] So C. Vaughan and T. D. Lea, *1 Corinthians*, Bible Study Commentary (Grand Rapids: Zondervan, 1983), 157. The conjunction εἶτα may indicate something subsequent or immediately consequent (so Robertson and Plummer, *First Corinthians*, 354).

[137] Gk. ὅταν. The temporal sequence is reversed logically; that is, Christ first destroys all hostile powers and then hands the kingdom over to the Father. The second clause explains what occurs in the deliverance of the kingdom. On the language of rule, authority, and power in Paul, see Rom 8:38; Col 1:16; 2:10–15; Eph 1:20–21; 3:10; 6:12; Titus 3:1.

[138] The grammar favors "Christ" who is clearly the subject of the verb in the first temporal clause, "When he hands over the kingdom to God the Father."

[139] So Ciampa and Rosner (*First Corinthians*, 766–67), who explain, "Paul may have been perfectly happy to express himself in such a potentially ambiguous manner, given his understanding (consistent with the psalm) that God acts through Christ and Christ is the agent of God's reign" (767; the comment is in reference to Ps 110).

[140] 15:25 begins with an explanatory γάρ.

5:14–21).[141] Paul conjoins the two psalms as the scriptural warrant for the destruction of all dominion, authority and power (15:24c; Ps 110:1) and the handing over of the kingdom to God the Father (15:24b; Ps 8:6).[142] Neither psalm is cited exactly or introduced by the quotation formula, "It is written," but both complement one another. The psalms are linked thematically by the phrase "under his feet," which implies reign.[143] Psalm 110 provides the term "enemies," which anticipates the key assertion of 15:26, "The last enemy to be destroyed is death,"[144] while Ps 8 provides the verb, "to subject"[145] that leads to the climax of 15:28 that describes the subjugation of all things to God. The New Testament makes ample Christological use of Ps 110:1 (see Matt 22:44; Mark 12:36; 14:62; Luke 20:42–43; 22:69; Acts 2:33–35; Rom 8:34; Eph 1:20; Col 3:1; Heb 1:3,13; 1 Pet 3:22). Psalms 8 and 110 also occur together in Eph 1:20–22.[146] Psalm 8 has in mind the Genesis account of the creation of mankind, while Ps 110 refers to the royal Davidic king. By combining the two psalms Paul is able to emphasize that what was lost in Adam is regained in Christ and fulfills God's intention for humanity.[147]

Verses 27b–28 follow through with the language of submission taken from Ps 8. Paul clarifies that "everything" put in submission to Christ does not include God himself, which would contradict the functional subordination within the Godhead (cf. 3:23; 11:3).[148] This is clear from the psalm itself. If God places everything under Christ, God is the exception. Instead, the Son himself is subjected to the one who puts all things under his feet (15:28).[149] The relational language of Father (15:24) and Son (15:28) underscores Christ the Son's redemptive work in accomplishing the will of God the Father (cf. John 5:19–30). The submission language is functional and does not imply that

---

[141] That Christ's reign begins at resurrection and ascension does not exclude a millennial perspective. So Kreitzer, *Paul's Eschatology*, 142–44. Heb 2:8 clarifies "In putting everything under him, God left nothing that is not subject to him. Yet at present we do not see everything subject to him."

[142] So Fee, *First Corinthians*, 755–58.

[143] Ps 8:6a reads, "You made him ruler over the works of your hands," and Ps 110:1a, "Sit at my right hand."

[144] 15:26 is emphatic. There is no participle or conjunction connecting the verse to 15:25, and "last enemy" occurs first in the sentence. The verb is present tense, "is being destroyed," and expresses certainty (so Thiselton, *First Corinthians*, 1234). J. P. Heil detects a chiasm in 15:24–28 with 15:26 at the center (*The Rhetorical Role of Scripture in 1 Corinthians*, Studies in Biblical Literature [Atlanta: Society of Biblical Literature, 2005], 213).

[145] Gk. ὑπέταξεν, aorist tense (NIV, "he put").

[146] Cf. also the close proximity of both Pss 8 and 110 in Hebrews (1:3,13; 2:5–8).

[147] See Thiselton, *First Corinthians*, 1235; Ciampa and Rosner, *First Corinthians*, 772–76.

[148] 3:22–23 anticipates the emphasis on death's defeat, "whether Paul or Apollos or Cephas or the world or life or death or the present or the future—all are yours, and you are of Christ, and Christ is of God."

[149] The Greek structure is emphatic, αὐτὸς ὁ υἱὸς (the Son himself).

the Son is inferior to the Father in essence of being.[150] The sovereignty the Father gives to the Son is for a definite purpose and time. "It is His work to put an end to all that opposes the sovereignty of God."[151] The final purpose clause explains the eschatological goal of the Son's subjugation to the Father, "so that God might be all in all." The phrase expresses "the unchallenged reign of God alone, in his pure goodness."[152] Paul uses similar terminology in 1 Cor 8:6a and Rom 11:36 (cf. also Eph 1:23; Col 3:11). Here the phrase should be understood in the context of death's defeat through resurrection (cf. 15:54–58). God's purposes take into account the whole of creation (Rom 8:19–25; Col 1:15–20; Eph 1:9–10,20–23). "All people, both the ungodly and the pious, all devils will be compelled by the work of Christ to recognize God as the One and Only."[153] In the end, Christ's work is for the glory of the Father (Phil 2:5–11).[154]

### 4. The Consequences of No Resurrection, Part 2 (15:29–34)

**[29]Now if there is no resurrection, what will those do who are baptized for the dead? If the dead are not raised at all, why are people baptized for them? [30]And as for us, why do we endanger ourselves every hour? [31]I die every day—I mean that, brothers—just as surely as I glory over you in Christ Jesus our Lord. [32]If I fought wild beasts in Ephesus for merely human reasons, what have I gained? If the dead are not raised**

**"Let us eat and drink,**
**for tomorrow we die."**

**[33]Do not be misled: "Bad company corrupts good character." [34]Come back to your senses as you ought, and stop sinning; for there are some who are ignorant of God—I say this to your shame.**

Paul's argument appears to transition abruptly from the climactic "so that God might be all in all" in 15:28 to an intriguing reference to baptism for the dead in 15:29. The structure of Paul's argument clarifies the shift, however, since 15:29–34 is clearly parallel to 15:12–19 and functions as the second

[150] The absolute use of the title "the Son" appears only here in Paul (noted by Garland, *First Corinthians*, 713; Fitzmyer, *First Corinthians*, 575). Collins (*First Corinthians*, 552) comments, "The title points to the unique relationship between Jesus and God and to God's unique act in raising Jesus from the dead, an act that inaugurates the eschatological scenario that culminates in Christ's handing all things over to God. At this moment when the kingdom is consummated the unique relationship between Christ and God is fully apparent. Christ will have completed the Father's work. The 'Son' title not only refers to the uniqueness of the relationship between the Father and the Son. It also expresses the idea that the Son has done the Father's work and states the relative subordination of the Son to the Father."

[151] Robertson and Plummer, *First Corinthians*, 335.

[152] Barrett, *First Corinthians*, 361.

[153] Robertson and Plummer, *First Corinthians*, 370.

[154] Cf. Rom 16:27; Gal 1:3–5.

refutation of the claim that there is no resurrection.[155] Baptism for dead is only the first of two examples that serve to show the absurdity of certain practices if the dead are not raised.[156] As in the first refutation of the view that there is no resurrection (15:12–19), the hypothetical scenario depicted by the conditional clause, "If the dead are not raised" occurs twice (15:29,32; cf. 15:13,16), yet Paul's argument moves in a different direction. Rather than continue with the theological consequences of no resurrection, Paul shows the incongruity of current practices among the Corinthians and the folly of apostolic suffering through a series of four rhetorical questions. Specifically, the practice of baptizing for the dead, whatever the phrase means, is nonsensical, and apostolic ministry, which entails unabating danger and daily death, is equally ludicrous if there is no resurrection of the dead.[157]

Verses 29–34 divide into three units. First, Paul calls into question the practice of those being baptized for the dead by posing two rhetorical questions (15:29): "What will those do who are baptized for the dead? If the dead are not raised at all, why are people baptized for them?" Second, using himself as a representative example of all apostles, Paul challenges the wisdom of the life of the apostles if there is no resurrection (15:30–32): "If the dead are not raised, 'Let us eat and drink, for tomorrow we die'" (15:32b). Third, Paul's probing questions lead to three exhortations: do not be deceived, become sober-minded, and do not sin (15:33–34). Paul underscores the urgency of the situation and scolds the Corinthians because "there are some who are ignorant of God."

**15:29** The question "What will they do?" is capable of different meanings such as "What do they hope to achieve or gain?" or "What will they do next?" Thiselton notes the vast semantic range of the verb "to do"[158] and suggests that the NIV translation "What will they do?" does not quite capture the subjective and logical force. He suggests as a more accurate translation, "What do those people think they are doing who . . . ?"[159] Garland finds the parallel in 15:32 helpful, "What does it profit me?", and thinks the question in 15:29 implies something like, "What good will it do them? If there is no resurrection of the dead, nothing could possibly accrue from that rite. They will be shown to be fools."[160]

---

[155] The section begins in Greek with the conjunction ἐπεί, translated by the NIV, "Now." The NASB translates, "Otherwise" (cf. 1 Cor 5:10; 7:14; 14:16). In context the meaning is, "If there is no resurrection from the dead" (so Robertson and Plummer, *First Corinthians*, 359). There is, therefore, a logical connection to the preceding material.

[156] So Fee, *First Corinthians*, 763; Garland, *1 Corinthians*, 715.

[157] Cf. 15:19, "If only for this life we have hope in Christ, we are to be pitied more than all men."

[158] Gk. ποιέω.

[159] Thiselton, *First Corinthians*, 1241.

[160] Garland, *1 Corinthians*, 716. Similarly Barrett (*First Corinthians*, 362), "What will they do next when it is discovered that the dead on whose behalf they have acted are dead and done with,

The history of interpretation attests to the ambiguity of Paul's reference to "those who are baptized for the dead."[161] Perhaps all exegetical options have been exhausted with no commanding consensus regarding its meaning. Fee quips, "One may consider it as axiomatic that when there is such a wide divergence of opinion, no one knows what in fact was going on."[162] Fee's point is well-taken, but there are reasonable interpretive options. Furthermore, the function of 15:29 is clear in context. Already Paul has demonstrated the disastrous theological consequences that ensue if the dead are not raised (15:12–19). Now he will show the senselessness of certain practices in light of the same hypothetical scenario. However obscure the notion of "baptism for the dead" may be, it is Paul's plain intention to take issue with those in Corinth who were saying, "There is no resurrection of the dead" (15:12).

Scholars often observe that the most natural reading of the text suggests a vicarious baptism of someone on behalf of, in the place of, and for the benefit of an unbaptized dead person. According to Hull, this view is "aptly labeled the 'majority reading.'"[163] Fee states that "this reading is such a plain understanding of the Greek text that no one would ever have imagined the various alternatives were it not for the difficulties involved."[164] Likewise Hays comments, "All of the numerous attempts to explain away the obvious sense of this verse are strained and unpersuasive."[165] Fee explains that if the vicarious view is correct, it likely "reflects some believers' being baptized for others who either were or were on their way to becoming believers when they died (e.g., as in 11:30), but had never been baptized," or "that it reflects the concern of members of households for some of their own number who had died before becoming believers."[166] In this view Paul does not necessarily commend the practice, but it serves the purpose of his argument that such a practice was inconsistent and contradictory for those who believed that there was no resurrection of the dead.[167] Demaris's study regarding the evidence

since there is no resurrection?", and Fee (*First Corinthians*, 763), "When they realize what they are doing and there is no real future for the dead, how will it affect them?"

[161] The most recent full-length study on this question is M. F. Hull, *Baptism on Account of the Dead (1 Cor 15:29): An Act of Faith in the Resurrection* (Atlanta: Society of Biblical Literature, 2005). See also B. M. Foschini's five-part series, "'Those Who Are Baptised for the Dead,' 1 Cor. 15:29; An Exegetical Historical Dissertation," *CBQ* 12 (1950): 260–76, 379–88; *CBQ* 13 (1951): 46–78, 172–98, 276–83; and the discussion in Thiselton, *First Corinthians*, 1242–49.

[162] Fee, *First Corinthians*, 762–63. Thiselton (*First Corinthians*, 1240) notes that "a vast literature stretches from the second century to the present day."

[163] Hull, *Baptism on Account of the Dead*, 11.

[164] Fee, *First Corinthians*, 764.

[165] Hays, *First Corinthians*, 267.

[166] Fee, *First Corinthians*, 767.

[167] So B. Witherington, "While Paul does not endorse this magical view of baptism's efficacy, he also does not see this as a serious enough aberration to debate the point; he simply uses it as part of his *ad hominem* argument" (*Conflict and Community in Corinth: A Socio-Rhetorical Commentary* [Grand Rapids: Eerdmans, 1994], 305–6). See also Blomberg, *1 Corinthians*, 299.

for a preoccupation with the dead in Corinthian culture supports the vicarious interpretation.[168] Collins accepts Demaris's argument and comments: "The practice of baptizing the living as a vicarious rite of passage to benefit the dead might have been a Christian response to this general concern. The intended beneficiaries would have been members of their families or catechumens who had not yet been baptized at the time of their deaths."[169] Collins concedes that there is little evidence that the practice existed in the early church but nevertheless concludes, "It is likely that the practice took place only in first-century Corinth, where religious syncretism was a fact of life even for Corinthian Christians. Paul's unusual use of the third person plural in a rhetorical question suggests that the practice may not have been widespread among the Corinthian Christians. Only a few of them may have practiced vicarious baptism on behalf of the dead."[170] Since the key preposition translated "on behalf of,"[171] when used of persons, normally suggests a vicarious effect, that is, the application of benefits, Collins thinks that other interpretations require a meaning that departs from Pauline usage.[172]

There are three main objections to the proxy, vicarious baptism view. First, there is no historical evidence for such a practice antecedent to 1 Corinthians, unless 15:29 provides such evidence. Second, vicarious baptisms did occur among Gnostic heretics who were condemned by the early Greek Fathers.[173] Third, such an understanding is out of step with Paul's own understanding of baptism elsewhere, and it is difficult to believe that he would mention an aberrant practice, however relevant to his argument, without condemning it. "To win one argument, he opens a Pandora's box of new theological problems."[174] The historical and theological problems with the vicarious baptism view have led to other explanations. Any interpretation has to address three key terms, namely, the meanings of the verb "to baptize," the preposition "for," and the substantival adjective "the dead."

---

[168] R. DeMaris, "Corinthian Religion and Baptism for the Dead (1 Corinthians 15:29): Insights from Archaeology and Anthropology," *JBL* 114 (1995): 661–82.

[169] Collins, *First Corinthians*, 556.

[170] Ibid., 557.

[171] Gk. ὑπέρ.

[172] Collins, *First Corinthians*, 559. Fitzmyer (*First Corinthians*, 578–80) also notes Demaris and concedes that the cultural context "might explain why Christians who lived there developed their own practice of showing concern for the dead." Regarding the preposition ὑπέρ, Fitzmyer concedes that we cannot rule out a causal sense, "baptized on account of the dead." Nevertheless, Fitzmyer concludes, "The explanation of vicarious or proxy baptism remains the most plausible, even though its meaning is not fully clear" (580).

[173] See Hull, *Baptism on Account of the Dead*, 40–42. Hull mentions Tertullian, Chrysostom, and Epiphanius. English contends that the Fathers merely mediated a view consistent with orthodoxy as defined by the church. See A. English, "Mediated, Mediation, Unmediated: 1 Corinthians 15:29: the History of Interpretation, and the Current State of Biblical Studies," *RevExp* 99 (2002): 419–28.

[174] Garland, *1 Corinthians*, 717.

Many follow the view of the Greek Fathers in retaining the normal sense of baptism as referring to Christian baptism and the usual meaning of the Greek preposition "for," as "on behalf of," yet understand "the dead" to refer metaphorically to the condition of believers who receive baptism.[175] This understanding complies with Pauline theology in that the one being baptized does so on behalf of their own bodies in the sense of being baptized for the part of them that is dying. Garland explains, "Paul interprets baptism as a symbol of death and resurrection, and 'the dead' either characterizes the individual's prebaptismal state or refers to the individual's soon-to-be dead body (cf. Rom 6:3–14; Eph 2:1,5; Col 2:13). Paul's specific statement in Rom. 8:10 that 'the body is dead because of sin' gives further credibility to this interpretation."[176] In other words, the expression "to be baptized for the dead" is theological shorthand for Christian baptism, which pictures death as the presupposition to resurrection. "Baptism connotes sharing Christ's death to share his resurrection."[177]

A third view that holds a significant place in scholarship takes the preposition "for" in a causal or referential sense, that is, "on account of/because of/with reference to/for the sake of." Thus, baptism is true Christian baptism, but those being baptized are baptized, in some way, "because of the dead." While the causal understanding of the preposition is the common element in this interpretive camp, there are different readings of the meaning of "the dead." One reading understands "baptism for the dead" to refer to something exceptional but not something that Paul would disapprove, such as a baptism out of affection or respect for the dead or a baptism in the hope of being reunited with a loved one. Such an attitude on behalf of the convert assumes resurrection.[178] In the most recent full-length scholarly treatment of this verse, Hull argues the thesis that "1 Cor 15:29 is a dual rhetorical question in which Paul holds up one group within the Corinthian community as a laudable example for the entire community."[179] Those being baptized do so as an act of faith in the resurrection of Christ, which guarantees the resurrection of all dead believers. "They undergo the rite of baptism 'on account of the dead'—on account of the fact that the dead are destined for life, having died hoping in the Lord's promise of salvation—on account of their faith in the fact that 'if there is no resurrection of the dead, then Christ has not been raised' (1 Cor 15:13)."[180] Ciampa and Rosner adopt this view and explain that "Paul is not interested in all dead

[175] So Chrysostom, *Hom. 1 Cor.* 40.2.

[176] Garland, *1 Corinthians*, 718.

[177] Ibid. See also J. C. O'Neil, "1 Corinthians 15:29," *ExpTim* 91 (1979): 310–11; R. P. Martin, *The Spirit and the Congregation: Studies in 1 Corinthians 12–15* (Grand Rapids: Eerdmans, 1984), 120–21; C. H. Talbert, *Reading Corinthians: A Literary and Theological Commentary on 1 and 2 Corinthians* (New York: Crossroad, 1987), 99.

[178] So Robertson and Plummer, *First Corinthians*, 359–60; Vaughan and Lea, *1 Corinthians*, 158; Thiselton, *First Corinthians*, 1248.

[179] Hull, *Baptism on Account of the Dead*, 3.

[180] Ibid.

people, but in those who will benefit from being raised to glory. That is, his references to 'the dead' have the righteous dead (i.e., dead who will be raised to glory) in mind."[181] They propose the following translation, "Now, if there is no resurrection, what will be accomplished by those who get baptized because of what they have heard about how our dead will be raised? If the dead are not raised at all, why are people undergoing baptism on account of them?"[182]

Two other views within this third line of interpretation deserve mention. White understands Paul's reference to "the dead" as a figurative caricature of apostolic suffering, which finds support in the verses that immediately follow: "And as for us, why do we endanger ourselves every hour? I die every day." The implication of 15:30–31 is that "Paul wants the Corinthians to understand him, in his role as an apostle, as being one of 'the dead' in 15:29."[183] Like other passages in the Corinthian correspondence (1 Cor 4:9; 2 Cor 2:14; 4:7–12; 6:1–10), in 1 Cor 15:29–32 Paul links death with apostolic ministry.[184] White explains, "Certain groups in Corinth were brought to faith and baptized 'on account of' some of the apostles, especially Paul and Apollos, to whom they subsequently and quite naturally felt an affinity, but their preferences resulted in the development of competitive allegiances to one or the other of the apostles. In our text, Paul points out the inconsistency of this fact with their denial of the resurrection. If 'truly dead' persons are not raised, what sense does it make for the Corinthians to be baptized on account of those who are 'dying all the time,' namely, the apostles?"[185] More recently, Patrick offers a variation of this view, agreeing that "the dead" refer to the apostles, yet not metaphorically but literally. The death of apostles known to the Corinthians (15:6) resulted in the practice of baptizing in honor of dead apostles whose testimony continued to bear fruit for the gospel.[186] White's view requires two different senses of "dead" in the same verse (metaphorical and literal), and Patrick's view falters in light of Paul's assumption that none of the Corinthians were baptized as an

---

[181] Ciampa and Rosner, *First Corinthians*, 783. Ciampa and Rosner note the strong ties of baptism to resurrection in Rom 6:3–13: "Baptism itself is tied to the resurrection hope by way of its integral role in the conversion experience. It is not that baptism per se brings salvation, but baptism is understood to be the initial confirmation of faith and act of initiation into the body of Christ. Certainly this text echoes the theme of other baptism texts that indicate that baptism is part and parcel of the process of entering into Christian life and fellowship" (784).

[182] Ibid., 784–85. Throughout 1 Cor 15 "the dead" is the subject of the verb "to be raised (15:15,16,29,32,35,52). Thus, Paul's focus is "on 'the dead' and what happens to them as his topic rather than merely reflecting a broad interest in the subject of the resurrection" (785).

[183] J. R. White, "'Baptized on Account of the Dead': The Meaning of 1 Corinthians 15:29 in its Context," *JBL* 116 (1997): 494.

[184] Ibid., 495. White draws from Hafemann's analysis of the theme of apostolic suffering in the Corinthian letters. See S. J. Hafemann, *Suffering and Ministry in the Spirit* (Grand Rapids: Eerdmans, 1990), 52–79.

[185] White, "'Baptized on Account of the Dead,'" 498.

[186] J. E. Patrick, "Living Rewards for Dead Apostles: 'Baptised for the Dead' in 1 Corinthians 15.29," *NTS* 52 (2006): 71–85.

act of allegiance to him or any other man (1 Cor 1:13–15). The other causal readings of 15:29 are more probable.

**15:30–32** The argument becomes increasingly more personal in 15:30–32 as Paul examines the logic of suffering for the gospel if there is no resurrection from the dead. Having questioned the practice of others who were being baptized for the dead, Paul now asks, "Why do *we* endanger *ourselves* every hour?" Paul then confesses, "*I* die daily," and asks of himself, "If *I* fought wild beasts in Ephesus for merely human reasons, what have *I* gained?"

The "we" in 15:30 has primary reference to the apostles,[187] although all who incur risks for the cause of the gospel could be included in the rhetorical question by way of extension (cf. Phil 1:29).[188] The verb translated "to be endangered"[189] occurs only here in Paul's letters, but the cognate noun is used eight times in the catalogue of sufferings in 2 Cor 11:26.[190] In context, the assertion, "I die daily," which Paul affirms with an oath,[191] "just as surely as I glory over you in Christ Jesus,"[192] does not refer metaphorically to "dying to self" but rather to the harsh realities of apostolic ministry (cf. 4:6–13; =:36; 2 Cor 1:3–11; 4:8–12; 6:1–10; 11:23–33; Gal 6:17). The affirmation is reminiscent of the prior description of the apostles as "men given over to death" (4:9). Thiselton captures the idea in his translation of 15:31a, "From day to day I court fatality."[193] Paul is referring to bona fide threats from real adversaries (cf. 16:8–9). Garland explains that Paul has in mind the death that "encompasses the sleepless nights, the hunger and thirst, the ceaseless labor, and being ill-clad, buffeted, reviled, persecuted, afflicted, beaten, imprisoned, and homeless" (cf. esp. 2 Cor 11:22–28).[194]

Paul's fourth rhetorical question calls attention to an example of his own suffering in Ephesus. He does not supply the details, only that he "fought wild beasts in Ephesus." The reference is surely metaphorical[195] but indicative nonetheless of real threats. Robertson and Plummer suggest Paul means that

---

[187] So Hays (*First Corinthians*, 268), who suggests that Paul's statement is an expansion of the ideas already expressed in 15:14–15,19.

[188] So Robertson and Plummer, *First Corinthians*, 361; Thiselton, *First Corinthians*, 1249; Fitzmyer, *First Corinthians*, 581.

[189] Gk. κινδυνεύω. The verb appears two times in Luke's writings (Luke 8:23; Acts 19:27,40).

[190] Gk. κίνδυνος.

[191] The Greek particle νή occurs only here in the New Testament (cf. also LXX Gen 42:15–16). BDAG, "marker pointing to the basis on which something is strongly affirmed, *yes indeed, by*."

[192] "Glory" is literally "boasting" (καύχησις), used here in a positive sense (cf. 1:31). Paul does not have a self-serving agenda but glories in the fruit of his apostolic labors among the Corinthians.

[193] Thiselton, *First Corinthians*, 1250.

[194] Garland, *1 Corinthians*, 719.

[195] Some have taken 15:32 as a denial by Paul of a tale about literally fighting wild beasts in Ephesus (so Conzelmann). See Garland (*First Corinthians*, 720) for a critique of the literal view; Acts mentions no such episode in Paul's life, and it is absent from the list of hardships in 2 Cor 11:23–29. Furthermore, Paul would not have suffered such fate as a Roman citizen and most likely would not have survived apart from miraculous deliverance.

"he was near being torn to pieces by infuriated men."[196] The image of fighting wild beasts is most likely a euphemism for contending with powerful antagonists, perhaps political opponents to the gospel. In 16:9 Paul mentions "many who oppose me." Since he is writing the letter from Ephesus, the opposition is fresh on his mind. Other texts bear witness to the difficulties Paul faced in this city (cf. Acts 19:23–41; Rom 16:3–4). Malherbe calls attention to the use of the metaphor of wild beasts in Greek moralistic literature as a euphemism for self-discipline in the struggle against human passions.[197] Williams also concurs with the metaphorical interpretation but proposes a Jewish apocalyptic conceptual background where the term "beasts" denotes evil spirits. According to Williams, "Paul viewed the confrontations and physical threats that he experienced in Ephesus as instigated by the evil spirits, or 'beasts,' at work in the demon-possessed, sorcerers, and idolaters of the city."[198] Williams' argument is twofold: (1) the common use of the "beast" image in the prophetic and apocalyptic literature of Judaism as a symbol of an evil spirit, and (2) the record of the book of Acts, which "remembers Paul's time in Ephesus as characterized by exorcisms, magical rivalries, and violent controversies regarding idolatry."[199] Ciampa and Rosner note the symbolic use of beasts or wild animals of pagan rulers in Dan 7.[200]

Whatever conceptual background informs the image, Paul uses the metaphor to denote extreme danger that brings the possibility of death, which is pointless if there is no resurrection of the dead. The phrase translated "for merely human reasons" stands first in the clause for emphasis. The Greek reads "according to man" and occurs in two other places in the letter.[201] Fee thinks the meaning of 3:3, "mere men," holds for 15:32, and that Paul is saying "if there is no hope in the resurrection, then his life or death struggle against the opponents of his gospel is carried on at the merely human level—he is nothing more than a 'mere man' among other 'mere humans.'"[202] Thiselton translates, "only with human horizons," that is, "with horizons that reach neither beyond the grave nor beyond human capacities to the power of God."[203] BDAG supports the meaning "like an ordinary man." The point is this—What is the profit, Paul asks, if I fought wild beasts in Ephesus only from an ordinary human perspective without any hope of resurrection?

[196] Robertson and Plummer, *First Corinthians*, 362. Paul uses the image of "biting and devouring one another" as a warning to believers in Gal 5:15.

[197] A. J. Malherbe, "The Beasts at Ephesus," *JBL* 87 (1968): 71–80. See also Collins, *First Corinthians*, 557.

[198] G. Williams, "An Apocalyptic and Magical Interpretation of Paul's 'Beast Fight' in Ephesus (1 Corinthians 15:32)," *JTS* 57 (2006): 45.

[199] Ibid.

[200] Ciampa and Rosner, *First Corinthians*, 789.

[201] Gk. κατὰ ἄνθρωπον (cf. also 3:3; 9:8; Rom 3:5; Gal 1:11; 3:15).

[202] Fee, *First Corinthians*, 771.

[203] Thiselton, *First Corinthians*, 1251.

The final occurrence of the conditional clause, "If the dead are not raised," appears in 15:32a, followed by the proverbial, "Let us eat and drink for tomorrow we die." Since the exact words appear in Isa 22:13 (LXX), Paul may be quoting the prophet, but Thiselton notes that the saying could equally originate from "an Epicurean slogan, or from an anti-Epicurean slogan which offers an ironic overstatement of Epicurean philosophy?"[204] Either way, the saying depicts the logical outcome and perspective of those who rule out any life beyond the grave. Hays thinks that Paul chooses the proverb for its use of "eating" and "drinking" language, which has been prominent in chaps. 8–10, that it is "a devastatingly apt characterization of these resurrection-denying Corinthians, whose own misbehavior has much to do with eating and drinking (1 Cor 10:21–22; 11:20–22)."[205] It is unlikely, however, that Paul intends such a subtle connection. Perhaps a better literary connection would be the stark contrast between those who seek satisfaction in this life alone with no hope of a life to come and the apostles, who presently "hunger" and "thirst" (4:11) but who do so as those identified with the crucified one who died and rose again (15:23).

**15:33–34** Paul concludes this unit with three imperatives followed by an explanation. The commands are (1) do not be misled, (2) come back to your senses as you ought, and (3) stop sinning. The reason given is, "For there are some who are ignorant of God." This, according to Paul, is a shameful matter.

The first command, "Do not be misled," is literally "Do not be deceived,"[206] or perhaps "Stop deceiving yourselves."[207] The warning against deception is followed by the proverbial saying "Bad company corrupts good character," which scholars recognize as a quote from the no longer extant comedy *Thais* by the Greek dramatist Menander (c. 292 BC). Menander may have adapted an already existing proverb that made its way into popular use. By the time of Paul the maxim was probably widespread.[208] Although the proverb itself can have a wide range of applications, Paul's use of it has the more specific focus of avoiding the corrupting influence of those who are denying the resurrection

[204] Ibid., 1252.

[205] Hays, *First Corinthians*, 268. Witherington (*Conflict and Community*, 306) connects the two proverbial sayings in 15:32b–33, "Let us eat and drink for tomorrow we die" and "Bad company corrupts good character." "Paul is alluding to where the 'some' who were denying the resurrection may have gotten their alternate eschatology: by dining in temples with those who espoused the imperial viewpoint. If so, then ch. 15 must be read in light of the whole discussion in chs. 8–10, which in turn suggests that the 'some' here are the same 'some' who are criticized there, namely certain reasonably well-to-do Gentiles (likely males) who were arguing for the right to dine in temples."

[206] The same construction appears in 6:9, which the NIV translates "Do not be deceived."

[207] If a middle voice and if we emphasize the present tense, μή plus the present imperative can denote the cessation of an action in progress (so the NIV on 15:34, "Stop sinning").

[208] Thiselton (*First Corinthians*, 1254) observes that "Jerome seems first to have attributed the quotation to Menander's comedy, but there is clear evidence that it had also become a popular maxim. Paul may well have heard it cited more than once as a maxim, and we may infer neither knowledge nor ignorance of Greek literature on Paul's part from this quotation."

from the dead.[209] Already he has clarified in 5:10 that believers are not to disassociate from the immoral people of this world but rather to disengage from those so-called believers involved in immoral practices (5:11). Though Paul does not explicitly call for disassociation here as he does in chap. 5, the language seems to imply it.[210] Like leaven that can infiltrate and corrupt the whole batch of dough (5:6), so also bad company can destroy good character.[211] The same verb refers to those who "destroy" the temple of God and who "will be destroyed" by God (3:17).[212] In 2 Cor 11:3 the verb refers to those who are "led astray" from sincere and pure devotion to Christ.[213] In 15:33 Paul is explicitly warning the Corinthians to avoid the corrupting influence of those who deny God by denying the resurrection and who will lead them astray from the purity of the gospel. Paul has already shown the disastrous theological implications of such belief (15:12–19), and it is possible that there is "a direct connection between much of the behavior being corrected by this letter and this denial of theirs."[214]

The command to "come back to your senses" is joined to the command to "stop sinning" by the coordinating conjunction "and."[215] The first command is an aorist imperative, stressing urgency.[216] The second is a present imperative and carries the idea of the cessation of action that is already occurring.[217] Although the command to stop sinning could apply to any number of things mentioned in the letter, the context suggests a more specific connection with the denial of resurrection and ethical decision-making that is guided by the attitude expressed in the proverb "Let us eat and drink for tomorrow we die" (15:32b).

An explanation follows from the three imperatives, "For there are some who are ignorant of God." In other words, as Collins explains, "Paul shares the Jewish view that idolatry and the failure to acknowledge the one God lead to immoral behavior (cf. 6:9–10; Rom 1:20–31; 1 Thess 4:5)."[218] The word

---

[209] So also Barrett, *First Corinthians*, 367.

[210] So Collins (*First Corinthians*, 571), "For Paul the well-being of the community (1:2) demands its radical separation from evil (cf. 5:5,6,9,13)."

[211] The word ὁμιλία (company) can also mean "conversation." If the word carries this sense here, then the meaning would be "Evil conversations such as those that deny the resurrection of the dead can only have a corrupting effect on your good character" (so Fee, *First Corinthians*, 773).

[212] Gk. φθείρω.

[213] Cf. also Eph 4:22. The cognate noun (φθορά) appears in 15:42,50 of the perishable body that must be transformed at resurrection. See also Rom 8:21; Gal 6:8.

[214] Fee, *First Corinthians*, 773.

[215] Gk. καί.

[216] This is the only use of the verb ἐκνήφω in the New Testament. Thiselton (*First Corinthians*, 1255) comments that its regular use in the LXX retains the sense of becoming sober after a state of drunkenness: "The metaphor requires an English rendering which somehow combines (a) waking to a clear mind after drunken stupor; (b) waking up to reality, i.e., coming to one's senses, in place of a fantasy, escapist world; (c) regaining a necessary, proper sobriety." For the metaphor of drunkenness in Paul, see Rom 13:11–13; 1 Thess 5:5–8.

[217] So the NIV translation, "Stop sinning."

[218] Collins, *First Corinthians*, 561.

"some" harks back to the "some" who deny the resurrection (15:12). They are one and the same group.[219] To deny the resurrection is to demonstrate a fundamental ignorance of God since resurrection is the climax of God's redemption of the world and the key event that culminates in his being "all in all" (15:28).[220] This is truly a matter of shame for the Corinthian community but especially for the arrogant "knowers" in the church who failed to grasp the most fundamental truth about God's person and power.[221] The same phrase occurs in 6:5, where Paul writes to shame those involved in lawsuits in light of the future role of believers in the eschatological judgment of the world. Such language would have constituted a sharp and powerful rebuke in an honor/shame culture.[222] Thiselton explains, "We have only to recall the importance of honor and self-praise, instantiated in rhetoric, benefactions, and monuments, to recall how sensitive the readers (esp. "the strong") would be to praise in their honor or to accusations which would bring shame."[223]

### 5. The Nature of the Resurrection Body (15:35–49)

**35But someone may ask, "How are the dead raised? With what kind of body
will they come?" 36How foolish! What you sow does not come to life unless it dies.
37When you sow, you do not plant the body that will be, but just a seed, perhaps of
wheat or of something else. 38But God gives it a body as he has determined, and to
each kind of seed he gives its own body. 39All flesh is not the same: Men have one
kind of flesh, animals have another, birds another and fish another. 40There are
also heavenly bodies and there are earthly bodies; but the splendor of the heavenly
bodies is one kind, and the splendor of the earthly bodies is another. 41The sun
has one kind of splendor, the moon another and the stars another; and star differs
from star in splendor.**

**42So will it be with the resurrection of the dead. The body that is sown is perishable, it is raised imperishable; 43it is sown in dishonor, it is raised in glory; it is
sown in weakness, it is raised in power; 44it is sown a natural body, it is raised a
spiritual body.**

**If there is a natural body, there is also a spiritual body. 45So it is written:
"The first man Adam became a living being"; the last Adam, a life-giving spirit.
46The spiritual did not come first, but the natural, and after that the spiritual.
47The first man was of the dust of the earth, the second man from heaven. 48As was**

[219] So also ibid.; Thiselton, *First Corinthians*, 1256. Collins comments, "The some who do not know God are those who deny the resurrection. The God who is known and experienced by his people is one who has raised Christ from the dead and promises resurrection to those who believe the kerygma. Those who deny the resurrection can be equated with people who have not experienced God (1 Thess 4:5), the living God who has raised Jesus from the dead."

[220] So Fee, *First Corinthians*, 774. Thiselton (*First Corinthians*, 1256) is correct in his assertion, "Knowledge of God is the linchpin of Paul's whole argument." Cf. esp. chap. 8.

[221] Cf. Jesus' confrontation of the Sadducees (Mark 12:24), who also denied the resurrection, "Are you not in error because you do not know the Scriptures or the power of God?"

[222] Cf. also 11:17–22.

[223] Thiselton, *First Corinthians*, 1257.

**the earthly man, so are those who are of the earth; and as is the man from heaven, so also are those who are of heaven. 49 And just as we have borne the likeness of the earthly man, so shall we bear the likeness of the man from heaven.**

In 15:35 the argument shifts from the fact of the resurrection to the nature of the resurrection body. Although bodily resurrection has been the issue all along, the term "body" appears for the first time in this chapter and becomes the dominant focus of 15:35–49.[224] The unit opens with two questions in the style of the Greek diatribe, a method of argumentation that employs a hypothetical opponent in order to address a real scenario: But someone may ask, "How are the dead raised? With what kind of body will they come?" Paul answers the questions by way of the Genesis creation narrative on the analogy of the seed (15:36–38) and the different kinds of earthly and heavenly bodies (15:39–44a), which prepares the way for another use of the Adam/Christ typology (cf. 15:22) that sets up the contrast between the natural body and the spiritual body (15:44b–49). The future resurrection body of believers is likened to the resurrection body of Jesus, the second man from heaven (15:49). The analogies draw from ordinary experience and do not attempt to prove bodily resurrection but rather offer a way to understand how bodily resurrection is possible.[225] Regarding the allusion to the Genesis account in this unit, Ciampa and Rosner observe that in the study of the beginning of creation we find keys to eschatology. "It is understood that in many ways the last things will be like the first things, only better."[226]

**15:35** The two questions of 15:35 could be interpreted as a sincere inquiry concerning bodily resurrection, that is, how it occurs and the nature of the resurrection body. The context, however, suggests a more hostile objector, one who Paul deems as ignorant of God and a matter of shame for the community (15:34) and to whom he replies immediately, "How foolish!"[227] Either Paul anticipates the objection of those who deny the resurrection or, more likely, he places the questions in the mouth of an imaginary objector based on what he already knows to be the case.[228] The argument carries more weight if this was the objection being raised in Corinth.[229] The epithet "fool" constitutes a particularly sharp rebuke in a letter where Paul has devoted such a large amount of space confronting those who deem themselves to be wise, knowledgeable, and spiritual.

---

[224] Gk. σῶμα, occurring nine times in 15:35–49.

[225] So Fitzmyer, *First Corinthians*, 586.

[226] Ciampa and Rosner, *First Corinthians*, 798–99.

[227] Lit., "You fool!" So NASB. Cf. also Jas 2:18–20.

[228] So also Fee, *First Corinthians*, 779. Either way, the "someone" is among those who deny the resurrection (15:12); so also Robertson and Plummer, *First Corinthians*, 368.

[229] Some think that Paul's method of argumentation softens his approach (Garland, *First Corinthians*, 277) or provides "a preemptive response to an objection that might already have been raised in Corinth" (Ciampa and Rosner, *First Corinthians*, 799).

Interpreters differ on whether the imaginary objector asks two different questions[230] or asks two questions that address essentially the same issue, that is, the first question, "How are the dead raised?", implies the second, "With what kind of body do they come?"[231] Even if the questions do not ask precisely the same thing, there is a very close correlation between the two. The second question clearly builds on the first and provides the focus of this section with its emphasis on the term "body." If bodies die and dissolve into the earth, then how is it possible and in what way can the same bodies reanimate and come back from the dead?[232] Fee suggests this is the chief problem for those who deny bodily resurrection, that "because they could not handle the *how,* they had given up the *that*—the resurrection itself. Having spoken at length with all of his rhetorical and theological skills to the latter question, he now turns to the former."[233] To some extent Paul has already addressed the question of how resurrection is possible by affirming the resurrection of Jesus, which some Corinthians denied by implication. Jesus was raised from the dead and others will follow (15:23). The possibility lies within God's power, who subjects all things to himself, including death (15:25–28). Resurrection does not entail the reanimation of dead corpses but rather the transformation of perishable bodies.

**15:36–38** Paul's response is sharp and abrupt, "How foolish!" "Fool" in the biblical sense denotes the person who denies God (cf. Pss 14:1; 52:1; 92:6).[234] Those who were denying the resurrection of the dead in Corinth supposed that they had raised a clever and insightful objection by asking about the possibility and nature of bodily resurrection. Paul will demonstrate that such a denial reveals a profound lack of insight into the diverse nature of God's creation and thus the lack of knowledge of God himself (15:34). The fool has only to consider the miracle of the harvest in order to recognize the creative power of God.[235] When planted the seed "dies" in the sense that it is transformed by the processes of nature under God's control into something quite unlike its original state. There is continuity yet complete transformation. Paul's descrip-

[230] So J. Jeremias, "Flesh and Blood Cannot Inherit the Kingdom of God," *NTS* 2 (1955): 151–59; Fitzmyer, *First Corinthians*, 586. The first question is taken up in 15:36–49 and the second in 15:50–57.

[231] So Fee, *First Corinthians*, 776; Garland, *1 Corinthians*, 727; Thiselton, *First Corinthians*, 1262.

[232] Paul addresses both the possibility of resurrection and its modality (so Collins, *First Corinthians*, 565).

[233] Fee, *First Corinthians*, 779. So also Hays (*First Corinthians*, 269), who suggests that the doubts expressed in the two questions are not doubts based on the possibility of supernatural events but "based on an aversion to the idea that the body could be reanimated after death. Such a turn of events would seem positively undesirable to ancient Hellenistic thinkers devoted to an ideal of spirituality that sought to transcend corporeality."

[234] The term "fool" (ἄφρων) occurs seventy-four times in Proverbs (LXX) alone. In the New Testament see also Luke 11:40; 12:20; Rom 2:20; 2 Cor 11:16,19; 12:6,11; Eph 5:17; 1 Pet 2:15.

[235] Paul has already used the analogy of the harvest in 3:6–8. Cf. also the similar saying of Jesus in John 12:24.

tion of the seed as "the body that will be" anticipates the full development of the analogy in 15:42–44. That the seed dies and is made alive recalls the Adam/Christ typology in 15:22, "For just as in Adam all die, even so in Christ all will be made alive."[236] To deny resurrection is to deny the fact that God does what he wills (15:38).

The purpose of the seed analogy is not to emphasize the necessity of death but rather to illustrate the principle of transformation (cf. 15:51).[237] The new living organism is not the old one reconstructed, although there is a necessary and close connection to the former. How they are connected remains a mystery.[238] Paul's purpose is not to explain the scientific details but to demonstrate continuity and transformation from creation itself.[239] No one unfamiliar with agriculture could ever imagine the utter difference between the seed planted in the ground and the glorious plant that emerges, each distinct to its own seed. For the believer, the fullness of life lies not on this side of the grave but in the glorious age to come. Resurrection entails new creation.[240] The key point is that God gives to each seed its own body as he has determined (15:38). The implication is that God will also give to each believer a resurrection body as he has determined. The language of God's determination echoes Paul's explanation of God's sovereign placement of the members of the body in 12:18. Thiselton rightly calls attention to the themes of God's sovereignty and grace conveyed by 15:38. It is God who determines the kind of body we will have, and it is God who gives.[241]

**15:39–41** Before applying the analogy of the seed that is sown and the body (plant) that is raised (15:36–37) directly to the "raising" of the believer's body in 15:42–44,[242] Paul introduces an additional analogy in 15:39–41, structured around the creation account of Gen 1:20–27. He presents earthly flesh in a descending order of complexity (men, animals, birds, and fish) and the heavenly bodies in a descending order of brilliance (sun, moon, and the stars). This builds on the analogy of the seed by showing that God gives to each kind of flesh or body its own unique glory. Furthermore, the polarity between what is earthly and what is heavenly sets the stage for the principle of transformation (15:40–42,50–57), which explains how the earthly body can enter into a

---

[236] On the use of the verb ζῳοποιέω (to make alive) in the New Testament, see John 5:21; 6:63; Rom 4:17; 8:11; 1 Cor 15:22,36,45; 2 Cor 3:6; Gal 3:21; 1 Pet 3:18. To bring something to life is an act of God.

[237] So Barrett, *First Corinthians*, 370; Thiselton, *First Corinthians*, 1264.

[238] Robertson and Plummer, *First Corinthians*, 369.

[239] Cf. Gen 1:11–13 and the creation of seeds and plant life on the third day.

[240] So Collins (*First Corinthians*, 564), "In 1 Corinthians Paul does not actually use the terminology of 'new creation' (cf. 2 Cor 5:17; Gal 6:15) when he writes about the resurrection of the body. There is, nonetheless, an analogy between the resurrection of the body and creation in that God, who gives bodies as he wills (v. 38), creates both the living body and the resurrected body."

[241] Thiselton, *First Corinthians*, 1265.

[242] Note the transition in 15:42a, "Thus also is the resurrection of the dead."

heavenly existence. Fee discerns a chiastic literary arrangement for 15:39–41 as follows.[243]

A Not all "flesh" is the same; [earthly bodies]

B People have one kind;
animals another;
birds another;
fish another;

C There are heavenly bodies [B']
There are earthly bodies [B]
C' The splendor of the heavenly bodies is of one kind;
The splendor of the earthly bodies is of another.

B' The sun has one kind of splendor;
The moon another kind of splendor;
The stars another kind of splendor;

A' And star differs from star in splendor [heavenly bodies]

This literary pattern emphasizes the different kinds of flesh and bodies in the original creation and introduces the key term "glory" (NIV, "splendor") at the peak of the chiasm in 15:40.[244] It also prepares the way for the sharp distinction between what is sown in the old creation and what will be raised in the new creation (15:42–44), namely, our earthly bodies patterned after Adam, the first man from the earth, and the body which is to come, that is, the body patterned after Christ, the second man from heaven (15:45–49). Earthly flesh is not the same and heavenly bodies are not the same, but each has its own distinct glory according to God's creative purpose.[245] Since heavenly and earthly bodies possess their own unique splendor (15:40), we can expect the same principle of diversity with respect to the resurrection body; that is, it will have its own glory according to God's purpose and will be well suited for its future existence in the new creation quite unlike our present bodies.[246] The different kinds of flesh and different kinds of celestial bodies of different brilliance underscores the point that God's creative purpose apportions different bodies suitable to their own habitat.

---

[243] Fee, *First Corinthians*, 783. Followed by Collins, *First Corinthians*, 565; Garland, *1 Corinthians*, 730.

[244] The term "glory" (Gk. δόξα) is a key term in the letter, occurring first in 2:7, which speaks of God's hidden wisdom destined for "our glory." In 2:9, Jesus is called the "Lord of glory." The command to "glorify God in your body" (NIV, "honor God with your body") occurs in a context that mentions resurrection (6:14). Cf. also the command to "do all to the glory of God" (10:31) and the "glory" language of 11:7–15.

[245] σάρξ (flesh) is used here in a neutral sense in order to emphasize the diversity of the material creation. "Body" calls attention to the diversities of form and character (so Thiselton, *First Corinthians*, 1267).

[246] Ciampa and Rosner (*First Corinthians*, 810) suggest that "the tie between resurrection bodies and the lights in the heavens was probably also encouraged or inspired by the most explicit passage on bodily resurrection in the Old Testament, Daniel 12:2–3."

**15:42–44a** The foregoing analogies of the seed, the different kinds of flesh, and the different celestial bodies build to the critical point of application in 15:42a: "So will it be with the resurrection from the dead."[247] The elaboration that follows returns to the comparison of what is sown to what is raised (15:36–37) by way of four antithetical statements that contrast the present earthly body and the future resurrection body.

| The earthly body is sown | It is raised |
|---|---|
| in corruption (NIV, "perishable") | in incorruption (NIV, "imperishable") |
| in dishonor | in glory |
| in weakness | in power |
| a natural body | a spiritual body |

The last pair, the natural body/spiritual body,[248] is a summary description of the contrasting bodies; that is, the natural body is the human body of this creation, which is corruptible, dishonorable, and weak; and the spiritual body is the resurrected body of new creation, which is incorruptible, glorious, and powerful. While Paul's language gives us a glimpse of the nature of the resurrection body, it still lies beyond our comprehension. What is clear, however, is that the essence of resurrection is the transformation of our earthly bodies (cf. Phil 3:20–21; Col 3:4; 1 John 3:2).

The language of "sowing" picks up on the metaphor of the seed that dies and comes to life (15:36–37) and may refer simply to the burial of the dead corpse in the ground.[249] Others argue, however, that Paul most likely is referring to the character of mortal life before death. In other words, the earthly body is distinguished by perishability, dishonor, and weakness, "qualities that are typically on greatest display as one passes from life to death."[250] Asher articulates a third view, namely, that Paul is referring neither to burial nor to all pre-resurrection human existence but employs the sowing metaphor to contrast human origins with the resurrection.[251] Both are creative acts of God

[247] The NIV supplies a future tense verb whereas in Greek the construction is verbless, "Thus also the resurrection of the dead."

[248] Gk. *σῶμα ψυχικός/σῶμα πνευματικός*.

[249] So Grosheide, *First Corinthians*, 383–84; W. F. Orr and James A. Walther, *1 Corinthians*, AB (Garden City: Doubleday, 1976), 343–47; S. J. Kistemaker, *1 Corinthians*, New Testament Commentary (Grand Rapids: Baker, 1993), 573.

[250] Ciampa and Rosner, *First Corinthians*, 811. So also Bruce, *1 & 2 Corinthians*, 152; Conzelmann, *1 Corinthians*, 283; Fee, *First Corinthians*, 784. Robertson and Plummer (*First Corinthians*, 380–81) think that Paul refers to the buried corpse but hint at the second view in their comment that the body "is in corruption before it reaches the grave" (372). Cf. also Barrett (*First Corinthians*, 372): "Paul does not mean only that the body placed in the grave is in a process of physical decomposition, though this is part of the truth and the clearest expression of it. Corruption is an evil power, by which the world is dominated in the old age (Rom 3:21). It affects not only human life, but the whole of creation."

[251] J. R. Asher, "ΣΠΕΙΡΕΤΑΙ: Paul's Anthropogenic Metaphor in 1 Corinthians 15:42–44," *JBL* 120 (2001): 102. Specifically, in 15:42–44 the verb "sowing" is "an anthropogenic metaphor describing the creation of the first human being, Adam." Asher provides instances of the use of

and receive further explication in the Adam/Christ typology of 15:44b–49. Although the metaphor of sowing could be used in this sense, we cannot know for sure whether Paul applies it in this way in 15:36–44.[252] On all accounts Paul's intent is to contrast present, earthly embodied existence with future, heavenly embodied existence.[253]

The meaning of "natural" body and "spiritual" body is worked out in further detail in the Adam/Christ typology of 15:44b–49. The two adjectives "natural" and "spiritual" have already been paired in contrast in 2:14–15 in delineating the natural man, who is governed only by fallen human impulses and who cannot accept or know the things of the Spirit, and the spiritual man, who is able to rightly appraise all things.[254] In principle, all believers are "spiritual" by virtue of their reception of the Holy Spirit (cf. 12:1–3,13), but what becomes clear in the present argument (15:44–49) is that believers have not yet received a "spiritual" body. It is possible that Paul uses the term "spiritual," in part, to remind those who deemed themselves to be "spiritual" (14:37), and who may have been among those denying the resurrection, that eschatology properly understood strips them of "their anti-somatic understanding of Christian existence."[255]

The terms "natural" and "spiritual" in this context do not mean "material" and "immaterial" but rather describe the present earthly body and the future

---

"sowing" to refer to human origins and generation in the Greco-Roman world (112–21). Garland (*First Corinthians*, 733–34) adopts Asher's argument. So also Heil (*Rhetorical Role of Scripture*, 239), "In these antitheses the verb 'it is sown' is synonymous with 'it is created,' but Paul prefers the metaphorical 'it is sown' because of the connotation that what is sown must die (15:36) before God gives it a body (15:38)."

[252] So Fitzmyer, *First Corinthians*, 595.

[253] Paul will elaborate further on the perishable/imperishable contrast in 15:50–54. Cf. Ps 8:5 for the possible influence of "glory" and "honor" language. On the liberation of creation from "corruption," see Rom 8:21. On the relation of glory, honor, and immortality to eternal life, see Rom 2:7 (cf. also 2 Tim 1:10). Regarding corruption and Jesus' resurrection see Acts 2:27–31; 13:35–37. Ciampa and Rosner (*First Corinthians*, 812) comment, "Although it was a corruptible body that was placed in Christ's tomb, it was not given the opportunity to experience corruption, but, as our bodies will also do (cf. vv. 53–54), it was clothed in incorruptibility. The undoing of the fall of humanity and of creation would be fully achieved only if corruption and decay were also completely overcome."

[254] Cf. also 3:1–4 where "spiritual" is set in contrast to other terms (made of flesh, fleshly [worldly], infant). Thiselton (*First Corinthians*, 1275) notes, "The contrast between ψυχικὸς ἄνθρωπος and ὁ δὲ πνευματικὸς in 2:14 and 15 (and πνεῦμα in 2:10–16) decisively prepares the ground for Paul's use of the two terms in 15:44." All occurrences of the term "spiritual" in 1 Corinthians include 2:13,15; 3:1; 9:11; 10:3–4; 12:1; 14:1,37; 15:44,46.

[255] Fee, *First Corinthians*, 785. Already in 2:6–3:4 and chaps. 12–14 Paul has reshaped the Corinthians' perspective on what it means to be "spiritual." Fee supposes that to describe the body as spiritual "must have been troublesome indeed." Cf. also Witherington (*Conflict and Community*, 309), "It would have been a jolt to the Corinthians for Paul to make clear that ultimately being *pneumatikos* had something to do with bodily existence, not merely with spiritual life as the believer now experiences it. In Paul's view, the truly 'spiritual' person is ultimately one who has the resurrection body."

transformed, resurrection body shaped in the image of Christ.[256] Paul derives the term "natural" from Gen 2:7, "The first man Adam became a living being."[257] Paul is not speaking of the composition of the body but rather the orientation or the animating power of the body.[258] In this present age the body is subject to the laws of physical life. In the age to come the body will be oriented and empowered by the Spirit in ways not possible in this present life.[259] To recall the analogy of 15:36–37, "The spiritual body will be to the animated body what the plant is to the seed, and there would be a certain continuity."[260] Garland describes the contrast between the natural and spiritual body as that which is "kindled by the soul" versus that which is "kindled by the Spirit." The natural body characterizes earthly life, while the spiritual body characterizes heavenly life. "The spiritual body is a body 'that eye has not seen and ear has not heard and has not entered the human mind' (1 Cor 2:9), that is transformed into the likeness of Christ (Phil. 3:21), and that is fitted for the new age."[261] Ciampa and Rosner explain, "To live in a resurrected body is to experience a new mode of existence, life directed and empowered by the Spirit, suitable to the age to come, in a body untainted by sin and death in any sense."[262] Thiselton points out that the traditions concerning the resurrection of Jesus in the Gospels confirm that "the spiritual body is more but not less than an earthly physical body."[263] In short, the resurrection body is that which is "adapted to eschatological existence under the ultimate domination of the Spirit."[264]

**15:44b–49** In 15:44b Paul repeats the antithetical contrast between natural/spiritual body in the form of a conditional clause in recognition of the proper eschatological order of things (cf. 15:23): "If there is a natural body, there is also a spiritual body."[265] This provides the thesis statement of the argument developed in 15:45–49 that explains the idea of the natural and spiritual body

---

[256] E.g., in 2:14–15, the "natural" and "spiritual" contrast does not mean "material" and "immaterial" but rather designates the guiding principle or power of one's life.

[257] "Being" translates the Greek ψυχή, which is cognate to the adjective ψυχικός.

[258] So Thiselton, *First Corinthians*, 1276–77.

[259] Robertson and Plummer, *First Corinthians*, 382. Believers are indwelt by and oriented to the Spirit in this present age (6:19) but in limited ways (cf. Rom 8:23; 2 Cor 1:22; 5:5; Eph 1:13–14; 4:30).

[260] Fitzmyer, *First Corinthians*, 596.

[261] Garland, *1 Corinthians*, 734.

[262] Ciampa and Rosner, *First Corinthians*, 817.

[263] Thiselton, *First Corinthians*, 1278. Thiselton points out that in the "resurrection traditions Jesus Christ was not always immediately 'recognized' (John 20:14,15; 21:12; Luke 24:13–20) but his personal identity was recognized in terms of sociophysical gestures and characteristics (Luke 24:31; John 20:16,20,27–28; action, voice, hands, side). In the tradition of Luke-Acts Jesus 'ascended' above the clouds (Acts 1:9,10), but in the Johannine tradition Jesus appears to have shared in the meal of fish (John 21:12,13)."

[264] Fee, *First Corinthians*, 785–86.

[265] The language of "first" and "last" gives cohesion to the unit (15:45,46,47). Paul's method of argumentation in 15:42–44 continues in 15:45–49 by developing the Adam/Christ contrast in a series of antithetical statements.

introduced in 15:44a.[266] Paul's argument in this paragraph is based on Gen 2 in another use of the Adam/Christ typology that harks back to 15:21–22 and the designation of Adam as the representative head of old creation, through whom came death, and Christ as the representative man of new creation, through whom comes the resurrection of the dead. Paul's primary concern is to answer the question of 15:35, "With what kind of body do they come?"

In order to further explain the polarity between the natural body and the spiritual body, Paul quotes Gen 2:7b, "The first man Adam became a living being," and then adds, "the last Adam, a life-giving spirit."[267] The connection of Paul's argument to the Genesis text is more apparent in Greek than in English since the phrase translated "living being" corresponds to the description of the present earthly body as "natural."[268] The phrase "life-giving spirit," on the other hand, describes the risen Christ, the last Adam, in his transformed state and corresponds to the description of the resurrection body as "spiritual." As with the term "spiritual," "spirit" does not mean "immaterial" but rather designates that which is the opposite of and belongs to a different order than the "natural." The modifier "life-giving" is a participle form of the verb meaning "to bring to life" that appears in 15:22 and 36.[269] In other words, just as the natural body came to all humans through Adam so also Christ became in resurrection a life-giving spirit (*pneuma*), that is, the source of life to all who are "in him."[270] The first Adam received life. The last Adam imparts life. Just as humans have a natural body after the pattern of Adam so also Christ is representative of all who will be raised and given a spiritual body. The framework of Paul's argument is representative, soteriological, and eschatological.[271]

In 15:46 Paul reasserts the principle of chronological order regarding the natural and the spiritual body (cf. 15:22–23) in order to reinforce yet again the polarity between our present state and the transformation that will occur at

---

[266] So Collins, *First Corinthians*, 568.

[267] Which Barrett (*First Corinthians*, 373) suggests is required in order to maintain the antithetical contrasts necessary for his argument. To the Genesis text Paul omits the initial "and" and adds "first" and the name "Adam." Otherwise, Paul quotes directly from the LXX. Ciampa and Rosner (*First Corinthians*, 820) suggest that the idea of "life-giving spirit" derives also from Gen 2:7 read in the light of Ezek 37, "In Genesis 2:7 it is when God breathed into the man that he came to life. In Ezekiel 37: 6,9,10,14 God repeatedly says, echoing Genesis 2, that it is by putting his breath or Spirit in his people that they would be brought to life. Ezekiel 37 describes 'a life-giving spirit' in the context of the resurrection of the dead, or the restoration of Israel described as a resurrection of the dead." Heil (*Rhetorical Role of Scripture*, 233) comments that 1 Cor 15:45b "resonates with LXX Gen 2:7a" (so also Fee, *1 Corinthians*, 788–89).

[268] Gk. ψυχή (being), ψυχικός (natural).

[269] Gk. ζῳοποιέω.

[270] On the close association between the Spirit and resurrection, see Rom 8:9–13 and 1 Pet 3:18 (cf. also John 5:21; 6:63; Rom 1:4).

[271] Commentators often note that Paul's concerns in 15:45–49 are primarily soteriological and eschatological rather than Christological (so Fee, *First Corinthians*, 787; Witherington, *Conflict and Community*, 309; Collins, *First Corinthians*, 568–69; Thiselton, *First Corinthians*, 1282).

resurrection. Just as old creation logically precedes new creation, so also the natural body precedes the spiritual body.[272] The comparison between Adam and Christ continues in 15:47–49 with a slight shift in terminology, from "first Adam/last Adam" to the "first man/second man" and the "man from earth/man from heaven." Genesis 2:7 is still the background text, "the LORD God formed the man from the dust of the ground," along with Gen 5:3, which refers to Adam bearing a son in his own image. The prepositional phrases "of the dust of the earth" and "from heaven"[273] could indicate either the origin or character of each representative man. Although the two are related, in context, the emphasis falls more on the latter; that is, the prepositional phrases "from earth" and "from heaven" are somewhat synonymous with "natural" and "spiritual" and carry a qualitative sense "having to do with *human* life that is characterized by being either 'of earth' or 'of heaven.'"[274] Since in the Greek of 15:47 there are no verbs, some think the meaning is that Adam came from the dust of the earth and Christ will come (future tense) from heaven. In other words, the reference to "the second man from heaven" is a reference to Christ's return.[275] If this is the case, then the emphasis falls on both origin and character.[276] Either way, humanity is marked by its relation to Adam or Christ. Those in Adam are "of the earth," and those who are in Christ are "of heaven" (15:48). Each bears the image (NIV, "likeness") of their respective representative head (15:49). While God created man in his own image (Gen 1:26–27), the background text to 15:49 is most likely Gen 5:3, which refers to Adam's descendants "in his own image." Humans continue to bear the image of God (Gen 9:6), even if altered by Adam's fall. The image of God "does not need to be regained, but to be perfectly restored/renewed."[277]

---

[272] Fee (*First Corinthians*, 791) speculates that Paul reasserts the chronology of "natural" and "spiritual" as a polemic against the Corinthians, "who assumed that they had already entered into the totality of pneumatic existence while they were still in their *psychikos* body." Others reject this perspective (so Garland, *First Corinthians*, 735, "Paul's argument in this passage has nothing to do with the Corinthians' self-centered spirituality but with their bewilderment over how a terrestrial body can be raised as a celestial body").

[273] Gk. ἐκ γῆς (of/from the earth) and ἐξ οὐρανοῦ (of/from heaven).

[274] Fee, *First Corinthians*, 792.

[275] On the phrase "from heaven," see also 2 Cor 5:2; 1 Thess 1:10. Cf. also Rom 10:6; 1 Thess 4:16–17; 2 Thess 1:7; Phil 3:20–21.

[276] So Robertson and Plummer, *First Corinthians*, 374; Barrett, *First Corinthians*, 375; Garland, *1 Corinthians*, 736. Cf. also Thiselton (*First Corinthians*, 1286), "The second man exhibits those qualities that come from heaven and shape the character and nature of the form in which those 'in' Christ will be raised."

[277] Ciampa and Rosner, *First Corinthians*, 824. Paul ties together image and glory in other texts (cf. 1 Cor 11:7; Rom 1:23; 2 Cor 3:18; 4:4). "The concepts of glory and image are probably linked throughout these texts such that we are to understand that the image of the earthly man lacks the glory with which it was previously created and is now an image of impermanence, weakness, ignobility, and of earthy humanness while the image of the heavenly man reflects God's glory in its incorruptible, powerful, honorable, and spiritual nature (cf. vv. 42–44). We spend these lives

Most English translations, including the NIV, go with the future indicative verb in 15:49b, "so shall we bear the likeness of the man from heaven," since this reading seems to fit the literary context of Paul's eschatological emphasis.[278] The better attested reading, however, is the subjunctive, as reflected in the NET, "let us also bear the image of the man of heaven." Paul concludes this portion of his argument with an exhortation "calling them to prepare now for the future that is to be."[279]

### 6. The Necessity of Transformation and Death's Final Defeat (15:50–58)

**50I declare to you, brothers, that flesh and blood cannot inherit the kingdom of God, nor does the perishable inherit the imperishable. 51Listen, I tell you a mys-
tery: We will not all sleep, but we will all be changed—52in a flash, in the twinkling
of an eye, at the last trumpet. For the trumpet will sound, the dead will be raised
imperishable, and we will be changed. 53For the perishable must clothe itself with
the imperishable, and the mortal with immortality. 54When the perishable has
been clothed with the imperishable, and the mortal with immortality, then the
saying that is written will come true: "Death has been swallowed up in victory."**

> **55"Where, O death, is your victory?**
> **Where, O death, is your sting?"**

**56The sting of death is sin, and the power of sin is the law. 57But thanks be to God!
He gives us the victory through our Lord Jesus Christ.**

**58Therefore, my dear brothers, stand firm. Let nothing move you. Always give yourselves fully to the work of the Lord, because you know that your labor in the Lord is not in vain.**

The final section of chap. 15 caps off Paul's lengthy discourse on the resurrection of the dead by summarizing some of the key emphases of the chapter and adding new information regarding those who are still living at the time of Christ's coming.[280] The language and imagery of 15:50–58 is characteristically apocalyptic in the mention of the kingdom of God, imperishability, immortality, and transformation. It resonates especially with 15:20–28 in the prior mention of the final events associated with Christ's coming, namely, the handing over of the kingdom and the subjection of all things to God the Father, including death,

in bodies that reflect Adam's state after the fall; we will spend the rest of eternity in bodies that reflect Christ's state after his resurrection from the dead" (cf. also 2 Cor 3:18; 4:4; Col 1:15; 3:10).

[278] So Robertson and Plummer, *First Corinthians*, 374–75; Barrett, *First Corinthians*, 377; Thiselton, *First Corinthians*, 1288–89.

[279] Fee, *First Corinthians*, 795. So also Collins (*First Corinthians*, 572), "The easiest reading of the text requires a future; by comparison the hortatory subjunctive is the *lectio difficilior.* The rhetorical analysis of ch. 15 shows, moreover, that Paul concludes each of his proofs (vv. 34,49) and his peroration (v. 58) with an exhortation. Hence, on the basis of the 'greatly preponderant external evidence' and the character of Paul's rhetoric, the subjunctive reading is to be preferred."

[280] The last specific mention of the dead being raised, which has been the theme of chap. 15, occurs in 15:52.

so that "God may be all in all." While in the previous section Paul explained that the transformation of believers' bodies will occur (15:42–49), he now insists that transformation must occur since the present human body is radically incompatible with God's imperishable kingdom (15:50–53).[281] In 15:54b–55, Paul triumphantly declares death's final overthrow by combining Isa 25:8 and Hos 13:14 into a single quote, linked by the catchwords "victory" and "death." Death still stings because of sin and the law, and death continues to reign over the believer in this age; but God promises the final victory through our Lord Jesus Christ (15:57; cf. 15:22–23).[282] For this reason, believers can confidently stand firm and abound in the work of the Lord (15:58). Verses 50–58 divide into three units: 15:50–53 stipulates the necessity of the transformation of the body for entrance into God's future kingdom; 15:54–57 reflects on death's defeat in the light of Scripture and the victory God gives in Christ; 15:58 concludes the discussion with an exhortation to prosper in the Lord's work.

**15:50** The solemn pronouncement "But this I say," along with the address "brothers," introduces the fundamental principle that the perishable body cannot inherit the imperishable kingdom. The phrase "flesh and blood" refers to the earthly human body, which is subject to sin and death.[283] Verse 50 exhibits a parallelism as follows:

| | |
|---|---|
| flesh and blood | will not inherit the kingdom of God |
| the perishable | will not inherit the imperishable |

Some argue that Paul has in mind two different groups; "flesh and blood" refers to those who are living at the time of Christ's coming and "the perishable" refers to those who have already died.[284] More likely, the parallelism is synonymous, meaning that "flesh and blood" refers to the perishable body.[285] Paul simply repeats the analogy of the seed in 15:42: "The body that is sown is perishable, it is raised imperishable."[286]

[281] Paul introduces the idea of the transformation of the living as a mystery (Gk. μυστήριον; cf. 2:1,7; 4:1; 13:2). Collins (*First Corinthians*, 575–76) notes how Paul's affirmation of the radical incompatibility of the present human body and the future resurrection body is a theme shared with Jewish apocalyptic literature.

[282] Our reading of 1 Cor 15:50–58 is greatly enhanced by 1 Thess 4:13–5:11 and 2 Cor 5:1–10.

[283] Cf. LXX Sir 14:18; 17:31; Matt 16:17; Gal 1:16; Eph 6:12; Heb 2:14.

[284] So Robertson and Plummer, *First Corinthians*, 376; Jeremias, "Flesh and Blood." This view holds that the parallelism is "synthetic" (complementary) rather than "synonymous."

[285] So Fee, *First Corinthians*, 798; Fitzmyer, *First Corinthians*, 603; Ciampa and Rosner, *First Corinthians*, 828. Although see Thiselton (*First Corinthians*, 1291), who asserts that the parallelism is more than merely synonymous. "Each part takes up (in inverse order) the two aspects of the change described in vv. 43–44. A σῶμα constituted by the presence and direction of the Holy Spirit entails: (i) holiness in place of sin (v. 50a); and (ii) the reversal of weakness, degeneration, and decay (v. 50b)."

[286] Garland (*First Corinthians*, 741) points out that one's view is related to the interpretation of the verb "to sow" in 15:42–44, which most likely refers to the living rather than to the dead corpse buried in the ground. "Perishable" is not equivalent to "dead." Collins (*First Corinthians*,

The kingdom of God in 15:50 is future, when those who belong to Christ will be raised and the Son hands the kingdom over to the Father (cf. 15:23–24). The phrase "kingdom of God" appears seven times in Paul's letters, five in 1 Corinthians (4:20; 6:9–10; 15:24,50; see also Rom 14:17; Gal 5:21). Whereas in 1 Cor 6:9–10 moral vices exclude one from an inheritance in the kingdom,[287] here the obstacle is one's present human condition, the perishable body. The verb "to inherit" occurs frequently in New Testament eschatological contexts (cf. Matt 5:5; 19:29; 25:34; Mark 10:17; Luke 10:25; 18:18; Heb 1:14; 6:12; 12:17; Rev 21:7). While the Old Testament speaks repeatedly of God's people inheriting the land, the concept broadens in the New Testament to inheriting the earth, the kingdom, and eternal life.[288] "Thus the promises about the land are swallowed up in the resurrection teaching so that all that was hoped for in terms of the restoration of Israel to the land and the restoration of the land (and all of creation) to an Edenic condition now finds its ultimate consummation in the resurrection of the dead and the complete renewal of creation that accompanies it."[289]

**15:51–53** The interjection, "Listen!"[290] calls for attention and introduces the "mystery"[291] that not all believers will die, but all will be changed. The verbs "to change"[292] (15:51,52) and "it is necessary"[293] (15:53) convey Paul's chief concern, which is to explain the material nature of the resurrection if "flesh and blood" cannot inherit the kingdom of God and the perishable cannot inherit the imperishable.[294] The believer's present body must be transformed, whether living or dead at Christ's return. Paul does not say anything more than he has already indicated in 15:42–49 about the precise nature of the change. His concern is to show that change is necessary for the living as well as the dead. Paul is not promising that some believers to whom he was writing would survive death but only indicates that some would be alive at the time of Christ's coming. Whether or not Paul expected to be alive at Christ's advent is an open question. Just as Paul uses the plural "we will not all sleep" here, he uses the plural in 6:14, "By his power God raised the Lord from the dead, and he will raise us also." Paul did not necessarily assume that he and the Corinthians belonged to the last generation of Christians. Paul's point is simple: even the living believers at the time of Christ's coming must undergo transformation in order to be fit for the age to come.

Three prepositional phrases indicate the character and the time of the resurrection: "in a flash," "in the twinkling of an eye," and "at the last trumpet."

579) suggests that with the parallelism "Paul has shifted from the language of Jewish apocalyptic to the language of Hellenistic philosophy and rhetoric."

[287] Cf. also Gal 5:21.

[288] Ciampa and Rosner, *First Corinthians*, 828–29.

[289] Ibid., 829.

[290] Gk. ἰδού. Only here in 1 Corinthians.

[291] Regarding the term "mystery" see discussion on 2:1–2.

[292] Gk. ἀλλάσσω.

[293] Gk. δεῖ.

[294] So Garland, *1 Corinthians*, 742.

Neither the expression "in a flash" nor "in the twinkling of an eye" occurs elsewhere in the New Testament or in the Septuagint. Both phrases imply an instantaneous transformation rather than a process, which is consistent with the Old Testament emphasis on God's sudden eschatological intervention to judge and to save.[295] The trumpet blast "intensifies the metaphor of suddenness, adding the dimension of divine decree and ordered signal."[296] The trumpet is the sign of the Day of the Lord (cf. Isa 27:13; Joel 2:1; Zeph 1:14–16; Zech 9:14; Matt 24:31; 1 Thess 4:16; Rev 8:2) and announces the moment of transformation.[297] "With the sound of the trumpet comes the passing of the present order of reality and the beginning of the kingdom of God."[298] With this revelation, building on 15:42–49, Paul answers decisively the questions of 15:35, "How are the dead raised? With what kind of body will they come?"

Verse 53 explains that transformation is essential (cf. 15:50) and describes the change using a clothing metaphor. Ciampa and Rosner note the link between the resurrection of believers and the restoration of creation (Rom 8:19–23) and suggest that Paul may have in mind Ps 102:26 (LXX Ps 101:27) in using the garment imagery, which is quoted also in Heb 1:11–12: "They will perish, but you remain; they will all wear out like a garment. You will roll them up like a robe; like a garment they will be changed." "If the old cosmos is to be exchanged for a new one as in putting on a new garment, it would be natural to assume that the same will take place with the bodies of the redeemed."[299] Paul employs the clothing metaphor numerous times in his letters (see Rom 13:12–14; 2 Cor 5:2–4; Gal 3:27; Eph 4:24; 6:11–14; Col 3:10–12; 1 Thess 5:8).[300] Like the analogy of the seed and the plant, the clothing imagery supports the idea of continuity between our present body and the resurrection body. To "put on the imperishable" recalls 15:42 and is another way of stating that "we will bear the image of the heavenly" (15:49).[301] As a good point of application, Thiselton observes, "In our own era after the turn of the millennium, when medicine has prolonged life beyond all earlier imagination, it is important not to lose sight of Paul's emphasis on release from degenerating capacities."[302]

[295] So Ciampa and Rosner, *First Corinthians*, 830 (cf. Isa 29:5–6; 48:3 and Mal 3:1; also Isa 30:13; 47:11; Jer 6:26; 15:8; 18:22; 49:19; 50:44; 51:8; Mark 13:36; Luke 21:34).

[296] Thiselton, *First Corinthians*, 1296.

[297] Other passages do not associate transformation with the trumpet call. This is the new element in 1 Cor 15:50–53.

[298] Collins, *First Corinthians*, 580.

[299] Ciampa and Rosner, *First Corinthians*, 831. Cf. also *1 Enoch* 62:15–16; *2 Enoch* 22:8–10.

[300] For a recent full-length treatment of the clothing imagery, see J. H. Kim, *The Significance of Clothing Imagery in the Pauline Corpus* (London: Clark, 2004).

[301] The Greek of 15:53 reads, "This perishable must put on . . ." and may refer to Paul's own mortal body (so Robertson and Plummer, *First Corinthians*, 377; Fitzmyer, *First Corinthians*, 605). The demonstrative pronoun "this" occurs four times in 15:53–54. Thiselton (*First Corinthians*, 1297) notes the significance of the repetition as indicating "clear continuity of identity (this body) even in the midst of radical transformation."

[302] Thiselton, *First Corinthians*, 1297.

**15:54–57** The argument now moves to the final stage. Verse 54, introduced by a temporal clause, repeats the parallelism of v. 53 and stipulates that when the transformation described in vv. 52–53 occurs the long-awaited promise of death's final defeat will come to pass. Death must be destroyed (15:26) so that "God may be all in all" (15:28).[303] In declaring death's destruction, Paul conflates portions of Isa 25:8 and Hos 13:14 into a single quotation, yet he does not cite either text exactly from the MT or the LXX.[304] The citation of Isaiah is closer to the MT in actual wording and context, although Paul could have drawn from other Greek versions.[305] Either way Paul casts anew the prophetic announcement that God "will swallow up death forever." Paul's use of Hosea is a fluid adaptation linked to Isa 25 by the key word "victory" in a mutually interpretive fashion. Collins explains that this method of citation is "akin to the way in which the Scriptures were used in rabbinic commentaries, in the Targums, and in the Qumran midrashim."[306] Paul interprets the Old Testament text "from the perspective of Christ's resurrection by turning it into a taunt. The rhetorical questions now sneer defiantly at death's impotence before the power and mercy of God, who wills to forgive sins (1 Cor. 15:3,17) and to raise the dead."[307] Thiselton keeps the interpretive task in focus by observing that the more technical questions about Paul's use of the Old Testament texts "should not distract us from engaging with the profound theological content which his citations serve to explicate. Paul projects an eschatological vision of a stingless death precisely because Jesus Christ has himself absorbed the sting on the basis of how his death and resurrection addresses the problem of human sin and the law (vv. 55–57)."[308]

In 15:56–57 Paul follows the citation of the biblical texts with commentary and puts the taunt of death into proper perspective. Death will not be destroyed

---

[303] Both 15:28 and 15:54 begin "but when" (Gk. ὅταν δέ).

[304] For a full discussion of the issues, see C. D. Stanley, *Paul and the Language of Scripture: Citation Technique in the Pauline Epistles and Contemporary Literature*, SNTSMS 74 (Cambridge: Cambridge University Press, 1992), 209–15.

[305] On the similarity of 1 Cor 15:54b to other Greek versions, see ibid., 210–11. The LXX of Isa 25:18 is markedly different from the MT, κατέπιεν ὁ θάνατος ἰσχύσας ("Having become strong, death swallowed up"). Hays (*First Corinthians*, 275) thinks that Paul is following the Hebrew textual tradition rather than the LXX. Ciampa and Rosner (*First Corinthians*, 832) suggest that "Paul was probably following a preexisting Greek text (Rev. 21:4 cites the same tradition)." Furthermore, the Isaiah text is frequently cited in the Rabbinic literature "where it is taken to be a divine promise that death would be no more in the age to come." Garland (*First Corinthians*, 745) prefers the explanation that Paul may have drawn on an idiom connected to the cognate Aramaic verb of the Hebrew adverb "forever" that means to "overcome" or "prevail."

[306] Collins, *First Corinthians*, 578. Hos 13:14 (LXX) reads, "O death, where is thy penalty?" (Gk. δίκη instead of νῖκος). Hays (*First Corinthians*, 276) suggests that Paul has altered "penalty" to "victory" in order to create a word-link with 1 Cor 15:57, but "it is also possible that the Isaiah citation supplies the word 'victory' to the Hosea text" (Ciampa and Rosner, *First Corinthians*, 833). Barrett (*First Corinthians*, 383) thinks that Paul is "writing freely, in scriptural language, of the ultimate victory over death."

[307] Garland, *1 Corinthians*, 745.

[308] Thiselton, *First Corinthians*, 1300.

until the end of all things (15:24–28) and so death still bears the sting of sin, which derives its power from the law (15:56). Paul does not elaborate further on the relationship between the triad of death, sin, and the law.[309] Undoubtedly the Corinthians "would understand this theological shorthand" based on prior instruction.[310] The details are worked out and preserved for us in other texts, especially Rom 5–7. Even though Paul's derision of death and his assertion of victory is in the present tense, the final victory awaits the return of Christ when those who belong to him will be raised (15:23). In other words, Paul contemplates death's defeat in the light of resurrection day. It is quite presumptuous to downplay the present reality of death and its power over humanity. We need not fear death (cf. Heb 2:14–15), but neither should we deny it (15:21–22; Rom 6:23). Paul faced death daily but with confidence in God who raises the dead (cf. 2 Cor 1:8–9; Rom 8:31–39). Thiselton explains, "Even if the last resurrection is still future, the basis of the victory is a present gift, providing grounds for present exultation and thanksgiving."[311] Paul's triumphant thanksgiving in 15:57 is recast similarly in Rom 7:24–25a: "What a wretched man I am! Who will rescue me from this body of death? Thanks be to God—through Jesus Christ our Lord!"[312]

**15:58** Paul concludes with an exhortation introduced by the affectionate address, "my beloved brothers."[313] His appeal to the Corinthians is to be steadfast and immovable, complementary terms qualified by the phrase "always abounding in the work of the Lord," and followed by the grounds "because you know that your labor in the Lord is not in vain." Paul's language harks back to the chapter's opening where he reminded them of the gospel they received and in which they stand and where he urged them to hold fast to the word he proclaimed to them lest they believed in vain (15:1–2). To "stand firm" in this context is to hold fast to the gospel and to the belief in the resurrection that the gospel proclaims. Otherwise they have believed in vain.[314] Having established the fact of resurrection as central to God's redemptive plan, Paul concludes by urging them to rid themselves of the belief that there is "no resurrection of the dead" and to prosper in the work of the gospel knowing that all such work is not in vain (cf. 15:10,14).[315]

---

[309] Fee (*First Corinthians*, 805) refers to 15:56 as a "brief compendium of his own theology."

[310] Garland, *1 Corinthians*, 746.

[311] Thiselton, *First Corinthians*, 1304.

[312] Paul's outburst of thanksgiving parallels the triumphal tone of 15:20–28 (cf. also 2 Cor 2:14; 8:16; 9:15). Thiselton (*First Corinthians*, 1303) identifies 15:57 as a speech-act, "a verbal equivalent to throwing one's arm around someone in gratitude."

[313] Cf. 4:17 and 10:14. Only here and in Phil 4:1 does "beloved" modify "my brothers."

[314] The adjective "steadfast" (Gk. ἑδραῖος) carries the sense of being established in the faith in Col 1:23. Cf. also Hays, *First Corinthians*, 277; Thiselton, *First Corinthians*, 1304–5.

[315] Collins (*First Corinthians*, 584) suggests that the language of 15:58 implies that the Corinthians continue Paul's work of evangelism (cf. the metaphor of building on Paul's foundation in 3:10–17).

## SECTION OUTLINE

VII. The Collection for the Saints in Jerusalem and Travel Plans (16:1–12)
   1. The Collection for the Jerusalem Saints (16:1–4)
   2. Travel Plans (Paul, Timothy, Apollos) (16:5–12)

## VII. THE COLLECTION FOR THE SAINTS IN JERUSALEM AND TRAVEL PLANS (16:1–12)

Paul brings the letter to conclusion by addressing several matters of practical concern and giving final exhortations.[1] At first glance the shift from the exultant tone of 15:50–58 regarding resurrection, transformation, and the defeat of death to the matter of the collection for God's people seems quite abrupt. Chapter 15 ended, however, with an exhortation to abound in the work of the Lord, and the collection is one way among others to do this very thing.[2] There is still much to attend to in this life, and Paul "must return to business."[3] In this final chapter Paul gives instructions for the collection for the saints in Jerusalem (16:1–4), announces his travel plans and the plans of Timothy and Apollos (16:5–12), and offers final exhortations, commendations, and greetings (16:13–24).

### 1. The Collection for the Jerusalem Saints (16:1–4)

**[1]Now about the collection for God's people: Do what I told the Galatian churches to do. [2]On the first day of every week, each one of you should set aside a sum of money in keeping with his income, saving it up, so that when I come no collections will have to be made. [3]Then, when I arrive, I will give letters of introduction to the men you approve and send them with your gift to Jerusalem. [4]If it seems advisable for me to go also, they will accompany me.**

---

[1] R. E. Ciampa and B. S. Rosner note that 1 Corinthians is distinct in the density of explicit references to particular Christian people or groups external to the Corinth church (Galatian churches, Jerusalem, Timothy, Apollos) and those who served as messengers of the church to others (Stephanas, Fortunatus, Achaicus) (*The First Letter to the Corinthians*, PNTC [Grand Rapids: Eerdmans, 2010], 839).

[2] In 16:10 Paul refers to Timothy who "does the work of the Lord as I also do." A. C. Thiselton (*The First Epistle to the Corinthians: A Commentary on the Greek Text*, NIGTC [Grand Rapids: Eerdmans, 2000], 1315) notes that the link with the historical witnesses to the resurrection underlines a "historical indebtedness" on the part of later Gentile Christians to the first witnesses and their communities.

[3] A. Robertson and A. Plummer, *A Critical and Exegetical Commentary on the First Epistle of St. Paul to the Corinthians*, ICC, 2nd ed. (Edinburgh: T&T Clark), 381.

The collection mentioned in 16:1–4 was a significant project for Paul that included other Gentile churches.[4] The context clarifies that the collection was an offering for believers in Jerusalem (16:3). Other New Testament passages provide a more complete picture of the offering and the reasons for it (see esp. Acts 24:17; Rom 15:25–31; 2 Cor 8–9; Gal 2:10). Each of these additional passages mention that the contribution was for the poor. The collection was a one-time gift, a voluntary contribution rather than a compulsory offering. One aspect of the gift was to alleviate human suffering, but there were theological motivations as well, namely, to solidify and strengthen the relationship between the Jewish and Gentile portions of the church thereby contributing to the unity of the church. It is possible that the offering was also rooted in the Old Testament eschatological expectation of a Gentile pilgrimage to Jerusalem, but Ciampa and Rosner caution that "there is no sufficient evidence to clearly affirm or deny the association."[5] In Rom 15:27, Paul mentions the willing participation of the churches of Achaia and Macedonia but also their obligation: "For if the Gentiles have shared in the Jews' spiritual blessings, they owe it to the Jews to share with them their material blessings." In this present paragraph Paul addresses both the method of collection (16:1–2) and the method of distribution (16:3–4).

**16:1–2** The phrase "Now about" translates the same Greek phrase used throughout the letter to indicate a question raised by the Corinthians in their letter to Paul.[6] Here the topic is the "collection for God's people," which reads more literally "the collection for the saints."[7] Since Paul mentions the collection rather abruptly with no elaboration other than to give instructions for its collection and distribution, this is surely a matter about which the Corinthians were already informed.[8] Here he does not mention the reason for the offering or its significance but simply insists that they proceed with the collection as the

[4] For specialist studies on the Jerusalem collection, see K. F. Nickle, *The Collection: A Study in Paul's Strategy*, SBT 48 (London: SCM, 1966); D. Georgi, *Remembering the Poor: The History of Paul's Collection for Jerusalem* (Nashville: Abingdon, 1992); D. J. Downs, *The Offering of the Gentiles* (Tübingen: Mohr, 2008).

[5] Ciampa and Rosner, *First Corinthians*, 842n8. Ciampa and Rosner note Isa 60:3–61:6; 66:20 as possible background texts. Nickle (*The Collection*, 100–143) discusses the theological significance of the collection in terms of Christian charity, unity, and eschatology.

[6] Gk. περί δέ. See 7:1,25; 8:1; 12:1. As noted previously 7:1 specifically indicates a question posed by the Corinthians and the formula most likely indicates the same elsewhere.

[7] Gk. περὶ δὲ τῆς λογείας τῆς εἰς τοὺς ἁγίους. J. A. Fitzmyer notes the occurrences of the term "saints" (holy people) with reference to the collection in 2 Cor 8:4; 9:1,12; Rom 15:25–26,31 (*First Corinthians: A New Translation with Introduction and Commentary*, AB 32 [New Haven: Yale University Press, 2008], 612).

[8] Paul does not indicate how the Corinthians were informed of the collection. If Paul himself did not inform them, then perhaps Titus (cf. 2 Cor 8:23). The collection may have originated in the Jerusalem Council (Acts 15:1–29; cf. Gal 2:10). There is an established pattern in 1 Corinthians of mentioning other churches (4:17; 7:17; 11:16; 14:33–34; 16:19).

churches of Galatia had been directed to do.[9] In 2 Cor 8–9 Paul devotes considerably more attention to the collection, which finds its theological basis in the generosity of Christ (2 Cor 8:9) and is itself an act of thanksgiving to God (2 Cor 9:12).[10] Presumably the Corinthians had asked Paul for further instructions, and he addresses the collection toward the end of the letter since he can do so briefly in relation to his travel plans. Paul is especially concerned that the collection is ready before he arrives in Corinth.

The term translated "collection" occurs only in this passage in the New Testament and is most likely a technical term used by the Corinthians in their letter to Paul regarding how to go about "collecting" the funds.[11] Although nonbiblical uses of the term denote the collection of money as a tax,[12] it does not carry such meaning in this context. Paul himself uses a wide variety of terms to refer to the collection,[13] which reflect his profound theological perspective on giving.[14] The collection is inextricably bound up in the nature of the gospel, "For you know the grace of our Lord Jesus Christ, that though he was rich, yet for your sakes he became poor, so that you through his poverty might become rich" (2 Cor 8:9). For Paul the collection was "an active response to the grace of God that not only ministered to the needs of God's people but also became a kind of ministry to God himself, which resulted in thanksgiving toward God and in a bond of fellowship between 'God's people' across the Empire."[15]

In 16:2 Paul lays out the instructions for the collection. On the first day of the week,[16] each person should set aside funds "in keeping with his income"[17]

[9] On the use of the verb διατάσσω (to direct/command) in 1 Corinthians, see also 7:17; 9:14; 11:34. Barrett raises the possibility that the Corinthians had been informed about the offering by some of the churches in Galatia (*A Commentary on the First Epistle to the Corinthians*, HNTC [New York: Harper & Row, 1968], 385). Fitzmyer (*First Corinthians*, 611) notes that Rom 15:25–31 exemplifies how Paul treats the topic when mentioned to his audience for the first time.

[10] So Thiselton, *First Corinthians*, 1316; R. F. Collins, *First Corinthians*, SP (Collegeville, MN: Liturgical Press, 1999), 586. Paul has urged the Corinthians to "imitate Christ" in 4:16–17 and 11:1. They can fulfill this exhortation, in part, by joyful participation in the collection.

[11] Gk. λογεία (16:1, 2). So G. D. Fee, *The First Epistle to the Corinthians*, NICNT (Grand Rapids: Eerdmans, 1987), 812.

[12] See Kittle, *TDNT* 4:282–83. See also Thiselton, *First Corinthians*, 1318.

[13] Such as grace (χάρις; 16:3; 2 Cor 8:6–7,19), sharing (κοινωνία; Rom 15:26; 2 Cor 8:4; 9:13), ministry or service (διακονία; Rom 15:25,31; 2 Cor 8:4; 9:1,12–13), blessing or bounty (εὐλογία; 2 Cor 9:5–6), service or help (λειτουργία; 2 Cor 9:12), and abundance (ἁδρότης; 2 Cor 8:20).

[14] Thiselton (*First Corinthians*, 1318) notes Paul's reference to the gospel as a "treasure" in 2 Cor 4:7.

[15] Fee, *First Corinthians*, 812.

[16] The reference to the first day of the week provides early evidence that believers gathered on Sunday, the day of Jesus' resurrection, for worship. See also Matt 28:1; Mark 16:2; Luke 24:1; John 20:1,19,26; Acts 20:7; Rev 1:10.

[17] BDAG renders the Greek (ὅ τι ἐὰν εὐοδῶται) as "save as much as he gains," but as Thiselton (*First Corinthians*, 1323) points out, this implies that one gives only when making a profit. "It seems most faithful to Paul's indefinite force to translate 'in accordance with how you may fare.'" Thiselton comments further, "In spirit, the tradition of the widow's mite lies behind Paul's phraseology: 'Whoever sows sparingly will also reap sparingly, and whoever sows generously will also

and save it until Paul arrives. Paul wisely urged the full participation of the whole church along with a systematic and orderly process of collection in order to yield maximum results. He did not want to solicit funds when he arrived in Corinth, nor did he want to make rushed or last-minute appeals.[18] He does not want to pressure them (2 Cor 9:7) but desires that they respond freely to the work of God's grace in their lives.[19] Paul's intent was to promote unity in the church and keep the needs of the Jerusalem saints before the Corinthians.[20]

The phrase translated "each one of you should set aside a sum of money"[21] suggests to some that the process involved each person privately setting aside funds at home until the designated time of collection.[22] Others feel the context indicates that a church treasury was involved since "Paul expressly deprecates the collecting of the money when he arrived (which would be necessary if they all had it at home)."[23] Ciampa and Rosner concur, "The mention of the first day of every week along with the purpose that when I come no collections will have to be made suggests that the setting aside of money would not be just the setting apart within one's own possessions but the setting aside of the money by presenting it to the leaders of the church (cf. Acts 4:34–5:2)."[24] Fitzmyer offers a balanced perspective by pointing out that Paul stresses individual contributions but says nothing about "where the collection of what is stored up should take place."[25] The situation of continuous and regular savings calls for the present imperative verb "one must put aside."[26]

**16:3–4** Having given instructions for the collection of the offering Paul now lays out a sensible and careful plan for its distribution. When he arrives in Corinth he will dispatch those approved by the Corinthians to take the gift to Jerusalem, along with personal letters of introduction.[27] If the circumstances are right for Paul to go along, then the letters will be unnecessary and he will travel with them to deliver the collection. The use of "letters of introduction"

reap generously. . . . God loves a cheerful giver . . .' (2 Cor 9:6,7; cf. 2 Cor 8:1–9:15)." Robertson and Plummer (*First Corinthians*, 385) comment, "In any case, the meaning is that the amount is to be fixed by the giver in proportion to his weekly gains; and there is no dictation as to the right proportion, whether a tenth, or more, or less. A tenth is little for some, impossible for others; but week by week each would see how much or how little he had got, and would act accordingly."

[18] So Robertson and Plummer, *First Corinthians*, 385.

[19] D. E. Garland, *1 Corinthians*, BECNT (Grand Rapids: Baker, 2003), 754.

[20] Witherington notes that Paul does not appeal only to the wealthy nor does he allow a few patrons to give large sums. He does not want to add to the social status of the well-to-do (*Conflict and Community in Corinth: A Socio-Rhetorical Commentary* [Grand Rapids: Eerdmans, 1994], 315.

[21] Gk. ἕκαστος ὑμῶν παρ' ἑαυτῷ τιθέτω ("Each of you must put aside for himself").

[22] So Robertson and Plummer, *First Corinthians*, 384; Fee, *First Corinthians*, 813; Thiselton, *First Corinthians*, 1323–24.

[23] L. Morris, *1 Corinthians*, TNTC (Grand Rapids: Eerdmans, 1985), 233.

[24] Ciampa and Rosner, *First Corinthians*, 843.

[25] Fitzmyer, *First Corinthians*, 614.

[26] Gk. τιθέτω. Noted by Thiselton, *First Corinthians*, 1323.

[27] This is Paul's second reference to his future plans to visit Corinth (cf. 4:18–21).

was common in the ancient world.[28] In this case the letters would verify the nature of the offering and introduce the contributors. But who would write the letters? The NIV opts for Paul, "I will give," but the ESV indicates the church, "those whom you accredit by letter." The NIV is likely the correct understanding, that is, the Corinthians would approve[29] trustworthy individuals to bear the offering to Jerusalem, but Paul would write the letters of introduction commending the Corinthian cohort to the believers in Jerusalem. Witherington notes that this too is a unifying strategy "since it will mean that the congregation as a whole must make a decision, and it wards off any hint that Paul might be indirectly trying to get funds for himself from the Corinthians."[30] According to Rom 15:25–33, Paul indeed made the trip and the offering was received.[31]

The phrase "If it seems advisable for me to go also" is capable of two different interpretations. The NIV rendering suggests that whether or not Paul will go to Jerusalem with the gift depends on his personal situation at the time. But since the word translated "advisable" is the Greek term often rendered "worthy,"[32] the phrase could imply, "If the gift is of a worthy amount," that is, if it is large enough.[33] The former is more likely, that Paul refers to his own personal situation and perhaps even the situation in Jerusalem.[34] Paul does not refer to the contribution as a "collection" in 16:3, as he does in 16:1–2, but rather as a "gift," which is the same word for "grace."[35] In laying out plans for the collection and distribution of the offering Paul wisely did not dictate a set amount nor did he choose those who would deliver the gift to Jerusalem.

## 2. Travel Plans (Paul, Timothy, Apollos) (16:5–12)

**[5]After I go through Macedonia, I will come to you—for I will be going through Macedonia. [6]Perhaps I will stay with you awhile, or even spend the winter, so that**

---

[28] The text reads, "through letters" (δι' ἐπιστολῶν), which most likely refers to what is known as "letters of introduction/recommendation." Cf. Acts 9:2,22–25; 15:23–29; 13:2–3; Rom 16:1–2; 2 Cor 3:1; 8:16–24. See Collins (*First Corinthians*, 589) for ancient sources.

[29] Gk. δοκιμάζω, which implies those who have stood the test and been approved (cf. 3:13). "Paul is alluding to the trusted integrity of those who can serve on behalf of a potentially suspicious congregation in which there are already 'splits' and perhaps competing patrons" (Thiselton, *First Corinthians*, 1324–25).

[30] Witherington, *Conflict and Community*, 315.

[31] Acts 20:3–21:17 describes a trip from Greece to Jerusalem. The evidence of 2 Corinthians suggests that the Corinthians initially failed to follow through and needed further motivation (2 Cor 8:10–11).

[32] Gk. ἄξιος. The term can carry the sense of what is "fitting" or "proper," thus the NIV translation "advisable."

[33] See Robertson and Plummer, *First Corinthians*, 385.

[34] F. W. Grosheide (*Commentary on the First Epistle to the Corinthians*, NICNT [Grand Rapids: Eerdmans, 1953], 398) explains that Paul means "if circumstances are such that the mission work demands my journeying to Jerusalem *they shall go with me*. Then letters will not be needed." So most recent commentators.

[35] Gk. χάρις.

**you can help me on my journey, wherever I go. [7]I do not want to see you now and make only a passing visit; I hope to spend some time with you, if the Lord permits. [8]But I will stay on at Ephesus until Pentecost, [9]because a great door for effective work has opened to me, and there are many who oppose me.**

**[10]If Timothy comes, see to it that he has nothing to fear while he is with you, for he is carrying on the work of the Lord, just as I am. [11]No one, then, should refuse to accept him. Send him on his way in peace so that he may return to me. I am expecting him along with the brothers.**

**[12]Now about our brother Apollos: I strongly urged him to go to you with the brothers. He was quite unwilling to go now, but he will go when he has the opportunity.**

The mention of the distribution of the offering for the believers in Jerusalem (16:3–4) compels Paul to lay out a more detailed itinerary for his impending visit to Corinth (16:5–9), along with information regarding the plans of Timothy (16:10–11) and Apollos (16:12).[36] Paul often includes a travelogue toward the end of his letters,[37] which express not only the places he intends to travel but also the people he desires to see and plans for the ministry of the gospel.[38] Here he states his intention of an extended visit to Corinth after passing through Macedonia. For the time being, however, he will remain in Ephesus because of pressing ministry opportunities. Plans changed, however, and did not pan out as Paul intended,[39] which evidently became a point of criticism from the Corinthians (see 2 Cor 1:15–2:4). In 16:10–11 Paul expresses concern over their reception of Timothy when he arrives and encourages the Corinthians to welcome him. Finally, in 16:12, Paul mentions that he strongly encouraged Apollos to visit Corinth, but for the time being Apollos is unable to go.[40]

**16:5–9** Passing through Macedonian on the way to Corinth was a more circuitous route than traveling by sea, but Macedonia, a Roman province, was the location of other Pauline churches (e.g., Philippi and Thessalonica). The

---

[36] Cf. 4:18–19. For a useful survey of the possibilities regarding Paul's travels in relation to the church at Corinth, see Murphy-O'Connor, *Paul: A Critical Life* (Oxford: Oxford University Press, 1996), 291–332.

[37] Cf. Rom 15:22–32; 2 Cor 12:14–13:1,10; 1 Thess 2:17–20; 3:11–13; Phlm 22.

[38] So Collins, *First Corinthians*, 591.

[39] We learn from 2 Corinthians that Paul made an unplanned visit to Corinth that developed into a major crisis resulting in the "letter of tears" (2 Cor 2:1–4). The exact opposite of what Paul planned happened (Fee, *First Corinthians*, 818). D. E. Garland notes, however, that Paul "appears to have followed the route proposed here at a later date when he traveled to Macedonia and then to Corinth (2 Cor. 2:12–13; 7:5; 8:1; 9:4; Acts 19:21; 20:1–3; see also Rom. 15:26; 16:1)" (*1 Corinthians*, BECNT [Grand Rapids: Baker, 2003], 757).

[40] Collins (*First Corinthians*, 595) notes that 1 Cor 4:17; 16:10–11; and 16:15–16 are crafted in a style that recalls features of the genre of the letter of recommendation mentioned in 16:3. However, since these passages are crafted into a longer letter they "lack the typical epistolary salutation and the epistolary closing that would be characteristic of a self-standing letter of recommendation." See C.-H. Kim, *Form and Function of the Familiar Letter of Recommendation*, SBLDS 4 (Missoula: Scholars Press, 1972).

term translated "to go through"[41] occurs frequently in Acts in reference to travel and may be a technical term for a missionary tour.[42] The present tense (lit. "I am passing through") in this context carries the force of firm intention.[43] Paul clarifies in 16:7 that he intends to remain in Corinth for an extended period of time,[44] hopefully spending the winter when travel would not be advisable, or perhaps not even possible. This is Paul's third mention in the letter of a future visit (cf. 4:18–21; 11:34).

The reason Paul gives for his extended visit is so that "you may send me on my way, wherever I may go" (16:6), which may refer to making provision for further missionary work.[45] If this is the case there is no conflict with Paul's prior refusal of financial support in ministry (cf. 9:1–18). This would not be a reversal of his prior policy of giving up his apostolic rights for the sake of the gospel but rather temporary assistance to get Paul to the next point of service and an opportunity for the Corinthians to participate in the larger missionary enterprise.[46] Paul's intentions represent both strategic insight and firm planning yet an openness to the contingencies of God's will: "If the Lord permits" (16:7).[47]

For the time being Paul plans to remain in Ephesus until Pentecost (16:8), a statement that provides both the location of the writing of the letter and a reference to a particular time of year (i.e., spring). Although a Jewish festival,[48] Pentecost no doubt held great significance for the church in light of the events described in Acts 2. In this context, however, Paul may be referring more to the season of Pentecost rather than to a specific day, much in the same way that people today might speak of remaining somewhere until "Christmas."[49] Either way, Paul explains that he intends to stay in Ephesus until mid-spring to early

---

[41] Gk. διέρχομαι (Acts 8:4,40; 9:32,38; 10:38; 11:19,22; 12:10; 13:6,14; 14:24; 15:3,41; 16:6; 17:23; 18:23,27; 19:1,21; 20:2,25).

[42] So Robertson and Plummer, *First Corinthians*, 387.

[43] So Barrett, *First Corinthians*, 389. The NIV translates the present as a future, "I will be going through." ESV, "I intend to pass through."

[44] The prepositional phrase "with you" (Gk. πρὸς ὑμᾶς) occurs three times in 16:5–7. The phrase means "to you" but in this context implies active interaction (so Robertson and Plummer, *First Corinthians*, 388; Thiselton, *First Corinthians*, 1328).

[45] So BDAG, who define προπέμπω ("to send") in this context, "to assist someone in making a journey; send on one's way with food, money, by arranging for companions, means of travel, etc." So also Fee, *First Corinthians*, 819; Thiselton, *First Corinthians*, 1328. The same verb is used in reference to Timothy in 16:11 (cf. also Acts 15:13; Rom 15:24; 2 Cor 1:16; Titus 3:13). Robertson and Plummer (*First Corinthians*, 388) question this meaning in this context, "He is not asking for money or provisions; the verb does not necessarily mean more than good wishes and prayers."

[46] So Fee, *First Corinthians*, 819.

[47] Cf. also Acts 18:21; Jas 4:15. The Greek phrase ἄρτι ἐν παρόδῳ ἰδεῖν is an idiom meaning "a fleeting visit; just while we happen to pass each other" (so Thiselton, *First Corinthians*, 1329).

[48] See Lev 23:15–21.

[49] So Fee, *First Corinthians*, 820; Garland, *1 Corinthians*, 758. Paul may mention Pentecost simply as an indication of a favorable season for travel (so Thiselton, *First Corinthians*, 1329–30). Hays, however, posits, "The reference to Pentecost is another indication, among many in his letter,

summer before traveling to Macedonia. His reason for remaining in his present location is that "a great door for effective work has opened to me."[50] The metaphor of an "opened door" refers to advantageous ministry opportunities, an opening for the preaching of the gospel (cf. also 2 Cor 2:12; Col 4:3).[51] Paul does not elaborate on the additional comment "and there are many who oppose me," but he has already mentioned fighting wild beasts in Ephesus in 15:32. The book of Acts provides further insight into the kinds of troubles Paul faced in Asia (see Acts 19:23–41; cf. also 2 Cor 1:8–11). Such is the case in every location where the undiluted gospel is preached. The gospel always elicits opposition yet cannot be hindered by it (Phil 1:12–14). Great opposition presents great opportunities for the proclamation of the gospel.[52]

**16:10–11** Already in 4:17–21 Paul explained that he sent Timothy to Corinth so that he might remind them of his ways in Christ. Here Paul expresses concern for how the Corinthians might receive his beloved son in the faith, which implies that the letter would arrive before Timothy. The NIV translation, "If Timothy comes," is a technically correct rendering of the Greek conditional clause,[53] which seems to indicate a measure of uncertainty about whether or not Timothy will actually arrive in Corinth. However, in light of 4:17, "the indefinite construction refers to the uncertainty not of the event, but of his time of arrival."[54]

Paul's directives regarding their reception of Timothy serve "to establish the role of Timothy among Paul's co-workers."[55] First, they are to "see to it that he has nothing to fear while he is with you."[56] While some think this statement refers to Timothy's youth and inexperience mentioned in the pastorals,[57] it is more likely that Paul is referring to the possibilities of being mistreated in Corinth. This is clarified by the explanatory clause and the next directive.

that Paul is still thinking in a Jewish frame of reference and expecting his Corinthian converts to do likewise" (*First Corinthians* [Louisville: John Knox, 1997], 285).

[50] Lit., "a great and effective door."

[51] At first glance the adjective "effective" doesn't seem appropriate to the door metaphor, but if "door" indicates opportunity, then "effective" carries the sense of an opportunity poised for results. See Robertson and Plummer (*First Corinthians*, 390), who note the similar phrase "our entrance to you" (1 Thess 1:9; 2:1). Collins (*First Corinthians*, 593) notes that the word "effective" (Gk. ἐνεργής), which occurs only here and Phlm 6, belongs to a word group commonly used by Paul to describe his proclamation of the gospel. The NIV translation captures the intent of the Greek well.

[52] So Hays, *First Corinthians*, 286.

[53] Gk. Ἐὰν δὲ ἔλθῃ Τιμόθεος.

[54] Thiselton, *First Corinthians*, 1330. So also Fee, *First Corinthians*, 821. So also ESV, TNIV, "When Timothy comes." Collins (*First Corinthians*, 596) comments, "Paul had sent Timothy to the Corinthians, but he seems not to have any knowledge of Timothy's having arrived."

[55] Thiselton, *First Corinthians*, 1331.

[56] "See to it!" translates βλέπετε, which can be admonitory (cf. 10:12, "Be careful").

[57] See 1 Tim 5:21–23; 2 Tim 1:6–8; 2:1–3,15; 4:1. Robertson and Plummer (*First Corinthians*, 390) suggest the meaning "take care that there is no painful awkwardness." For a different perspective on Timothy, see C. R. Hutson, "Was Timothy Timid? On the Rhetoric of Fearlessness (1 Corinthians 16:10–11) and Cowardice (2 Timothy 1:7)," *BR* 42 (1997): 58–73.

Timothy does the work of the Lord just as Paul does. This may be a not-so-subtle warning that Timothy is Paul's representative while in Corinth and the manner in which they treat him is, in effect, how they are treating Paul.[58] In the second directive Paul warns, "No one . . . should refuse to accept him," which reads more literally, "No one should despise him."[59] Finally, Paul encourages the Corinthians to "send him on his way in peace so that he may return to me."[60] "To send" is the same verb used in 16:6 and, in this context, may imply the supply of provision for Timothy's return trip to Paul. Paul concludes his remarks concerning Timothy with the statement, "I am expecting him along with the brothers." As Robertson and Plummer point out, the meaning could be, "I am expecting him and so are the brothers," in which case "the brothers" are the same group mentioned in 16:12. But it is equally possible, and more likely, that Paul is referring to Timothy's traveling companions.[61]

**16:12** Apollos figured prominently in the first major section of the letter in relation to Paul's discussion of the problem of divisions in the church (see 1:12; 3:4–6,22; 4:6). Although Apollos was apparently held in high esteem by some in Corinth, it is crystal clear from what Paul says about him here and in the first four chapters that Apollos was not responsible in any way for the factions that had developed in Corinth. The final occurrence in 16:12 of the formula "Now about"[62] may indicate that the Corinthians had specifically asked Paul in their letter to send Apollos, but we cannot know for sure. Garland explains, "It may be the case that they made no inquiry about Apollos in their letter, and Paul simply anticipates their disappointment that Apollos had not returned and averts any suspicion that somehow he had prevented him from returning."[63] Either way, Paul strongly encouraged Apollos to return to Corinth, but at the present time he was "quite unwilling to go." There is no indication from Paul's brief comments of why the Corinthians desired a visit from Apollos and no indication of why Apollos refused to come at the present time. Some surmise that Apollos did not return due to his disgust with the

[58] As Hays (*First Corinthians*, 287) explains, "The most direct way for any Corinthians who are offended by Paul's letter to demonstrate their displeasure will be to attack Timothy. Paul anticipates this difficult situation and calls on the Corinthian church to 'send him on his way in peace,' with support rather than hostility." So also Collins (*First Corinthians*, 596), "If the Corinthians were negatively disposed toward Timothy, this may have been because of Timothy's association with Paul. Timothy may have been a victim by transference; he may have been presumed 'guilty' by association."

[59] Gk. ἐξουθενέω, the same term used in 1 Cor 1:28; 6:4.

[60] Garland (*First Corinthians*, 761) notes that sending "in peace" is a traditional formula: see Exod 4:18; 1 Sam 20:42; 2 Kgs 5:19; Acts 15:33; 16:36; Jas 2:16.

[61] Acts 19:22 mentions that only Erastus is with Timothy, but there were surely others that Luke does not mentioned (so Fee, *First Corinthians*, 822).

[62] Gk. περὶ δὲ.

[63] Garland, *1 Corinthians*, 761.

perpetuation of factions in his name.[64] Paul's strong encouragement to Apollos to visit Corinth shows the strength of Paul's character and his absolute commitment to partnership in ministry. No jealousy existed between the two.

[64] So Robertson and Plummer (*First Corinthians*, 393), "Although St Paul was not afraid that Apollos would join the Apollos party, Apollos may have been afraid that this party would try to capture him," and "Apollos will not come while there is an Apollos party in opposition to the Apostle." So also Ciampa and Rosner (*First Corinthians*, 853), "It does seem remarkable that Paul gives no indication that Apollos sent greetings to the Corinthians, unlike Aquila and Priscilla (cf. v. 19). This lends some support to the idea that he recognized that his oratorical gifts had created a personality cult, contributing to harmful divisions that should not be reinforced." See also Thiselton, *First Corinthians*, 1332; Fitzmyer, *First Corinthians*, 623.

## SECTION OUTLINE

VIII. Letter Closing (16:13–24)
1. General Exhortations (16:13–14)
2. Commendation of the Household of Stephanas and Others (16:15–18)
3. Greetings (16:19–20)
4. Paul's Greeting and Conclusion: Warning and Affirmation of Love (16:21–24)

## VIII. LETTER CLOSING (16:13–24)

The formal letter closing includes general exhortations (16:13–14), a commendation of the household of Stephanas and the mention of two additional men (Fortunatus, Achaicus) who ministered to Paul (16:15–18), greetings from churches and individuals (16:19–20), and Paul's personal greeting and benediction (16:19–24).[1] This particular letter closing is unique among Paul's other letters in its emphasis on love (16:14,22,24),[2] the inclusion of an anathema (16:22), and the postscript following the final grace benediction (16:24).[3] Scholars debate the extent to which this section gathers up and recapitulates major themes in the letter.[4] Clearly love has been a major emphasis and explains its strong presence here. Furthermore, Paul's exhortation to submit to people like those of the household of Stephanas who exemplified such love in their devotion to the service of the saints (16:15) and the encouragement to recognize Stephanas, Fortunatus, and Achaicus as co-laborers in the gospel (16:17–18) coheres with the imitation motif so prominent in the letter (cf. esp. 4:16–17; 11:1) as well as the emphasis on unity (cf. 1:10–17).[5] The other

---

[1] On the use of the verb παρακαλῶ (16:15; "I urge you") in other Pauline letter closings see Rom 16:17–20; 1 Thess 5:12–14 (cf. also Phil 4:2–3). Cf. also 1 Cor 1:10 and 4:17.

[2] The emphasis on love in 16:14 and 22–24 brackets the letter closing.

[3] Noted by A. C. Thiselton, *The First Epistle to the Corinthians: A Commentary on the Greek Text*, NIGTC (Grand Rapids: Eerdmans, 2000), 1334.

[4] Hays comments, "At first glance, this looks like boilerplate material, for all of these admonitions could be addressed to any church anywhere. On closer inspection, however, we can see that Paul may have chosen at least some of the words in verses 13–14 with an eye towards the particular needs of the Corinthian community" (*First Corinthians* [Louisville: John Knox, 1997], 288). For an account of the rhetorical function 16:13–24 as a recapitulation of the main themes of the letter, see A. Eriksson, *Traditions as Rhetorical Proof: Pauline Argumentation in 1 Corinthians*, ConBNT 29 (Stockholm: Almqvist & Wiksell International, 1998), 284–98. For a more cautious appraisal, see D. E. Garland, *1 Corinthians*, BECNT (Grand Rapids: Baker, 2003), 764; R. E. Ciampa and B. S. Rosner, *The First Letter to the Corinthians*, PNTC (Grand Rapids: Eerdmans, 2010), 855.

[5] So Witherington, who sees 16:15–18 as "a final exhortation, a final attempt to end factiousness in the Corinthian congregation, and amplifies some key points that Paul wishes to reiterate"

exhortations (16:13) are more general and would be appropriate and applicable to a wide audience.

### 1. General Exhortations (16:13–14)

**[13]Be on your guard; stand firm in the faith; be men of courage; be strong. [14]Do everything in love.**

The first four imperatives evoke the image of the soldier who is alert, steadfast, courageous, and strong in preparation for conflict.[6] The commands "all reflect the kinds of things a general might say to his troops before they enter into battle,"[7] and, as Fee observes, they are "related in that they all call for watchfulness and steadfastness as to the faith itself (cf. 15:58)."[8] The fifth command clearly picks up on the major emphasis of love in the letter (cf. esp. 13:1–13).

The first command, "Be on your guard,"[9] appears frequently in eschatological contexts in calling for alertness and watchfulness in the light of the coming of the Lord. The verb appears frequently on the lips of Jesus toward the close of his ministry.[10] Eschatological watchfulness may also be the primary emphasis here (cf. esp. chap. 15),[11] although in light of the full context of the letter, Fee suggests the broader meaning of watchfulness regarding the enemy (1 Pet 5:8) and corrosive influences (Acts 20:31).[12] The second command, "stand firm in the faith," recalls 15:1–2,58 and is the only imperative of the first four qualified by the phrase "in the faith."[13] The meaning could be either "stand firm in *your* faith"[14] or "stand firm in *the* faith." In other words, the faith here could be understood as one's own personal faith or "the faith" in the sense of the

(*Conflict and Community in Corinth: A Socio-Rhetorical Commentary* [Grand Rapids: Eerdmans, 1994], 318).

[6] On concluding imperatives in Paul's letters see also Rom 16:17–19; 2 Cor 13:11; Phil 4:8–9; 1 Thess 5:12–22.

[7] Ciampa and Rosner, *First Corinthians*, 855.

[8] G. D. Fee, *The First Epistle to the Corinthians*, NICNT (Grand Rapids: Eerdmans, 1987), 827. Cf. 15:1, "Now, brothers, I want to remind you of the gospel I preached to you, which you received and on which you have taken your stand."

[9] Gk. γρηγορεῖτε.

[10] For all uses of the term in the New Testament, see Matt 24:42–43; 25:13; 26:38,40–41; Mark 13:34–35,37; 14:34,37–38; Luke 12:37; Acts 20:31; 1 Cor 16:13; Col 4:2; 1 Thess 5:6,10; 1 Pet 5:8; Rev 3:2–3; 16:15. On the theme of eschatological watchfulness, see also Rom 13:11–14.

[11] So Hays, *First Corinthians*, 288; R. F. Collins, *First Corinthians*, SP (Collegeville, MN: Liturgical Press, 1999), 599.

[12] Fee, *First Corinthians*, 827. So also Thiselton (*First Corinthians*, 1335), "The exhortation to keep alert need not be understood as primarily or exclusively referring to eschatological watchfulness (as in 1 Thess 5:6, 10; cf. Mark 14:34–38; Matt 24:42–43; 25:13). Paul diagnoses much of the problem of misperception of the resurrection as caused by an absence of alert, coherent reflection (15:2, 33–34). Once they have given alert attention to such matters, they must stand firm or stand fast in the gospel."

[13] Gk. στήκετε. Cf. also Gal 5:1; Phil 1:27; 4:1; 1 Thess 3:8; 2 Thess 2:15.

[14] So NRSV.

gospel traditions received. Although the latter may be the primary meaning,[15] we need not drive a wedge between the two as though they are mutually exclusive. Holding firmly to received traditions entails personal commitment and behavior.[16]

The third and fourth commands, "be men of courage" and "be strong," are complementary. The verb translated "be men of courage" occurs only here in Paul and means "to act like men." At key points in the letter Paul has reminded them of their childish behavior.[17] While some in Corinth operated under the false pretense of maturity and strength, Paul now exhorts all to be courageous and strong in the truest sense of the terms. To be strong and courageous is a common Old Testament theme.[18] As Garland explains, "This scriptural echo calls for the Corinthians to be valorous and not cowardly and reflects Paul's conviction that Christians, who are set apart to be holy (1:2; 6:11), must stand over against the extraordinary pressures of their pagan society. Acting out the convictions of their faith will lead inevitably to severe testing (cf. 10:13)."[19]

The last command, "Do everything in love," is the crowning exhortation. As Paul reminded the Corinthians so eloquently in 13:1–3, all things achieved without love are for naught. In a very real sense this fifth command "distills the message of the letter into a single sentence."[20] "All things" occurs first in the sentence for emphasis. Love, biblically defined (13:4–7), holds the key to every relational problem mentioned in the letter. Love is an especially prominent theme in chaps. 8–14, and Paul's final words of the letter are an affirmation of his love for them (16:24).

## 2. Commendation of the Household of Stephanas and Others (16:15–18)

**[15]You know that the household of Stephanas were the first converts in Achaia, and they have devoted themselves to the service of the saints. I urge you, brothers,**

---

[15] So Fee, *First Corinthians*, 828; Thiselton, *First Corinthians*, 1335.

[16] So Ciampa and Rosner (*First Corinthians*, 855), who see an element of both strong doctrinal conviction and personal behavior, "to persist in acting in a way that is consistent with faith in Christ." J. A. Fitzmyer understands the meaning as standing firm "in one's fundamental commitment to the gospel" (cf. Phil 1:27) (*First Corinthians: A New Translation with Introduction and Commentary*, AB 32 [New Haven: Yale University Press, 2008], 624). Faith is one's response to the preaching gospel. Garland (*First Corinthians*, 766) offers a balanced perspective, "In the immediate context, 'faith' refers to the traditions about Christ's death and resurrection that Paul delivered to the Corinthians (1 Cor. 15:3–5; cf. 15:14,17), but it also applies to the belief in one God over all the earth, a jealous God (8:4–6), who prohibits all forms of idolatry and sexual immorality."

[17] So also Thiselton, *First Corinthians*, 1336. Cf. 3:1; 13:10–11; 14:20.

[18] Fee (*First Corinthians*, 828) suggests that Paul recalls the language of Ps 31:24 (LXX 30:25), "Be strong and take heart, all you who hope in the LORD." The LXX employs the same two verbs, ἀνδρίζομαι and κραταιόω. Cf. also LXX Deut 31:6–7,23; Josh 1:6,9,18; 2 Sam 10:12; 1 Chr 22:13; 28:20; 2 Chr 32:7; Pss 26:14; 30:25; Dan 10:19.

[19] Garland, *1 Corinthians*, 767.

[20] Hays, *First Corinthians*, 289.

**[16]to submit to such as these and to everyone who joins in the work, and labors at it. [17]I was glad when Stephanas, Fortunatus and Achaicus arrived, because they have supplied what was lacking from you. [18]For they refreshed my spirit and yours also. Such men deserve recognition.**

In Greek, 16:15 begins with the word translated "I urge you,"[21] which the NIV relegates to the end of the verse since the content of the exhortation is given in 16:16: "to submit to such as these and to everyone who joins in the work, and labors at it."[22] In the Greek sentence structure the exhortation is followed by an explanatory parenthesis giving the reason why the Corinthians should submit to people such as those who belong to the household of Stephanas, namely, because "they have devoted themselves to the service of the saints." The first exhortation of the letter called for unity (1:10), and the parallel use of the same verb urged the Corinthians to become imitators of Paul (4:16). Here, Paul similarly enjoins the Corinthians to acknowledge those who work together and labor for the cause of the gospel. This exhortation follows hard on the fifth imperative in 16:14, "Do everything in love." Stephanas and others, who devote themselves to the service of the saints, are personal, living examples of those who genuinely care for others and who are worthy of emulation. Throughout the letter Paul has offered himself as an example marked by the values of the cross. Now he identifies others who also labor together with him in ministry. To submit to someone as Paul advises implies learning from, following, and patterning one's life accordingly. In describing the devotion of Stephanas and his household, Paul's wording is a bit unusual in the Greek and reads literally, "They appointed themselves unto the ministry of the saints."[23] But as Thiselton points out, the sense of the verb as used here, followed by the reflexive pronoun, is that "they set themselves aside" for the work. "Today we might speak of their loyal commitment to this work of service and ministry."[24] Respected leaders legitimate their spiritual authority through their service in the gospel.[25]

In his explanatory aside (16:15) Paul recalls that the household of Stephanus was among the firstfruits of Achaia; that is, they were among the first converts in this Roman province.[26] Paul mentioned in 1:16 that he personally

---

[21] Gk. παρακαλέω, the same verb used in 1:10; 4:16.

[22] Cf. also 1 Thess 5:12–13. Collins (*First Corinthians*, 605) takes note that in both places Paul describes the leader's work and toil (cf. also Rom 16:6,12; Gal 4:11; Phil 2:16; 1 Thess 3:5).

[23] The Greek verb is τάσσω, used by Paul only here and Rom 13:1 in the sense of governing authorities established by God.

[24] Thiselton, *First Corinthians*, 1339.

[25] So Hays, *First Corinthians*, 290. Paul does not offer specifics regarding their service. Apparently, their labor in the gospel was well known. The mention of their "service of the saints" recalls the mention of the collection for the saints in 16:1, but the two are probably unrelated as Barrett (*First Corinthians*, 394) notes, "Stephanas has already begun his ministry to them, whereas the collection for the Jerusalem saints is only at this point being set in motion."

[26] This does not mean that Stephanas was the very first convert, only that he was among the first of Paul's missionary efforts in Corinth, which is why he baptized them. As the "firstfruits" Stephanas and his household were harbingers of things to come. On "firstfruits" see the discus-

baptized Stephanus and his household. Stephanas was the probable bearer of the Corinthian letter to Paul and the one who would return to Corinth with Paul's response (our 1 Corinthians).[27] Stephanus may have been Paul's primary source of knowledge of many of the Corinthians' problems. The mention of Stephanas' household probably indicates that he was a person of considerable financial means. Not all wealthy members of the church were to be blamed for the rifts between the rich and the poor. Some were exemplary and worthy of recognition.[28]

Finally Paul reports that Stephanas, Fortunatus, and Achaicus arrived in Ephesus and "supplied what was lacking from you" (16:17). Robertson and Plummer capture the sense of Paul's meaning: "You cannot all of you come to me; but these excellent delegates will do quite well."[29] Or as Thiselton observes, "In modern English idiom Paul seems to say that they compensate for his missing his dear Christian brothers and sisters there."[30] These three men represented the believers in Corinth, and Paul rejoiced when they arrived. Just as these godly men were a blessing to the Corinthians, so also they refreshed Paul's spirit.[31] We do not know anything further about Fortunatus and Achaicus since there is no other mention of them in the New Testament. Great is the tribe of the "unknowns" in the kingdom of God.

### 3. Greetings (16:19–20)

**19The churches in the province of Asia send you greetings. Aquila and Priscilla greet you warmly in the Lord, and so does the church that meets at their house.**
**20All the brothers here send you greetings. Greet one another with a holy kiss.**

The letter concludes with standard greetings (16:19–22), a grace benediction (16:23), and a postscript (16:24). The final greetings in Paul's letters reveal his considerable support network in ministry.[32] First Paul conveys greetings from the

sion on 15:20,23. Thiselton (*First Corinthians*, 1338) reminds that the term firstfruits derives its main significance not primarily from being first in sequence but first in the sense of constituting a sample, pledge, or promise of more to come.

[27] So A. Robertson and A. Plummer, *A Critical and Exegetical Commentary on the First Epistle of St. Paul to the Corinthians*, 2nd ed. (Edinburg: T&T Clark, 1914), 396. This is, of course, not absolutely certain. Sosthenes is also a candidate (1:1).

[28] Witherington (*Community and Conflict*, 321) points out, "It is a mistake to assume that early Christianity only appealed to and converted the poor, slaves, and other oppressed minorities in the Greco-Roman world, especially if one is talking about Roman Corinth." Furthermore, "The Good News that Paul preached was for all people, but it often required the greatest sacrifices of the socially better-off, since they had more to give and the most to lose in honor, power, and social position by converting to a new minority religion."

[29] Robertson and Plummer, *First Corinthians*, 396.

[30] Thiselton, *First Corinthians*, 1340.

[31] See 2 Cor 7:13; Phlm 7,20.

[32] Cf. Rom 16:16–23; 2 Cor 13:12; Phil 4:21; Col 4:10–14; 2 Tim 4:21; Phlm 23. Paul does not send greetings in Galatians or 1 and 2 Thessalonians. Collins (*First Corinthians*, 607) observes

churches of Asia, Aquila and Priscilla, the church that meets in their house, and a general greeting from "all the brothers," followed by the exhortation, "Greet one another with a holy kiss." Greetings provide Paul with another means of keeping "the churches aware of, and thus in relationship to, one another."[33]

The greeting from the churches of Asia[34] provides the Corinthians with one final reminder of their solidarity with other churches, that they are one assembly of believers among many (cf. 1:2; 4:17; 7:17; 11:16; 14:33–36; 16:1). This is the only place in Paul's letters where he sends a collective greeting from all churches in one province.[35] Since pride nurtures a destructive self-sufficiency and autonomy, throughout the letter Paul "has worked to encourage the Corinthians not to think of themselves as an independent group but as an organic part of a larger movement with some common traditions, values, and practices."[36] The sooner they can recapture a wide vision of the work of the gospel, the better off they will be.

Aquila and Priscilla add their personal greetings along with the church that meets in their house.[37] Their greeting is "in the Lord," which denotes "the sphere or element in which anything exists or takes place."[38] Aquila and Priscilla are the only persons Paul mentions by name in these greetings, other than himself. They were former Corinthians of the same trade as Paul (Acts 18:1–3) who accompanied him in missionary travel (Acts 18:18). In Rom 16:3–4 Paul refers to the couple as "my fellow workers in Christ Jesus" and as those who "risked their lives for me."[39] In Acts 18:24–19:1 Luke records the interaction of Priscilla and Aquila with Apollos in providing him with more precise instruction in the Christian faith. Throughout the New Testament we find this couple in different locations. Aquila and Priscilla were already in Corinth when Paul arrived, having moved from Italy because Claudius had banned all Jews from Rome (Acts 18:2).[40] When Paul wrote 1 Corinthians they were in Ephesus,

"the greetings in 1 Corinthians are the most complex series of final greetings in all of Paul's letters" since we find greetings in the first (16:21), second (16:20b), and third person (16:19–20a).

[33] Fee, *First Corinthians*, 835.

[34] For other references to Asia in Paul's letters, see Rom 16:5; 2 Cor 1:8; 2 Tim 1:15.

[35] Noted also by Fee, *First Corinthians*; Garland, *1 Corinthians*, 771.

[36] Ciampa and Rosner, *First Corinthians*, 861.

[37] Cf. also Rom 16:5. Fitzmyer (*First Corinthians*, 628) notes the ambiguity of the Greek phrase, τῇ κατ' οἶκον, which could mean "according to their household," that is, the church made up of the household of Aquila and Priscilla, or their material house. "The latter sense is more likely, and it is to be located probably in Ephesus itself."

[38] Robertson and Plummer, *First Corinthians*, 398.

[39] Ciampa and Rosner (*First Corinthians*, 861) note that both Luke and Paul refer to Priscilla first in two out of their three references to the couple (Acts 18:2,18,26; Rom 16:3; 1 Cor 16:19; 2 Tim 4:19), "presumably because she was a woman of unusual social stature and means and/or because of her unusual gifts and abilities as a Christian leader." The only two women mentioned by name in 1 Corinthians are Priscilla and Chloe (1:11).

[40] Garland (*First Corinthians*, 771) speculates that they settled in Corinth due to promising job prospects with the Isthmian games.

presumably joining Paul in missionary work. Later they returned to Rome (Rom 16:3) and then back to Ephesus (1 Tim 4:19). In both Rome and Ephesus a church met in their house. Like Stephanas, Priscilla and Aquila were people of financial means, which enabled them to serve the church in the capacity of a patron.[41] Thiselton provides a good summary of the contribution of this outstanding couple, "In Aquila and Prisca we see a combination of true Christian devotion and sacrifice, a vision for the spread of the gospel, deep affection for Paul, and affection for communities of Christians in a network of locations that was growing into a worldwide church."[42]

The greeting from "all the brothers" is ambiguous. Fitzmyer equates the phrase with "all the Christians of Ephesus."[43] Fee thinks "it refers to Paul's various coworkers and traveling companions."[44] In some contexts in 1 Corinthians the title "brother" seems to carry a technical sense. In the letter opening and letter closing Paul identifies Sosthenes and Apollos as "the brother" (1:1; 16:12).

The final command "to greet one another with a holy kiss" represented a common practice in Paul's world. This kiss was a gesture of respect and affection and served as a outward symbol of unity among believers.[45] Paul distinguishes the kiss as "holy," signifying the status of believers in Christ (1:2). Like the command to "do everything in love" (16:14) "this is a command to get rid of their unhappy divisions and jealousies. The solemn kiss was a token of the love for one another which all Christians ought to regard as a debt (Rom. 8:8)."[46]

### 4. Paul's Greeting and Conclusion: Warning and Affirmation of Love (16:21–24)

**[21]I, Paul, write this greeting in my own hand.**
**[22]If anyone does not love the Lord—a curse be on him. Come, O Lord!**
**[23]The grace of the Lord Jesus be with you.**
**[24]My love to all of you in Christ Jesus. Amen.**

The final greeting of the letter is Paul's, which he writes with his own hand. Presumably he used a secretary, possibly Sosthenes (1:1), for the actual writing

---

[41] Fitzmyer (*First Corinthians*, 628) observes that the "house-church was one of the factors in early Christianity that aided the spread of the gospel and contributed to the growth of the church, its structure, and its life. The mention of such house-churches also implies the centrality of the home in early Christian life."

[42] Thiselton, *First Corinthians*, 1344.

[43] Fitzmyer, *First Corinthians*, 628. So also Robertson and Plummer, *First Corinthians*, 398.

[44] Fee, *First Corinthians*, 836.

[45] See Rom 16:16; 2 Cor 13:12; 1 Thess 5:26; 1 Pet 5:14 (cf. also Mark 14:45; Luke 7:45; 15:20; Acts 20:37; Phil 4:21).

[46] Robertson and Plummer, *First Corinthians*, 399. Fee (*First Corinthians*, 836) notes that in the Old Testament background the kiss was the evidence of reconciliation (Gen 33:4).

of the rest of the letter.[47] The personal signature may have been a means of authentication (cf. 2 Thess 2:1)[48] or a gesture of his love and concern for the Corinthians.[49] Paul follows his greeting with a pronouncement of curse on those who do not love the Lord (16:22a), an invocation for the Lord to come (16:22b), a grace benediction (16:23), and a final affirmation of his love for them (16:24).

Paul's firm denunciation of those who do not love the Lord strikes sensitive modern ears as rather strong, but such is the exclusivity of gospel. Christians fundamentally affirm that there is only one God, the Father, and one Lord, Jesus Christ (8:6). Paul is "perfectly clear that one's attitude toward and relationship with the Lord is of ultimate significance."[50] The curse language "Anathema!" recalls the use of the same word in 12:3, where Paul clarified that no one speaking by the Spirit of God calls Jesus "accursed." In Gal 1:8–9 Paul states twice that any who preach another gospel, including an angel from heaven or even himself, is accursed.[51] Love is the hallmark of the Christian community, yet it is a discerning love that derives its content from a commitment to the Lordship of Christ.[52] Eph 6:24 states the opposite of 1 Cor 16:22, "Grace to all who love our Lord Jesus Christ with an undying love." Whether one stands under God's curse or under his grace has to do with one's love for the Lord, which manifests itself in obedience.[53] Love for God is a central biblical theme (Deut 6:4–5; Matt 22:36–40; Rom 8:28; 1 Cor 2:9; 8:3; Eph 6:24; Jas 1:12; 2:5).

The NIV translation "Come, O Lord!" (16:22b) renders a Greek transliteration of Aramaic.[54] Since the phrase follows closely on the curse pronounced

---

[47] Cf. Rom 16:22, where Tertius identifies himself as the letter's scribe.

[48] Fee (*First Corinthians*, 837) thinks the signature "related to the questioning of his authority by some in this church."

[49] So Thiselton, *First Corinthians*, 1347; Ciampa and Rosner, *First Corinthians*, 864.

[50] Ibid. Ciampa and Rosner (865) further note the comparable Old Testament context of Ps 2:1–12, which warns the enemies of the promised Davidic king, "Kiss the Son, lest he be angry and you be destroyed in your way, for his wrath can flare up in a moment. Blessed are all who take refuge in him" (cf. also 15:24–28).

[51] The NIV translates ἀνάθεμα in Gal 1:8–9, "eternally condemned." In Rom 9:3 Paul states that he could wish himself to be accursed from Christ for the sake of his fellow Israelites.

[52] The word for love in 1 Cor 16:22 is φιλέω rather than ἀγαπάω, which is more typically of Paul (φιλέω occurs only here and Titus 3:15 in Paul's letters). This may suggest that Paul repeats a formulaic traditional saying (so Fitzmyer, *First Corinthians*, 629) but we cannot know for sure. The semantic difference between the two terms is often exaggerated. Paul's use of it here may be due to the use of the cognate term "kiss" (φίλημα) in 16:20 (so Robertson and Plummer, *First Corinthians*, 400).

[53] So Fee (*First Corinthians*, 837), "To insist on human wisdom over against the gospel of the Crucified One is to 'not love the Lord'; so with living in incest, attendance at idol feasts, and so forth. The ultimate issue for Paul, therefore, is not their obedience to his word, but their love, or lack thereof, for the Lord himself. Failure to obey him is lack of love for him; to reject him in this way is to place oneself under the *anathema*."

[54] Gk. μαράνα θά. There are different ways to understand the phrase: "Our Lord, come!"; "Our Lord has come (i.e., he is present)"; "Come, O Lord!" (NIV), that is, an eschatological prayer similar in intent to Rev 22:20.

on those who do not love the Lord (16:22a), it probably represents a fervent eschatological prayer that looks to the Lord's final triumph over all enemies. As Hays explains, "The prayer addresses the risen Lord and implores him to return—thus bringing about the consummation that Paul sketched in 15:20–28: the resurrection of the dead, the subjugation of all hostile powers, and the final triumph of God."[55] Since Paul utters the prayer, it inherently warns the Corinthians "that at any moment they may have to answer for their shortcomings."[56]

Paul began the letter by extolling God's grace, and he concludes the letter with a grace benediction.[57] The gospel, from beginning to end, is about God's grace in Christ to the undeserving. Genuine love flows from grace, and Paul's last word to the Corinthians is that he loves them.[58] He has been quite sharp and confrontational with them at various points in the letter, but along the way, he has reminded them that they are his "beloved" (4:14; 10:14; 15:58), and he wants them to know, one final time, that he loves them all, not just a select few. Paul has warned them precisely because he loves them, and if they will receive the letter as children from a loving father, they will know that Paul loves them and the Lord, for he has shown, by his own example, how to live as God's holy people (1:2) for God's glory (10:31).

---

[55] Hays, *First Corinthians*, 292.

[56] Robertson and Plummer, *First Corinthians*, 401. So also Fee, *First Corinthians*, 839.

[57] Paul always concludes his letters with a grace benediction. This differs markedly from other Hellenistic letters, which normally close with a simple, "Farewell."

[58] Cf. the similar but not identical expressions in 2 Cor 13:14; Eph 6:23.

# Selected Bibliography

## Commentaries


Allo, Ernest B. *Saint Paul: Première Épitre aux Corinthiens*. Paris: Gabalda, 1956.

Bachmann, Philipp. Der erste Brief des Paulus an die Korinther (Leipzig: Deichert, 1921).

Barclay, William. *The Letters to the Corinthians*. Philadelphia: Westminster, 1975.

Barnett, Paul. *1 Corinthians*. Fearn: Christian Focus, 2000.

Barrett, C. K. *A Commentary on the First Epistle to the Corinthians*. HNTC. New York: Harper & Row, 1968.

Blomberg, Craig L. *1 Corinthians*. NIVAC. Grand Rapids: Zondervan, 1994.

Bruce, F. F. *1 and 2 Corinthians*. NCB. Grand Rapids: Eerdmans, 1971.

Calvin, John. *The First Epistle of Paul the Apostle to the Corinthians*. Translated by John W. Fraser. Grand Rapids: Eerdmans, 1996.

Ciampa, Roy E., and Brian S. Rosner. *The First Letter to the Corinthians*. PNTC. Grand Rapids: Eerdmans, 2010.

Collins, Raymond F. *First Corinthians*. SP. Collegeville, MN: Liturgical Press, 1999.

Conzelmann, Hans. *1 Corinthians: A Critical and Historical Commentary on the Bible*. Translated by J. Leitch. Hermeneia. Philadelphia: Fortress Press, 1975.

Edwards, T. C. *A Commentary on the First Epistle to the Corinthians*. 2nd ed. London: Hodder & Stoughton, 1885.

Ellicott, Charles J. *St. Paul's First Epistle to the Corinthians: With a Critical and Grammatical Commentary*. London: Longmans, Green, and Co., 1887.

Fee, Gordon D. *The First Epistle to the Corinthians*. NICNT. Grand Rapids: Eerdmans, 1987.

Findlay, George G. "St. Paul's First Epistle to the Corinthians." 2:727–953 in *The Expositor's Greek Testament*. Edited by W. R. Nicholl. Grand Rapids: Eerdmans, 1961.

Fitzmyer, Joseph A. *First Corinthians: A New Translation with Introduction and Commentary*. AB 32. New Haven: Yale University Press, 2008.

Garland, David E. *1 Corinthians*. BECNT. Grand Rapids: Baker, 2003.

Godet, Frederick L. *Commentary on the First Epistle to the Corinthians*. 2 vols. Edinburgh: T&T Clark, 1886–87.

Grosheide, F. W. *Commentary on the First Epistle to the Corinthians*. NICNT. Grand Rapids: Eerdmans, 1953.

Hays, Richard B. *First Corinthians*. Louisville: John Knox, 1997.

Héring, Jean. *The First Epistle of Paul to the Corinthians*. Translated by A. W. Heathcote and P. J. Allcock. London: Epworth, 1962.

Hodge, Charles. *An Exposition of the First Epistle to the Corinthians*. Grand Rapids: Eerdmans, 1976.

Horsely, Richard A. *1 Corinthians*. ANTC. Nashville: Abingdon, 1998.

Kistemaker, Simon J. *Exposition of the First Epistle to the Corinthians*. New Testament Commentary. Grand Rapids: Baker, 1993.

Lightfoot, Joseph B. *Notes on the Epistles of St. Paul*. Grand Rapids: Zondervan, 1957.

MacArthur, John. *1 Corinthians*. Chicago: Moody Press, 1984.

Mare, W. H. "1 Corinthians." Pages 173–297 in *The Expositor's Bible Commentary*. Edited by Frank E. Gaebelein. Grand Rapids: Zondervan, 1976.

Meyer, H. A. W. *Critical and Exegetical Handbook to the Epistles to the Corinthians*. Winona Lake: Alpha, 1979.

Moffatt, James. *The First Epistle of Paul to the Corinthians*. MNTC. New York: Hodder & Stoughton, 1938.

Morris, Leon. *1 Corinthians*. TNTC. Grand Rapids: Eerdmans, 1985.

Murphy-O'Connor. *1 Corinthians*. New York: Doubleday, 1998.

Parry, R. S. J. *The First Epistle of Paul to the Corinthians*. Cambridge: Cambridge University Press, 1937.

Patterson, Paige. *The Troubled Triumphant Church: An Exposition of First Corinthians*. Fort Worth, TX: Seminary Hill Press, 2011.

Robertson, Archibald, and Alfred Plummer. *A Critical and Exegetical Commentary on the First Epistle of St. Paul to the Corinthians*. 2nd ed. ICC. Edinburgh: T&T Clark, 1914.

Schrage, Wolfgang. *Der Erste Brief an die Korinther*. 4 vols. Zurich: Benziger, 1991–2001.

Talbert, Charles H. *Reading Corinthians: A Literary and Theological Commentary on 1 and 2 Corinthians*. New York: Crossroad, 1987.

Thiselton, Anthony C. *The First Epistle to the Corinthians: A Commentary on the Greek Text*. NIGTC. Grand Rapids: Eerdmans, 2000.

———. *First Corinthians: A Shorter Exegetical and Pastoral Commentary*. Grand Rapids: Eerdmans, 2006.

Thrall, Margaret E. *1 and 2 Corinthians*. Cambridge: University Press, 1965.

Vaughan, Curtis, and Thomas D. Lea. *1 Corinthians*. Bible Study Commentary. Grand Rapids: Zondervan, 1983.

Weiss, Johannes. *Der Erste Korintherbrief*. Göttingen: Vandenhoeck & Ruprecht, 1910.

Witherington, Ben. *Conflict and Community in Corinth: A Socio-Rhetorical Commentary*. Grand Rapids: Eerdmans, 1994.

## Articles, Essays, Dictionaries, Monographs, and Other Works

Ackerman, David A. *Lo, I Tell You a Mystery: Cross, Resurrection, and Paraenesis in the Rhetoric of 1 Corinthians*. Princeton Theological Monograph Series 54. Eugene, OR: Pickwick, 2006.

Adams, Edward, and David G. Horrell. *Christianity at Corinth: The Quest for the Pauline Church*. Louisville: WJK, 2004.

Allard, Robert E. "'Freedom on Your Head' (1 Corinthians 11:2–16): A Paradigm for the Structure of Paul's Ethics." *WW* 30 (2010): 399–407.

Arzt, Peter. "The 'Epistolary Introductory Thanksgiving' in the Papyri and in Paul." *NovT* 36 (1994): 29–46.

Asher, Jeffrey R. "ΣΠΕΙΡΕΤΑΙ: Paul's Anthropogenic Metaphor in 1 Corinthians 15:42–44." *JBL* 120 (2001): 101–22.

Aune, David E. *Prophecy in Early Christianity and the Ancient Mediterranean World*. Grand Rapids: Eerdmans, 1983.

Bahr, G. J. "Paul and Letter Writing in the First Century." *CBQ* 28 (1966): 476–77.

Bailey, K. E. "The Structure of 1 Corinthians and Paul's Theological Method with Special Reference to 1 Cor 4:17." *NovT* 25 (1983): 152–81.

Barnett, Paul. *Paul: Missionary of Jesus*. Grand Rapids: Eerdmans, 2008.

Barré, Michael L. "To Marry or To Burn: πυροῦσθαι in 1 Cor 7:9." *CBQ* 36 (1974): 193–202.

Bartchy, S. S. Μᾶλλον χρῆσαι*: First-Century Slavery and the Interpretation of 1 Corinthians 7*. SBLDS 11. Missoula: Society of Biblical Literature, 1973.

Barton, S. C. "Paul's Sense of Place: An Anthropological Approach to Community Formation in Corinth." *NTS* 32 (1986): 225–46.

Beale, Gregory K. *The Temple and the Church's Mission: A Biblical Theology of the Dwelling Place of God*. Downers Grove: InterVarsity Press, 2004.

Bedale, Stephen. "The Meaning of *Kephalē* in the Pauline Epistles." *JTS* 5 (1954): 211–15.

BeDuhn, Jason David. "'Because of the Angels': Unveiling Paul's Anthropology in 1 Corinthians 11." *JBL* 118 (1999): 295–320.

Bernard, J. H. "The Connexion Between the Fifth and Sixth Chapters of 1 Cor." *ExpTim* 7 (1907): 433–43.

Bjerkelund, Carl J. *Parakalō: Form, Funktion und Sinn der parakalō–Sätze in den paulinischen Briefen*. Oslo: Universitetsforlaget, 1967.

Black, David Alan. *Paul, Apostle of Weakness: Astheneia and Its Cognates in the Pauline Literature*. Rev. ed. Eugene: Wipf and Stock, 2012.

Blue, Bradley. "The House Church at Corinth and the Lord's Supper: Famine, Food Supply, and the Present Distress." *CTR* 5 (1993): 221–39.

Bullmore, Michael A. *St. Paul's Theology of Rhetorical Style: An Examination of I Corinthians 2.1–5 in Light of First Century Graeco-Roman Rhetorical Culture*. San Francisco: International Scholars, 1995.

Burk, Denny. "Discerning Corinthian Slogans Through Paul's Use of the Diatribe in 1 Corinthians 6:12–20." *BBR* 18 (2008): 99–121.

Byrne, Brendon. "Sinning Against One's Own Body: Paul's Understanding of the Sexual Relationship in 1 Corinthians 6:18." *CBQ* 45 (1983): 608–16.

Byron, John. "Paul and the Background of Slavery: The *Status Quaestionis* in New Testament Scholarship." *CurBS* 3.1 (2004): 116–39.

Callan, Terrance. "Prophecy and Ecstasy in Greco-Roman Religion and in 1 Cor." *NovT* 27 (1985): 125–140.

Campbell, Barth. "Flesh and Spirit in 1 Cor. 5:5: An Exercise in Rhetorical Criticism of the NT." *JETS* 36 (1993): 331–42.

Campbell, R. Alastair. "Does Paul Acquiesce in Divisions at the Lord's Supper?" *NovT* 33 (1991): 61–70.

Caragounis, Chrys C. "'Fornication' and 'Concession'?: Interpreting 1 Cor 7, 1–7." Pages 543–49 in *The Corinthian Correspondence*. Edited by Reimund Bieringer. Leuven: University Press, 1996.

Carson, D. A. *Showing the Spirit: A Theological Exposition of 1 Corinthians 12–14*. Grand Rapids: Baker, 1987.

———. "Silent in the Churches: On the Role of Women in 1 Corinthians 14:33b–35." Pages 140–53 in *Recovering Biblical Manhood and Womanhood: A Response to Evangelical Feminism*. Edited by John Piper and Wayne Grudem. Wheaton: Crossway, 1991.

Chance, J. Bradley. "Paul's Apology to the Corinthians." *PRSt* 9 (1982): 145–55.

Chester, Stephen J. "Divine Madness? Speaking in Tongues in 1 Corinthians 14.23." *JSNT* 27 (2005): 417–46.

Cheung, Alex T. *Idol Food in Corinth: Jewish Background and Pauline Legacy*. JSNTSup 176. Sheffield: Sheffield Academic Press, 1999.

Chow, John K. *Patronage and Power: A Study of Social Networks in Corinth*. JSNTSup 75. Sheffield: Sheffield Academic Press, 1992.

Ciampa, Roy. "Revisiting the Euphemism in 1 Corinthians 7:1." *JSNT* 31 (2009): 325–38.

Ciampa, Roy E., and Brian S. Rosner, "The Structure and Argument of 1 Corinthians." *NTS* 52 (2006): 205–18.

Clarke, Andrew D. *Secular and Christian Leadership in Corinth: A Socio-Historical and Exegetical Study of 1 Corinthians 1–6*. AGJU 18. Leiden: Brill, 1993.
Collier, G. D. "'That We Might Not Crave Evil': The Structure and Argument of 1 Corinthians 10:1–13." *JSNT* 55 (1994): 55–75.
Collins, A. Y. "The Function of 'Excommunication' in Paul." *HTR* 73 (1980): 251–63.
Colson, F. H. "μετασχημάτισα in I Cor. iv. 6." *JTS* 17 (1916): 379–84.
Corley, Jeremy. "The Pauline Authorship of 1 Corinthians 13." *CBQ* 66 (2004): 256–74.
Cotterell, Peter, and Max Turner. *Linguistics and Biblical Interpretation*. Downers Grove: InterVarsity, 1989.
Cullmann, Oscar. *Christ and Time*. London: SCM, 1951.
———. *The Christology of the New Testament*. 2nd ed. London: SCM, 1963.
Dahl, Nils A. "Paul and the Church at Corinth According to 1 Corinthians 1:10–4:21." Pages 313–35 in *Christian History and Interpretation: Studies Presented to John Knox*. Cambridge: University Press, 1967.
Davidson, Richard M. *Typology in Scripture: A Study of Hermeneutical Typos Structures*. Berrien Springs, MI: Andrews University Press, 1981.
Davies, Rupert E. *Studies in 1 Corinthians*. London: Epworth, 1962.
Dawes, Gregory W. "'But If You Can Gain Your Freedom' (1 Corinthians 7:17–24)." *CBQ* 52 (1990): 681–97.
———. "The Danger of Idolatry: First Corinthians 8:7–13." *CBQ* 58 (1996): 82–98.
Deissmann, Adolf. *Light from the Ancient Near East*. London: Hodder & Stoughton, 1927.
Delobel, J. "1 Cor 11:2–16: Towards a Coherent Explanation." Pages 369–89 in *L'Apôtre Paul: Personnalité, style et conception due ministère*. BETL 73. Edited by A. Vanhoye. Leuven: Peeters, 1986.
DeMaris, Richard. "Corinthian Religion and Baptism for the Dead (1 Corinthians 15:29): Insights from Archaeology and Anthropology." *JBL* 114 (1995): 661–82.
Deming, Will. *Paul on Marriage and Celibacy: the Hellenistic Background of 1 Corinthians 7*. 2nd ed. Grand Rapids: Eerdmans, 2004.
Derrett, J. D. "Paul as Master-Builder." *EQ* 69 (1997): 129–37.
Dickson, J. P. *Mission Commitment in Ancient Judaism and in the Pauline Communities*. Tübingen: Mohr-Siebeck, 2003.
Dodd, Brian J. "Paul's Paradigmatic 'I' and 1 Corinthians 6:12." *JSNT* 59 (1995): 39–58.
Donfried, Karl P. "Justification and Last Judgment in Paul." *Int* 30 (1976): 140–52.
Downs, David J. *The Offering of the Gentiles*. Tübingen: Mohr, 2008.
Dunn, James D. G. *Jesus and the Spirit*. London: SCM, 1975.
———. "How Are the Dead Raised? With What Body Do They Come? Reflections on 1 Corinthians 15." *SwJT* (2002): 4–18.
Ekem, John D. K. "Does 1 Cor 11:2–16 Legislate for 'Head-Covering'?" *Neot* 35 (2001): 169–76.
Ellington, Dustin Watson. "Imitating Paul's Relationship to the Gospel: 1 Corinthians 8:1–11:1." *JSNT* 33 (2011): 303–15.
Elliott, J. K. "In Favour of *Kauthesomai* at 1 Corinthians 13:3." *ZNW* 62 (1971): 297–98.
———. "Paul's Teaching on Marriage in 1 Cor: Some Problems Considered." *NTS* 19 (1973): 219–25.
Ellis, E. Earle. *Prophecy and Hermeneutic in Early Christianity*. Grand Rapids: Eerdmans, 1978.
———. "Traditions in 1 Corinthians." *NTS* 32 (1986): 481–502.
———. *The Old Testament in Early Christianity*. Grand Rapids: Baker, 1991.
Engels, Donald. *Roman Corinth: An Alternative Model for the Classical City*. Chicago: University of Chicago Press, 1990.

English, Adam. "Mediated, Mediation, Unmediated: 1 Corinthians 15:29: the History of Interpretation, and the Current State of Biblical Studies." *RevExp* 99 (2002): 419–28.

Enns, P. E. "The 'Moveable Well' in 1 Cor 10:4: An Extrabiblical Tradition in an Apostolic Text." *BBR* 6 (1996): 23–38.

Eriksson, Anders. *Traditions as Rhetorical Proof: Pauline Argumentation in 1 Corinthians*. ConBNT 29. Stockholm: Almqvist & Wiksell International, 1998.

Exler, F. X. J. *The Form of the Ancient Greek Letter of the Epistolary Papyri*. Washington: Catholic University of America, 1923.

Fiore, Benjamin. "'Covert Allusion' in 1 Corinthians 1–4." *CBQ* 47 (1985): 85–102.

Fishbane, Michael. "Through the Looking Glass: Reflections on Ezek 43:3, Num 12:8, and 1 Cor 13:8." *HAR* 10 (1986): 63–75.

Fisk, Bruce N. "Eating Meat Offered to Idols: Corinthian Behavior and Pauline Response in 1 Corinthians 8–10." *TrinJ* 10 (1989): 49–70.

———. "*Porneuein* as Body Violation: The Unique Nature of Sexual Sin in 1 Corinthians 6.18." *NTS* 42 (1996): 540–58.

Fitzgerald, J. T. *Cracks in an Earthen Vessel: An Examination of the Catalogues of Hardships in the Corinthian Correspondence*. SBLDS 99. Atlanta: Scholar's Press, 1988.

Fitzmyer, Joseph A. "Another Look at *Kephalē* in 1 Corinthians 11:3." *NTS* 35 (1989): 503–11.

Forbes, Christopher. *Prophecy and Inspired Speech in Early Christianity and Its Hellenistic Environment*. WUNT 75. Tübingen: Mohr, 1995.

Fotopoulos, John. *Food Offered to Idols in Roman Corinth: A Social-Rhetorical Reconsideration of 1 Corinthians 8:1–11:1*. WUNT 151, Tübingen: Mohr Siebeck, 2003.

———. "The Rhetorical Situation, Arrangement, and Argumentation of 1 Corinthians 8:1–13: Insights into Paul's Instructions on Idol-Food in Greco-Roman Context." *GOTR* 47 (2002): 165–98.

Francis, James. "As Babes in Christ—Some Proposals Regarding 1 Cor. 3:1–3." *JSNT* 7 (1980): 41–60.

———. *Adults as Children: Images of Childhood in the Ancient World and the New Testament*. Religion and Discourse 17. Oxford: Peter Lang, 2006.

Frid, Bo. "The Enigmatic ἀλλά in 1 Cor 2:9." *NTS* 31 (1985): 603–11.

Furnish, V. P. *The Theology of the First Letter to the Corinthians*. New Testament Theology. Cambridge: Cambridge University Press, 1999.

Gagnon, Robert A. J. *The Bible and Homosexual Practice: Texts and Hermeneutics*. Nashville: Abingdon, 2001.

Gardner, Paul D. *The Gifts of God and the Authentication of a Christian: An Exegetical Study of 1 Corinthians 8–11:1*. Lanham, MD: University Press of America, 1994.

Georgi, Dieter. *Remembering the Poor: The History of Paul's Collection for Jerusalem*. Nashville: Abingdon, 1992.

Gill, David. W. J. "The Importance of Roman Portraiture for Head-Coverings in 1 Corinthians 11:2–16." *TynBul* 41 (1990): 245–60.

———. "Corinth: A Roman Colony in Achaea." *BZ* 35 (1991): 233–41.

Gillespie, Thomas. W. *The First Theologians: A Study in Early Christian Prophecy*. Grand Rapids: Eerdmans, 1994.

Gladd, Benjamin. *Revealing the Mysterion: The Use of Mystery in Daniel in Second Temple Judaism with Its Bearing on First Corinthians*. BZNW 160. Berlin: Walter de Gruyter, 2008.

———. "The Last Adam as the 'Life-Giving Spirit' Revisited: A Possible Old Testament Background of One of Paul's Most Perplexing Phrases." *WTJ* 71 (2009): 297–309.

Gooch, Peter. *Dangerous Food: 1 Corinthians 8–10 in its Context*. Waterloo, ON: Wilfrid Laurier University Press, 1993.

Goppelt, Leonard. *Typos: The Typological Interpretation of the Old Testament in the New*. Grand Rapids: Eerdmans, 1982.

Greenbury, James. "1 Corinthians 14:34–35: Evaluation of Prophecy Revisited." *JETS* 51 (2008): 721–31.

Grindheim, S. "Wisdom for the Perfect: Paul's Challenge to the Corinthian Church (1 Corinthians 2:6–16)." *JBL* 121 (2002): 689–709.

Grudem, Wayne. A. *The Gift of Prophecy in 1 Corinthians*. Lanham, MD: University Press of America, 1982.

———. "Does *Kephalē* (Head) Mean 'Source' or 'Authority over' in Greek Literature? A Survey of 2,336 Examples." *TrinJ* 6 (1985): 38–59.

———. "The Meaning of *Kephalē* ('Head'): A Response to Recent Studies." *TrinJ* 11 (1990): 3–72.

———. "1 Corinthians 14.20–25: Prophecy and Tongues as Signs of God's Attitude." *WTJ* 41 (1979): 381–96.

Gupta, Nijay K. "Which 'Body' Is a Temple (1 Corinthians 6:19)? Paul Beyond the Individual/Communal Divide." *CBQ* 72 (2010): 518–36.

Gundry, Robert H. *Sōma in Biblical Theology with Emphasis on Pauline Anthropology*. Cambridge: Cambridge University Press, 1976.

Gundry-Volf, Judith. M. "Gender and Creation in 1 Corinthians 11:2–16: A Study in Paul's Theological Method." Pages 151–71 in *Evangelium, Schriftauslegung, Kirche*. Edited by Jostein Edna, Scott Hafemann, Otfried Hofius, and Gerlinda Feine. Göttingen: Vandenhoeck & Ruprecht, 1997.

Hafemann, Scott J. *Suffering and Ministry in the Spirit*. Grand Rapids: Eerdmans, 1990.

Hall, David R. "A Disguise for the Wise: ΜΕΤΑΣΧΗΕΜΑΤΙΣΜΟΣ 1 Corinthians 4:6." *NTS* 40 (1994): 143–49.

Hall, Robert G. "Epispasm: Circumcision in Reverse." *BRev* 8 (1992): 52–57.

Harris, W. V. "'Sounding Brass' and Hellenistic Technology: Ancient Acoustical Device Clarifies Paul's Well-Known Metaphor." *BAR* 8 (1982): 38–41.

Hays, Richard B. *Conversion of the Imagination: Paul as Interpreter of Israel's Scripture*. Grand Rapids: Eerdmans, 2005.

Heil, John P. *The Rhetorical Role of Scripture in 1 Corinthians*. Studies in Biblical Literature 15. Atlanta: Society of Biblical Literature, 2005.

Hengel, Martin. *Crucifixion in the Ancient World and the Folly of the Message of the Cross*. Translated by J. Bowden. Philadelphia: Fortress Press, 1977.

Hensley, Adam D. "*Sigaō*, *Laleō*, and *Upotassō* in 1 Corinthians 14:34 in Their Literary and Rhetorical Context." *JETS* 55 (2012): 343–64.

Hill, C. E. "Paul's Understanding of Christ's Kingdom in 1 Corinthians 15:20–28." *NovT* 30 (1988): 573–89.

Hiu, Elim. *Regulations Concerning Tongues and Prophecy in 1 Corinthians 14:26–40: Relevance Beyond the Corinthian Church*. LNTS 406. London: T&T Clark, 2010.

Hodgson, R. "Paul the Apostle and First Century Tribulation Lists." *ZNW* 74 (1983): 59–80.

Hofius, O. "The Lord's Supper and the Lord's Supper Tradition: Reflections on 1 Corinthians 11:23b–25." Pages 75–115 in *One Loaf, One Cup: Ecumenical Studies of 1 Cor 11 and Other Eucharistic Texts*. Edited by B. F. Meyer. Macon, GA: Mercer University Press.

Holladay, Carl R. "1 Corinthians 13: Paul as Apostolic Paradigm." Pages 80–98 in *Greeks, Romans, and Christians: Essay in Honor of A. J. Malherbe*. Edited by David Balch, Everett Ferguson, and Wayne Meeks. Minneapolis: Fortress, 1990.

Hollander, Harm W. "Seeing God 'in a Riddle' or 'Face to Face': an Analysis of 1 Corinthians 13.12." *JSNT* 32 (2010): 395–403.

Hooker, Morna. "'Beyond the Things Which Are Written': An Examination of 1 Cor. iv.6." *NTS* 10 (1963):

———. "Authority on Her Head: An Examination of 1 Cor. xi.10." *NTS* 10 (1966): 410–16.

———. "Hard Sayings: 1 Cor. 3:2." *Theology* 69 (1966): 19–22.

Horrell, David G. *The Social Ethos of the Corinthian Correspondence: Interests and Ideology from 1 Corinthians to 1 Clement*. Edinburgh: T&T Clark, 1996.

———. "Theological Principle or Christological Praxis? Pauline Ethics in 1 Corinthians 8:1–11:1." *JSNT* 67 (1997): 83–114.

Horsely, Richard A. *Wisdom and Spiritual Transcendence at Corinth: Studies in First Corinthians*. Eugene: Cascade Books, 2008.

Hoskins, Paul M. "The Use of Biblical and Extrabiblical Parallels in the Interpretation of First Corinthians 6:2–3." *CBQ* 63 (2001): 287–97.

Hull, Michael F. *Baptism on Account of the Dead (1 Cor 15:29): An Act of Faith in the Resurrection*. Atlanta: Society of Biblical Literature, 2005.

Hultgren, Stephen J. "The Origin of Paul's Doctrine of the Two Adams in 1 Corinthians 15:45–49." *JSNT* 25 (2003): 343–70.

Hurd, J. C. *The Origin of 1 Corinthians*. New York: Seabury, 1965.

Hurley, James B. "Did Paul Require Veils or the Silence of Women: A Consideration of 1 Cor 11:2–16 and 14:33b–36." *WTJ* 35 (1973): 190–220.

Hutson, Christopher Roy. "Was Timothy Timid? On the Rhetoric of Fearlessness (1 Corinthians 16:10–11) and Cowardice (2 Timothy 1:7)." *BR* 42 (1997): 58–73.

Instone-Brewer, David. *Divorce and Remarriage in the Bible: The Social and Literary Context*. Grand Rapids: Eerdmans, 2002.

Isaksson, Abel. *Marriage and Ministry in the New Temple: A Study with Special Reference to Mt. 19.13–12 [sic] and 1 Cor. 11.3–16*. ASNU 24. Lund: Gleerup, 2002.

Jeremias, Joachim. "Flesh and Blood Cannot Inherit the Kingdom of God." NTS 2 (1955): 151–59.

———. *The Eucharistic Words of Jesus*. London: SCM, 1966.

Johanson, B. C. "Tongues, a Sign for Unbelievers." *NTS* 25 (1979): 180–203.

Johnson, Luke Timothy. *The Writings of the New Testament: An Interpretation*. Rev ed. Minneapolis: Fortress Press, 1999.

Jones, Peter R. "1 Corinthians 15:8: Paul the Last Apostle." *TynBul* 36 (1985): 3–34.

Judge, Edwin A. *The Social Pattern of the Christian Groups in the First Century*. London: Tyndale, 1960.

Kelly, J. N. D. *Early Christian Creeds*. London: Longmans, 1950.

Kempthorne, R. "Incest and the Body of Christ: A Study of 1 Corinthians vi. 12–20." *NTS* 14 (1967): 568–74.

Kim, Chan-Hie. *Form and Function of the Familiar Letter of Recommendation*. SBLDS 4. Missoula: Scholars Press, 1972.

Kim, Jung Hoon. *The Significance of Clothing Imagery in the Pauline Corpus*. London: Clark, 2004.

Kinman, Brent. "'Appoint the Despised as Judges!' (1 Corinthians 6:4)." *TynBul* 48 (1997): 345–54.

Klein, George L. "Hosea 3:1–3—Background to 1 Cor 6:19b–20?" *CTR* 3 (1988): 373–75.

Klein, William M. "Noisy Gong or Acoustic Vase: A Note on 1 Corinthians 13:1." *NTS* 32 (1986): 286–89.

Kloha, Jeffrey. "Idols, Eating, and Rights (1 Cor. 8:1–11:1): Faithful and Loving Witness in a Pluralistic Culture." *Concordia Journal* (2004): 178–202.
Klutz, Todd E. "Re-reading 1 Corinthians after Rethinking 'Gnosticism'." *JSNT* 26 (2003): 193–216.
Koet, Bart J. "The Old Testament Background to 1 Cor 10,7–8." Pages 607–15 in *The Corinthian Correspondence*. BETL 75. Edited by Reimund Bieringer. Leuven: University Press, 1996.
Kovacs, Judith L. *1 Corinthians: Interpreted by Early Christian Commentators*. The Church's Bible. Grand Rapids: Eerdmans, 2005.
Kreitzer, L. Joseph. *Jesus and God in Paul's Eschatology*. JSNT 19. Sheffield: JSOT Press, 1987.
———. "1 Corinthians 10:4 and Philo's Flinty Rock." *CV* 35 (1993): 109–126.
Kubo, Sakae. "1 Corinthians 7:16: Optimistic or Pessimistic?" *NTS* 24 (1977): 539–44.
Kuck, David W. *Judgment and Community Conflict: Paul's Use of Apocalyptic Judgment Language in 1 Corinthians 3:5–4:5*. NovTSup 66. Leiden: Brill, 1992.
Kurek-Chomycz, Dominika A. "Whose Control over Whose Will? 1 Cor 7:36–38 in Patristic Exegesis." Pages 245–52 in *Studia Patristica*. Leuven: Peeters, 2006.
Lakey, Michael J. *Image and Glory of God: 1 Corinthians 11:2–16 as a Case Study in Bible, Gender and Hermeneutics*. London: T&T Clark, 2010.
Lampe, Peter. "Theological Wisdom and the 'Word about the Cross': The Rhetorical Scheme in 1 Corinthians 1–4." *Int* 44 (1990): 117–31.
Lanci, J. R. *A New Temple for Corinth: Rhetorical and Archaeological Approaches to Pauline Imagery*. New York: Lang, 1997.
Lanier, David E. "With Stammering Lips and Another Tongue: 1 Cor 14:20–22 and Isa 28:11–12." *CTR* 5 (1991): 259–85.
Litfin, Duane A. *St. Paul's Theology of Proclamation: 1 Corinthians 1–4 and Greco-Roman Rhetoric*. Cambridge: Cambridge University Press, 1994.
Lösch, Stefan. "Christliche Frauen in Corinth (1 Cor 11.2–16): Ein neuer Lösungsversuch." *TQ* 127 (1947): 216–61.
MacGregor, Kirk R. "1 Corinthians 15:3b–6a, 7 and the Bodily Resurrection of Jesus." *JETS* 49 (2006): 225–334.
Malherbe, A. J. "The Beasts at Ephesus." *JBL* 87 (1968): 71–80.
Malone, Andrew S. "Burn or Boast? Keeping the 1 Corinthians 13, 3 Debate in Balance." *Bib* 90 (2009): 400–406.
Marshall, I. Howard. *Last Supper and Lord's Supper*. Grand Rapids: Eerdmans, 1981.
Marshall, Peter. *Enmity in Corinth: Social Conventions in Paul's Relation with the Corinthians*. WUNT 23. Tübingen: Mohr, 1987.
Marshall, William W., Craig Blomberg, and Robert L Hubbard Jr. *Introduction to Biblical Interpretation*. 2nd ed. Nashville: Thomas Nelson, 2003.
Martin, Dale B. "Tongues of Angels and Other Status Indicators." *JAAR* 59 (1991): 547–89.
Martin, Ralph P. *The Spirit and the Congregation: Studies in 1 Corinthians 12–15*. Grand Rapids: Eerdmans, 1984.
Martini, Jeromey. "An Examination of Paul's Apocalyptic Narrative in First Corinthians 15:20–28." *CTR* 8 (2011): 57–70.
Massey, Preston T. "The Meaning of κατακαλύπτω and κατὰ κεφαλῆς ἔχων in 1 Corinthians 11.2–16." *NTS* 53 (2007): 502–23.
Meeks, Wayne A. "'And Rose Up to Play': Midrash and Paraenesis in 1 Cor 10:1–22." *JSNT* 16 (1982): 64–78.
———. *The First Urban Christians: The Social World of the Apostle Paul*. New Haven: Yale University Press, 1983.

Meggit, Justin J. *Paul, Poverty, and Survival*. Edinburgh: T&T Clark, 1998.

Merkle, Benjamin L. "Paul's Arguments from Creation in 1 Corinthians 11:8–9 and 1 Timothy 2:13–14: An Apparent Inconsistency Answered." *JETS* 49 (2006): 527–48.

Mitchell, Alan Christopher. "Rich and Poor in the Courts of Corinth: Litigiousness and Status in 1 Cor 6:1–11." *NTS* 39 (1993): 562–86.

Mitchell, Margaret Mary. "Concerning περὶ δὲ in 1 Corinthians." *NovT* 31 (1989): 229–56.

———. *Paul and the Rhetoric of Reconciliation: An Exegetical Investigation of the Language and Composition of 1 Corinthians*. Louisville: Westminster John Knox, 1991.

———. *Paul, the Corinthians, and the Birth of Christian Hermeneutics*. Cambridge: Cambridge University Press, 2010.

Moiser, Jeremy. "A Reassessment of Paul's View of Marriage with Reference to 1 Cor 7." *JSNT* 18 (1983): 103–22.

Munck, Johannes. "The Church without Factions." Pages 135–67 in *Paul and the Salvation of Mankind*. Translated by Frank Clarke. London: SCM, 1959.

Murphy-O'Connor, Jerome. "Corinthian Slogans in 1 Cor 6:12–20." *CBQ* 40 (1978): 391–96.

———. *St. Paul's Corinth: Texts and Archaeology*. Glazier: Wilmington, 1983.

———. "Interpolations in 1 Cor." *CBQ* 48 (1986): 81–94.

———. "1 Corinthians 11:2–16 Once Again." *CBQ* 50 (1988):

———. *Paul: A Critical Life*. Oxford: Oxford University Press, 1996.

———. "Interpolations in 1 Corinthians." Pages 257–87 in *Keys to First Corinthians: Revisiting the Major Issues*. New York: Oxford University Press, 2009.

———. *Keys to First Corinthians: Revisiting the Major Issues*. Oxford: Oxford University Press, 2009.

Neirynck, F. "The Sayings of Jesus in 1 Corinthians." Pages 141–76 in *The Corinthian Correspondence*. Edited by Reimund Bieringer. BETL 75. Leuven: University Press, 1996.

Newman, Cary C. *Paul's Glory-Christology: Tradition and Rhetoric*. Leiden: Brill, 1992.

Niccum, C. "The Voice of the Manuscripts on the Silence of Women: The External Evidence for 1 Cor 14:34–35." *NTS* 43 (1997): 242–55.

Nickelsburg, George W. E. "An ἔκτρωμα, Though Appointed from the Womb: Paul's Apostolic Self-Description in 1 Corinthians 15 and Galatians 1." *HTR* 79 (1986): 198–205.

Nickle, Keith F. *The Collection: A Study in Paul's Strategy*. SBT 48. London: SCM, 1966.

O Brien, P. T. *Introductory Thanksgivings in the Letters of Paul*. Leiden: Brill, 1977.

O'Day, Gail R. "Jeremiah 9:22–23 and 1 Corinthians 1:26–31: A Study in Intertextuality." *JBL* 109 (1990): 259–67.

O'Neil, J. C. "1 Corinthians 15:29." *ExpTim* 91 (1979): 310–11.

Odell-Scott, D. W. "Let the Women Speak in Church: An Egalitarian Interpretation of 1 Cor 14:33b–36." *BTB* (1983): 90–93.

———. "In Defence of an Egalitarian Interpretation of 1 Cor 14:34–6." *BTB* 17 (1987): 100–103.

Orr, William F., and James A. Walther. *1 Corinthians*. AB 32. Garden City: Doubleday, 1976.

Ortlund, Dane. "'Power Is Made Perfect in Weakness' (2 Cor. 12:9): A Biblical Theology of Strength through Weakness." *Presb* 36 (2010): 86–108.

Oster, Richard. "When Men Wore Veils to Worship: The Historical Context of 1 Corinthians 11.4." *NTS* 34 (1988): 481–505.

Paige, Terrence. "1 Corinthians 12:2: A Pagan Pompe?" *JSNT* 44 (1991): 57–65.

Pao, David W. *Thanksgiving: An Investigation of a Pauline Theme*. Edited by D.A. Carson. New Studies in Biblical Theology. Downers Grove: InterVarsity Press, 2002.

Pascuzzi, Maria. "Baptism-Based Allegiance and the Divisions in Corinth: a Reexamination of 1 Corinthians 1:13–17." *CBQ* 71 (2009): 813–29.

Patrick, James E. "Living Rewards for Dead Apostles: 'Baptised for the Dead' in 1 Corinthians 15.29." *NTS* 52 (2006): 71–85.

Patterson, Stephen J. "A Rhetorical Gem in a Rhetorical Treasure: the Origin and Significance of 1 Corinthians 13:4–7." *BTB* 39 (2009): 87–94.

Payne, P. B. "Fuldensis, Sigla for Variants in Vaticanus, and 1 Cor 14:34–35." *NTS* 41 (1995): 240–62.

Perriman, A. C. "The Head of a Woman: The Meaning of *Kephalē* in 1 Cor 11:3." *JTS* 45 (1994): 602–22.

Petzer, J. H. "Contextual Evidence in Favor of καυχήσομαι in 1 Corinthians 13:3." *NTS* 35 (1989): 229–53.

Pfitzner, Victor C. *Paul and the Agon Motif: Traditional Athletic Imagery in the Pauline Literature*. Leiden: Brill, 1967.

Phipps, W. E. "Is Paul's Attitude toward Sexual Relations Contained in 1 Cor. 7.1?" *NTS* 28 (1982): 125–31.

Pickett, R. *The Cross in Corinth: The Social Significance of the Death of Jesus*. JSNTSup 143. Sheffield: Sheffield Academic Press, 1997.

Pogoloff, Stephen M. *Logos and Sophia: The Rhetorical Situation of 1 Corinthians*. Atlanta, GA: Scholars Press, 1992.

Porter, Stanley E. "Peace, Reconciliation." Pages 695–99 in *Dictionary of Paul and His Letters*. Edited by Gerald F. Hawthorne, Ralph P. Martin, and Daniel G. Reid. Downers Grove: InterVarsity, 1993.

Portier-Young, Anathea. "Tongues and Cymbals: Contextualizing 1 Corinthians 13:1." *BTB* 35 (2005): 99–105.

Prior, Michael. *Paul the Letter Writer*. JSNTSup 23. Sheffield: JSOT Press, 1989.

Richards, E. Randolph. *The Secretary in the Letters of Paul*. WUNT 2:42. Tübingen: Mohr, 1992.

Richardson, Peter. "'I Say, Not the Lord': Personal Opinion, Apostolic Authority, and the Development of Early Christian Halakah." *TynBul* 31 (1980): 65–86.

———. "Judgment in Sexual Matters in 1 Corinthians 6:1–11." *NovT* 25 (1983): 37–58.

Robinson, J. A. T. *The Body: A Study in Pauline Theology*. London: SCM, 1966.

Rosner, Brian S. "'οὐχὶ μᾶλλον ἐπενθήσατε': Corporate Responsibility in 1 Corinthians 5." *NTS* 38 (1992): 470–73.

———. "A Possible Quotation of Test. Reuben 5:5 in 1 Corinthians 6:18a." *JTS* 43 (1992): 123–27.

———. *Paul, Scripture and Ethics: a Study of 1 Corinthians 5–7*. AGJU 22. Leiden: Brill, 1994.

———. *Greed as Idolatry: The Origin and Meaning of a Pauline Metaphor*. Grand Rapids: Eerdmans, 2007.

Sanders, Todd K. "A New Approach to 1 Corinthians 13:1." *NTS* 36 (1990): 614–18.

Sandnes, K. O. "Prophecy—a Sign for Believers (1 Cor 14, 20–25)." *Bib* 77 (1996): 1–15.

Savage, Timothy B. *Power Through Weakness: Paul's Understanding of the Christian Ministry in 2 Corinthians*. SNTSMS 86. Cambridge: Cambridge University Press, 1996.

Schatzmann, Siegfried S. *A Pauline Theology of Charismata*. Peabody, MA: Hendrickson, 1987.

———. "Purpose and Function of Gifts in 1 Corinthians." *SwJT* 45 (2002): 53–68.

Schreiner, Thomas R. *Paul, Apostle of God's Glory in Christ: A Pauline Theology*. Downers Grove: InterVarsity, 2001.

Schreiner, Thomas R., and Matthew R. Crawford, eds. *The Lord's Supper: Remembering and Proclaiming Christ Until He Comes*. NAC Studies in Bible and Theology. Nashville: B&H, 2010.

Schreiner, Thomas R., and Shawn D. Wright, eds. *Believer's Baptism: Sign of the New Covenant in Christ*. NAC Studies in Bible and Theology. Nashville: B&H, 2006.

Schubert, P. *Form and Function of the Pauline Thanksgivings*. BZNW 20. Berlin: Topelmann, 1939.

Schwiebert, Jonathan. "Table Fellowship and the Translation of 1 Corinthians 5:11." *JBL* 127 (2008): 159–64.

Shogren, Gary S. "How Did They Suppose 'the Perfect' Would Come? 1 Corinthians 13:8–12 in Patristic Exegesis." *Journal of Pentecostal Theology* 15 (1999): 99–121.

Sigountos, James G. "The Genre of 1 Corinthians 13." *NTS* 40 (1994): 246–60.

Smit, Joop F. M. "Two Puzzles: 1 Corinthians 12.31 and 13.3: A Rhetorical Solution." *NTS* 39 (1993): 246–64.

———. "Tongues and Prophecy: Deciphering 1 Cor 14, 22." *Bib* 75 (1994): 175–90.

———. "'Do Not Be Idolaters': Paul's Rhetoric in First Corinthians 10:1–22." *NovT* 39 (1997): 40–53.

———. "The Rhetorical Disposition of First Corinthians 8:7–9:27." *CBQ* 59 (1997): 476–91.

———. *"About the Idol Offerings": Rhetoric, Social Context, and Theology of Paul's Discourse in 1 Corinthians 8:1–11:1*. CBET 27. Leuven: Peeters, 2000.

———. "'What Is Apollos? What Is Paul?' in Search for the Coherence of First Corinthians 1:10–4:21." *NovT* 44 (2002): 231–51.

Smith, Barry D. "The Problem with the Observance of the Lord's Supper in the Corinthian Church." *BBR* 20 (2010): 517–43.

Smith, Jay E. "Slogans in 1 Corinthians." *BSac* 167 (2010): 68–88.

Son, Sang-Won. *Corporate Elements in Pauline Anthropology: A Study of the Selected Terms, Idioms, and Concepts in the Light of Paul's Usage and Background*. AnBib 148. Rome: Editrice Pontificio Istituto Biblico, 2001.

Stendahl, Krister. "Glossolalia—the NT Evidence." Pages 109–24 in *Paul Among Jews and Gentiles*. London: SCM, 1977.

Stewart, David R. "A Conciliatory Principle in 1 Cor. 4:6." *NovT* 29 (1987): 320–46.

South, James T. "A Critique of the 'Curse/Death' Interpretation of 1 Cor. 5:1–8." *NTS* 39 (1993): 539–61.

Stanley, Christopher D. *Paul and the Language of Scripture: Citation Technique in the Pauline Epistles and Contemporary Literature*. SNTSMS 74. Cambridge: Cambridge University Press, 1992.

Still, E. Coye. "Divisions over Leaders and Food Offered to Idols: The Parallel Thematic Structures of 1 Corinthians 4:6–21 and 8:1–11:1." *TynBul* 55.1 (2004): 17–41.

Still, Todd D. *Jesus and Paul Reconnected: Fresh Pathways into an Old Debate*. Grand Rapids: Eerdmans, 2007.

Stowers, Stanley K. *Letter-Writing in Greco-Roman Antiquity*. Philadelphia: Westminster, 1986.

———. "Paul on the Use and Abuse of Reason." Pages 253–86 in *Greeks, Romans, and Christians: Essays in Honour of J. Malherbe*. Edited by D. L. Balch, Everett Ferguson, and Wayne Meeks. Minneapolis: Augsburg, 1990.

Sweet, J. P. M. "A Sign for Unbelievers: Paul's Attitude to Glossolalia." *NTS* 13 (1966): 240–57.

Terry, Ralph B. *A Discourse Analysis of First Corinthians*. Dallas: University of Texas Press, 1995.

Theissen, Gerd. *The Social Setting of Pauline Christianity: Essays on Corinth*. Translated by J. H. Schutz. Philadelphia: Fortress Press, 1982.

Thielman, Frank. *Theology of the New Testament: A Canonical and Synthetic Approach*. Grand Rapids: Zondervan, 2005.

Thiselton, Anthony C. "The Meaning of ΣAPX in 1 Corinthians 5:5: A Fresh Approach in the Light of Logical and Semantic Factors." *SJT* 26 (1973): 204–28.

———. "Realised Eschatolgy in Corinth." *NTS* 24 (1978): 510–26.

Toussaint, S. D. "1 Corinthians Thirteen and the Tongues Question." *BSac* 120 (1963): 311–16.

Treier, Daniel J. "Typology." Pages 823–27 in *Dictionary for Theological Interpretation of the Bible*. Edited by Kevin J. Vanhoozer, Craig G. Bartholomew, Daniel J. Treier, and N. T. Wright. Grand Rapids: Baker, 2005.

Verbrugge, Verlyn. "1 Corinthians." Pages 239–414 in *Galatians-Romans*. Expositor's Bible Commentary. Edited by Tremper Longman and David E. Garland. Rev. ed. Grand Rapids: Zondervan, 2008.

Via, Dan Otto, and Robert A. J. Gagnon. *Homosexuality and the Bible: Two Views*. Minneapolis: Fortress Press, 2003.

Waaler, Erik. *The Shema and the First Commandment in First Corinthians: An Intertextual Approach to Paul's Re-reading of Deuteronomy*. WUNT 253. Tübingen: Mohr Siebeck, 2008.

Walker, William O. "1 Cor. 2:6–16: A Non-Pauline Interpolation?" *JSNT* 47 (1992): 75–94.

———. *Interpolations in the Pauline Letters*. JSNTSup 213. London: Sheffield Academic Press, 2001.

———. "1 Corinthians 15:29–34 as a Non-Pauline Interpolation." *CBQ* 69 (2007): 84–103.

Wallace, Daniel B. *Greek Grammar Beyond the Basics: An Exegetical Syntax of the New Testament*. Grand Rapids: Zondervan, 1996.

Welborn, L. L. *Politics and Rhetoric in the Corinthian Epistles*. Macon, GA: Mercer University Press, 1997.

Wenham, David. "Whatever Went Wrong in Corinth?" *ExpTim* 108 (1997): 137–41.

White, J. L. *Light from Ancient Letters*. FF. Philadelphia: Fortress Press, 1986.

White, Joel R. "'Baptized on Account of the Dead': The Meaning of 1 Corinthians 15:29 in Its Context." *JBL* 116 (1997): 487–99.

Widmann, Martin. "1 Kor 2 6–16: Ein Einspruch gegen Paulus." *ZNW* 70 (1979): 44–53.

Williams, Guy. "An Apocalyptic and Magical Interpretation of Paul's 'Beast Fight' in Ephesus (1 Corinthians 15:32)." *JTS* 57 (2006): 42–56.

Williams, H. H. Drake. *The Wisdom of the Wise: The Presence and Function of Scripture within 1 Cor. 1:18–3:23*. AGJU 49. Leiden: Brill, 2001.

Willis, Wendell. *Idol Meat in Corinth: The Pauline Argument in 1 Corinthians 8 and 10*. Chico, CA: Scholars Press, 1985.

———. "'The Mind of Christ' in 1 Corinthians 2, 16." *Bib* 70 (1989): 110–22.

———. "1 Corinthians 8–10: A Retrospective after Twenty-Five Years." *ResQ* 49 (2007): 103–12.

Winter, Bruce W. "The Lord's Supper at Corinth: An Alternative Reconstruction." *RTR* 37 (1978): 73–82.

———. "Secular and Christian Responses to Corinthian Famines." *TynBul* 40 (1989): 86–106.

———. "Civil Litigation in Secular Corinth and the Church: The Forensic Background to 1 Cor 6:1–8." *NTS* 37 (1991): 559–72.

_____. *Seek the Welfare of the City: Christians as Benefactors and Citizens*. First-Century Christians in the Graeco-Roman World. Grand Rapids: Eerdmans, 1994.

———. "The Achaean Federal Imperial Cult II: The Corinthian Church." *TynBul* 46 (1995): 169–78.

———. "1 Corinthians 7:6–7: A Caveat and a Framework for 'The Sayings' in 7:8–24." *TynBul* 48 (1997): 57–65.

———. *Philo and Paul among the Sophists*. SNTSMS 96. Cambridge: Cambridge University Press, 1997.

———. "Puberty or Passion? The Referent of ὑπέρακμος in 1 Corinthians 7:36." *TynBul* 49 (1998): 71–89.

———. *After Paul Left Corinth: The Influence of Secular Ethics and Social Change*. Grand Rapids: Eerdmans, 2001.

Witherington, Ben. "Not So Idle Thoughts about Eidolothuton." *TynBul* 44.2 (1993): 237–54.

Wolter, Michael. "Let No One Seek His Own, but Each One the Other's (1 Corinthians 10, 24): Pauline Ethics According to 1 Corinthians." Pages 199–217 in *Identity, Ethics, and Ethos in the New Testament*. Berlin: Walter de Gruyter, 2006.

Wright, N. T. *The Climax of the Covenant: Christ and the Law in Pauline Theology*. Minneapolis: Fortress Press, 1991.

———. *The Resurrection of the Son of God*. Minneapolis: Fortress Press, 2003.

Wuellner, Wilhelm. "The Sociological Implications of 1 Corinthians 1:26–28 Reconsidered." Pages 666–73 in *Studia Evangelica*. Edited by E. A. Livingstone. Berlin: Akademie Verlag, 1973.

Yarbrough, O. Larry. *Not Like the Gentiles: Marriage Rules in the Letters of Paul*. SBLDS 80. Atlanta: Scholars Press, 1985.

Zaas, P. "Catalogues and Context: 1 Corinthians 5 and 6." *NTS* 34 (1988): 622–29.

# Name Index


Ackerman, D. A. *438*
Adams, E. *18, 48, 75, 438*
Allard, R. E. *438*
Allo, E. B. *437*
Arzt, P. *438*
Asher, J. R. *405–6, 438*
Aune, D. E. *290, 438*

Bachmann, P. *437*
Bahr, G. J. *36, 438*
Bailey, K. E. *47, 438*
Barclay, W. *437*
Barnett, P. *437–38*
Barré, M. L. *171, 438*
Barrett, C. K. *22–24, 45, 54, 57, 60, 65, 67–68, 70–73, 88, 95, 97, 118, 121, 126, 132, 134, 136, 143–44, 149–50, 153, 167–69, 171–72, 175, 177, 179–81, 185–86, 188, 191, 201, 210, 214, 219, 221, 223, 227–28, 231, 240, 242, 244, 247, 259, 263, 272–73, 282, 287–88, 295, 297, 304, 306–7, 312, 314, 319, 327, 331–32, 338, 341, 344, 351, 353, 362–63, 370, 376, 382, 388, 390–91, 399, 403, 405, 408–10, 414, 419, 423, 437*
Bartchy, S. S. *438*
Barton, S. C. *439*
Baur, F. C. *48*
Beale, G. K. *102, 105, 439*
Bedale, S. *258, 439*
BeDuhn, J. D. *263, 439*
Bernard, J. H. *142, 439*
Bjerkelund, C. J. *51, 439*
Black, D. A. *81, 439*
Blomberg, C. L. *22, 88, 151, 161, 179, 184, 191, 201, 211, 229, 251, 253, 257, 263, 283, 297, 299, 301, 358, 361, 373, 392, 437*
Blue, B. *186, 439*
Bruce, F. F. *77, 86, 88, 98, 136, 153, 171, 176, 212, 250, 259, 263, 266, 301, 386, 405, 210*
Bullmore, M. A. *439*
Burk, D. *439*
Byrne, B. *151, 159, 439*
Byron, J. *181, 439*

Callan, T. *439*
Calvin, J. *437*
Campbell, B. *138, 439*
Campbell, R. A. *269, 439*
Caragounis, C. C. *164–65, 167, 439*
Carson, D. A. *316, 356–59, 439*
Chance, J. B. *49, 439*
Chester, S. J. *344–45, 439*
Cheung, A. T. *195, 198, 201, 238, 246, 248–49, 439*
Chow, J. K. *133, 439*
Ciampa, R. E. *22–23, 34, 36, 38–41, 44, 46–47, 50–51, 53, 55–57, 59–60, 62–64, 66–72, 74, 78, 85–86, 88, 90, 95, 98, 102–3, 105, 108–9, 118, 133–34, 138–41, 146, 151, 155–58, 160, 163–67, 170, 176–77, 180–81, 185, 187, 189, 191, 193, 200, 203–4, 206, 208, 212, 214, 216–19, 221, 226, 229, 231, 234, 238–43, 246, 248, 250, 253, 256–59, 261–66, 272, 275, 277–78, 282, 290–91, 295–96, 299–300, 303, 307–9, 312–16, 318–19, 322–23, 325, 327, 329–30, 334, 336, 338–41, 344, 349–53, 358, 360–62, 365–68, 372–73, 375–76, 385, 388–89, 394–95, 397, 401, 404–9, 411–14, 417–18, 420, 426–29, 432, 434, 437, 439*
Clarke, A. D. *133, 440*
Collier, G. D. *225–26, 230–31, 233–34, 440*
Collins, A. Y. *440*
Collins, R. F. *22, 34–35, 37, 40, 42, 44–45, 51–54, 56–57, 60, 63, 70, 74, 80, 96, 107, 109–11, 117, 120, 122, 129, 138, 150–51, 154–55, 158, 170, 172–73, 177, 180, 193, 221, 234, 238, 240, 242, 246–48, 261, 264, 284, 294, 300, 303, 305–12, 314–15, 318, 328, 333, 336, 338, 340, 343, 345, 347–49, 352, 354, 357, 363, 366–67, 374–75, 377, 381, 384–85, 390, 393, 397, 399–400, 403–4, 408, 410–11, 413–15, 419, 421–22, 424–25, 428, 430–31, 437*
Colson, F. H. *440*
Conzelmann, H. *57, 84, 86, 118, 123, 136, 153, 163, 170, 176, 193, 210, 222, 327, 348, 371, 396, 405, 437*
Corley, J. *440*
Cotterell, P. *259, 440*

Crawford, M. R. *270, 447*
Cullmann, O. *88, 284, 440*

Dahl, N. A. *48, 440*
Davidson, R. M. *226, 440*
Davies, R. E. *101, 440*
Dawes, G. W. *178, 199, 440*
Deissmann, A. *74, 440*
Delobel, J. *254–55, 265, 440*
DeMaris, R. *393, 440*
Deming, W. *161, 440*
Derrett, J. D. *440*
Dodd, B. J. *153–54, 440*
Donfried, K. P. *138, 440*
Downs, D. J. *418, 440*
Dunn, J. D. G. *284, 440*

Edwards, T. C. *263–64, 437*
Ekem, J *440*
Ellicott, C. J. *437*
Ellington, D. *440*
Elliot, M. *309*
Elliott, J. K. *440*
Ellis, E. E. *84, 226, 290, 440*
Engels, D. *18–19, 440*
English, A. *393, 441*
Enns, P. E. *441*
Eriksson, A. *206, 427, 441*
Exler, F. X. J. *33, 441*

Fee, G. D. *19, 22, 35–37, 40, 42, 44–45, 48–49, 51, 53, 55, 57–58, 61–62, 64–65, 67–71, 76, 80, 84, 88–94, 97–99, 102, 105–6, 111–14, 116–27, 131–32, 134–35, 137–39, 141, 143, 145–49, 153–57, 161, 164, 167, 169–71, 174, 176, 179–81, 184–85, 187, 189, 193, 200, 203–4, 210, 212, 221, 226–27, 231, 235–36, 239–42, 245–46, 259, 266–68, 271, 275, 277–78, 280–82, 284, 286–87, 290, 295–96, 297, 299, 303–4, 307–8, 311–14, 316, 318, 322, 324, 327, 329–30, 332, 334–35, 339, 342, 344–46, 355–57, 362–63, 366–67, 369–71, 373–76, 378, 380–83, 389, 391–92, 397, 399–402, 404–11, 415, 419–20, 422–23, 424–25, 428–29, 432–35, 437*
Findlay, G. *437*
Fiore, B. *116–17, 441*
Fishbane, M. *318, 441*
Fisk, B. N. *157–58, 200, 204, 441*
Fitzgerald, J. T. *121–22, 441*
Fitzmyer, J. A. *38, 40–41, 45, 48–49, 55, 63–64, 70, 80, 87–90, 92, 112, 114, 116, 119, 121–22, 138, 153, 158, 193, 258–59, 263–64, 303–4, 315, 318, 324–25, 331–32, 334–35, 339–40, 349–50, 357, 363, 366–67, 369–70, 373, 375–77, 380, 383, 390, 393, 396, 401–2, 406–7, 411, 413, 418–20, 426, 429, 432–34, 437, 441*
Forbes, C. *290–91, 351, 360, 441*
Foschini, B. M. *392*
Fotopoulos, J. *198, 201–3, 208, 238, 240, 246, 441*
Francis, J. *99, 441*
Frid, B. *90, 441*
Furnish, V. P. *155, 441*

Gagnon, R. *148, 441, 448*
Gardner, P. D. *441*
Garland, D. E. *22, 34–35, 43, 50, 54–57, 62–66, 68–70, 75, 79–80, 83, 85, 87–90, 92–97, 99, 101, 103–6, 108, 111–14, 116–18, 120–23, 125–26, 129, 131–35, 138, 140–42, 144–47, 152, 154–57, 161, 163–64, 166–73, 175–77, 179, 181, 185–87, 189–90, 193, 199–200, 204, 210–12, 217, 219–21, 223, 227, 229, 231–34, 236–40, 242–43, 245, 247, 249, 254–59, 261, 263–64, 266, 269–270, 272–73, 275–78, 281, 283–85, 287–88, 290, 294–99, 303–5, 308–10, 312–14, 316, 318–19, 322–23, 325, 329, 331, 334, 340–42, 344–45, 347–49, 351–52, 354–55, 357, 360, 363, 368, 370–76, 379–80, 382, 385, 387–88, 390–91, 393–94, 396, 401–2, 404, 406–7, 409, 411–12, 414–15, 420, 422–23, 425, 427, 429, 432, 437*
Georgi, D. *418, 441*
Gill, D. *18, 261, 441*
Gillespie, T. W. *366, 441*
Gladd, B. *80, 441*
Godet, F. L. *437*
Gooch, P. *248, 442*
Goppelt, L. *226, 442*
Greenbury, J. *361, 442*
Grindheim, S. *442*
Grosheide, F. W. *73, 139, 153, 157–58, 163–64, 167, 171, 186, 330–31, 334, 380, 405, 421*
Grudem, W. A. *258–59, 283, 290–91, 327, 341, 356, 359, 442*

Gundry, R. H. *153, 442*
Gundry-Volf, J. M. *253, 442*
Gupta, N. K. *442*

Hafemann, S. J. *217, 395, 442*
Hall, D. R. *117, 442*
Hall, R. G. *180, 442*
Harris, W. V. *306, 442*
Hays, R. B. *39, 50, 57, 63, 103, 118, 127, 134, 164, 170, 172, 175, 178, 180–82, 185–86, 198, 200, 206, 212, 214, 220, 228–29, 231, 234–35, 241, 256, 268–69, 273, 311–13, 325–29, 334, 346, 351, 355, 358, 363, 380, 382, 384, 387, 392, 396, 398, 402, 414–15, 423–25, 427–30, 435, 437, 442*
Heil, J. P. *63, 66–67, 74, 90, 96, 264–66, 389, 406, 408, 442*
Hengel, M. *64, 442*
Hensley, A. D. *442*
Héring, J. *437*
Hill, C. E. *388, 442*
Hiu, E. *361, 442*
Hodge, C. *437*
Hodgson, R. *122, 442*
Hofius, O. *266, 271–72, 442*
Holladay, C. R. *305, 442*
Hollander, H. *443*
Hooker, M. *99, 118, 263, 443*
Horrell, D. G. *18, 48, 56, 75, 202, 204, 207, 211, 269, 438, 443*
Horsely, R. A. *142, 269, 437, 443*
Hoskins, P. M. *145, 443*
Hubbard, R. L., Jr. *151*
Hull, M. F. *392–94, 443*
Hultgren, S. J. *443*
Hurd, J. C. *151, 185, 200, 256, 443*
Hurley, J. B. *260, 443*
Hutson, C. R. *424, 443*

Instone-Brewer, D. *176, 443*
Isaksson, A. *260, 443*

Jeremias, J. *402, 411, 443*
Johanson, B. C. *342, 443*
Johnson, L. *255, 443*
Jones, P. R. *375, 443*
Judge, E. A. *74, 443*

Kelly, J. N. D. *372, 443*
Kempthorne, R. *158, 443*
Kim, C.-H. *422, 443*
Kim, J. H. *413, 443*
Kinman, B. *146, 443*
Kistemaker, S. J. *217, 325, 336, 363, 405*
Klein, G. L. *443*
Klein, W. M. *306, 443*
Klein, W. W. *151, 159, 444*
Kloha, J. *444*
Klutz, T. E. *444*
Koet, B. J. *232–33, 444*
Kovacs, J. L. *444*
Kreitzer, L. J. *388–89, 444*
Kubo, S. *444*
Kuck, D. W. *100, 105, 111, 118–19, 121, 444*
Kurek–Chomycz, D. A. *444*

Lakey, M. J. *444*
Lampe, P. *62, 444*
Lanci, J. R. *109, 444*
Lanier, D. E. *444*
Lea, T. D. *98, 178, 187, 203, 212, 242, 258, 296–97, 302, 388, 394, 438*
Lightfoot, J. B. *437*
Litfin, D. A. *60, 69, 79, 81, 444*
Lösch, S. *260, 444*

MacArthur, J. *242, 437*
MacGregor, K. R. *444*
Malherbe, A. J. *397, 444*
Malone, A. S. *444*
Mare, W. H. *437*
Marshall, I. H. *271, 444*
Marshall, P. *56, 66, 119–20, 444*
Martin, D. B. *444*
Martini, J. *444*
Martin, R. P. *444*
Massey, P. T. *260, 263, 444*
Meeks, W. A. *56, 74, 225, 444*
Meggit, J. J. *74, 445*
Merkle, B. L. *255, 445*
Meyer, H. A. W. *438*
Mitchell, A. C. *143, 445*
Mitchell, M. M. *22, 39, 50–51, 56, 105, 130, 160, 211, 222, 256, 266, 294, 304, 329, 445*
Moffatt, J. *180, 438*
Moiser, J. *170, 173, 445*
Morris, L. *69, 85, 88, 90, 92, 101–2, 114, 135, 140, 149, 153, 156, 163, 167, 170–71, 175–78, 180, 182, 184, 187, 212, 214, 226, 247, 258–59, 268, 272, 276, 280, 283–84, 287–88, 302, 331, 369–70, 420, 438*
Munck, J. *48, 51, 445*

Murphy-O'Connor, J. *18–21, 37, 58, 84, 154–55, 247, 263, 422, 438, 445*

Neirynck, F. *123, 445*
Newman, C. C. *90, 445*
Niccum, C. *357, 445*
Nickelsburg, G. *372, 376–77, 445*
Nickle, K. F. *418, 445*

O'Brien, P. T. *34, 41–44, 46, 445*
O'Day, G. R. *74, 445*
Odell-Scott, D. W. *357, 445*
O'Neil, J. C. *394, 445*
Orr, W. F. *405, 445*
Ortlund, D. *81, 445*
Oster, R. *260, 445*

Paige, T. *284, 445*
Pao, D. W. *41, 445*
Parry, R S. J. *438*
Pascuzzi, M. *446*
Patrick, J. E. *395, 446*
Patterson, P. *438*
Patterson, S. J. *446*
Payne, P. B. *357, 446*
Perriman, A. C. *255, 259, 446*
Petzer, J. H. *306, 308, 446*
Pfitzner, V. C. *222, 446*
Phipps, W. E. *446*
Pickett, R. *446*
Plummer, A. *45, 50, 55–58, 65, 70, 95, 98, 105, 116–17, 121, 126, 130, 144–45, 147, 149, 151, 153–56, 158, 161, 163–64, 167–69, 172–73, 176, 184, 189, 200–201, 209, 221, 227–30, 235–37, 240, 248, 264–65, 268, 271–72, 277, 282–83, 285, 288, 303, 315, 319, 326, 329, 334, 348, 350–53, 358, 363, 370–72, 374–76, 379–82, 384, 386–88, 390–91, 394, 396–97, 401, 403, 405, 407, 409–11, 413, 417, 420–21, 423–26, 431–35, 438*
Pogoloff, S. M. *59–60, 446*
Porter, S. E. *446*
Portier-Young, A. *306, 446*
Prior, M. *37, 446*

Richards, E. R. *36, 446*
Richardson, P. *142, 174, 446*
Robertson, A. *45, 50, 55, 57–58, 65, 70, 95, 98, 105, 116–17, 121, 126, 130, 144–45, 147, 149, 151, 153–56, 158, 161, 163–64, 167–69, 172–73, 176, 184, 189, 200–201, 209, 221, 227–30, 235–37, 240, 248, 264–65, 268, 271–72, 277, 282–83, 285, 288, 303, 315, 319, 326, 329, 334, 348, 350–53, 358, 363, 370–72, 374–76, 379–82, 384, 386–88, 390–91, 394, 396–97, 401, 403, 405, 407, 409–11, 413, 417, 420–21, 423–26, 431–35, 438*
Robinson, J. A. T. *153, 446*
Rosner, B. S. *22–23, 34, 36, 38–41, 44, 46–47, 50–51, 53, 55–57, 59–60, 62–64, 66–72, 74, 78, 85–86, 88, 90, 95, 98, 102–3, 105, 108–9, 118, 130, 133–34, 138–41, 146, 151, 155–58, 160, 163–67, 170, 176–77, 180–81, 185, 187, 189, 191, 193, 200, 203–4, 206, 208, 212, 214, 216–19, 221, 226, 229, 231, 234, 238–43, 246, 248, 250, 253, 256–59, 261–66, 272, 275, 277–78, 282, 290–91, 295–96, 299–300, 303, 307–9, 312–16, 318–19, 322–23, 325, 327, 329–30, 334, 336, 338–41, 345, 349–53, 358, 360–62, 365–68, 372–73, 375–76, 385, 388–89, 394–95, 397, 401, 404–9, 411–14, 417–18, 420, 426–29, 432, 434, 437, 439, 446*

Sanders, T. K. *446*
Sandnes, K. O. *342, 446*
Savage, T. B. *81, 446*
Schatzmann, S. *446*
Schrage, W. *438*
Schreiner, T. R. *228, 270, 290–91, 446–47*
Schubert, P. *41, 447*
Schwiebert, J. *447*
Shogren, G. S. *447*
Sigountos, J. G. *304, 306, 308–12, 447*
Smith, B. D. *447*
Smith, J. E. *151, 447*
Smit, J. *447*
Smit, J. F. M. *198, 304, 339, 343–44*
Son, S.-W. *447*
South, J. T. *132, 136–37, 447*
Stanley, C. D. *63, 67, 90, 414, 447*
Stendahl, K. *335, 447*
Stewart, D. R. *447*
Still, E. C. *197, 447*
Still, T. D. *447*
Stowers, S. K. *33, 79, 447*
Sweet, J. P. M. *341, 447*

Talbert, C. H. *285, 394, 394*

Terry, R. B. *22, 447*
Theissen, G. *74, 203, 448*
Thielman, F. *23, 448*
Thiselton, A. C. *18, 20, 23, 34, 36–42, 44–45, 48–49, 52–53, 55, 57–58, 61, 63–66, 68–72, 75–77, 79–80, 84–85, 87–88, 90–91, 94–99, 102–7, 113–15, 118–19, 121, 125–27, 132, 135, 137–38, 143, 148, 150, 152–53, 155, 157–59, 164, 168–71, 174–76, 179, 184, 187, 189, 193, 197, 203–4, 207, 211, 220–21, 224, 226–28, 232, 234–35, 237, 241, 243, 252, 258–59, 264–70, 274–76, 278, 280–84, 290–91, 298–99, 301, 304, 313, 320–25, 329–30, 332–34, 336–42, 345, 348–52, 359–60, 363, 369–71, 373–77, 380–82, 385–87, 389, 391–92, 394, 396–400, 402–4, 406–11, 413–15, 419–21, 423–24, 426–31, 433–34, 417, 438*
Thrall, M. E. *359, 438*
Toussaint, S. D. *316, 448*
Treier, D. J. *226, 448*
Turner, M. *259, 440*

Vaughan, C. *98, 178, 203, 212, 242, 258, 296–97, 302, 388, 394, 438*
Verbrugge, V. *331, 342, 357, 448*
Via, D. O. *148, 448*

Waaler, E. *448*
Walker, W. O. *21, 84, 448*
Wallace, D. B. *105, 175, 297, 316*
Walther, J. A. *405, 445*
Weiss, J. *438*
Welborn, L. L. *118, 448*
Wenham, D. *448*
White, J. L. *33, 448*
White, J. R. *395, 448*
Widmann, M. *84, 448*
Williams, G. *397, 448*
Williams, H. *63, 67, 78, 87, 90–92, 95, 448*
Willis, W. *22, 87, 96, 198–99, 241, 448*
Winter, B. W. *18, 51, 60, 74, 79, 117, 142–43, 160, 168, 180, 183–84, 186, 193, 254–55, 257, 261, 268, 278, 284–85, 448*
Witherington, B. *22, 34, 36, 38, 49–51, 60, 75, 108, 200, 203, 235, 240, 303–5, 329, 358, 392, 398, 406, 408, 420–21, 427, 431, 438–49*
Wolter, M. *449*
Wright, N. T. *206, 449*
Wright, S. D. *228, 447*
Wuellner, W. *74, 449*

Yarbrough, O. *449*

Zaas, P. *140, 449*

# Subject Index


### A

Adam/Christ typology *385, 408–10*
Anathema *434*
angels *145*
Apollos *20, 54–55, 425–26*
apostles *301–2*
apostleship, Paul's *35–36*
arrogance *116, 119, 124, 126*

### B

baptism *58–59, 227–28*
baptism for the dead *390–92*
beginnings of the church at Corinth *19–20*
boasting *120, 217*
bodily resurrection *28–29*

### C

calling *75*
Cephas *55*
charisma *43–44*
Chloe *52–53*
Christ in the wilderness *228–29*
church *38*
church at Thessalonica *34*
church discipline *136–38, 140–41*
church the body of Christ *294–302*
circumcision *180–81*
Corinth *17–18*
courage *429*
crucifixion *64*

### D

Day of the Lord *45, 108*
death *414–15*
divorce *172–77*

### E

eschatology *29, 235–36*
eschatology, over-realized *44*

### F

faithfulness of God *46*
fellowship *46*
1 Corinthians
    occasion *21*
    structure *21–29*
firstfruits *385*
food sacrificed to idols *27, 198–209, 243–44*
fornication *154*
freedom *210–21*

### G

gift of prophecy *290–91, 327, 345–46, 348, 350–52*
gift of tongues *291–93, 320, 323–46, 349–50*
gospel, the *369–78*
grace, theology of *76*

### H

head covering *260*
headship *257–66*
holiness *37–38*
Holy Spirit *332*
homosexuality *148*
human wisdom *67–69, 93, 106*

### I

idolatry *231–32, 238–44*
incest *132*
*inclusio* *47*

### J

judging *114–15*
Julius Caesar *18*

### K

kingdom of God *412*
knowledge *204–5*

### L

lawsuits *142–48*
Lord's Supper *239–42, 268–77*
love *303–319*

### M

marriage *162–68*
maturity *87–88*
mystery *80, 86, 89*

### N

natural man *94–95*

### O

offerings for the poor *418–21*

### P

power *65–66*
prostitution *156–59*

purity *25–26*

## R

resurrection of Christ *369–78, 380–90*
resurrection of the body *379, 386–90, 401–10, 412–13*
reward *104, 108, 113*

## S

*sarkinos/sarkikos* *97–99*
self-confidence *236*
servants of God *101–5, 112*
sex in marriage *166–67*
sexual immorality *132, 232–33*
slavery *181–82*
Sosthenes *36–37*
Spirit baptism *297*
spiritual gifts *28, 282–92, 300–302*
spiritual man *94–95*
Stephanas *430–31*
stewards *112–13*

## T

teachers *302*
temple of God *108–9*
temptation *237*
testing Christ *233*
thanksgiving *24, 33, 41–46*
Timothy *424–25*
transformation of the body *412*
travel plans *422–24*
typology *230–31, 235*

## U

union with Christ *156–57*
unity *50–52*

## W

weak *220*
wisdom *59–60*
wisdom of God *25, 61–64, 72, 77, 83, 85, 89, 107, 124*
wisdom of the world *110*
women in the church *354–60*
worship *27–28*

# Scripture Index


## Genesis

1–2 *359*
1:11–13 *403*
1:20–27 *403*
1:26–27 *262, 409*
1:27 *262*
2 *162, 408*
2:7 *407–9*
2:7a *408*
2:7b *408*
2:18 *162*
2:18–23 *262*
2:21–22 *258*
2:24 *153, 157, 162, 166, 295*
5:3 *409*
6:1–4 *263*
6:2 *263*
9:6 *409*
12:7 *374*
15:8 *175*
17:3 *346*
17:7 *175*
17:10–14 *180*
18:26 *175*
21:9 *232*
22:4 *373*
26:8 *232*
26:14 *103*
26:24 *374*
33:4 *433*
35:9 *374*
39 *158*
39:17 *232*
40:8 *93*
40:22 *93*
41:12 *93*
42:15–16 *396*
42:18 *373*
48:3 *374*

## Exodus

3:13–14 *39*
4:18 *425*
4:22 *40*
6:3 *374*
7:3 *70*
12:6 *139*
12–14 *226*
12:14 *273*
12:15–19 *139*
12:23 *136, 234*
13:7 *139*
13:21–22 *226–27*
14:13–31 *226*
14:19–20 *227*
14:24 *227*
14:31 *227*
15:20 *260*
16:1–36 *229*
16:3 *234*
16:10 *374*
17:1–7 *226*
17:1–17 *229*
17:2–7 *233*
17:6 *229*
19:5–6 *39*
19:11 *373*
19:15 *167*
19:16 *373*
20:5 *244*
20:16 *381*
21:10–11 *166*
22:19 *136*
22:20 *136*
22:28 *384*
23:19 *384*
24:8 *272*
25:2–3 *384*
25:8 *108*
29:45 *108*
32 *232–33*
32:1–5 *232*
32:6 *226, 228*
32:6a *232*
32:6b *231*
32:17–19 *232*
32:28 *233*
32:31c *232*
32:35 *277*
34:14 *244*
34:15 *248*
35:5 *384*
36:6 *384*
39:1 *384*

## Leviticus

2:12 *384*
7:6–10 *215*
7:14 *215*
7:28–36 *215*
9:23 *374*
15:18 *167*
18:7–8 *132*
18:22 *148*
19 *27, 195*
19:1–2 *39*
19:18 *196*
20:13 *148*
22:12 *384*
23:9–14 *384*
23:10 *384*
23:15–21 *423*
26:11–12 *108*

## Numbers

4:18 *136*
5:9 *384*
5:22 *333*
6:24–26 *40*
8:19 *277*
11 *226, 231–34*
11:4 *231*
11:4–34 *226, 231*
11:29 *325*
11:33 *277*
11:34 *231*
12:6 *318*
12:6–8 *318*
12:8 *318*
12:12 *375*
14 *234*
14:10 *374*
14:11 *311, 70*
14:14 *227*
14:15–16 *234*
14:16 *230*
14:20–30 *237*
14:22 *70*
15:20–21 *384*
16 *234*
16:19 *374*
16:30 *312*
17:7 *374*
18:8 *384*
18:11–12 *384*
18:29–30 *384*
18:32 *384*
20:1–13 *226*
20:1–16 *226*
20:2–13 *229*
20:6 *374*
20:11 *229*
20:24 *312*
21 *233*
21:4–9 *233*
21:16–20 *229*
25 *233*
25:1–9 *232*
25:2 *232*
26:65 *225*
31:29 *384*
32:11–12 *225*

## Deuteronomy

1:34 *311*
4:10 *38*
4:34 *70*
5:9 *244*
6 *27, 195*
6:4 *195, 206*
6:4–5 *205, 434*
6:5–6 *195*
6:13 *157*
6:14–15 *244*
6:16 *233*
7:6 *39*
7:7 *76*
7:9 *41*
9:7 *312*
9:8 *312*
9:8–16 *232*
9:10 *38*
9:18–21 *232*
10:17 *206*
10:20 *157*
11:22 *157*
12:6 *384*
12:11 *39, 384*
12:15 *229*
12:17 *384*
12:21 *39*
12:26 *39*
14:22–26 *241*
14:23–24 *39*
16:2 *39*

16:4 *139*
16:6 *39*
17:7 *141*
17:8 *39*
17:12 *141*
18:4 *384*
18:16 *38*
18:20–22 *291*
18:22 *352*
19:19 *141*
21:21 *141*
21:22–23 *64*
22:21–22 *141*
22:24 *141*
23:2–4 *38*
23:9 *38*
24:1–4 *172*
24:7 *141*
24–25 *214*
25:1 *215*
25:4 *213–14*
26:2 *39, 384*
26:10 *384*
26:19 *39*
27:15 *333*
27:15–26 *136*
28:37 *318*
28:46 *70*
28:49 *339*
28:60 *157*
31:6–7 *429*
31:20 *312*
31:23 *429*
31:30 *38*
32 *226, 229, 243–44*
32:4 *229*
32:5–20 *40*
32:15 *229*
32:17 *205, 243–44*
32:18 *229*
32:21 *205*
32:24 *277*
32:30 *229*
32:31 *229*
32:35 *312*
33:21 *384*
34:11 *70*

**Joshua**

1:6 *429*
1:9 *429*
1:18 *429*
2:22 *373*
3:2 *373*
3:10 *136*
7:25 *136*
8:35 *38*
22:17 *277*
24:19–20 *244*

**Judges**

2:17 *232*
4:4 *260*
7:15 *93*
16:25 *232*
20:2 *38*
21:5 *38*

**1 Samuel**

2:10 *74, 77*
2:29 *384*
10:4 *384*
20:42 *425*
21:4–6 *167*
10 2 Kings
5:19 *425*

**2 Samuel**

1:21 *384*
10:12 *429*
12:22 *177*
13:1–4 *303*

**1 Kings**

3:5 *374*
9:2 *374*
10:1 *318*
11:2 *157*
12:28 *232*
13:34 *136*
14:22 *244*
15:4 *175*

**2 Kings**

1:18 *157*
3:3 *157*
18:6 *157*
22:14 *260*
23:1–23 *138*

**1 Chronicles**

16:27 *256*
16:36 *333*
22:13 *429*
28:20 *429*
29:2 *105*

**2 Chronicles**

1:7 *374*
3:1 *374*
7:12 *374*
9:1 *318*
29:5 *138*
29:30 *138*
29:35 *138*
31:5 *384*
31:10 *384*
31:12 *384*
31:14 *384*
32:7 *429*
34:22 *260*
35:1–19 *138*

**Ezra**

6:13–22 *138*
8:25 *384*
8:32 *373*
10:3 *174*
10:6 *134*
10:19 *174*

**Nehemiah**

1:4 *134*
5:13 *333*
6:14 *260*
8:6 *333*
8:9 *134*
9:16–18 *232*
10:38 *384*
10:40 *385*
12:44 *385*
13:5 *385*

**Esther**

4:14 *177*
5:1 *373*

**Job**

1:12 *137*
2:6 *137*
3:16 *375*
5:12 *73*
5:13 *110*
12:17 *68*
27:6 *114*
28:12–28 *90*

**Psalms**

2:1–12 *434*
6:10 *76*
8 *264, 373, 384, 389*
8:3–5 *262*
8:5 *406*
8:6 *389*
8:6a *389*
9:25 *312*
14:1 *402*
16:8–11 *373*
18:2 *229*
24:1 *199, 247–48*
26:5 *38*
26:14 *429*
29:3 *89*
30:25 *429*
31:17 *76*
31:24 *429*
33:10 *67*
35:4 *76*
35:26–27 *76*
40:15 *76*
50:12 *247*
52:1 *402*
56:13 *373*
69:23–24 *71*
75 *226*
77:18 *233*
77:51 *385*
78:15–16 *229*
78:18 *233*
78:23–29 *229*
78:24 *228*
78:58–64 *244*
83:16–18 *76*
89:11 *247*
89:34 *67*
92:6 *402*
93:11 *73*
94:1 *312*
94:11 *110*
95:8–11 *233*
98:6 *39*
102:26 *413*
104:36 *385*
105 *226, 234*
105:39 *227*
106 *226*
106:19–23 *232*
106:21 *232*
106:37 *244*
110 *373, 388–89*
110:1 *373, 384, 388–89*

110:1a *389*
116:8 *373*
135:9 *70*
136:2–3 *206*
138:1 *264*
144:13 *41*

**Proverbs**

1:6 *318*
5:3 *158*
5:15–20 *166*
6:7 *103*
6:23–7:27 *158*
9:12 *103*
24:5 *103*
24:30 *103*
31:16 *103*

**Ecclesiastes**

3:5 *167*
6:3 *375*

**Song of Songs**

15:3 *385*

**Isaiah**

3:3 *105–6*
5 *103*
5:2 *103*
6:2 *264*
6:8–9 *35*
8:3 *260*
8:14 *71*
8:18 *70*
19:11–12 *68*
19:12 *68*
22:13 *398*
25 *414*
25:8 *411, 414*
25:18 *414*
26:19 *368*
27:13 *413*
28 *340–41*
28:9–10 *341*
28:11 *320, 339*
28:11–12 *329, 336–37, 339–41, 344*
28:12 *340*
28:16 *69–70*
29:5–6 *413*
29:13 *67*
29:13–14 *67*
29:14 *61–62, 67–68, 90*
29:14b *67*
30:13 *413*
33:18 *68*
37:4 *175*
37:19 *205*
40:1–11 *95*
40:13 *84, 95, 337*
40:13a *95*
41:11 *76*
44:25 *68*
45:13 *336*
45:14 *337, 346*
47:11 *413*
48:3 *413*
48:6 *90*
49 *376*
49:1–5 *35*
49:4 *377*
49:7 *41*
49:23 *346*
52:7 *59*
52:11a *373*
52:13–15 *90*
52:15 *90*
53 *373*
53:6 *272*
53:6–12 *272*
60:3–61:6 *418*
60:10–16 *346*
63:16 *40*
64:3 *90*
64:4 *90*
64:8 *40*
65:16 *90*
65:17 *90*
66:15 *107*
66:20 *418*

**Jeremiah**

1:5 *35*
1:10 *105*
2:3 *39*
2:26 *76*
2:30 *136*
3:16 *90*
3:19 *40*
5:6 *136*
6:26 *413*
9:22–23 *61, 73–74*
9:23–24 *77*
15:8 *413*
18:9 *103, 105*
18:22 *413*
22:7 *136*
24:6 *103, 105*
28:23 *103*
28:55 *136*
29:23 *66*
31:3 *136*
31:8 *136*
31:9 *40*
31:31 *272*
31:32 *136*
32:31 *136*
32:36 *136*
49:19 *413*
50:44 *413*
51:8 *413*

**Ezekiel**

6:14 *136*
8:3 *244*
11:16 *108*
14:16 *136*
20:31 *385*
20:40 *385*
36:9–10 *103*
37 *408*
37:1–34 *368*
37:6 *408*
37:9 *408*
37:10 *408*
37:14 *408*
37:26–28 *108*
41:6–7 *385*
43:3 *318*
44:30 *385*
45:1 *385*
45:13 *385*
45:16 *385*
48:8–10 *385*
48:12 *385*
48:18 *385*
48:20–21 *385*

**Daniel**

2 *90, 307*
2:19–23 *90, 92, 307*
2:20–22 *72*
3 *308*
4 *307*
5:8 *93*
5:12 *93*
7 *397*
7:9–10 *107*
7:18–27 *39*
7:22 *145*
8:23 *318*
10:2 *134*
10:19 *429*
12:1–3 *368*
12:2 *386–87*
12:2–3 *404*

**Hosea**

3:1–3 *159*
3:2 *373*
8:5 *311*
11:1–11 *40*
13:14 *411, 414*

**Joel**

2:1 *413*
2:14 *177*
2:16 *167*
2:28 *260, 354*
2:28–32 *39*
2:32 *45*
3:5 *39*

**Amos**

4:11 *108*
5:18–20 *45*
7:14–15 *35*

**Obadiah**

1:13 *136*

**Jonah**

1:7 *373*
3:9 *177*

**Nahum**

1:2 *244*

**Habakkuk**

2:18 *205*

**Zephaniah**

1:14 *244*
1:14–16 *413*
1:18 *244*

**Zechariah**

4:6 *78*
4:6–10 *78*
8:13 *336*
8:17 *312*

8:22–23 *346*
9:14 *413*
10:3 *311*
12:1 *92*
12:12–14 *167*

**Malachi**

1:11 *39*
2:15–16 *157*
3:1 *413*
3:1–3 *107*
3:2–3 *105*
3–4 *105*
3:8 *385*
4:1 *107*

**Matthew**

2:11 *346*
3:10–12 *107*
3:11 *297*
4:7 *233*
4:9 *346*
4:14–20 *269*
5:1–11 *116*
5:4 *134*
5:5 *412*
5:18 *339*
5:22 *107*
5:32 *172*
5:44 *123*
7:1–4 *115*
7:19 *107*
7:21–27 *224*
9:6 *263*
9:10–13 *76*
9:15 *134*
9:16 *52*
10:10 *216*
10:21 *272*
11:8 *148*
11:20 *76*
11:25 *68, 76*
11:25–27 *76*
12:28–42 *70*
12:31 *158*
13:9–13 *269*
13:11 *80*
13:40 *107*
13:42 *107*
13:50 *107*
15:18–19 *67*
16:6 *139*
16:17 *411*
16:21 *374*
16:27 *104*
17:15 *107*
17:19–20 *307*
17:22–23 *272*
17:23 *374*
18:8–9 *107*
18:10–14 *76*
18:15 *218, 345*
18:15–17 *147*
18:26 *346*
18:32 *166*
19:1–10 *172*
19:5 *157*
19:18 *381*
19:28 *145*
19:29 *412*
20:1–16 *76*
20:18–19 *272*
20:19 *374*
21:12–13 *138*
21:21 *307*
21:28–41 *76*
21:42 *373*
22:1–10 *76*
22:30 *184*
22:36–40 *27, 195, 303, 319, 434*
22:44 *389*
24:9 *272*
24:31 *413*
24:38 *184*
24:42–43 *428*
25:13 *428*
25:16–22 *218*
25:34 *412*
25:40–45 *209*
25:41 *107*
26:2 *272*
26:26–28 *271*
26:29 *273*
26:38 *428*
26:40–41 *428*
27:26 *272*
27:52 *194*
27:64 *374*
28:1 *419*
28:13 *194*
28:16 *374*
28:52 *388*

**Mark**

1:8 *297*
1:24 *88*
1:34 *88*
2:15–17 *76*
2:21 *52*
4:11 *80*
7:1–8 *76*
7:6–7 *67*
7:14–23 *247*
8:11 *76*
8:31–38 *76*
9:31 *272*
9:43 *107*
9:48–49 *107*
10:2–12 *172*
10:9 *173*
10:17 *412*
10:19 *381*
10:23–27 *76*
10:33 *272*
10:45 *218*
11:15–18 *138*
11:22–24 *307*
12:1–2 *76*
12:6 *124*
12:19–25 *190*
12:24 *400*
12:25 *184*
12:36 *389*
12:42 *373*
13:12 *272*
13:17–20 *186*
13:34–35 *428*
13:36 *413*
13:37 *428*
14:22–24 *271*
14:34 *428*
14:34–38 *428*
14:37–38 *428*
14:45 *433*
14:62 *389*
15:15 *272*
16:2 *419*
16:10 *134*
16:17 *292*
16:20 *43*

**Luke**

2:36 *260*
3:9 *107*
3:16 *297*
3:16–17 *107*
3:19 *345*
4:12 *233*
5:4 *316*
5:29–32 *76*
6:28a *123*
7:25 *148*
7:36–50 *76*
7:45 *433*
8:10 *80*
8:23 *396*
8:24 *316*
9:22 *374*
9:54 *107*
10:7 *216*
10:21–22 *76*
10:21–23 *76*
10:25 *233, 412*
10:26 *339*
10:29–37 *76*
11:1 *316*
11:40 *402*
11:45–53 *76*
12:15 *190*
12:16–21 *190*
12:20 *402*
12:37 *428*
12:42 *112*
12:49 *107*
14:12–24 *76*
14:15–24 *190*
15:1–32 *76*
15:20 *433*
16:1 *112*
16:17 *339*
17:6 *307*
17:26–37 *190*
17:27 *184*
17:29 *107*
18:2 *124*
18:2–6 *145*
18:4 *124*
18:9–13 *76*
18:18 *412*
18:20 *381*
18:24–27 *76*
18:32–33 *272*
18:33 *374*
19:17 *263*
19:45–47 *138*
20:13 *124*
20:26–27 *122*
20:35 *184*
20:42–43 *389*
21:16 *272*
21:23 *186*
21:34 *413*

22:17 *273*
22:17–20 *271*
22:25–27 *101*
22:30 *145*
22:45 *194*
22:69 *389*
23:34 *89, 312*
24:1 *419*
24:7 *272, 374*
24:13–20 *407*
24:16 *318*
24:20 *272*
24:21 *374*
24:25–27 *373*
24:31 *318, 407*
24:32 *373*
24:44–46 *374*
24:46 *374*

## John

1:33 *297*
2:13–22 *138*
2:19–22 *374*
3:20 *345*
3:21 *313*
5:4 *356*
5:16–19 *40*
5:19–30 *389*
5:21 *403, 408*
5:29 *387*
6:30 *70*
6:63 *403, 408*
7:40–43 *52*
7:49 *339*
7:53–8:11 *356*
8:12 *272*
8:21–24 *382*
8:34 *154*
8:46 *345*
9:16 *52*
9:18 *342*
10:9 *272*
10:11–14 *125*
10:19–21 *52*
10:20 *345*
10:34 *339*
11:11 *194*
12:24 *402*
12:34 *339*
15:6 *107*
15:25 *339*
16:8 *345*
19:16 *272*
20:1 *419*
20:14 *407*
20:15 *407*
20:16 *407*
20:19 *419*
20:20 *407*
20:26 *419*
20:27–28 *407*
21:12 *407*

## Acts

1:5 *297*
1:6–11 *375*
1:9 *407*
1:10 *407*
1:21–22 *212*
2 *292, 423*
2:4–11 *291–92*
2:14–21 *260*
2:18 *354*
2:21 *39*
2:24–31 *373*
2:27–31 *406*
2:32 *212*
2:33–35 *389*
2:37 *346*
3:15 *212*
3:17 *88–89*
3:24 *79*
4:2 *79*
4:4–5 *209*
4:5 *88*
4:8 *88*
4:13 *333*
4:25–28 *89*
4:26 *88*
4:28 *89*
4:33 *212*
4:34–5:2 *420*
4:36–37 *213*
5:1–11 *136*
5:6 *189*
5:17 *269*
5:42 *316*
6:13 *316*
7:2 *89*
7:39–43 *232*
7:60 *194*
8:4 *423*
8:16 *227*
8:37 *356*
8:40 *423*
9:1–5 *377*
9:1–20 *35*
9:2 *421*
9:14 *38*
9:15 *36*
9:21 *38*
9:22–25 *421*
9:26–28 *213*
9:32 *423*
9:38 *423*
10:25 *346*
10:38 *423*
10:40 *374*
10:44–48 *292*
10:46 *292*
10:46b–47 *292*
11:16 *297*
11:19 *423*
11:19–26 *213*
11:22 *423*
11:28 *291*
12:6 *194*
12:10 *423*
12:14 *318*
12:15 *345*
12:23 *264*
13:1 *302*
13:1–3 *291*
13:2–3 *421*
13:5 *79*
13:6 *423*
13:10 *316*
13:14 *423*
13:36 *194*
13:38 *79*
14:3 *307*
14:4 *213*
14:14 *213, 375*
14:24 *423*
15 *198, 201, 220*
15:1–29 *418*
15:3 *423*
15:5 *269*
15:13 *423*
15:20 *151*
15:23 *39*
15:23–29 *155, 200, 421*
15:33 *425*
15:36 *79*
15:36–41 *213*
15:41 *423*
16:1–3 *219*
16:6 *423*
16:16–24 *307*
16:17 *79*
16:21 *79*
16:25–34 *174*
16:36 *425*
17:3 *79*
17:11 *351*
17:13 *79*
17:16 *200, 311*
17:23 *79, 423*
18 *19–20*
18:1–3 *432*
18:1–11 *36*
18:2 *19, 432*
18:4 *19–20*
18:5 *20*
18:6 *20*
18:7–8 *20*
18:8 *54*
18:9 *200*
18:9–10 *81*
18:11 *20, 103*
18:12 *19*
18:12–17 *18*
18:12–18 *144*
18:15–16 *144*
18:17 *36*
18:18 *20, 74, 432*
18:21 *423*
18:23 *423*
18:24 *54*
18:24–19:1 *54, 432*
18:26 *432*
18:27 *423*
19 *292*
19:1 *103, 423*
19:1–7 *292*
19:5 *227*
19:11 *307*
19:21 *422–23*
19:22 *425*
19:23–41 *397, 424*
19:27 *396*
19:32 *38*
19:39 *219*
19:39–40 *38*
19:40 *396*
20:1 *316*
20:1–3 *422*
20:2 *423*
20:3–21:17 *421*
20:7 *419*
20:25 *423*

20:31 *124, 316, 428*
20:37 *433*
21 *198*
21:7 *260*
21:9 *354*
21:10–11 *291*
21:23–26 *219*
21:32 *316*
22:1–21 *35*
22:7–8 *377*
22:14 *212*
22:16 *149*
22:21 *36*
23:1 *207*
23:21 *342*
24:5 *269*
24:14 *269*
24:16 *207*
24:17 *418*
25:4 *342*
26:2–23 *35*
26:5 *269*
26:14–15 *377*
26:16 *212*
26:17 *36*
26:23 *79*
26:24–25 *345*
28:3–6 *307*
28:5 *342*
28:22 *269*

**Romans**

1:1 *35*
1:1–5 *36*
1:2 *35, 373*
1:2–7 *35*
1–3 *346*
1:3 *242*
1:4 *408*
1:5 *377*
1:6 *71*
1:8 *41, 79–80*
1:9 *46*
1:11 *44–45, 228*
1:13 *227, 283*
1:16 *66, 71*
1:18 *313*
1:18–31 *69*
1:18–32 *19*
1:20–31 *399*
1:21–23 *240*
1:23 *409*
1:25 *333*
1:26 *265–66*
1:26–27 *148*
1:27 *311*
1:28 *223*
1:29 *53*
1:32 *173, 312, 318*
2:4 *309–10*
2:6 *104*
2:7 *406*
2:8 *313*
2:14 *265*
2:15 *207*
2:16 *115*
2:18 *334*
2:19 *312*
2:20 *402*
2:25–29 *181*
2:27 *265*
2:28–29 *242*
3:3 *315*
3:3–7 *89*
3:4 *156*
3:5 *145, 397*
3:6 *156*
3:19 *339*
3:21 *384, 405*
3:25 *272*
3:30 *206*
3:31 *156, 315*
4:1 *242*
4:1–12 *312*
4:11 *227*
4:14 *315*
4:17 *72, 403*
4:24 *381*
4:25 *272, 369*
5 *385–86*
5:2–3 *308*
5:5 *304*
5:6 *220*
5:6–8 *372*
5–7 *415*
5:8 *58*
5:9 *65, 272*
5:9–10 *65*
5:10 *172, 381*
5:11 *172*
5:12–16 *385*
5:12–20 *385–86*
5:12–21 *383*
5:14 *226, 385*
5:14–21 *386, 388*
5:15 *385*
5:15–16 *44, 279*
5:18–19 *385*
5:21 *386*
6:2 *156*
6:3 *227*
6:3–4 *369*
6:3–7 *58*
6:3–11 *228*
6:3–13 *395*
6:3–14 *394*
6:4 *40, 58, 90, 156, 373*
6:4–6 *89*
6:6 *64, 168, 295, 315*
6:8 *90*
6:10 *381*
6:12 *295*
6:12–13 *155*
6:12–14 *328*
6:14–15 *219*
6:15 *156*
6:17 *257, 327*
6:19 *155*
6:22 *384*
6:23 *44, 279, 415*
7:2 *176, 187, 190*
7:2–3 *157*
7:4 *295*
7:6 *315, 384*
7:7 *156*
7:13 *118, 156*
7:14 *98, 228*
7:24 *295*
7:24–25a *415*
8 *304*
8:1–4 *181*
8:2 *220*
8:4 *180, 242*
8:5–17 *137*
8:8 *433*
8:9 *280, 297*
8:9–11 *157*
8:9–13 *408*
8:10–13 *295*
8:11 *156, 403*
8:12 *242*
8:13 *242*
8:14 *280*
8:15 *40*
8:16 *331*
8:17 *64*
8:18 *382*
8:19 *44*
8:19–23 *413*
8:19–25 *390*
8:21 *399, 406*
8:23 *44, 137, 155, 295, 384–85, 407*
8:24 *65, 318*
8:25 *44*
8:28 *72, 434*
8:29 *89, 46*
8:30 *72*
8:31–39 *224, 304, 415*
8:32 *58, 272, 372*
8:33 *45*
8:34 *389*
8:35 *122*
8:38 *186, 388*
8:38–39 *110*
9:1 *207*
9:3 *242, 434*
9:5 *242, 333*
9:7 *72*
9:12 *72*
9:14 *156*
9:24–26 *72*
9:27 *65*
9:30–31 *322*
9:33 *70–71*
10:1–13 *181*
10:6 *409*
10:9 *65, 207*
10:12–13 *38*
10:13 *39, 65*
10:14 *342*
10:15 *59*
11:1 *156*
11:11 *156*
11:11–12 *71*
11:13 *36*
11:14 *65*
11:15 *172*
11:16 *175, 384–85*
11:17 *221*
11:21 *265*
11:24 *265*
11:25 *80, 122, 227, 283, 307*
11:26 *65*
11:29 *279*
11:33 *92*

11:34 *95*
11:36 *206, 333, 77*
12:1 *155*
12:2 *87*
12:3 *41, 120*
12:3–6 *377*
12:3–8 *294*
12:4–6 *295*
12:6 *41, 279, 290, 351*
12:6–8 *288*
12:9–21 *309*
12:13–14 *322*
12:14 *123, 146*
12:15 *190, 300*
12:16 *122, 238*
12:17 *147*
12:17–21 *123*
12:20 *258, 261*
13:1 *356, 430*
13:1–7 *143*
13:3 *88*
13:4 *101, 371*
13:5 *186, 207*
13:7 *166*
13:8 *180*
13:8–10 *181, 196, 304*
13:11–12 *190*
13:11–13 *399*
13:11–14 *190, 428*
13:12 *107*
13:12–14 *413*
13:13 *53, 88*
14 *198, 247*
14:3 *146*
14:4 *113*
14:7 *246*
14:10 *146*
14:13 *115*
14:13–15 *247*
14:14 *207*
14–15 *200, 207*
14:15 *58*
14:17 *149, 412*
14:19 *322–23*
15 *198*
15:2–3 *246*
15:3 *90*
15:4 *124, 226, 373*
15:6 *40*
15:8 *43, 101*
15:15 *41*
15:15–19 *377*
15:16 *37*
15:19 *307, 362*
15:21 *90*
15:22–32 *422*
15:24 *423*
15:25 *419*
15:25–26 *354, 418*
15:25–31 *418–19*
15:25–33 *421*
15:26 *419*
15:27 *98, 228, 418*
15:31 *354, 418–19*
15:33 *333, 352*
16:1–2 *421*
16:2 *274*
16:3 *104, 432–33*
16:3–4 *397, 432*
16:3–5a *74*
16:5 *384, 432*
16:6 *377, 430*
16:7 *213, 301, 375*
16:9 *104*
16:12 *377, 430*
16:16 *433*
16:16–23 *431*
16:17 *327*
16:17–19 *428*
16:17–20 *427*
16:21 *104*
16:22 *37, 434*
16:23 *20, 54, 74, 112*
16:25 *80, 45*
16:27 *333, 390*

## 1 Corinthians

1:1 *20–21, 50, 433*
1:1–2 *61, 125*
1:1–9 *51*
1:2 *34–35, 38, 51, 65, 75, 139, 174, 378, 429, 432, 435*
1–3 *85*
1–4 *74, 310–11*
1:4 *34*
1:4–9 *314*
1:5 *34, 42*
1:6 *34*
1:7 *44, 279*
1:7–8 *188*
1:8 *45, 107*
1:9 *34, 61, 71–72, 75, 314*
1:10 *47, 50–52, 427*
1:10–4:21 *19, 23, 33, 36, 47, 281*
1:10–6:20 *21*
1:10–9 *23*
1:10–17 *47, 49, 51, 297, 427*
1:11 *20–21, 50*
1:11–12 *380*
1:12 *20, 49, 51, 53, 168, 213, 425*
1:13 *51, 64*
1:13–15 *396*
1:13b–16 *297*
1:14 *20, 227, 320*
1:16 *20*
1:17 *35–36, 43, 60–61, 63, 79, 215, 301, 333, 365–66*
1:17–3:23 *59*
1:17–4:21 *366*
1:17–18 *306*
1:17–25 *79, 336, 369*
1:18 *60–61, 65–66, 85, 289, 329, 382, 386*
1:18–3:4 *49*
1:18–3:23 *49*
1:18–4:13 *48, 50*
1:18–19 *381*
1:18–25 *63, 277, 336*
1:19 *25, 49, 65, 90, 339, 352*
1:20 *65, 68*
1:21 *65, 69, 72, 83, 230, 379*
1:21–24 *70*
1:22 *65, 69*
1:23 *65, 250*
1:23–24 *69*
1:24 *46, 61, 65–66, 72, 75, 85, 289*
1:25 *65–66, 73, 299*
1:26 *50, 66, 73, 180, 242*
1:26–31 *19–20, 73–74*
1:27 *73, 299*
1:28 *366, 425*
1:29 *33*
1:29–31 *308, 310*
1:30 *42, 65, 159, 369*
1:31 *25, 33, 49, 51, 133, 339, 352*
2 *90*
2:1 *50, 60, 79–80, 307, 326*
2:1–2 *412*
2:1–5 *24, 36, 60, 63, 79, 306, 326, 333, 352, 369–70*
2:2 *79, 130, 250, 326*
2:4 *23, 59–60, 79, 85, 379*
2:4–5 *289–90*
2:5 *44, 281, 326, 329*
2:6 *61, 68, 76, 98, 337*
2:6–3:4 *23, 72, 283, 317, 337, 406*
2:6–7 *327*
2:6–8 *62, 90*
2:6–9 *188, 366*
2:6–10 *281*
2:6–16 *21, 28, 44, 60, 63, 65, 84, 327*
2:7 *80, 307, 404*
2:7–8 *85*
2:7–13 *35*
2:8 *275, 366*
2:9 *25, 49, 337, 339, 404, 407, 434*
2:9–16 *337*
2:10 *327*
2:10–5 *59*
2:10–11 *90*
2:10–12 *332*
2:11 *292*
2:12 *281*
2:12–13 *327*
2:12–16 *351*

2:13 *23, 60, 79, 228, 279, 281, 406*
2:13–3:4 *337*
2:14 *281*
2:14–15 *115, 130, 346, 407*
2:15 *23, 228, 281, 406*
2:16 *25, 35, 49, 52, 64, 337*
3 *246*
3:1 *23, 50, 228, 281, 338, 406*
3:1–4 *63, 87, 98*
3:3 *53, 305*
3–4 *101*
3:4 *49*
3:4–5 *49, 56*
3:4–6 *20, 53, 425*
3:4–9 *53, 55*
3:4–15 *281*
3:5 *85, 115*
3:5–4:13 *49*
3:5–9 *56*
3:5–17 *63*
3:6 *36, 54, 78, 106*
3:6–8 *402*
3:7 *341*
3:7–9 *85*
3:8 *115, 377*
3:9 *281*
3:10 *36, 41–42, 78, 115, 281, 377*
3:10–11 *24, 78*
3:10–15 *70, 188, 246*
3:10–17 *415*
3:12 *281*
3:12–15 *366*
3:12–17 *44*
3:13 *52, 115, 224, 421*
3:13–15 *143*
3:14 *281*
3:15 *65*
3:16 *43–44, 204, 256*
3:16–17 *26, 133, 281*
3:17 *77, 399*
3:18 *24, 84, 87, 148, 236*
3:18–23 *49, 53, 97, 304*
3:19 *339*
3:19–20 *25, 49, 73*
3:21 *33, 49, 51, 133, 310*
3:21–23 *265*
3:22 *20, 53, 55–56, 186, 213, 425*
3:23 *49, 53, 56, 64, 389*
4:1 *78, 80*
4:1–2 *185*
4:1–5 *44, 85, 104, 188, 218, 338, 345, 366, 381*
4:1–13 *63, 143*
4:3–4 *94, 346*
4:3–5 *130*
4:4 *235*
4:5 *106, 130, 345*
4:6 *20, 23, 26–27, 33, 49–50, 53, 55–56, 133, 146, 305, 310, 340, 352, 425*
4:6–13 *36, 44*
4:7 *33, 40, 42, 130, 276*
4:8–10 *64*
4:8–13 *42*
4:9 *36, 395*
4:9–13 *78*
4:9–15 *85*
4:10 *239, 299*
4:11 *398*
4:12 *322*
4:14 *435*
4:14–15 *24, 78, 370*
4:14–16 *50*
4:14–21 *47, 97, 338*
4:15 *36, 215*
4:16 *34, 36, 47, 50–51*
4:16–17 *24, 47, 64, 78, 201, 369, 427*
4:17 *20, 24, 38, 353, 378, 415, 418, 422, 427, 432*
4:17–21 *424*
4:18 *119, 305, 310*
4:18–19 *23, 26–27, 33, 133, 326*
4:18–21 *420, 423*
4:19 *329*
4:20 *66, 412*
4:21 *78, 326*
5:1 *21, 26, 305, 336*
5:1–5 *44, 143*
5:1–6:11 *196*
5:1–7:40 *23*
5:1–13 *19, 26, 33, 126, 285, 305, 311–12, 327, 366, 380*
5:2 *23, 26–27, 33, 119, 141, 310*
5:3 *142*
5:3–5 *25, 115, 242, 281*
5:4 *50, 198*
5:5 *65, 107, 141, 188, 399*
5:6 *43, 109, 204, 256, 399*
5:7 *25, 42, 58, 64, 141*
5:7–8 *242, 369*
5:7a *24*
5:8 *64, 190*
5:9 *20, 190, 399*
5:9–10 *245*
5:9–11 *19*
5:10 *175, 190, 196, 391*
5:11 *399*
5:12–13 *142*
5:13 *399*
5:18 *314*
6:1 *340*
6:1–3 *44, 142, 188, 366*
6:1–8 *311*
6:1–11 *26, 33, 285, 305, 312, 336*
6:2 *43, 142*
6:2–3 *109, 204, 256*
6:3 *43*
6:4 *38, 142, 425*
6:5 *119, 276, 400*
6:6 *142, 248*
6:7 *131*
6:7–8 *64*
6:9 *43, 109, 217, 256, 398*
6:9–10 *42, 127, 188, 196, 399, 412*
6:9–11 *19–20, 224, 366*
6:11 *25, 42, 50, 65, 77, 139, 174, 281, 369, 429*
6:12 *95, 245, 252, 280, 357*
6:12–14 *137*
6:12–20 *19, 33, 86, 196, 295, 305*
6:13 *26, 76, 84, 132*
6:14 *38, 44, 188, 366, 404, 412*
6:15 *28, 43, 109, 296*
6:15–16 *204, 256*
6:15–17 *295*
6:16 *43, 109*
6:17 *25, 281*
6:18 *26, 132*
6:19 *25, 43–44, 92, 109, 204*
6:19–20 *42, 295*
6:20 *25, 58, 64, 77, 86, 281, 369, 373*
7:1 *21, 195, 256, 357, 367, 418*
7:1–7 *157*
7:1–16:4 *22*
7:1–40 *196*
7:2 *26, 129, 132, 150, 161*
7:4 *154, 157*
7:7 *279*
7:8 *161, 168*
7:8–10 *336*
7:10 *161, 216, 352*
7:10–16 *35*
7:11 *161, 171*
7:12 *168*
7:12–15 *248*
7:12–16 *157, 161, 336*

7:14 *38, 175, 391*
7:14–15 *157*
7:15 *72*
7:17 *24, 38, 125, 378, 418–19, 432*
7:17–18 *72*
7:20 *75, 171*
7:20–22 *72*
7:21 *146*
7:22 *86*
7:23 *25, 42, 58, 64, 77, 369, 373*
7:24 *50, 72, 171*
7:25 *22, 35, 52, 160, 195, 352, 418*
7:25–38 *310*
7:26–27 *161*
7:27–28 *119*
7:29 *50, 168*
7:29–31 *129*
7:31 *44, 65, 367*
7:32–35 *157*
7:35 *252*
7:36 *310*
7:37 *161, 186, 263*
7:38 *341*
7:39 *187, 384*
7:40 *25, 35, 52, 92, 161, 171, 281, 362*
8:1 *22–23, 28, 33, 43, 106, 119, 160, 198, 246, 249, 256, 281, 289, 305, 310, 319, 321, 334, 352, 367, 418*
8:1–11 *64*
8:1–11:1 *19, 23, 33, 86, 282*
8:1–13 *200, 280*
8:2 *24, 121, 236*
8:3 *27, 434*
8:4 *195, 198, 249*
8:4–6 *27, 241*
8:4–8 *243*
8:6 *77, 110, 228, 265, 390, 434*
8:6–13 *340*
8:7 *198, 204, 207, 249, 289*
8:7–11 *281*
8:7–13 *249, 352*
8:9 *106, 212, 236*
8:9–10 *119, 300*
8–10 *201*
8:10 *106, 198, 207, 249, 281, 319, 323*
8:10–11 *289*
8:11 *25, 58, 369, 373, 381*
8:12 *207*
8:13 *238, 324*
8–14 *25*
9:1 *228*
9:1–2 *36, 301, 370, 374*
9:1–5 *85*
9:1–6 *54*
9:1–18 *24, 36, 423*
9:1–27 *305*
9:3 *94, 111, 212, 346*
9:5–6 *375*
9:8 *356*
9:9 *339*
9:11 *23, 98, 145, 228, 281, 406*
9:12 *313*
9:13 *43, 109, 204, 256*
9:14 *79, 352, 419*
9:15–18 *180*
9:16 *35, 186*
9:17 *85*
9:17–18 *104*
9:19–23 *59, 154, 280, 336, 360, 367, 369*
9:20–23 *345*
9:22 *177, 300, 324*
9:22–24 *177*
9:24 *43, 109, 204, 256*
9:24–25 *104*
9:24–27 *44, 81, 108, 367*
9:26 *328*
10:1 *50, 256*
10:1–6 *58*
10:1–13 *109*
10:2 *59*
10:3–4 *23, 281, 406*
10:4 *272*
10:7 *339*
10:8 *314*
10:8–10 *137*
10:9–10 *381*
10:10 *136*
10:11 *44, 124*
10:12 *106*
10:13 *41, 46, 429*
10:14 *158–59, 415, 435*
10:14–22 *140, 156, 200, 229, 295*
10:15 *122*
10:16 *46, 295*
10:16–22 *108*
10:17 *295*
10:18 *106*
10:19 *198, 241*
10:19–21 *205*
10:20 *46, 256*
10:21–22 *398*
10:23 *106, 133, 154, 192, 196, 280–81, 319, 334, 357*
10:23–24 *287*
10:23–33 *177, 280–81*
10:24 *324, 329, 340*
10:25 *94, 207, 346*
10:27 *72, 94, 336, 346*
10:27–29 *207*
10:27–30 *336, 345*
10:29 *340*
10:30 *248*
10:31 *84, 146, 159, 248, 404, 435*
10:31–11:1 *347*
10:31–33 *154, 287, 336*
10:32 *38*
10:33 *192, 324, 329*
10:46 *292*
11:1 *36, 50, 224, 427*
11:2 *34, 64, 271, 352, 370, 372*
11:2–14:40 *23*
11:2–16 *21, 124, 300, 311, 319, 355–56, 358*
11:2–34 *22*
11:3 *355, 389*
11:4–5 *290, 324*
11:4–6 *319*
11:5 *358–59*
11:6 *355*
11:7 *84, 409*
11:7–15 *404*
11:8–9 *359*
11:15 *84*
11:16 *24, 38, 121, 125, 236, 353, 358, 378, 418, 432*
11:17–18 *345, 348*
11:17–22 *74, 300, 310*
11:17–34 *19, 64, 311, 319, 358*
11:18 *21–22, 38, 51*
11:20 *345, 348*
11:20–22 *398*
11:21–22 *180*
11:22 *38, 311, 319, 331*
11:22–27 *124*
11:23 *35, 352, 372*
11:23–24 *373*
11:23–26 *172, 369*
11:24 *58, 64*
11:24–26 *25*
11:26 *44, 79*
11:27 *341, 367*
11:27–31 *229*
11:28 *56*
11:29 *119, 295*
11:30 *136, 194, 380, 384*
11:31 *119*
11:33 *50, 146*
11:33–34 *345, 348*
11:34 *419, 423*
12:1 *22–23, 50, 93, 160, 227–28, 256, 281, 317, 322, 337, 365, 367, 406, 418*
12:1–3 *19, 362*

12:1–13 *256*
12:1–14:40 *23, 33, 64*
12:2 *20, 43, 336, 343*
12:3 *38, 93, 207, 352, 368*
12:4–6 *40*
12:4–11 *43*
12:4–31 *320, 322*
12:7 *102, 154, 252, 280, 324, 338, 352*
12:7–10 *320, 348*
12:7–11 *319, 350*
12:8 *43–44*
12:8–10 *327*
12:10 *291, 330, 351–52*
12:11 *102, 354*
12:12 *57, 156*
12:12–13 *108*
12:12–14 *58, 153*
12:12–27 *348*
12:13 *59, 227*
12–14 *25*
12:14 *156*
12:18 *102, 288, 384*
12:18–20 *156*
12:22 *156*
12:25–27 *156*
12:27 *108, 153*
12:28 *38, 321, 327, 351*
12:28–29 *290*
12:29–30 *320, 345*
12:30 *93*
12:31 *321, 330, 363*
12:31b *321*
13 *204*
13:1 *93*
13:1–3 *288–89, 429*
13:1–13 *280, 352, 428*
13:2 *80, 202, 327*
13:3 *326*
13:4 *23, 33, 119*
13:5 *193, 246, 329, 356*
13:8 *43, 76, 202, 327*
13:8–11 *84, 337*
13:8–12 *44*
13:8–13 *205*
13:9 *290*
13:10 *87*
13:10–11 *76*
13:11 *93, 98, 338*
13:13 *384*
14:1 *23, 228, 281, 290, 323, 363, 406*
14:1–4 *234*
14:1–5 *293*
14:1–19 *281*
14:1–25 *280*
14:2 *80, 292*
14:2–6 *93*
14:3 *281*
14:3–5 *290, 352*
14:4 *106, 281*
14:4–5 *38*
14:5 *256, 281, 291*
14:6 *50*
14:9 *93*
14:11 *93, 234*
14:12 *38, 281, 352*
14:12–19 *234*
14:13 *93, 291*
14:13–19 *291*
14:14 *52*
14:15 *52*
14:16 *333, 391*
14:16–17 *119*
14:17 *106, 281, 340, 352*
14:18–19 *93*
14:19 *38, 52, 125, 256*
14:20 *87, 98, 146, 317*
14:20–25 *177, 281*
14:21 *93, 356*
14:22–23 *234*
14:22–24 *248*
14:23 *38, 93, 280, 348*
14:24 *94, 290, 345*
14:25 *336, 346*
14:26 *50, 236, 260, 280–81, 348, 352*
14:26–27 *234*
14:27–29 *93*
14:28 *38, 291*
14:29 *119, 276, 290–91*
14:30 *291*
14:31 *290*
14:32 *290*
14:33 *378*
14:33–34 *418*
14:33–35 *38*
14:33–36 *21, 125, 432*
14:33–38 *366*
14:33b *24*
14:33b–36 *260*
14:34 *255*
14:34–35 *93*
14:35 *255–56, 355*
14:36 *24*
14:36–38 *234*
14:37 *23–24, 95, 121, 228, 236, 281, 283, 290, 317, 406*
14:38 *279, 365*
14:39 *50, 93, 290*
14:40 *260*
15 *25*
15:1 *50, 372, 428*
15:1–2 *217*
15:1–3 *271*
15:1–4 *35*
15:1–11 *63, 85, 113*
15:1–58 *22–23, 59*
15:2 *65*
15:3 *25, 58, 63–64, 352, 414*
15:3–5 *429*
15:5 *55*
15:5–9 *301*
15:6 *194*
15:8 *212*
15:8–10 *372*
15:9 *38, 72, 323*
15:9–10 *36, 372*
15:9–11 *36*
15:10 *42, 377*
15:11 *24, 85*
15:12 *21–22, 33, 257*
15:12–58 *155*
15:13 *394*
15:14 *429*
15:17 *414, 429*
15:18 *194*
15:20 *156, 194*
15:20–28 *44, 92, 110*
15:20–58 *137*
15:22 *403*
15:24 *76, 127, 412*
15:24–26 *84*
15:26 *76*
15:27–28 *355–56*
15:28 *46, 206, 265*
15:29 *58–59, 131*
15:31 *50*
15:32 *191, 222*
15:33 *109, 139*
15:34 *369*
15:36 *119, 369, 403*
15:40–43 *84*
15:44 *23, 228, 281, 406*
15:44–45 *157*
15:44–46 *228*
15:45 *339, 386, 403*
15:46 *23, 228, 281, 406*
15:49 *262*
15:50 *50, 127, 168, 188, 412*
15:51 *80, 194, 369*
15:52 *328*
15:57 *41–42*
15:58 *50, 369, 377, 435*
16:1 *22, 38, 146, 160, 354, 432*
16:1–12 *23*
16:2 *326*
16:3 *42*
16:5 *326*
16:5–9 *126*
16:8 *159*
16:10 *20*
16:10–11 *422*
16:11 *146*
16:12 *20, 22, 53, 56, 160, 433*
16:13 *146, 428*
16:13–24 *23*

16:15 *50–51, 385*
16:15–16 *356, 422*
16:16 *355, 377*
16:17 *20–21, 54, 159*
16:19 *38, 418*
16:21–23 *44*
16:22 *434*

## 2 Corinthians

1:1 *35, 126*
1:3–7 *33*
1:3–11 *396*
1:8 *227, 283, 432*
1:8–9 *415*
1:8–11 *424*
1:11 *279*
1:12 *78, 81*
1:12–14 *108*
1:14 *107*
1:15–2:4 *422*
1:15–17 *126*
1:16 *423*
1:17 *242*
1:18 *46, 237*
1:20 *333*
1:21 *43, 46*
1:22 *385, 407*
1:24 *104*
2:1–4 *422*
2:1–11 *20*
2:4 *190*
2:5–11 *138, 312*
2:12 *424*
2:12–13 *422*
2:13 *331*
2:14 *39, 122, 308, 395, 415*
2:17 *81*
3:1 *421*
3:2–3 *36*
3:3 *98*
3:5 *377*
3:6 *403*
3:7 *315*
3:7–18 *89*
3:11 *315*
3:13–14 *315*
3:13–16 *261*
3:17 *157*
3:18 *90, 318, 409–10*
4:1 *185*
4:2 *81*
4:4 *68, 409–10*
4:6–7 *65*
4:7 *81, 419*
4:7–10 *66*
4:7–12 *64, 121, 395*
4:7–16 *382*
4:8–10 *122*
4:8–12 *396*
4:9 *323*
4:10–11 *122*
5:1–10 *411*
5:2 *409*
5:2–4 *413*
5:5 *385, 407*
5:7 *318*
5:10 *45*
5:11 *81*
5:14–15 *58, 372*
5:16 *242*
5:17 *403*
5:18–19 *172*
5:18–20 *172*
5:19 *312*
6:1 *377*
6:1–10 *395–96*
6:3–10 *382*
6:4 *186*
6:4–5 *122*
6:4–10 *64, 121*
6:6 *309–10*
6:8–10 *122*
6:9 *278, 318*
6:10 *42*
6:13 *124*
6:14–7:1 *156*
6:16–18 *108*
7:1 *81*
7:2 *109*
7:5 *422*
7:6–7 *387*
7:13 *331, 431*
7:15–16 *138*
8:1 *41, 422*
8:1–9:15 *420*
8:4 *354, 418–19*
8:6–7 *419*
8:7 *34, 329*
8–9 *418–19*
8:9 *42, 204, 419*
8:10–11 *421*
8:16 *415*
8:16–24 *421*
8:19 *419*
8:20 *419*
8:23 *104, 221, 301, 418*
8:24 *308*
9:1 *354, 418–19*
9:4 *422*
9:5 *112*
9:5–6 *419*
9:6 *168, 420*
9:7 *186, 420*
9:12 *418–19*
9:12–13 *419*
9:13 *419*
9:15 *415*
10:1 *50*
10:2 *143, 242*
10:3–4 *81*
10:3–6 *328*
10:7–11 *55*
10:8 *106*
10:10 *54, 79, 146, 387*
10:12 *93, 143*
10:13–14 *36*
10:13–16 *36*
10:17 *77*
11:2 *109, 157, 183*
11:3 *399*
11:4 *55*
11:5 *377*
11:6 *333*
11:7–9 *213*
11:13–15 *117*
11:15 *101, 104*
11:16 *402*
11:16–30 *116*
11:18 *242*
11:19 *238, 402*
11:21 *143*
11:22 *219*
11:22–28 *396*
11:23 *55, 377*
11:23–29 *121–22, 308, 382, 396*
11:23–33 *396*
11:24 *219*
11:24–29 *64*
11:26 *396*
11:29 *171, 300*
12:2 *158*
12:6 *402*
12:7 *136*
12:9 *81*
12:10 *122, 186, 308*
12:11 *402*
12:12 *36, 307*
12:13 *213*
12:14 *124, 246*
12:14–13:1 *422*
12:19 *106*
12:20 *53, 88, 352*
12:21 *132, 134*
13:3–5 *224*
13:4 *66*
13:5–7 *223*
13:10 *106, 422*
13:11 *52, 352, 428*
13:11–13 *304*
13:12 *431, 433*
13:13 *46*
13:14 *435*

## Galatians

1 *372*
1:1 *35*
1–2 *375*
1:3 *35*
1:3–4 *40*
1:3–5 *390*
1:4 *58, 68, 186, 372*
1:5 *333*
1:6 *72, 379*
1:6–7 *154*
1:6–9 *39*
1:6–10 *33*
1:8–9 *434*
1:11 *372, 397*
1:11–17 *35*
1:12 *35, 271, 372*
1:13 *323*
1:13–14 *372*
1:15 *72, 212, 230, 372, 376–77*
1:15–2:21 *372*
1:15–16 *185*
1:16 *411*
1:17–19 *375*
1:19 *301, 375*
1:23 *323*
2 *55*
2:1–10 *52*
2:2 *108, 377*

2:3–5 *217*
2:6 *217*
2:7 *36*
2:7–8 *55*
2:7–9 *377*
2:9 *41*
2:10 *418*
2:11 *377*
2:15 *265*
2:17 *156*
2:19 *64*
3:1 *79, 81*
3:4 *370–71*
3:5 *290*
3:6 *312*
3:10–14 *64*
3:13 *137*
3:14 *118*
3:15 *397*
3:17 *168, 315*
3:18 *180*
3:20 *206*
3:21 *156, 403*
3:23 *219*
3:27 *227, 58*
3:28 *178*
3:29 *242*
4:2 *112*
4:4–5 *219*
4:5 *118*
4:6 *40*
4:8 *265*
4:9 *205*
4:11 *108, 370–71, 377, 430*
4:12 *125, 342*
4:14 *146*
4:19 *124*
4:21 *219*
4:23 *242*
4:25–26 *242*
4:29 *242, 323*
5 *88, 99*
5:1 *146, 153, 428*
5:1–2 *246*
5:4 *315*
5:5 *44*
5:5–6 *304*
5:6 *180–81*
5:8 *72*
5:9 *139*
5:11 *64, 315, 323*
5:13 *72, 203, 237*
5:14 *180, 196, 304*
5:15 *397*
5:16–26 *314*
5:17 *242*
5:18 *95, 219*
5:19 *99, 132*
5:20 *53, 88, 269*
5:21 *149, 412*
5:22 *309–10*
5:22–23 *280*
5:23 *349*
5:24 *137*
6:2 *180, 220*
6:6 *334*
6:8 *399*
6:12 *64, 217, 323*
6:14 *64, 156*
6:15 *180–81, 403*
6:16 *242, 352*
6:17 *122, 396*
6:18 *331, 333*

## Ephesians

1:1 *35*
1:3 *333*
1:3–14 *33*
1:5 *89, 230*
1:6 *256*
1:7 *272*
1:9 *80, 230*
1:9–10 *390*
1:11 *89*
1:12 *256*
1:13–14 *407*
1:14 *256, 385*
1:15–23 *33*
1:16 *316*
1:20 *389*
1:20–21 *388*
1:20–22 *389*
1:20–23 *390*
1:22 *258*
1:23 *390*
2:1 *394*
2:1–3 *40*
2:1–5 *382*
2:3 *265*
2:5 *394*
2:8 *65*
2:8–9 *77*
2:13 *272, 384*
2:15 *315*
2:16 *64, 172*
2:19–22 *106*
2:20 *106, 290, 301*
3:1 *58*
3:2 *218*
3:2–5 *86*
3:2–13 *80*
3:3–4 *80*
3:5 *35, 290*
3:8 *92, 377*
3:8–13 *92*
3:9 *80, 218*
3:9–13 *85*
3:10 *88*
3:13 *58*
3:21 *333*
4:1 *72, 274*
4:1–2 *310*
4:2–5 *304*
4:4 *72*
4:5 *58*
4:6 *206*
4:11 *290, 301*
4:11–12 *288*
4:13 *87, 236*
4:15 *258*
4:17 *168*
4:22 *109, 399*
4:24 *313, 413*
4:30 *407*
4:32 *310*
5:1–2 *310*
5:2 *372*
5:3 *132*
5:4 *311*
5:5 *149*
5:11 *146, 345*
5:13 *345*
5:15–16 *190*
5:17 *402*
5:19 *348*
5:21 *356*
5:21–24 *360*
5:22–6:9 *166*
5:22–33 *162*
5:23 *258*
5:24 *356*
5:25–32 *295*
5:26–27 *118*
5:32 *80, 157*
5:33 *112, 264*
6:4 *124, 235*
6:5 *242*
6:10–12 *88*
6:10–20 *328*
6:11–14 *413*
6:12 *282, 388, 411*
6:19 *80*
6:23 *435*
6:24 *434*

## Philippians

1:1 *35, 101, 126*
1:3 *41*
1:3–6 *224*
1:5 *34, 221*
1:5–7 *221*
1:6 *41, 45, 107*
1:6–10 *45*
1:7 *221*
1:10 *44–45, 107, 250*
1:11 *256*
1:12–14 *424*
1:14 *143*
1:15 *53*
1:17–18 *79*
1:18 *190*
1:20 *155*
1:26 *387*
1:27 *274, 428–29*
1:27–30 *328*
1:29 *396*
1:29–30 *121*
2:1 *46*
2:1–5 *96*
2:1–7 *246*
2:1–11 *38*
2:2 *52*
2:5 *64*
2:5–8 *52, 218*
2:5–11 *64, 90, 285, 390*
2:6–11 *385*
2:8 *64*
2:11 *40*
2:12 *81, 387*
2:13 *230*
2:14–16 *140*
2:16 *45, 107–8, 222, 308, 377, 430*
2:17 *123*
2:20 *246*
2:25 *104, 301*
2:29 *217*
3:3 *242*

3:3–17 *35*
3:6 *114, 323*
3:6–9 *377*
3:7–21 *224*
3:8 *218–19*
3:9 *224*
3:10 *64*
3:10–11 *382*
3:11 *236*
3:12 *323*
3:12–14 *87, 120, 323*
3:12–15 *87*
3:13–14 *222*
3:14 *223, 323*
3:15 *87*
3:17 *125, 224, 226, 231*
3:18 *64*
3:20 *44*
3:20–21 *405, 409*
3:21 *90, 117*
4:1 *223, 415, 428*
4:1–2 *64*
4:2 *96*
4:2–3 *427*
4:3 *104*
4:4 *146, 190*
4:4–9 *352*
4:8–9 *428*
4:9 *352*
4:10–20 *213, 216*
4:20 *40, 333*
4:21 *431, 433*
4:23 *331*

**Colossians**

1:1 *35*
1:3 *41*
1:4 *34*
1:4–5 *304*
1:4–6 *41*
1:7 *101*
1:9 *316*
1:10 *274*
1:13 *137, 149*
1:15 *410*
1:15–20 *390*
1:16 *388*
1:16–17 *206*
1:18 *258, 386*
1:19 *230*
1:20 *64, 172, 272*
1:22 *45, 172, 384*
1:23 *415*
1:24 *58, 85*
1:24–28 *80, 92*
1:25 *218*
1:25–29 *85*
1:26 *85, 88, 91*
1:26–27 *80*
1:27 *85, 382*
1:28 *79, 85, 87, 124*
1:28–29 *85*
1:29 *85, 377*
2:1 *58*
2:2 *80, 88*
2:5 *134, 363*
2:6 *354*
2:7 *43, 106*
2:10 *258*
2:10–15 *388*
2:12 *58*
2:13 *382, 394*
2:14 *64*
2:15 *88*
2:16–19 *115*
2:19 *258*
2:20–21 *163*
3:1 *389*
3:4 *405*
3:5 *132, 137*
3:10 *410*
3:10–12 *413*
3:11 *390*
3:12 *309–10*
3:15 *72, 146*
3:16 *124, 348*
3:18 *356, 360*
3:18–19 *162*
3:22 *242*
4:2 *428*
4:3 *80, 424*
4:5 *141*
4:10–14 *431*
4:11 *104*
4:12 *87*

**1 Thessalonians**

1:1 *126*
1:2 *41*
1:3 *34, 304*
1:4–9 *44*
1:5 *43, 81, 127*
1:6 *34*
1:6–8 *34*
1:6–9 *34*
1:7 *226, 231*
1:8 *39*
1:9 *200, 424*
1:10 *44, 369, 372, 409*
2:1 *377, 424*
2:2 *222*
2:4 *112, 114*
2:4–6 *381*
2:5–10 *213*
2:7 *98*
2:9 *377*
2:11 *124*
2:12 *44, 72, 149, 274*
2:13 *41, 271*
2:17–20 *422*
2:19 *223, 308, 387*
2:19–20 *108*
3:1–5 *313*
3:2 *45, 104*
3:5 *108, 377, 430*
3:7 *186*
3:8 *428*
3:11 *40*
3:11–13 *44, 422*
3:13 *40, 45, 333, 387*
4:1 *271*
4:3 *132*
4:5 *399–400*
4:6 *312*
4:7 *72*
4:11 *172*
4:12 *141*
4:13 *227, 283*
4:13–5:11 *411*
4:13–15 *194, 384*
4:13–18 *380, 387*
4:14 *372*
4:15 *387*
4:16 *328, 413*
4:16–17 *409*
5:2 *107*
5:3 *136*
5:4 *107*
5:5–8 *399*
5:6 *428*
5:8 *328, 304*
5:10 *372, 428*
5:12 *124, 377*
5:12–13 *102, 430*
5:12–14 *427*
5:12–22 *428*
5:14 *124, 309*
5:15 *147, 323*
5:19–21 *351*
5:19–22 *291, 315*
5:20 *146, 290*
5:20–21 *351*
5:22 *146*
5:23 *45, 137, 352, 387*
5:24 *41, 46, 72, 237*
5:26 *433*

**2 Thessalonians**

1:1 *35*
1:3 *41*
1:3–4 *34*
1:6–10 *44*
1:7 *409*
1:7–8 *107*
1:9 *136*
2:1 *387, 434*
2:1–11 *388*
2:2 *107, 186*
2:7 *80, 307*
2:8 *315, 387*
2:8–14 *89*
2:12 *312*
2:13 *41, 384*
2:14 *72*
2:15 *257, 428*
2:15–3:6 *352*
2:17 *45*
3:3 *41, 45, 237*
3:4 *172*
3:6 *172, 257, 271*
3:7–9 *125, 213*
3:9 *226, 231*
3:10 *172*
3:12 *172*
3:14 *124, 140*
3:15 *124, 140*

**1 Timothy**

1:1 *35*
1:2 *39*
1:3 *172*
1:4 *218*
1:5 *207*
1:10 *148*
1:12 *113*

1:12–16 *35, 42*
1:13–16 *377*
1:15 *65*
1:17 *333*
1:18 *222, 290*
1:19 *207*
1:20 *278*
2:5 *206*
2:8 *39*
2:8–15 *254*
2:11 *359*
2:11–15 *355, 360*
2:12 *358*
2:13 *359*
2:13–14 *255*
3:7 *141*
3:8 *101*
3:9 *80, 207*
3:10 *45*
3:12 *101*
3:19–20 *137*
4:1 *244*
4:2 *207*
4:3 *163*
4:6 *101*
4:7 *222*
4:10 *377*
4:11 *146, 172*
4:12 *226*
4:14 *279, 290*
4:19 *433*
5:7 *172*
5:17 *377*
5:20 *345*
5:21–23 *424*
5:22 *146*
6:2 *146*
6:4 *53*
6:9 *136*
6:11 *323*
6:12 *72*
6:13 *172*
6:16 *333*
6:17 *172*

## 2 Timothy

1:1 *35*
1:1–7 *33*
1:2 *39*
1:3 *207*
1:6 *279*
1:6–8 *424*
1:7 *424*
1:9 *65, 72*
1:10 *315, 406*
1:15 *432*
2:1–3 *424*
2:5 *222, 224*
2:6 *377*
2:13 *46, 237*
2:15 *424*
2:17–18 *367*
2:19 *205*
2:22 *38, 323*
2:25 *278*
3:1 *186*
3:8 *223*
3:12 *237, 323*
4:1 *424*
4:2 *327, 345*
4:6 *114*
4:6–8 *224*
4:7 *222, 328*
4:8 *223*
4:10 *303*
4:14 *104*
4:18 *65, 333*
4:19 *432*
4:21 *431*
4:22 *331*

## Titus

1:1 *35*
1:6–7 *45*
1:7 *112*
1:9 *327, 345*
1:13 *345*
1:15 *207*
1:16 *223*
2:5 *356, 360*
2:7 *226*
2:8 *124*
2:9 *356*
2:11–13 *41*
2:12 *278*
2:14 *372*
2:15 *345*
3:1 *356, 388*
3:5 *65*
3:9 *53*
3:10 *124, 141, 235*
3:10–11 *140*
3:13 *423*
3:15 *434*

## Philemon

1 *104, 126*
4 *41*
5–6 *41*
6 *424*
7 *431*
10 *125*
14 *186*
17 *221*
18 *146*
20 *431*
22 *422*
23 *431*
24 *104*
25 *331*

## Hebrews

1:1–4 *206*
1:3 *389*
1:11–12 *413*
1:13 *389*
1:14 *412*
2:3 *43*
2:5–8 *389*
2:8 *389*
2:10–14 *89*
2:14 *411*
2:14–15 *415*
4:12 *346*
5:12–14 *98*
6:5 *275*
6:8 *223*
6:10–12 *304*
6:12 *412*
7:16 *98*
9:9 *207*
9:14 *207*
9:28 *44*
10:2 *207, 316*
10:22 *207*
10:23 *46*
11:13–16 *122*
11:28 *136, 234*
12:4–10 *278*
12:5 *345*
12:17 *412*
13:9 *43*
13:18 *207*
13:21 *333*
13:25 *333*

## James

1:1 *39*
1:2–15 *237*
1:12 *223, 382, 434*
1:18 *384*
2:1 *89*
2:1–13 *267*
2:5 *76, 382, 434*
2:8–13 *304*
2:9 *345*
2:14–26 *224*
2:16 *425*
2:18–20 *401*
3:7 *265*
3:13–18 *64*
3:15 *94*
3:16 *352*
4:4 *158, 238, 303*
4:9 *134*
4:11–12 *114*
4:12 *67*
4:13 *218*
4:13–17 *190–91*
4:14 *190*
4:15 *423*
5:7–9 *190*

## 1 Peter

1:2 *39*
1:3–8 *304*
1:7 *256*
1:17 *104*
2:2 *98*
2:5 *228*
2:15 *402*
2:19 *207, 237*
2:19–21 *147*
2:23 *123*
3:1 *218*
3:1–6 *177, 360*
3:9 *123*
3:10 *316*
3:15–16 *123*
3:16 *207*
3:18 *403, 408*
3:20 *44*
3:20–21 *227*
3:21 *207*
3:22 *389*
4:1 *316*
4:10 *44, 112, 279*
4:11 *333*
5:4 *223*
5:8 *428*
5:11 *333*
5:14 *433*

## 2 Peter

1:2 *39*

1:4 *265*
2:1 *269*
3:12 *107*

## 1 John

1:6 *357*
1:8 *357*
1:10 *357*
2:3–5 *224*
2:9 *269*
2:15–17 *65*
2:17 *191*
3 *357*
3:1 *304*
3:9 *357*
3:18 *313*
4:1 *95, 351*
4:7 *205*
4:7–12 *304*
4:16 *319*
5:7–8 *356*
5:16–17 *137*
5:21 *240*

## 3 John

3 *39*
6 *274*
8 *104*

## Jude

13 *311*
15 *345*
19 *94*
20 *106*
25 *333*

## Revelation

1:4 *39*
1:6 *333*
1:8 *386*
1:9 *221*
1:10 *270, 419*
1:20 *80*
2 *198*
2:10 *223*
2:14 *151, 233*
2:21 *233*
2:23 *104*
3:2–3 *428*
3:3 *342*
3:19 *345*
4:10 *346*
5:14 *346*
7:11 *346*
7:12 *333*
8:2 *413*
10:7 *80*
11:6 *263*
11:16 *346*
14:4 *384*
14:18 *263*
16:9 *263*
16:15 *428*
17:5 *80*
17:7 *80*
18:11 *134*
18:15 *134*
18:19 *134*
19:4 *346*
19:10 *346*
20 *387*
20:4 *145*
20:5–6 *388*
20:6 *263*
20:12–13 *104*
21:7 *412*
22:8 *346*
22:12 *104*
22:20 *434*